Poems and Stories
for Overcoming Idleness

KOREAN CLASSICS LIBRARY: HISTORICAL MATERIALS

Poems and Stories for Overcoming Idleness

P'ahan chip *by Yi Illo*

translated, annotated, and with an introduction by
Dennis Wuerthner

University of Hawai'i Press/Honolulu
Korean Classics Library

© 2024 The Regents of the University of California
All rights reserved
Printed in the United States of America

First printed, 2024

Library of Congress Cataloging-in-Publication Data

Names: Yi, Il-lo, 1152–1220, author. | Würthner, Dennis, translator,
  annotator.
Title: Poems and stories for overcoming idleness : P'ahan chip by Yi Illo /
  Dennis Wuerthner.
Other titles: P'ahanjip. English | P'ahan chip by Yi Illo
Description: Honolulu : University of Hawai'i, [2024] | Series: Korean
  classics library; Historical materials | Includes bibliographical
  references and index.
Identifiers: LCCN 2023035269 (print) | LCCN 2023035270 (ebook) | ISBN
  9780824897246 (hardback) | ISBN 9780824897338 (epub) | ISBN
  9780824897345 (kindle edition) | ISBN 9780824897321 (pdf)
Subjects: LCSH: Yi, Il-lo, 1152–1220. | Yi, Il-lo, 1152–1220. P'ahan chip.
Classification: LCC PL987.Y53 P3413 2024 (print) | LCC PL987.Y53 (ebook)
  | DDC 895.71/1—dc23/eng/20231120
LC record available at https://lccn.loc.gov/2023035269
LC ebook record available at https://lccn.loc.gov/2023035270

Korean Classics Library: Historical Materials

Series Editors:
John B. Duncan, University of California, Los Angeles
Namhee Lee, University of California, Los Angeles
Robert E. Buswell, Jr., University of California, Los Angeles

Series Editorial Board:
Donald Baker, University of British Columbia
Sun Joo Kim, Harvard University
James B. Lewis, Oxford University
A. Charles Muller, Tokyo University
Young-chan Ro, George Mason University
Kenneth R. Robinson, International Christian University, Tokyo
Edward Shultz, University of Hawai'i, Mānoa

Senior Editor: Jennifer Jung-Kim, University of California, Los Angeles

*This work was supported by the English Translation of 100 Korean Classics program through the
Ministry of Education of the Republic of Korea and the Korean Studies Promotion Service of the Academy
of Korean Studies (AKS-2014-KCL-2130001).*

University of Hawai'i Press books are printed on acid-free paper and meet the guidelines for
permanence and durability of the Council on Library Resources.

Contents

Acknowledgments	vii
Conventions	ix
Part I. Translator's Introduction	1
Part II. Translation	69
Fascicle 1	71
Fascicle 2	97
Fascicle 3	129
Epilogue	163
Glossary of Names, Titles, and Terms	169
Abbreviations	199
Notes	201
Bibliography	429
Index	443

Acknowledgments

I would first like to express my profound gratitude to my teachers and friends Marion Eggert and Thorsten Traulsen of Ruhr University Bochum, without whom none of this would ever have been possible. Thank you for all the years of guidance, support, and friendship.

I am thankful to the Academy of Korean Studies for providing me with both generous support and patience. I want also to express my gratitude to the researchers at the University of California, Los Angeles for their continuous assistance. For his precious help, I sincerely thank Robert Buswell. I owe a great debt to Jennifer Jung-Kim, who offered invaluable guidance and encouragement during this book's publication process. I am grateful as well for the pointed and stimulating remarks made by the unknown reviewers. Thank you very much to my copy editor, Eileen Chetti, whose careful comments and thoughtful suggestions were immensely instructive and helpful. Thank you, too, to Stephanie Chun of the University of Hawai'i Press for shepherding this project to its completion.

A special thank-you to my senior colleagues at Boston University, who have been such a great pleasure to work with: Sarah Frederick, Abigail Gillman, Jungsoo Kim, Heeju Lee, Petrus Liu, Margaret Litvin, Roberta Micallef, Jaemin Roh, Peter Schwartz, Sunil Sharma, Keith J. Vincent, William Waters, Yoon Sun Yang, Catherine Vance Yeh, and Anna Zielinska-Elliott.

Thank you also to Bergen Grant for his meticulous help in finishing up the manuscript.

My deepest gratitude goes to my parents and sisters for everything they have done for me. And in the end, thank you to Oh Jungsik, my late best friend.

To my wife, Jiwon, the love of my life, and our awesome children, Joan, Lian, and Taean.

This translation is offered not only in the hope that it will make a small contribution to the study of premodern Korean and East Asian history, literature, and thought but also with the profound wish that it be of value and, most importantly, joy to academic and nonspecialist readers alike.

Conventions

Korean and Literary Chinese (K. *hanmun*) used in Korean sources are romanized according to the McCune-Reischauer system. When citing secondary sources, I follow the romanization style used by the sources' authors or editors. For Chinese and Japanese proper nouns and terms, I have used the pinyin and Hepburn systems, respectively. Birth, death, and reign dates are given for historical figures; at times, the sobriquets are named as well. In translated passages and quotes from other sources, my interpolations are within square brackets.

In the source, the individual episodes are unnumbered and untitled, but for practical reasons, in the translation I have identified the relevant fascicle and entry number before each entry as follows: [1:1], [2:1], [3:1], and so on.

All translations are my own, unless otherwise indicated.

I. Translator's Introduction

Translator's Introduction

In the realm of Korean literature, this book is something special, for it counts among the oldest extant Korean sources, and it is one of the rare original works allowing a direct glimpse into medieval Korea, the time of the Koryŏ dynasty (918–1392).

While an abundance of linguistically, stylistically, and thematically diverse official and private writings from the Chosŏn dynasty (1392–1897) have been transmitted to us in various printed and manuscript forms, often providing us with a layered understanding of many phases and developments in premodern and early modern Korea and East Asia, surviving sources created during medieval times, especially the early and middle stages of the Koryŏ dynasty, are quite limited. This scarcity of remaining Koryŏ source material can be attributed to a number of factors: the Imjin War (1592–1598) certainly marked a sad climax in terms of the destruction and disappearance of cultural heritage.[1] Yet preceding periods of crisis and transformation, such as the attacks of Khitan Liao (916–1125) in 1011,[2] or the calamitous invasions of the Mongols or the Red Turbans during the thirteenth and fourteenth centuries,[3] also brought about the demolition of libraries and archives, and ultimately the irretrievable loss of works of literature and thought from Koryŏ.

As recent studies have shown, however, a substantial number of late Koryŏ dynasty books and documents—in fact, as many as some ten thousand volumes[4]—were still extant and circulating during the first decades after the Koryŏ–Chosŏn transition. These were of relevance when, a few decades into the new dynasty, high-ranking scholar-officials were royally commissioned with assembling—essentially creating—an official history and literary canon of Koryŏ; the eventual results of this undertaking were such monumental works as *Koryŏsa* (History of the Koryŏ dynasty, completed in 1451) and *Tongmunsŏn* (Selections of refined literature of Korea, completed in 1478).[5] Yet these large-scale early Chosŏn book projects geared toward the generation of a Koryŏ history and canon can serve to verify an

3

4 POEMS AND STORIES FOR OVERCOMING IDLENESS

important point: that next to the late Koryŏ material inherited by Chosŏn after the dynastic divide, literary and historiographical sources created as early as the twelfth or early thirteenth century must likewise have been readily available (at least to a certain few) in mid- to late-fifteenth-century Korea. Clearly, leading scholar-officials involved in the creation of *Koryŏsa, Tongmunsŏn,* or *Sinjŭng tongguk yŏji sŭngnam* (Revised augmented survey of the geography of Korea, 1530) had both access to and intimate knowledge of one of these mid-Koryŏ works, specifically the book at hand: *P'ahan chip* (Collection [of poems and stories] for overcoming idleness)[6] by Yi Illo (Yi In-ro; 1152–1220, courtesy name Misu, child name Tŭgok).[7]

Yi Illo, the author and compiler of *P'ahan chip,* was a late-twelfth–early-thirteenth-century scholar-official who was active at the prestigious Hallim-wŏn (Royal Academy of Letters), the highest-ranking academic institution in the country, which offered literary and scholarly assistance to the ruler and the government, as well as at the courts of several Koryŏ kings. He was also a member of the celebrated poets' societies Chungnim Kohoe (High Gathering of the Bamboo Grove) and Haedong Kirohoe (Assembly of Elders of [the Country] to the East of the Sea). As a well-known intellectual of his time, his biography is featured in *Koryŏsa,*[8] and more than a hundred of his poems can be found in *Tongmunsŏn.*[9]

In a nutshell, *P'ahan chip* is a work consisting of a multitude of poems and short nonfictional narratives.[10] In most cases, the prose passages offer the relevant contexts for the verse compositions.

In its oldest extant version, containing all together eighty-three untitled entries divided over three fascicles (K. *kwŏn*),[11] the poetry and prose in *P'ahan chip* are composed in Literary Chinese, the *scriptura franca* of the premodern East Asian "Sinographic Sphere" (the cultures of China, Korea, Japan, and Vietnam, which traditionally relied on this Chinese script and literary language). There is no preface to the collection, but an epilogue, penned by one of Yi Illo's sons, is featured at the end of the oldest surviving edition.

In premodern times *P'ahan chip* was occasionally categorized under the catchall term *sosŏl* (C. *xiaoshuo*), "trivial anecdotes,"[12] but because of its pervasive primary focus on poetry, it has generally come to be viewed as belonging to the genre of *sihwa* (C. *shihua*), "remarks on poetry," or "poetic criticism." An offshoot of the relatively broad literary form of the "brush note" or "miscellany" (C. *biji*), the *sihwa* form and genre originated in Northern Song dynasty China (960–1127) with Ouyang Xiu's (1007–1072) *Liuyi shihua* (Remarks on poetry from the Retired Scholar with Six Things, 1071), then continued and flourished with such works as *Wengong xu shihua* (Continuation of remarks on poetry from Wengong) by Sima Guang (1019–1086), *Houshan shihua* (Remarks on poetry from Houshan) by Chen Shidao (1053–

1102), *Shilin shihua* by Ye Mengde (1077–1148), *Suihantang shihua* (Remarks on poetry from Suihantang) by Zhang Jie (n.d.), and later *Canglang sihua* (Remarks on poetry from Canglang) by Yan Yu (1191–1241). A Northern Song invention, *sihwa* grew to be the dominant form of literary criticism during Southern Song (1127–1279) and later imperial China.[13] While Ouyang Xiu was the originator of the overall literary form, Yi Illo's *P'ahan chip* is generally considered the first work of *sihwa* from Korea.[14] As the literary historian Cho Tongil states in the chapter "Pip'yŏng ŭisik-ŭi sŏngjang" (The development of a critical consciousness) of his seminal historiography of Korean literature, *Han'guk munhak t'ongsa* (A universal history of Korean literature), "Genuine [poetic] criticism emerged only in the latter half of the Koryŏ dynasty, and *P'ahan chip* by Yi Illo can be named as its first example."[15]

Unlike its various Chinese literary predecessors as well as a number of Korean successor works, *P'ahan chip* does not feature the genre appellation *sihwa* (coined by Ouyang Xiu) in its title. This indicates that the aspect of "remarks on poetry after casual conversations," which is one essential characteristic of early Northern Song *sihwa* collections, is not as pronounced in Yi Illo's work. While it is true that many of its episodes are written in an anecdotal narrative literary style (K. *irhwa*), Yi's compositions certainly do not give the impression of having been written on a whim, of being overly spontaneous and tentative, or of having been "composed much as talk is uttered."[16] It can be said that most of the entries in *P'ahan chip* maintain a well-considered content and tone while carrying productive value and factual reliability.

While the genre appellation is commonly rendered as "talks on poetry," "remarks on poetry," or "comments on poetry," in relation to *P'ahan chip* I understand *sihwa* more as *si* and *hwa,* that is, as "poems and [contextualizing] stories." *Si* (C. *shi*), poetry composed in Literary Chinese, is at the literary heart of the collection, just as it was at the heart of premodern East Asian literature as a whole, or at the center of the official and social life in premodern Korea. Without doubt, Yi Illo used *P'ahan chip* as a platform to showcase his own poetry and lyrical talent, but the collection also includes a wide array of mainly pentasyllabic and heptasyllabic verse compositions written by a vast multitude of other poets.[17] Yi's poetry appears chiefly in fascicle 1 (in fact, in twenty-two of the twenty-five episodes),[18] while in fascicles 2 and 3 (which feature only one and five of his own compositions, respectively) he focused on quoting and integrating poems written by people of diverse backgrounds. These are, on the one hand, Korea's high and (intellectually) mighty: influential Confucian scholar-officials and literati, eminent Buddhist masters, erudite Daoist hermits, and even several Koryŏ kings. On the other hand, Yi also recorded — and thereby essentially rescued — the poetry

6 POEMS AND STORIES FOR OVERCOMING IDLENESS

of overlooked or forgotten men: lower-level academicians, petty officials, unemployed intellectuals, and rural scholars from the Korea of his day and age, people whose poetry was well composed but still would have sunk into oblivion if Yi had not chosen to incorporate it into his *P'ahan chip*.[19] In addition, the work features citations, discussions, and evaluations of poems and poetic lines by Chinese model and master poets particularly of the Tang and Northern Song eras, such as Du Fu (712–770; courtesy name Zimei), Han Yu (786–824), and Bai Juyi (772–846) of the Tang, and Ouyang Xiu, Su Shi (1037–1101; pen name Dongpo), and Huang Tingjian (1045–1105) of the Northern Song. Of these, Du Fu's poetry is clearly made out by Yi Illo to be the supreme ideal of poetic writing (see 1:21, 2:4), yet it is especially the poetry of Su Shi, the ultimate Song dynasty scholar-aesthetic, and that of Huang Tingjian that Yi Illo appears to have been drawn to on a personal level (though both of these intellectual giants did not create works of *sihwa* themselves).[20] Extant sources suggest that Yi had access to the collected writings of Su and Huang,[21] although it is certain that he also received their poetry and thought through later miscellany collections, especially *Lengzhai yehua* (Night chats from chilly hut, 1121) by the Chan monk Juefan Huihong (1071–1127), which served as a major source and (structural) model for *P'ahan chip*. At the same time, traditional, formal poetry models, especially the classics of Chinese antiquity such as the *Shijing* (Book of songs) or the *Chuci* (Lyrics of Chu), are of little importance in Yi Illo's more informal *sihwa* collection.[22] Accordingly, 2:4 begins, "From the time when the *Odes* ["Xiaoya" and "Daya" of the *Shijing*] waned and the *Airs* ["Guofeng" of the *Shijing*] were lost [as poetic models], poets all believed that Du Zimei strode alone as [an exemplar of peerless poetic brilliance]."

Though generally not addressed explicitly, a number of vital issues pertaining to the characteristics, roles, and functions of poetry in medieval Korea and premodern sino-centric East Asia are implicitly raised throughout *P'ahan chip*. For instance, almost all poems in the collection illustrate the multiple sophisticated ways in which verse compositions written in Literary Chinese could develop meaning, authority, and substance through open or covert citations and allusions, repetitions, or subtle transformations of predecessor texts. In a premodern Korean reading environment, references to works of ancient or more recent Chinese and Korean literature and thought did not need to be specifically marked by the authors, because an intended readership (literati, scholar officials, or government clerks) was able — and certainly expected — to immediately recognize them on the basis of their extensive learning. This interplay of allusion, creativity, and readership awareness is raised in a highly entertaining way, for example, in 3:11. The episode tells of an obviously rather self-assured young scholar by the name of No Yŏngsu (n.d.), who one night sets afloat a skiff and, rowing upstream amid the descending darkness, starts singing the following short poem at the top of his lungs: "Winds howling, the Yi River is cold; / in a solitary boat I went off alone." The first line is a quotation from the *Yishui ge* (Song of the Yi River), contained in "Cike liezhuan" (Biographies of the assassin-retainers) of the first universal history of ancient China, the *Shiji* (Records of the Grand Historian). In the Chinese source, the poem reads: "Winds howling, the Yi River is cold; / a brave man, once gone, will not return." Over the further course of the episode, however, it becomes very clear that No Yŏngsu was by no means as brave a man as he obviously meant to make himself out to be through the citation. A knowing readership aware of the original poem from the *Shiji* will, I believe, have found the allusion to this specific Chinese poem about bravery embedded in the narrator Yi Illo's description of the overall scene hilariously funny.

Furthermore, *P'ahan chip* offers the opportunity to contemplate the matter of the actual space and location where poetry was composed: for example, while a number of episodes (1:18, 2:25, 3:1) illustrate how poetry was an essential medium of communication between the ruler and his ministers at the court, an entry such as 1:7 can give us a sense of how during mid-Koryŏ times Buddhist temples not merely were sites of religious practice but also served as centers of cultural and intellectual exchange, as a space where literati and (poet-)monks creatively interacted with one another in a mutually stimulating environment. In addition, the specific situation described in 1:7 suggests a certain spontaneity in the creation of poetry. This on-the-spot creativity, the ability to activate poetic knowledge and skill without preparation, is one characteristic feature of the creation of poetry described throughout *P'ahan chip*.

A fine example for an entry apt to raise awareness of the multifaceted functions of poetry during mid-Koryŏ is 2:6, the beginning of which deals with an international diplomatic exchange that took place in 1102 between the young Korean literatus Kim Yŏn (d. 1127; also widely known today as Kim Injon) and a Khitan Liao envoy by the name of Meng Chu (n.d.), who is a case in point of a foreigner in Koryŏ remembered only through his mentions in Korean sources, not those of his native country. The two people, who were quite different in terms of age, status, and origin, come to engage in a poetry competition. On the one hand, 2:6 serves to demonstrate how important poetry composed in Literary Chinese was to the system of diplomatic and tributary relations, for it illustrates that poetry was the common ground upon which scholar-diplomats of vastly different backgrounds could jointly operate and actually come together. We can see in this episode how poetry functioned as the vehicle by which meaningful relationships

8   POEMS AND STORIES FOR OVERCOMING IDLENESS

between both individuals and states were forged, and it becomes clear that in these politically sensitive situations of comparatively rare direct transnational contact, the creation of verse compositions on the basis of a collective knowledge of an array of classical texts and written in the mutually shared *scriptura franca,* Literary Chinese, was anything but a trivial pastime. This holds true not only for the Liao-Koryŏ diplomatic exchange in 2:6, but also for episode 2:2, where the Koryŏ envoy Kim Puŭi (1079–1136) builds diplomatic bridges with Northern Song scholars and even Emperor Huizong through poetry when staying at the Song Chinese court. On the other hand, the poetry competition between the diplomats Kim Yŏn and Meng Chu in 2:6 can also be viewed as an expression of the cultural competition that often took place during such diplomatic encounters. It is clear that the Liao envoy wants to test the artistic, intellectual competencies of the young Korean and essentially means to prove and underscore a cultural supremacy of the Liao over Koryŏ. The fact that Kim Yŏn readily responds and thereby asserts his equivalence in learning and erudition serves to portray Koryŏ as at least equal (perhaps even superior, given Kim's young age) to the Liao. Yi Illo's narration of this event lets us know that Kim Yŏn's quick-witted, poetically beautiful (though, admittedly, in terms of allusions to classical literature, seemingly inferior) response was viewed as a badge of honor not only for himself but also for his home country. In addition, Meng and Kim's poetic exchange is interesting in terms of practical communication and spoken language. For one must note that when Meng and Kim present their lines, the source has *ch'ang* (C. *chang*), "to sing out" or "to chant," again implying that the poetic lines were composed and presented spontaneously. It is well known that conversations and poetry competitions among Korean and foreign literati, who spoke different languages but were both well-versed in Literary Chinese, were commonly conducted in written form, often through so-called brush talks (K. *p'ildam;* C. *bitan*). Yet the word *ch'ang* as well as the overall setting of the poetic exchange — two people sitting atop their horses in a vast frozen landscape entirely covered in snow — suggest that the lines were presented verbally on the spot, and thus one cannot but wonder whether an interpreter obviously well trained in the classics was present at this occasion (generally it is believed that interpreters were inferior in classical learning in comparison to the scholars whose words they were to translate, which often led to difficulties in communication).[23] What is more, the exchange between these intellectuals from Liao and Koryŏ is thought-provoking with regard to the perception of self and other by the interlocutors, as well as the representation thereof through the narrating brush/voice of Yi Illo. At the end of 2:6, Yi tells how Kim Yŏn composed a farewell poem upon being sent to the northwestern frontier regions in 1117. In this poem,

TRANSLATOR'S INTRODUCTION   9

Kim, referring to the Liao, states that he intends "to sweep away barbarian [Khitan] filth." Though it is commonly believed that Koreans regarded the Khitan with hostility and considered them far more "barbaric" (C. *hu*) than themselves,[24] the beginning of the episode in question, that is, the portrayal of the cultured, well-learned Liao envoy Meng Chu and the developing friendship between the Khitan and the Korean, presents a much more positive image of the roughly contemporaneous evaluation of the northern neighbor. Then again, the meeting between Meng Chu and Kim Yŏn took place in 1102, while Kim's poem was composed roughly fifteen years later, during a time when the power structures north of the Korean border were dramatically in flux, the Jurchen Jin (1115–1234, Later Jin) were on the rise after having proclaimed their own independent imperial dynasty,[25] the Liao were rapidly losing ground, and Koryŏ, after having shifted its alliances in favor of the newly emerging suzerain of Jin, was primarily interested in sweeping the Khitan "barbarians" out of the Ŭiju border area and nearby Liaodong, the territory that had once been ruled by Koguryŏ and which by many in Koryŏ was still considered ancestral (home)land.[26]

In this same context yet on a different note, the poem appearing at the end of episode 3:19 furthermore allows us to hypothesize regarding yet another facet of mid-Koryŏ self-perception or self-evaluation, namely, that vis-à-vis the Song dynasty. The relevant poem reads:

> Master Su [Dongpo's] literary works were even heard of overseas,
> but the Song dynasty's Son of Heaven put fire to his writings.[27]
> Literary works can be turned into ashes and embers,
> yet his wide-spreading, mighty name — how could it ever be burned?

There is the interesting idea here that the value and beauty of Su Shi's poetry is being acknowledged and valued to a greater extent in Koryŏ than in China, and that it is the poets of Koryŏ, not those of Song, who ought to be considered the true successors to Su's literary legacy. A clear-cut Korean identity vis-à-vis the Song (which also clearly shows in 2:18), as well as perhaps the notion of a self-perceived cultural superiority of Koryŏ over China, could be read into these lines and into the fact that Yi Illo specifically chose to cite them at the end of an episode opening with the statement that "the brush technique of [calligrapher] Kim Saeng, a man from Kyerim [Silla], was ingenious, splendid, and not even people of Jin or Wei could have hoped to keep pace with it." These are just a few examples indicating how various entries in *P'ahan chip* can offer textual bases for the discussion of broader issues connected to Literary Chinese poetry in the premodern Sinographic Sphere.

10 POEMS AND STORIES FOR OVERCOMING IDLENESS

Poetry thus constitutes the core of the collection. Yet in this work of *sihwa,* the *si* never appear alone, independently, but are always embedded in and entwined with the *hwa* (C. *hua*), the, in my understanding, "nonfictional narratives," "anecdotes," or "stories." In this book, I render *hwa* as "story," meaning a narrative recounting of a series of nonfictional events told through the reliable narrating voice of the author, Yi Illo, not a sequence of *imagined* events that need to be reconstructed by a reader from the arrangement of a narrative plot.[28] No entry in *P'ahan chip* features only freestanding poetry, but a few entries in the particularly prose-heavy second fascicle consist entirely of prose (2:11, 2:18).[29] For the most part, however, there is a productive interplay of poetry and prose, as the stories serve to offer the suitable, required contexts and settings for the poems. These narrative "jottings"[30] are fairly short but, on the level of storytelling (again, simply the narrative recounting of a series of events), rather elaborate, very readable, instructive, entertaining, and oftentimes quite humorous. While drawing substantially on outside material, many parts are also based on Yi's personal experiences, emotions, and knowledge and thereby constitute both a broader, as well as an eyewitness, approach to literature, historiography, or official and social life in mid–Koryŏ dynasty Korea. This dual character of closeness and remoteness, in turn, is reflected in the varying perspectives of the narrator: some of the episodes involving Yi Illo or his acquaintances were written immediately after the relevant events had taken place, and there is little distance; other stories are told from memory, and sometimes Yi even narrates from the perspective of an old man looking back on things that transpired during much earlier phases of his life. What is more, multiple episodes deal with past or contemporaneous events that Yi was not even personally involved in, but which must have been relayed to him either verbally or through the reading of texts.

It is important to understand that the stories and anecdotes are by no means limited to a decorative function — they are not superfluous, but rather give the poems coherence and deeper meaning, and frequently serve to elucidate external sources. And since it may be surmised that even most contemporaneous readers will in many instances quite possibly have lacked the necessary knowledge to fully grasp the meaning of *all* the poems or otherwise inserted texts (such as intricate compositions in the service of political communication), the framing, guiding narratives enable the reader to recognize and understand foundations and links, and ultimately take more pleasure in the reading of the collection.

The prose passages deal (in accordance with the guidelines of the *sihwa* genre) to a considerable degree with clarifications, analyses, and commentaries of the aesthetics, theoretical bases, compositional backgrounds, or specific technical aspects of entertaining, generally well-crafted, relatively recent Korean and Chinese poetry composed in Literary Chinese (choice of words, use of allusions, rhyme patterns, line composition, etc.). In addition, they pertain to a wide range of other topics. One may say that, besides poetry, the second focal point of the collection is people. We encounter (auto)biographical information on Yi Illo and many of his acquaintances and friends, but also on various other contemporaneous and historical figures of diverse origins. Many of these men are mentioned time and again throughout the collection, often appearing in more than one episode. Furthermore, the narratives presented contain not seldom meandering, yet purpose-driven and astonishing in their eventual focal points, musings on a variety of other subjects: these comprise portrayals of ancient and recent episodes of Silla and Koryŏ history (not of the other earlier Korean states of Kaya, Koguryŏ, Paekche, or Parhae);[31] notes on Korean customs, manners, habitual practices, and social life of old and new (again, only from Silla, which Yi Illo portrays as the charter state of his own dynasty, as well as from Koryŏ itself); descriptions of the court and administrative institutions, bureaucratic life, or official procedures (especially the civil service examinations and the structure of the recruitment system), festivals, and events; observations of Korean approaches to foreign policy and diplomacy; discussions of books and the overall circulation of literature and knowledge; remarks on the creation, particularities, and relevance of calligraphy and painting; introductions to poetic theory through Buddhist thought; reflections on the roles and the plight of women in the world of high-ranking men; and portrayals of places such as famous mountains, lakes, ravines, or buildings such as temples, pavilions, palace halls, and (at times ramshackle) scholars' studies and dwellings, many of which have long since vanished.

P'ahan chip is thus marked by the creative blending of poetry and prose, or put differently, the high and the low, for while poetry was always viewed as the premier literary form, prose was traditionally held in comparatively low regard for most of the premodern period in Korea. Yet this aspect of merging is visible on other levels, too. For instance, reflecting the intellectual and religious climate and structure of the mid-Koryŏ state and society, *P'ahan chip* vividly shows the stimulating, productive interaction of Buddhism, Daoism, and Confucianism. Moreover, one striking characteristic of *P'ahan chip,* and something that clearly sets it apart from foundational Northern Song *sihwa* collections, is its transnational, intercultural hybridity: on the one hand it is a decidedly Korean work, unquestionably a direct product of the author's personal (private and official) situation as well as of specific cultural, political, and social developments in mid–Koryŏ dynasty Korea,

12   POEMS AND STORIES FOR OVERCOMING IDLENESS

but at the same time it is deeply rooted in (and requires a considerable amount of knowledge of) Chinese language, literature, history, and thought. Fusion is thus a key facet of *P'ahan chip,* but so is fragmentation, meaning the unique characters of each individual episode. One may say that with its multifaceted yet harmonious perspectives on aspects of history, literature, culture, religion, aesthetics, and intellectual and ordinary life in mid-Koryŏ, *P'ahan chip* bears a resemblance to a literary mosaic. A well-constructed mosaic must have the individual pieces; the seemingly random, yet in fact thoroughly thought-through placement of pieces; and a final, fully complete image. Certainly, the fragments can be regarded, studied, and enjoyed individually, yet the beholder is also meant to appreciate the entirety, for the actual beauty arises from the harmonious union, the artistic, technically sound assemblage and fusion of the individual pieces.[32] In the literary mosaic *P'ahan chip,* each episode retains its distinct content and identity, yet when seen from afar and put into a broader context (for instance, with the contemporaneous zeitgeist, political and cultural developments, or the life experiences of the author), they blend together into a coherent, meaningful entity.

This idea of the ostensibly unorganized but in reality carefully arranged artistic form of the mosaic leads me to the issue of the inner structure of *P'ahan chip.* Certainly, the arrangement of the episodes seems, at a first and fleeting glance, not to adhere to any strict compositional pattern and may therefore strike a reader, especially a modern one, as somewhat random and disconnected. This element of outward randomness, which does provide the overall work with an anecdotal, lighthearted, by-the-way charm, has been identified as one distinctive characteristic of the *sihwa* genre.[33] Yet it is hard to imagine that Yi Illo, a literatus highly trained in the rules and regulations of classical Chinese literature, put the collection together without paying any mind to a sound inner structure. Regarding the character of each of the three fascicles, Yi Sangik has observed that "fascicle 1 is concerned with his [Yi Illo's] own poetry, fascicle 2 is characterized by storytelling [K. *sŏrhwa*], and fascicle 3 deals with other people's poetry — this is the way [*P'ahan chip*] is arranged."[34] Still, I think it is possible to identify even deeper levels of composition. In line with (at least partly) comparable East Asian poetry-prose pieces from roughly the same period, such as *Ise monogatari* (The tales of Ise), the first Japanese work of *uta monogatari* (poem-tales), it seems reasonable to assume that many of the entries in *P'ahan chip* must be viewed, in one way or another, as interrelated pairs, or even sequences of several interconnected episodes.[35] One must bear in mind, of course, that (as is explained later in this introduction) the extant manuscript in three stacked parts did not come to the woodblock printer by Yi Illo's hand, but only after passing through the hands of his son, who owned them after Yi's death, as well as those of a certain surveillance commissioner. This, in turn, leaves room for the theory that the sequence of the individual episodes in each *kwŏn* may be a side effect of a later reconstruction. However, identifiable subtextual links between many of the episodes strongly suggest that their arrangement was indeed consciously, purposefully designed by the author. Allow me to briefly share my thoughts on possible connections between some of the entries in the three fascicles.

In fascicle 1, episodes 1:1 through 1:4 may be viewed as setting the tone for the entire collection: 1:1 in a political/social sense, 1:2 in a structural sense, and 1:3 and 1:4 in the sense of Yi Illo's guiding role model, Su Shi (1:3 and 1:4 both deal with the fabrication and appreciation of objects of material/writing culture, and both are based on Su Shi's views concerning the relationship between literature and certain "crafts"); 1:8 and 1:9 are linked through the institution of the Hallim-wŏn, for here Yi describes the beginning (1:8) and the end (1:9) of his career as an academician; 1:9 is furthermore related to 1:10 through the figure of Kim Kunsu (n.d.); while 1:10 and 1:11 deal with ink-bamboo painting, these two episodes are also essentially concerned with artistic/literary collaborations of different scholars in painting and poetry. Experiences of travel to mountainous regions, as well as the poetry Yi wrote during these journeys with friends and family, can be seen as a thread binding 1:13 and 1:14 together. Yet in these two episodes we can also sense similar critical undercurrents pertaining to certain Buddhist and Daoist practices: a slightly teasing, mocking undertone directed at quixotic Buddhist monks, who must abstain from alcohol, reflects in the graffiti-like drinking poem Yi stealthily scribbles onto the door of a hall at Ch'ŏnsu Temple in 1:13; and the Daoist ideal of withdrawing from the world and finding individual freedom in reclusion is portrayed as a mere pipe dream in 1:14. Episodes 1:17 and 1:18 both depict the creation of verses on the subject of flowers; 1:21 and 1:22 tackle the issue of the enormous effort and dedication needed to write high-quality poetry, yet while 1:21 offers relevant examples of master poets from China (e.g., Jia Dao or Du Fu), 1:22 shows comparable literary figures dealing with similar troubles from contemporaneous Koryŏ (e.g., Chŏng Chisang or Kang Iryong).

In fascicle 2, the first eleven entries can be read as a larger block of episodes surrounding major intellectual figures from early- to mid-twelfth-century Koryŏ who represent the three spheres of the pluralist state: Confucianism, Daoism, and Buddhism. High-ranking Confucian ministers and scholar-officials are depicted in 2:1 through 2:7, Daoist masters in 2:8 and 2:9, and leading Buddhist monks (all disciples of Ŭich'ŏn) in 2:10 and 2:11. The quantitative focus lies on the representatives of Confucian learning

14   POEMS AND STORIES FOR OVERCOMING IDLENESS

and statecraft, and this can yet again be taken as a reflection of Yi Illo's personal prioritization regarding these three systems of thought. Entries 2:12 and 2:13 are built in a similar manner, with two short verses by two different poet-monks (K. *sisŭng*) per entry; 2:14 and 2:15 tell of close friends of Yi Illo and their poetry; 2:16 and 2:17 share the aspect of presenting the process of the collaborative creation of a single verse composition by a number of poets; direct Chinese influences on the construction of Korean Buddhist temples, as well as these temples' beautiful surrounding scenery, serve as the underlying themes of 2:18, 2:19, and 2:20; the setting of both 2:20 and 2:21 is Ch'ŏnsu Temple; 2:21 and 2:22 are held together by the common component of poetry written by Yi Illo's close relatives, that is, his son and his great-grandfather; and 2:23 and 2:24 are concerned with the lives and literatures of two major figures of the Silla dynasty, Ch'oe Ch'iwŏn (b. 857) and Kim Yusin (595–673; here one must note that Ch'oe appears in a much more favorable light than Kim). While the final entry of fascicle 2, episode 2:25, appears to stand alone at first, one could argue that it should be viewed as interconnected with the fascicle's first entry. Entries 2:1 and 2:25 may be hypothesized to serve as a frame, for both episodes are concerned with people from the inner circle of King Myŏngjong who each had an enormous influence on Yi Illo's life, namely, his mentor in 2:1 and his foster father in 2:25. This idea of a frame consisting of episodes 1 and 25 might also be applied to fascicle 1, for here we have a man of the military being ridiculed for his lack of literary education in 1:1, and the description of actual advanced practices of poetic training designed for civil officials at a Confucian academy in 1:25. If understood this way, the contrast in the first fascicle's frame could subtly underscore the idea that only those who have received a proper (civil) education can go on to produce serious works of literature.

In the case of fascicle 3, however, it is more complicated to identify an overarching frame, because (as explained later in the introduction) it is not entirely clear which episode marked the original final entry of the collection. Yet 3:1 and 3:2 are bound together by the cultured ruler King Yejong (r. 1105–1122), while 3:2 and 3:3 are connected by the portrayal of two gifted young scholars with rather unusual starts to their respective official careers; 3:4 and 3:5 discuss master poets of China (Su Shi and Hwang Tingjian) and contemporaneous Koryŏ poets who can be considered to be on par with them (Im Ch'un and O Sejae); 3:8 and 3:9 discuss Im Ch'un and Paegunja Sinjun, who in a later episode (3:18) even appear together and were thus most likely viewed by Yi Illo as a pair of like-minded intellectuals; 3:10 and 3:11 depict aspiring scholars and their participation in the civil service examinations; 3:11 and 3:12 both amusingly portray men who pretend to be

TRANSLATOR'S INTRODUCTION   **15**

something they clearly are not (brave and rich), as well as people who expose the braggers' true selves (cowards and beggars); 3:12 and 3:13 mutually tell of cultured people living in abject poverty; 3:15 and 3:16 may together be understood as entries dealing with poems on mountains; 3:17 and 3:18 clearly address the issue of talented intellectuals not (or almost not) being recognized and utilized by the government; 3:19, 3:20, and 3:21 debate the literature and theories of Chinese model poets (Su Shi, Huang Tingjian, Han Yu, Ouyang Xiu); episodes 3:22 through 3:26 address the defects and specificities of the contemporaneous recruitment system; and both 3:29 and 3:30 may be taken as dealing with dissident intellectuals and their poetry.

The entries in *P'ahan chip* must have been composed over a period of several years, even decades, perhaps, for at times Yi Illo refers to events that must have occurred many years before the collection's actual collation as having taken place "yesterday" (e.g., 2:15) or "recently" (e.g., 1:9). Yet the collection was finalized and assembled sometime in the second decade of the thirteenth century, during the final stage of Yi Illo's life. Extant sources strongly suggest that the bulk of the entries was assembled in or around 1211, shortly before King Hŭijong (r. 1204–1211), who had purportedly been involved in a plot to assassinate the then de facto military ruler Ch'oe Ch'unghŏn (1149–1219), was dethroned and exiled.[36] The deportment of Hŭijong, whom (as alluded to in the epilogue and hinted at in 3:24) Yi Illo had meant to offer the work up to, may have led to *P'ahan chip* not being carved on woodblocks and printed during Yi's lifetime. Yet *P'ahan chip,* in fact, may also have been either supplemented or finalized a few years later, around 1216 or 1217, during the early reign of King Kojong (r. 1213–1259), a king not talked about in *P'ahan chip* at all. This is a possible (though admittedly not very likely) scenario, because in the collection's last entry Yi Illo writes of the death of Wang Ŭi (d. 1216), eldest son of Prince Yangyanggong (himself the brother of King Hŭijong). Here it says, "Such a pity! Heaven did not give him many years, and suddenly he had to heed the call [to write a record on the] Jade Tower [up there in Heaven]." Deriving from a tale about the Tang dynasty poet Li He (790–817), the term *ongnu* (C. *yulou*), "jade tower," refers to a marvelous young poet's premature death.[37] This sentence consequently implies that the final entry must have been written (and maybe also included) directly after Wang Ŭi's death, in other words, after 1216. It has convincingly been argued, however, that this final entry was not inserted into the original *P'ahan chip* manuscript by Yi Illo himself, but rather that it was added by another person at a much later point in time, in the late 1250s, when the work was first carved on woodblocks.[38] If one does consider 3:33 to be a later addition, the original manuscript would have ended on the notion that the ability to create superb literature

16   POEMS AND STORIES FOR OVERCOMING IDLENESS

cannot be learned, but that one simply has to be born with supreme literary and intellectual capacities (the idea of an overarching frame, consisting of episodes 1:1 and 3:32, might again be applicable in this case).

Before it was woodblock printed and thereby fixed, *P'ahan chip* circulated in manuscript form for several decades in mid-thirteenth-century Korea, and it was read, discussed, copied, and passed around by the literati even during this war-ridden era of the initial Mongol attacks on Koryŏ (1231, 1235, 1239), when the dynasty was thrust into chaos and the government was forced to move the capital to Kangdo (1232). Scholar-poets and high-ranking members of the ruling elite are known to have enjoyed, wrestled with, and even disparaged specific entries and poems contained in *P'ahan chip,* which in turn reveals that they must have had intimate knowledge of its content. For instance, particular passages from Yi Illo's collection are referred to, criticized, and in turn also defended in the seventh entry of the lower fascicle of *Pohan chip* (Collection of supplementary writings [for overcoming] idleness, 1255) by Ch'oe Cha (1188–1260):

> Lecturer Ha Ch'ŏndan visited me [Ch'oe Cha], saying, "Kang Iryong once wrote the following on the topic of the egret: 'It flies, slicing an emerald mountainside.' He made painful efforts to chant more, but didn't manage to come up with a corresponding line. Later, Misu [Yi Illo] supplemented it, saying, 'It occupies, nesting in high treetops' [a reference to 1:22]. This is contained in *P'ahan.* Generally, continuing and supplementing [an unfinished poem] is a good thing, but if one can't manage to obtain a beautiful line [to complete a couplet], one ought to just let it be. How come Misu lowered himself to produce something [as coarse] as this? Sir, you ought to just remove it." I answered, "*P'ahan* also features [the passage on] Drafter Chŏng [Chisang] who returned [to the Eight-Foot Room] after having already reached the gates of the capital [also 1:22], as well as [the anecdote on] Hwang Pinbin who cried bitterly as he descended from the tower [a reference to 2:22] — it seems like those were mistakes! However, the words of him who anticipates and first comes up with something, one shouldn't dare to peremptorily call them wrong. Even more so in the case of 'It nests high' in relation to 'It slices emerald' — for this indeed is masterful! Why remove it?" When I refused, Ha became furious and dashed out the door.[39]

It was one of Yi Illo's (most likely illegitimate) sons, Yi Sehwang (n.d.), who appears to have been in possession of the original handwritten manuscripts of his father's unpublished works, and according to his epilogue, he stored them at his own house after Yi Illo's death. More importantly, however, Yi Sehwang, who served as an official at the court during the chaotic era of the initial Mongol invasions, when countless books and objects of cultural heritage were irreversibly destroyed in the abandoned capital of Kaesŏng, was in the actual position to carry along and safeguard his father's writings when following the king's retinue and escaping to Kanghwa Island. In the epilogue, Yi states that he valued the box holding his father's manuscripts "like a basket full of gold" while fearing "that but a single word contained therein might be lost," and so it can be argued that both Yi Sehwang's personal commitment as well as his official and social position (illegitimate sons were not as strongly discriminated against in Koryŏ as they were later during the Chosŏn dynasty) were key factors in *P'ahan chip* surviving these years marked by the large-scale obliteration of Korean cultural products in the 1230s.

P'ahan chip was first printed in 1260 on the initiative of one Duke Taewŏn (or perhaps Taewŏn Wang gong, with the last name being Wang), possibly a descendant of King Hŭijong and Wang Ŭi.[40] In the late 1250s, this person is said to have served as surveillance commissioner, and in Kijang Lesser Prefecture happened to meet Yi Sehwang, who had just been demoted and sent to the deep south. When they sat together and chatted, their conversation touched upon Yi Illo, and Yi Sehwang took out a stack of three hundred poems as well as the original manuscript of *P'ahan chip* and showed it to the surveillance commissioner. Duke Taewŏn thereupon had a skilled craftsman carve the work into printing blocks. The printed version finally appeared in 1260 — tellingly, one might add, merely one year after the rule of the Ch'oe family had collapsed in the wake of immense pressure from both inside and outside (the last of the Ch'oe rulers had been murdered in 1258, and a peace agreement with the Mongols had been reached in 1259).

Unfortunately, this initial print version of *P'ahan chip* has not been transmitted. One must note that extant sources leave room for the hypothesis that the 1260 woodblock print was not entirely congruent with Yi Illo's original 1211 handwritten manuscript. For in *Pohan chip* 3:21, Ch'oe Cha (who did not yet have access to a printed edition of *P'ahan chip* and must have worked with a manuscript) writes, "Misu included Im Chongbi's couplet *Kollyun'gang-sang* [Upon the ridges of Mount Kunlun] into his *P'ahan*, but I didn't take [and include] it for this [here *Pohan chip*]."[41] Neither a couplet by Im Chongbi (n.d.) under the mentioned title, nor a contextualizing narrative passage are contained in the still-existing oldest version of *P'ahan chip* from 1659, and it may well be that the poem and the story were already excluded prior to the work's initial 1260 woodblock printing.[42] In addition, one anecdote that much later, in the nineteenth century, was claimed to have featured in a "collection" (K. *chip*) by Yi Illo,

18 POEMS AND STORIES FOR OVERCOMING IDLENESS

can likewise not be found in the 1659 version of *P'ahan chip*. This information, and even a citation of the relevant episode, appear in *Oju yŏnmun changjŏn san'go* (Scattered manuscripts of glosses and comments of Oju, 1837, vol. 47, *Ransaeng pyŏngjŭngsŏl*) by Yi Kyugyŏng (1788–1856):

> In a collection by Misu Yi Illo of Koryŏ it says, "Director of the Chancellery Kim Pusik [1074–1151] early on went to the court in [the capital of] Song China [on an official mission around 1116]. When he [and the other Korean envoys] arrived at Youshen-guan, the hall for guardian deities, he spotted a hall in which a statue of a female deity was on display. Their escort Wang Fu said to them, 'This here is a deity of your distinguished country—do you gentlemen know about her?' Eventually he explained, 'In ancient times there was a woman of the [Chinese] imperial house. Without even having a husband she got pregnant, and when she consequently became the object of everyone's suspicion, she [escaped,] floated across the ocean, and came to stay in [the state of] Chinhan [on the Korean Peninsula]. She then gave birth to a son, who became the first king of the Country East of the Sea.[43] Later he became a celestial deity, and the imperial woman became a terrestrial deity, who for a long time dwelled on Mount Sŏndo. This here is a statue of her.'"

It may be that Yi Kyugyŏng had access to a different version of *P'ahan chip*, perhaps one that was closer to the original version of 1211. Alternatively, this story may have featured in one of Yi Illo's other collections (although it is believed that all of his other works had vanished by the nineteenth century). Or he simply may have made a mistake, erroneously establishing a connection between this story, which is actually a commentary by Kim Pusik at the end of the Silla annals of *Samguk sagi* (History of the Three Kingdoms),[44] and Yi Illo.

In any case, the oldest surviving edition of *P'ahan chip* (which served as the primary source for this book's translation) is a mid-Chosŏn recut copy (K. *chunggan-pon*) of an earlier edition. The template edition used for this 1659 reprint was in all likelihood a 1493 woodblock-print edition that had been commissioned and handed up to King Sŏngjong (r. 1469–1494) by the high-ranking official Yi Kŭkton (1435–1503), who in 1484 had worked with Sŏ Kŏjŏng on the compilation of the *Tongguk t'onggam* (Complete mirror of the Eastern Country) and who was in the early 1490s serving as provincial governor (K. *kamsa*) of Kyŏngsang.[45] Yi Kŭkton, who as a historian was quite critical of the quality of such major works as Kim Pusik's *Samguk sagi*,[46] obviously valued *P'ahan chip* highly enough to consider it adequate reading material for the king of Chosŏn (as the relevant entry from the *Veritable Records*, quoted in the following section, "*P'ahan chip* in Chosŏn, Colonial Times, and the Koreas," shows, this opinion was not shared by all of the officials at court). The extant 1659 version was fittingly carved and printed in the Kyŏngsang city of Kyŏngju, and prepared on the initiative of the governor of Kyŏngju (K. Kyŏngju *puyun*), Ŏm Chŏnggu (1605–1670). Ŏm had obtained *P'ahan chip* from the renowned scholar-painter Cho Sok (1595–1668), whose family the book had apparently belonged to for a long time.[47] This edition bears a seal of the Sigang-wŏn, the Office of Royal Lectures, indicating that this copy was stored at the library of an heir apparent, most likely the later King Sukchong (r. 1674–1720).[48] It may therefore be argued that *P'ahan chip* only survived through the Imjin War and was passed on into late Chosŏn and modern times because of the good fortune that copies of it not only were part of the royal holdings in Hanyang but also were being kept in private collections owned by scholars residing in the countryside.

As shown in figure 1, the poems in every entry of the 1659 woodblock print are marked with punctuation, comma-like black dots handwritten in the lower right-hand margin of every second word, starting with the first character. These consistent dots, which (as the color indicates) were inserted not by the copier but by a secondary person who used the text at a later stage, obviously do not have the function of marking characters as erroneous, they do not indicate derivative readings of characters, and their location is monotonous (in a Korean reading environment, there was of course no need for the indication of tone). They simply appear to have been put down in the poems as separation marks, perhaps as reading aids for a novice unable to parse the text, though the syntactic, semantic caesuras of the poetic lines (in five-character poetry usually after the second word, in seven-character poetry after the second and/or fourth word) were obviously not taken into consideration. Also, whereas in Chinese texts the first word of a poem is usually not marked, curiously, in *P'ahan chip* we find the punctuation sign next to the initial character of every poem. The reader may have meant to highlight the importance of the poems. Or the procedure may have had a didactic function. Yet what exactly could be learned from it is unfortunately not entirely clear to me.

In addition, the extant copy contains a number of inserted sheets of paper: on one of these we do find a brief explanatory annotation to the relevant *P'ahan chip* content (on the slip of paper sticking to the page of 1:22, there is a scribbled note on Kiji Im Ch'un and his poem in that episode). Other sheets seem to lack readily discernable content-related connections to the work. For instance, in between the pages of 3:32, an episode dealing with

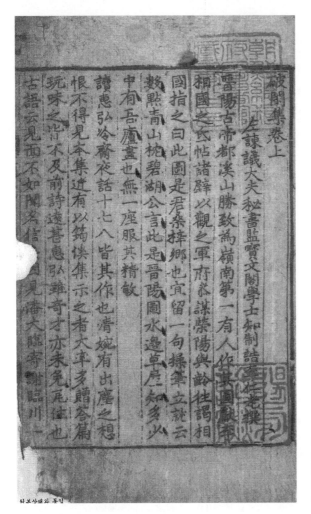

Figure 1: First page of *P'ahan chip* from the 1659 woodblock-print edition. National Library of Korea. #Ko 3648-62-377. https://www.nl.go.kr.

the poetry of Sŏ Munwŏn and Kwŏn Tollye, we find an inserted slip (which at one point was apparently pasted onto the page) with a handwritten quote of a passage on a certain procedure to bring the dead back to life (write the word *kwi*, "ghost," onto the dead man's forehead with the blood drawn from the corpse's ring finger; see fascicle 3, note 304) from the fourth volume of Ŏ Sukkwŏn's (fl. 1525–1554) *P'aegwan chapki* (A storyteller's miscellany) on it. In front of the epilogue are more inserted pages densely covered with handwritten text on the lives of the late Koryŏ scholar-officials Chŏng Kasin (1224–1298), Kim I (1265–1327), and Yi Chonyŏn (1269–1343)—naturally, none of these men appear anywhere in *P'ahan chip*. Similar pages can also be found at the very end of the book.

P'ahan chip in Chosŏn, Colonial Times, and the Koreas

P'ahan chip was composed in the tradition and style of Chinese literary predecessors, which Yi clearly must have had access to. But the work itself also sparked an ensuing process of *sihwa* writing in Korea, for during later Koryŏ times, *P'ahan chip* came to serve as a primary model for several Korean collections of remarks on poetry. Most prominently, the aforementioned *Pohan chip* was from the very beginning designed as its direct sequel, and, accordingly, *Pohan chip* was also referred to as *Sok P'ahan chip* (Sequel to *P'ahan chip*). *Pohan chip* was carved on woodblocks and printed in the cyclic year ŭlmyo, 1255, five years prior to the publication of the initial woodblock print of its underlying model, *P'ahan chip*, when the Ch'oe regime was already weak but still in charge. In his preface to this follow-up collection, entitled *Sok P'ahan chip sŏ* (Preface to the sequel to *P'ahan chip*), Ch'oe Cha writes,

> However, from the various renowned worthies [of our dynasty] of old and new, only seven or eight got to have their *munjip* [collected writings] put together, while the rest of the famous literary writings and exquisite poetic lines all vanished and were never heard of again. The academician Yi Illo roughly gathered some of them and completed a piece, which he called *P'ahan*. Chinyang-gong [Ch'oe U (d. 1249)], however, believed that this book was not yet wide-ranging enough,[49] and thus he ordered me to continue and supplement it.[50]

Another late Koryŏ collection influenced by and belonging to the peer group of *P'ahan chip* is the nowadays quite prominent *Yŏgong p'aesŏl* (Fictional narratives by Old Man "Oak") by Yi Chehyŏn (1287–1367).

Like many of his contemporaries, Yi Illo was a very productive writer, and he is known to have composed several voluminous pieces of poetry and prose. These books were all apparently still available to a literati readership in early Chosŏn, for at the end of his biography in *Koryŏsa* it says, "Of what he brought forth, the *Ŭndae chip* [Collection of Silver Terrace] in twenty volumes, the *hujip* in four volumes, the *Ssangmyŏng-jae chip* [Collection of Ssangmyŏng Studio; according to the epilogue of *P'ahan chip* a collection of miscellaneous writings from Yi Illo's time as a member of the Haedong Kirohoe] in three volumes, and the *P'ahan chip* in three volumes are circulating in the world."

An entry in the eighth volume of *Yongjae ch'onghwa* (Yongjae narratives), a privately written literary miscellany by the scholar-official Sŏng Hyŏn (1439–1504), likewise reveals that three works by Yi Illo were still extant in late-fifteenth-century Korea. At the same time, however, this source may serve to explain why so many books from Koryŏ and early Chosŏn vanished during the Imjin War: there often existed no more than a single copy of them, and once this lone copy was destroyed, the work was lost forever. In *Yongjae ch'onghwa* it says, "Of the *Ŭndae chip* there exists only a single cased copy [K. *chil*]; then there is the *Ssangmyŏngjae*, which is extant in one cased copy, and the upper and lower cased copies [K. *sang ha chil*][51] of *P'ahan chip* — all of these were written by Yi Illo."[52] Early Chosŏn scholars having had access to Yi Illo's collection is also evidenced by other extant sources. The collection is, for example, recurrently referred to in Sŏ Kŏjŏng's (1420–1488) *Tongin sihwa* (Poems and stories by Easterners [Koreans], 1474), and in Kang Hŭimaeng's (1424–1483, styled Sasukchae) preface to this fifteenth-century *sihwa* collection, the *Tongin sihwa sŏ* (Preface to *Tongin sihwa*), it says,

> In our Eastern Region [Korea], poetry greatly flourished, [...] but only with the composition of such works as *Yŏgong p'aesŏl* by Teacher Ikchae [Yi Chehyŏn] or *P'ahan chip* by Grand Master of Remonstrance [K. Taegam] Yi [Illo] there was an investigation into the essence of our Eastern Region's poetry. Yet hereafter there was no one to carry on [this careful examination of our literature] for hundreds of years — how could this not be cause for great lamentation?[53]

As an example for a reference to *P'ahan chip* in one of the entries of *Tongin sihwa*, we may look at the twenty-eighth entry of the first fascicle, where Sŏ Kŏjŏng writes,

> Early on I asked the teachers at the Hallim Academy,[54] "[...] Among the ancients there were many who really liked their own literary writings. There is, for instance, Cai Mengzhai's [Cai Zhengsun (1239–after 1300)] *Lianzhu shige* [A string of pearls in poetic form], or Grand Master of Remonstrance Yi Illo's *P'ahan chip* — all of them were fascinated by their own poetry, and the ancients' genuine frankness can be seen herein." The various teachers replied, "The poems of Confucius aren't arranged in the *Guofeng* ["Airs of the States" of the *Shijing*], and the compositions by Zhao Ming [of the Shang dynasty] aren't compiled in the *Wenxuan* [Selected literature] either. Whether that's good or bad we cannot know with certainty."[55]

P'ahan chip served as a source for another major book and canonization project of early Chosŏn, namely, the *Tongmunsŏn*. For if we consider fascicle

TRANSLATOR'S INTRODUCTION   23

1 of *P'ahan chip* alone, a substantial number of its poems reappear (furnished with new — or perhaps original — titles) in the *Selections of Refined Literature of Korea:* there is the poem by Chŏng Yŏryŏng (n.d.) from 1:1, which features under the title "Chinju sansu to" ([Poem on a] painting of the landscape of Chinju) in *TMS* 19:21a–b; Yi Illo's poem from 1:3 appears under the title "Ch'odo Maengju — chogong muk ch'ŏ" (Upon first arriving in Maengju — the place where I produced tributary ink) in *TMS* 20:1b; Yi's poem from 1:7 is contained in *TMS* 13:7b; the poem on the leaf floating forth from the royal palace from 1:12 features under the title "Che ch'osŏ chokcha" (Written on scrolls of draft script) in *TMS* 20:1a; his poem from 1:14 is contained under the title "Yu Chiri-san" (Roaming the Chiri Mountains) in *TMS* 13:6b–7a; his poem from 1:15 appears under the title "Ha Im sangguk munsaeng Cho Sasŏng Ch'ung ryŏng munsaeng hŏnsu" ([Written] to congratulate Rector Cho Ch'ung, graduate of Minister of State Im, who led on his own graduates to wish [Im Yu] a long life) in *TMS* 13:6b; and the two palindrome poems from 1:16 feature under the titles "Kamch'u hoemun" (Stirred by autumn, a palindrome) and "Hyŏn sijae hoemun" (Presented to the grand councilor of the time, a palindrome) in *TMS* 9:3a–b and *TMS* 9:7a–b.[56]

P'ahan chip is also referred to in two passages from an official Chosŏn document, namely, the *Sŏngjong sillok* of 1493. The first relevant entry from the *Veritable Records* of King Sŏngjong casts a light on how *P'ahan chip* was printed, annotated, and circulated (only on a very small scale at the court) toward the end of the fifteenth century, a time when some of the figures discussed in Yi Illo's work obviously no longer belonged to the realm of shared knowledge and needed explaining by experts in Korean history. It says,

> Kim Sim [1445–1502], first councilor in the Office of Special Councilors [K. Hongmun-gwan Pujehak], presented an abbreviated memorial [K. *ch'aja*], saying "I have heard the following: Recently, when Yi Kŭkton became provincial governor of Kyŏngsang, and Yi Chongjun [1458–1499] became office manager [K. *tosa*], they proceeded to have the *Youyang zazu* [Miscellaneous morsels from Youyang], the *Tang Song shihua* [Remarks on poetry from the Tang and Song dynasties], the *Yishan yuefu* [Yishan's songs of the music bureau], as well as the *P'ahan*, the *Pohan chip*, the *Taep'yŏng t'ongjae* and other books printed, and to have these handed up to the throne. Order was then given to ultimately store these [printed books] at the Ministry of the Royal Household [K. Naebu] [for the king to read]. In turn, *Taep'yŏng t'ongjae, P'ahan, Pohan* and other collections were handed down again, and we ministers were commanded to briefly annotate the era names of the successive ages and the origins of the people [mentioned in these works], and to bring them forth [so that they may be read by the king]."[57]

24 POEMS AND STORIES FOR OVERCOMING IDLENESS

However, as can be seen in the second relevant entry from this *sillok*, Kim Sim and the other ministers were in no hurry to add the requested annotations, for they opposed the king of Chosŏn spending his time perusing noncanonical, and in their eyes irrelevant and distracting, books such as *P'ahan chip*. King Sŏngjong, however, vehemently defended his desire as well as his right and obligation to read these works. Parts of this second entry read:

> First Councilor Kim Sim and others came, announcing the following: "It has been said that we ministers loathe the task of annotating collections such as the *Tang Song shihua*, the *P'ahan*, or the *Pohan*. Before, however, we had already been told to proofread and correct this here [encyclopedia] *Shiwen leiju* [Classified collection based on historical facts and on literature], and for this reason we did not annotate [those other pieces] straightaway. Yet we ministers received the royal command [to add the relevant annotations], and even if we had to wade through boiling water or walk through raging fire, we would never dare shun [His Majesty's orders]. Moreover, this is only about some trifling matter of literary writing, so how could we feel any sort of loathing with regard to this? We ministers harbor no such emotions whatsoever. We ministers are equipped with inferior abilities—in our positions as attendants [K. *sijong*] we look upon the study of poetry as a secondary matter for [a person as important as] the ruler of men, and we always fear that Your Sagely Highness may give too much thought to these [ancient, distracting collections]. [Yi] Kŭkton, a great minister who has knowledge of the principle, presented these nonclassical, ludicrous books [such as the *P'ahan* or the *Pohan*] to the court, and from the bottom of our hearts we ministers truly considered this to be wrong. [...]"
>
> The king's response was transmitted in the following way: "It's not that I didn't understand the meaning of what you lot are saying. Though the *Youyang zazu* and the other books certainly are miscellanies with noncanonical narratives, [a canonical work such as] the *Guofeng* [of the *Shijing*] likewise contains obscene words—in the lectorium of classics [C. *jingyan*] there clearly were those [eminent scholars] who demanded that it ought not to be brought forth when lecturing [the ruler], and men in aftertimes often discussed its wrongs. Yet the ruler of men must observe both good and bad in order to make exhortations or warnings. If it was as you lot are saying, then what about the recently printed *Shiwen leiju*? Are there no noncanonical narratives in that book? Are we supposed to search out and exclude all of these books from the Ministry of the Royal Household, so that the lord of men can read nothing but the Four Books and Five Classics

[C. *sishu wujing*] anymore? I ordered you to annotate these books in the eighth month, and as of yet you haven't written or brought forth anything at all — the blame for this is going to come back to you."[58]

P'ahan chip was read by intellectuals such as Kim Sisŭp (1435–1493) in the middle of the fifteenth century,[59] and it may even be hypothesized to have served as one inspiration for *Kŭmo sinhwa* (New tales of the golden turtle, ca. 1460s), Kim's now famous collection of strange tales (C. *chuanqi*, K. *chŏn'gi*).

In early-sixteenth-century Chosŏn, too, literati had access to *P'ahan chip* and were familiar with individual entries. This is evidenced by Kim Allo's (1481–1537) collection of "unofficial stories" (K. *yadam*) *Yongch'ŏn tamjŏk ki* (Records of Mr. Dragon Spring's talks in solitude) from 1525, where *P'ahan chip* is mentioned in relation to the painter Yi Nyŏng (n.d.), who lived during the reign of King Yejong of Koryŏ (r. 1105–1122), and his painting *Ch'ŏnsu-sa nammun to* (Painting of the southern gate of Ch'ŏnsu Temple), which in *P'ahan chip* is discussed in 2:20. Kim Allo writes,

> The matter of *Ch'ŏnsu-wŏn to* [Painting of Ch'ŏnsu Monastery] by Yi Nyŏng of the Koryŏ dynasty being seen and praised in China is spoken of in detailed fashion in *P'ahan chip*. But how come his traces have been transmitted to merely such a small extent? Pihaedang [sobriquet of Anp'yŏng taegun (1418–1453), the fourth son of King Sejong] simply loved old paintings, and he had expertise in [painting] techniques. Whenever he heard that someone possessed [such an ancient painting], he would go out and get it, even if he had to pay double the [adequate] price. Thus he collected exhaustively for a number of years, and all in all [his collection] contained several hundreds of painting scrolls. Ancient objects of the Tang and the Song dynasties, even though they may have been damaged, thinned-out, faded, or in bad condition, he would spend fortunes on them and there was nothing he would not get. Now, Yi Nyŏng was a [Korean] man of recent times, and if [his artistic work] had really been considered valuable and precious [during previous ages], how is it possible that one cannot find any mention of it in Pihaedang's painting records? This person [Yi Nyŏng] passed away not too long ago, but still [his paintings] have entirely vanished and nothing has been transmitted — that, in fact, may be considered quite suspicious."[60]

In Ŏ Sukkwŏn's *P'aegwan chapki* it says, "In our Eastern Country there have been few works of 'trivial anecdotes' [K. *sosŏl*]. From Koryŏ there is only *P'ahan chip* by Grand Master of Remonstrance Yi Illo, *Pohan chip* by Chorong Ch'oe Cha, and *Yŏgong p'aesŏl* by Ikchae Yi Chehyŏn. [...]"[61] Another major

26 POEMS AND STORIES FOR OVERCOMING IDLENESS

book project of the early sixteenth century, *Sinjŭng tongguk yŏji sŭngnam*, cites extensively from *P'ahan chip*.[62]

Yet different from the majority of official and private Koryŏ writings that must have circulated during early Chosŏn (such as the *Ŭndae chip* and the *Ssangmyŏngjae chip*), *P'ahan chip* did not vanish in the wake of the Imjin War, but was rather continuously passed on, referenced, and cited during the latter half of the Chosŏn dynasty. In "Che *P'ahan chip*" (Written onto *P'ahan chip*) from Pak T'aesun's (1653–1704) *Tonggye chip* (Collection of Tonggye, 1736), it says,

> *P'ahan chip* was compiled by the Koryŏ academician Misu Yi Illo. Misu gave off a sound with his literary writing during the middle period of the Koryŏ dynasty. Regarding the poetry and prose he brought forth, much of it has vanished, little has been transmitted, and it is only this here collection [*P'ahan chip*] which is being printed and circulated in the world today.[63]

P'ahan chip is listed furthermore in An Chŏngbok's (1712–1791) survey of Korean history, *Tongsa kangmok* (Major and minor points about the history of Korea, written between 1756 and 1758), and here we find a reference to *P'ahan chip* 2:24 in an account of the Silla general and statesman Kim Yusin, entitled "Kim Yusin Ch'ŏn'gwan ki sa" (The matter of Kim Yusin and the courtesan Celestial Official). It says,

> The basic transmission of the *History of the Three Dynasties* contains many numinous, strange matters [in relation to Kim Yusin]. And the *Tongguk [t'ong]gam*, too, is often cited, but since there is nothing [significant] to take over from all of these [tales of the strange in the older histories], I left them all out. Only the one incident with the singing girl Ch'ŏn'gwan, that was a deed of merit [Kim] Yusin achieved in his latter days, and generally speaking it derived from [his will] to overcome his own private [desires] as well as his ambition to achieve merit [as a pious son] — thus, although [this anecdote] cannot be spotted in the original histories, I shall now follow the [*Sinjŭng tongguk yŏji*] *sŭngnam* and the *P'ahan chip* and insert it here [in *Tongsa kangmok*].[64]

P'ahan chip is quoted in such works as *Maeho yugo* (Posthumous manuscripts of Maeho, 1784)[65] and Yi Yuwŏn's (1814–1888) *Imha p'ilgi* (Jottings by Imha),[66] and there is also a text entitled *Che P'ahan chip hu* (Inscribed on the back of *P'ahan chip*) by Yi Chonghwi (1731–1797).[67] Moreover, there exists a manuscript version of *P'ahan chip* from the nineteenth century, which is currently being stored at the University of California, Berkeley Library and which was apparently prepared by Sŏ Yugu (1764–1845). All this serves to show that *P'ahan chip* was continuously published, circulated, and read in late Chosŏn Korea.

Astonishingly, extant sources even suggest that the work was known in nineteenth-century China. For when in 1831 the Chosŏn envoy Hong Sŏkchu (1774–1842) was staying in the Chinese capital, the Qing antiquarian scholar Liu Xihai (1793–1852) asked him whether there still existed a woodblock-print version (K. *kakpon*) of *P'ahan chip,* and Hong replied that there in fact still were such books to be found in Korea, but that by this point in time they had become very rare (K. *man'gyŏl*).[68]

With *P'ahan chip* being both accessible and discussed in the closing stages of the Chosŏn dynasty, it comes as no surprise that Yi Illo's collection of *sihwa* was of interest to Japanese and Korean intellectuals when they, naturally for very different reasons, both set out to construct the narrative of a singular Korean literary history and its teleology in the early decades of the twentieth century. And as an (at least by Korean standards) ancient work written by a single identifiable author, Yi Illo's *P'ahan chip* could not avoid being established as a core piece of a Korean canon during the foundational phase of a national Korean literature.

It was printed by the Chōsen Kosho Kankōkai (Society for the Publication of Old Korean Books), an organization that was under the patronage of Japanese authorities, in the newly introduced metal type, which made profitable reproduction and the mass circulation of books possible. The Chōsen Kosho Kankōkai began reprinting old Korean texts in Kyŏngsŏng (Seoul) in 1909 and reprinted dozens of books of Korean literature and history in three phases (24 books from 1909 to 1911, 28 books from 1911 to 1913, 24 books from 1913 to 1916). *P'ahan chip* was printed in 1911 (Meiji 44) as part of the nineteenth volume of the series alongside other collections such as *Pohan chip, Ikchae chip,* Chŏng Yagyong's *P'irŏn kakbi,* and *Tongin sihwa.*[69] Different from the 1659 woodblock-print version, the 1911 metal-type version contains punctuation, which unquestionably simplifies the reading.

A reference to *P'ahan chip* 2:20 can be found in an annotation to a poem by Kim Yunsik (1835–1922) in *Unyang chip* (Collection of Unyang) from 1914,[70] and in November of 1929, *P'ahan chip* was serialized in its *hanmun* original (not like other classical works in Japanese or vernacular Korean translation)[71] over several weeks in the daily newspaper *Chungoe ilbo* (Home and abroad news, 1926–1931). It was here published in a three-week-long series entitled "Tongguk myŏngga *sihwa* chip" (Illustrious *sihwa* collections of the Eastern Country [Korea]; next to *P'ahan chip,* this series also features entries from *Pohan chip*). In the relevant *Chungoe ilbo* issues, various

28 POEMS AND STORIES FOR OVERCOMING IDLENESS

P'ahan chip entries appear partly in full, partly in an abridged form in direct succession and new order (i.e., not the original order of the episodes in the source). The entries were selected, arranged, and commented upon by one Chŏng Insŏ.[72]

In 1926 there was also the interesting case of one poem originally contained in *P'ahan chip* being singled out and presented independently. It is Kim Yŏngbu's (1096–1172) poem *Yugam*, "Stirred by something," from 2:4, which deals with the rise and military expansion of the Jin dynasty, and with a Korean perceiving the Jurchen as an imminent threat to the integrity of the state of Koryŏ. The poem reads:

> Recently I've heard that a neighboring dynasty's power will become
>   dangerous,
> that an expansion of its territory, an extension of its boundaries is
>   imminent.[73]
> My white hair is wind-tossed, frost and snow fall;
> my loyal heart is devoted, ghosts and spirits know.
> Lian Po could still eat [large amounts of rice in his old age], and it
>   wasn't without purpose;[74]
> [Huo] Qubing rejected a mansion, and there was action in that, too.[75]
> Hush, hush, for these innermost thoughts, there is no place to
>   tell them;
> each time I encounter a mug of ale, I get drunk as mud.

This medieval piece dealing with the danger of a perceived "barbarian" neighboring state's aggressive expansion of territory and a Korean's desire to fight for the survival of his country even in old age tellingly features as a representative example for *P'ahan chip* in a mid-1920s issue of the journal *Tonggwang* (Eastern brightness, vol. 7 (1926/11/01): 80), where it appears under the heading "Chasan *sihwa*" (*Sihwa* [collated by] Chasan). Chasan was the sobriquet of colonial modernity literary scholar An Hwak (1886–1946), who authored the first historiography of Korean literature, *Chosŏn munhaksa* (A history of Korean literature, 1922). One might say that it is difficult not to take An's decision to select and cite this specific poem from *P'ahan chip* as a subtle form of criticism vis-à-vis Japanese colonial aggression during the so-called era of Cultural Rule (J. Bunka Seiji).[76]

P'ahan chip is moreover mentioned in the landmark historiography of Korean narrative literature *Chosŏn sosŏlsa* (A history of Korean narrative literature),[77] where Kim T'aejun (1905–ca. 1950) describes the work as a representative example of the "golden era" of Koryŏ literature (this *hwanggŭmgi* being, in Kim's eyes, the reign of King Kojong). Yet similar to the preceding

Chosŏn dynasty sources, which predominantly tend to depict and utilize the collection simply as an old reservoir for miscellaneous information on poetry, people, customs, cultural characteristics, or picturesque spots of Korea's early dynasties, in the *Chosŏn sosŏlsa* chapter "Koryŏ-ŭi p'aegwan munhak-kwa pulgyo munye" (Fictional literature and Buddhist literary art of Koryŏ) Kim T'aejun in the early 1930s likewise did not see the necessity to offer any deeper interpretation of *P'ahan chip* or its author. He writes,

> *P'ahan chip,* just as the title says, is a play with words of a man of letters eliminating idleness. By and large, it may be called [a piece of] *sihwa,* but since [throughout the collection] the old customs of Silla as well as the contemporaneous sceneries and things of Sŏgyŏng [P'yŏngyang] and Kaegyŏng [Kaesŏng] were recorded here and there, as a reader you get drawn into the realm of perfect composition [K. *sammae*].[78]

However, as a number of available sources suggest, only some twenty-odd years later, after liberation, division, and war, when national canonization processes and the study of Korean literature were driven forward independently on both sides of the demarcation line, the way in which both Yi Illo and *P'ahan chip* were academically discussed changed considerably. This change eventually took place in both Koreas, but it happened, one may venture to say, noticeably early in North Korean literary studies. As evidenced in a variety of publications from the time when the *juche* (*chuch'e,* "self-reliance") ideology took form in the late 1950s and early 1960s, North Korean historiographies of Korean literature not only treated Yi Illo's life in a much more detailed, extensive fashion, but increasingly interpreted his writings against the backdrop of biographical, political, and social developments.[79] These literary-historiographical works, in line with the dictated North Korean ideological guidelines of the time, stressed the expression of resistance and struggle against "feudal structures" as a major determining factor for the quality and value of a piece of premodern Korean literature. Some post–Korean War scholars increasingly established a connection between Yi Illo's literature and the political/social transformations that took place in the wake of a decisive event of Koryŏ history: the military coup d'état of 1170 (generally referred to in Korea as *musin chŏngbyŏn* or *kyŏngin ran*). In the autumn of the cyclic year *kyŏngin* (1170), a number of elite members of Koryŏ's stratum of military officials (K. *muban*), joined by some disgruntled civil officials (K. *munban*), turned their long-felt dissatisfaction with the established political and social order into violent dissent by launching an insurrection that swiftly led to the banishment (and eventual assassination) of the reigning King Ŭijong (r.

1146–1170), the first son of King Injong (r. 1122–1146), and the subsequent enthronement of Ŭijong's brother, Myŏngjong (r. 1170–1197), a puppet-king with apparently little authority. When the *muban* thereupon overthrew the government and system traditionally controlled and operated by the civil elites, it was the beginning of a century of military dominion over Koryŏ politics, which ended only with the final acceptance of Mongol supremacy over Koryŏ in 1270.[80] According to lore (substantiated by entries in *Koryŏsa*), the military revolt of 1170 was literally "sparked" by one specific fiery incident: Kim Tonjung (d. 1170), the son of Kim Pusik, is said to have lit up the beard of General Chŏng Chungbu (1106–1179) with a candle in an act of mockery. This humiliating affront is said to have constituted the final, decisive insult after centuries during which military officials had been sidelined by an all-dominant, apparently tyrannical, arrogant civil elite and had been discriminated against in terms of influence, official posts, salaries, and property.[81] Moreover, the beard-burning incident was carried out by none other than the son of Kim Pusik, who as the dominant civil figure in the capital of Kaesŏng in the 1130s had triumphantly led government forces to put down the rebels surrounding the monk Myoch'ŏng in 1135, which led to the prestige of the military establishment having been at a low ebb.[82] Kim Tonjung's barefaced mockery of Chŏng seems to have dynamically mobilized the upper echelons of the military community, and in their resistance to the long-established political and social structures, the *muban* community at first stood together, thereby becoming stronger. Moreover, they built connections with the opposing group by joining forces with certain *munban* and by maintaining the overall administrative structures of the civil state. Thereby they succeeded in creating a movement that shaped power structures in Koryŏ and which eventually proved to endure across an entire century. In the immediate aftermath of the 1170 coup, however, almost three decades of political chaos followed, with different generals and military strongmen vying for power, fighting and murdering one another while gutting the state coffers. Especially in the 1180s, military strongmen of seemingly inferior education, standing, and purportedly also character rose to power, such as Yi Ŭimin (d. 1196), who has come to be viewed as the epitome and embodiment of the treachery and random violence that engulfed the kingdom during that time. Then, in 1196, General Ch'oe Ch'unghŏn seized power and stabilized the dynasty with an iron hand. The house of Ch'oe, first under Ch'oe Ch'unghŏn and then under his son Ch'oe U, eventually went on to de facto rule the dynasty until 1270.

The military revolt of 1170 marked the end of an era, and for the civil elites who were caught in between the ages of civil and military rule, the effects must have been enormous. For many of these intellectuals-in-

TRANSLATOR'S INTRODUCTION   31

between,[83] that is, scholars in a transition state who had grown up acquiring an education and identity during the heyday of traditional civilian rule but spent the rest of their working lives under various *muban* regimes, the sudden loss of power to the military must have been accompanied by a keen sense of loss of dignity. They would not merely have felt alienated from and frustrated by the novel sociopolitical order, but must have experienced a deep estrangement from both values and knowledge of old and new (very similar developments and sentiments we find, I would argue, again among Korean intellectuals during the transitional period in East Asia at the end of the nineteenth century). And in order to come to terms with the abrupt, violent death of their era and the rise of new sociopolitical realities, Yi Illo and other representatives of these mid-twelfth-century "intellectuals-in-between" (who must be separated from younger literati of that century, such as Yi Kyubo [1168–1241], who was born only two years before the coup, came to maturity under military rule, and identified to a much stronger degree with the prevailing political culture) turned to literature, the means of expression they knew best.

A connecting line between the 1170 military revolt and the literature of this age, especially that of Yi Illo and the other members of the Chungnim Kohoe, is, for instance, drawn in the influential historiography of Korean literature *Chosŏn munhak t'ongsa* (A universal history of Korean literature, 1959).[84] Regarding Yi Illo it says,

> However, what is most precious in Ri Illo's poetry, what makes us identify most with it, is his humanitarian pathos [K. *indojuŭijŏk ppap'osŭ*]. Naturally, many works in his poetic oeuvre reveal an escapist tendency influenced by Buddhism and Daoism, but even in the case of these works, his dissident ideas and emotions vis-à-vis the conflict-ridden contemporaneous sociopolitical realities serve as the underlying foundation.[85]

There is, of course, not enough space here to do justice to the complex and complicated subject of how premodern Korean literature was interpreted, evaluated, and translated in the foundational phase of North Korean literary studies.[86] Yet it must be stated that, however agenda- and policy-driven it may have been, the (as far as I can tell) novel approach of regarding Yi Illo essentially as an oppositionist, a dissenter, and interpreting his extant literary works primarily as expressions of his resistance against contemporaneous political rulers and sociopolitical realities — an interpretation, one must note, that was later likewise established in South Korean academia — is thought-provoking.[87] This holds true especially if we take into account that Yi, at least according to all relevant sources on his life, was a conformist

32   Poems and Stories for Overcoming Idleness

and careerist. Moreover, throughout premodern, early modern, and colonial times, the history of the reception of *P'ahan chip*, the only extant cohesive work featuring Yi's original writings, suggests that the collection was by and large read only as a work of literary criticism — that is, criticism *of* literature, not *through* literature. In his "Sŏ *P'ahan chip* hu — *imo*" (Written at the end of *P'ahan chip* — in the cyclic year *imo* [1762]), the eighteenth-century scholar Kim P'irhyŏng (1725–1800) even went so far as to say, "He [Yi Illo] personally experienced the revolts of the cyclic years *kyŏng*[*in*] [1170] and *kye*[*sa*] [1173], and witnessed the changes at court after the drowning in the lake [of King Ŭijong, 1173], but in this book [*P'ahan chip*] there isn't even a single word or half a line [on these tumultuous events]."[88]

Nevertheless, Yi lived during a unique phase in Korean history that saw fundamental transformations of long-established power and status structures, and it is clear that dissent, both open and hidden, forms where power, status, and privileges are challenged and in motion. In light of the source, that is, certain actors, narratives, and poems in *P'ahan chip*, as well as against the backdrop of the kind of people he is known to have socialized with, and the writings some of these close friends and literati acquaintances produced, there are good reasons to examine extant literary works that were, in one way or another, produced by Yi Illo under the aspect of dissent and military-system critique. This approach, which I (with a few small innovative twists) mean to predominantly pursue in the course of this introduction, offers a biographical and historical context against which certain readings of Yi's extant work(s) become possible. Yet this approach is also apt to touch on broader, more persistently relevant issues, which may carry meaning for our age as well.

For one, it can lead to considerations of the advantages of conformity, avenues for nonviolent dissent, and specific modes of (literary) critique vis-à-vis a reigning power elite; moreover, it raises questions regarding the (possibly conflicting) roles and obligations imposed on an individual in a specific society: what economic or political factors, what social pressures or benefits, determine whether a person turns into a conformist, a dissenter, or something in between, someone who intends to express a dissenting private opinion while leading a compliant public life? Moreover, it can cast a light on the relevance of networks, especially literary networks, and the impact of male friendships in a (medieval Korean) society. And it can touch on more general matters related to literature, such as impetuses for the composition, compilation, publication, and circulation of books and collections; the way in which reader- or listenership's levels of (literary) knowledge and experience (or lack thereof) gear the understanding and evaluation of texts; and, connected to this, how the reception and impact of

TRANSLATOR'S INTRODUCTION   33

a book are dependent on original/intended or later/detached audiences and reading environments.

Military Revolt and Military Regimes, a Life of Service in the Center, and a Life of Suffering on the Margins

Yi Illo was a distant relative of the influential high-ranking minister Yi Chayŏn (1003–1061),[89] who was the brother of Yi Illo's great-great-grandfather Yi Chasang, as well as the later infamous Yi Chagyŏm (d. 1126). A member of a branch of the Inju Yi-*ssi*,[90] in-laws of the royal house and for a time one of the most powerful lineages of early Koryŏ, Yi Illo was born in 1152 in the Koryŏ capital of Kaesŏng. For several generations, members of his family had verified their intellectual abilities by having passed the increasingly important civil service examinations in first place as *changwŏn*, "principle graduates," also referred to as *yongdu*, "Dragon Heads" (see 3:10). Yi Illo was born into seemingly ideal social conditions, but in his early youth he also had to deal with a stroke of fate, for his parents are known to have passed away when he was a mere child.

Yi mentions several members of his family in *P'ahan chip*. In 2:18 he relates an anecdote about Yi Chayŏn, while in 2:3 he mentions Yi Chagyŏm (though he only refers to his notorious ancestor as the Duke of Chosŏn). It is known that the high official Yi O (1042–1110; see 2:22) was Yi Illo's great-grandfather,[91] but *Koryŏsa* does not mention the names of either Yi's grandfather or his father. According to the *Inju Yi-ssi sebo* (Genealogy of the Yi family of Inju), however, Yi Illo's grandfather's name was Yi Ŏllim, his paternal uncle (K. *paekpu*) was Yi Kwangjin (d. 1178), and his father's name was Yi Paeksŏn. Yi Kwangjin (see 3:13), who served, for example, as *ch'amji chŏngsa* (assistant executive in political affairs) at the beginning of Myŏngjong's reign, had six sons—Yi Yuin, Yi Yuŭi, Yi Yujik, Yi Yuryang, Yi Yugyŏng, and Yi Yuon. In 3:20, Yi Illo mentions Yi Yugyŏng and refers to him as his "paternal younger male cousin"; other people who are talked about as "cousins" are a chief monk, Ch'ŏllim, as well as a certain minister of state, Ch'oe (see 1:14). Another uncle of Yi Illo's was the poet-monk Yoil (n.d.; see 2:24), who also served as his foster father after the early death of his parents. By the time he was thirty years of age, Yi Illo must have been married, though not a single word pertaining to his wife can be found in any of the extant sources. It is known, however, that his father-in-law was a person by the name of Ch'oe Yŏngyu (n.d.), who in 1182 went as felicitation envoy on the occasion of the New Year (K. Hajŏngsa) to the Jurchen Jin dynasty. According to a poem titled *Chŭng Misu che sŭng Ch'anji* (Presented

34   POEMS AND STORIES FOR OVERCOMING IDLENESS

to Misu's younger brother, the monk Ch'anji), which was written by Yi's close friend Im Ch'un (n.d.), Yi Illo had a younger brother who at one point was a Buddhist monk and went by the dharma name of Ch'anji. Moreover, as can be seen in episode 3:10, Yi had three legitimate sons, Chŏng, Yang, and On. He had additional (perhaps illegitimate) sons in Yi Kyun and Yi Sehwang (the person who penned the epilogue of *P'ahan chip* and with whose help the collection was first printed in 1260), who are mentioned neither in *P'ahan chip* nor in *Koryŏsa*.[92] In addition, in the epilogue to *P'ahan chip* it also says that Yi Illo had a young granddaughter who was staying at his house when he passed away in Hongdojŏng Village.

Thus, his family background reveals that Yi, the offspring of a lineage of privileged, well-to-do metropolitan intellectuals, grew up in a hybrid environment marked by Buddhism, a pillar of Koryŏ society and the primary foundation of religious legitimation of the dynasty, but also characterized by thorough Confucian education and learning (see 3:28), with all efforts and labors geared toward success in the prestigious civil service examinations, which served as one gateway to officialdom and political participation. In these surroundings, he naturally came into contact with and befriended other young men who had similar regional, social, and educational backgrounds and who were in a similar life situation. *P'ahan chip* bears witness to this, for one of its most striking features is the various entries dealing with the lives and literatures of Yi Illo's friends from the early stages of his life, in other words, the other members of the Chungnim Kohoe.

This now famous group of literati friends who were different in age and social position but had mutual ideas and visions of poetry was also known as Haejwa Ch'irhyŏn, "Seven Worthies from [the Country] Left of the [Yellow] Sea," and Kangjwa Ch'irhyŏn, "Seven Worthies from [the Country] Left of the [Yalu] River."[93] The designation "High Gathering of the Bamboo Grove" derived from the poet society's model organization, Zhulin Qixian, the "Seven Worthies of the Bamboo Grove," from third-century China.[94] Besides Yi Illo himself, members of the Chungnim Kohoe were O Sejae (b. 1133), Im Ch'un, Cho T'ong (n.d.), Hwangbo Hang (n.d.), Ham Sun (n.d.), and Yi Tamji (n.d.).[95] Yi Illo appears to have been quite close with all of them, but his dearest friend was undoubtedly Im Ch'un.

The exact dates of Im Ch'un, courtesy name Kiji, are unknown, yet he is generally thought to have been born at the beginning of the reign of Ŭijong, around 1148, and to have died around the twentieth year of the reign of Myŏngjong, at the age of approximately forty.[96] Im Ch'un, almost two hundred of whose pieces—poems, letters, discussions, and even prose works[97]—are extant today, was hailed as a prodigious poet in his youth, but his literary works, in fact, survived and were transmitted to posterity

TRANSLATOR'S INTRODUCTION   35

only through the efforts of Yi Illo, who more than two decades after Im's death assembled his friend's texts and put them together into a collection of six volumes, the *Sŏha sŏnsaeng chip* (Collected works of Teacher Sŏha), also known as *Im Sŏha chip* (Collected works of Im Sŏha; *ISC*) or simply *Sŏha chip* (Collected works of Sŏha).

That Yi Illo and Im Ch'un were very close shows in the fact that in *P'ahan chip* Im Ch'un is regularly affectionately referred to as *ou* Kiji, "my friend Kiji."[98] Yi and Im were from the same Kaesŏng circles of well-learned, well-off civil officials, they had devoted their childhoods and teenage years to the diligent study of poetry and classical literature, and both surely envisioned successful futures for themselves, smooth roads to office, active political participation, and also, of course, personal wealth. Yet their lives and careers were (at least in part) derailed when, from one day to the next, the political and social power relations in Koryŏ were turned upside down in the wake of the military revolt of the cyclic year *kyŏngin,* and there arose an unstable era in which the dynasty time and again stood at the brink of complete disintegration and utter chaos. In the aftermath of the initial 1170 coup, when the military officials were out for revenge for decades of marginalization and mockery by the literati officials, many of the members of the civil elite were attacked, ousted, killed, or forced to go into hiding. Yi Illo and Im Ch'un were no exceptions in this regard.

In Yi Illo's biography in *Koryŏsa* it says that "during Chŏng Chungbu's revolt he cut off his hair [and became a Buddhist monk] in order to escape [the dangerous situation in the capital], but when the revolt was pacified he returned to the mundane world." It seems as though his family was spared during the insurrection on account of having acted in a more measured, respectful manner toward the men of the military in the years leading up to the coup (see 3:13). Still, when civil officials were being hunted down in Kaesŏng during the upheaval, Yi fled to take shelter with the person who had raised him and who certainly embodied a father figure, namely, his deceased father's younger brother, the monk Yoil, abbot of Hŭngwang Temple, who hid his now hairless stepson for several years in the safety of high Buddhist circles and the seclusion of a mountain temple.[99] Yoil is known to have been a close acquaintance, longtime adviser, and distant relative of King Myŏngjong (see 2:25), and due to these connections was apparently able to offer his nephew protective shelter.

Yet after having spent a few years in hiding, Yi Illo reemerged: in 1175 he passed the examination at the National University (K. Kukchagamsi), studied at the National Academy (K. Kukhak), and in 1180, at the age of twenty-nine, passed the metropolitan civil service examinations with highest honors as Dragon Head. Yi Illo was thereby recognized as the country's

36   POEMS AND STORIES FOR OVERCOMING IDLENESS

premier young poet of his class. The examination was presided over by Min Yŏngmo (1115–1194). Though Yi Illo was his *munsaeng* (examination passer), Min Yŏngmo, Yi's *chongbaek* (examination administrator), is mentioned in neither *P'ahan chip* nor any of Yi Illo's other extant writings from *Tongmunsŏn*.[100]

Shortly after his great success in the examinations, Yi was appointed to his first office as Kyeyang *kwan'gi* (secretary of Kyeyang; modern-day Puch'ŏn). Thus, from the beginning of the second decade of military rule, he ventured forth on the path of officialdom. A bit earlier, in 1182, he was even granted the honor of going north to the Jurchen Jin as a member of the retinue of his father-in-law, Ch'oe Yŏngyu. He did so in the official position of *sŏjanggwan* (document officer), and, at least according to Yi Sehwang's epilogue, as a poet left such a lasting impression on the literati of the Northern dynasty that later Jin envoys to Korea would regularly ask about his life and career. To be able to embark on a journey beyond the borders of Korea and enter into foreign lands was an extraordinary event in the life of any scholar in premodern times, and it can be surmised that Yi, who was still a relatively young man at this point, gathered many unique impressions and experiences in the polyethnic Northern dynasty. Here one must note that his visit to the Chinese (i.e., not very tribal Jurchen) environment of the Central Capital (modern Beijing, which served as the Jin capital from 1153 to 1214) coincided with the relatively peaceful, politically stable period of the so-called High Jin, the era of the reign of Emperor Shizong (r. 1161–1189), during which learning, culture, and belles lettres flourished and some of the dynasty's greatest literati were educated.[101] There certainly could not have been a better time for a Koryŏ intellectual to travel there.

Yi Illo was first appointed to serve at the prestigious Hallim Academy in 1185, then was reappointed in 1189. He stayed there until 1194, then advanced to the higher-status office of *yebu* wŏnwoerang (vice director of the Ministry of Rites) during the reign of King Sinjong (r. 1197–1204), in other words, the early stage of the de facto rule of Ch'oe Ch'unghŏn. In 1199 he returned to the Hallim-wŏn, though it is unclear whether he served at the academy while simultaneously being employed at the Ministry of Rites. Yi's career hereafter appears to have taken a hit, for he subsequently served as magistrate of Maengsŏng in P'yŏngan Province, most likely from 1203 to 1205, when the Ch'oe regime had consolidated its power. This appointment to govern a place in the deep north, where he was even forced to perform exhausting manual labor (see 1:3), may well have been a demotion, perhaps even a form of political exile (in 3:14, for instance, being sent out to govern a faraway region is clearly portrayed as a banishment in disguise). In the final passage of 2:21, Yi leaves no doubt that this time away from the capital and his family weighed heavily on him. Years later, in 1212, when he was already in his early sixties, Yi was appointed *nangjung* (office chief). Thereafter, during the reign of King Kojong, he served in such offices as *pisŏgam* (director of the Palace Library) and *chwa kanŭi taebu* (left grand master of remonstrance),[102] thereby eventually reaching rank 3. In this final phase of his life he was also *pomun-gak haksa* (academician of the tower of precious letters) and worked at the Office for Drafting Proclamations, where he served as *chijego* (drafter of proclamations), an office in which he formulated the official proclamations of the king. In addition, it is known that he was to serve as examiner in the civil service examinations but that he passed away before this could be realized.

Curiously, in his biography in *Koryŏsa* it says, "He was famous for his poetry during that time, but by nature he was partial [or narrow-minded] and impetuous [K. *p'yŏn'gŭp*], and since he stood in opposition [K. *o; C. wu*] to the contemporaneous world, he was not made great use of." His official career, however, does show that he progressively rose in rank and that by the time of his death in 1220, Yi had offered continuous service to different military regimes and strongmen in various mid- to higher-level positions of the upper echelons of Koryŏ bureaucracy for almost forty years. His life path, I think, contradicts the statement from *Koryŏsa*. Certainly, especially bearing in mind that early in his career he was selected principal graduate (K. *changwŏn*), it does seem curious that he never reached any of the truly powerful offices. All in all, however, one may say not only that Yi weathered the political storm of 1170 more or less unscathed, but also that in terms of official service and accumulated merit he indeed flourished under the new conditions and decision makers. However, during this age of military domination, the road back to the capital was not as smooth for all of the literati who had met disaster during the early 1170s.

Let us, for instance, examine the case of Im Ch'un. Though Im's clan may not have been as prestigious as that of his friend Yi Illo (he was a clansman of the Yech'ŏn Im-*ssi*), he was nevertheless from a family of civil officials based in Kaesŏng. Yet when he was around the age of twenty, many of his closest relatives were purged and killed in the wake of the military coup.[103] The Im family's wealth and land were quickly expropriated after the revolt by the new rulers, and as a result, Im Ch'un was plunged into abject poverty. In contrast to Yi Illo, however, Im Ch'un did not leave the capital helter-skelter to flee to a safe hideout in the mountains, but is known to have stayed on for another four or five years, after which he was finally forced to make his escape to the south of the Korean Peninsula, around 1175. What might have prompted him to linger in Kaesŏng in the face of life-threatening danger and poverty? For one, he may have meant to bide his time and simply

38   POEMS AND STORIES FOR OVERCOMING IDLENESS

hold out, perhaps expecting military rule to crumble as a result of either the peasant and slave uprisings that erupted between 1172 and 1176[104] or the turf wars that incessantly raged among the various military leaders pursuant to the takeover. On the other hand, some of his poems seem to suggest that he was, in one way or another, involved in the growing anti-military-government movement of the early 1170s, perhaps even in the countercoup attempts that repeatedly took place during that time.[105] As violence by the military begat violence by certain civil elites, in 1173 an armed uprising led by Kim Podang (d. 1173), who had intended to kill the two generals Chŏng Chungbu and Yi Ŭibang (d. 1174) and envisioned restoring the authority of both the toppled King Ŭijong and the civil elites, took place in the northeastern border region.[106] Kim Podang's revolt was quickly suppressed and the rebel leaders executed. The same happened in a subsequent revolt led by Cho Wich'ong (d. 1176) in 1174, who also mustered troops in the northern region and attempted to fight the new Kaesŏng government but was swiftly repressed as well.[107] When these rebellions were quashed, numerous civil officials involved in the incidents, and even high ministers such as Han Ŏn'guk (d. 1173), were killed. As extant sources clearly show, the situation for individuals who had supported or actively participated in the attempted overthrows, or intellectuals openly critical of the military regime, became unbearably perilous. For instance, with regard to Kim Podang's attempted countercoup, the purging of civil officials and their families, as well as the overall violent, retaliatory atmosphere of the years after the military coup, Yi Chehyŏn writes the following in the first entry of the second fascicle of *Yŏgong p'aesŏl:*

> In the final year of King Ŭi[jong], Chŏng Chungbu, Yi Ŭibang, and Yi Ko [d. 1171] staged a revolt and moved the king to Kŏje. Among the [civil] ministers at court, many met disaster. Also, when their [the civil officials'] families were about to be slain [by the military officials], General-in-Chief [K. Taejanggun] Chin Chun [d. 1179] said, "Those [civil officials] who we [men of the military] hated and utterly despised were Han Noe [n.d.], Yi Pokki [d. 1170], and a few others — but, really, all in all they weren't more than four or five people. With regard to the killing of the guiltless [ministers], it has already been excessive — but now you even want to kill their wives and children?" And using his powers, he forbade it. Four years later, Kim Podang mustered troops, planning a restoration [of Ŭijong], but he failed. And again, all of the men of letters [K. *munsa*] were sought out and murdered — both center and periphery roiled in turbulence, and no one was safe both day and night. Assistant Commander [K. Nangjang] Kim Pu [n.d.] thereupon said to Chŏng [Chungbu] and Yi [Ŭibang], "Heaven's will

cannot be known, and the heart of the people cannot be fathomed. Since we have simply relied on force and not considered righteousness, we have indiscriminately slaughtered numerous caps and gowns [civil officials] — in the world, how then could [vengeful literati such as] Kim Podang be few in number [under such violent circumstances]? Those among us [men of the military] who have sons and daughters ought to be commanded to form marriage ties with the houses of scribal clerks [K. *munsa; C. wenli*; meant are the *mun'gwan* (C. *wenguan*), the civil service officials] in order to set their minds at ease. That would be a path which could be walked upon for a very long time." The group [of generals] followed his words. Only hereafter did this catastrophe slowly come to an end.[108]

It can be presumed that in these years marked by unrest and violent antagonism, Im Ch'un was an oppositionist intellectual who had in some form joined the restorationist, anti-government movement, and this may also explain why, as can be seen in the following quote, no one was willing to offer him help or shelter in the mid-1170s, why even his remaining relatives shied away from him. He simply appears to have been dangerous company. In the letter *Yŏ Hong Kyosŏ sŏ* (Letter given to Hong Kyosŏ) Im writes,

> From the time I experienced calamity, many a time I trod forward and stumbled backward, went into hiding, sought refuge with people, and asked for help! But they all treated me like a dog or a swine, and disregarded me entirely. For this reason, when I lived in the capital, for five years the hunger and cold became worse and worse. Even among my next of kin there wasn't anyone who would have opened his door for me. Eventually I took my family and went east with them.[109]

Many years later, when Im had already been dead for more than two decades, Yi Illo set out to gather Im Ch'un's literary works and collate the *Sŏha chip,* and, next to a preface he also composed, and included a sacrificial address to his friend, the *Pu Yi Misu che Im sŏnsaeng mun* (Attached sacrificial address of Teacher Im by Yi Misu), which reveals that Yi had been well aware of the difficult circumstances his closest friend had been plunged into after his flight from the capital. He writes,

> Wherever you dwelled, you never had a blackened chimney,[110] and when you were traveling you wailed at the end of each trail.[111] But you didn't let poverty and peril alter any of your standards. [...] Dark anger filled your chest, meanderingly entwined like clouds and rainbows. [...] The anger and resentment over you not having been granted the red cassia

40   POEMS AND STORIES FOR OVERCOMING IDLENESS

[i.e., success in the civil service examinations] shall remain until the end of Heaven and earth.[112]

As is evidenced in these lines, even throughout the years of exile and hardship in the south of the Korean Peninsula, Im Ch'un never gave up hope of fulfilling his life's preeminent goal, namely, successful participation in the civil service examinations, and by that a definite verification of his value and standard as a scholar and intellectual. According to his letter *Yŏ Wang Yakchu sŏ* (Letter given to Wang Yakchu), Im returned north to Kaesŏng to take part in the 1180 civil service examinations, but in the end was unable to do so on account of some alleged illness.[113] He voiced his frustration with this situation in the poem *Pyŏngjung yu kam* (Stirred by something while in sickness), which reads,

> Year after year, the examinations are opened but passed by in vain;
> as I'm approaching old age, I'm still hale and hearty.
> [Success in] the civil service examinations has always been obtained
>   by eminent scholars;
> among the high lords of state, who'd be willing to recommend an un-
>   talented one [like me]?
> The long behemoth wants to rouse [the waters], but the waves and
>   billows have already run dry;
> the ailing crane longs to fly [up into the sky], but its wings are already
>   broken.
> It has been there all along, the region east of the river where I lived in
>   seclusion;
> I pity myself — my hair is all white, and now I'm going back there.[114]

At the same time, Yi Illo, who had reemerged a few years earlier, not only passed these very same national examinations, but did so in the highly prestigious rank of principle graduate.[115] Im congratulated Yi on his success with a poem titled *Chaksi ha Yi changwŏn Misu* (Composing a poem to congratulate Principal Graduate Yi Misu), but in this piece he also bemoans his own failure, noting that while Yi rises like the majestic Peng in the north (i.e., Kaesŏng), he himself must take flight like a magpie and escape toward the mountains of the south.[116] Overall, Im Ch'un, who was later famed as one of the finest poets of the entire Koryŏ period, failed three times in the field of literary composition (K. *chesulgwa*) in the civil service examinations and was never successful.[117]

Yet although their lives developed in radically different directions, Im and Yi stayed lifelong friends, and there are quite a number of poems and letters by both Kiji and Misu that display their mutual deeply felt affection. For instance, there is Im's poem *Yuhoe Misu* (Misu on my mind), which reads in part, "It has been such a long time since we parted, / but everywhere I go I have to bear that sorrow [of missing you]."[118] Yi Illo, on the other hand, composed the poem *Chŭng sau* (Presented to my four friends; these friends are Im Ch'un, Cho T'ong, Yi Tamji, and a monk by the dharma name of Chongnyŏng), in which he speaks about their shared past and present, writing the following about Im, his "friend in poetry" (K. *si u*):

> Long ago we belonged to the [capital's] literary circles,
> competing for fame, bravely you sought [to make a name for
>   yourself] first.
> I had early on escaped the sharp-edged spear-tip;
> and you, too, got enough of the venomous hand.[119]
> These days you loathe spears and shields,
> and when we meet, we only call for ale.
> Should make the pair of birds stop crying;
> ought to remember the two tigers fighting.
> > > *[The poem] to the right [in the source] is for Im Kiji,*
> > > > *my friend in poetry.*[120]

When Im lived "in the southland," meaning predominantly in the Kyŏngsang area, Yi Illo appears to have frequently visited him, and the two friends seem to have enjoyed discussing and drinking together.[121] Nevertheless, Yi does not seem to have had any means to help or support his friend with regard to a better life, financially or in terms of social standing, before Im's untimely death, which may well have been caused by the harsh conditions he had lived under. Against this backdrop, one cannot but wonder what Yi Illo felt vis-à-vis his best friend (before and after his passing), with whom he claimed to be "like glue and varnish" but from whom, at the same time, he was also far apart in many respects. Did he feel sorry for neglecting his friend, for having been unable to improve Im's situation while he was still alive? Yi Illo did hold comparatively high offices and was part of a network of influential civil government representatives for about ten years before Im passed away, but he never seems to have been in a position to assist in his recovery and social/official reintegration (according to O Sejae's biography in *Koryŏsa*, Yi Illo did try his best to heave O into office, but without success; see fascicle 3, note 204). Or, perhaps keenly aware that Im had been sidelined on account of his participation in the civil resistance movements, did he feel embarrassed for having holed up at his uncle's mountain monastery, only to resurface and blithely pursue a career under the later infamous military

42   POEMS AND STORIES FOR OVERCOMING IDLENESS

regime of the 1180s controlled by Yi Ŭimin? Or was he perhaps guilt-ridden for having, in fact, profited from the 1170 military revolt, which essentially led to the elimination of numerous capable literati such as Im Ch'un, who— if they had been granted the time, leisure, and material security to continue focusing on their studies under the guidance of a well-connected mentor in the same way Yi had done in the calm, safe surroundings of Hŭngwang Temple—unquestionably could have posed as serious rivals in the civil service examinations and, ultimately, in the race for the few well-paying, leading positions in the central bureaucracy? Since appointments to office (let alone high office) were rare, the competition among the scores of successful examination passers must have been fierce (a situation Yi describes in detail in 3:23).[122] And one has to bear in mind that many potential competitors for the limited government positions that could actually be obtained through success in the civil service examinations (and not through the *ŭm*-system of inheritance of posts)[123] had left the capital after the military revolt and were later, like Im Ch'un, continuously disregarded in the examinations or, like O Sejae,[124] ignored in the process of appointment to office despite having passed the *kwagŏ*.

The case of Yi Illo is murky, indistinct—there seems to have existed a tension between his official loyalties and obligations and his personal convictions and bonds. He certainly profited from the overall political and bureaucratic transformations, quietly played along, and steadily rose in rank. Then again, while as a minister he "did what the others did," as a poet and author he appears to not have "thought what the others thought."[125] For in much of his extant literature, a decidedly dissident stance and tone can be detected. Against the backdrop of some of his poetry and prose, Yi can be claimed to have held critical views concerning the political developments and the contemporaneous recruitment system similar to those of Im Ch'un (see 2:3), and it may be surmised that these shared sentiments bridged the gaps in geography and lifestyle, and perhaps served as the foundation for their persistent friendship. In *Tongmunsŏn* we find, for example, the poem *Sok haengno nan* (Hard traveling—a continuation [of Li Bai's poem by the same title]), where in the third stanza Yi laments that refined scholars (here embodied by Yan Hui, the favorite disciple of Confucius) have to live in misery and poverty while uncivil men (represented by the greedy, violent Robber Zhi from *Zhuangzi* who disregarded all proper human norms and even threatened to butcher Confucius into mincemeat if he dared to linger on) live a haughty life of power and luxury during a thoroughly crooked age:

> Yan [Hui], out in a back alley, with his arm as a pillow and but a
>   single bamboo plate of food,[126]

[while atop Mount] Dongling, [Robber Zhi][127] minced and munched a
   human liver in broad daylight.
All that happens in this day and age is truly wistful and sad;
the upright Way has always caused men difficulties.[128]

Rebellious Ministers, a Painting of Chinyang, and Oxen in the Red Room

Yi Illo's criticism is also reflected on multiple levels in *P'ahan chip*. As a work
from the *sihwa* genre, *P'ahan chip* is of course, first and foremost, a work of
poetic criticism. Yet its criticism is not limited to the realm of literary writing
alone. For in *P'ahan chip*, which, as I argue in the following paragraphs, was
geared toward a readership with a very specific educational and social back-
ground, one can discover quite a number of entries, passages, and poems
that may be interpreted as indirect, veiled critiques of contemporaneous
political and social issues, people, and institutions. Here one must bear in
mind that *P'ahan chip* was regarded as belonging to a genre of informal, an-
ecdotal literature. The seemingly random, casual literary *sihwa* form, which
was accepted to contain the expression of individual experiences and per-
sonal opinions, offered him a suitable literary framework to subtly present
his criticism in a by-the-way, ostensibly trivial manner. We see this, for
example, in 3:24, where he casually writes about plants (specifically a tan-
gerine tree from the southland that he happened to catch a glimpse of in the
royal flower garden) and then skillfully weaves his criticism of the selection
and treatment of officials into the flow of the narration.

Yi's critical attitude can be detected in both *si* and *hwa* of *P'ahan chip*. For
instance, his dissatisfaction with the situation in the capital and his desire to
leave behind the burdensome, stressful official society under military rule
are reflected in his highly interesting palindrome poem in 1:16 (in which
he compares himself to the slowly drying, dying fish from *Zhuangzi* 26.2),
in his poem composed upon a monk's request at Angam Temple in 1:7, or
in the contextualizing story of 1:14, which today counts among the most
well-known episodes of the entire collection. Apparently unable to bear the
pressure in Kaesŏng any longer, in 1:14 Yi describes how as a young man
he traveled with his cousin to the Chiri Mountains in the southwest of the
Korean Peninsula, determined to shun the degenerate world. At Chiri-san he
had envisioned finding and then escaping to Ch'ŏnghak Grotto, a legendary
paradisiacal realm equal to the fabulous land behind the Peach Blossom
Spring, a hidden place of bliss and righteousness to which, according to Tao
Yuanming's (365–427) famous *Taohuayuan ji* (A record of Peach Blossom
Spring), people of the Qin dynasty (221–207 BCE), worn out by the chaos of

44   POEMS AND STORIES FOR OVERCOMING IDLENESS

their war-ridden era, had once fled in the hope of finding protection from sorrow and suffering. Yet after having roamed the gorgeous mountains with their secluded valleys and raging waterfalls for some time, Yi finally realizes that Ch'ŏnghak Grotto simply cannot be found, that it is as imaginary as that spring in Wuling, that an otherworldly sphere where intellectuals can take shelter does not exist, and that consequently escape from the apparently crooked, violent age is impossible. "When I had read this [*Taohuayuan*] *ji* [before], I hadn't yet been mature enough," he remarks in a somewhat disillusioned manner after rereading the Chinese work at the end of the episode, thereby admitting that while he had taken Tao Yuanming as his guiding mentor at a younger age (just as Yi Illo's model Su Shi, himself a dissident poet, intellectual, and scholar aesthetic,[129] had done), he now understood that he must integrate himself into the prevalent society and perhaps look for other paths to express his criticism.

But Yi does not speak only about himself: at various points throughout the collection, he also discusses the literatures and lives of people known to have stood in opposition to the governments or rulers of their respective times. Some of these rebellious ministers either lived before him or died when Yi Illo was still young. For instance, though he is apparently reluctant or by convention not allowed to mention his full name, Yi praises the poetry of Chŏng Chisang (see 1:22, 3:30), who was alleged to have been involved in the rebellion of the monk Myoch'ŏng staged in P'yŏngyang and who was executed in 1135; he admiringly recounts anecdotes about the upright, frank minister Kim Sinyun and cites Kim's poetry critical of the state of the dynasty under Ŭijong (see 2:29); he writes about the counterrevolutionary Han Ŏn'guk, at whose old study on Mount Yong he even says he spent a night while on his way to take up his first official position in Kyeyang some ten years after Han's execution (see 1:24); he brings to mind the remonstrance of his benefactor Mun Kŭkkyŏm (1122–1189), who criticized the administrative performance, political decisions, and general quality of government of Ŭijong, an apparently bon vivant king allegedly prone to bad habits who might have averted the military revolt if he had only listened to Mun's advice (see 2:1); he tells of the sad life and bitter literature of Paegunja Sinjun, a dissident Confucian official who turned his back on Chŏng Chungbu's military regime and chose to spend the rest of his life as a Buddhist monk in the mountains (see 3:9, 3:18); and he generally paints a rather grim picture of the standard of living of many lower-level or unemployed literati who must eke out a living in poverty (see, for example, 3:13).

Let us now take a closer look at some of the poetry cited in *P'ahan chip*. The first poem in the collection is, in fact, a verse composed *by* a military official, an otherwise completely unknown person by the name of Chŏng

Yŏryŏng, who served in the position of *kunbu ch'ammo*, "counselor in military command." Episode 1:1 shows this aide to a military commander composing a poem on a painting of Chinyang at the house of Yi Chijŏ (1092–1145), a "great minister" of the early twelfth century (see 2:5) who was famed for his upright character, his refusal to subordinate himself to opportunistic, unworthy leaders, and his opposition to some of the most politically powerful people of his time. Yet as elucidated in the quote that follows, this poem by the military man Chŏng in 1:1 turns out to be clumsy and inept.[130] Yet Yi Illo, tongue in cheek, goes on to say that "all in attendance [Yi Chijŏ included] were awed by his [Chŏng's] exquisite poetic finesse and his superb literary skillfulness."[131] That Chŏng's poem must really have been considered a rather crude piece of amateurism can be deduced from a remark in the thirteenth volume of *Chibong yusŏl* (Classified essays of Chibong; completed in 1614) by Yi Sugwang (1563–1628), for here it says,

> In Koryŏ, Chŏng Yŏryŏng was a person from Chinju. Early on he had seen a painting of Chinju on the wall of somebody's house. He wrote the following poem: "Dots of green mountains pillowed on an emerald lake; / the master says, 'This here's a painting of Chinyang.' / Thatched huts by the water — who knows how many? / In their midst is my cottage, but on the painting — it's not there!" During that age it was referred to as a beautiful composition, but the second line isn't beautiful at all.

Aside from the fact that the poem's second line, *kong ŏn ch'a si chinyang-do*, probably just was not the most refined line in the eyes of a Chosŏn literatus, this statement may also have to be read against the backdrop of information given earlier in the relevant *P'ahan chip* entry, namely, the military man's failure to recognize and respond to an allusion to a *Shijing* passage made by Yi Chijŏ (who does not simply say, "This here's a painting of Chinyang," but rather alludes to the "homeland of mulberry and catalpa"). Chŏng is thereby clearly made out as uneducated in the authoritative Confucian classics. Interestingly, in the scholarship, the initial *P'ahan chip* entry has generally been taken at face value. For instance, in his seminal *Han'guk munhak t'ongsa*, Cho Tongil offers the following interpretation:

> In this book [*P'ahan chip*] there is no preface. [Yi Illo] did not put up any general discussion at the beginning of the text, but straightaway enters with an anecdote. A person by the name of Chŏng Yŏryŏng, who is otherwise not known to us at all, views a painting of the scenery of his homeland and impromptu writes a well-structured poem, making renowned scholars of that age sigh in admiration. If one wants to ascribe

46   Poems and Stories for Overcoming Idleness

> any hidden meaning to an opening such as this, it would have to be that it is impossible to pass judgment on literary talent by the outer appearance [of a person] alone.[132]

In view of the previously quoted text from *Chibong yusŏl,* however, this evaluation of the quality of Chŏng Yŏryŏng's verse, as well as the overall theory regarding Yi's thought process behind his decision to open his collection with this specific episode, can indeed be called into question. For against the backdrop of *P'ahan chip* as a whole, it seems much more likely that this entry constitutes blatant irony, that Yi—emulating Yi Chijŏ—really meant to ridicule the simpleminded, unlearned, pretentious military official in the most prominent position of all, at the very beginning of his work. Yet there may be another layer of critical meaning here: for the topic of Chŏng's poem, the region of Chinyang (present-day Chinju in Southern Kyŏngsang Province, South Korea) was actually the *sigŭp* (salary land) of Ch'oe Ch'unghŏn and his family, that is, the people who de facto ruled Koryŏ during the time when Yi Illo finished and collated *P'ahan chip.* The area of Chinyang was formally granted to Ch'oe Ch'unghŏn by the king in 1205, and this *sigŭp* was later even passed on to his son and successor, Ch'oe U (who was invested Chinyang-hu, "Marquis of Chinyang"). Since taxes and labor service were paid directly to the *sigŭp* holder and not to the throne, the area not only made the Ch'oes rich but also made the family financially independent from the state. Chinyang, where Ch'oe Ch'unghŏn also must have trained and stationed his private army, thus essentially formed the clan's power base and economic foundation, and it became a major factor during the solidification of Ch'oe rule in the 1210s.[133] That Chinyang, albeit decades prior to becoming Ch'oe Ch'unghŏn's stronghold, serves as the setting and underlying topic of the initial entry of *P'ahan chip* is certainly no coincidence. Like Yi Chijŏ, Yi Illo shows up a man of the military as ignorant and incompetent, and by explicitly linking this mockery to the region of Chinyang (which in the first sentence Yi announces to be an "ancient imperial capital"), by extension he can be argued to have attacked the ruling Ch'oe Clan through a benign-seeming, wolf-in-sheep's-clothing text (which, just as in the case of the *Shijing* line quoted by Yi Chijŏ, the *muban* would not be able to understand).[134] Thereby, I think, he essentially sets the tone for the entire collection in the very first entry (in the second entry he straightaway establishes a connection with the collection's underlying structural model, *Lengzhai yehua*). Moreover, this first entry may also be viewed in relation to the supposed original final entry, 3:32, at the end of which he says that, as a civil official, he possesses innate brilliant abilities in the composition of literature—abilities that could never be acquired by a man of the military.

Another poem cited by Yi that can be read as veiled criticism of the *muban* per se and perhaps the Ch'oe Clan in particular is the first of the anonymous verse compositions featured in 2:13:

> Pyŏngna noin Kŏbi said to me, "Once I spotted a quatrain written on the wall of a post pavilion.
>
> > The sun in autumn as radiant and warm as the sun in spring,
> > bamboo-leaves and plantains set off against a whitewashed wall.
> > Don't you boast toward this gentleman about the size of your leaves,
> > for this gentleman shall laugh at you when the frost is near."

Traditionally, the bamboo serves as a symbol for the cultured scholar-offi-cial, the literatus, or simply the "gentleman." Plantains, on the other hand, are in some Chinese texts associated with soldiers and military invasions.[135] This lyrical work could thus be taken as an allusion to the military officials in power, who, like the plantains, are excessively boastful about their self-presumed might, and the subdued stratum of civil officials, represented by the bamboo. The anonymous poet here may have insinuated that, as the (political) climate changes, the plantains/military, which appeared so powerful and grand at one point, will inevitably wither, while the resilient bamboo/literati, which may seem frail at first but does not easily break or perish, will eventually have the last laugh.

But Yi Illo went a step further, for some of his own poetry in *P'ahan chip* may also be interpreted as critiques of contemporaneous political and social developments. For instance, his "poem on historical themes" (K. *yŏngsa si*) from 1:12 seems to have served as a means to "merge tears with ink," to ar-tistically camouflage his disapproval of the state of affairs at court under military domination while still making his dissent "plain to see" for any educated contemporary reader.

Of relevance in this framework is also episode 1:20, which deals with a poetry competition held on the occasion of an auspicious blue cow having been presented to the court by the stationmaster of Ch'ŏnggyo Postal Relay Station. Here it says,

> At the beginning of the reign of King Ŭi[jong], the stationmaster of Ch'ŏnggyo Postal Relay Station had raised a blue cow, the appearance of which was unique and unusual. And so, he presented it to the court.
>
> The king commanded all of the rhetorical ministers close by to compose rhapsodies and poems [on the topic of this auspicious animal] and come up with rhymes, but the [complicated] rhyme pattern put [the literati

48   POEMS AND STORIES FOR OVERCOMING IDLENESS

officials] in a precarious position, and there was no one who didn't seem embarrassed. Kim Hyosun of the Eastern Bureau then won first place, while Sin Ŭngnyong of the Jade Hall came next. [...]

Sŏha Im Chongbi, likewise, was a gifted scholar. When he heard about this he gave a sigh, saying, "If I'd been made to participate in this venue, I should've written the following:

> In Peach Grove you were let loose in spring, then marched into the
> Red Room."

Yet in the end he did not manage to come up with a corresponding line. Now I mean to emulate and continue it.

> On the isles of the Silver Stream you pursued an immortal woman;
> the black peony flower reached Snow Hall.[136]
> On Hangu [Pass] you returned at dawn, floating along in purple
> vapors;
> in Peach Grove you were let loose in spring, then marched into the
> Red Room.

Yi's poem can be read in different ways: on the one hand, simply as a piece filled with allusions to cow-related episodes from ancient Chinese history and literature, yet on the other hand also as a lyrical expression of Yi Illo's intellectual dissent vis-à-vis the initial leaders of the military revolt who had stormed the palace, overthrown the king, and ousted or made compliant the civil officials in 1170. The information given in the surface narration that causes a reader to stumble and which can therefore be viewed as an indicator, a trigger for an underlying subtext, is the sudden appearance of Im Chongbi, who heaves a deep sigh when thinking of Ŭijong's verse competition (clearly in disapproval, not admiration). The Hallim academician Im Chongbi, who most likely died during the 1170 military revolt, was the uncle and personal tutor of Im Ch'un, and thus one may surmise that the line "in Peach Grove you were let loose in spring, then marched into the Red Room" was recited to Yi Illo by Im in a private setting. One could consequently detect two layers in this episode: a surface layer depicting an official realm at Ŭijong's court, and a subsurface layer relating to a private sphere. On this subtextual level, the cow in its various forms in the episode's second part would stand in for the intruding military officials rushing in like raging bulls, while the Weaver Maid (i.e., a cultured woman), Su Shi's studio Snow Hall (C. Xuetang; i.e., a place where distinguished intellectuals gathered to create and discuss poetry and historiographical writings), and the Red Room (i.e., the royal palace) would represent the invaded court and the subdued class of literati officials. One can assume that Yi recognized a critical undercurrent in Im Chongbi's line—for one must note that in premodern Korea, oxen and cows were traditionally viewed as the most stupid among the domestic animals, while ignorant people (who are too stupid to tell a cow's head from its behind) were sometimes likened to them[137]—and it seems likely that he felt the need to double down on the hidden meaning, to pick up Im's line about dumb animals on the loose that trample into and invade a refined place, and to add three more similar lines of his own. On the surface, Yi Illo thus produced a laudatory poem—on the subtext level, however, his poem could be interpreted as constituting the exact opposite, criticism of the tumultuous political takeover by the wild, cowishly ignorant men of the military, and the lack of action and reaction of the majority of civil officials.[138]

The Cure for an Illness, the Question of Audience and Readership, and the Destruction of Old Men's Idleness

Allow me to briefly focus on another interesting aspect, for an additional point that may support the understanding of *P'ahan chip* as a critical work designed to break open encrusted structures is its title.

As can be seen on the cover as well as the first page of the 1659 edition (where the title features at the upper right margin; figure 1), in late Chosŏn Korea the work was known under the title *P'ahan chip*. Yet as evidenced through a number of sources, the collection's original title, which Yi is said to have chosen himself, was simply *P'ahan* (he personally also may have referred to his work as a *kajip*, a "collection of family writings").[139] This is demonstrated, for example, in a passage from Yi Sehwang's epilogue, where it says, "Eventually he gathered poems on set topics from home and abroad which could be taken as model works, arranged them, and put them in order. He made three fascicles, and titled [the collection] *P'ahan*." In a later part of his epilogue, however, Yi Sehwang himself refers to the work as *P'ahan chip*, and this expanded, new title with the supplemented character *chip* (which may have initially been added by either the printer, Duke Taewŏn, or Yi Sehwang to bring Yi Illo's work in line with the earlier printed *Pohan chip*) later simply seems to have stuck. In the fifteenth-century sources *Koryŏsa* and *Tongmunsŏn*, for instance, it is referred to and categorized as a *chip*, a "collection." It is important to note, of course, that *P'ahan chip* is not a *chip* in the common, established sense, not a collection of the author's entire collected writings.

Figure 2: Cover of *P'ahan chip* from the 1659 woodblock-print edition. National Library of Korea. #Ko 3648-62-377. https://www.nl.go.kr.

Yet viewed against the backdrop of the majority of titles of Song Chinese collections of miscellanies, which conventionally feature the author's sobriquet and an indication that the work constitutes an informal collection (e.g., *Liuyi shihua*),[140] even Yi Illo's original title, *P'ahan*, is rather unusual. In terms of wording, *p'a* (C. *po*), can mean "to dispel," "to relieve," or "to overcome" (which is particularly fitting in the perhaps more playful and buoyant context that *p'a* appears to acquire when matched with "idleness"), but it can likewise mean the more forceful "violent destruction of concrete objects of any kind," "smashing things to pieces."[141] The word *han* (C. *xian*) can refer to an "enclosure" (for animals), a "boundary line," a "barrier," or a certain kind of "standard." In *Shuowen jiezi* (Explaining simple and analyzing compound characters), the oldest character dictionary of ancient China, the word is used in a verbal sense in the explanation, "*Lao*, this is a pen to enclose and raise oxen and horses" (C. *lao, xian yang niuma juan ye*), and also as a noun in the short clarification, "*Xian* is a barrier [or a fence]" (C. *xian, lan ye*). In the

TRANSLATOR'S INTRODUCTION   51

sense of "standard" it appears in *Lunyu* 19.11, where it says that one is not to transgress the *norms* of Great Virtue.[142] To the best of my knowledge, the collection's title has hitherto not been understood or translated in this way anywhere else, but viewed purely from a linguistic standpoint, as well as against the backdrop of the above-cited classical Chinese sources and the fact that we can encounter this notion of "breaking (free from) the cage and the norms of late-twelfth century society under military rule" in a number of Yi's autobiographical episodes, I do believe that the original title *P'ahan,* which was consciously established by the author and first compiler himself, could justifiably be rendered "Breaking norms," "Overcoming barriers," or even "Destroying the cage." This more radical layer of the title's meaning (which in turn appears to be watered down when paired with the word *chip*) seems, albeit uncommon, quite sensible to me.

Then again, one must note that an important passage from the work's epilogue (quoted later in this introduction) strongly suggests that *han* ought to be taken in its other primary (and in *P'ahan chip* studies entirely established) sense, namely, as "to be unengaged in irrelevant duties," to "be free and easy," or to "feel at leisure."[143] In the English-speaking world, *leisure* is often taken as a well-earned repose, as positively elevating, ultimately productive, and thus desirable unoccupied time; *idleness,* on the other hand, particularly if imposed upon a person by outside forces such as prolonged illness, delayed convalescence, political exile, or the loss of an occupation, is usually understood as leading to degeneration, shiftlessness, a deadening of the spirit, and moral deterioration. (As will hopefully become clear through the discussion that follows, this is why I have chosen the term "idleness" over the term "leisure" as the translation for the word *han* in *p'ahan.*)[144]

Yet in Chinese tradition, *xian* also often denotes a specific form of leisure/idleness, as it is generally associated with elderly men's high-minded aloofness from worldly affairs, as well as with their drinking of alcohol, playing of music, and composition of poetry.[145] As a case in point, Bai Juyi's *Er shun yin* (On being sixty) says, "In leisure [or perhaps idleness] I open new ale and taste a few cups; / in drunkenness I recall old poems and sing a whole volume."[146] I could not find the term *p'ahan* (C. *poxian*), "break / destroy / overcome idleness" or "broken / destroyed / overcome idleness" (clearly, if it needs to be broken, it cannot be fruitful "leisure" but must be harmful "idleness" or "indolence"), in any relevant classical texts of Chinese antiquity, but it does appear in verbal usage sporadically in Chinese and Korean poetry roughly contemporaneous with *P'ahan chip.* For instance, the poem *Chunri* (A spring day) by Southern Song poet Lu You (1125–1210) says, "To relieve [*p'a*] a lingering guest's idleness [*han*], one strikes up a game of

52   POEMS AND STORIES FOR OVERCOMING IDLENESS

chess." And in the poem *Amsŏ* (Lodging on a cliff) by the late Koryŏ poet Yi Saek (1328–1396), the first lines read,

> The man of the Way now has quit learning,
> the thatched cottage stands facing green mountains.
> Picking up leaves, in the morning he stokes a cooking-fire;
> viewing the scriptures, during the day he overcomes idleness
> [*p'ahan*].[147]

Traditional interpretations of the title *P'ahan chip* are based on the epilogue to the collection written by Yi Sehwang, a text that in itself is rather problematic in terms of authenticity and completeness. For it was written forty years after Yi Illo's death and almost fifty years after the collation of *P'ahan chip* by a person not mentioned in any of the relevant sources, who claims to be Yi Illo's son. In the middle of this epilogue, Yi Illo is quoted on the issue of the meaning of his collection and its title:

> Eventually he [my father Yi Illo] gathered poems on set topics from home and abroad which could be taken as model works [for future works of poetry], arranged them, and put them in order. He made three fascicles, and titled [the collection] *P'ahan*.
>
> Also, he said to his peers, "When I speak of a man with leisure [K. *hanja*],[148] I mean someone who established merit and achieved fame, then eventually retired on his own accord,[149] [built a hut] in the green fields, [a man who] in his heart has no more longings for outside things. Moreover, I mean someone who conceals his traces in mountains and forests, who eats when he's hungry and sleeps when he's tired. Only then, [after reaching self-chosen retirement and the resulting loss of worldly ambitions] this leisure can be achieved and become whole. However, if [such a man] viewed this here [*P'ahan*], the wholeness of this [pure, positive] kind of leisure [*han*] which he may have achieved — it would be shattered [*p'a*] [by reading my text, because the reading of it would stir this man in such a way that he would become actively involved again].
>
> Yet [on the contrary,] when it comes to someone who is submerged in the fatiguing mundane toils and troubles [of politics and officialdom], always works laboriously for fame and high official position, keeps close [to powerful men like swallows] to the heat, who [diligently] rushes east and races west [when ordered to do so] — if [such a man] one morning suffers a loss [of his position and is forced into retirement], then by his outer appearance he may well look as though he possessed this [positive, pure] kind of leisure, but his heart really roils in turbulence. That's exactly

the moment when idleness will turn into an illness. However, if [such a man] views this here [*P'ahan*], the [harmful] illness of idleness [K. *han-ji pyŏng*] which he will likely have contracted — it will be cured [by reading my text]. And wouldn't that be even better than [squandering time by] playing board games [C. *bo*] or chess [C. *yi*][150] or something?"[151] Those who had listened to him at the time collectively said, "That's true!"

This source has generated certain standardized interpretations of the title *P'ahan chip*, which usually home in on Yi Illo and his own alleged condition of leisure as a basis for writing,[152] or which take it as meaning "for leisurely reading."[153] Focusing on the first part of the previous quotation, some scholars have also suggested that with the title, Yi implied one must first acquire total peace of mind and then have this leisure shattered in order to reach a stage enabling one to produce serious literature.[154] The word *han* has conflicting connotations in the opposing parts of Yi's statement: while signifying a praiseworthy, pure kind of leisure in the first part, it clearly has the negative meaning of "enforced upon idleness" in the closing passage (the same, in fact, can be seen in the poems by Yoil and King Myŏngjong in 2:25, where it is the final word of both verse compositions). While this may seem puzzling, Yi's contradictory use of *han* is in line with the diverging good or bad implications the term has in classical texts. In *Zhuangzi* 2.2, for instance, it prominently appears as *hanhan* (C. *xianxian*) and is directly set against the related and homophone *hanhan* (C. *xianxian*): "Comprehensive understanding is idle [*hanhan*], petty knowledge is pedantic [*hanhan*]," or, as in Richard Wilhelm's wonderful German *Zhuangzi* translation *Das wahre Buch vom südlichen Blütenland*, "Große Weisheit macht sicher und frei, kleine Weisheit ist Tyrannei [Great wisdom makes you secure and free, small wisdom is tyranny]."[155] The dual nature of *han*, which can be either positive or negative depending on the person and context, is visible in other classical sources as well. In *Xunzi* (Master Xun) 21.11, a well-educated man "living in leisure [K. *han'gŏ*] and pondering in quietude" acquires "complete understanding,"[156] while in *Lunheng* (Discursive weighing) 85.5, Wang Chong "living in [forced-upon] leisure" prompts him to get creative and produce a piece of literature on common morals to rouse the public conscience. On the flip side, the commentary to *Daxue* (Great learning) says, "When the inferior man is living in leisure, there is no limit to the extent of his evil."[157] Hence, in his use of *han*, Yi Illo clearly builds on this two-sided understanding in foundational Chinese texts. But, in my view, the closing part of his statement is especially significant, for here, *P'ahan chip* is proclaimed by the author himself to aptly serve as a remedy, a cure for this negative form of *han*,[158] that is, a harmful kind of involuntary inactivity imposed from above onto eager, obedient civil officials, a kind of idleness causing pent-up anger that can be neither released nor publicly vented.

The central question here is, of course, which audience Yi Illo was speaking to. Who were his addressees, those who after his speech collectively agreed that his words were correct and, as a result, most likely put down their *yi* pieces and picked up Yi's *P'ahan chip* instead? In the epilogue, Yi Illo's speech is preceded by a paragraph in which Yi Sehwang alleges that *P'ahan chip* was created primarily for conservatory reasons, to preserve outstanding ancient Korean poetry, during the time when his father participated in the Chungnim Kohoe together with Im Ch'un and O Sejae. This poets society existed during the late 1180s and early 1190s, after Yi had returned from Kyeyang and was serving as *chiksagwan* (intendant of the Bureau of Historiography) in the capital. Yet there can be no doubt that the bulk of *P'ahan chip* was put together in or around 1211, a time when core members of the Chungnim Kohoe were long dead and Yi, in turn, was actively involved in the Haedong Kirohoe, an exclusive club of elderly, by then mostly retired civil officials. The Haedong Kirohoe members may also be considered "intellectuals-in-between in a time of transition," because they had not only been active during Myŏngjong's reign, but had likewise played vital roles in Ch'oe Ch'unghŏn's endeavor to stabilize the dynasty in the immediate wake of his 1196 coup. At the outset of Ch'oe Ch'unghŏn's rule, these experienced civil officials had been in charge of reforming the recruitment system to generate a new cadre of young, loyal civil officials for the Ch'oes (see the role of the Haedong Kirohoe member Paek Kwangsin [n.d.] as described in 3:26).[159] Yet the early years of Ch'oe rule marked a time when the established old elites of the twelfth century were gradually being pushed aside to make room for those unconditionally loyal to the house of Ch'oe. And while some of these old elites and elderly civil associates close to the military ruler may have been allowed to retire on their own initiatives and terms, extant sources suggest that in this period of political and bureaucratic transition, many of the older officials did not give up their hard-earned positions wholly voluntarily. As evidenced in *Koryŏsa*, in 1199, for instance, Ch'oe Tang, quasi as a farewell present, was promoted to the position of *munha sirang p'yŏngjangsa* (vice director of the Chancellery) only to retire directly afterward, while at the same time another twenty officials were simultaneously made to retire "although they had not requested it," meaning that they were "ordered to retire" (K. *myŏng sajik*) entirely against their will.[160] While these officials would most likely have been financially compensated, they may still have held grudges against the Ch'oe regime, which had sidelined and excluded them. Thus, when Yi Illo here states that his collection ought to be read by those who are idle on the outside but inwardly embittered for having been forced into retirement, it makes perfect sense to assume that he was addressing certain members of the Haedong Kirohoe, not those of the Chungnim Kohoe (the prominent members of which had been poor social outcasts and had not served in office at all). The majority of Chungnim Kohoe members, most of whom were in their mid- to late thirties when the club existed, would at that point in their lives certainly not have taken Yi's words as pertaining to themselves, while some of the aged and maybe cast-aside Haendong Kirohoe members would surely have felt spoken to. Hence, it is reasonable to conclude that there is an error, an inconsistency in Yi Sehwang's text,[161] or that perhaps a passage about the Haedong Kirohoe in the original 1260 epilogue was lost over time.

Let us for a moment consider the possible link between *P'ahan chip* and the Haedong Kirohoe a bit further. The assembly was initiated and organized by Ch'oe Tang, and it is known to have comprised Ch'oe Sŏn (d. 1209),[162] Chang Yunmun (d. 1211), Yi Chunch'ang (n.d.), Paek Kwangsin, Ko Yŏngjun (d. 1208), Yi Sejang (n.d.), Hyŏn Tŏksu (d. 1215), Yi Illo, Cho T'ong, and Pak Insŏk (d. 1212). The club began meeting at Ch'oe Tang's studio in 1203, and Yi Illo must have been invited to join a few years after that.[163] He may have been asked to become part of the group to function as a kind of chronicler, someone who recorded what was said and done at Ssangmyŏng Studio (one final product of this must have been the *Ssangmyŏng-jae chip*).

Much later, at the beginning of the Chosŏn dynasty, the influential thinker Kwŏn Kŭn (1352–1409), whose interest in and private collection of the works of earlier intellectuals played a crucial role in the preservation of Koryŏ literature, described Ch'oe Tang's association of intellectuals in his *Hu-Kiyŏnghoe sŏ* (Preface for the latter assembly of elderly excellencies), stating,

> That the [original] Kiyŏnghoe [Kirohoe] assembly took place a long time ago. Bai Letian [Bai Juyi] of the Tang dynasty and Wen Lugong [Wen Yanbo, 1006–1097] of the Song dynasty both had assemblies [of contemporaneous elderly intellectuals] in the capital. At the time they were praised as beautiful, and paintings were created to transmit it. In our Eastern Region, when the previous dynasty [Koryŏ] was at its height, Defender-in-Chief [K. T'aewi] Master Ch'oe Tang, whose sobriquet was Ssangmyŏngjae, together with seven other scholar-officials who had withdrawn on their own accord due to old age, admired what these two [Tang dynasty] masters [Bai Juyi and Wen Yanbo] had done. So they started the Haedong Kiyŏng-ji Hoe, the "Assembly of Elderly Excellencies of the Country East of the Sea," and they would get together on every tenth day of each month. They [the original members of the Haedong Kirohoe]

56 POEMS AND STORIES FOR OVERCOMING IDLENESS

> would simply amuse themselves with the drinking [of ale] and the recit-
> ing [of poetry], and their words never reached [any serious topics such as]
> whether [the times and the government] were good or bad, or [whether
> there were fellow scholars whose lives had been] a success or a failure
> [K. *changbu tŭksil*]. Later, those who succeeded them turned [the assem-
> bly] into a place for the veneration of the Buddha, and they succeeded in
> getting the elders to worship as well.[164]

Kwŏn Kŭn here states that the Haedong Kirohoe initially started out as
a decidedly nonpolitical, nonreligious gathering of elder statesmen who,
perhaps meaning to forget about suffered wrongs, strove to simply spend
their twilight years in drunken leisure with games and music (so, basically
the traditional activities pursued by those who have *han*),[165] but that the asso-
ciation's character changed decidedly after the younger members, in all like-
lihood particularly Yi Illo and Cho T'ong, who had not retired and were still
in office at the time in question, joined the group and eventually succeeded
in getting Ch'oe Tang and the others to participate in more meaningful activ-
ities they devised. This appears to have been related primarily to a religious
sphere, but hidden under the guise of religious practice there might also
have existed a political one (as was so often the case in Korean history both
old and new). Yet due to a number of factors, one can assume that Yi would
not have planned to rouse the old men to any action that could have resulted
in serious consequences (especially for himself): for one, Ch'oe Ch'unghŏn
had a firm grip on the dynasty in the early 1200s; some of the foundational
members of the Haedong Kirohoe had close connections with the Ch'oe
regime; financially, the old men were in comfortable, secure positions; Yi Illo
himself acted, at least outwardly, in a submissive way and appears to have
adapted to the new order; moreover, throughout his life he seems to have
faced authority as well as political and social pressure in a rather cautious
manner. Nevertheless, when confronted with the dull inactiveness of these
former ministers, who had withdrawn and seemingly fully surrendered to
the new civil and military power structures of the age, who had settled into
the role of civil mascots of the military regime, and who merrily idled away
their time in untroubled, inebriated ease while fellow members of the pre-
1200 literati stratum had not long ago been purged, pushed aside, and in
some instances even killed, Yi may have felt the urge to shake (if not to say
wake) them up. And, as can be seen in his earlier cited words, he must have
anticipated that underneath the old men's outward complacency lay inner
unrest, perhaps wrath and fury about the way some of them may have been
sidelined in spite of their merits and eagerness to serve.

Since *P'ahan chip* was in all probability produced by Yi Illo during his time as a "young" participant in this elite circle of retired literati, I think it is obvious that during the association's meetings at Ssangmyŏng Studio, that is, a narrow but nevertheless public space,[166] the Haedong Kirohoe members functioned as the initial readership of the original manuscript. Yi Illo may have envisioned presenting the final version of his *P'ahan* to King Hŭijong[167] — a ruler, one must bear in mind, who so deeply opposed the political string-puller Ch'oe Ch'unghŏn that he allegedly meant for him to be assassinated. Yet one may venture to say that the retired high-level civil officials of the Kirohoe were both the work's first recipients and it's intended readership. These old-timers (most of them were born in the 1130s and 1140s) constituted a knowing readership, because many of the people discussed in the collection had been actual acquaintances, colleagues, or adversaries of Kirohoe members. As a group of similarly educated peers from old-established lineages, they shared identity, experience, and knowledge with the author. With *P'ahan chip*, Yi Illo was speaking *to* this group and *for* this group. In contrast, the military officials in charge, as well as the "youngsters" of the post-1200 civil elite, would have constituted an unknowing, unfamiliar readership.

Thus, when perusing, reading aloud, or listening to the episodes of Yi Illo's collection during their regularly held Kirohoe get-togethers, which may have constituted the original reading environment, the various poems and anecdotes are likely to have caused the old men to reminisce, to have made them reconsider the upheavals of the past years and their consequences, to have incited them to converse about their relationships or conflicts with the scholars and civil officials appearing in Yi's manuscript, and to have provoked them to think about their own (mis)conduct, their complicity, and the fate of their own status group under the new sociopolitical realities of Ch'oe rule in the early thirteenth century.[168] These collective acts of reading, listening to, and speaking about the poems, people, and events contained in his collection may have been what Yi Illo alluded to when he spoke of *P'ahan chip* as a cure for their harmful "illness of idleness." *P'ahan chip* may have functioned as a spark for a shared critical culture of remembrance, as a basis for memorialization, and it also may have rekindled a *munban* — perhaps "us versus them" — conscience among the old civil officials (vis-à-vis both the *muban* and the new and upcoming civil elites). Besides rescuing and preserving the knowledge and standards of a bygone era at a point in time when military rule seemed stronger and more secure than ever, this formation or strengthening of a shared memory and identity may have been one of Yi's primary objectives.

Hence, it appears permissible to read the collection's original title *P'ahan* not in relation to Yi Illo himself, but rather in relation to the intended

58 POEMS AND STORIES FOR OVERCOMING IDLENESS

original readership, the members of the Haedong Kirohoe, whom Yi may have wanted to "break the cage," be more engaged, more conscious, more actively defiant, instead of squandering their time "by playing *bo* or *yi* or something." Thereby, Yi may have meant to have the old men "overcome idleness [caused by having been shut out]." And, in the end, the intellectual-in-between Yi Illo (who belonged to that peer group of pre-1200 officials but who was nevertheless still active and employed after the turn of the thirteenth century) does seem to have struck a chord with the idle old-timers, for all who heard his words and obviously must have had the manuscript of "this here [*P'ahan*]" right in front of their eyes, affirmatively replied with *yŏn* (C. *ran*), "That's true."[169]

Walking Cane and Frosty Sword, Opposing Roles and Conflicting Obligations, and the Appropriation of a Dead Man's Poetry

From among the various individuals of bygone or contemporaneous times treated in *P'ahan chip,* this initial reader- or listenership may have been particularly moved to read or hear about Yi Illo's emotional accounts of his "friend Kiji," who was forced to "rove the southland." In *P'ahan chip,* Im Ch'un is portrayed as a brilliant poet, but also as an embittered, unrecognized, largely forgotten intellectual (see 3:18). Yet one must note that Im Ch'un's own poetry as it appears in his collected writings, *Sŏha chip,* is at times much more angry and aggressive than the few poems of his included in *P'ahan chip*. Various pieces in *Sŏha chip* illustrate the degree to which Im despised the unlearned men of the 1170s and 1180s military who ruled without experience and traditional legitimacy and who had destroyed his aspirations, career, family, and livelihood. And since he was neither physically in the capital nor employed in any office, from his outsider's position he did have a certain degree of liberty to not follow the crowd, to write against the ruling authorities, and to wear opposition as a personal badge.

A prime example for such a literary product of Im Ch'un's dissent, as well as for his meandering, allusion-heavy style of poetry, is *Kabonyŏn ha p'iji kangnam p'ayu yuri-ji t'an inbu changdan'ga myŏngji wal "Changgŏm haeng"* (In the summer of the year *kabo* [1174], as I sought refuge in the southland, I very much sighed over roaming in dire straits; thus I composed a lengthy song, calling it *Changgŏm haeng,* "Walking while using my sword as a cane"). Tellingly, this piece is the final entry of the first volume of *Sŏha chip,* concluding the section on the first phase of Im's life in Kaesŏng. In the poem he writes about the political, social, and bureaucratic changes during a time when "waves and billows raged," condemns the "lot of vulgar men" who "lick the rulers' piles" (i.e., the opportunistic civil officials who served the men of the military, much the same way Yi Illo did), alludes to possible participation in the countercoups of the early 1170s, hints at his far-reaching, probably counterrevolutionary plans (which no one yet knows about), threatens that his "journey isn't about finding a field to farm" but rather about "executing treacherous barbarians," and asserts that, drawing his three-foot sword and turning it from a harmless walking cane into a deadly weapon, he will fight to avenge the dynasty until the very end. The poem reads:

A filthy six-foot body, once plunged down between Heaven and
> earth.
[The master of the archers] took a bow of mulberry wood and arrows
> of the wild rebus, shooting toward the four cardinal points;[170] the
> man-child had gall [fighting spirit] as big as a ladle.
Even more so when wild winds howled, when waves and billows
> raged all over the sea-girt world.
Horned dragons, fish and turtles, all were yet uneasy; came out of
> their holes, in utter confusion, and lost their dwellings.
At the time, there were no scholars of heroic mold;[171] who hurried to
> [join] gatherings of deed and fame?
Ah! I was a [useless] gourd hung [on a string];[172] was berated [and
> sank into] abject poverty, [cast] far beyond the ends of the earth.
Amid the dust of Chang'an [Kaesŏng], I had lain resting aloof for five
> years.
Constantly feeling so hungry that my facial color had turned ashen, [I
> had soothed] my hollow, dreary insides with a thousand books.
It was enough for me when my shinbones were warm, for when my
> belly was full, I wished for nothing more.
Laughable, literary writing doesn't generate any cash — how
> could Emperor [Wu of Han] ever have read the *Zixu* [*fu*] [and
> immediately employed Sima Xiangru]?[173]
It's [not the cultured men of letters who are rewarded and employed
> for their writings but rather] the lot of vulgar men of this age
> in turmoil, who lick piles and get thirty carriages for it [in
> payment].[174]
I wanted to go spit in their faces; [only then would I,] floodlike, have
> rhapsodized and [had a will to] return [home].[175]
Ceased going to the village gate,[176] this old body of mine; was like a
> bird in a cage, a fish in a pond.
The entire household had to travel ten thousand leagues,[177] but
> neighing was but a single donkey.

60   POEMS AND STORIES FOR OVERCOMING IDLENESS

Around the home of the mountains, as [I see] rushing autumn wind
rise, a cup of water-shield broth would taste just fine.[178]

Moving along slowly, I turn my head and gaze back into the distance
toward the central plain; it's a pity how long it's been an [uncultured, rugged] land of wind and waves.

A yellow rooster crows out at night, it's not a disagreeable sound; get
up and dance, and heroic intentions shall arise by themselves.[179]

Who says that a wife can't support her clothes? Far-reaching schemes
and valiant plans, but no one has any knowledge of them yet.

[Zhang Liang] manufactured a hammer but failed when attacking
[the First Emperor of] Qin, then had to take refuge in Xiapi.[180]

At ease he knelt and fetched a shoe from [underneath] the bridge; one
really cannot move backward the old man's promise.[181]

And I laugh! [General Xiang Yu's] strength to move mountains,[182] it
was snatched by a little child.

Once he encountered the prominent nose in the dragon
countenance;[183] ten thousand households enfeoffed to the
marquis, the emperor was teacher.

A great man's accomplishments are inherently like this;[184] why
should begging for rice be an object of derision?

A single reed [boat] on the river's sunny side; going back I'll have to
pound grain where I stop for the night.[185]

Clouds and mists like in a painting; plants and trees as if adorned.

Floating family and a drifting abode, for all my life; still in the
bosom, naturally there's nothing but [the thought of returning
back] home.

This journey isn't about looking for a field to farm — [my intention
is to execute treacherous barbarians and expose their bodies to
public view!] I just fear that Scholar Zu [Ti] will bring out his
whip before [me].[186]

Deeply moved, I am without words, as tears are streaming down;
vast and vague beyond those birds, the empty, lengthy sky.

Inside its case is my frosty sword, [it's blade of steel is] cold and
three-feet long; [this] bold man has a heart, and to the very end
he will repay his debt to the dynasty.[187]

In light of a poem such as this, Im Ch'un can unquestionably be called a dissident, even subversive intellectual, someone who in a poetic way spoke (his personal) truth to power, challenging the political and social structures of this period. One must keep in mind, however, that the majority of his remaining works and epistles are specifically addressed to his close friends, which implies that only a very small circle of people actually had access to his original works. Often even the physical spots where he chose to put down his poetry were decidedly private, as evidenced through the title of a poem he wrote on a wall of his friend's dwelling, the *Sŏ Tamji ka pyŏk* (Written on a wall of [Yi] Tamji's house). Portraying the high-status men and women of his time as indulging in their fattening desires while upright scholars (such as himself) have to eke out a meager existence, Im writes, "And I ask: as chicks and dogs grow fat, / how come phoenixes and cranes grow gaunt?"[188] Clearly, though he lived on the fringes of society, he could not have publicly disparaged the military rulers' usurpation of power, for that would have made him a political threat, a danger the officials in charge would undoubtedly have dealt with quickly and severely. Thus, except when writing together with friends or sending his poetry and letters to the people he knew well, he had no chance to voice his biting criticism of the political and personal circumstances. Had he done so in the open, one could assume that people in the capital region would have been aware of his (notorious) name. But as hinted at in 3:25, after years of his absence, people in Kaesŏng were more or less oblivious to the poet Im Ch'un by the mid-1180s. Yi Illo, on the other hand, was by then a well-known, well-connected official. And while dissent usually implies externality, Yi lived and worked in the center. Therefore, publicly siding with Im Ch'un, lamenting his friend's plight, or autonomously voicing any sort of disapproval vis-à-vis the ones in power, those who had, in fact, heaved him into the prestigious institutions and authoritative positions he was serving in, would unquestionably have jeopardized his career, maybe even his life. And in all likelihood not just his own, but also those of his three legitimate sons, Chŏng, Yang, and On, who had all passed the civil service examinations and were busy climbing up the official and social ladders. Nonetheless, Yi had experienced the 1170 military revolt at a decisive, formative age, and he had directly witnessed its devastating effects on his peer group and inner circle of acquaintances.

Thus, it is hypothesized here that Yi, an intellectual-in-between, for the better part of his life was caught in a struggle to reconcile fundamentally conflicting roles and diametrically opposed obligations. These comprise, on the one hand, the obligations to fulfill the role of the filial (foster) son of a well-off metropolitan family who was reared by someone from King Myŏngjong's inner circle and who was expected to continue the line of successful members of the lineage; the role of the diligent Confucian scholar who masters the civil service examinations, has a dutiful sense of required social participation, and offers his learning and knowledge in the service of the ruling government; the role of the *munsaeng* and protégé who profits from his examiners' and benefactors' advocacy and needs to prove that he was worthy of his patrons' and teachers' trust and lobbying;[189] the role of the dependable royal subject and representative of the prestigious Hallim Academy; and the role of the proud father and responsible husband who can provide for his family and pave or at least not block the way to officialdom for his sons.

On the other hand, Yi's literature in both *P'ahan chip* and *Tongmunsŏn* reflects the importance that friendship and the upkeep of close personal relationships despite possible geographical or social gaps had for him. Thus, he must have felt a deep obligation to also fulfill the role of the friend— especially in relation to Im Ch'un.[190] Here one must remember that in premodern sino-centric East Asia, male friendship, the only nonhierarchical bond of the Five Cardinal Relationships that constituted the very core of Confucian society and thought,[191] was generally of high importance to the cultured literati. According to *Lunyu* 1:8, friendship can only exist between those who are equally morally good and righteous, for noble men should "have no friends who are not of equal (moral) caliber."[192] In the Confucian view, virtue was the basis of friendship between cultivated men, and vice versa, friendship between cultivated men was always closely connected to the notion of mutual moral betterment, of friends serving as role models for the realization, improvement, and refinement of one's own cultured character and conduct. A friend was someone who Yi—as a Confucian and, of course, also as a Buddhist[193]—had to be true to even in the most dire circumstances, someone whom he had to strive to live up to.[194] Im Ch'un, as a master poet and wronged but righteous, unyielding intellectual, would undoubtedly have served as a major (and quite possibly burdensome) source of both inspiration and obligation for his friend Yi Illo.

In addition—and this can be deduced from the structure and content of *P'ahan chip*—he must have felt the responsibility to carry the torch and shine a light on the once mighty though now disempowered old status group of late-twelfth-century civil officials while keeping the merits of the military men and the new civil elites in the dark. For while *P'ahan chip* discusses the deeds and literatures of many figures from the civil and religious realms of the pre-Ch'oe Ch'unghŏn era, the collection is essentially void of entries dealing with young civil elites as well as men of the military. Though the Ch'oe Clan of Chinyang is certainly hinted at in 1:1, neither Ch'oe Ch'unghŏn nor his son and political heir, Ch'oe U, are specifically mentioned by name anywhere in *P'ahan chip,* and one may well interpret their absence as a form of subtle dissent, as *criticism through omission* (in this respect, *P'ahan chip* constitutes the exact opposite of its proclaimed "sequel," *Pohan chip*).[195] Viewed from outside, Yi Illo appears to have been on friendly terms with Ch'oe Ch'unghŏn, to whose home he was invited and for whom he is known to have composed verses during one of Ch'oe's poetry gatherings (K. *sihoe*).[196] Yet bearing in mind that Yi's foster father, Yoil, by all indications was a sworn enemy of Ch'oe Ch'unghŏn (who had dethroned Myŏngjong), one may conclude that the uncle would have passed on the aversion toward the Ch'oe house (and perhaps even inside knowledge regarding plans to assassinate Ch'oe Ch'unghŏn) to his nephew and quasi stepson.[197] But since undisguisedly voicing this aversion was impossible under the circumstances, Yi could be hypothesized to have chosen to give voice to his criticism in *P'ahan chip* by simply not wasting a single word on the Ch'oes at all, while simultaneously lauding Ch'oe Ch'unghŏn's adversaries.[198] Also disregarded are the prior military regimes of Chŏng Chungbu and Yi Ŭimin, the latter of which was in fact toppled by Ch'oe Ch'unghŏn.[199] Historically, Ch'oe's accession to power marked a caesura, and one should make clear distinctions between the 1170 coup, its tumultuous aftermath, the decades of political chaos that unfolded until 1196, and the stabilized conditions under the rule of the Ch'oe. Yet if Yi had bluntly disparaged the military authorities and the treatment of able intellectuals and civil officials during the 1170s and 1180s, by extension he would also have called into question the legitimacy of the rule of the Ch'oe house. Notably, what is essentially also ignored in the Silla-legacy-heavy *P'ahan chip* is the ancient state of Koguryŏ (and that of Parhae) — in a time when, as Michael C. Rogers has pointed out, the new consciousness of the military dictatorship period only recognized Koguryŏ successionism and the military rulers moreover supported "progressive" literati whose writings could serve to reinforce the idea of Koguryŏ as the dynasty's legitimate progenitor state (such as Yi Kyubo's *Tongmyŏng-wang p'yŏn*, "Ode to King Tongmyŏng"),[200] the striking absence of Koguryŏ-related material in *P'ahan chip* may well be interpreted as yet another form of silent criticism by the intellectual-in-between Yi Illo. Still, the obligations to fulfill his roles as a loyal friend and member of the established yet continuously marginalized old stratum of civil officials appear to have weighed heavily on Yi, especially as he was approaching the end of his life. And while he silenced himself in his role as an official and in his own literature was forced to intentionally omit or write between the lines to avoid incurring danger, he might have felt a pressing need for a more direct, explicit mode for the expression of his opposition. After all, dissent simply does not work in silence — it must materialize, must become known, must make a mark.

Therefore, I suggest the following theory: instead of poking his head above the surface and exposing himself by using his own literary works to publicly attack the military authorities and unavoidably suffer the dire consequences, he consciously, purposefully chose to make use of the more openly dissident literature of Im Ch'un, who had died many years before

64   POEMS AND STORIES FOR OVERCOMING IDLENESS

and whose family had by now crumbled and could thus not be punished any further. One may assume that for this reason, Yi Illo started rummaging through his stacks of letters and poems, contacting mutual acquaintances (or their children) as well as people he knew Im to have corresponded or socialized with, and progressively gathered and collated the stray handwritten or perhaps copied manuscripts of his friend's poems and texts to eventually piece together Kiji Im Ch'un's *munjip,* the *Sŏha chip.* Yi wrote a preface to the collection, the "Sŏha sŏnsaeng chip sŏ," where he states the following about the process of collecting and editing:

> Now I have obtained the poems he left behind by [listening to] what the later-born recite, have roughly categorized them, and made them into a work of six volumes, which I called *Sŏha sŏnsaeng chip.* I commanded the child Pi to proofread the handwriting, and it shall be carved on woodblocks, so that the work will be transmitted. It is so sad that Heaven did not grant more years, and while what he wrote does not amount to much in number, catching a glimpse of a single feather of a phoenix is enough to give an understanding of the auspiciousness of this nine-colored [majestic bird]. The deceased teacher's name was Ch'un, his courtesy name was Kiji, and his education he is said to have obtained from his uncle, the academician [Im] Chongbi."[201]

Though Yi here writes that he meant to have the work put on woodblocks, it is known that after finishing the *Sŏha chip* in the late 1210s, Yi stored the original collection at his own house. It simply seems as though he did not have the financial wherewithal to realize this costly undertaking. Yet his wish for publication and circulation of Im's works in the end did come true, for, amazingly, the *Sŏha chip* was in fact initially printed in 1222, only two years after Yi Illo's own death, that is, an age in which printing was reserved for a very limited number of authoritative (often religious) texts. And perhaps even more amazingly, the collected writings of the dissident outcast Im Ch'un were printed on the initiative of none other than Ch'oe U, the paramount military leader of Koryŏ who de facto governed the dynasty for several decades from 1219 on. This 1222 original woodblock-print version of *Sŏha chip* is unfortunately not entirely extant today (only volumes four and five are in the collection of the Harvard Yenching Library), but Ch'oe U himself penned an afterword (K. *husŏ*), in which he explains his reasons for having Im Ch'un's collected works printed:

> [...] Teacher Sŏha Im Ch'un, he was a giant of a talent. [...] Recently I had heard that Great Remonstrance Official Yi Misu had sought and

obtained leftover and withered remnants [of Im Ch'un's writings] from people of the younger generation, and that he had edited them to turn them into six volumes all together. Though he had stored it at his house, he had bemoaned not having the means to have [Im Ch'un's works] carved on woodblock [to have it printed and circulated]. [Eventually the collection had been hidden away] like a [precious] mirror inside an old dressing case. [...] Fearing that, on another day, [Im's works] would turn to dust and simply melt away, that they would not be transmitted to later generations, I took hold of the original [from Yi Misu's place of dwelling]. Thereafter, I had it officially sent to the various academies [K. *chehagwŏn*] in the Western Capital [P'yŏngyang] in order for it to be put on woodblocks. When these [woodblocks] were finished, I had them moved to the capital, had them delivered to the Printing House [K. Sŏjŏkchŏm], and [finally] had [the finished printed books] disseminated widely into the world, to set a standard for the later-born.[202]

Ch'oe U here asserts that he went through the trouble of having the collection of a person who had received almost no recognition during his day put on woodblocks in P'yŏngyang and printed in Kaesŏng in order for Im's literature not to be lost and for it to serve as a model for later generations of poets.[203] Conservation of Im's literature may have been one incentive, and possibly there was even demand for this specific work from intellectuals of the time. Yet Ch'oe U may also simply have intended to improve his own image, and simultaneously disparage the uncultured rule of the military dictators preceding that of his own family. He might have meant to cast an unfavorable light especially on the low-born Yi Ŭimin, who had dominated the court during the 1180s and early 1190s and had failed to value and employ intellectuals such as Im Ch'un before being overthrown by Ch'oe Ch'unghŏn in 1196 (he did, of course, value and employ Yi Illo). In turn, by recognizing the literary brilliance of Im Ch'un and validating it by means of an expensive woodblock print produced in P'yŏngyang and Kaesŏng, Ch'oe U might have striven to give his own reign, which in 1222 was still at a very early stage, a more refined, cultured appearance.[204] Following his father's example, he understood the importance of positioning himself as a supporter, a guardian of the arts and the literati, whom he most likely meant to appease and keep in line with such demonstrative measures of cultural policy. By printing a work containing an abundance of poems and letters critical of recent political issues and military leaders, Ch'oe may have meant to suggest to the civil officials that, under his watch, remonstrations and the public articulation of productive criticism (*jian*, "remonstrance," generally being a core feature of institutionalized Confucianism) would be

66   POEMS AND STORIES FOR OVERCOMING IDLENESS

permissible (albeit, in truth, only if voiced by someone who was long dead), that a culture of serious debate would be established, that they could write at ease without having to fear a loss of recognition and support, and that, consequently, there would be no need for any real dissatisfaction and anger (let alone potential uprisings) from their side. The printing of the *Sŏha chip* may thus be viewed as an attempt by Ch'oe U to win over and lull the civil officials at the outset of his rule.[205] Ch'oe U would have had his reasons for commissioning a carving and print of the *Sŏha chip*, just like Yi Illo would have had his reasons for gathering or copying the original texts (most of which, according to Ch'oe U, were already in a fairly bad state) decades after his friend's death and editing Im's collection.

The compilation of a person's *munjip* was, generally speaking, a posthumous affair and also a self-conscious act by the compiler. Reasons for the collection and collation of a late scholar's writings were certainly manifold. As exemplified in Ch'oe U's text, *munjip* were at times put together on royal (or other authoritative) order to preserve someone's writings for posterity. Mostly, however, it was family members, students, or disciples who collected their descendant's or teacher's writings in order to assemble, put in chronological or generic order, pass on, and oftentimes even mingle with someone's literary oeuvre (i.e., simply add texts or extract those perceived to be inept). Moreover, by means of a *munjip*, especially a printed one, it was possible to establish the literary value of a person's writings and fortify the author's name. Especially during the Koryŏ dynasty, when printing was not generally done for commercial or personal reasons but still mostly in order to fix or stress a text or an interpretation's significance and prestige, the carving on woodblock was an act that ascribed the utmost importance to pieces of writing. And while there was certainly the aspect of preventing a writer's name and works from sinking into oblivion, there was also the aspect of editors or printers striving to position themselves as saviors of a deceased intellectual's works.[206]

Issues surrounding the author certainly also played a role in the case of the compilation of *Sŏha chip*. Yi Illo, who himself was apparently well organized when it came to manuscripts of his own compositions,[207] meant to preserve Im Ch'un's writings for posterity, bring structure to Im's posthumous manuscripts, and establish his friend's name as a master poet. But in this case it does seem worthwhile to turn the situation upside down and briefly focus on the editor and his personal motives. Yi's act of putting together Im's oftentimes undisguisedly critical poems and texts into the six volumes of *Sŏha chip* could in itself be understood as an elusive expression of dissent directed against the leading status group of Yi's time, an act of rebellion that may have been designed to escape the unlearned military officials' attention while being plain to see for the *Sŏha chip*'s intended readership, the learned literati who were actually able to disentangle the complex networks of complicated allusions that Im's poetry was famous for (see 3:4). One must keep in mind that Yi Illo, who was then in the final stage of his life, edited the *Sŏha chip* some twenty-odd years after Im's death, which implies that it was not a rash decision made under emotional distress in the immediate wake of Im's passing, but obviously a deliberate, long-planned act. In his epilogue to *Sŏha chip,* Ch'oe U states that Yi Illo eagerly wanted Im Ch'un's poems to be printed and published (which is already evidenced by the fact that for *Sŏha chip,* unlike in the case of *P'ahan chip,* Yi wrote a preface), but that he lacked the financial means for such a costly undertaking, which, as he says, troubled Yi. If Yi himself had been able to publish and thereby widely distribute the collection, he could have openly expressed his subjective sentiments of dissent through the brush of Im Ch'un and may have inspired his peers to understanding or even action. Yet this would still not have posed any immediate threat to either Yi or his sons—for it would have been another man's writings, a dead man's poetry. Im had passed away more than two decades before, and viewed from an outsider's perspective, the collation of an old friend's writings would not have been anything out of the ordinary.

The collation, and to a certain degree the appropriation, of Im Ch'un's writings may thus be viewed as a subtle, intricate expression of dissent by Yi Illo designed for a knowing readership of similarly educated peers. And this is, in turn, essentially consistent with his method of formulating and sending criticism to a specific readership in *P'ahan chip.*

Yet while this dissident facet of *P'ahan chip* can be assumed to have been recognized by intended readers who had personally known many of the figures appearing in the work, it seems to have been lost during the early Chosŏn dynasty, when the collection's deeper layers dealing with contemporaneous issues became less and less relevant in a new, detached reading environment, and the work came to serve primarily as a repository for miscellaneous information and data, amusing anecdotes, historical narratives, ancient customs and cultures, and architectural features and scenic landscapes of old Korea.

At the end of his epilogue to the 1260 woodblock-print edition of *P'ahan chip,* Yi Sehwang voices his hope that his "[father's writings] may become treasures for descendants of myriad generations." Those people hereby imagined to cherish Yi Illo's literature in a faraway future are us. To twenty-first-century readers who are about to delve into this translation of an early Korean work of *sihwa,* the collection offers a precious glimpse into the lit-

68   POEMS AND STORIES FOR OVERCOMING IDLENESS

erature, arts, society, religion, and politics of the mid-Koryŏ era, a time for which authentic sources are exceedingly scarce.

Yet *P'ahan chip* also gives us the rare opportunity to traverse a literary bridge over the flood of time, and to experience, share, and personally connect to the lives, thoughts, and emotions of human beings who lived and wrote literature in Korea more than eight hundred years ago.

II. Translation

P'ahan chip — Fascicle 1

Composed in writing[1] by the
> Chwa Kanŭi Taebu, "Left Grand Master of Remonstrance,"[2]
> Pisŏgam, "Director of the Palace Library,"
> Pomun-gak Haksa, "Academician of the Tower of Precious Letters,"[3]
> Chijego, "Drafter of Proclamations,"[4]

> Yi Illo.

[1:1]

Chinyang is an ancient imperial capital.[5] The surpassing scenery of its glens and mountains is the very best in Yŏngnam.[6] Somebody once created a painting of this place, and presented the work to Minister of State[7] Yi Chijŏ,[8] who pasted it on walls, just to admire it.

When Counselor in Military Command [Chŏng] Yŏryŏng of the Rongyang [Chŏng Clan] came to pay his respects, the minister of state pointed at it, saying, "This painting is of your homeland of mulberry and catalpa.[9] You ought to leave a line on it."

[Chŏng Yŏryŏng thereupon] wielded his brush, rose, and approached [the painting]. [His poem read,]

> Dots of green mountains pillowed on an emerald lake;
> the master says, "This here's a painting of Chinyang."
> Thatched huts by the water — who knows how many?
> In their midst is my cottage, but on the painting — it's not there![10]

All in attendance were awed by his exquisite poetic finesse and his superb literary skillfulness.

[1:2]

I read Huihong's *Lengzhai yehua*, "Night Chats from Chilly Hut."[11] Seven or eight [volumes] out of ten were entirely his own creations.[12] [This collection of anecdotes, poetics, and poetic criticism is] pure and graceful, and there is a level of imagination that rises from the common dust.[13] Regrettably, I didn't get to see the original collection.[14]

Recently there was somebody who showed me [another one of Huihong's works,] the *Yunxi ji*, "Collection of Yunxi,"[15] which, by and large, contains many pieces of presentation-and-response poetry. Taking them in slowly, I got the impression that they don't even come close to the earlier poems [contained in *Lengzhai yehua*]. Though Huihong had rare talents, [in the case of the poetry contained in *Yunxi ji*] he just couldn't escape what happens when you're "betting for tiles."[16] That old saying, "Meeting someone face-to-face isn't as good as knowing him only by his repute"[17] — well, it is credible![18]

[When reading through the *Lengzhai yehua*] I came across a single line that Pan Dalin[19] had once sent to Xie [Yi] of Linchuan.[20] I will now make a supplement for it.[21]

> Wind and rain filled the city, the Double Yang was near;[22]
> frosted leaves flying about, chrysanthemums half yellow.
> I sensed vulgar vapors, as he came and ruined my ideas;
> only have a single line to send to the autumn light.[23]

[1:3]

Munbang sabo, the "four treasures of a scholar's studio" [paper, brush, ink stone, and ink],[24] are all things Confucians are in need of. The manufacture of ink is the most difficult, but since the metropolitan area is a place where ten thousand treasures are amassed,[25] finding it is easily achieved. That's why no one thinks of it as precious.

After I had been sent out to govern Maengsŏng,[26] I suddenly received order[27] from Area Command[28] to produce and hand up five thousand sticks of ink for royal use.[29] Since they had to be presented for acceptance by the first month of the following spring, riding [the chariot][30] I hastened to arrive in Kongam Village, where I spurred the people and had them pick [enough twigs and roots] for a hundred bushels[31] of pine soot,[32] assembled skilled craftsmen [to carry out the manufacture], and personally supervised the work process myself.

"Finished!" I cried after a full two months. My face, my clothes — everything was the color of soot and coal. I removed [the black filth] right away at another place, but the washing and bathing was terribly arduous. Only then did I return to the city.

Ever since those days, when I catch sight of an inkstick, even if it's just a tiny chunk, I value it as heavily as a thousand pieces of gold, and never dare to look at it with indifference. Hence, when you think about what people commonly use — rattan paper,[33] Qi bamboo,[34] Shu brocade,[35] Wu silk[36] and the like — they really all belong to this very same category.

An ancient once remarked: "In the poem *Mei nong,* "Pitying the farmer,"[37] it says,

Who knows that for the meal inside his bowl,
grain for grain was all toil and hardship?[38]

These were the words of an earnest, benevolent one." I managed to write a single quatrain in Maengsŏng, which read,

Zhichuan wore a sash around his waist, by the white clouds' edge;[39]
while picking cinnabar grains, he meant to learn about immortals.[40]
I smile at myself over the startled snake, for the old habit's still
    there;[41]
had received the left half of a tally,[42] but ended up in charge of dark
    green pine soot.[43]

[1:4]

Kim Saeng[44] of Kyerim[45] used the brush like a spirit, his was neither [ordinary] draft nor running script,[46] and [in terms of innovation] his own calligraphic style far surpassed the fifty-seven model styles of the various masters [collected in the *Chunhuage fatie,* the "Model calligraphies from the Imperial Archives of Chunhua Pavilion"].[47]

In our dynasty,[48] Hwaŏm taesa[49] Kyŏnghyŏk[50] and Master Kim Ipchi[51] of the Security Council[52] gained fame on account of their draft script, but still they couldn't escape the inelegant commonness of Zhong Yi or Zhou Yue.[53]

In the final year of the reign of King Ŭi[jong],[54] the vigor of the brush of the Great Jin[55] envoy Ge Yi[56] was considered remarkably untrammeled.

74   POEMS AND STORIES FOR OVERCOMING IDLENESS

Ch'oe Tang[57] of the Qinghe [Ch'oe Clan] purchased [one of Ge Yi's] pieces of calligraphy and regularly hung it up on a wall to admire it. But then there was somebody who borrowed the work, just to look at it. [Later, however,] that person simply held back the original and returned a copy [of the authentic piece]. Academician [Ch'oe Tang hereupon] recited from a poem by Dongshan,[58] saying,

> A rice-cake drawn on the ground doesn't necessarily have to bear a
>   resemblance [to the original],[59]
> to make a foolish child's mouth water in yearning.[60]

[Ch'oe Tang] thus laughed it off and didn't demand an explanation from him.[61] When I heard about this, I playfully composed the following quatrain.

> As Ziyun's spring worms sluggishly form a line,[62]
> Drunken [Huai]su's startled snake[63] has vanished into the hazy
>   distance.[64]
> Woke from a dream not knowing who had taken his deer;[65]
> many forks in the road, and in vain he sighed over having lost his
>   sheep for good.[66]

[1:5]

When Chajin[67] of Hangyang [County] was sent out to take his position as local magistrate in Kwandong,[68] his wife, a woman from the Min Clan, flew into an incomparable fit of jealousy. For he had a maidservant who was an astonishing beauty, and [his wife] forbade him to [take her with him or even] go anywhere near her.

"But that's very easy!" Chajin said, and with someone from the district he traded the maidservant for a cow, which he then raised.[69] When I heard about this, I playfully completed a quatrain.

> On the lake, an oriole flew off into the distance, never to return;[70]
> on the river floodplain, jade pendants tinkled crisply; strove to find
>   them, but it is hard.[71]
> Peach in the garden and willow of the lane, where are they now?[72]
> Left is only a black peony by the balustrade.[73]

Since the roads were blocked, however, I didn't manage to put [the letter containing this poem] in the postbox.

Some twenty years later, when Chajin built a new house [and became my next-door neighbor] in Hongdojŏng Village,[74] he and I linked walls and connected lanes, and the two of us were together from morning to night. When one day he requested to see some of my poetry sketches,[75] I just took out the entire stack and showed it to him.

After having read through about half of them, he came upon that very poem entitled *Mun uin wi kun'gun sobak ich'ŏp hwanu*, "Written upon having heard about a friend who became the victim of his wife's oppression when she made him trade his concubine for a cow."

Chajin was stunned.

"Who is this about?" he asked slowly.

"But, Master, it's about you, of course," I replied, chuckling all the while.

"Indeed, that's what happened," Chajin replied, "but [my wife and I] were really just kidding around in our own bedroom. Though not mocking or judging [such a private affair] would really be the right thing to do, if it wasn't for this, how else could I help you win everlasting fame as a poet?"

His wife from the Min Clan died before Chajin. He lived as a widower for eight years, but never even went near any attractive woman. One may say he was a nobleman who earnestly practiced [the way to be sincere].[76]

[1:6]

When in mid-autumn Principal Graduate[77] Hwang Pinyŏn[78] was on [night] duty in the Jade Hall,[79] there were no clouds in the infinite sky and the moon's radiance was as bright as the light of day. He composed a poem and showed it to O Semun,[80] who was in the same office as himself.

The first day in between *ji* and *meng*;[81]
hot then cold, the weather has evened out.
Spring nights, how come they are so quiet and calm, while
autumn eves alone are so clamorous and raucous?
The moonlight's just as it always is —
the human mind's what makes it [feel] so [very differently].
I know that you, sir, can settle the matter —
which of these sceneries, really, is to take precedence?

Taking it in slowly, I felt that deep down there was principle and charm, and since I didn't see a companion piece, I made use of its meaning and answered it myself.

76 Poems and Stories for Overcoming Idleness

In one year the full moon
orbs ten and two times.
Why then, when autumn draws toward its half,
does [the moonlight] flow through the sky [so brilliantly] that
    shadows slant all by themselves?
Autumn winds brush aside covering veils,[82]
jade dews wash it clean in gorgeous ways.
For this reason [autumn eves] are different from nights in spring;
relying on a poem, I transmit it in detail.

[1:7]

Angam Temple[83] lies in the north of Tan Prefecture.[84] Though it's not at all far from the Imperial Capital, here the mountains are extraordinary and the waters different, it lies deep and secluded, and there is a dark, peculiar atmosphere about the place.

Early on, Tamji[85] of the Longxi [Yi Clan] and I once stayed there [for a while] to read, and every day at sunset we would lean against the railing and let our gazes wander freely: fishermen's fires flickering, clouds quietly descending, mists tranquilly drifting, thatched huts huddled together — it was as if we were by the spring in Wuling.[86]

When we were about to head back [to the capital], the abbot elder, pulling my robe, asked me to leave a word. He did so diligently and cordially, and thus I wrote the following poem on a wall:

Pressed by gray waves ahead, kingfisher-blue cliffs behind;
whistling winds in reeds and [forests] half of pines and of firs.
Master Xie's wanderlust, he only had a pair of clogs;[87]
Zhang Han's homesickness, [winds] filled a sail entirely.[88]
If only one could ride a hoary crane on Mount Gou;[89]
one mustn't wet the blue coat with tears in Penpu.[90]
The ten continents and three isles I [long to] rove extensively;[91]
ashamed I am as swiftly my bones will be exchanged.[92]

Twenty years later, when Chajin was sent out to conduct an inspection in a southern prefecture, he became weary of the journey and entered this temple to take a rest. The wall with the poem on it had already half crumbled, it was covered with filth, moss had sprouted on it, and it had become almost impossible to read my words.

"Although [the monks] failed to cover this poem with [green] gauze to preserve it,"[93] Chajin remarked to the person standing next to him, "at least they didn't cover it with plaster. How fortunate!"

And straightaway he put up a poetry board [onto which he copied my poem], personally wrote a colophon, and advised the temple-head to make sure that this board would neither fall down nor be lost.

[1:8]

On the night of the fifteenth of the first month, lanterns sewn of gauze are arranged in front of the ruler's seat, which is ornamented with axes.[94] The [academicians of the] Hallim-wŏn are commanded to compose lantern poems,[95] bring them forth, and present them; craftsmen are ordered to use gold foil,[96] cut out the Chinese characters of the poems, and paste them onto the lanterns. All of the rhapsodies have to treat the sceneries of the night of the fifteenth of the first month.

During the reign of King Myŏng[jong], I entered service at the Jade Hall. Thus I composed [a poem for the royal lantern festival] and brought it forth.

Winds are soft, do not cause golden ashes to fall;[97]
as night hours stretch out, gradually I see a jade worm's birth.[98]
You must know, a single loyal heart is present;
wants to help, that he with double pupils may shine as brightly as
sun and moon.[99]

The king greatly conferred praise and reward upon me, and later, when all [Hallim academicians] were to chant their poems on the lanterns, it began with mine.

[1:9]

Long ago, at the beginning of the reign of King In[jong], Vice Director of the Royal Secretariat and Chancellery[100] Hŏ Hongjae,[101] as head of the Golden Roster,[102] entered service at the Jade Hall.

After King Ŭijong had ascended the throne, Master Yu Hŭi[103] and Master Hwang Pinyŏn entered [the Hallim Academy] in succession.

When King Myŏng[jong] let the world be,[104] it was Master Yi Sunu[105] who was first called.[106]

I, untalented as I may be, followed in succession after him.[107]

Recently it was Master Kim Kunsu[108] who yet again followed after me

78 POEMS AND STORIES FOR OVERCOMING IDLENESS

and entered [the Hallim Academy as principal graduate]. With a quatrain I congratulated him.

> Ten years I held the brush, spelling out imperial cords;[109]
> many cultured men have entered in succession, and now spring is in
>   the Jade Hall.
> These days I begin to grasp the preciousness of the flower-patterned
>   paving stones;[110]
> all are the principal people[111] of [those who passed] the Dragon Gate.[112]

[1:10]

Apart from his mastery in the literary arts of phrase and brush, Kim Ipchi [Tonjung] of the Security Council was supremely skilled in [painting the] ink gentleman.[113]

Early on he [had painted a picture on the theme of] *Sangan ryangch'ong*, "Two shrubs of [mottled] bamboo by the banks of the Xiang,"[114] which he presented to his examination administrator,[115] Minister of State Ch'oe.[116] He then composed a quatrain to thank him.[117]

> His late Majesty in his years was praised a "live bamboo";[118]
> how often have I thought back on it, holding my feelings within?
> When two shrubs of [mottled] bamboo suddenly stood facing the
>   western balcony,
> I only feared a trunk [severed] from its roots would grow forth from
>   the ground.[119]

Principal Graduate Kim Kunsu is Kim Tonjung's son. He received instruction in the family practices and his [skill in ink painting] is quite marvelous. Once, when Kunsu and I were at the Surveillance Office together,[120] there stood a white screen in the office. Various masters asked [him] to paint [at least] a single [bamboo] culm [onto the screen], while they urged me to write a colophon for it. So, I wrote the following:

> The Hermit of Snow Hall gave off a sound with his poetry,[121]
> yet his ink-play's elegance was likewise an imitation of life.[122]
> Distantly imagining Wen Xiaoxiao of Jiangnan,[123]
> who needed to divide his school [of ink bamboo painting] and send
>   [the gentlemen] to Pengcheng.[124]

[1:11]

Pyŏngna noin[125] early on presented me with a small screen onto which Su kŏsa [An Ch'imin] had painted an ink bamboo.[126] One line of a poem by Bai Fu[127] was written on the back:

> Administrating fine winds and mists,
> humiliating common plants and trees.[128]

The brushwork was ingenious, splendid, and I savored and studied it ceaselessly — whenever I came upon a piece of paper, a white screen, or a hanging scroll, I would always whirl [the brush] and spatter [ink] until I myself could say that I had managed to achieve at least some vague resemblance with [Su kŏsa's style].[129] For this reason I composed the following poem:

> Lingering ripples still reach the emerald bamboo;[130]
> suspect that in a previous life I was Wen Xiaoxiao.

However, I honestly wasn't skilled enough, and merely managed to obtain some rough likeliness of form.

Chief monk Ch'ŏllim,[131] my older cousin, once presented me with a paper folding screen and requested [me to paint an ink bamboo on] it. I painted only a single culm diagonally across the four panels, but wasn't up to the task of [painting] the leaves. [Later] there was a painting master[132] who caught sight of it and said, "This culm, those joints — a mediocre one wouldn't have been capable [of painting this]. There's the elegance and vigor of Dongshan's ink play in it." When he then turned to calmly [paint] eight or nine leaves in between, it did seem as though there was a serene air [to the finished composition].

In the long ago, Pan Yue[133] obtained Yue Guang's ideas and sewed them together to complete an outstanding piece of brush writing.[134] [Zichan of] East Village,[135] Grand Councilor of the State of Zheng,[136] still marked [diplomatic orders] with his own unique style [even after they had already been drafted, critiqued, discussed, edited, and ornamented by Bi Chen and Shi Shu].[137]

Now, regarding this bamboo [painting], the composure of him who carves and chisels, and the artistry of him who sits with outstretched legs,[138] they blended into each other so harmoniously that it seemed as though it

80   POEMS AND STORIES FOR OVERCOMING IDLENESS

had all originated from a single hand holding both the bellows and the hammer.[139] One may speak of this as "converging spirits"! There was someone who praised it, saying,

> Heaven and earth have a single energy,
> Hu and Yue have the very same heart.[140]
> The ultimate of everything marvelous,
> and no traces can be found.[141]

[1:12]

Early on I caught sight of two scrolls of draft script hanging on the wall of a noble house. They had been sooted by smoke rising from a cooking fire, stained by rainwater that had leaked through the roof, and both [the calligraphy's] form and color appeared oddly ancient. The poem read,

> Inscribed on a red leaf, a poem came floating forth from inside the
>   Phoenix City;[142]
> tracks of tears merged with ink, but still clear to see.
> The rushing waters in the palace canal were murky, elusive;[143]
> yet they washed up a sliver of a palace lady's true condition.[144]

The guests in their seats all put their heads together and stared intensely at it, saying, "This has got to be the brushwork of someone from Tang or Song times." In confusion [they debated controversially among one another about the creator of the calligraphy as well as the poem] but weren't able to get to the bottom of it. After a while they came up to me, asking me what I considered to be its real substance.

"These are traces of my very own handwriting," I answered slowly.

Taken aback, the other guests exclaimed, "Since there are traces of grease splats on torn, wrinkled silk,[145] it seemed to us not like a recent but rather an ancient work!"

"This is a piece from my poems on historical themes," said I.[146] "See, I never write in draft script unless the poems are my own compositions."[147]

[1:13]

When Yŏngnak [Cho T'ong][148] of the Tianshui [Cho Clan] was about to take his position as magistrate of Yang Prefecture,[149] Chajin and I braved [the dim, frigid hours of] dawn and arrived at the gates of Ch'ŏnsu Temple,[150] where we had planned to hold a parting feast for him. Yŏngnak, however, was held up by a companion [in the capital].

When he still hadn't gotten there by noon, with slow steps the two of us wandered around [the temple grounds] and eventually swung by one of the monks' residences. All was quiet, nobody was there—so I stealthily jotted the following poem with pale ink onto a wooden door [of the Buddhist Hall]:

> Waiting for a friend,[151] but the friend hasn't arrived yet;[152]
> looking for a monk, but there're no monks here either.
> Only a bird beyond the forest
> calling a tune, urging us on: *che-ho,* "lift the jug."[153]

About twenty years later I happened to meet a monk at Chajin's house. His appearance of a man of the Way was imposing and rather unusual. He bowed to me, saying, "In the past, I once was granted the honor of seeing a superb piece of your poetry, but only here and now do I get the chance to express my gratitude for it." I was puzzled and didn't really understand, but then the monk recited this very poem, and [with a twinkle in his eye] he remarked, "I was the abbot of the monastery back then." Together we laughed wholeheartedly. Eventually I added [both the poem and the story] to the collection of family writings.[154]

[1:14]

Mount Chiri is by some referred to as Turyu[-san], "[Mount] Headstop."[155] Rising from Mount Paektu in [the territory of] the Northern dynasty,[156] the bud-like peaks and calyx-like valleys [of the T'aebaek mountain range] spread out and continue on [southward] until they reach Taebang County,[157] coiling in knots and knots for thousands of leagues, circling around, and occupying some ten prefectures. It would take ten months to get from one boundary to the other.

Old-timers [in the capital] used to tell the following story among each other: "In [the Turyu Mountains] lies Ch'ŏnghak-tong, "Blue Crane Grotto."[158] The path that leads you there is extremely narrow, barely admitting a single man to pass through. You have to lie flat on your belly and slowly crawl forward for a number of leagues, but eventually you'll get to a wide-open space where there're rich fields and fertile soils in all four corners, and these're just perfect for sowing and planting.[159] Only blue cranes nest and rest there, and that's why it's named after them. In times of old, those who

82   POEMS AND STORIES FOR OVERCOMING IDLENESS

had retreated from the world used to dwell at this place,[160] and crumbled walls and earthen moats still exist beneath heaps of thorns and brambles."[161]

Long ago, I and Minister of State Ch'oe,[162] who is my older cousin, had our minds set on brushing off our robes and departing for good.[163] Then we promised each other that we would [venture out into those mountains in the deep south and] find this grotto, thinking that if we entered it with a bamboo-cage holding two or three calves, it would be possible for us to [live there in reclusion and] not hear anything of the vulgar men of the world anymore.[164] Eventually, we set off from Hwaŏm Temple,[165] reached Hwagae Lesser Prefecture,[166] and then spent the night at Sinhŭng Temple.[167] Wherever we passed, there was nothing that wasn't like the immortals' realm: a thousand cliffs vying for resplendent beauty, ten thousand ravines quarrelling over the flow [of their magnificent waterfalls], thatched cottages nestling behind bamboo fences, peach and apricot trees setting each other off—this, it seemed to me, was not the human world [but rather an enchanting, otherworldly sphere]. Yet the place [those old-timers] had spoken of as "Blue Crane Grotto," ultimately we didn't find it there. And so, I left a poem on the rocks of a cliff.

> Mount Turyu lies remote, twilight clouds hang low;
> ten thousand ravines and a thousand cliffs, resembling [Mount]
>   Kuaiji.[168]
> Went out with the cane, intending to find Blue Crane Grotto;
> from afar beyond the forest, in vain we hear white monkeys howl.[169]
> [Stone] towers and terraces in the hazy distance, the three mountains
>   far away;[170]
> moss-covered and obscured are those four characters inscribed.[171]
> Should you ask: "The immortals' spring, where's it at?"[172]
> Falling petals and rushing waters had us humans lose the way.[173]

Yesterday, at my studio, by chance I perused the *Wuliu xiansheng ji,* the "Collected works of Master Five Willows,"[174] and there was the *Tao[hua] yuan ji,* "The Record of Peach Blossom Spring." I looked at it over and over again, [reading the following story]:

People of the Qin dynasty,[175] worn out by the chaos [of their war-ridden era], led their women and children to a deeply hidden, inaccessible realm, surrounded by [impenetrable] mountains, hemmed in by [raging] streams—they made a place their home that not even the wood- and grass-gatherers could have hoped to reach. Then, during the Taiyuan era of the Jin dynasty,[176] a fisherman once reached it by a stroke of good fortune, but [upon having left it] he immediately forgot the way, and never found it again.

In later ages there were those who painted pretty pictures of it, as well as those who sang songs to transmit the story, and always Peach [Blossom] Spring was taken as a world of immortals, the capital of those who ride feathered carriages and stormwind chariots, those who enjoy longevity and everlasting vision.[177]

When I had read this [*Taohuayuan*] *ji* [in my younger years, before traveling to Mount Chiri,], I hadn't yet been mature enough. Truly, there's no difference [between the legendary Peach Blossom Spring and] Blue Crane Grotto. How could even a high-minded scholar like Liu Ziji[178] have gone out once and discovered it?[179]

[1:15]

On the basis of their [submitted] literary writings, *munsaeng*[180] obtain reflections on their literary knowledge from the *chongbaek*,[181] and, what's more, they receive special regard in the realm of Blue Clouds.[182] It's what the ancients referred to as an "encounter of [Zhong Zi]qi and [Bo]ya."[183] Thus, if [a *munsaeng*] takes office—even if he reaches a position [as high and prestigious as] guardian of measure[184]—he'll still be nothing more than a youngster in terms of hierarchy, and for him, no one would ever dare conduct the rituals proper [for the *chongbaek*].

In the long ago, Pei Hao of the Later Tang[185] had served three times as examination administrator during the Tongguang era.[186] When his examination passer Ma Yisun[187] then presided over the civil service examination, [Ma] pulled along the various scholars of the new [Golden] Roster,[188] to go and pay respect [to Pei Hao]. [Thereupon Pei Hao] composed the following verse:

> Three times I took charge of the Rites Apartment, and I am eighty
> years old;
> below my disciple's gateway I get to see his disciples.[189]

In our dynasty, [the civil service examination and recruitment system] began during the time of King Kwang[jong], with [presented] scholars[190] being selected on the basis of their submitted poems and rhapsodies.[191] Yet at this early stage, there were never any *chongbaek* who got to see their *munsaeng* be in charge of examinations and selections themselves.

84   POEMS AND STORIES FOR OVERCOMING IDLENESS

At the beginning of the reign of King Myŏng[jong], Academician Han Ŏn'guk[192] led on his *munsaeng* to pay respect to Minister of State Ch'oe Yuch'ŏng,[193] and he, too, composed a poem:

> Attached in lines they come to pay me a visit, and what an honor it is for me;
> glad to see my disciple's gateway pupils.

This, while being based on the ancient example set by Master Pei, was by all who heard it referred to as a "magnificent assembly."

It has been eight years now since our current king ascended the throne.[194] [This year,] assistant headmaster of the National Academy[195] Cho Ch'ung,[196] too, pulled along his *munsaeng* until they all reached [the house of] Minister of State Im Yu,[197] where he meant to express his gratitude. Yet Master [Im Yu], as director of the Chancellery,[198] is currently still on duty at the Chancellery. This is something that has never happened in old and new! It was a rare thing, indeed![199] I composed a poem to record this outstanding, astonishing [incident].

> Ten years in the Yellow Cabinet,[200] he assisted in finding peace;
> three times he opened the Spring Apartment,[201] presiding over the association alone.[202]
> A gentleman of the state, as always, repays like a gentleman of the state;[203]
> a disciple has now, too, obtained his disciples.
> Wind and clouds in motion, the Kun [has become the] Peng, rippling [the waters];[204]
> linen and kudzu in profusion, [among them] swans and egrets shining brightly.[205]
> [Offered a toast with] a cup of golden liquor:[206] May the Master live long!
> With a jade pipe[207] one ought to play the tune of "Xi qian ying."[208]

[1:16]

Hoemun si, "palindrome poems,"[209] which originated during Qi-Liang times,[210] are a lyrical form of playing around with written words, and that's really all there is to it. In the long ago, after [Su Hui], the wife of Duo Tao, had woven [a palindrome poem] into brocade,[211] the weaving-loom remained as it was,[212] and the Three Sages of Song[213] were likewise all skilled in it. The *Nanxu ji,* "Collection of Xu [Ling] from the South,"[214] contains the [palindrome] poem *Panzhong ti,* "Style of [the poem on] a tray,"[215] and even if one reads it in continuous spirals, it can be divided into forty different verses. Its rhymes are then still harmonious, but its blood vessels aren't connected anymore.[216]

In our dynasty, Academician Yi Chisim[217] was once stirred by autumn. He composed the following twin-rhyme palindrome poem in a rather skilled manner:

> Vanishing summer heat, I know autumn is early;
> [summer is] drifting away, gradually feeling agony.
> Wind-tossed pines, like green awnings toppling;
> rushing waters, like emerald vines twining.
> Ridges are distant, converging mists white;
> towers are high, dispersing breezes cool.
> Halfway in the sky, the shining moon is splendid;
> a dark room, illuminated by a shimmering glow.
>
> [A glowing shimmer illuminates a room's dark,
> as the splendid moon is shining in the sky halfway.
> Cool breezes, dispersing by high towers,
> white mists, converging by distant ridges.
> Like twining vines, emerald waters rushing;
> like toppling awnings, green pines wind-tossed.
> Agonized feelings are gradually drifting away;
> in early autumn, I know summer heat has vanished.][218]

I, too, once emulated the style of this poem [and composed the following *hoemun si*], which I presented to the grand councilor of the time.

> In my youth I studied, longed for wandering in officialdom;
> [all those] poems' completion—it was painstaking hardship.
> An old man's recollections, like spring catkins flying wildly;
> thin hair, like daybreak's hoarfrost so new.
> A toppled cauldron, the morning's cooking fire has died out;
> an empty stomach, at night it rumbled on and on.
> To requite kindness the heart is earnest;
> who'll be there to save a drying fish?[219]
>
> [A fish is drying, to save it who will be there?
> In earnest, a heart's kindness shall be requited.

86   Poems and Stories for Overcoming Idleness

> On and on it rumbled, at night the stomach was empty;
> a died-out cooking fire, in the morning a cauldron toppled over.
> Like new hoarfrost, at daybreak the hair is so thin;
> wildly flying catkins, in spring there's a recollecting old man.
> In hardship, painstakingly I completed [all those] poems;
> in officialdom I wander, longing for the studies of my youth.]

See, palindromes must be harmonious and easy when read forward, but if read backward there likewise mustn't be anything sounding uneven, anything troublesome or coarse. Both words and meaning have to be equally marvelous. Only then can it be called [a *hoemun si* composed] in a skillful manner.

[1:17]

The chrysanthemum has many different variations, and although one cannot possibly enumerate them all, yellow should naturally be considered its proper color. For this reason, the ancients said,

> Of the five colors,[220] [yellow] is most precious;
> after a thousand flowers [have already withered], [chrysanthemums]
>   alone shall be revered.[221]

Yesterday I went to the studio of [Master] Ch'oe of the Security Council,[222] where in the rear garden the yellow flowers were in full bloom, their golden hue dazzling the eye.

"I've been waiting for you," Master [Ch'oe] called out to me, all the while pointing at the flowers, "because I wanted to trouble you to chant just a single verse [on the topic of these chrysanthemums]. But now it's already too late in the evening, so let's just agree to do it another day." Hence, we had a few rounds of ale, after which I departed.

By chance, as I was riding atop my horse, some long lines came to my mind. I shall present them to him on a future occasion.

> On the pond of Han, an auspicious [yellow] swan's wings were
>   firstly preened;[223]
> when [Fu] Fei of the Luo [River] returned home,[224] dust was stirred
>   by her slippers.[225]
> You should know that an immortal's character, even in old age,
>   doesn't wither,

even if whistling autumn winds enter into the flowers' bones.
Let the charm remain, and pick one to make three springs return;[226]
this poet would be glad to see just a single stalk plucked,
to have it float in a golden goblet, and wait for times to come,
for in the lord's home, there's no need to fear the chills of ice and
   frost.

[1:18]

King Ye[jong], by his Heaven-endowed nature, loved learning, and he revered the Confucian scholars' elegance. He had especially opened Ch'ŏngyŏn-gak, the "Tower of Pure Debate,"[227] and each day he critically discussed the prescripts and canons[228] with the academicians [of the Hallim Academy] there.[229]

Early on, [King Yejong] was present at the Sa-ru, the "Sedge-Grass Tower."[230] In front of [this building] the peonies had just opened in full bloom,[231] and thus [the king] commanded the various Confucian scholars of the [six] Inner Palace Offices[232] to write poems of seven words and six rhymes [on the subject of these pretty peonies] within the [time limit set by a] marked candle.[233] Eastern Palace Household Administration Secretary An Porin[234] became the winner [of this poetry competition], and based on the candidates' rank, grace was bestowed very generously.

Back then, Teacher Kang Iryong's fame as a poet had stirred all under heaven,[235] and the king had made up his mind to wait and take a look at his composition. Yet by the time the candle had burned all the way down to the mark, [Kang Iryong] still had only managed to write but a single couplet. Concealing his piece of paper [he ran out in shame,] hiding himself in the palace canal. The king thereupon ordered some of the junior attendants at the yellow gates[236] to hurry out after him and retrieve [the poem]. [Kang Iryong had] written the following:

His head white, Old Drunkard glanced [at them] from behind the
   main hall;[237]
his eyes sparkling, Confucian Elder leaned [toward them] beside his
   fence.[238]

Since his use of allusions was as refined and magnificent as this, the king sighed in admiration and praised it without cease, saying, "To something like this, the ancients would have said, 'If, on a head like a mortar, flowery hairpins entirely adorn the face, it still won't be anything like Xi Shi's face

88   POEMS AND STORIES FOR OVERCOMING IDLENESS

with makeup only half-applied.' "[239] Thus he consoled him and sent him on his way.[240] Now I intend to supplement what was missing.

> A single bloom, gorgeously red, worth ten thousand cash;
> light shadows [of clouds and faint rain] — exactly the right weather
>   for cultivating flowers.[241]
> [Wears the] immortals' makeup, doesn't need to borrow rouge
>   to dye;
> the tidings of spring, it has already leaned on a *jiegu* to
>   transmit them.[242]
> According to Chu custom, fragrant times approached on the one
>   hundred and fifth;[243]
> in the palace of Han, new favorites were worn on the headdresses of
>   the three thousand.[244]
> In the morning, it's the sunshine that already turns it toward
>   drunkenness;
> at night, it's the fear of the wind's cold that won't let it fall asleep.
> His head white, *and the above words*[245]
> As the candlelight slowly faded, chanting became ever more
>   distressing —
> he picked remaining charm, put it in a single couplet.

[1:19]

Skillfulness or clumsiness in poetry are neither determined by [whether poems are written] slowly or rapidly, nor by [whether poets write] before or after.[246] Nevertheless, he who sings a poem is in front, while he who harmonizes with it is always behind. He who sings sojourns at perfect ease, is at leisure and relaxed, with nothing weighing him down, while he who harmonizes with it cannot avoid being pulled along by force, and being left in a tight spot.[247] Thereby, when someone continues a person's rhyme — no matter how famous or talented he may be — there's always something he won't match. On principle, that's just the way it is!

Chulao [Wang Anshi][248] once happened to see Meishan [Su Dongpo's][249] rhapsody on snow, a poem of [an intricate] rhyme pattern with the [final] character *cha*, "fork."[250] Loving [Su's] ability to make use of rhymes, [Wang] had already composed one piece to harmonize with it,[251] but in his heart he still felt dissatisfied, and thus he continued it with yet another five pieces of his own.[252] Although he made use of allusions in an even more peculiar way, and coughed up expressions in an even more complex fashion — aiming to press [Su Shi's poems] down by means of the strangeness and complexity [of his allusions] — he still couldn't avoid the [general] limitations [of the response poem] mentioned above. As it is said in military treatises: "It is better for me to oppress a man than to have that man oppress me." That is credible!

This morning I went up to the studio when snow had just ceased to fall. Thereupon I remembered the two elders' poems, and to harmonize I completed two companion pieces. Yet I also couldn't avoid being pulled along by force, and I hope that those who will view [my poems] may forgive me for it.

A thousand trees in falling darkness, upon them perching crows;[253]
radiant the bright [moon] pearl, still shedding its light onto the cart.[254]
Immortal bones, together amazed there is something like the
    virgin girl;[255]
spring winds, have no way of controlling the madly [scattering]
    flowers.[256]
Faint sounds of drizzling rain rustling a window's paper;[257]
the cold pulling on a traveler in sorrow til he reaches a wine house.[258]
For ten thousand leagues and all around,[259] silver is the world;[260]
mire on the road's entry, burying its three forks.[261]

A clear sky's biting cold will surely rouse the [perching] crows;
claps of thunder rumbling, trailing [A] Xiang's cart.[262]
As the cold creeps into greenish wine, it can hardly rouse [warming]
    dizziness;
as [the cold] threatens the reddish lamp, it can barely blossom its
    [shining] flower.
One stroke of the oars as it is time to leave, I understand the guest's
    impulse;[263]
a solitary thread of smoke rising from somewhere, I recognize my
    mountain house.
Shut the gates, lie down on high — no one ever reaches [this studio];
saved some copper coins, hang them on a painting fork.[264]

[1:20]

At the beginning of the reign of King Ŭi[jong],[265] the stationmaster[266] of Ch'ŏnggyo Postal Relay Station[267] had raised a blue cow,[268] the appearance of which was unique and quite unusual. And so, he presented it to the court.

90   POEMS AND STORIES FOR OVERCOMING IDLENESS

The king commanded all of the rhetorical ministers[269] close by to compose rhapsodies and poems [on the topic of this auspicious animal] and to come up with rhymes. But the [complicated] rhyme pattern put [the literati officials] in a precarious position, and there was no one who did not seem embarrassed.

Kim Hyosun[270] of the Eastern Bureau[271] won first place, while Sin Ŭngnyong of the Jade Hall came next. Kim [Hyosun] had written:

Phoenixes, observing virtue, are ashamed to come and nest at the
    tower [in the presence of the blue cow];[272]
horses, replete with essence, are embarrassed to ascend and respond
    to the room [in the presence of the blue cow].[273]

Sin [Ŭngnyong] had written:

He struck your horn—thus long ago you sighed when [King Huan of
    Qi] encountered Master Ning;[274]
he was about to ritually anoint a bell with your blood—thus now you
    avoid being led past the halls of Qi.[275]

"Although his use of allusions to ancient matters is quite skilled," said the king upon having read [Sin Ŭngnyong's poem] several times over, "his words really verge on being disrespectful. That's why I think this poem ought to take second place." [King Ŭijong] bestowed upon them wine of the highest quality as well as bolts of silk, each in accordance with his placing.

Sŏha Im Chongbi was a gifted scholar, too.[276] When he heard about this he gave a sigh, saying, "If I'd been made to participate in this venue, I would've written the following:

In Peach Grove you were let loose in spring,[277] then marched into the
    Red Room."[278]

Yet in the end he didn't manage to come up with a corresponding line. Now I mean to emulate and continue it.

By the banks of the Silver Stream you pursued an immortal woman;[279]
the black peony flower reached Snow Hall.
On Hangu [Pass] you returned at dawn, floating along in purple
    vapors;[280]
in Peach Grove you were let loose in spring, then marched into the
    Red Room.

[1:21]

As for the techniques of polishing [poetic] lines,[281] Shaoling [Du Fu] alone fully mastered their marvelousness. This is evidenced, for example, in lines of the following kind:

> Days and months, a bird in a cage,
> Heaven and Earth, a duckweed on the waters.[282]

Or

> Ten summers in the homespun of Mount Min,
> three frosts among the pounding blocks of Chu homes.[283]

Also, since man's talents are [as assorted and diverse] as household utensils, some square and some round, it's simply impossible to have all of them proper and prepared. And the strange sights and extraordinary enjoyments under heaven, those by which one can please both the heart and the eye, are exceedingly manifold.

Yet if ability and talent fall short of one's ambitions, then, just to use a comparison, it's the same as a worn-out nag trotting along on that thousand-league-long road between Yan and Yue[284] — you can crack the whip all you like, it'll never reach that faraway place.

Thereby, people of old, even if they possessed unworldly talent, didn't dare to rashly set about [considering a poem finished] — they necessarily first added their skill of refining and polishing, and only then would they have attained enough to put down those rainbows that would cast their glow for all of time. It got to a point where they would forge a poem for ten days straight, refine it for an entire season, chant it in the morning and sing it at night, stroke their whiskers while hardly feeling comfortable with a single word — in a whole year they'd barely finish three pieces! [Jia Dao was undecided whether] a hand should "knock on" or "push" [a gate under the moon], and [lost in thought, from time to time imitating these gestures of knocking and pushing,] he inadvertently blundered into [the retinue of] Metropolitan Governor [Han Yu].[285] [And paying no mind to anything other than] chanting an accomplished poem, [Du Fu] became wretchedly thin while passing by Boiled [Rice] Mountain.[286] They had the ambition to [poetically] exhaust the [splendor of the] western peaks,[287] or the striking of the bell at midnight[288] — poems such as these, it's impossible to list them all.

Getting to Su [Shi] and Huang [Tingjian], with them the use of allusions

92   POEMS AND STORIES FOR OVERCOMING IDLENESS

became increasingly precise, and their carefree, unrestrained spirits revealed themselves on an even wider scale. Regarding the marvelousness of their polished lines, they surely ought to be considered on par with Shaoling.[289]

[1:22]

Academician [Kim] Hwangwŏn[290] of our dynasty wrote the following poem on his studio in the province:[291]

> In a mountain city, rains are fierce — suddenly turning to hail;
> in a marshy land, shadows are abundant — frequently setting free
>   rainbows.

When Yi Sunu of the Crape Myrtle [Secretariat][292] was sent out to guard Kwandong, he wrote the following:

> Inside the Thin Willow Camp, a new general;[293]
> below the Crape Myrtle Flower, a former secretary.

[When I became principal graduate in the civil service examinations,] my friend Kiji presented me with [a poem]:

> The wind blows hard as the Peng of the Oblivion rises from the north;
> the moon shines bright as the startled magpie cannot rest on a branch.[294]

The rectifier of omissions of the Rongyang [Chŏng Clan][295] once happened to travel to the Eight-Foot Room [in Kaesŏng Temple][296] on Mount Ch'ŏnma.[297] All evening long he made painful efforts to [come up with and] chant a poem, but eventually wasn't yet able to assemble his thoughts. At dawn, as he started on his way back, he went on reciting, loosely holding on to his horse's reins. When he had almost reached the gates of the capital, he suddenly happened to hit upon a single couplet, which went as follows:

> At the top of the rocks, a pine ages under a single sliver of moon;
> at the end of the earth, a cloud descends upon a thousand dots of
>   mountains.[298]

Whipping the lame horse, he rushed back [to Kaesŏng Temple], rattled the doorknob [of the Eight-Foot Room] with his hands, stormed into the temple room,[299] roused his brush, hastily scrawled these lines onto a wall, and only then he returned [to the capital].

Also, there was Teacher Kang Iryong, who wanted to write on the subject of the "Egret." Braving the [heavy] rain, time and again he ventured out to arrive above the creek south of Ch'ŏnsu Temple. Finally, as he was observing the birds, he suddenly happened to hit upon a single line:

It flies, slicing an emerald mountainside.

And forthwith he spoke to the people, "Today, at last I got to reach a place even the ancients never reached.[300] Later there certainly shall be someone with rare talents who will be able to continue it."

When I think about this line, I honestly don't consider it to be as brilliant as those by the poets of earlier generations, but that [Kang Iryong] said this must've simply been due to the fact that he had had to make such painful efforts to be able to chant it in the first place. I made the following supplement to it:

It occupies, nesting in high treetops;
it flies, slicing an emerald mountainside.

Well, if a single line such as this is put amid a poet's collected pieces, the entire rest may well be coarsely prepared. It's precisely like,

Where there are pearls, plants do not wither;
where there is jade, streams are naturally beautiful.[301]

[1:23]

U-hu, "Behind the Cow," was the milk name[302] of Hwawŏnok,[303] a flower of the Bureau of Music.[304] In terms of beauty and artistry she was the finest at one point in time. Principal Graduate Hwang[305] composed the *U-hu ka,* the "Song of U-hu," which, in substance, went as follows:

[Her parents] bemoaned that the moth-eyebrows had to die before
 the horses;[306]
meaning to exhort her, in turn [they] named her "Behind the Cow."[307]

Principal Graduate Yu Hŭi wrote,

94 POEMS AND STORIES FOR OVERCOMING IDLENESS

The cow's heart, it should only be offered to me, Xizhi.[308]

"I'm sure they meant for her to follow [a devoted, loving husband like] the Cowherd up there in Heaven,"[309] said my friend Kiji, "and that's why they took *u*, "cow," and *hu*, "behind," as the characters for her [milk] name." Then he asked me to rhapsodize with him [on the subject of the singing girl and her name].[310] [The poem I wrote went as follows.]

Haven't you seen
how Shi Chong rode upon a cow, so fast as if in flight,[311]
or how Lüzhu's splendid substance was more resplendent than the
   numinous mushroom and orchid?[312]
And haven't you seen
how the Duke of Wei read his books, riding on a cow all the while,[313]
or how Xue'er's exquisite singing was clearer than even the highest
   clouds and wisps?[314]
From ancient times girls in patterned silk[315]
have dwelled behind the cow.
With this I ask Behind the Cow —
"what they call you, is it in line with my ideas or not?"[316]
Smiling sweetly, she tilts her head slightly,
[and sings] a single tune worth a thousand in gold, for my long life.

[1:24]

Long ago I went out to assist in Kyeyang,[317] and upon having received a surveillance commissioner's call,[318] I arrived at Mount Yong,[319] where I spent the night at the [old] study of Minister of State Han Ŏn'guk.

The peaks and ridges, winding and coiling, were shaped like a gray-green serpent, and the study was squatting directly on [the mountainous animal's] forehead. The current of the [Han] River flows up to the foot [of Mount Yong], splits there, and forks in two.[320] [Out toward the west,] beyond the [two forks of the] river, distant pinnacles stand [in a straight line], and gazing down upon this [from the studio] it all looked to me like the word *san* 山, "mountain." I chanted a poem with a clear voice, then rose and trusted my brush to write it on a wall.

Two rivers, billowing, billowing, split like a swallow's tail;
   three mountains, faint, faint, carried away on turtles' heads.[321]

In those years, if I'd been allowed to accompany [him holding] the
  turtledove cane,[322]
together we'd have headed toward gray waves, grown familiar with
  white gulls.[323]

Yŏngnak [Cho T'ong] of the Tianshui [Cho Clan] was a *munsaeng* of Minister of State Han.[324] Once he visited the minister of state, and happened to recite this very poem as they were having a round of ale. The minister of state put down his cup, chanted the poem and finally spoke, "Fifty years have passed since I last sojourned in Hanyang![325] But now, upon hearing just a single line, the glimmer of its mountains and the colors of its river are laid out so clearly, it's as if everything was right before my eyes! That's exactly what an ancient meant when he wrote *sijung hwa*, 'in poems, there are paintings.' "[326]

[1:25]

On a day in the fourth month of the cyclic year *kyehae*, the third year of the Huangtong reign [of the Jurchen Jin emperor Xizong],[327] Commissioner Kim[328] received the royal will to command two ministers[329] to go to Naksŏngjae Study Hall[330] at Irwŏl Temple,[331] where they were to debate and practice[332] with the various scholars.

At the beginning of the intercalary fourth month, on the eighth day, [the ministers and scholars composed] linked verses.[333] Palace Attendant Ch'oe Sanbo[334] called out the word *kye*, "brook," whereupon the following was written:

Brooks trickle down, gurgling, murmuring, always studying
  the sea;[335]

—*Myŏngjong*[336]

in a dream the soul is startled, happily gazing toward Heaven.

—*Kim Sukch'ŏng*

The word *sa*, "thread," was then called out, and the following was written:

Like a thread so straight stands a weeping willow by a field lane in
  spring;

—*Myŏngjong*

like a brow so fine hangs a new moon by the clouds' edge in twilight.

—*Kim Chach'ing*

96   POEMS AND STORIES FOR OVERCOMING IDLENESS

Brook waters sounding through forests, coming from distant valleys;
—*Sang Yŏnggong, "First Minister"*

mountain clouds brushing over rocks, amassing above lofty peaks.
—*Kim Sangsun*

Peaks and ridges, pointed, pointed, close-rowed spears and halberds;
—*Sang Yŏnggong, "First Minister"*

poplars and willows, swaying, swaying, hanging skeins and threads.

The following day, King [Injong] entered the inner palace and perused them.

P'ahan chip — Fascicle 2

[2:1]

The wise man sees what hasn't yet taken form, while the fool calls it a nonexistent matter, complacently not considering it as anything to worry about. Only after calamity has already struck will he become anxious and labor with all his might, longing to be saved from it — but what good will this do in terms of whether he lives or dies, succeeds or fails? It was for this reason that Bian Que didn't get to save Marquis Huan from his illness.[1] In the long ago, during the time of Emperor Wen of Han,[2] all within the sea-girt world was structured and peaceful, the people lived in abundance and wealth, but Jia Yi still lamented bitterly.[3] After Emperor Wen of Tang had founded the dynasty,[4] he became more cautious and fearful with each passing day, and while he wasn't yet the least bit lazy, Wei Zheng[5] nonetheless submitted the *Shijian* [*shu*], the "[Memorial of the emperor's] ten lapses."[6] For this reason the following has been transmitted: "He who remonstrates tackles the source and does not let [harmful developments] unfold any further. He who warns of [solid] ice when there is only hoarfrost[7] prevents [the craving for] jade-cups when only lacquerware [is being produced]."

Long ago, King Ŭi[jong] ascended the throne after several dozens of generations had been marked by plentifulness and peace,[8] and he came into a structured government. The days of his reign went by, and whichever matter it may have been, there was nothing he did not handle. Everybody said, "The achievements of this great era of peace are more stable than Mount Tai!" and no one ever dared to utter any words [of criticism regarding the king and the court]. Only Censor Mun Kŭkkyŏm directly knocked on the palace doors,[9] pulled a memorial to the throne out of a black silken bag, and what it stated exposed the entire sickness of the age.[10] People said to this that "a phoenix had sung toward the early

98   POEMS AND STORIES FOR OVERCOMING IDLENESS

sun,"[11] but when [the Son of] Heaven heard it, he didn't yet consider [Mun Kŭkkyŏm] loyal.[12] The master thus took off his court robe, returned to his home, and composed the following poem.

> Zhu Yun breaking the balustrade — it was not out of yearning for
>   praise;[13]
> Yuan Ang standing in the carriage's way — how could it have been
>   for his personal sake?[14]
> A single fraction of loyal earnestness, [August] Heaven has not yet
>   shone His light upon it;
> a horse, severely whipped and beaten, withdraws reluctantly.[15]

When King Myŏng[jong] ascended the throne, [Mun Kŭkkyŏm] was chosen to serve as [the king's] throat and tongue in the land.[16] Regarding such issues as to whether the dynasty was in peace or in peril, the people at ease or in sickness, the literati officials diligent or unworthy — he communicated everything for the [Son of] Heaven to hear, and there wasn't the smallest thing he would have concealed or ignored. To this day, relations with neighboring countries have been fine, interior and exterior have been calm and free of troubles, and this, truly, is due to the influence of Master [Mun Kŭkkyŏm].

When holding the position of chancellor, he recommended me, and I entered service at the Jade Hall.

At the beginning of the new year, Master [Mun Kŭkkyŏm] passed away.[17] Thereupon I composed the following elegy.

> Early, at Changhe,[18] he cried out, pushing away [menacing] clouds;[19]
> late, at Yuyuan, he held on to the [setting] sun, [making every effort
>   to] turn it around.[20]
> The cinnabar phoenix, long it bathed upon the [Phoenix] Pool;[21]
> the white chicken, why did it hurry him inside his dreams?[22]

"When Master [Mun Kŭkkyŏm] served at the court, there were major crises[23] from beginning to end," people of the times said, "but nothing about that is brought forth in these two [initial] lines. One could say [it's not a lyrical elegy,] it's a 'Veritable Record.'"

Yesterday I passed by the master's former country residence, where plants and trees were graying with age and spring water was gushing forth from cracks in rocks. Earlier this had been the spot where the master had sojourned and feasted. I lingered on with a heavy heart, unable to leave, and eventually composed an impromptu poem, which I left upon a wall.

From below the rocks, cold cold waters
swirl and whirl, as if there were thoughts.
Who knows if those currents of [melted] ice and snow
are still winding around the Phoenix Pool?[24]
The Eastern Tower, I peered at it once more, stayed on for a little
      while;[25]
the Western Gate, it's where I meant at sundown
to inscribe a poem and leave it in the middle of the wall,
to send it off to the Nine Springs,[26] just to let it be known.[27]

[2:2]

Kim Puŭi[28] of the Security Council was the younger brother of Director of the
Chancellery Master Munyŏl [Kim Pusik].[29] Both had stood out on account
of their achievements in literary writing.

Early on, when [Kim Puŭi], carrying royal staff and tally, had gone to
the Central dynasty as an envoy,[30] [Emperor] Zhenzong[31] loved his talent,
and even met him with the proper rites.

When [the emissaries] were on the premises of the official guesthouse
[where our dynasty's embassy was stationed in the Song capital of Bianjing],
two men suddenly entered to have a little drink with them.[32] They [eventually
passed the time with] a drinking game of fine phrases,[33] and the first phrase
called out was:

In the heavens there are three hundred sixty degrees;[34]
in the stars there is the one who herds oxen.

The next phrase called out was:

On a Qi-board there are three hundred sixty intersections;[35]
there are horses but no oxen.[36]

Master [Kim Puŭi] then straightaway called out:

In a year there are three hundred sixty days;
on the first day of spring one uses clay oxen.[37]

Everyone present was awed by his superb literary skillfulness.

Earlier, when attending the emperor's banquet, as the guests were
becoming increasingly tipsy, the emperor had taken a poem of long lines and

100 POEMS AND STORIES FOR OVERCOMING IDLENESS

six rhymes and showed it to them, whereupon he had sent out his attendants to urgently order each of the attending guests to write a companion piece and bring it forth. The master, without even having to think hard about it, simply picked up his brush, [finished the poem in no time,] and rose right away. It roughly said the following:

> Beside Chenxiang Pavilion I hear a new melody;[38]
> before Lili Gate I congratulate the age of great peace.[39]
> No way to repay the virtue of Heaven and earth even a tiny bit;
> have only my drunken brush to express gratitude for birth and growth.

The emperor had sighed, praising it without cease, whereupon he had bestowed [Kim Puŭi] with gifts even more generously.

In the final year of Huizong's reign, however, the Jurchen Jin brought about the fall of Bianjing, captured the two emperors [Huizong and Qinzong], and returned with them to the north.[40] [After the establishment of the Southern Song,] the Prince of Kang[41] inherited the throne and dispatched the envoy Yang Yingcheng to come [to our dynasty].[42] [Yang] subsequently requested to borrow an [eastern] passage [to Huining, the Upper Capital of Jin,][43] and asked [our court to be allowed] to go and pay his respects to the two [captured] emperors in their provisional place of residence.[44] In the discussions at court, however, [the king and his officials][45] made the firm decision that this should not be allowed.[46] [The king] hereupon ordered Master [Kim Puŭi] to compose a memorial to answer [Emperor Gaozong of the Southern Song].[47] [In the missive] it said:

> The benevolence of Heaven and earth brings each of the myriad things to completion. The virtue of emperors and kings should not hold the multitude of [base] people responsible for what causes them difficulties.

Also, it said:

> They are many, we are few[48] — this already makes it hardly possible for us to engage in battle with them. And if the lips are missing, the teeth will be cold — again, how do we know this will not turn out to be a blessing [for the Southern Song]?[49]

Also, it said:

> Leading the vassal lords and honoring the kings of Zhou — we dare not agree [to emulate] the old example of Qi and Jin.[50] Defining the land and

creating the Tribute of Yu — we hope not to lose the ancient righteousness of Jing and Xu.[51]

Since Master Munyŏl had already entered the Secretariat, [his younger brother Kim Puŭi] had to stay at the Security Council for more than ten years.[52]

By nature, [Kim Puŭi] was addicted to reading, and thus he opened a separate room where he always discussed literary writings with other scholar officials. Even his wife and concubine hardly ever caught sight of his face.

When it happened that [Kim Puŭi] had to take to his bed with an illness, some scholar at court dreamed that horse droppings were falling from the clouds above. [A dream-reader] was questioned [about the possible meaning of this strange dream, and] he said, "Today, Kim [Puŭi] of the Security Council put on heavenly [immortal's] clothes, [for he has passed away]." The world referred to him as Ch'ŏnsŏng-ji Chŏng, "Essence of the Stars in Heaven."

If a child of a wealthy, noble family isn't born with innate abilities and a natural liking [for learning], he will hardly become a person skilled in literary writing. Although Kim [Puŭi] of the Security Council clearly was from a family as precious as the Eight Petals of the Xiao Clan,[53] he nevertheless abandoned the old habits of the elegant, fancy life and actually sat down properly all day long to read his books.

He wasn't fond of writing essays and poetry, but whenever there was an occasion at which he had to compose them, he would necessarily cleanse his brush in a bowl of ice,[54] and only then would he proceed to it. For this reason, not many of his pieces have been transmitted in the world, but those works which actually were passed on invariably constitute audacious lines. For instance, when he was on his way to China as an envoy, he wrote the following quatrain in a guest lodge in Yŏmju:[55]

Dreamless under mandarin-duck blankets, the night is dull, so dull;
the autumn moon, full of passion, illuminates the painted eaves.
Calling it "Salt Prefecture" truly is a grave mistake,
for the entire prefecture's pretty things are thoroughly "saltless."[56]

[2:3]

King In[jong] ascended the throne when he was just a child,[57] and thus his senior maternal uncle, the Duke of Chosŏn [Yi Chagyŏm], dominated the court.[58]

102   POEMS AND STORIES FOR OVERCOMING IDLENESS

The medical official Ch'oe Sajŏn[59] walked and talked in the midst of [Chen] Ping and [Zhou] Bo, who in the end secured the throne of Han.[60] By way of this, his portrait was painted on Qilin [Tower],[61] and he rapidly ascended to the office of grand councilor. At the time, the drafter of proclamations Kim Chonjung[62] composed the following royal proclamation:

> Mang Heluo bumping into a precious lute [reveals:] a turn of events
>   can arise most suddenly;[63]
> Xia Wuqie blocking [Jing Ke's dagger] with a bag of medicine
>   [reveals:] in his intentions there was loyalty and righteousness.[64]

At the time, people said that it corresponded with principle, and [the king] bestowed grace upon him in great fashion.

[Ch'oe Sajŏn] had two sons: one was named Pyŏn, the other was named Yŏl. The master had given a gilded vase to each of his sons,[65] but after having abandoned the building,[66] his beloved concubine stole one of them.[67] The older brother was wrathful and sought to flog her, but the younger brother argued, "She's our late father's beloved concubine. Giving away some of the family funds to help her out would naturally be the right thing to do! All the more in the case of an object such as this! Because the gilded vase that I received is still here, isn't it? Please let me pass it on to you, and don't be too hard on this concubine."

When King In[jong] heard about this incident, he said, "This may be called 'filial' [K. *hyo*] and 'benevolent' [K. *in*]." And straightaway he used his royal brush to bestow upon him the name Hyoin, "He who is filial and benevolent." His establishment of a great standard at court can be viewed herein.

Early on, [Ch'oe Hyoin] had resigned as audience usher in the Office of Ceremonies[68] to be able to partake in the civil service examinations. By doing so, he had meant to follow the command left to him by his late father, but he had not yet received a positive result. Hence he constantly thought it disgruntling without end. His friend Minister Kim Sinyun[69] composed a hexasyllabic poem and presented it to him.

> In a selection with dice there are always gains and losses;[70]
> inside a yellow millet dream there is always rise and fall.[71]
> An expression of eagerness,[72] but in a life's hundred, how long can
>   it last?
> How come you burden your heart over this?[73]

[2:4]

From the time when the *Odes* waned and the *Airs*[74] were lost [as poetic models], poets all believed that Du Zimei strode alone as [an exemplar of peerless poetic brilliance]. Yet it wasn't just because the words he set up were exquisite and solid, or because his poetry encompassed the essential splendor of Heaven and earth. Not even during a single meal would he forget his lord, and firm was the standard of his loyalty and righteousness, which had their roots on the inside and their manifestations on the outside. Line after line there was nothing which wouldn't also have flown forth from the mouths of [Hou] Ji and Qi.[75] Reading [Du Zimei's poetry] is enough to make the weak develop resolution,[76] and [Yang Xiong's statement], "When the tinkling sound is *linglong*, crystal clear, how can the substance be anything but jade,"[77] can certainly be used in relation to it.

Yesterday I caught a glimpse of the poem *Yugam*, "Stirred by something," by Minister of State Kim Yŏngbu,[78] which read:

> Recently I've heard that a neighboring dynasty's power will become
>   dangerous,
> that an expansion of its territory, an extension of its boundaries is
>   imminent.
> My white hair is wind-tossed, frost and snow fall;
> my loyal heart is devoted, ghosts and spirits know.
> Lian Po could still eat [large amounts of rice in his old age], and it
>   wasn't without purpose;
> [Huo] Qubing rejected a mansion, and there was action in that, too.
> Hush, hush, for these innermost thoughts, there is no place to
>   tell them;
> each time I encounter a mug of ale, I get drunk as mud.

The older he got, the stronger the sincerity of his earnest concern for our dynasty became—it was as towering as Mount Tai and Mount Hua, quarreling over their height.[79] Truly admirable!

Throughout his life, whenever the master gave himself up to drink, he would develop a wild temper, and then even kings, lords, and great men were scared of him. When he was young, [one night] he had dreamed that he was roaming around in the royal palace, then had strolled out to the polo grounds, where hundreds of jugs of ale had stood prepared in dense rows. Two or three of these jugs, however, had slanted and tipped over, and he

104   POEMS AND STORIES FOR OVERCOMING IDLENESS

had asked someone about this. "That ale will be drunk by Licentiate Kim Yŏngbu," [was the answer he received]. Master Zhang's money from the thirty-six braziers, it was credible![80]

[2:5]

King In[jong] divined, obtaining [the prophecy] that the [terrestrial] force needed for the Restoration and Great Flowering [of the country] was to be found in the Western Capital.[81] Therefore he newly opened Yongŏn Tower.[82]

When the Phoenix Carriage was on a royal tour of the west, the king held a feast for the crowds of officials. On this occasion he commanded Academician Yi Chijŏ to compose something on the spot. In substance, he wrote:

> The Divine Ruler comes forth in *Zhen,* riding to *Qian;*[83]
> then again, it may be said: It corresponds to the fortune of the time.
> The king is at home in Hao, and he is drinking his wine;[84]
> indeed, it is appropriate: Doing this together with the crowds.[85]

Also, he wrote:

> They congratulated each other in their chambers, saying:
> We have waited for our prince; the prince is come, and we revive![86]
> Hearing His Majesty's pipes and flutes,
> they say to each other: Our king is capable in musical performances.[87]

Also, he wrote:

> Traveling and being delighted are what sets the standard for the
>   various lords —
> thus it coincides with an adage of the Xia.[88]
> Food and drink are what fills the loyal ministers' hearts —
> it stands in harmony with the chant of the people of Zhou.[89]

His parallel clauses were exact and clear-cut, and indeed there were no scars left behind by the hatchet or the chisel. When Master Munyŏl caught a glimpse of them, he sighed in admiration, exclaiming, "Those ministers nowadays who write clauses in the four-six style, in terms of the skillfulness of their [poetic] structures they can in no way compare to this."

Master [Yi Chijŏ] was the son of the director of the Chancellery, [Yi]

Kongsu.[90] At the age of eighteen he was chosen as Dragon Head, was then selected into high office, and before long was appointed high state councilor. His appearance was like that in a masterful painting, he did not presumptuously glance around [to see if anyone was watching him], and even when new students and the later-born came to see him he always treated them like high guests. His loyal words of advice and his excellent plans were enough to be considered equal to Yi Yin's "Yixun" or Fu Yue's "Yueming" [from *Shujing*]. Truly, what they used to refer to as a "great minister" in ancient times — it was him. To this very day his former place of dwelling is called Chŏngdang ri, the "Chancellery [Scholar's] Village."

Early on he had been sent on a mission to the Eastern Capital,[91] where he playfully wrote the following poem.

> Magnificently drunk, drowsy dozy, tumbling in and out of dreams at dawn;
> unaware of a jade-like beauty sleeping [next to me] beneath the curtains.
> Bystanders, don't you laugh at me for the meagerness of my elegant expressions;
> I can rhapsodize a piece to the melody of *Xijiang yue,* "West River Moon."[92]

[2:6]

Director of the Chancellery Kim Yŏn[93] was the son of Manager of Affairs [Kim] Sanggi.[94] He became illustrious on account of his literary writings in his early years, and even before reaching the age of thirty he took a small carriage, ventured out to the borderland, and served [as escort commissioner][95] to accompany the Great Liao envoy Meng Chu on his way [to the capital].[96]

[Meng] Chu saw the young man and figured that he would be pretty easy to deal with. As they rode to the outskirts of the city one day, the bridles of their horses side by side, snow [ceased to fall] and the skies suddenly cleared. They looked around in all four directions, but everything was a vast white blur, nothing could be made out clearly, and the only sound was the horses' hooves stomping the snow-covered ground. [Meng] Chu let his sleeves hang down, intoned faintly, and sang out the following:

> Horses' feet stomping the snow, in heaven Thunder is moving.[97]

106   POEMS AND STORIES FOR OVERCOMING IDLENESS

Master [Kim Yŏn], on the spot, responded in the following way:

Banners' tassels fluttering in the wind, [it is as if] blazing fires flew.

Astonished, [Meng] Chu said, "Truly, you possess heavenly endowed talents!"[98] By way of this, the affection they felt for one another grew deeper with each passing day, and both were saddened that they had come to know one another so late. When [Meng Chu] had to return to the Liao court, he took an ornament made from the "Horn for the Communication with Heaven"[99] off his girdle and gave it to [Kim Yŏn] as a present.[100]

When Master [Kim Yŏn] was at the Censorate,[101] everything he submitted [to the king] was in line with far-sighted plans designed to properly govern the dynasty, and while at first his memorials may have seemed pedantic, benefits arising from his work shall exist hundreds, thousands of years from now.

During the time of the reign of King In[jong], powerful ministers gained control over the court, and when [Kim Yŏn] heard [derogatory] nursery rhymes he pretended to be sick, so that he would be allowed to return home.[102] After the restoration of the correct government,[103] however, he was yet again summoned and made grand councilor. In his conduct and habits, much was related to the supernatural and extraordinary, and nobody during his age was really able to fathom any of this.

His three sons[104] all reached the office of grand councilor on account of their writings, and at the time they were considered comparable to the [Langya] Wang [Clan] and the [Chenjun] Xie [Clan] from Jiangzuo [Eastern Jin].[105]

Early on,[106] upon being sent out to guard [the frontier region of] Yong-man [during the turbulent times of the final confrontations between the Khitan Liao and the Jurchen Jin], he composed a poem, which he showed to his examination passers [as he was about to set out on the road to the deep north].[107] It read:

For ten years in the Halls of State[108] I held reeling silk in the palm of
    my hand;[109]
today I was turned into a minister [controlling what lies] beyond the
    city gates.[110]
In the Remonstrance Bureau I could not submit honest arguments;
in the Frontier Office I shall sweep away barbarian filth.
The hair on my temples has turned white so early, because I worry
    for the dynasty;
the tears are hard to hold back, as I yearn for my father.

Many thanks to all disciples in my school,[111]
[who raise] a hundred jars of purest wine at a farewell banquet for a
traveling man.[112]

[2:7]

In Minister Kim Chaŭi's[113] unbendingly righteous nature there was
remarkable moderation.

Early on he had taken up the struggle in the art of composition at the
Department of Spring.[114] [Just around this time], in a dream the king had seen
a person being picked out for the ranks,[115] and his name was Ch'ang.[116] When
[in reality] he then opened the paste-sealed envelope [containing the list of
successful examination passers], Master [Kim Chaŭi] was in second place,
and his name was Chŏng. Astounded, the king thought this quite peculiar.[117]

When [Kim Chaŭi] stood in court, in his stalwart, honest conduct and
speech there was the serious air of a frank, remonstrating minister. But
by nature he craved the ale, and when he was drunk he would rise, dance
around, and sing all kinds of songs from all over the world right there and
then.[118] Yet [even in a state of utter drunkenness,] everything he said was
related to questions of political order in the dynasty and at the court. At the
time people used to say, "We'd rather run into a tiger or a wild ox than meet
Master Kim when he's drunk."

When he was just about to go out to conduct an inspection in the
southland, the king warned him from atop the balcony, saying, "Regarding
Your Excellency's writings, your ambitions, as well as your moral principles,
there's no shame in comparing them to those of the ancient sages, yet only
your drinking of ale is so excessive, it's actually a flaw. After having had
three cups, be careful not to have any more of it touch your mouth!"

When [Kim Chaŭi] thereupon roamed all around the prefectures and
counties he had to inspect, he regularly did so clearheadedly, as he didn't
drink [alcohol in unreasonable quantities anymore].

On his way he swung by a Buddhist monastery in the mountains,
where he paid a visit to an old monk whom he had known for a long time.
Clasping hands they chatted about their memories, and when later they
were about to part, [the old monk] bought some ale, meaning to arrange a
farewell banquet for him.

[Kim Chaŭi] stepped out through the temple gates, squatted down on
a mossy boulder, and eventually said, "A while ago, when I left the capital,
there was a royal decree forbidding me to drink more than three cups of
ale. So, go on and fetch that iron alms bowl you use when venerating the

108   Poems and Stories for Overcoming Idleness

Buddha,[119] and then come back here." And so, he served himself three times and left. This alms bowl, however, could hold about a gallon. That's how bold he usually was.

Early on, saddened by Minister of State Ch'ŏk [Chun'gyŏng's] banishment to the south,[120] he had written the following quatrain.

> Heroic manner of dragon and tiger, guts of iron and stone;
> strove to be loyal and righteous, to serve his lord and king.
> Only when the [lofty] birds are gone, the [good] bow is put away;[121]
> it wasn't [the Marquis of] Huaiyin who revolted against the Emperor
>   of Han.[122]

[2:8]

Master Chillak [Yi] Chahyŏn had risen in a family of ministers,[123] yet even when holding high office, he always envisioned escaping to the realm of purple-tinted clouds.[124] As a young man he had sojourned in the Golden Chambers,[125] had followed the Daoist Ŭn Wŏnch'ung,[126] and had privately asked [Master Ŭn] for advice concerning scenic spots of glens and mountains that could serve as suitable places to live in reclusion.

"Up Yangja River,"[127] Master Ŭn had responded, "there's one bend of green mountains — that truly would be a region where one could completely withdraw from the profane world." After hearing this, [Ŭn Wŏnch'ung's words] had always hung in his heart.

At the age of twenty-seven he was appointed director of the Office of Music,[128] but suddenly he suffered the disaster [that had made Zhuangzi] drum on a basin [and sing, for his wife passed away].[129]

Thereupon he brushed off his official robe and departed for good, eventually entering Mount Ch'ŏngp'yŏng,[130] where he restored Munsu Monastery to reside there.[131] He was very fond of the theories of the Buddhist Sŏn [C. Chan; J. Zen] school, and if a student happened to come along he would immediately enter a dark room with him to sit in an upright position of meditation all day long and forget words.[132] Time and again he would bring up and discuss the cardinal meanings of the patriarchs of yore, and by way of this, the Dharma of his mind disseminated in the Country East of the Sea. Both Hyejo and Taegam,[133] two state preceptors,[134] were his disciples.

In a grotto, at a dark, secluded place, he built the Sigam, the "Retiring One's Cloister,"[135] which was oval like a swan's egg and so narrow that he barely managed to spread both knees. Silently he would sit inside of it for days on end, not stepping out at all.

FASCICLE 2   109

When his friend Kwak Yŏ,[136] who had passed the civil service examinations in the same year as himself,[137] received a tally and went out to take up his new appointment in Kwandong,[138] he paid [Yi Chahyŏn] a visit. Then [Kwak Yŏ] presented [Yi Chahyŏn] with a poem, which read as follows:

The scenery of Ch'ŏngp'yŏng resembles the banks of the Xiang;
unexpectedly we met, and I'm seeing a man of old.
Thirty years ago, together we passed the civil service examinations;[139]
then were a thousand leagues apart, each lodging for himself.
The drifting clouds enter the grotto, already I am free from affairs;[140]
the bright moon is in the brook, not sullied by profane dust.
With eyes locked we're without words, and thus long we remain,
calmly reflecting to each other our old feelings and spirits.

Master [Yi Chahyŏn] matched this rhyme in the following way:

Warmth pressing onto brooks and mountains, the season has
    imperceptibly changed to spring;
suddenly turning the immortal's cane, you came to visit a man of
    reclusion.
That [Bo]yi and [Shu]qi hid away from the world was only to keep
    their nature intact;[141]
that [Hou] Ji and Xie diligently served their countries was not for
    themselves.[142]
Receiving the summons, now it may seem like tinkling pendants
    of jade;
hanging up your official cap, when will you brush off your robe all
    the profane dust?
When will you stay here in this place, so that together we can lodge
    in hiding,
to cultivate what has always been, our undying spirits?[143]

King Ye[jong], thirsting for and looking up to his honest, elegant bearing, repeatedly summoned him to court, yet when facing the royal messengers, [Yi Chahyŏn] told them, "When I first stepped out of the gates of the capital, I swore that I would never set foot upon its marvelous grounds again. I do not dare heed this summons." Eventually, he sent along a memorial, [an abstract of] which reads,

In the age of Tang and Yu, Yao and Shun's ministers Kui and Long[144]
expounded the plans of the court, while Chao and Xu[145] showed the

noble determination to live in mountain forests [rather than succeed the emperor]. To nourish a bird as a bird should be nourished, one must strive to eliminate its fear of bells and drums.[146] [Your Majesty,] see a fish and know [the happiness of] a fish,[147] enable me to proceed according to my nature in rivers and lakes,[148] [forget about me and let me transform along my own course].[149]

The king knew full well that [Yi Chahyŏn] would never bend, and thus he especially went on a royal tour to the Southern Capital after having summoned [Yi Chahyŏn] to meet him there.[150] [When they finally sat face-to-face], [King Yejong] asked him about the essentials of cultivating the self and nourishing life, and [Yi Chahyŏn] replied, "The ancients said, 'For nourishing life, nothing is better than having few desires.'[151] Your Majesty ought to keep this in mind."

The king sighed and praised him without cease, saying, "Words can be heard, but the Way cannot be transmitted; the body can be seen, but the will cannot be bent. Truly, you are in the tradition of [Xu You and Chao Fu of] the Ying River."[152] Thereupon [the king] presented him with tea and medicine and sent him back into the mountains.[153]

When [Yi Chahyŏn] passed away, the posthumous name [bestowed upon him] was Chillak Kong, "Master Truest Joy." His deeds and achievements can be viewed in Minister of State Kim's *Chungch'ang ki,* the "Records of Reconstruction."[154]

[2:9]

When King Ye[jong] was still at the Spring Palace [as crown prince], the hermit Kwak Yŏ served as his tutor, and when he ascended the eastern steps [and became king], [Kwak Yŏ] hung up his official cap and departed for good. [Yejong later] bestowed upon him one peak of Mount Yaktu, a mountain located to the east of the capital, where he opened a summer residence named Tongsan-jae, "East Mountain Studio."[155]

A black scarf wrapped around his head and a crane-feather cape on his shoulders, [Kwak Yŏ] had walked in and out of the palace apartments, and at the time people had referred to him as the "Feathered Guest of the Golden Gates."[156]

Early on, during a banquet in the inner palace, the king had bestowed upon him a single flower, which he placed on his hat. Thereupon he had commanded [Kwak Yŏ] to bring forth a poem.

Who cut red gossamer to make a peony?
The fragrant heart has not yet fully opened, for it dreads the cold of
spring.
[The beauties] of the six palaces, wearing powder and kohl, all look at
each other, saying,
"why's the palace flower atop that Daoist's cap?"

Also, following the royal carriage, [Kwak Yŏ] had once gone to Changwŏn
Pavilion.[157] The king had ascended the tower to gaze into the distance at
nightfall, and down in the fields there had been an old man, riding his ox
alongside a brook, on his way home. Thus, [the king] had commanded
[Kwak Yŏ] to compose an impromptu poem [on this scenery].

An appearance of great peace, riding his ox as he pleases;
half wet by a misty drizzle, passing over the field-boundary slopes.
I know that by the water his house must be close by;
he's following that setting sun, a brook's currents by his side.

But how could it merely have been [Kwak Yŏ's] immortal-like elegance or
his Daoist rhymes that captivated and stirred the mind of the ruler of men? In
terms of literary writing he was likewise strong and nimble beyond compare.
The king's regard and concern for him were most remarkable, and none of
the ministers at court could rival him.

Early on, the king had left [incognito] through the northern gates [of the
palace] and, leading on a group of several dozens of guards of the Yellow
Gates while calling himself Chongsil Ryŏrhu, "Marquis of the Royal House,"
had visited Tongsan-jae. The hermit [Kwak Yŏ], however, was presently
staying in the city and hadn't yet returned to his studio. The king lingered
around for quite some time, and eventually created a poem entitled *Hach'ŏ
nanmang chu*, "Wherever, [whenever,] it's hard to forget the ale,"[158] which
he wrote on a wall with his very own imperial brush before going back to
the palace. At the time, everyone said, "The words of white clouds by the
Emperor [Wu] of Han[159] and the brush of dancing phoenixes of the Sovereign
of Tang [Taizong], both are truly brought together herein. [Such an amazing
combination of content and style] has never existed in old and new." The
words [of King Yejong's poem] went as follows:

Wherever, [whenever,] it's hard to forget the ale;
sought the genuine one, but without having met him I must turn
round.

The study's window casts back the light [of the setting sun];
the jade seal script [on the lid of the cinnabar stove] conceals leftover
    ashes.
Fangzhang,[160] no one's here to guard it;
the immortal's door, all day long it stood open.
In the garden, orioles sing on ancient trees;
in the yard, cranes doze on gray-green moss.
The flavor of the Way, who am I to talk to about it?
The teacher, he left and hasn't yet come.
Deep longing has me drenched in emotions;
turning my head, again I linger on.
Pick up my brush, leave a poem on a wall;
cling to the railing, reluctantly descend from the terrace.
Many moods that help intoning,
every place I encounter is cut off from the dust of the profane world.
Sultry heat diminishes below the trees,
gentle breezes waft in through the hall's corner.
If there wasn't a single cup [of ale] at a time like this,
washing away my troubles and woes, how could it be done?

Master [Kwak Yŏ later] wrote the following in response.

Wherever, [whenever,] it's hard to forget the ale;
in vain, the precious carriage had to turn round.
[Behind] the crimson gates I went after small banquets;[161]
[inside] the cinnabar stove crumbled cold ashes.[162]
The local libation lasted all night before it ended,
the imperial gate waited til dawn before it opened.
Staff in hand,[163] I returned on the narrow paths of Pengdao,[164]
my wooden clogs, smeared with Luo[yang] city moss.[165]
A blue-clothed child[166] spoke from below the trees,
"The Jade Emperor, from amid the clouds He did come."
The Turtle Palace,[167] all had been gloomy and still,
the Dragon Coach,[168] long it lingered on.
With an intention, still He took the brush;
without a companion, alone He ascended the terrace.
Failed to peer at Sun and Moon,[169]
how sad! That I had moved toward the dust of the profane world.
Scratching my head, I stand below the stairs,
full of anguish, I lean against a rock's corner.

If there wasn't a single cup [of ale] at a time like this,
how should I ever soothe an inch of my heart?[170]

[2:10]

T'aebaek-san-in Kyeŭng[171] was the rightful successor of State Preceptor
Taegak [Ŭich'ŏn].[172] As a child he had temporarily stayed at a monks'
residence, where he had read his books. One day, after hearing the sound
[of him reciting the scriptures] from the opposite side of a wall, Taegak
exclaimed, "This [boy] truly is a dharma-vessel!"[173] Thus [Taegak] urged
him to have his head shaved and become his disciple. Kyeŭng henceforth
studied diligently, intensively both day and night, and in a state of excellence
he entered the inner chambers.

Succeeding Taegak [as state preceptor], he extolled the Great Dharma
for some forty years, and since he had become a person the king held in high
esteem, he was never allowed to leave the capital.[174] Yet after repeatedly
handing in requests [in poetic form,] he eventually returned to the T'aebaek
Mountains.[175]

With his own hands he established Kakhwa Temple,[176] and when he
greatly clarified the Buddhist teachings there, students came flocking in
from all directions, no less than hundreds, thousands of them each day.
Hence, he came to be referred to as Pŏphae Yongmun, "Venerable Master
of the Dharma Sea."

During that time, in Hŭngwang Temple[177] there lived [a monk by the
dharma name of] Chisŭng who was fond of learning and thus went out to
study under [Kyeŭng's] wing, [paying his teacher respect by] lifting the
front of his garment.[178]

Yet upon entering the new year, [Chisŭng] requested to return to
his mountain [and go back to Hŭngwang Temple]. [Kyeŭng thereupon]
composed a poem to send him off.

Those who love learning, today they're certainly few;
those who forget appearances, of old they've also been rare.
Looking back, what was it that I had
for you to come and lean on me?
In a barren valley we spent three months of winter together;
the breezes of spring blow one day, and you go back.
Leaving and staying, both are beyond the mundane world;
no need for tears to moisten my robe.[179]

114   Poems and Stories for Overcoming Idleness

Well, the words of those who have obtained the Way are carefree, leisurely, and tranquil, and their profound principle is deep and wide. Even the loftiness and magnificence of [the poet-monk] Chanyue [Guanxiu],[180] or the purity and gracefulness [of the verses written by] Canliao [Daoqian],[181] how could they have ever surpassed [that of Kyeŭng]? About [a person such as Kyeŭng] the ancients would have said, "When the wind blows upon the water, patterns will arise naturally."[182]

[2:11]

The monk Hyeso[183] of Sŏho [Temple][184] was erudite in both inner and outer canons,[185] supremely skilled in poetry, and his brushwork was wonderful, too.

Early on he had taken State Preceptor Taegak as his teacher and become his leading disciple. When the state preceptor urged him to attend the Clergy Appointment,[186] he replied, "How could I be a horse in the royal stables, with [the king] examining my every step?"

Always he would follow wherever the state preceptor would go, continuously engaging in critical discussions about literary writings with him. When the state preceptor passed away, he compiled [Ŭich'ŏn's] records of activities in ten volumes,[187] of which Director of the Chancellery Kim [Pusik] then selected [certain passages for the creation of] the memorial stele [for Ŭich'ŏn].[188]

When [Hyeso] resided at Kyŏnbul Monastery of Sŏho, his abbot's chamber was still and silent. In it he had put nothing but a dark blue schist plate the size of a mat, and from time to time he would dash off and write freely on it, just to get out what stirred him.

After the director of the Chancellery had retired from office, riding on a donkey he often visited [Hyeso at Kyŏnbul Temple], and together they chatted about the Way all evening long.[189]

The king had long since heard of his reputation and sought to install him as head of the Place of Practice in the Inner Palace.[190] He eventually had him lecture on the *Hwaŏm-kyŏng,* the "Avataṃsaka-sūtra," and bestowed upon him silver in large quantities.

The teacher used all of that silver to buy a hundred lumps of granulated sugar, which he lined up both inside and outside his home. When people asked him about the reason for this, he replied, "My entire life I've been addicted to sugar. If perchance the merchant ships don't come next spring, how am I supposed to get a hold of it?" Those who heard him all laughed about his sincerity and frankness.

[2:12]

In the region of Kŭmnan[191] lies Hansong Pavilion,[192] where the Four Immortals[193] sojourned so long ago. Their three thousand followers each planted a tree here, and to this day these trees have grown in thickest green so very high that they seem to brush the clouds. Below [the pines' lush foliage] lies Ta-jŏng, "Tea Well."[194] When the monk and state preceptor Kyeŭng stayed here, he left the following poem.

> In days past, the sons of whose houses were
> the three thousand that planted the emerald pines?
> While these men's bones have long since putrefied,
> the pines' leaves still retain a lush appearance.

The companion piece [by Hyeso] read:

> Days of yore, the immortals' excursions so far away,
> and in thickest green only remain the pines.
> All that's left is the moon at the bottom of the spring;
> helps me vaguely envisage the ancient appearance.

Those who discussed the poems believed that the structure of the teacher's [reply] poem was skillful, but that its natural charm wasn't like that of the first piece.[195]

[2:13]

Pyŏngna noin Kŏbi[196] said to me, "Once I spotted a quatrain written on the wall of a post pavilion.

> The sun in autumn as radiant and warm as the sun in spring,
> bamboo-leaves and plantains set off against a whitewashed wall.[197]
> Don't you boast toward this gentleman about the size of your
>   leaves,[198]
> for this gentleman shall laugh at you when the frost is near."

Also, Teacher Kwangch'ŏn of Wangnyun [Temple][199] chanted a poem in the recent style, which went as follows:

116   POEMS AND STORIES FOR OVERCOMING IDLENESS

> What I lost through my indolence in spring, whom am I to tell?
> Back then, I may have heard an oriole, but then said I misheard.[200]
> Laughable, someone who's so troubled by the nature of things
>   as me;
> peony heads hang heavy, noon breezes are gentle.

For neither of the two poems do we have the creators' names, but the word pattern isn't different from that of someone from the Tang or Song dynasty. The two teachers both followed renowned worthies of our Country East of the Sea, sojourned with them, and necessarily there must have been something they carried along. For this reason, I noted both of them down, to wait for someone who may have knowledge [of their origins and creators].

[2:14]

Teacher Kwangch'ŏn of the Punhwang School[201] was tranquil and broad-minded, and he just didn't guard his behavior in trivial matters.

Early on he had once gone to the Place of Practice in the Inner Palace. Having become magnificently drunk, he had slumped over and dozed off, with snivel and snot dribbling down onto his chest. Therefore, he became the subject of punishment by some officer in charge, and in the end, they expelled him.

When Chogam[202] heard about this incident he said, "[King Wen of Zhou, who could drink] a thousand goblets of ale, was a sage, [and Confucius, who could drink] a hundred glasses of ale, was a worthy, too. One can pile up mash to form a mound, but it won't cause any harm to a perfect being. What's more, Buddhists roam and play in self-contentment, and certainly they cannot but test the limits." Then he composed a Buddhist *gāthā*.

> Pattra leaves rolled to make cups for bamboo-leaf [ale];[203]
> heavenly flowers have all fallen,[204] eye-flowers in full bloom.[205]
> The land of drunkenness is vast,[206] the mortal world is narrow;
> who knows old man Wanhui,[207] who feigned insanity?[208]

[2:15]

When Hwaŏm wŏlsa was young,[209] he used to follow me on my travels, styling himself Koyang ch'wigon, "Baldheaded Drunkard of Gaoyang."[210] In the poetry he composed there was the elegance and vigor of [poems written by the Tang dynasty poet-monk] Jia Dao.[211]

Yesterday I took him along when I paid Kiji of Sŏha a visit,[212] and while the two of them met for the very first time, it seemed as though they were old companions. [Kiji] addressed [Hwaŏm wŏlsa], saying, "You, teacher, have been praised by Master Yi for such a long time! How come we necessarily had to wait until after we clasped hands and talked about becoming friends, and only then got to know each other?"

And right on the spot where he was sitting, [Kiji] lifted his brush, wrote a poem and presented it to him.

Long ago there was the Buddhist Huiqin, an able poet,
who always kept close companionship with an Old Drunkard.[213]
Like Misu of the present day, a truly extraordinary scholar,
who boasted to me that in Gaoyang he'd obtained a bare head.
Long it grieved me that I had heard your name but hadn't yet laid
   eyes on you;
now that we've met I wish to converse, but have forgotten words.
Pure poetry and sturdy brush, why need I ask?
For tales have been told ever since he became principal graduate.

[2:16]

When Hwang Pinyŏn of the Jiangxia [Hwang Clan] hadn't yet passed the civil service examinations, he used to read books with two or three of his friends at Kamak Temple in Tan Prefecture.[214]

Tonggak Kim Sinyun, a famous scholar during that age, had used mad words [of criticism] while being drunk on ale, offending noble vassals of the time.[215] After having been forced to walk out of the capital on foot as a consequence of this, he had passed by Kamak [Temple], where he told [the residing monks and scholars] the following about himself: "I'm an old soldier on my way back home, and I ask permission to spend the night here." [Hwang] Pinyŏn, feeling pity for the man's old age and his apparent distress, assented to this.

[Kim Sinyun] stayed beneath the blanket all day long, not uttering a single word, but then happened to pick up a fire tong, with which he scribbled some Chinese characters into the ashes. Those sitting close by all pointed and glanced at them, saying, "Look, that old-timer seems to understand writing pretty well."[216]

118 POEMS AND STORIES FOR OVERCOMING IDLENESS

The following morning the master's son, [Kim] On'gi,[217] who by then had already passed the civil service examinations, came looking for [his father], carrying a jug of ale and having brought two or three blue-capped servants with him.

"Yesterday my father stepped out through the gates of the capital and then reached this place. Is he present here at the moment?" he asked someone upon arriving at the gates [of the temple].

"There's only an old soldier who came and spent the night. How could [anyone as prestigious as] Kim Tonggak be here?" the person replied.

[Kim] On'gi, however, immediately rushed inside and prostrated himself in the courtyard. [Hwang] Pinyŏn, feeling deeply ashamed, then also threw himself on the ground and apologized [for his rude misconduct].

Master [Kim Sinyun] smiled, saying, "Young scholar, how could you have known that Fan Sui has already become grand councilor in Qin?"[218]

Thereupon they ascended to the northern summit [of Mount Kamak], sat down on a rock beneath a pine, drank together, and enjoyed themselves to the utmost. [Kim Sinyun eventually] ordered his fellow travelers to create a rhapsody on the theme of *Song p'ung*, "The Wind in the Pines."

> Cutting it off, then sending it off — the black gibbon howls;
> lifting it up, then raising it up — the white crane dashes.
> *—Pinyŏn*

> Weary of its noise, a traveler rests on a pillow;
> scared of its cold, a child gathers dry branches.
> *—Chongnyŏng*[219]

> Feeding on the cool [wind] on [Mount] Guye;[220]
> a sudden gust of wind sweeps over the Terrace of Chu.[221]
> *—Anonymous*

> A crane is freezing, can hardly fall asleep;
> a monk is meditating, alone, as though he was deaf.
> *—Tonggak*

That evening they drank heavily, and when they were done, [Hwang] Pinyŏn kowtowed and proclaimed that he wished to receive instructions [from Kim Sinyun]. So, he stayed on for several months, and they read the *Qian Hanshu*, the "History of the Former Han," together. [Kim Sinyun] only returned after they were finished.

This is still a popular story among the literati to this very day.[222]

[2:17]

Academician Kim Hwangwŏn,[223] Bureau Director of the Left Yi Chungyak,[224] and the hermit Kwak Yŏ were all extraordinary scholars. In their youth they had become friends on the basis of their literary writings, and were then referred to as *sin'gyo*, "divine friends."

The two masters [Kim Hwangwŏn and Kwak Yŏ] had early on visited the dwelling of the bureau director of the left, and their pure conversations were carried out so busily, they didn't even realize that the sun had already set. The moon came out in an instant, the clouds cleared, and the dark blue sky resembled water. Together they ascended to the top of the southern tower, had a little drink, suggested a rhyme pattern, and then each of them composed one part of a linked verse. Yi hastily wrote,

> A strong atmosphere arising unseen, a sword beyond the
> firmament;[225]
> a grand strategy turning secretly, a plan inside the tent.[226]

Kwak's poem read,

> Those in their seats [as pure as] ice and snow, guests of the Three
> Mountains;[227]
> those small weights atop the scale, marquis of ten thousand
> households.[228]

When hereafter it was [Kim] Hwangwŏn's turn, he said to them, "I would choose to do something quite different from any of the other three."[229] Eventually he took a full cup of ale and chanted the following in a clear voice.

> As the sun sets, birds' songs hide in the dark-green trees;
> as the moon brightens, people's talks float up the high tower.

Without even noticing it, the two other masters leaned forward on their knees, then said, "How could even the ancients have come this far?" Eventually they brought their gathering to a conclusion.

My friend [Yi] Tamji is a direct descendant of the bureau director of the left, and early on I caught a glimpse of genuine pieces [of Yi Chungyak's writings]. His drunken ink [style of calligraphy] was intense and clear, and they are genuine treasures of the [Yi] house.[230]

[2:18]

Master Ch'anghwa Yi Chayŏn,[231] carrying royal staff and tally, once went to the Southern dynasty as an envoy,[232] and there he climbed up to Ganlu Temple [on Mount Beigu] in Runzhou.[233]

Having fallen in love with the scenic beauty of the lakes and mountains [surrounding the temple], he said to the steersman[234] who had accompanied him on his travels [to the Central dynasty], "You ought to take a careful look at these mountains, streams, and towers, behold their shapes and forms, and carry them in your heart. You mustn't miss the slightest thing."

"I shall do as you have commanded," the boatman replied.

After their return to our dynasty he made an agreement with the steersman, saying, "You see, between the earth and the sky, generally all things that have a physical form are alike in one way or another. For instance, the nine [peaks of Nine Doubt] Mountain by the banks of the Xiang River are so much alike that wayfarers get confused by them;[235] the [Yellow] River flows in nine bends, and the Southern Sea likewise has nine curving bays. Consequently, if you look at it that way, the natural dispositions in the shapes of mountains and the forms of rivers are just like the facial features of human beings — though they're unique in a thousand ways and diverse in myriad manners, among them there's inevitably always something in which they're all the same. What's more, our Eastern Country isn't far away from Mount Penglai, and the purity and magnificence of our mountains and streams is a million times superior to that of the Central dynasty. Therefore, in terms of its spots of splendid scenic beauty, how could there not be something that comes close to Jingkou?[236]

You ought to take your skiff with the short oars, sail on and on, drift and sink along with ducks and wild geese — no place should be too out-of-the-way for you to reach, no place too far away for you to find. See if you can discover [a spot resembling Runzhou] for me. You may take ten years, so be mindful not to act too hastily in this matter."

"Yes," replied the steersman.

It took the winters and summers of six years until he first discovered [the landscape he had been asked to look for,] by the Western Lake near the capital. [Hurriedly] he ran to inform Master [Yi Chayŏn], saying, "I have just discovered [the place you ordered me to find]! We could return there in three meals' time. Though it may be troublesome, I hope you will come along to take a look at it yourself."[237]

When eventually they ascended [a hill] together and had a bird's-eye view over the land, [Yi Chayŏn] happily glanced over at the man. "See,

Ganlu Temple in the Southern dynasty is extraordinary and beautiful beyond compare," he said, "but really it is only the skillfulness of its buildings' structures as well as the artistry of its paintings and decorations that make it such a particularly surpassing sight. In terms of the natural forms brought forth by Heaven and created by earth, the difference is truly no more than one hair of nine oxen, [not even worth mentioning]."

Right away, he spent gold and silk to have lumber and tiles prepared. Overall, the architectural style of the towers, pavilions, pools, and terraces was modeled exactly after Ganlu Temple in the Central dynasty. When it was finished, the name he put on the board, of course, read *Kamno*[-*sa*], "Sweet Dew [Temple]."[238] Directing and planning the operation had gone smoothly, there had been no need to use the whip, and everything had worked out by itself.

Later, the poet-monk Hyeso [first] chanted [a congratulatory poem], and Director of the Chancellery Kim Pusik concluded it.[239] Those who heard it all composed companion pieces, so that there were several thousands of them in the end.[240] Eventually, they were put together in a large collection.

[2:19]

Anhwa Temple, located in a valley north of the Phoenix City,[241] was originally established by King Ye[jong].[242] By means of his divine sageliness and eminent virtue, King Ye[jong] served the Great Song without ever contravening the rites. Emperor Xianxiao,[243] thinking him excellent, bestowed upon him praise and reward: he especially gave him works of exemplary calligraphy, famous paintings, as well as rare and exquisite items in incalculable quantities. Upon hearing that [King Yejong] had established this temple, [Emperor Xianxiao] specially dispatched an envoy equipped with treasures for the main prayer hall as well as statues, which he sent along. With his imperial brush he then personally wrote a plaque [carrying the inscription *Nŭngin* (Śākyamuni)-*ji chŏn*, "Hall of the Buddha,"] for the main prayer hall, and commanded [Grand Preceptor] Cai Jing[244] to inscribe a board for the gate [with the words *Chŏngguk Anhwa-ji sa*, "Temple of Tranquility in the Peaceful Country"].[245]

Its decorative paintings and the structures of its buildings make [Anhwa-sa] the most prestigious in our Country East of the Sea.[246] Stepping out through the temple gates one reaches the [temple compound's] Royal Flower Garden, which is some six, seven leagues away.[247] Cinnabar cliffs and emerald ridges stretch out wide and long on both sides, and there is a brook running alongside a path through the rocks, with a sound like tinkling jade pendants. All around only pines and cypresses soar into the sky, and even at the height of summer it always seems [as cool and refreshing] as in early autumn. Those coming and going appear as though they were inside a painting on a screen, and in the world, it is referred to as the place of dwelling of the immortals and genuines of Yŏnha-dong, the "Grotto of hazes and auroras."[248]

Long ago, Minister of State [Yun] Ŏni lodged here for fasting,[249] and in a dream he caught sight of the Academician Hu Zongdan aboard a leaf-sized boat, gliding toward him.[250] They met in front of Chach'wi-mun, "Purple Emerald Gate," where he composed the following quatrain.

> The place deep amid five-colored clouds,[251] it is my home;
> where mists envelope towers and terraces, where days and months
>   are long.
> Turning my head [to look back] at years gone by — my friend,
> these days you're constantly toiling, even in the field of your dreams.

Chach'wi-mun is located at [Anhwa] Temple.

[2:20]

Ch'ŏnsu Temple lies east of the capital, about a hundred paces outside the city gates. Linked peaks rise up behind it, level rivers stream by before it, hundreds of wild cinnamon trees cast their shadows upon the narrow path, and people traveling from the southland to the Imperial Capital cannot but take a rest underneath them. Wagon wheels and hooves rumble and stomp on and on, the sounds of fishermen's songs and woodcutters' flutes continue without cease, cinnabar pavilions and emerald towers half shimmer through mists and haze in forests of pines and fir. When the princes and nobles bring [their beautiful women with] pearls and kingfisher-blue [ornaments in their hair], leading on [those singing girls with] their reed instruments and songs, their welcomes and farewells necessarily take place by the temple gate.[252]

Long ago, during the time of King Ye[jong], Yi Nyŏng[253] of the Department of Painting[254] was supremely skilled in landscape painting. He had once given one of his paintings to a Song merchant, and when long thereafter the king demanded a famous [Chinese] painting from that same Song merchant,[255] [he simply] took out this very painting and presented it to him. The king then summoned numerous officials [of the Department of Painting] and [proudly] showed it to them. At this point, Yi Nyŏng stepped forth and remarked, "Well, this is actually my painting *Ch'ŏnsu-sa nammun to*, 'Painting of the southern gate of Ch'ŏnsu Temple.'" He peeled a layer off the back, they all took a look, and there was the mark [of Yi Nyŏng] written down in every detail. Only then did they grasp what a fine painter he really was.

[2:21]

In the seventh year of the reign of King Sin[jong],[256] I was sent out to govern Maengsŏng, while my son Adae[257] at the same time rushed to take office in Chindong.[258]

My friend [Yi] Tamji said to Ham Chajin, "The son of Yi of the Jade Hall has received a bamboo slip and will proceed to his new post in a southern prefecture, while our companion [his father Yi Illo] will be staying far away from him in [the northern region of] Maengsŏng. The two of us ought to go and arrange a farewell banquet for his [son]."

Both brought their own sons along, and when they reached the western peak by Ch'ŏnsu Temple, they spread out mats, talked about the impending separation, and had eight or nine rounds of ale. Chajin eventually called out to his son Pŏmnang, telling him to compose a single line as a farewell present for the traveler, and [Pŏmnang] straightaway said:

Red trees of the home-journey, lush they shall stand.[259]

Adae continued it, saying:

Green mountains of the homeland, distant they shall grow.

As the sun slanted, they concluded [the farewell banquet].

After Adae had reached his office, he narrated the entire story in great detail in a letter he sent to me over the distance of a thousand leagues to Maengsŏng. When I was handed the letter, I couldn't help but laugh out loud, and even among the house servants or the local officials there wasn't anyone who did not clap his hands in delight and excitement. [My son's portrayal of] the appearance of the capital region's mountains and streams, [his depiction of] my old friends and former companions' laughter and talk, and [his description of] the crisscrossing of the parting feast's cups and goblets—all of this was so vivid, it seemed to be right in front of [my and everyone's] eyes.

The sorrow of the [lone] travels and the [dire] situation of having had to wander far [from the capital, my home, and my family] melted away like snow in boiling water, and [it felt as though] in my beard and on my temples

124   POEMS AND STORIES FOR OVERCOMING IDLENESS

a strand or two of [grayish] hair had turned black again. Eventually I noted down the date to record in memory the happiness [of that day].

[2:22]

The southern buildings of Yŏngmyŏng Temple[260] in the Western Capital[261] are a superb site under heaven. [Yŏngmyŏng-sa was] originally constructed by Master Hŭng. To the south it overlooks the Tae[dong] River, and beyond the river lie broad plains, vague and vast, the borders of which cannot be made out. Only to their eastern edges is there one line of shore, and far in the distance small peaks rise and sink, now there, now gone.[262]

Long ago, when King Ye[jong] once went on a royal tour of the western region, he held a feast at this spot with a crowd of his ministers. They drank together, chanted back and forth, and while the poems they composed were large in number, each and every one of them was carved on metal and stone or played as silk-bamboo music,[263] to be transmitted by the Music Bureau.

Just at that time, my ancestor, Vice Director of the Royal Secretariat and Chancellery Yi O, who was then present at the Jade Hall, was a member of the entourage following the king when he climbed up and looked out.[264] He ordered the building to be called Pubyŏng-nyo, "Hut of Floating Emerald,"[265] composed a poem, and recorded the event from beginning to end in great detail. The serene air of the mountains and rivers [spreading out in front of Pubyŏng-nyo] is apt to vie with that of Dishu Pavilion in the Central dynasty, but in terms of elegance and beauty [Pubyŏng-nyo] even surpasses it.

Yet when Academician Kim Hwangwŏn made a stop in the Western Capital, he climbed up [to Pubyŏng-nyo] and ordered the petty officials to collect all of the poetry boards left behind [at the pavilion] by the scores of wise men of old and new, and to have them all burned.[266] Thereupon he leaned against the railing and tried his best to chant [a self-composed poem]. By sunset his voice was properly strained—he sounded like a monkey howling at the moon—but he had only been able to come up with a single couplet:

> On the one side of the long wall—ripples and ripples of water;
> on the eastern rim of the great plain—dots and dots of mountains.

Then his imagination dried up and he didn't manage to come up with any more words [for the second couplet]. Wailing bitterly, he descended.[267]

A few days later he finished a piece, which even to this day is considered a peak of poetic perfection.[268] At the time the people said, "Long ago we heard that Song Yu[269] was saddened by the breath of autumn,[270] and now we see [Kim] Hwangwŏn wailing at the evening sun."[271]

[2:23]

The courtesy name of Master Munch'ang Ch'oe Ch'iwŏn was Koun, "Lonely Cloud."[272] He entered the court of the Central dynasty [of Tang] as a guest and tributary [scholar of Silla], was picked out for the ranks [in the guest and tributary examinations],[273] and later sojourned at Gao Pian's headquarters.[274] The realm was in turmoil during those days, and all of [General Gao Pian's] letters and written commands came out of [Ch'oe Ch'iwŏn's] hands.[275]

When he was about to return home [to Silla],[276] [his friend the Tang poet] Gu Yun,[277] who had passed the civil service examinations in the same year [that Ch'oe Ch'iwŏn had], created the *Koun p'yŏn*, the "Lonely Cloud Piece," to send him off.

> On the winds you left across the ocean,
> accompanying the moon, you arrived in the mortal world.
> Lingered on but could not stay;
> far and wide, again you return east.[278]

Master [Ch'oe Ch'iwŏn] also related the following himself:

> At the age corresponding with the number of layered peaks of Wu Gorge,[279]
> [wearing] cotton I entered the Central Efflorescence.
> In my year corresponding with the number of constellations in the Silver Stream,[280]
> [wearing] brocade I reentered the Eastern Country.

Already aware that the dragon of our [dynasty's founder] T'aejo would arise,[281] [Ch'oe] presented a letter and personally brought it forth,[282] but his heart to serve as an official [under T'aejo] turned to ashes, and he sited a dwelling to live in reclusion on Mount Kaya.[283] One morning he rose early and walked out the door—no one knows where he went off to, but since he left his cap and shoes in the forest, he might well have become an [immortal] guest on high. The monks of [Haein] Temple took that day to offer prayers for his postmortem merit.

Master [Ch'oe Ch'iwŏn] had a cloud beard, jade cheeks, and always

126   POEMS AND STORIES FOR OVERCOMING IDLENESS

there was the cover of a white cloud hovering above him. His portrait was kept at his Tŏksŏ-dang, his "Reading Hall,"[284] and it has remained there to this very day.

From his Tŏksŏ-dang it is about ten leagues to Munŭng Tower, which is located at the mouth of the grotto.[285] [In this picturesque area] there are cinnabar cliffs and emerald ridges, pines and juniper trees standing azure on azure, winds and waters arousing one another, and naturally there are sounds of metal and stone.

Early on, Master [Ch'oe Ch'iwŏn] had written a quatrain [onto a rock at this place]. Its drunken ink [style of calligraphy] was of transcendental ease, and people passing by all point at the inscription, saying, "It was Master Ch'oe who wrote that poem on the rock." His poem reads:

> Mad spurting over rocks in folds, roaring over ridges in layers;
> here, people's talk is hard to discern, even from a foot away.[286]
> Always fear that the sound of disputes may reach my ears,
> thus I had roaring waters embrace the mountain.[287]

[2:24]

Kim Yusin was a man from Kyerim. His accomplishments were brilliant, and they are exhibited in the *kuksa,* the "Histories of the [Three] States."[288]

It is said that when he was a child, his mother [Manmyŏng], the wife [of Kim Sŏhyŏn], instructed him more strictly with each passing day to not engage in reckless social intercourse.[289]

One day, after he had accidentally spent the night at the house of a woman of lower status, his mother faced and reprimanded him, saying, "I'm already old! Day and night, I hope that you grow up to establish merit and fame, and bring honor to both your lord and father. But now you associate with the little children of lowly butchers and wine sellers, and amuse yourself in lewd establishments and liquor stores?" When she then cried and sobbed without cease, [Kim Yusin fell onto his knees] in front of his mother and of his own accord swore that he would never ever pass by the door [of that very disreputable house] again.

One day, as he was on his way home, drunk on ale, his horse followed along the old road, and by mistake arrived at the house of the singing girl. Both delighted and resentful, with tears streaming down her face, she stepped out to greet him. It was only then that Master [Kim Yusin] grew aware of what had actually transpired. So, he chopped off the head of the horse he had ridden, discarded the saddle, and went home on foot. The woman thereupon composed a *yuan ci,* a "Song of resentment," which she transmitted to him.

In the Eastern Capital lies Ch'ŏn'gwan-sa, the "Temple of the Celestial Official," [which was built at] the [same] spot where [the singing girl's] house [once stood].[290] When Minister of State Yi Kongsŭng[291] early on went to take his post as Eastern Capital secretary,[292] he composed the following poem:

> The temple being called Ch'ŏn'gwan, there is a cause for it from
>   long ago;
> when suddenly I heard they'd commenced to build [a temple there],
>   it left me gloomy.
> The young noble, full of passion, he sojourned beneath the blossoms;
> the fair woman, harboring resentment, she wept before the horse.
> The red-maned [animal], with passion it went back on the road it
>   knew so well;
> the gray-turbaned [servant], for what crime did he mindlessly crack
>   the whip?
> Only left is a single tune, its lyrics marvelous:
> "I slept with the moon"[293] — for all eternity it shall be transmitted.[294]

Ch'ŏn'gwan, "Celestial Official," was this girl's sobriquet.[295]

[2:25]

During the time of Emperor Myŏng,[296] my uncle,[297] Monk Superintendent Yoil,[298] went in and out of the Forbidden Rooms [of the royal palace], disregarding left and right for more than twenty years.[299] Always he would write [the same] poem in which he asked to be allowed to retire from the court [and return to the mountains]. This he brought forth as a memorial to the throne. It read:

> Dreams fading away at the fifth watch, leaning against pinewood
>   gates;[300]
> ten years in the Purple Precincts, lingered there.[301]
> Early on, [my] tea faintly contained the phoenix's shadow,
> as peculiar fragrances freshly vaporized in the [black-glazed teacup
>   with] partridge feather design.[302]
> How pitiful, the gaunt crane has soared off into the cinnabar
>   firmament;

128   POEMS AND STORIES FOR OVERCOMING IDLENESS

for long the hungry monkey was made resentful on an emerald
    mountain.[303]
Wish that for my twilight years I may return to my old place of
    reclusion,
and to not be commanded to hang around like a white cloud by a
    cliff's edge in idleness.

The king greatly gave praise [to my uncle's poem], but then spoke to the
teacher, "Long ago, someone said, 'Don't be astounded if I go back early one
morning, goosefoot-staff in hand; it's because my [home] mountain is idly
holding back a cloud above a brook.'[304] One may dare say that this person
of previous times had already obtained the teacher's rare zest." Thereupon
the king wrote a reply poem in order to bestow it upon him.

The patriarch's mind-seal[305] manufactures the main gates,[306]
thus comprehending true emptiness,[307] in an instant it is there.
Sitting at ease, bits of aloeswood [incense] pile inside the brazier;
welcoming a guest, the Qiong-bamboo staff breaks [the teacup with]
    purple moss design.
It's fine if scriptures and treatises are transmitted to monks and nuns,
but don't take moving forward or holding yourself in reserve when
    remembering your old mountain.[308]
Evening bell and morning incense, diligently apply yourself to
    chanting the rites;
We beseech you to let the ignorant and base obtain peace and leisure.

If we survey both old and new, we shall find many instances in which
renowned [black-clothed] Buddhist masters and superior [patchwork-
robed] monks received the favor of a lord or king, or in which [royal] pieces
of writing were bestowed upon them! Yet [for a king] to especially match
the rhymes [of a simple monk's poem] and [for His Majesty] to express his
own intentions in such an affectionate, dense manner — never has there been
anything like it.

Yesterday I visited my uncle's abbot chamber, and he showed me this
piece written by His Majesty. The imperial brush had moved as if in flight,
scents of orchid and musk emitted sweetly from it, and thus I adjusted
my cap, put on a solemn countenance, knelt down, and read the poem. It
was the same as looking up to the sun in the sky beyond the clouds, as an
auspicious gleam of wonderful colors gloriously flooded my eyes. Truly, it
was awe-inspiring![309]

P'ahan chip — Fascicle 3

[3:1]

It was ancient custom in Kyerim to select men of beautiful looks and elegant bearing, adorn them with pearls and kingfisher-blue [ornaments], and refer to them as *hwarang*, "flower boys."[1] The people of that dynasty all held them in high esteem. Their followers were more than three thousand in number, and [they were all trained and educated in a] similar way to how [the Lord of Ping]yuan, [the Lord of Meng]chang, [the Lord of Chun]shen, and [the Lord of Xin]ling had bred their troops.[2] After those standing out from the crowd had been chosen, they were given high rank at the court, yet [from among these chosen few] it was only the disciples of the Four Immortals,[3] being most accomplished, who were allowed to erect steles [on which their masters' heroic deeds were retold].[4]

After the dragon of our [founder] T'aejo [Wang Kŏn] had risen [and our dynasty was established], he believed that the traditional ways of the old dynasty [Silla] hadn't yet [entirely] broken away! Thus, in a winter month he opened the P'algwan Sŏnghoe, the "Magnificent Assembly of the Eight Commandments,"[5] selected four sons of good families, clothed them in rainbow-colored robes,[6] and had them dance in rows in the courtyard.

Edict Attendant Kwak Tongsun,[7] in lieu [of those who had long ago participated in this Festival of the Eight Commandments at T'aejo's court], composed a laudatory memorial, which read as follows:

> Since Fuxi-shi became king under Heaven,[8] there has been nothing higher than the Three Han of T'aejo. On distant Mount Guye lived a Spirit-Man,[9] he must have been like the four sons of Wŏlsŏng.[10]

He also wrote:

130   POEMS AND STORIES FOR OVERCOMING IDLENESS

Peach blossoms on flowing waters have vanished into the distance: [there once was another cosmos,] yet real traces of it are hard to find.[11] Venerable families and surviving customs of earlier times persisted;[12] certainly August Heaven would not let them perish.[13]

He also wrote:

It may not have been the courtyard of [Emperor] Gao [Yao],[14] but they got to go in rows of the various animals leading one another to dance.[15] All the scholars of Zhou sang the stanza of how "young men made [constant] attainments [through him]."[16]

[Kwak] Tongsun was the nephew of the hermit Kwak [Yŏ], and in his youth he had had talent and fame. One time, when the hermit was staying at Sanho Pavilion in the Grand Interior,[17] [Kwak] Tongsun had gone to pay his respects [to his uncle]. Their pure conversation[18] was relaxed and unhurried, and when the sun went down he stayed the night there.

Around midnight the moonlight resembled white silk, and King [Yejong], who had gone out for a stroll, arrived at Sanho Pavilion. The hermit ordered Tongsun to step outside and prostrate himself.

"Who is this man?" the king inquired.

"Just my nephew so-and-so," [Kwak Yŏ] replied. "I had not seen his face in a long time, but today, fortunately, we got a chance to chat freely after having suffered separation for so long. When he was about to go back out, the palace gates had already been lowered. I am guilty of a crime deserving death, a crime deserving death!"

"For me, too, it's been a long time since I last heard of him," replied the king.

The hermit offered a toast to [the king's] longevity, and impromptu wrote the following poetic line:

The rays of the moon slant to find the Son of Heaven's throne.

He ordered Tongsun to continue it, who thus fell onto his knees and presented the following:

The dew on the flowers still moistens the attendant official's robe.

The king greatly conferred praise and reward upon him, saying, "Your talents being such as this, how could even Emperor Ming [of Tang] have borne to throw you out?"[19] That night, [King Yejong] had him take night duty at the Golden Gates.

[3:2]

King Ye[jong] held Confucian scholars in high esteem. Thus, every other year he personally selected worthy and good men [from among the candidates of the civil service examinations],[20] and by inspecting the accepted examination papers in advance, he would gain an understanding of their talents.

The candidate in the departmental examinations[21] Ko Hyoch'ung was a famous scholar,[22] but he had composed a poem entitled *Sa muik si,* "Poem on the four ineffectivenesses,"[23] by which he had publicly criticized his lord's mistakes — even a sagely ruler [like King Yejong] couldn't have been empty of concern [when faced with such impudence].

When the [metropolitan civil service examinations] were held in the Halls of Spring, it was ordered that the attendant official Im Kyŏngch'ŏng[24] was to go to the examination mats straightaway, expel Ko Hyoch'ung, and only then disclose the topic [of the examination].

Academician Hu Zongdan thereupon hurriedly ran to the Halls to present an abbreviated memorial to the throne,[25] by which he got [the king] to pardon [Ko's] crime.

Hereafter [Ko Hyoch'ung] again took part in the civil service examinations,[26] and when he gave his examination paper to the minister of spring, the first lines read:

> In these scrolls I am sending word: poems, rhapsodies, discussions —
> our parting, gentlemen, shall take place this coming spring.
> You shall become everlasting treasures in the Imperial Archive,
> I shall turn into the leading man in the Blue Clouds.

Indeed, he was selected Dragon Head, and as he was soaring high in the Inner Palace he spoke honestly, all the while having the elegant manner of a remonstrating minister. Wherever he went, people all pointed at him, saying, "That's the one who early on composed the *Sa muik si!*"

[3:3]

When the scholar Pak Wŏn'gae was in his youth,[27] he was intelligent and not like others. At just eleven years of age he had composed an announcement,[28] which he presented to Chancellor Ch'oe Yunŭi,[29] begging him to award an office to his father. It read:

132   POEMS AND STORIES FOR OVERCOMING IDLENESS

There is one man who has not been granted your grace — it is only my
  father;
he who can make all things obtain their proper place — truly, it is
  only you.

When Minister of State [Ch'oe Yunŭi] read this, he suspected that someone
else must have written [this well-phrased announcement in the young boy's]
stead, and therefore he made up his mind to test him face-to-face.

[Eventually he said to Pak Wŏn'gae,] "I'd like to drink a cup of tea right
now. You, child, shall apply the characters *hyang*, "fragrance," and *wang*,
"king," as rhymes,[30] and write a poem on the subject of *Chŏngjung chagyak*,
"The Chinese peony in the courtyard." Do it before I've finished my tea."
[Pak Wŏn'gae] on the spot responded [with the following quatrain]:

On the Chinese peony still linger the colors of spring;
in front of the porch it emits a peculiar fragrance.
The tree peony,[31] if it was by its side,
would surely be ashamed for being called the "hundred
  flowers' king."

The minister of state ceaselessly sighed in astonishment, exclaiming, "You'll
most certainly become a leader of the later-born."

When [Pak Wŏn'gae] grew up he took part in the triennial lower civil
service examinations,[32] and the disclosed examination topic was *Kukcha
chigong-ji ki*, "The country must be a perfectly impartial vessel." [Pak
Wŏn'gae] wrote:

Yao and Shun could hardly transmit [the world] to their
  [unworthy] sons;[33]
Shang and Zhou obtained [the world] by merit.[34]

Since he had employed allusions in such an exquisite and marvelous way,
he was indeed picked out for the ranks, and became a much-heard-of person
for a while.[35]

[3:4]

When composing poetry, a poet oftentimes employs allusions [to people
and matters of yore], and one refers to this as "Ghost Registers."[36] [The

Tang dynasty poet] Li Shangyin made use of allusions that were rugged and remote, [and lyrical works modeled after Li Shangyin and composed in the poetic style nowadays] called the "Xikun Style,"[37] they're all literary writings suffering from that very same disease.[38]

Recently, Su [Dongpo] and Huang [Tingjian] have rushingly risen [to fame and popularity], and while they also followed and revered this technique [of utilizing intricate allusions to ancient works and people], the way they arranged their words was so much more skilled [than that of the poets contained in *Xikun chouchang ji*, the "Collection of verses on the same themes from Western Kunlun Mountain"]. [In the poetry by Su Dongpo and Huang Tingjian] there are no marks left behind by the hatchet or the chisel at all. Thus, one may say that [Su Dongpo and Huang Tingjian's poetry] is bluer than indigo![39] [This is evidenced,] for instance, in [the following examples by Su] Dongpo:

> I saw the tale of a man astride a whale, roaming through the vast and
>   boundless;[40]
> I recall [the tale] of a man picking lice [from his clothes], chatting
>   about his bitter misery.[41]

> Long nights, I'm longing for my home, where might it be?
> remaining years, I know what the feeling must be for you coming
>   so far.[42]

The technique of line composition [makes these lines appear] as if they had been brought to life naturally by transformative creation, and whoever reads them cannot possibly know which [ancient] matters [Su Dongpo] was alluding to. [Or, take the following lines by] Shangu [Huang Tingjian], where it says,

> There is little piquancy in language because there is none of *this* in it;[43]
> he who can look back at ice and snow is only this gentleman.

> My eyes look on human nature as Rolling a Five;[44]
> my heart knows that worldly matters equal Three in the Morning.[45]

There are many poems such as these [in the collections of Huang Tingjian].

My friend Kiji, too, has mastered the marvelous [technique of making use of difficult but meaningful allusions, as can be seen in verses] such as the following ones:

134 POEMS AND STORIES FOR OVERCOMING IDLENESS

[The quick passing of] years and months often has me stunned, like
    when a sheep's shoulder blade was well cooked [so rapidly];[46]
with ancient-style poetry we get together again,[47] as the high skies
    are cold.[48]

In the belly: early I knew that the spirit is full there;
in the bosom, then: nothing vulgar is born there at all.[49]

These verses were all dispersed through people's mouths, and really one
ought not to feel ashamed even when comparing them to the ancients.

[3:5]

As a child I once climbed up Mount Ch'ŏnma, which lies north of the capital.
There [I wandered around], seeking the odd and choosing the extraordinary
without omission. Eventually I spotted a poem someone had left on the wall
of a sequestered temple.[50] It read:

Who ever named it "Heavenly Grindstone Ridge"?[51]
Skimming the void, with massed azure floating [above and around it].
Only a hand's width apart from the sky;
    the hanging moon [above the mountain], how many autumns [has
        it seen]?
The path is rugged, drooping like the arm of a monkey;
the poem is aslant, tilting like the head of a crane.

Below there was yet another line, but so washed away that it was impos-
sible to decipher. The poet's name was nowhere to be found, yet it certainly
must have been someone who had fled the world of the vulgar to cultivate
the Way amid valleys and cliffs, for the words he had written were pure
and bitter.[52]

[3:6]

The music register[53] of a southern prefecture[54] contained [the name] of a
singing girl whose beauty and artistry were equally amazing. And there
was a county magistrate — I've forgotten his name — who had fallen madly
in love with her.

    It happened around the time when his term in that post was coming to an end and he was to take the carriage back [to the capital]: all of a sudden, he got magnificently drunk and slurred to some bystander, "The moment I step out of this county by a mere few strides, she'll immediately be with some other guy."

Then he promptly proceeded to scorch both her cheeks with a wax-torch, and there wasn't a patch of skin [on her face] left unmarred.

Later, [Chŏng] Sŭmmyŏng of the Rongyang [Chŏng Clan][55] passed by this area, carrying royal staff and tally. When he caught sight of this singing girl, the sadness and anger he felt were infinite. Thus, he took out two pieces of the finest paper patterned with clouds of indigo,[56] wrote a quatrain on them in his very own handwriting, and gave them to her.

> Amid the shrubs of a hundred flowers, a serene, blossoming
>   countenance;
> suddenly struck by maddest wind, bereaved of its deepest red.
> Even otter marrow could not mend her cheeks of jade;[57]
> noble sons of Wuling, boundless ought to be your efforts.[58]

Thereupon he urged her, saying, "Whenever a government official on a mission stops by here, you must take out this poem and show it to him."

The singing girl diligently complied with his instructions, and every time somebody saw the poem he would at once present her with alms and care, for they all wanted the [high minister and adviser to King Injong,] Master Rongyang [Chŏng Sŭmmyŏng,] to hear about their [charitable and praiseworthy] deeds.

By way of this she obtained profit, and eventually became twice as rich as before.[59]

[3:7]

Master Hwang Sunik possessed rare talents,[60] and when he was in his youth he sojourned at the National Academy, reading his books. As it happened, he [later] came to suffer from a [chronically] dry mouth. Once he asked someone for Jian[zhou] tea,[61] and with an announcement he expressed his appreciation for it:

> After Censor Meng had sent it to Lu Tong, swiftly purest winds rose
>   beneath his two arms.[62]
> After Minister of State Wang had given it to Pingfu,[63] a round
>   emerald moon fell from the nine-tiered heavens.[64]

136 POEMS AND STORIES FOR OVERCOMING IDLENESS

Also, in reply to someone else's poem on cranes he wrote:

> Treading, firmly, over a trail's moss, pine-like legs are strong;
> dancing, flappingly, under a courtyard's moon, snow-like garments
> are cool.

Since his talents were as outstanding as this, the literati of that age all respected and revered him.

Often he would visit Kim Chonjung of the Security Council, and on one occasion there was someone who offered pine-mushrooms [to Kim Chongjung] as a present. The minister of state requested that [Hwang Sunik] take these mushrooms as a lyrical subject and write a poem. Thus, he rose and straightaway wrote the following:

> Last night my eating-finger moved,
> and this morning I got to taste something exquisite.[65]
> Originally, it is not being cultivated on small hills;
> rather it has the aroma of China-root-fungus.

[Hwang Sunik] craved ale and had little sense of self-regulation. He hung around in petty offices for a long time and could never manage to get promoted.

Suddenly one evening, when the weather was frigid and he was thoroughly drunk, he slumped over his desk and drifted off to sleep. That night his neighbor dreamed that he caught sight of the teacher unfolding a white silken parasol [used during funeral processions], appearing as if he was about to return to his former place of dwelling on Mount Paektu. At dawn, he went over to pay him a visit, but [Hwang Sunik] had already passed away! In the world they called him Paektu-*chŏng*, "Essence of Paektu."

[3:8]

When Sŏha Kiji got weary of journeying, he settled down in Sŏngsan County.[66] The county chief had often heard his name and therefore sent him a singing girl who was to share the pillow with him. Late that night, however, she ran off and went back. Downhearted, Kiji composed a poem.

> Climbed up the tower, but she failed to act as the partner who blows
> the pipe;[67]

escaped to the moon, to no good purpose she became the immortal
who stole the elixir.[68]
Unafraid of the senior official's stern command;
upset over a bad fated relationship with an [ugly old] wayfarer.[69]

His use of allusions was superb, and this is something to which the ancients would have said, "Embroidered with golden thread, yet not a trace of it anywhere."

[3:9]

After Paegunja Sinjun[70] had hung up his [Confucian] cap on Sinho [Gate],[71] he returned to his mountain estate in Kong Prefecture to live in seclusion. The county magistrate sent his son to receive [the former minister's] teachings, and [the young man was educated by Paegunja Sinjun] for years. [When the magistrate's son eventually set out to] take part in the civil service examinations in the capital, [Paegunja Sinjun] sent him off with a quatrain.

Ducal Son Xinling mustered his finest soldiers,
set off afar to Handan, to establish great fame.[72]
All the heroes of the world went to follow the ruler's carriage;
how pitiable! Wiping away his tears was old Hou Ying.[73]

[3:10]

My ancestors have succeeded one another with [brilliant] literary writings for generations on end, and eight slips of red paper have already been transmitted [to members of my family] by now![74] I'm not talented, but by chance I got to dwell in front of many scholars [and was selected principle graduate].

My eldest son, Chŏng, was put in fourth place; next, my second son, Yang, was put in third place; next, my third son, On, was put in second place. They are all exceptional, their talents outstanding at a young age, and their examination ranks were majestic — still they weren't able to supremely reside in the spot of principle [Dragon] Head, thereby obtaining the same rank as their father.

Koyang wŏlsa [Kakhun][75] composed a poem to congratulate me [on the success of my sons]:

138   POEMS AND STORIES FOR OVERCOMING IDLENESS

Three sons' stringed pearls,[76] all continuing their father's elegance;
four branches on the immortal's cassia, all inside a single house.[77]
They may have occupied the Golden Roster for years on end,
yet they kept away from the Dragon Head, yielding it to their
    Old Man.

[3:11]

Some forty leagues west of the capital there is a place of slow currents and
gentle waves, where [the stream] is so clear and emerald that one can see all
the way to the bottom. Distant peaks and faraway summits together reach
the sky, and truly there is no difference to the splendid atmosphere of Xixing
as described in the collections of Su [Dongpo] and Huang [Shangu].[78]

The young scholar No Yŏngsu was skilled in verse making.[79] Once, at
sundown he set afloat a skiff, rowed upstream, and traveled on, for he meant
to spend the night at a temple by the lake. Mid-stream he whistled for a long
while, and, absentmindedly, came up with a verse:

Winds howling, the Yi River is cold;
in a solitary boat I went off alone.

He had chanted at the top of his voice, but, regretfully, there was no one to
continue it.

Suddenly, however, from in between the reeds [by the riverbank],
from amid a deep darkness veiled by wafts of fog, a responding voice
sounded:

Mists engulfing, the Chu sky is vast;[80]
traveler, where are you off to?

When Master No heard this, he was so shocked and terrified, he really
couldn't get a hold of himself.

"No human being dwells inside [those murky, foggy reeds]," he stam-
mered, "so it must've either been an immortal or a perfected being."[81] He
halted the oars, quite incapable of going any farther.

When the night was advancing toward its half, he carefully glanced all
around, but there was no human sound far and wide. Only the waning stars
and the crescent moon mirrored upturned in the frosty waves. Eventually,
he somehow managed to go back.

The following day there was a commotion in the capital, for word had spread that a celestial immortal had descended by the western lake.

A month or so later I heard this: Ryu Su,[82] having passed the civil service examinations, had spent that night in a fishing boat.

[3:12]

Lord Pak Kongsŭp lived in abject poverty,[83] yet he craved the wine. One time, when a visitor came around, there was nothing to drink, so he asked the monks of Yŏngt'ong Temple for some wine.[84] [The monks] used a white, bellied-mountain-bottle, filled it to the brim with spring water, sealed it very tightly with cord, and sent it to him.

When Master Pak first laid eyes upon it he was delighted, exclaiming, "This vessel can easily hold two gallons! Long ago, the King of Chen feasted in Pingle [Hall] with wine worth ten thousand cash per gallon,[85] and Du Zimei likewise said,

> You must come over swiftly to drink a gallon;
> I just now happen to have three hundred copper coins.[86]

Now the two of us haven't even spent a single coin, and still we've obtained this excellent wine. If we each drink a gallon, our drunken, carefree merriment won't be any less than that of those men of old!"

With this he [hastily] opened [the bottle], peeked at [the liquid contained inside] — and it was water.

Regretting that he had been so shortsighted, that he had fallen for the old [monks'] scheme, he composed a poem, which he sent to them.

> A guest came passing by,
> in his purse not a single coin.
> When he asked them to share Luyue wine,[87]
> all he got was Huishan spring water.[88]
> What looked like a tiger was a rock in a forest,[89]
> what seemed like a snake was a bowstring on a wall.[90]
> Chomping away [when standing in front of] a butcher shop,[91]
> but how much more so when standing in front of a wine bottle?[92]

When the monks saw his poem, they again recompensed him with excellent wine.

[3:13]

Academician P'aeng Chojŏk[93] had an obsessive desire for books. His hut was made of a few beams thatched with reeds, with wind and rain blowing in from all sides, and for him, [purchasing firewood was as unaffordable as] buying cassia wood [would have been for others], while [cooking rice was as rare a thing as] cooking up jades.[94] Still, [if he had his books,] he was always content and at ease.

Whenever he produced a piece of literary writing, it invariably possessed deep roots, and readers [of his texts] would regularly come upon lines that they would find difficult to comprehend.

In the final years of King Ŭi[jong], Minister of State Yi Kwangjin[95] had been humble and respectful, diligent and cautious, and thus he did not experience any hardships [during the military revolt].[96] Master [P'aeng Chojŏk] was then at the Garden of [Silken] Threads,[97] and he composed the following royal proclamation, [which the king bestowed upon Yi Kwangjin]:

> Perils and hardships, you have experienced them in full measure! And one may say, you are in danger! You obtained it [your current official position] by being courteous, refined, respectful and restrained.[98] To the end, you were without guilt.

At the beginning of the reign of King Myŏngjong, the examination administrator Han Ŏn'guk pulled along the various scholars of the new [Golden] Roster to pay his respects to his mentor, Minister of State Ch'oe [Yuch'ŏng], and then composed a poem to thank him. Master [P'aeng Chojŏk][99] matched this poem with one of his own, the opening of which read:

> A superior man made fully human a superior man; continuing on, he [too] obtained blooming talents.
> Below the *munsaeng* are the *munsaeng;* jointly standing in rows, expressing their appreciation.

Also, it said:

> Inside the lion-leader cave are lion-leaders,[100] the same in their roars.
> Below the cassia-bough forest are cassia-boughs,[101] no duality in their aromas.

Thus was his [poetry's] strangeness and ruggedness.

In his twilight years, [P'aeng Chojŏk] was exceedingly fond of the canonical Buddhist scriptures, and under Hwaŏm Master Changgwan[102] he studied the [Hwaŏm] pŏpkye kwanmun, the "Discernments of the Dharmadhatu of Avatamsaka."[103] He composed a poem of one hundred rhymes to thank him, and in the world [this poem] was referred to as Chojŏk posal song, "Chojŏk's Bodhisattva hymn."

[3:14]

After Academician Kim Hwangwŏn had been appointed grand master of remonstrance, he offered his medicine time and time again,[104] but as he failed to change Heaven's powerful [will],[105] he was eventually sent away to govern Sŏngsan.

The road took him out to Punhaeng Relay Station,[106] where he happened to meet Yi Chae[107] of the Celestial Institute,[108] who was presently on his way back to the court upon his return from a southern state.[109] Since [the two old friends] had met at this relay station entirely by chance, [Kim Hwangwŏn] wrote a poem and presented it to [Yi Chae].

Atop Punhaeng Tower,[110] how could there not be a poem?
Leaving it for the glorious envoy,[111] conveying what is on my mind.
Reeds and rushes rustling bleakly in the land of the autumn waters,
rivers and mountains shimmering vaguely in the hour of the
    evening sun.
With the ancients not in sight, in the present age I sigh in vain;
bygone matters hard to amend, and grief is all that's left.
Who'd believe[112] that the traveler was demoted to Changsha's [grand
    tutor],[113]
and that with low office and old age his hair will grow thin?

Members of the gentry all wrote companion pieces,[114] and they amounted to about a hundred poems. These were all put in order, and [the entire collection] was titled Punhaeng chip, "Collection of Punhaeng."[115] Academician Pak Sŭngjung produced a preface,[116] and Lord Taewŏn had [the Punhaeng chip] carved on woodblocks,[117] for it to be circulated.

Throughout his life, whenever he composed a poem, Master [Kim Hwangwŏn] would invariably use the two words sŏk yang, "evening sun." Minister of State Kim Puŭi recorded in [Kim Hwangwŏn's] epitaph that he believed this [sŏgyang] to have been a prognostication for [the poet's] rise to a prestigious, reputable position late in life.

142   POEMS AND STORIES FOR OVERCOMING IDLENESS

[3:15]

> Thatched cottage in autumn, the seventh month;
> rain on *tong* trees at night,[118] the third watch.
> Resting on pillows, travelers without dreams;
> behind the window, insects with sounds.
> On shallow grass, water-drops spraying in confusion;
> on cold leaves, pure [raindrops] sprinkling in profusion.
> To me it has a serene charm,
> I know the way you feel tonight.[119]

This is a composition by Academician In Pin.[120] That the academician's name shook the Country East of the Sea like thunder, it was essentially because of this very poem.

Long ago, when I assisted in Kyeyang Commandery, one day I was rowing my boat, going from Kongam Lesser Prefecture[121] to the southern lake of Haeng Prefecture.[122] [On the way] I caught sight of a sharp slope [by the riverbank], [shooting up] like wild rice, and there were eight or nine pines and firs, densely standing off to one side, as well as the remnants of walls and crumbled fences.

Those passing by all pointed at it, saying, "This is the old site of Master In's thatched cottage."

I moored my boat, unable to go any farther. Eventually I lingered on, [strolled around,] and with a long whistle I pictured this person in my mind. Then I came upon a small trail, which I ascended all the way up to the southern tower of Sohwa Temple.[123] There I spotted a poem on a wall, all covered in moss and darkish, but with vague traces of pale ink still barely discernable. Stepping closer I inspected it—it had been inscribed by Master In [Pin].

> Plantains resounding beyond the reed-screen, I know it is the mountain rain;
> sails emerging atop the mountain-peak, I see it is the ocean wind.[124]

One may say: beneath a [famous] name there is no hollow scholar!

[3:16]

Kaegol, "All-bone," are the famous mountains of Kwandong.[125] Their peaks and ridges, their grottoes and ravines—nothing but rock. Gazing at them from a distance, it's as though they [were splattered onto the horizon with the] splashed ink [painting technique]. The people roosting on these [precipitous, barren] cliffs all fill up cracks and crevices with [fertile] soil brought from faraway places, and only then do they get to plant and grow wild rice and fruits to eat.

With royal staff and tally, Chŏn Ch'iyu[126] of the Jade Hall once passed through these mountains, and he inscribed the following poem:

> Plants and trees growing sparsely, like the hair [sprouting on a]
>   bald head;
> mists and auroras curling halfway, like a garment [exposing] bare
>   shoulders.
> Looming high are the all-bone [mountains], all alone in their solitary
>   purity,
> surely laughing at the meaty mountains, in all their big fatness.

[3:17]

That the Eastern Bureau is "Mount Penglai," while the Jade Hall is called "Turtle Head,"[127] is because both are offices for spirits and immortals. In accordance with our dynasty's time-honored system, even the Son of Heaven may not act solely on his own authority when it comes to promotion or demotion [in these two offices]. If there is a vacant spot [in the Eastern Bureau or the Jade Hall], a candidate necessarily has to be recommended by the various Confucian scholars of the [six] Inner Palace offices, and only then can he be appointed. If there is no praise of him being a "Three Often,"[128] or of him having the [literary] talent of [composing a poem in] seven paces,[129] then everyone in the world will say, "In such a [prestigious official] position he certainly won't be able to avoid being mocked as one with 'bloody fingers and a sweaty face.'"[130]

During the reign of King Ye[jong], Chŏng Sŭmmyŏng, an impoverished and unsuccessful scholar[131] from the southland,[132] possessed rare talents and great capacities, yet he waded through the world without finding a ford. Early on he had rhapsodized on the subject of *Sŏkchukhwa*, the "China pink flower."

> People love the peony's red,
> plant and cultivate it lavishly inside their gardens.
> Who knows that in a field of wild weeds,
> there too stands one fine flowery shrub?

144   POEMS AND STORIES FOR OVERCOMING IDLENESS

> Its color permeating the moon in a village pond,
> its aroma carried on the wind in the hilltop trees.
> The place is remote, young nobles are few,
> its lovely charm belongs to an old man in the fields.[133]

At the time, there was a grand porter[134] who happened to recite this very poem [at the court], and thereby it reached the Blessed Percipience.[135] "If not for the keeper of the hounds," said the king, "how should I have known that [Sima] Xiangru was still around?" And he immediately ordered [Chŏng Sŭmmyŏng] to be appointed to the Jade Hall.[136]

At the beginning of the reign of King Ŭi[jong], the Worthy and Excellent[137] Hwangbo T'ak was selected principle graduate after having taken the state examinations *ten* times.[138] Earlier, the king had happened to sojourn in the Royal Forest [behind the palace], where he admired the Chinese peonies. Eventually he had completed a single poetic piece [on the subject of this flower],[139] but among the attendant officials no one had been able to compose a response to the royal verse [when commanded to do so]. Thereupon the Worthy and Excellent [Hwangbo T'ak] had brought forth a single poem:

> Who says flowers have no lord,
> when the royal countenance bestows favor on them every day?
> Surely they welcome the beginning of summer,
> alone they guard the last of spring.
> Midday slumber, winds blowing fresh wake them from it;
> morning toilet, rains washing down make it anew.
> Palace girls, don't you envy them —
> though you're much alike, in the end, they're just not real.[140]

The king had greatly conferred praise and reward upon him. When hereafter the Selection Ministry[141] had brought him forth as someone scheduled to fill some [minor] post at the bureau, the king spotted his name. "Isn't that the one who earlier brought forth a command poem to my own composition on the Chinese peony?"[142] he inquired, and right away marked [Hwangbo's] name with his imperial brush, sending him straight to the Eastern Bureau.[143]

Master Chŏng [Sŭmmyŏng] later entered the Security Council[144] and dwelled there as [the king's] throat and tongue. He received the final commands [of Injong], assisted the [young] lord [Ŭijong as royal tutor], spoke out boldly with words of reason, and had the elegance of an upright minister of the king.[145]

Master Hwangbo [T'ak], too, was in charge of [drafting] royal edicts and pronouncements, going in and out of the halls of state for more than ten years.

Ah! Those were conjunctions of winds and clouds,[146] about which the ancients said they occurred only once in a thousand years. But when I now look at these two masters, they were both, in fact, recognized [by their respective kings] on the basis of merely a single poem — there was no need for [auspicious] dreams or divinations,[147] as these unions took place naturally. The encounter of an enlightened [king] and a good [minister], how could it ever happen by chance?

[3:18]

After Paegunja had thrown away his Confucian scholar's cap, he studied the teachings of the Buddha. With a bag tied to his waist he roved extensively through all the famous mountains [as a wayfaring monk].[148]

[One day], as he was walking along on the road, he was emotionally stirred upon hearing an oriole sing, and he completed the following quatrain:

> Boasting with the loveliness of your crimson beak and yellow robe,
> you ought to be calling out from within red walls and light green
>   trees.[149]
> Why then are you in this tumbledown village, in this still and
>   dreary land?
> From afar beyond the forest at times sending two, three cries.[150]

When my friend Kiji felt depressed, he roved the southland.[151] Upon hearing an oriole, he too composed a poem.

> By a farming home, mulberries ripen as barley gets dense;
> from among the light green trees I first hear the yellow bird.
> As if it knew the traveler [who once was a guest] under the flowers in
>   Luoyang,[152]
> it solicitously warbles, never taking a rest.[153]

Poets of old and new have relied on animals to give expression to their thoughts, and there are many poems of the same kind as the above quoted. The two masters' compositions — while it is not as though they had been arranged to go together from the very beginning, it still seems as though

146   POEMS AND STORIES FOR OVERCOMING IDLENESS

these spat-out lamentations of gloom and regret were uttered by the mouth of one and the same person.[154]

[Paegunja and Kiji both] had talent, but they weren't made use of [as officials during their times]. Their drifting about at the ends of the earth, the way they voyaged and how they were swept along—it's all clearly visible within those few words. Hence, when it is said, "A poem's source lies in the heart-mind"—it is credible!

[3:19]

The brush technique of Kim Saeng, a man from Kyerim, was ingenious, splendid, and not even people of Jin or Wei could have hoped to keep pace with it.

Reaching our dynasty, only State Preceptor Taegam as well as Academician Hong Kwan[155] have made names for themselves [in terms of calligraphy], and generally the inscriptions on the horizontal plaques in the palace halls and flower pavilions, or the mottoes and admonitions on the folding screens, were all the products of these two masters' brushes.

When Master Chillak [Yi Chahyŏn] of [Mount] Ch'ŏngp'yŏng passed away, the monk Hyeso of Western Lake composed a sacrificial address,[156] the state preceptor [Taegam] wrote it down [in his magnificent calligraphic style], and they even spared no efforts to have [his calligraphy] engraved in stone to transmit it [to posterity]—in the world, this was referred to as the "Three Perfections."[157] Indeed, it wasn't like that lot of Ch'oes and Yangs [of present times], for what they have achieved [in calligraphy] has fat flesh [on the outside] but brittle bones [on the inside]. At the time, there was a commentator who remarked, "Pulling iron to make sinews, breaking mountains to create bones; [the calligraphy's] strength could bend the yoke of a carriage, its sharpness could pierce the scales of armor."[158]

Among the people of Song there was one who sought to obtain a piece in the state preceptor's handwriting in exchange for exquisite silk and magnificent ink. He asked Academician Kwŏn Chŏk[159] to compose two quatrains, which he then copied and sent along. [One of them read:]

> Master Su [Dongpo's] literary works were even heard of overseas,
> but the Song dynasty's Son of Heaven put fire to his writings.
> Literary works can be turned into ashes and embers,
> yet his wide-spreading, mighty name—how could it ever be burned?

The other piece has been lost.

[3:20]

My younger cousin, Minister [Yi] Yugyŏng,[160] is the son of a grand councilor's family. From an early age he has prided himself on his elegance, and for those who sojourn with him it must certainly feel as though they were moving alongside a mountain of jade.

Early on he had entered Sangch'un Pavilion while being drunk on ale[161] and had chanted upon admiring a tree peony. Yi Yangsil of the Security Council watched him from the side and, loving his elegance and rhymes, presented him with a poem.[162]

> A single sliver of the Longxi moon[163]
> came flying, shining its light on the city of Luo.[164]
> When we part — [miserable,] as if there were long rains;
> where we meet — [elated,] as though the skies freshly cleared.

The rhymes were manifold, and I can't possibly note them all down.

In the long ago, Shangu [Huang Tianjing] discussed poetry, saying, "Not changing the [poetic] meaning of the ancients when creating one's own [poetic] expressions — this [technique] is referred to as *huangu*, 'swapping the bones'; imitating the [poetic] meaning of the ancients while giving it [new] shape — that [technique] is referred to as *duotai*, 'appropriating the embryo.'"[165] This, while being as far away from simply "stripping off an animal's hide and eating it raw"[166] as the sky and the deep blue sea are apart from each other, in fact cannot avoid being little more than the skill of nimbly plundering and stealthily stealing in order to [act as if one had] created [something entirely new]. How could one claim to be so marvelous as to bring forth new meaning from where even the ancients couldn't arrive at? When I received the above-quoted poem, I said, "This verse has obtained meaning from the ancients."

Yesterday, at Ssangmyŏng Studio,[167] I met Mister Yi of the Security Council to discuss poetry, and our conversation turned to this poem.

[Former] Minister Yi Chunch'ang[168] thereupon said with a troubled, altered expression, "My late father gave this poem to me as a present."[169]

I was stunned and sighed without cease, then said to the seated guests, "If one inserted this poem in the *Xiaodu ji*,[170] who'd ever know that it wasn't [one of Du Mu's pieces]?"

148 POEMS AND STORIES FOR OVERCOMING IDLENESS

[3:21]

Shigu, the [ancient] "Stone Drums,"[171] were put in place in the Confucian Temple in Qiyang [during the Tang dynasty].[172] From the Zhou dynasty, [when these Stone Drums were purportedly created], to the Tang dynasty, [when they were discovered and relocated,] for roughly two thousand years [some of the Stone Drum inscriptions] had been transmitted by the *Shi*[*jing*] and the *Shu*[*jing*],[173] but as for the various histories [of later times] or the works by the Hundred Schools of Thought, in fact none of them transmitted any of [the inscriptions]. In addition, the two masters Wei [Yingwu][174] and Han [Yu][175] both had broad knowledge of ancient matters—yet [in their songs on the Stone Drums,][176] what exactly was it that made them speak of [these artifacts] as the "Drums of King Xuan of the [Western] Zhou,"[177] or write on the songs' words, dissecting them without omission? Master Ouyang [Xiu], too, believed that there were three reasons for concern when it came to these matters.[178]

Yesterday I was in my library,[179] and it so happened that I read these texts [by Wen Yingwu, Han Yu, and Ouyang Xiu again]. Something about them struck my core, and I chanted a poem of twenty rhymes. I shall await [evaluations by] noblemen of later generations.

> Wooden shoes were passed on, becoming treasures for ten thousand
> generations;[180]
> Classics from the Wall, too, have been on all the Confucians' tongues.[181]
> Massive, bulging Stone Drums, from ancient times they were called
> unique,
> and were even made objects in the Master's Dark Palace.[182]
> Xuan of Zhou in olden days initiated a restoration,
> Fang [Shu][183] and Zhao [Hu][184] wielded their battle-axes in
> succession.
> With three thousand war chariots, like a hawk in flight,[185]
> to the north to subjugate the Xianyun,[186] to the south to restrain
> the Yue.[187]
> Expanded the territory, already reclaimed the basis once established
> by Wen and Hu;[188]
> the glorious achievement, appropriately to be performed with
> zithers.
> With a lighter sound he led the troops back,[189] singing the *Cai qi;*
> cautiously handling all the tiny matters, yet again obtaining a
> lucky day.[190]

Surely one must remember the earnestness of the generals back then,
but for how many years have scabbard and bow-case produced
  nothing but lice and nits?
An oath [as everlasting as] rivers and mountains,[191] never to fade;
[their] figures drawn on whitewashed walls, likewise not to be
  erased.
How could the moon-axe thumping down on the cloud-roots[192]
be anything like the fine inscriptions of victorious expeditions with
  the peculiar tadpole script?[193]
These words are blending and beautiful, simple and pure;
the profound principle ought to have been contained in the *Airs* and
  in the *Odes*.
How could the song collectors have seen but not collected them?[194]
On the shores of the gray sea they were left behind like Bright Moon
  [Pearls].
Ah! More than a thousand years since those times of Zhou;
rain-beaten and windswept, many [of the inscriptions] were
  worn away.
What remained were a dozen or so words in one line;
a single scale of a [coiling] serpent-dragon,[195] who again will
  cherish it?
"Our chariots are well crafted, our horses are well matched" —
these words are interrelated with the *Shi*[*jing*].[196]
Master Han [Yu] certainly also had deep [knowledge] of the *Shi*[*jing*],
read it once and recognized Xuan of Zhou's ardor.
Wind and clouds entered his brush, which rushed off to write the
  mighty verse,
dissecting it all, unwilling to leave behind the finest details.
Otherwise, this Writing of Ours[197] would have completely turned to
  cold ash;
how would it have gotten to stand in line with the "Songgao" [of the
  Shijing]?
As if sojourning at the Emperor's place amid a dream,
or briefly hearing the *Juntian* — all is pure and surpassing.[198]
Now that I've chanted, I mean to supplement them,
but since my fine-haired brush's already dull, it is difficult to bind
  together.
If one dipped a finger in them, one would discover the taste of the
  Nine Cauldrons;
a bird in flight — how could I supplement a single word that once
  was lost?[199]

150   POEMS AND STORIES FOR OVERCOMING IDLENESS

[3:22]

As to the affairs of the world, the only thing not separated into high or low by being either noble or common, rich or poor, is literary writing. In fact, the creation of literary writing is [a natural process], much like the sun and the moon clinging to Heaven,[200] or the clouds and the mists gathering or scattering in the Great Void. Those who have the eyes for it, there's nothing they couldn't see, for nothing can be covered or obscured to them. Therefore, even [poor, unemployed] scholars dressed in linen and kudzu can sufficiently shed rays of light to bring forth rainbows. The nobleness of [Chief Minister] Zhao Meng,[201] his mighty power, how could it not have been enough to make prosperous the country and plentiful the families? But when it comes to his literary writing, one simply cannot praise him for it. Therefore, it may be said: literary writing has a set value of its own, and the wealthy can't diminish it. For this reason, Ouyang Yongshu[202] remarked, "If later generations hadn't been fair [in the judgment of Confucius's and Mencius's literary writing], there wouldn't be any Sages left in our day and age."[203]

[O] Sejae of the Puyang [O Clan] was a gifted scholar.[204] [In the prime of his life] he repeatedly took part in the civil service examinations but didn't get to pass a single one of them.[205] Then, all of a sudden, he came to suffer from ailing eyes, whereupon he wrote the following poem:

> Old age and sickness accompany each other;
> I finish out the year, still in commoners' clothes.
> Black blossoms have more and more obscuring shadows;[206]
> purple stones have less and less glowing light.[207]
> Afraid of staring at words before the lamp;
> ashamed of looking at sunglow behind the snow.
> Waited to see the Golden Roster finished;
> close my eyes, forget [all lofty] plans.[208]

[O Sejae] had married three times, but he abandoned [each of his wives] and left.[209] He had no children to support him, no land to stick an awl in, while rice and water were irregular commodities for him. Only after reaching the age of fifty did he finally succeed in the civil service examinations,[210] [but since even then he was not appointed to any office], he eventually traveled to the Eastern Capital as a visitor, and there he passed away.[211] Getting to his literary writing, how could one ever discard it simply because he lived in poverty and stumbled [through life]?[212]

[3:23]

In the world, scholars have been chosen by means of the civil service examinations for a very long time! Starting from times of Han and Wei, then passing through the Six Dynasties, [the examination system] achieved its highest level of sophistication during Tang and Song. In accordance with this model [set by the Tang and Song recruitment systems], in our dynasty, too, civil service examinations are conducted once every three years,[213] and in old and new, after thousands of years, those who by means of their literary productions have picked up the green or purple [robes of ordinary or mid-level officials][214] are simply beyond recording. Yet from among the many preceding scholars [who successfully passed the civil service examinations], those who were later actually awarded high official positions have been exceedingly few.

In general, literary writings are obtained through Heaven-endowed nature, while rank and emolument are what people have at their disposal. If one sought it by means of the Way, one may say it was easy! Nonetheless, Heaven and earth do not let the myriad creatures obtain only their beautiful things—for this reason, [the beast that is endowed with] horns is deprived of sharp teeth, [the bird that is endowed with] wings has only two feet,[215] famously pretty flowers bear no fruit, and bright-colored clouds scatter all too swiftly.

With people it is like that, too. Those endowed with rare talents and luxuriant artistic gifts are shunned from scholarly honors and are not granted [access to high office]—in principle, that's just the way it is! We have this starting with Kong[zi], Meng[zi], Xun[zi], or Yang[zi],[216] and find it even when reaching Han [Yu], Liu [Zongyuan],[217] Li [Bai], or Du [Fu]—their literary writings and virtuous reputes may have been sufficient to create sensations throughout the ages, but in terms of official posts they didn't even ascend to ministers or grandees! Hence, those who are capable of being selected into the high first appointments of Dragon Heads and then get to walk on to become grand councilors, truly they're the ones who the ancients referred to as "those who ride a crane to Yangzhou."[218] How would it be possible for many to achieve such a [rare and exceptional] thing? In the case of our dynasty, eighteen people have entered the office of grand councilor [after having passed the civil service examinations] as principle graduates.

Today [Principle Graduates] Ch'oe Hong'yun and Kŭm Kŭgŭi have succeeded one another in getting to the Yellow Door [of the Prime Minister Room in the Chancellery],[219] while I myself and Vice Director Kim Kunsu

152 Poems and Stories for Overcoming Idleness

together sojourned at the Garden of Proclamations.[220] Other [Dragon Heads] who have obtained ranks in prestigious key positions comprised yet another fifteen people—how abundant they are!

Now it is the cyclic year *kisa*, it has been six years since our king ascended the throne,[221] and Master Kim [Kunsu] went out to govern a southern prefecture. Thus, various masters, [all of them principal graduates,] assembled in Hoe Village to see him off,[222] and in the world they referred [to us] as a *Yongdu hoe*, an "Assembly of Dragon Heads."[223] Gazing at [this assembly] from a distance, it looked like [a gathering of] ascending immortals. I wrote a piece to commemorate it.

> A dragon flies to the position of Fifth Nine;[224]
> below, a flock of dragons has gathered.
> Swallows and spits out the Bright Moon Pearl,
> soars and leaps up the Blue Cloud Road.
> Has already ascended to Li Ying's Gate;[225]
> shall serve to shower down the Yin Grand Councilor's
> [copious] rain.[226]
> Only precious is Hua Xin the Head;
> the Belly and the Tail, how'd they be worth comparing?[227]

The words of this verse may be excessive and inept, but still I hope it will make later generations fully understand that not even [the age of the sage-kings] Tang [Yao] and Yu [Shun] could have matched our dynasty in terms of its abundance of brilliantly qualified people.

[3:24]

The following has been transmitted:

> If it stands in the south, it will become a [delicious thin-skinned]
> tangerine;
> if it stands in the north, it will become a [bitter thorny-skinned]
> orange.[228]

Generally, when plants and trees are not in their natural soil, they can in no way flourish in accordance with their true nature. Yesterday, however, I walked out of the Golden Boudoir[229] and arrived at the Royal Flower Garden, where I saw a tangerine tree, about a fathom in height, which bore an enormous amount of fruit. When I asked a garden-keeper about this, he replied, "The tree was donated by someone from a southern region. Every morning I take salt water and pour it over its roots. That's why it grows so flourishingly."

Ah! Plants and trees are, of course, non-sentient objects — nevertheless, through the powers of watering and cultivation they get to reach this [lush, fruitful] state. Even more does this apply when the ruler of men employs his people: when he does not quibble over them being from far or near, distant or close by;[230] when he binds them by means of grace and care; when he rears them by means of rank and salary — how, then, could there be anyone [among both the military and civil officials] lacking in loyalty and devotion to aid the dynasty?

On that account I have written twelve rhymes, hoping that the person collecting the poem shall make use of this dust and have it read by His Majesty.[231]

Who took the seedling of the fiery prefecture,[232]
and transplanted it beside the forbidden royal stockade?
Escaped from the southern seashore,[233]
suddenly settled close to the palace wall.
Thin as jade, its shrub full of thorns;
abundant as clouds, its leaves have awns.
When carrying blossoms in spring, it's lined with white;
when bearing fruit in autumn, it's imbued with yellow.
Heavy dews congeal, becoming the kernels;
raw silk is used, separating the pulp.
As for picking, it'll surely trouble white hands;
as for ripening, it'll certainly take clear frost.
Spewing out mists, it moistens our gowns and sleeves;
gushing out waterfalls, it rinses our lungs and bowels.
It may have crossed the Huai's waters from afar,[234]
but that didn't diminish the fragrance [of the sweet tangerines] from
    Dongting.
Its aromatic flavor contains the immortal's realm;
its sound separates me from my old [earthly] home.
Though they may say: this isn't the soil [complying with its] nature —
[the tree still flourishes,] and it is only by [His Majesty's] gracious
    brilliance.
Ashamed to stand side by side with a "thousand [wooden] slaves";[235]
only serving as the four hoary-haired's hideout.[236]

154   POEMS AND STORIES FOR OVERCOMING IDLENESS

Just look at the old man [sitting] on Yi [bridge],
how he abandoned [Western] Chu to assist Emperor Gao.[237]

[3:25]

After Kiji had sought refuge in the southland for about ten years, he took
his sick wife and returned to the capital.[238] There, however, he had no land
to stick an awl in anymore. One day, as he was roaming about, free from
cares, he came upon a secluded monastery. Blithely he wetted a towel and
wrapped it around his head, sat down in an upright position, and whistled
lengthily.

"Sir, who're you to behave in such an unrestrained, jaunty manner?"
a monk questioned him.[239] [Kiji] thereupon wrote a poem of twenty-eight
words.[240]

Early on, my literary writings stirred the Imperial Capital;
[but today,] in Heaven and earth I'm merely some old scribbler.
Just now I've come to understand the [superior] meaning of the Gates
    of Emptiness;
in this crowded monastery, there's no one who'd recognize
    my name.[241]

[3:26]

Academican Paek Kwangsin[242] presided over the civil service examinations
[together with Im Yu during the reign of King Sinjong].[243] When it was over,
the various scholars of the new [Golden] Roster collectively held a celebra-
tory banquet [in his honor], offering prayers for [their examiner's] long life
and good fortune.

Then they went to pay their respect to the academician at Oksun
Pavilion,[244] [where Paek Kwangsin and his *munsaeng*] had a little drink
together. [Paek Kwangsin eventually] wrote a quatrain and showed it
to them.

Long life or early death have always been obtained from Heaven;
it is not through prayer that one could alter or prolong one's years.
Sleeping drunk last night, I had the strangest of dreams —
know it was your collected sincerity that made me feel this way.

[3:27]

In the long ago, [after breaking his Buddhist vow and begetting Sŏl Ch'ŏng,] the Great Sage Wŏnhyo mixed with butchers, [wine] merchants, [and other ordinary folk].[245] Early on, beating on a [mask made of an uncanny-looking] crookneck bottle gourd, he sang and danced on markets. [The mask] he named *Muae*, "Unhindered."[246]

Hereafter there were some enthusiasts[247] who attached golden bells to the top [of similar gourd masks] and hung bright-colored silk at the bottom, considering them ornamentations. Then these people would strike [the gourds], move forward and backward, and all was done to a rhythm. They would pluck something from the scriptures and treatises[248] to compose Buddhist *gāthās*,[249] which they would call *Muae ka*, "Songs of the Unhindered." [These songs] even reached the old men in the fields, who would then likewise emulate them, considering them something to play around with.[250]

State Preceptor Muaeji [Kyeŭng] made an attempt at writing the following:

This object, for long, was in use as something useless;[251]
the ancients, after all, named by something nameless.[252]

Recently, there was the mountain man Guanxiu,[253] who created the following *gāthā*:

Waving two sleeves was to break off the Two Hindrances;[254]
three times lifting the feet was to go beyond the Three Realms.[255]

Both compared [Wŏnhyo's gourd-mask dance] by means of the true principle. I also looked at his dance and created the following praise:

The belly [hollow], resembling a cicada's in autumn,
the neck [outstretched], like a turtle's in summer.[256]
Through its crookedness it could follow people,
through its emptiness it could hold things.
Didn't get obstructed by a hard stone-kernel,
didn't get laughed at by a mallow pot.
Han Xiang[zi] contained the entire world in it,[257]
Old Man Zhuang floated through the lakes and rivers in it.[258]
Who made a name for it?

156   POEMS AND STORIES FOR OVERCOMING IDLENESS

It was the Humble Householder.[259]
Who made a praise for it?
It was the Hunchbacked Yi of Longxi.[260]

[3:28]

When I was eight or nine years of age, I practiced reading under an old Confucian. Early on he taught me to read an aphorism by someone from ancient times.

> Flowers are laughing before the railing, but their sounds cannot be
>> heard;
> birds are crying amid the forest, but their tears are hard to see.[261]

"Ultimately, this isn't anything like,

> The willow knits its brows outside my gate, but its intentions are
>> hard to fathom,"

said I. "Now this verse is quite magnificent in terms of wording and meaning."[262]
    The old Confucian was flabbergasted.[263]

[3:29]

King Ŭi[jong] issued a royal command to the Five Circuits and Two Border Regions in the East and the West,[264] ordering them to distribute and dispatch officials to exhaustively record all of the poetry that had been written in the academies and shrines as well as the post and relay stations, and bring them to the Royal Archive.[265] Then he carefully investigated the local folk songs[266] in terms of the benefits or harms for the people and creatures [mentioned therein]. Thereupon he selected renowned passages and outstanding words, had them compiled and submitted, to be made into an anthology of poetry.
    There was, for instance, the following poem, which an impoverished, unsuccessful scholar had written on the wall of a postal relay station:

> All day long the sun scorched my back as I was plowing,
> but still there's not a single peck of millet for me.

Fascicle 3   **157**

If I could transform and was sat down in an ancestral hall,
I'd get to eat grain well up to ten thousand bushels.[267]

After Minister Kim Sinyun had been sent out to guard headquarters in [the northern frontier region of] Yongman [Ŭiju], he had also created a poem:

Gutting the people and flattering the high has long since become a
    habit;
the entire country flooded by the wily and obsequious.[268]
Abundant salary and high office, though they may be lusted for,
the bright sun in the blue sky indeed is hard to deceive.
The illness of the King of Qi, if it could have been treated,
[Wen] Zhi being boiled alive, how could he have dared to refuse?[269]
I am sending word to my companions — don't you laugh at me;
I was straight, and even if it wasn't enough — I was a real man.

Back then, the officials had recorded these two pieces together and brought them forth. The king examined the poems, and when he came upon these two, he read them with a darkening expression, silently brooding over them for quite some time. The ministers to his left and right were all terrified, unable to fathom [what had so infuriated the king and what was about to unfold].

In autumn, [King Ŭijong] ordered Master [Kim Sinyun] to move camp to the eastern frontier, and the following year he had him rush back to the headquarters [of the western border region] in Yongman. Three times [Master Kim Sinyun] received the order to carry the banners [and relocate to the opposite frontier] — a rather unusual thing for a member of the court.

[3:30]

In times of old, the Western Capital served as the capital of Koguryŏ.[270] It is embraced by mountains and rivers, the atmosphere and scenery are vigorous and extraordinary, and since ancient times many unique people and extraordinary scholars have come from here.

During the time of King Ye[jong], [in P'yŏngyang] there lived an exceptionally talented man by the surname of Chŏng — his given name has slipped my mind.[271] He was a mere child when he wrote the poem *Song uin*, "Sending off a friend,"[272] which read as follows:

158   POEMS AND STORIES FOR OVERCOMING IDLENESS

As rains subside over the long embankment, plants' colors are
    plentiful;
as I'm sending you off [on your journey of] a thousand leagues, I'm
    moved to sorrowful singing.
The waters of the Taedong River, when will they be at an end?
My tears of parting, year after year they shall add to and make rise its
    waves.[273]

Also, he wrote the following poem:

Peach and plum are without words, yet butterflies naturally linger on;
wutong trees are aloof and serene, yet phoenixes come and display
    themselves.
If non-sentient beings attract sentient beings,
how then could humans not associate and be dear to each other?
From afar you came to this district;
we met unforeseen, it was good karmic attraction.
In the seventh and eighth month, when the weather was cool,
we shared bedclothes and pillow for not even a full ten days.
To me we were like Chen and Lei, like glue and varnish;[274]
now you've left me behind, like some rotten mat.
My parents are alive, I may not travel far;[275]
meant to follow you but couldn't — still, in my heart I am far, far away.
Before the eaves are nesting swallows, male and female;
upon the pond are mandarin ducks, floating in pairs.
Who will chase away those birds,
to ease my sorrows of parting?[276]

Hereafter he hastened down to the capital[277] to take part in the civil service
examinations. Going in and out of the Inner Palace, he boldly spoke his mind
and had the elegance of an upright minister from ancient times.

Once, he had joined the entourage following the king to Changwŏn
Pavilion,[278] and he wrote the following poem:

Winds sending off a traveler's sails, wisps of clouds;
dews freezing on the palace's tiles, scales of jade.
By the light-green willows are eight, nine houses, their doors shut;
under the bright moon are two, three people, leaning in a tower.[279]

His words, graceful and rising from the common dust, were all of the same
kind as these.

He composed a sacrificial address for Teacher Chinjŏng of Tongsan-jae [Kwak Yŏ],[280] and the king moreover commanded him to write a *Tongsan-jae ki*, an "Account of Eastern Mountain Studio." He composed a memorial, in which it said:

On a crane's back he ascended to perfection,
riding through white clouds to the faint and the remote.
Recorded these matters on a hornless dragon's head,[281]
unrolled the urging of a purple royal command.

Also, it said:

His age exceeding seventy,
he had not yet left the faction of Medium Longevity.[282]
His merits filling triple thousands,[283]
he will certainly be summoned by Unsurpassed Purity.[284]

Also, it said:

And that I went in and out of the teacher's gate,
it has been such a long time now!
Even more, as I raise the Son of Heaven's command,
there is nothing to refuse it.

Even today it's on everybody's lips, and there is simply no end to it.

[3:31]

The literary writings by Kyerim Suong[285] of the Crape Myrtle were so towering and outstanding, he strode alone during his moment in time. Innately he had a good eye for people. He regularly had to go out to conduct inspections in the southern prefectures, and once, upon reaching Wansan,[286] he caught sight of one [young] minor clerk by the name of Ch'oe Ku,[287] whose ironish face was stern and cold, and who, as a person, was so sunk in contemplation, taciturn, straightforward, and reticent that he seemed to possess far-reaching, thorough abilities.[288] [Kyerim Suong] brought him to the capital, where he reared him like his own son, educating him with books and histories and instructing him in the general standards of literary composition. [After some time, Ch'oe Ku] was brilliant [in completing writings][289] and accomplished [in learning], as both his words and his brush were vigorous

160   POEMS AND STORIES FOR OVERCOMING IDLENESS

and strong. At the age of twenty he took the civil service examinations [conducted on the palace grounds] and reached the *pyŏng*-grade.[290] Thereupon he sojourned in the Stone Canal [Pavilion][291] and entered the Golden Horse [Gate]. Always he was loyal in the face of adversity,[292] never acting with a view to his own advantage but merely desiring to apply himself for the good of the dynasty in times of need.

Early on he had written a companion piece in reply to a friend's *Yŏngnyu si*, a "Poem on the willow,"[293] in which it says,

> Xizi's brows were long,[294] she was skilled in making eyebrow black;
> Xiaoman's waist was slender,[295] she was of unrivaled charm.[296]

Also, he had written the following on the topic of a hitherto unbloomed peony:

> Leaning over the garden wall, peeping at Song Yu;[297]
> beyond the wall, seduced by [Sima] Xiangru.[298]

His words and expressions, fluent and gorgeous, were all of the same kind as these.

[3:32]

Scholar Sŏ Munwŏn[299] and Master Kwŏn Tollye[300] had been friends since their youth. Both were the sons of Confucian families, and because they were similar in talent and age, the two of them were like brothers. It often happened that one of them would present the other with a piece of poetry, and this would then in turn be answered. Master Sŏ composed a poem, which read:

> When you, Master Kwŏn, replied to my piece,
> you omitted three, four couplets.
> What kind of words were contained therein?
> To think of it frustrates me in vain.
> For instance, perhaps: in mid-autumn, the night of the Sixteenth,
> when the full bright moon had waned just a tiny bit,
> its gleam and shine seemed most adorable.
> Or, perhaps: when Taizhen had just finished bathing in the hot
>   spring,[301]
> her hair was disheveled, her hairpin askew,

her heavy makeup was slightly smeared — still, in her bearing was
   enduring charm.
Line after line the clinking sound of jades, moving on the paper;
yet I'm afraid they flew away, turning into clouds and mist.
Or was it because you think me a longtime wayfarer who's easily
   stirred and pained,
that you refrained from having precarious expressions, bitter words,
   transmitted in their entirety?

Well, what is bestowed by Heaven, one is born with it, one simply has it —
it can't be altered by anything. For this reason, when Zhongni [Confucius]
was born he played with sacrificial bronze vessels, and when King Wen was
born he did not trouble his teacher — all this simply came naturally to them.
The inherent cannot be rectified by [wearing] hide-strips or bow strings [on
one's feet].[302] Therefore, when it was said that "[a floodlike qi] cannot be ob-
tained by a seizure of righteousness,"[303] that's exactly what was meant.[304]

[3:33]

Now, Minister of Works[305] so-and-so was the eldest son of the Mighty Sover-
eign's younger brother, [Prince] Yangyanggong.[306] He was refined from the
time he was weaned, and early on read books and histories simply for his
personal pleasure. When he walked, he chanted; when he sat, he recited — his
eyes never registered anything [but poetry]. When growing up, in learning
there was nothing he did not encompass, and as for the principle, there was
nothing he did not comprehend — [his erudition] was vast and flooding, like
when one looks out onto rivers and lakes that never reach a shore! As for
poetic expositions, he was skilled in that, too; his use of the brush was ex-
quisite. His talents were outstanding, and when looking at him in terms of
the civil service examinations, he was someone whose name would certainly
have been in the competition for first or second rank. The world thought
him a signpost of the royal house.

   Such a pity! Heaven did not give him many years, and suddenly he
had to heed the call [to write a record on the] Jade Tower [up there in
Heaven].[307]

   Kwano, a man of the mountains,[308] had early on spent some time in his
mansion, looking for surviving manuscripts. That way he obtained eight
or nine pieces of poetry composed in the recent style, and he was overjoyed
that in them he found the two beauties [of his outstanding lyrical compo-
sition and his superior writing style]. [Kwano] showed them [to me], and

162   POEMS AND STORIES FOR OVERCOMING IDLENESS

there was the wind-tossed, cloud-topping vigor and style [of the eldest son of Yangyanggong, the nephew of King Hŭijong].

[I] shall have [these verses] carved on woodblock,[309] to transmit them to posterity. For this reason [I] briefly wrote a preface, stating the following:

> From times of old, relatives of the royal house have inherited earth wrapped in rushes in their swaddling clothes.[310] Their eyes indulge in pearls and kingfisher-blue splendor, their ears are used to take pleasure in silk-bamboo music—and seldom there is one among them who gives any thought to literary writing. Now, Minister of Works so-and-so, by his Heaven-endowed nature, enjoyed learning, and from the time when he was not yet seven or eight years in age he was already so incredibly fond of books and histories that even with food and drink placed in front of him, the sound of him reciting and singing would not cease and could even be heard outside.

P'ahan chip — Epilogue

In the *Nanhuapian,* the "Pure Classic of Nanhua,"[1] it says, "A father does not serve as a matchmaker for his own son, which means that it is better for another man to praise the son than for his own father to do so."[2] Why would that be? One might say it is because those who hear [a father laud his own son] may well have their doubts [about such praises]. And when a son does something for his father, it is quite similar. For if a son takes what his father has done and extols [his father's will and actions] as something beautiful in his own writing, he will only attract criticism toward himself. Then again, it is not as if he was not the son. Yet in the *Daijing,* the "Records of the Rites of the Elder Dai,"[3] it says, "The father sets him up, the son continues his ways."[4] In the past, the child [Yang] Wu's participation in the [composition of the] [*Tai*]*xuan*[*jing*], the "Classic of Supreme Mystery," was such a case.[5] Moreover, in the *Lulun,*[6] the "*Lun*[*yu*] of Lu," it says: "When your father is alive, observe his will; when your father is dead, observe his former actions."[7] Thus, when it comes to a father's will and his actions, how would a stranger ever be capable of describing them in any way similar to what they were really like? It is no one but the son who is capable of doing so. If one adheres to the suspicion toward the father as brought forth in the *Nanhua,* turns one's back on the obligation of the son as preset in the *Daijing* or the *Lulun,* refrains from recording a father's will and his actions, and consequently does not transmit them to posterity — where then would the obligation to regard a father's [will and actions] be?

My deceased father was born in the cyclic year *imsin* [1152], the fourth year of the Tiande era of the Great Jin.[8] Early on he lost his parents, and he had nothing to rely on or go back to. Yet there was his paternal uncle, Hwaŏm Monk Superintendent Yoil, who consoled and raised him. He never had him stray from his side, and his instructions and teachings were very sincere — the *sanfen wudian,* the "Three prescripts and five canons" [of the Three Augusts and Five Thearchs], or the entire writings of the

164 POEMS AND STORIES FOR OVERCOMING IDLENESS

Hundred Schools of Thought, there was nothing the two of them did not read thoroughly.

In the summer of the cyclic year *ŭlmi* [1175] they put his name down in the state-level examination roster, and in the autumn of the following year he entered the highest sphere of worthies [at the National Academy], where he subsequently passed the aptitude examinations. Moreover, he became principal graduate in the civil service examinations held in the spring of the cyclic year *kyŏngja* [1180], and the sound [of his name] stirred the Forest of Scholars.

His father-in-law, Director of Studies[9] Master Ch'oe Yŏngyu, was appointed felicitation envoy on the occasion of the New Year, and [my father accompanied him] as document officer, thus becoming part of the voyage [to the Northern dynasty].

On the twenty-seventh day of the twelfth month of that year they arrived at Emao Temple in Yuyang, the place where [An] Lushan had once trained his troops [before launching his rebellion against Tang Emperor Xuanzong]. Thus, [my father] left the following poem:

> Hibiscus flowers set off against an emerald mountaintop;
> morning wine firstly flushed the face of white jade.
> The dancing was done, but the melody of *Rainbow Skirts* hadn't yet
> ended,
> when one morning, thunder and rain accompanied the pig-dragon.[10]

When they entered the capital of Yan on New Year's Day,[11] he wrote a Spring Welcoming Message for a tablet that was to be hung above the gate of the official hostel [where the embassy was stationed]. It read:

> Dark brows curving charmingly — it's the willow by the road;
> white snows wafting fragrantly — it's the plum on the ridge.
> My house and garden are thousands of leagues away, yet I know
> they're well,
> for the winds of spring have already come from East of the Sea.

Not long after he had written this poem, he was already famous all over the Chinese court.

Upon his return [to our dynasty] he left the court and became secretary of Kyeyang. A short while thereafter he entered [the capital and court again, as he] came to fill a vacancy at the Hallim [Academy], and various words [by the king] as well as many memorials came from his hands. Later, whenever academicians from the Chinese court met with emissaries of our dynasty, they would recite the aforementioned poems and ceaselessly ask, "What office does he currently hold?" From the time my deceased father began serving at the Hal[lim]-wŏn until he reached the Office for Drafting Proclamations, he spelled out the [sovereign's] cords for some fourteen years.

Whenever he encountered a scenic spot in his spare time, he would put his brush to paper, and his words would spout forth like spring water, always without the slightest hindrance. The people at the time all pointed at [his spontaneously composed verses, which had emerged seemingly fully formed], calling them "belly drafts."

Every day my father would spend with Sŏha [Im] Kiji, Pogyang [O] Sejae, and others, [and since they all shared mind and heart,] they promised one another that [the focus of their friendship would be sharp enough to cut through] metal and [that the words emitting from their combined mind would have a fragrance like that of an] orchid.[12] Mornings among the flowers or nights underneath the moon, there was not a time when they were not together, and the world referred to them as the Chungnim Kohoe, the "High Gathering of the Bamboo Grove."

[One day,] as they were getting a little drunk, [my deceased father] said to them, "By the shores of the Li River, there definitely is gold dust;[13] below Mount Jing, how couldn't there be beautiful jade?[14] Our country borders on [the otherworldly realms of] Penglai and Yingzhou, and from ancient times it has been called a 'country of spiritual immortals'. Its concentrated numinousness has brought forth its superiority, and every five hundred years it has given birth [to a sage].[15] [There are people of our dynasty] who made a fine appearance in China: Academician Koun Ch'oe [Ch'iwŏn] set the tone from the front, while Executive Vice Minister Pak Illyang[16] replied from the back, and distinguished Confucians or poet-monks skilled in verses on set topics whose names sped through foreign regions, we've had them generation after generation. As for our own group, if we don't gather and record [what was said and written by those great poets of old and new] to transmit [their poems and stories] to later ages, then [their outstanding literary writings] shall be buried and washed away, and they will not be passed on—there's no doubt about that!" Eventually he gathered poems on set topics from home and abroad that could be taken as model works, arranged them, and put them in order. He made three fascicles, and titled [the collection] *P'ahan.*

Also, he said to his peers, "When I speak of a man with leisure, I mean someone who established merit and achieved fame, then eventually retired on his own accord, [built a hut] in the green fields, [a man who] in his heart has no more longings for outside things. Moreover, I mean someone who conceals his traces in mountains and forests, who eats when he's hungry

166 POEMS AND STORIES FOR OVERCOMING IDLENESS

and sleeps when he's tired. Only then, [after reaching self-chosen retirement and the resulting loss of worldly ambitions] this leisure can be achieved and become whole. However, if [such a man] viewed this here [P'ahan], the wholeness of this [pure, positive] kind of leisure that he may have achieved—it would be shattered [by reading my text, because the reading of it would stir this man in such a way that he would become actively involved again].

"Yet [on the contrary,] when it comes to someone who is submerged in the fatiguing mundane toils and troubles [of politics and officialdom], always works laboriously for fame and high official position, keeps close [to powerful men like swallows] to the heat, who [diligently] rushes east and races west [when ordered to do so]—if [such a man] one morning suffers a loss [of his position and is forced into retirement], then by his outer appearance he may well look as though he possessed this [positive, pure] kind of leisure, but his heart really roils in turbulence. That's exactly the moment when idleness will turn into an illness. However, if [such a man] views this here [P'ahan], the [harmful] illness of idleness that he will likely have contracted—it will be cured [by reading my text]. And wouldn't that be even better than [squandering time by] playing board games or chess or something?" Those who had listened to him at the time collectively said, "That's true!"

The collection was already finished, but [my deceased father] had not yet had the chance to bring it to the attention of the king.[17] Then he unfortunately contracted a minor disease and [unexpectedly] passed away in his home in Hongdojŏng.

Earlier, his young granddaughter, who was then staying at the house, had seen the following scene amid a dream: a group of fifteen blue-clothed children, carrying blue banners and azure umbrellas, were banging on the door, calling and shouting, while the house servants were trying to hold the door shut with all their might. Suddenly the door lock burst open by itself— the blue-clothed children leaped inside, quickly congratulated one another, dispersed, and then they were gone. Before long, my father passed away. How are we to know if he was not summoned to write a record on the Jade Tower [in Heaven]? On the evening of the day he ascended to the realm of the immortals, a single wisp of glowing red mist hung between Oxherd and Dipper, and it did not fade away all night long. Those who gazed at it were all amazed by the sight. This is, by and large, my deceased father's past.

[My deceased father] had confidence in the strength of his literary writings, but he was saddened on account of his never having been put in the position of assessor [of candidates in the civil service examination],[18] and he always dwelled in a melancholy state of mind [because of this appalling disregard]. After having ascended to the position of left grand master of remonstrance he had finally received the command to select the talented, but even before he could open the examinations, Heaven did not lend him more time, and he suddenly passed away. Who knows, it might have been that force of pent-up anger from inside his breast which soared up high into the sky [to hover as red mist in between the stars that night he died].

Woe! What he brought forth throughout his life comprise five rhapsodies in the ancient style, as well as about 1,500 poems of ancient regulated verse. With his own hands he created the *Ŭndae chip*; also, he created miscellaneous writings from among the Kirohoe, which he turned into the *Ssangmyŏng-jae chip*. Hong Sayun of the Security Council was related by marriage to Master Defender-in-Chief Ssangmyŏng [Ch'oe Tang]. Early on he was in charge of Hŭngwang Monastery, and eventually received a royal decree to have [the *Ssangmyŏng-jae chip*] put on woodblocks at the Kyojang-dang, the "Directorate for Buddhist Scriptures,"[19] and to have the work transmitted to the world. The rest [of my father's manuscripts] had not yet been printed, but instead simply rotted away in a storage room of my house for many, many years.

In early autumn of the Water Dragon Year [the cyclic year *imjin*, 1232], the northern [Mongol] army started a massive invasion [of our dynasty]. They plundered Songdo and created utter chaos inside the city, forcing [our king and court to abandon the capital and] enter Kangdo.[20] At the time, heavy rains poured down ceaselessly for months on end, one had to carry the young and support the old, nobody had any idea where to go, and many people must have died somewhere in the gorges and ravines.

I was serving as an instructor [at the National Academy] during this time. Following in the retinue of the king's carriage [to Kangdo], trudging along in dire straits by water and land, I always carried my [father's] surviving manuscripts with me. Not merely valuing them like a basket full of gold, my only fear was that but a single word contained therein might be lost. Awake or asleep, for fifty years now I have upheld the hope that his writings may become treasures for descendants of myriad generations!

A while ago I was expelled from the Eastern Pavilion because of some incident, was fined, and demoted to be stationed in Kijang Lesser Prefecture.[21] Duke Taewŏn,[22] who was then serving as surveillance commissioner, happened to take a rest at the village where I was stationed. As he inquired about the people [of this region], our conversation touched upon the topic of my deceased father's surviving manuscripts. Pitying that I was too weak [and poor,] and that I had not yet been able to fulfill [my father's] wish [of having his works printed], he commanded me to bring him three hundred miscellaneous writings as well as the three fascicles of *P'ahan chip*.[23] After

168 POEMS AND STORIES FOR OVERCOMING IDLENESS

having inspected them personally, he commanded a craftsman to carve them into printing blocks — by way of this he not only shone a bright light into [my father's] dark palace,[24] but also had my personal misery melt away like ice in the morning. Do I not have to record the course of events in every detail to present [and preserve this good deed] for all eternity?

That which has yet to be finished — I will leave it to my descendants to put in order. If they carry on my intention, have [my deceased father's remaining manuscripts] printed with woodblocks, and thereby transmit them [to later generations], they will be in line with what was explained in the *Daijing* and the *Lulun,* and may also become mirrors for all of time.

On a day in the third month of the cyclic year *kyŏngsin* [1260],
this was respectfully noted down by the unworthy son,
the Audience Usher[25]

[Yi] Sehwang.

Glossary of Names, Titles, and Terms

Adae	阿大	*baiwu*	百五
ado	阿堵	*baiyuan*	白猿
adomul	阿堵物	*bajiao*	芭蕉
ae	礙	*banzhu*	斑竹
aesa	哀詞	Baopuzi	抱朴子
Akhak kwebŏm	樂學軌範	*Baopuzi neipian*	抱朴子內篇
Allyŏmsa	按廉使	Baqiong ren	巴邛人
Amsŏ	巖棲	Beigu-shan	北固山
Anch'alsa	按察使	*Benshishi*	本事詩
An Ch'imin	安置民	Bianjing	汴京
An Chŏngbok	安鼎福	*Biannian tongzai*	編年通載
An Ch'uk	安軸	Bian Que	扁鵲
Angam-sa	仰嵓寺	*biji*	筆記
Angyŏp ki	盎葉記	*bilanggan*	碧琅玕
Anhwa	眼花	*Bingong ke*	賓貢科
An Hwak	安廓	*Bingzhu*	冰柱
Anhwa-sa	安和寺	Binlao	邠老
An kŏsa mukchuk ch'an	安處士墨竹贊	*Bizixing zheng Bi Yao*	偪仄行贈畢曜
An kŏsa Sunji	安居士淳之	*bo*	博
An Lushan	安禄山	*Bomen*	撥悶
Annam *Tohobusa*	安南都護府使	Boya	伯牙
An Porin	安寶麟	Boyi	伯夷
Anp'yŏng taegun	安平大君	Bunka Seiji	文化政治
Anren	安仁	Cai Jing	蔡京
Ansang	安詳	Cai Mengzhai	蔡蒙齋
apkaek	狎客	*Cai qi*	采「
Arun	遏雲	*Cai shiguan*	採詩官
awŏn	亞元	Cai Zhengsun	蔡正「
A Xiang	阿香	*Canglang sihua*	滄浪詩話
baichi	白癡	Canliao	參寥
Bai Fu	白傅	Cao Cao	曹操
Bai Juyi	白居易	Cao Zhi	曹植
Bai Letian	白樂天	*cha*	叉

169

GLOSSARY

Chabi-ryŏng 慈悲嶺
Chach'ŏn 子千
Chach'wi-mun 紫翠門
Ch'ae Chegong 蔡濟恭
chaeho 齋號
Chaeip Oktang yujak sŏ pyŏksang 再入玉堂有作書壁上
Ch'ae Pomun 蔡寶文
Chaesang 宰相
chaesin 宰臣
chagoban 鷓鴣斑
chagŭm 紫禁
chagyak 芍藥
Chaha-dong 紫霞洞
Ch'a Hansong-jŏng un 次寒松亭韻
ch'aja 箚子
Chajin 子眞
chak / ch'ang 作 / 漲
Chaksi ha Yi changwŏn Misu 作詩賀李壯元眉叟
ch'a kun 此君
ch'amgun 參軍
chami 紫薇
Ch'amji chŏngsa 參知政事
ch'an 撰
chanam hwan 自南還
chang / chang (staff) 仗 / 杖
ch'ang 昌
ch'ang ("sing") 唱
changbu 丈夫
changbu tŭksil 臧否得失
Chang Chamok 張自牧
Changch'ŏng 長清
Changgwan 壯觀
Changgyo 將校
Changgyŏng kongju 長慶宮主
changhae 瘴海
Changhe 閶闔
Changhen ge 長恨歌
Changhwa 章和
Ch'anghwa 昌華
Changje-gun 長堤郡
Chang Mun'gyŏng 張聞慶
Changnak-chŏn 長樂殿

ch'ang nokp'a 漲綠波
ch'angnyŏ 娼女
changsaeng kusi 長生久視
Changsŏgi 掌書記
Chang Sunsŏk 張純錫
changun chup'il 唱韻走筆
changwŏn 壯元
Changwŏn-jŏng 長源亭
ch'angye ch'wiok 爨桂炊玉
Chang Yunmun 張允文
Ch'anji 纘之
Chanyu Dashi 禪月大師
Chanyue Guanxiu 禪月貫休
Chanyue ji 禪月集
Chao Fu 巢父
Chao Gongwu 晁公武
Cha O nangjung Semun ka pang Kwangmyŏng-sa Mun changno ch'aun Mun-gong 自吳郎中世文家訪廣明寺文長老次韻文公
chapki 雜記
Ch'arwŏn 察院
Chasan sihwa 自山詩話
Chasŏ 字書
chasŏk 紫石
Ch'aun O tonggak Semun chŏng kowŏn che haksa sambaek un si 次韻吳東閣世文呈誥院諸學士三百韻詩
Ch'aun tongnyŏn Mun Wŏnwoe che Kamno-sa 次韻同年文員外題甘露寺
Chayu 子由
che 車
Chech'ap'aŭi-hyŏn 齊次巴衣縣
Che ch'osŏ chokcha 題草書簇子
Chedo ch'albangsa 諸道察訪使
Che gong 車攻
chehagwŏn 諸學院
Che Hansong-jŏng 題寒松亭
cheho ("lift the jug") 提壺
cheho ("pelican") 鵜鶘
cheil in 第一人

GLOSSARY 171

Che Im sŏnsaeng mun 祭林先生文
Che i p'yo 第二表
Che Kaya-san Toksŏ-dang 題伽倻山讀書堂
chemun 祭文
Che Naju kwan 題羅州館
Chen Dezhi 陳德之
Chengdi 成帝
Chenjun Xie-*shi* 陳郡謝氏
Chen Ping 陳平
Chen Shidao 陳師道
Chen wang 陳王
Chenxiang-ting 沉香亭
Chen Zhong 陳重
Che P'ahan chip 題破閒集
Che P'ahan chip hu 題破閒集後
cheryun 帝綸
Chesi-sŏk 題詩石
chesulgwa 製述科
Che Taebugyŏng Yi-gong Yugyŏng mun 祭大府卿李公惟卿文
chi 尺
chi 之
Chibi fu 赤壁賦
Chibong yusŏl 芝峰類說
Chi ch'umilwŏnsa 知樞密院事
Chi chunggunbyŏng masa 知中軍兵馬事
Chi chusa 知奏事
Chidal 怛怛
chi gonggŏ 知貢舉
Chiin 之印
Chi Injŏng 智仁挺
Chijego 知制誥
Chikchae 直哉
chikkang 直講
chiksagwan 直史館
chil 帙
Chillak 眞樂
ch'imsuk maek changjo 椹熟麥將稠
Chin Chun 陳俊
Chindŏkchae 進德齋
Chindong 珍洞
Chin'gam sŏnsa pi 眞鑑禪師碑

Chin'gang 晉康
chin'gong 眞空
Chinhan 辰韓
Chinhŭng 眞興
Chin Hwa 陳澕
Chinjŏng 眞靜
Chinju-*mok* 晉州牧
Chinju sansu to 晉州山水圖
chinsa 進士
chinsagwa 進士科
Chinsan 珍山
ch'insi 親試
chinsin 縉紳
Chinyang 晉陽
Chinyang-gong 晋陽公
chip 集
chipsarang 執事郎
Chiri 地理
Chiri-san 智異山
Chiri-san Ch'ŏnghak-tong ki 智異山靑鶴洞記
Chisa 知事
chisang sŏn 地上仙
Chisŏ 知瑞
Chi sŏbukmyŏn Pyŏngmasa 知西北面兵馬事
Chi sŏbungmyŏn Yususa 知西北面留守事
Cho Ch'ung 趙沖
chodae 措大
Chodojae 造道齋
Ch'odo Maengju — chogong muk ch'ŏ 初到孟州造貢墨處
Ch'oe Cha 崔滋
Ch'oe Ch'iwŏn 崔致遠
Ch'oe Chŏngbun 崔正份
Ch'oe Ch'ung 崔沖
Ch'oe Ch'unghŏn 崔忠獻
Ch'oe Ch'ungsu 崔忠粹
Ch'oe Chunong 崔俊邕
Ch'oe Hae 崔瀣
Ch'oe Ham 崔諴
Ch'oe Hong'yun 崔洪胤
Ch'oe I 崔頤

Glossary

Ch'oe Ku 崔鉤
Ch'oe Kyun 崔均
Ch'oe P'och'ing 崔襃稱
Ch'oe Sajŏn 崔思全
Ch'oe Samun 崔思文
Ch'oe Sanbo 崔山甫
Ch'oe Sarip 崔斯立
Ch'oe Sŏn 崔詵
Ch'oe Sŏn 崔璿
Ch'oe Tang 崔讜
Ch'oe U 崔瑀
Ch'oe Yŏngyu 崔永濡
Ch'oe Yuch'ŏng 崔惟清
Ch'oe Yunŭi 崔允儀
Ch'oe Yusŏn 崔惟善
Ch'ŏhu 處厚
Cho Hyomun 曹孝門
Ch'ŏk Chun'gyŏng 拓俊京
ch'ŏlbal 鐵鉢
Chŏlchi 節之
chŏl kyeji 折桂枝
Chŏlla-do 全羅道
chŏlli 傳吏
Ch'ŏllim 千林
chŏm chakp'a 添作波
Chŏmgwi pu 點鬼簿
ch'ŏm nokp'a 添綠波
Ch'ŏmsabu chubu 詹事府注簿
Ch'ŏmsabu roksa 簷事府錄事
Cho Munbal 趙文拔
ch'omyŏng 初名
ch'ŏn 賤
ch'ŏn (Heaven) 天
Chŏn Ch'iyu 田致儒
Chŏnda-jŏng 煎茶井
chŏng (measure) 挺
chŏng 晶
Chŏng 程
Chŏngan 靖安
ch'ongchae 冢宰
Chŏng Chisang 鄭知常
Chŏng Chungbu 鄭仲夫
ch'ŏngdam 清談
Chŏngdang munhak 政堂文學

ch'ŏngdong 青童
Chŏngguk Anhwa-sa 靖國安和寺
Chŏngguk Anhwa-ji sa 靖國安和之寺
Ch'ŏnggyo-yŏk 青郊驛
Ch'ŏnggyŏng 清卿
Ch'ŏnghaja 青霞子
Ch'ŏnghak-tong 青鶴洞
Chŏnghyŏn 定玄
Chŏng Insŏ 鄭寅書
Chŏng Io 鄭以吾
Ch'ŏngjanggwan chŏnsŏ 青莊館全書
chongjiu 重九
Chŏngjong 定宗
Ch'ŏngju 菁州
Chŏngjung chagyak 庭中芍藥
Chŏng Kasin 鄭可臣
Chŏng Kongbun 鄭公賁
Chŏng Kŭgyŏng 鄭克永
Chŏng Kŭn 鄭僅
Ch'ongnang 摠郎
Chongning 崇寧
Chongnyŏng 宗聆
Ch'ŏngp'yŏng-san 清平山
Ch'ŏngp'yŏng-san 清平山文殊
   Munsu-wŏn ki   院記
chŏngŏn 正言
Chŏng Pangu 鄭邦祐
Cho Sik 曹植
Cho Sin 曹伸
ch'osŏ 草書
Chongsil ryŏrhu 宗室列侯
ch'ŏngsam 青衫
Chŏng Sŏn 鄭僎
Chŏng Sŭmmyŏng 鄭襲明
ch'ŏngu 青牛
Ch'ŏngun 青雲
Ch'ŏn'gwan-sa 天官寺
Chŏng Yagyong 丁若鏞
Chongyang 重陽
Ch'ŏngyŏn-gak 青宴閣
Ch'ŏngyŏn-gak 清燕閣
Ch'ŏngyŏn-gak ki 清讌閣記
Chŏng Yŏryŏng 鄭與齡
Ch'ŏnhwa 天花

Chŏnjung naegŭpsa	殿中內給事	*Chujung chup'il chŭng*	醉中走筆 贈李
Ch'ŏnma-san	天摩山	*Yi Ch'ŏnggyŏng*	清卿
ch'ŏnmin	賤民	*Ch'uksa*	祝史
ch'ŏnmin	天民	Chulao	楚老
Ch'ŏnmin	天民	*ch'uljin*	出塵
ch'ŏnno	千奴	*Ch'uljin Yongman ch'a*	出鎮龍灣次示
Ch'ŏn-sa	闡師	*simunsaeng*	門生
Ch'ŏnsŏng-ji chŏng	天星之精	*Ch'umilsa*	樞密使
Ch'ŏnsu-mun	天壽門	*Ch'umirwŏn*	樞密院
Ch'ŏnsu-sa	天壽寺	*Ch'umirwŏn pusa*	樞密院副使
Ch'ŏnsu-sa nammun to	天壽寺南門圖	*chumun*	朱門
Ch'ŏnsu-wŏn	天壽院	*Ch'unbang sihak*	春坊侍學
Ch'ŏnsu-wŏn to	天壽院圖	*chung*	眾
Ch'ŏnt'ae-chong	天台宗	*Chungch'ang ki*	重刱記
chonwang	尊王	*chungch'un*	仲春
ch'ŏnwŏn	天院	*Chungch'uwŏn*	中樞院
chŏnye	戰藝	*Chungch'uwŏn pusa*	中樞院副使
Chŏppansa	接伴使	*chungdong*	重瞳
Chorong	拙翁	*chunggan-pon*	重刊本
chosam mosa	朝三暮四	Ch'unghŭi	冲曦
ch'ŏsa pang	處士牓	*Chŭng Kim kong*	贈金公君綏
Chōsen Kosho	朝鮮古書刊	*(Kunsu)*	
Kankōkai	行會	*Chŭng Misu che sŭng*	贈眉叟弟僧
Cho Sok	趙涑	*Ch'anji*	纘之
Cho Sŏk	趙奭	*ch'ungmun*	祝文
Chosŏn	朝鮮	Chungnim Kohoe	竹林高會
Chosŏn hanmunhaksa	朝鮮漢文學史	*Chungoe ilbo*	中外日報
Chosŏn kong	朝鮮公	*Chŭng sau*	贈四友
Chosŏn kukkong	朝鮮國公	*chungsŏ*	中書
Chosŏn munhaksa	朝鮮文學史	Chungsŏ Munhasŏng	中書門下省
Chosŏn sosŏlsa	朝鮮小說史	Ch'ungsŏn	忠宣
Cho T'ong	趙通	*Chungsŏryŏng*	中書令
Cho Wi	曺偉	*Chungsŏ sain*	中書舍人
Cho Wich'ong	趙位寵	*Chungsŏsirang*	中書侍郎平
Cho Yŏngin	趙永仁	*p'yŏngjangsa*	章事
chu	州	*Chungsŏsŏng*	中書省
ch'uaek	樞掖	*chungsu*	中壽
chuanqi	傳奇	*Chungsundang chip*	中順堂集
Ch'ubu	樞府	*Chŭng Taegwang-sa*	贈大光寺堂頭
Chubut'o-gun	主夫吐郡	*tangdu*	
Chuci	楚辭	*Chŭng Tamji*	贈湛之
ch'ugwang	秋光	*chunguan*	春官
chuhyang	醉鄉	*Chunhuage fatie*	淳化閣法帖
Chuixiang	垂象	*Chunhuage tie*	淳化閣帖

Glossary

chunjae	俊才	Dazhong xianfu	大中祥符
chunniu	春牛	*deng longmen*	登龍門
Chunri	春日	*Dengtuzi haose fu*	登徒子好色賦
Chunwei	春闈	Deng Yu	鄧禹
chunyin	春蚓	*Diao Qu Yuan fu*	吊屈原賦
chusa	舟師	*diqi*	地氣
chuswi	州倅	*Dishi-jing*	帝釋經
chu u	酒友	*Dongguan Kaogong ji*	冬官考工記
chuzi	處子	*dongtian*	洞天
chwa	坐	*dontian fudi*	洞天福地
chwabu	左符	*dou*	斗
chwa chŏngŏn	左正言	Doulu	都盧
Chwaeju	祭酒	*Duange xing*	短歌行
chwaju	座主	Du Fu	杜甫
Chwa kanŭi taebu	左諫議大夫	*Du Meishan ji ai qi*	讀眉山集愛其
Chwa sagan	左司諫	*xueshi neng yongyun*	雪詩能用
Chwa sarangjung	左司郎中	*fu ciyun yishou*	韻復次韻
Chwa sŭngsŏn	左承宣		一首
chwa sŭpyu	左拾遺	*Du Meishan ji ciyun*	讀眉山集次韻
Chwauwi roksa	左右衛錄事	*xueshi wushou*	雪詩五首
Ch'wisu sŏnsaeng	醉睡先生	Du Mu	杜牧
Ch'wi Yi	醉李	Duo Tao	竇滔
Cike liezhuan	刺客列傳	Dushun	杜順
Ciyun Mi Fu er Wang	次韻米黻二	*emei*	蛾眉
shu bawei ershou	王書跋尾	*ershiba xiu*	二十八宿
	二首	*Er shun yin*	耳順吟
cuigui	催歸	Fan	范
cuihua gu	催花鼓	Fang Shu	方叔
cuta	蹴踏	Fangzhang	方丈
Da'an	大安	Fanke-shan	飯顆山
dabi	大比	Fan Li	范蠡
Dadai liji	大戴禮記	Fansu	樊素
Dai Andao	戴安道	Fan Sui	范睢
Daijing	戴經	Fan Zhixu	范致虛
Dai Kui	戴逵	*fatie*	法帖
dajin	大金	*Fayan*	法言
Dajin Gaoli guoxinshi	大金高麗國	Fayun	法雲
	信使	*Feibai dazi shufu*	飛白大字數幅
dan	石	*feigong*	匪躬
Danzhu	丹朱	*feiran*	斐然
Daodejing	道德經	*fendian*	墳典
Daoqian	道潛	*feng*	風
Dasheng	達生	*Feng fu*	風賦
Daya	大雅	*Fengji Gao changshi*	奉寄高常侍

GLOSSARY

Fengji zhouzhong fuzhen shuhuai sanshiliuyun fengcheng Hunan qinyou 風疾舟中伏枕書懷三十六韻奉呈湖南親友

Fengqiao yebo 楓橋夜泊

fu 符

fu 賦

Fuchou 復愁

Fu Fei 宓妃

Funiao fu 鵩鳥賦

Fuxi 伏羲

Fu Yue 傅說

fuyi 韍辰

fuzi 夫子

fuzuo 韍座

Ganlu-si 甘露寺

Gaoli tujing 高麗圖經

Gao Pian 高駢

Gaoyang Jiutu 高陽酒徒

Gaoyi 高逸

Gaozong 高宗

Ge Hong 葛洪

Ge Yi 蓋益

gu 骨

guangming 光明

Guanxiu 貫休

guisui 詭隨

Guming 顧命

Guofeng 國風

Guo Han 郭翰

guoshi 國士

Guo shihuang mu 過始皇墓

Hach'ŏ nanmang chu 何處難忘酒

Ha Ch'ŏndan 河千旦

Hadong-gun 河東郡

Haechwa ch'irhyŏn 海左七賢

haedong 海東

Haedong-chong 海東宗

Haedong Kirohoe 海東耆老會

Haedong kiyŏng-ji hoe 海東耆英之會

haedong kongja 海東孔子

Haedong kosŭng chŏn 海東高僧傳

Haedong munhŏn ch'ongnok 海東文獻總錄

Haedong pirok 海東秘錄

Haein-sa 海印寺

haengjang 行藏

haengnonk 行錄

haengsŏ 行書

Haeyang-do 海陽道

Ha Im sangguk mun-saeng Cho Sasŏng Ch'ung ryŏng mun-saeng hŏnsu 賀任相國門生趙司成冲領門生獻壽

Hajŏngsa 賀正使

hak 學

hak hae 學海

hakkwan 學官

hallim haksa 翰林學士

hallim sidok haksa 翰林侍讀學士

Hallim-wŏn 翰林院

Ham Su 咸修

Ham Su myojimyŏng 咸脩墓誌銘

Ham Sun 咸淳

Ham Yuil 咸有一

han 閑

Han Anin 韓安仁

Han Feizi 韓非子

han'gŏ 閑居

Hangu guan 函谷關

Hangyang 恒陽

hanhai 瀚海

hanhan / hanhan 閑閑 / 開開

Han Huang 韓滉

hanin 閑人

hanja 閑者

han-ji pyŏng 閑之病

hanju 寒具

Han Kwangyŏn 韓光衍

Han Kwŏn 韓卷

Han Kyoyŏ 韓皦如

Hanlin daizhao 翰林待詔

hanmun 漢文

Han Munjun 韓文俊

Hannam 漢南

Han Noe 韓賴

Han Ŏn'guk 韓彦國

Han Ŏn'guk kanggŏ 韓相國江居

176 GLOSSARY

Hanshi Jie 寒食節
Hanshu 漢書
Hansong-jŏng 寒松亭
Han Sun 韓恂
Han Wudi 漢武帝
Han Xiangzi 韓湘子
Han Xin 韓信
Han Xizai 韓熙載
Han Yan 韓衍
Hanyang 漢陽
Han Yu 韓愈
Han Yuch'ung 韓惟忠
haojie zhi shi 豪傑之士
Haojing 鎬京
Hapch'ŏn-gun 陜川郡
Hechu nanwang 何處難忘酒
  jiu – qishou 七首
hei mudan 黑牧丹
Hengzhou song Li daifu 衡州送李大夫
  qizhang mian fu 七丈勉赴
  Guangzhou 廣州
heshan daili 河山帶礪
heshan zuoshi 山河作誓
He Wang You 和王斿
Hobu sangsŏ 戶部尙書
Hŏ Chigi 許之奇
hoe 灰
Hoemun si 回文詩
Hoe-ri 檜里
Hŏ Hongjae 許洪材
Hŏ Kŏt'ong 許巨通
Hŏ Mok 許穆
Homuk koje 好墨古製
hongbang 紅房
Hong Chabŏn 洪自藩
Hong Chae 洪載
hongci 宏辭
Hongdojŏng pu 紅桃井賦
Hongdojŏng-ri 紅桃井里
hongji 紅紙
Hong Kan 洪侃
Hong Kwan 洪瓘
Hong Manjong 洪萬宗
Hongmun-gwan 弘文館

Hongmun-gwan 弘文館副提學
  Pujehak
Hongnyu-dong 紅流洞
hongp'ae 紅牌
hongqiang 紅墻
Hong Sŏkchu 洪奭周
Hongye tishi 紅葉題詩
hosaja 好事者
Hou Chibi fu 後赤壁賦
Houshan shihua 後山詩話
Hou Ying 侯嬴
Hu 胡
Hu (personal name) 煦
hu (bushel) 斛
hua 花
Huainanzi 淮南子
Huaisu 懷素
Huang Chao 黃巢
Huangchao cilin diangu 皇朝詞林典故
Huang Dazhong 黃大忠
Huangdi neijing suwen 黃帝內經素問
huanghua 皇華
Huanghuangzhe hua 皇皇者華
Huanghu ge 黃鵠歌
Huang Shigong 黃石公
Huang Shigong sanlue 黃石公三略
Huang Tingjian 黃庭堅
Huangtong 皇統
huanqi 喚起
Huan Tan 桓譚
Huan Wen 桓溫
Huan Xuan 桓玄
Hua Xin 華歆
Hua Xin zhuan 華歆傳
Huayan fajie guanmen 華嚴法界觀門
huazhuan 花磚
Hu chip 後集
hŭi 羲
hŭi (play) 戲
Huihong 惠弘
Huihong 惠洪
Hŭiija 希夷子
Hŭijong 熙宗
Hŭijŭng Ch'ŏn sa 戲贈闡師

GLOSSARY

Hŭijŭng Milchu swi	戲贈密州倅	Hwaŏm taesa	華嚴大士
Huishan *quan*	惠山泉	Hwaŏm wŏlsa	華嚴月師
Hui Xiu	惠休	Hwaŏm wŏlsujwa	華嚴月首座
Huiyuan	慧遠	*hwarang*	花郎
Huizong	徽宗	*hwasa*	畫史
Hu-Kiyŏnghoe sŏ	後耆英會序	Hwasa	畫師
hŭk moktan	黑牧丹	Hwawang kye	花王戒
Hŭngwang-sa	興王寺	Hwawŏnok	花原玉
huobo shengtun	活剝生吞	Hwawŏnok	花園玉
Huo Qubing	霍去病	*hyang*	香
Hu-Paekche	後百濟	*hyangak*	鄉樂
husŏ	後序	Hyejo	慧照
husŏl	喉舌	Hyejong	惠宗
Hu Zhai	胡仔	Hyeryang	惠亮
Hu Zongdan	胡宗旦	Hyeso	惠素
hwa	話	*hyo*	孝
hwa (flower)	花	*hyŏlchi hanan*	血指汗顏
hwa (blossom)	華	*hyŏllyang*	賢良
hwach'a	畫叉	*hyŏnch'a*	懸車
Hwagae-hyŏn	花開縣	*hyŏng*	衡
hwagak	畫角	*hyŏngbŏp*	刑法
Hwaguk	畫局	*Hyŏngbu sirang*	刑部侍郎
hwaji wi pyŏng	畫地爲餠	*hyŏngsŭng*	形勝
hwalchuk	活竹	Hyŏnjong	顯宗
Hwangbo Hang	皇甫沆	Hyŏnjŏng *sŏnsaeng*	玄靜先生
Hwangbo Kwan	皇甫瓘	Hyŏnjun	賢俊
Hwangbo T'ak	皇甫倬	*Hyŏn sijae hoemun*	獻時宰回文
Hwang *changwŏn*	黃壯元	Hyŏn Tŏksu	玄德秀
Hwang Chullyang	黃俊良	*Ibu wŏnoerang*	吏部員外郎
hwangdae che	皇大弟	*idu*	螭頭
Hwangdo	皇都	*igung*	離宮
Hwanggak	黃閣	*ijang*	二障
hwanggŭmbang	黃金榜	Ijo	吏曹
hwanggŭmgi	黃金期	*Ikchae chip*	益齋集
Hwangjŏn ri	黃田里	*Ilchae ki*	逸齋記
hwangmun	黃門	Ilchae Kwŏn Han'gong	一齋 權漢功
Hwang Munbu	黃文富	*ilgwan*	日官
Hwang Munjang	黃文莊	*ilp'yŏn tansim*	一片丹心
Hwang Pinyŏn	黃彬然	Im Chongbi	林宗庇
Hwang Sunik	黃純益	Im Ch'un	林椿
hwan'gwan	宦官	*Imha p'ilgi*	林下筆記
hwangyŏp	黃葉	Im Kwang	林光
Hwaŏm-kyŏng	華嚴經	Im Kwangbi	林光庇
Hwaŏm-sa	華嚴寺	Im Kyŏngch'ŏng	林敬淸

Glossary

Im Minbi	林民庇	*Jiegu lu*	羯鼓錄
Im-*saeng*	林生	Ji Kang	嵇康
Im Sŏha chip	林西河集	*ji meng*	季孟
im taebo	臨大寶	Jin	金
Im Wan	林完	*jinbo*	金薄
Im Wŏnae	任元數	*jindai*	金帶
Im Yu	任濡	Jing	青
Im Yujŏng	林惟正	Jing Ke	荊軻
Im Yumun	林有文	Jingkou	京口
Im Yu munsaeng	任濡門生	*Jingshi tongyan*	警世通言
in	仁	*Jingui*	金閨
Indam	印淡	*jingyan*	經筵
Injong	仁宗	*Jingyin*	京尹
Inju Yi-*ssi*	仁州李氏	Jingyun	景雲
Inju Yi-ssi sebo	仁州李氏世譜	*jingzhou yin*	京兆尹
		jinlei	金罍
In Pin	印份	*jinluan*	金鑾
Inye T'aehu	仁睿太后	*jinma men*	金馬門
Ipchi	立之	Jin Midi	金日磾
Ip Ch'ŏnghak-tong pang Ch'oe Koun	入青鶴洞訪崔孤雲	*Jinshi*	金史
		Jinshu	晉書
Ipchong kalmunwang	立宗葛文王	*jinshui*	金水
irhwa	逸話	*jinye*	金液
irwŏl	日月	*Ji ri*	吉日
Irwŏl-sa	日月寺	*jishizhong*	給事中
Ise monogatari	伊勢物語	Jiuquan	九泉
ji	集	Jiuyi-shan	九疑山
jia	家	*jiyou*	己酉
Jia Dao	賈島	*ju*	句
Jia Langxian	賈浪仙	Juan a	卷阿
jian	諫	*jue*	絶
Jiancha	建茶	Juefan	覺範
Jiangfei ernü	江妃二女	Juefan Huihong	覺範惠洪
Jiang han	江漢	*jueju*	絶句
Jiang Ning	蔣凝	*juling*	酒令
jianjian	謇謇／蹇蹇	Ju Meng	劇孟
Jian jin jiu	將進酒	*juntian*	鈞天
Jianyan jiadao Gaoli lu	建炎假道高麗錄	*Junzhai dushu zhi*	郡齋讀書志
		Kabonyŏn ha p'iji	甲午年夏 避地
Jianzhang Gong	建章宮	*kangnam p'ayu*	江 南頗有
Jianzhou	建州	*yuri-ji t'an inbu*	流離之歎因
Jia Yi	賈誼	*changdan'ga myŏngji*	賦長短歌
Jicha yu Pingfu	寄茶與平甫	*wal "Changgŏm*	命之曰杜
jie	界	*haeng"*	劍行
jiegu	羯鼓	*kado*	假道

GLOSSARY

Kaebaek-hyŏn	皆伯縣
Kaegol	皆骨
kaek	客
Kaesŏng	開城
Kaesŏng-sa	開聖寺
Kaesŏng-sa p'alch'ŏk-pang	開聖寺八尺房
Kagwŏl	覺月
Kaifeng	開封
Kaiyuan Tianbao yishi	開元天寶遺事
kajip	家集
kak	閣
kakch'ok	刻燭
Kakhun	覺訓
Kakhwa-sa	覺華寺
kakpon	刻本
Kamch'al	監察
Kamch'u hoemun	感秋回文
Kamno-sa ch'a Hyewŏn un	甘露寺次惠遠韻
kamsa	監司
Kangdo	江都
Kang Hŭimaeng	姜希孟
Kang Iryong	康日用
Kangjong	康宗
Kang-ju	康州
Kangjwa ch'irhyŏn	江左七賢
Kangmun chihu	閣門祇候
Kangnam	江南
Kangnam-do	江南道
kangsŭp	講習
Kanō Sanraku	狩野山楽
kansin	姦臣
kanwŏn	諫垣
kapkwa	甲科
kari	伽梨
Kaya yŏnmaeng	伽倻聯盟
kedou	科斗
Keshan	柯山
ki	機
Kiam kŏsa	棄菴居士
Kigŏju	起居注
Kigŏryang	起居郎
Kigŏ sain	起居舍人
kigwan	機關
Kijang *hyŏn*	機張縣
Kiji	耆之
Kil In	吉仁
Kim Allo	金安老
Kim Chach'ing	金子稱
Kim Chaŭi	金子儀
Kim Ch'ŏn	金闡
Kim Chonjung	金存中
Kim Chujŏng	金周鼎
Kim Ch'wiryŏ	金就礪
Kim Hwangwŏn	金黃元
Kim Hyosun	金孝純
Kim Hyu	金烋
Kim I	金怡
Kim In'gyŏng	金仁鏡
Kim Injon	金仁存
Ki Misu ku ch'osŏ	寄眉叟求草書
Kim kŏsa chip	金居士集
Kim Kunsu	金君綏
Kim Kŭkki	金克己
Kim Kŭn	金覲
Kim Kyŏngsu	金敬守
Kim Manjung	金萬重
Kim On'gi	金蘊琦
Kim P'irhyŏng	金弼衡
Kim Podang	金甫當
Kim Pu	金富
Kim Puil	金富佾
Kim Pup'il	金富弼
Kim Pusik	金富軾
Kim Pusu	金富脩
Kim Puŭi	金富儀
Kim Saeng	金生
Kim Sanggi	金上琦
Kim Sangsun	金尚純
Kim Sijung sŭngno pang kangsŏ Hyeso sangin	金侍中乘驢訪江西惠素上人
Kim Sim	金諶
Kim Sinyun	金莘尹
Kim Sisŭp	金時習
Kim Sukch'ŏng	金淑清
Kim Sukhŭlchong	金肅訖宗
Kim Sun	金順
Kim T'aehyŏn	金台鉉

Glossary

Kim T'aejun	金台俊	Koryŏng Kaya	古寧伽倻
Kim Tan	金端	*Koryŏsa*	高麗史
Kim Tonjung	金敦中	*Koryŏsa chŏryo*	高麗史節要
Kim Un'gyŏng	金雲卿	*Koryŏ-ŭi p'aegwan*	高麗의 稗官文
Kim Ŭiwŏn	金義元	*munhak-kwa pulgyo*	學과 佛教
Kim Yŏn	金緣	*munye*	文藝
Kim Yŏngbu	金永夫	kosa	高士
Kimyŏng sŏl	忌名說	kosigwan	考試官
Kim Yunsik	金允植	*Kosŏk Pyŏngna-jŏng si ki*	孤石碧蘿亭
Kim Yusin	金庾信		詩記
Kim Yusin Ch'ŏn'gwan	金庾信天官	Koun p'yŏn	孤雲篇
ki sa	妓事	Kowŏn	誥院
Kiŏn	記言	Koyang Ch'wigon	高陽醉髡
Kirin-gak	麒麟閣	Koyang-gun	高陽郡
Kirohoe	耆老會	Koyong-gun	古龍郡
kisa	己巳	Ko Yŏngjun	高瑩中
kisaeng	妓生	*kŏja*	舉子
kisim	機心	Kŏt'a	居陁
Ki Taesŭng	奇大升	Kŏyŏl-sŏng	居列城
ko	高	Ku	玖
Koaesa	告哀使	*ku* (maternal uncle)	舅
Kobong chip	高峯集	Kuaiji-shan	會稽山
Kobong-hyŏn	高峯縣	*kuangcao*	狂草
ko chedo	古帝都	Ku Chagyun	具滋均
Ko Hyoch'ung	高孝冲	*kugam*	龜鑑
kojŏk	古蹟	*Kŭgam*	戟巖
Kojong	高宗	Kui	虁
Kokchu	谷州	Kujae Haktang	九齋學堂
Kollyun'gang-sang	崑崙岡上	*kujang*	鳩杖
Kongbi zhong jing	孔壁中經	*ku-ji mun*	丘之門
Konghou yin	箜篌引	*Kukcha chigong-ji ki*	國者至公之器
Kongje	公濟	Kukchagamsi	國子監試
kongmun	空門	Kukchagam taesasŏng	國子監大司成
kongmun u	空門友	*Kukch'ang yugo*	菊窓遺稿
kongno	鵁鷺	Kukhak	國學
kong ŏn ch'a si	公言此是晉	*kuksa*	國師
chinyang-do	陽圖	*kuksa* (Histories of the	國史
kongsik	公式	[Three] States)	
Kongzi shijia	孔子世家	*kuksŏn*	國仙
kon-oe sin	閫外臣	*kŭmbang su*	金榜首
Koryŏ	高麗	Kŭm Ch'o	今初
Koryŏguk Ogwan-	高麗國五冠山	Kŭmgang kŏsa	金剛居士
san Taehwaŏm	大華嚴靈通	*kŭmgyu*	金閨
Yŏngt'ong-sa chŭngsi	寺贈謚大覺	*kŭmin*	金印
Taegak kuksa pimyŏng	國師碑銘	Kŭm Kŭgŭi	琴克儀

Kŭmkye chip	錦溪集	*kwŏn*	卷
kŭmmun	金門	Kwŏn Chŏk	權廸
kŭmnae	禁內	Kwŏn Chŏk	權適
Kŭmnan	金蘭	*kwŏn chung*	卷中
Kŭmnan ch'ongsŏk- *chŏng ki*	金蘭叢石亭記	*kwŏn ha*	卷下
		Kwŏn Kŭn	權近
Kŭmodae	金吾臺	*kwŏn sang*	卷上
Kŭmo sinhwa	金鰲新話	Kwŏn Tollye	權惇禮
kŭmp'ung	金風	*kye*	溪
kŭmsang	今上	*kyech'un*	季春
kŭmsin	金燼	*kyehae*	癸亥
kŭmsŏ cheyu	禁署諸儒	Kyerim	鷄林
Kŭm Ŭi	琴儀	*Kyerim hwangyŏp*	雞林黃葉鵠嶺
kun	鯤	Kongnyŏng	青松
kun	君	*ch'ŏngsong*	
Kunbu ch'ammo	軍府參謀	*kyesa*	啓事
kung	窮	*kyesong*	偈頌
kunja	君子	Kyeŭng	戒膺
kunje	郡齋	Kyeŭng	繼膺
Kŭpkodang	汲古堂	*Kyewŏn p'ilgyŏng*	桂苑筆耕
kŭpkŭp	汲汲	Kyeyang	桂陽
Kurye-gun	求禮郡	Kyeyang-gu	桂陽區
kuŭi	摳衣	Kyeyang *Kwan'gi*	桂陽管記
Kuunmong	九雲夢	Kyeyang tohobu	桂陽都護府
Ku Zhang Houyu ci	哭張后餘辭	*Kyobang*	敎坊
kwa	科	*kyobang hwa*	敎坊花
kwae kwan	掛冠	*kyŏgo*	格五
Kwak Tongsun	郭東珣	Kyoha-gun	交河郡
Kwak Yŏ	郭璵	Kyojang-dang	敎藏堂
kwan	館	Kyojang togam	敎藏都監
Kwanbuk-kung	館北宮	Kyoju-do	交州道
Kwandong	關東	*kyŏllyonggun*	牽龍軍
Kwangch'ŏn-sa	光闡師	Kyŏnbul-sa	見佛寺
kwan'gi	官妓	*kyŏngch'aek*	警策
kwangje ammun	廣濟嵒門	*kyŏngdo*	京都
Kwangji	廣智	*kyŏnggi*	京妓
Kwangji taesŏnsa Chiin myojimyŏng	廣智大禪師之 印墓誌銘	Kyŏnhwŏn	甄萱
		Kyŏnghyŏk	景赫
Kwangjong	光宗	*Kyŏngin*	庚寅
Kwanhyŏnbang	管絃房	*kyŏngin ran*	庚寅亂
Kwannae chŏngsa	關內程史	Kyŏngju *puyun*	慶州府尹
Kwano	觀悟	*kyŏngnon*	經論
Kwansŭng	貫乘	Kyŏngŏpchae	敬業齋
Kwa Ŏyang	過漁陽	*kyŏngsa*	京師
kwibu	龜趺	*kyŏngsa* (startled snake)	驚蛇

182 GLOSSARY

kyŏngsa ip ch'o 驚蛇入草
Kyŏngsang-do 慶尙道
Kyŏngse yup'yo 經世遺表
Kyŏngsisŏ 京市署
kyŏngsŏng 京城
Kyŏn Yujŏ 甄惟底
Kyosŏgwan 校書館
Kyunhyŏng 鈞衡
Langya Wang-*shi* 琅琊王氏
lao, xian yang niuma 牢,閑養牛馬
  juan ye 圈也
Laoxue an biji 老學庵筆記
Lari you Gushan fang 臘日遊孤山訪
  Huiqin Huisi erseng 惠勤惠思
  二僧
Lei Yi 雷義
Lengzhai yehua 冷齋夜話
li (Chinese mile) 里
Li 離
Liang ch'ŏnmun 梁千文
liang zhe 兩浙
Lianju 聯句
Lian Po 廉頗
lianxing 鍊形
Lianzhu shige 聯珠詩格
Li Bai 李白
Libu shilang 禮部侍郎
Liexian zhuan 列仙傳
Lie Yukou 列御寇
Liezi 列子
Li Ge 李革
Li Gongzuo 李公佐
Li Guang 李廣
Li He 李賀
Li Heng 李衡
Liji 禮記
Lili-wen 立禮門
Li Mi 李密
Li Mixun 李彌遜
Li Shangyin 李商隱
Li Shen 李紳
Li Shimin 李世民
Lishui-xian *wei* 溧水縣尉
Li Tong 李侗

Liu Bang 劉邦
liubo 六博
Liu Cha 劉叉
Liu Kun 劉琨
Liu Ling 劉伶
Liu Xie 劉勰
Liu Xihai 劉喜海
Liu Xiu 劉秀
Liu Xun 劉訓
Liu Yelang Yonghuasi ji 流夜郎永華
  Xunyang qunguan 寺寄潯陽
  群官
Liu Yiqing 劉義慶
Liuyi shihua 六一詩話
Liu Yong 柳永
Liu Zihou 柳子厚
Liu Ziji 劉子驥
Liu Zongyuan 柳宗元
Liwei 禮闈
Li Yiji 酈食其
Li Ying 李膺
Liyi zhong 禮儀中
Li Zhexian zuicao he 李謫仙醉草嚇
  Man shu 蠻書
longfu 龍腹
longtou 龍頭
longwei 龍尾
Longxi 隴西
luchui 鑪錘
Lu Ji 陸機
Lu Jia 陸賈
Lulun 魯論
lun 綸
Lunheng 論衡
Lunyu 論語
Lunyu sinǔi 論語新義
Luocheng 洛城
Luo Congyan 羅從彥
Luo fei 洛妃
luoshen 洛神
Luoshen fu 洛神賦
Lu Tong 盧同
Luye *jiu* 盧岳酒
Lu You 陸游

GLOSSARY 183

Lu You	陸遊	*Moch'un mun aeng*	暮春聞鶯
Lu Yü zhuan	盧毓傳	Mongdŭk	夢得
Lüzhu	綠珠	*Mongmin simsŏ*	牧民心書
ma	馬	*mongno*	木奴
maegye ch'wiok	買桂炊玉	*mongnol*	木訥
Maeho yugo	梅湖遺稿	*moran*	牡丹
mae kanse	每間歲	*mu*	武
maengch'un	孟春	*muae*	無寻
Maengju	孟州	Muaeji	無寻智
Maengju sŏngnang	孟州城廊	Muaeji *kuksa*	無寻智國師
Maengsan-gun	孟山郡	*muban*	武班
Maengsŏng	孟城	Mubi	無比
Maewŏltang chip	梅月堂集	Mudang	無黨
Ma Heluo	馬何羅	*mukkun*	墨君
ma-jŏn	馬前	Mulan-yuan	木蘭院
Mang	莽	*mun*	文
man'gyŏl	漫缺	*munban*	文班
Manp'ok-tong	萬瀑洞	*munbang sau*	文房四友
Mawei-yi	馬嵬驛	*munbŏl sahoe*	門閥社會
Ma Yisun	馬裔孫	*Munch'ang-hu*	文昌侯
Mei nong	燜農	Mundŏk-kak	文德閣
Meishan	眉山	*mun'gwan*	文官
Mei Yaochen	梅堯臣	*munhasaeng*	門下生
Meng Haoran	孟浩然	*Munha sijung*	門下侍中
Meng Qi	孟棨	*Munha sirang*	門下侍郎平
Mengyou Tianmu yin	夢游天姥吟	*p'yŏngjangsa*	章事
liubie	留別	Munhasŏng	門下省
Mengzi	孟子	Munhŏn	文憲
migwang	未廣	*munhyŏng*	文衡
mijŭng hyu	未曾休	Munjong	文宗
Min	閩	Munjŏng	文貞
Mingdu pian	名都篇	Mun Kongin	文公仁
Ming *huang*	明皇	Mun Kongyu	文公裕
Mingzong	明宗	Mun Kŭkkyŏm	文克謙
Min lao	民勞	*munsa*	文士
Min Sap'yŏng	閔思平	*munsa* (scribal clerks)	文吏
minŭng hyu	未能休	*munsaeng*	門生
Min Yŏngmo	閔令謨	Munsuk	文淑
Misu	眉叟	Munsu-wŏn	文殊院
Misu pang yŏ	眉叟訪予於開	*Mun Tamji t'akche, i si*	聞湛之擢第 以
ŏ-Kaeryŏng i arijiju	寧以鵝梨旨	*haji*	詩賀之
wi hyang; chaksi saji	酒爲餉作詩	*Mun uin wi kun'gun*	聞友人爲郡君
	謝之	*sobak ich'ŏp hwanu*	所迫以妾
mo	某		換牛

184 GLOSSARY

Munŭng-gyo	武陵橋	*nangdo*	郎徒
Munŭng-nu	武陵樓	*Nangjang*	郎將
Munyŏl	文烈	*Nangjung*	郎中
musin chŏngbyŏn	武臣政變	*Nanhuapian*	南華篇
musin chŏnggwŏn	武臣政權	*Nanhua zhenjing*	南華真經
mu so aejang	無所礙障	*Nanke taishou zhuan*	南柯太守傳
Muyŏl	武烈	*nanp'a*	蠻坡
Myoch'ŏng	妙淸	*Nanxu ji*	南徐集
myoho	廟號	Nan Zhuo	南卓
myŏng	鳴	*napkwŏn*	納卷
myŏnggong	令公	*neidian*	內典
myŏnggyŏnggwa	明經科	*Neize*	內則
Myŏnghwang	明皇	Ning Qi	寧戚
Myŏngjong	明宗	Ningzi	寗子
Myŏngjong taewang-ttae	명종대왕때 그	Niulang	牛郎
kŭ-ŭi samch'on in	의 삼촌인	Niu Sengru	牛僧孺
chung Ryoil	중 료일	*no*	奴
Myŏngju-do	溟州道監倉使	No Insu	盧仁綏
Kamch'angsa		*noksa ch'amgunsa*	錄事參軍事
myŏng sajik	令致仕	No Sasin	盧思愼
Myŏng-*wang*	明王	No Yŏngsu	盧永綏
myŏngyu	名儒	*o*	忤
Naebu	內府	Obong-san	五峯山
Naedojang	內道場	*ŏbu*	御府
Naesaryŏng	內史令	O Chŏngsŏk	吳廷碩
Naesi	內侍	*odo*	五道
Naesi roksa	內侍錄事	*Odo anch'alsa*	五道按察使
Naesi-wŏn	內侍院	*Odo yanggye to*	五道兩界圖
naeŭi	內醫	*ogung*	鼇宮
Naewŏn	來遠	*ogyo*	五教
Nagun	樂雲	*ogyŏng*	五更
Na Hŭngyu	羅興儒	O Hangnin	吳學麟
Naksŏngjae Haktang	樂聖齋學堂	Ŏhwawŏn	御花園
Namdo	南都	*Oju yŏnmun changjŏn*	五洲衍文長箋
namguk	南國	*san'go*	散稿
Namho	南湖	*okch'ung*	玉虫
namjo	南朝	Ok Hwau	王和遇
namju	南州	*Oksŏnmong*	玉仙夢
nammu	男巫	*oksun*	玉筍
Namnang	南郎	Oksun-jŏng	玉筍亭
namp'o	南浦	*oktang*	玉堂
Namwŏn-gun	南原郡	*Oktang paek pu*	玉堂栢賦
Namwŏn sogyŏng	南原小京	Ŏm Chŏnggu	嚴鼎耉
Nanchao	南朝	*ŏmuk*	御墨

GLOSSARY

On	榲	Pak Kongsŭp	朴公襲
ongnu	玉樓	Pak Kyŏngjak	朴景綽
ŏru	御樓	Pak Sŭngjung	朴昇冲
Orŭng	五陵	Pak Sŭngjung	朴昇中
Ŏsa chungsŭng	御史中丞	Pak T'aesun	朴泰淳
Ŏsadae	御史臺	*Palchi*	拔之
Osaeng	悟生	P'alch'ŏk-pang	八尺房
ose	五歲	*p'algwan hoe*	八關會
O Sejae	吳世才	*p'algwan sŏnghoe*	八關盛會
Ŏsŏwŏn	御書院	*panbak*	盤薄
Ŏ Sukkwŏn's	魚叔權	Pan Dalin	潘大臨
ou kiji	吾友耆之	*pang*	房
oun	五雲	*pang* (Roster)	榜
Ouyang Xiu	歐陽脩	*Pang Ham Chajin san'gŏ*	訪咸子眞山居
Ouyang Yongshu	歐陽永叔	Pangjang	方丈
O Yŏnch'ong	吳延寵	*pan'gung*	泮宮
p'a	破	P'an'gwan	判官
p'ae	佩	*Pang Yu Milchik Pŏn.*	訪柳密直藩歸
Paegunja	白雲子	*Kwi-i yuyŏng*	而有詠
P'aegwan chapki	稗官雜記	P'an sŏbukmyŏn	判西北面兵
paegya	白夜	*Pyŏngmasa*	馬事
paekchŏpsŏn	白摺扇	Panwŏlsŏng	半月城
Paek Kwangsin	白光臣	Pan Yue	潘岳
paekpu	伯父	*Panzhong shi*	盤中詩
Paek Sŏnyŏn	白善淵	*p'asu*	破睡
Paek Suhan	白壽翰	Pei Hao	裴皞
Paeksun-gung	百順宮	Pei Zan	裴瓚
Paektu-*chŏng*	白頭精	*peng*	鵬
P'aeng Chojŏk	彭祖逖	Penglai	蓬萊
P'aeng Chojŏk, Chang	彭祖逖, 蔣劇	*pi*	婢
Kŭngmaeng	孟	Pihaedang	匪懈堂
P'aeng Hŭimil	彭希密	*p'ilbop*	筆法
Paengnyŏn ch'ohae	百聯抄解	*p'ildam*	筆談
paeun	排雲	*p'ilgi sosŏl*	筆記小說
p'ahan	破閑	Pingfu	平甫
P'ahan chapki	破閑雜記	*pingsŏl p'a*	氷雪派
P'ahan chip	破閑集	*Pipa xing*	琵琶行
Pak Chiwŏn	朴趾源	Piro-bong	毘盧峯
Pak Ho	朴浩	*P'irŏn kakbi*	卮言覺非
pakhŭp	博洽	*P'irwŏn chapki*	筆苑雜記
Pak Illyang	朴寅亮	Pisŏ	秘書
Pak Illyang-gwa Kim	朴寅亮곽 金仁	Pisŏ-gak	祕書閣
Injon (Yŏn)	存(緣)	*Pisŏgam*	秘書監
Pak Insŏk	朴仁碩	*p'ogal*	布葛

186 GLOSSARY

poguk	報國	Punhwang-*chong*	芬皇宗
pogŭn	卜隱	*Pu Yi Misu che Im*	附李眉叟祭林
Pogwŏl	補闕	*sŏnsaeng mun*	先生文
Pogyang *sŏnsaeng*	濮陽先生	*p'yojŏn*	表箋
Pohan chip	補閑集	*pyŏkkyŏng*	壁經
Pohyŏn-wŏn	普賢院	*Pyŏlgŏn'gon*	別乾坤
Pojŏng-mun	保定門	*Pyŏljwa*	別坐
P'oju	抱州	*pyŏnggwa*	丙科
Pokch'i-san	伏雉山	*p'yŏngjang*	平章
Pomun-gak	寶文閣	*P'yŏngjangsa*	平章事
Pomun-gak *haksa*	寶文閣學士	*Pyŏngjung yu kam*	病中有感
Pomun-gak *taeje*	寶文閣待制	*Pyŏngmasa*	兵馬使
Pŏnam chip	樊嚴集	*Pyŏngmok*	病目
Ponghwang Chi	鳳凰池	*pyŏngna noin*	碧蘿老人
pong myŏng	鳳鳴	*p'yŏn'gŭp*	偏急
pongsŏng	鳳城	*p'yŏnjŏn*	便殿
ponjo	本朝	Qi	碁
p'o paekp'il	布百匹	*qiao*	敲
pŏpchu	法酒	"Qi ao"	淇奧
Pŏphae yongmun	法海龍門	*Qibu shi*	七步詩
pŏpki	法器	Qichun	蘄春
Pŏpsŏng-*chong*	法性宗	Qincheng bajiao	秦城芭蕉
Poyo *sŏnsa*	普耀禪師	*Qingping diao*	清平調
pu	符	*qingtan*	清談
Pubyŏk-chŏng	浮碧亭	Qingxian	慶先
Pubyŏng-nu	浮碧樓	*qingyun*	青雲
Pubyŏng-nu si	浮碧樓詩	Qin Shihuangdi	秦始皇帝
Pubyŏng-nyo	浮碧寮	Qinzong	欽宗
pukcho	北朝	*Qiu feng ci*	秋風辭
pulman ki ŭi	不滿其意	*qiushe*	秋蛇
Pulsaŭi-bang	不思議房	Qizhou	蘄州
P'ungak	楓嶽	*Qizhou fangyushi*	齊州防禦使
p'ungjin	風塵	Qizhu	蘄竹
P'ung Ŭijong mihaeng si	諷毅宗微行詩	*Quanjiu shisi shou*	勸酒十四首
p'ungyo	風謠	*Quan Tangshi*	全唐詩
Punhaeng-nu	分行樓	*Rangjung*	郎中
Punhaeng-yŏk	分行驛	*Ransaeng pyŏngjŭngsŏl*	卵生辨證說
Punhaeng-yŏk ch'a	分行驛次板上	*ri*	吏
p'ansangun ŏkku	韻憶舊	*Ron chup'ilsa yagŏn*	論走筆事略言
Punhaeng-yŏk ki	分行驛寄忠州	Rongsŏja	隴西子
ch'ungju chasa	刺史	Rongsŏ t'ari	隴西駝李
Punhaeng-yŏk rusang	分行驛樓上次	Rong Yu	戎昱
ch'a Kim haksa	金學士黃文	Ruan Ji	阮籍
Hwangmun siun	詩韻	Ruan Xian	阮咸

Ruan Yue	阮閱	sang ha chil	上下帙
Ruizong	睿宗	Sangha panmannyŏn-ŭi	上下半萬年의
Ruolan	若蘭	uri yŏksa – c'hong-	우리 歷
Ryu Su	柳脩	ŭro pon Chosŏn-ŭi	史—縱으로
sa	絲	charang	본 朝鮮의
sa (teacher)	師		자랑
sa cheil kye	四第一偈	sangjae hyang	桑梓鄉
sadae	事大	Sangjŏnggwan	詳定官
sadaebu	士大夫	Sangjŏng kogŭm yemun	詳定古今禮文
sagan	司諫	Sang Min Sangsi Sik sŏ	上閔上侍湜書
sagi	私妓	sang mun	相聞
Sagong	司空	San'gŏ	山居
Sagwan	史館	sangong	三公
Sahan	史翰	sangp'i	相避
Sahŏnbu	司憲府	Sangsŏ chwabokya	尙書左僕射
Sain	舍人	Sangsŏ-jang	上書莊
saja	師子	Sangsŏsŏng	尙書省
saja	獅子	Sanguo yanyi	三國演義
saja (four sons)	四子	Sang Weihan	桑維翰
Sajik	司直	Sang Yŏnggong	上令公
sa kunja	四君子	Sang Yu Yangyang	上柳襄陽陳情
samasi	司馬試	chinjŏng sŏ (Chahan)	書自漢
samch'ŏn	三千	Sanho-jŏng	山呼亭
samch'ŏn'gye	三千界	sanin	山人
samch'un	三春	sansu u	山水友
samda	三多	Saŏp	司業
Samguk sagi	三國史記	sa-ru	莎樓
Samguk yusa	三國遺事	sa-ru (Gauze Tower)	紗樓
samgye	三界	saryun	絲綸
Samhan kugam	三韓龜鑑	Sa Sangju Chŏng Sŏgi	謝尙州鄭書記
samjang	三場	So kye	紹啓
samjŏl	三絕	Sasin	詞臣
sammae	三昧	sasŏn	四仙
samno	三老	sasŏn-bi	四仙碑
Samsin-tong	三神洞	Sasŏng	司成
samsŏng	三省	Sasukchae	私淑齋
samwŏl maek ch'ojo	三月麥初稠	Saŭnsa	謝恩使
Sanch'on haedang	山村海棠	Sejo	世祖
sanfen wudian	三墳五典	Shangjun	商均
Sangan ryangch'ong	湘岸兩叢	shangshe sheng	上舍生
sangch'ŏng	上淸	Shangu	山谷
Sangch'un-jŏng	賞春亭	Shanmu	山木
Sangdo	上都	Shan Tao	山濤
sangguk	相國	shanteng	剡藤

188 GLOSSARY

Shanxi	剡溪	*sigo*	詩藁
Shanzhong wenda	山中問答	*sigŭp*	食邑
Shaoling	少陵	*Sigyŏngam*	息影庵
Shelong	蛇龍	*siho*	詩號
sheng	笙	*sihoe*	詩會
shenghuang	笙簧	*sihwa*	詩話
Shen Jiji	沈既濟	*sije*	試題
Shenxian zaji	神仙雜記	*Sijong*	侍從
Shenyi ji	神異記	*sijung hwa*	詩中畫
Shi Cangshu	石蒼舒	*sik*	軾
Shi Chong	石崇	*sikchi*	食指
shier zhang	十二章	Silla	新羅
Shigu	石鼓	Sima Guang	司馬光
shiguan	詩官	Sima Qian	司馬遷
Shigu ge	石鼓歌	Sima Xiangru	司馬相如
Shiguo	十國	*simin*	心印
Shihua zonggui	詩話總龜	*sinch'ong*	宸聰
Shiji	史記	*sindong*	神童
Shijian shu	十漸疏	Sinho-mun	神虎門
Shi Jie	石介	Sinhŭng-sa	神興寺
Shijing	詩經	Sinjong	神宗
Shi jizhuan	詩集傳	Sinjun	神駿
Shilin shihua	石林詩話	*Sinjŭng tongguk yŏji*	新增東國輿地
Shilong	士龍	*sŭngnam*	勝覽
Shimen wenzi chan	石門文字禪	*sinp'il*	神筆
Shiqu ge	石渠閣	*sinsan*	神山
Shishou xinyu	世說新語	*sinsŏn*	神仙
Shiwen leiju	事文類聚	Sin Ŭngnyong	愼應龍
shiyi	詩意	*sip'an*	詩板
shizhou sandao	十洲三島	*Sirang p'yŏngjangsa*	侍郎平章事
Shujin	蜀錦	*sishu wujing*	四書五經
Shujing	書經	*sisŭng*	詩僧
Shu Mojie 'Lantian	書摩詰藍田煙	*si u*	詩友
yanyu tu'	雨圖	*siwŏn*	詩垣
shuo	朔	*sŏbong*	西峰
Shuogua zhuan	說卦傳	*Sŏbungmyŏn pyŏngma*	西北面兵馬
Shuoshan xun	說山訓	*pusa*	副使
Shuowen jiezi	說文解字	*Sogak*	俗樂
Shuqi	叔齊	*Sŏgi*	書記
shushi	術士	*sŏgyang*	夕陽
Sibido	十二徒	*Sŏgyŏng*	西京
sida meiren	四大美人	Sŏhae-do	西海道
Sidok	侍讀	*Sŏha sŏnsaeng chip*	西河先生集
Sigam	息庵	*Sŏha sŏnsaeng chip sŏ*	西河先生集序
Sigang-wŏn	侍講院	*So hwangmun*	小黃門

GLOSSARY 189

Sohwa-sa	小華寺	*Song p'ung*	松風
soin	小人	Sŏngsan	星山
soja	小字	Song Sanxian	宋三賢
Sŏjanggwan	書狀官	*Song Tamji sa pukcho*	送湛之使北朝
Sŏjŏkchŏm	書籍店	*songyŏnmuk*	松煙墨
Sŏk Chongnyŏng Chogam	釋宗聆足菴	Song Yu	宋玉
sŏk chŏng	夕情	*sŏnje*	先帝
Sŏkchukhwa	石竹花	*sŏnjin*	仙眞
Sok haengno nan	續行路難	Sŏnjo	宣祖
sŏkkŏ	石渠	Sŏ *P'ahan chip* hu — *imo*	書破閑集後壬午
Sŏ Kŏjŏng	徐居正	*sŏp'an*	書板
Sok P'ahan chip	續破閑集	*sŏrhwa*	說話
Sok P'ahan chip sŏ	續破閑集序	*sŏru*	書樓
Sok U-hu ka yŏ Misu tongbu	續牛後歌與眉叟叟同賦	*so-sa*	蕭寺
Sŏldang	雪堂	*sŏsan*	西山
Solsŏngjae	率性齋	*sosŏl*	小說
sŏm	蟾	Sosŏng kŏsa	小性居士
Somun swaero	謏聞鎖錄	*Sŏ Tamji ka pyŏk*	書湛之家壁
Sŏ Munwŏn	徐文遠	Sŏ Yugu	徐有榘
somyŏng	小名	Ssanggye-sa	雙溪寺
sŏnbae	先輩	Ssangmyŏng-jae	雙明齋
Sŏnbu	選部	*Ssangmyŏng-jae ki*	雙明齋記
Song An'guk	宋安國	*Ssangsong si*	雙松詩
Song Chisŭng	送智勝	*su*	粟
Songch'un si	送春詩	Su Boyu qi	蘇伯玉妻
Songdo	松都	*Sŭbyu*	拾遺
Songgao	崧高	Su Hui	蘇蕙
Song gaoseng zhuan	宋高僧傳	*Suihantang shihua*	歲寒堂詩話
songgwan	松關	Su-ju	樹州
Song Ham Sun pu Ingnyŏng sŏ	送咸淳赴翼嶺序	*Suk Han Ŏn'guk sŏjae*	宿韓相國書齋
Sŏngho sasŏl	星湖僿說	Su kŏsa	睡居士
Sŏng Hyŏn	成俔	*Suk Yŏnho-sa sa chae ruhu*	宿煙湖寺寺在樓後
Song in	送人	Sullang	述郎
Sŏngjong	成宗	Sun Bin	孫臏
Sŏngjong sillok	成宗實錄	*sŭng*	乘
Sŏngju	星州	*sun'gaeng*	蓴羹
Sŏngju-*mok*	星州牧	*sun'gaeng nohoe*	蓴羹鱸膾
Song Kong Chaofu xiebing guiyou Jiangdong jian cheng Li Bai	送孔巢父謝病歸遊江東兼呈李白	*sŭngbo si*	陞補試
		Sungmun-gwan	崇文館
		Sŭngso Man	勝小蠻
Song Misu	送眉叟	*Sŭngsŏn*	承宣
Sŏngmyŏngjae	誠明齋	*sŭngsŏn*	僧選
		sŭngt'ong	僧統

190 GLOSSARY

Sŭngt'ong Ŭich'ŏn t'ammyŏng	僧統義天塔銘	*Taixuanjing*	太玄經
		Taixue	太學
Sungŭi-jŏn	崇義殿	Taiye Chi	太液池
Sunji	淳之	Taiyuan	太元
suryŏng	守令	*Taizhen*	太眞
Susan chip	修山集	*Taizi binke*	太子賓客
Su Shi	蘇軾	Taizong	太宗
susin / susin	誰信 / 須信	*Ta-jŏng*	茶井
Su Yijian	蘇易簡	*T'akche*	擢第
Su Zhe	蘇轍	Talbu	達夫
Su Zizhan	蘇子瞻	*talsu*	獺髓
ta	踏	Tamin	淡印
Ta Chi	多智	Tamyak	湛若
Taeakkuk	大樂局	Tan Daoluan	檀道鸞
Taeaksa	大樂司	*tan'gan*	斷簡
Taeaksŏ ryŏng	大樂署令	*tangdu*	堂頭
T'aebaek-san-in	太白山人	*tanghyŏng*	堂兄
Taebang-gun	帶方郡	*tangje*	堂弟
Taebingjae	待聘齋	*Tangshu*	唐書
Taebugyŏng	大府卿	*Tang Song shihua*	唐宋詩話
Taech'uk	大祝	*Tangsŏ purip Ch'oe Ch'iwŏn yŏlchŏn ŭi*	唐書不立崔致遠列傳議
Taegak	臺閣		
Taegak *kuksa*	大覺國師	Tang Wenhuang	唐文皇
Taegam	大諫	Tang Yanqian	唐彥謙
Taegam	大鑑	*Tang zhiyan*	唐摭言
t'aehak paksa	太學博士	*tanjo*	丹竈
taehon	大閽	Tan-ju	湍州
Taehwajae	大和齋	Tansok-sa	斷俗寺
t'aehwang che	太皇弟	*Taohuayuan ji*	桃花源記
t'aeja	太子	*taolin*	桃林
Taejanggun	大將軍	Tao Yuanming	陶淵明
Taeje	待制	*Tao Yuanming ji*	陶淵明集
taejŏl	大節	*Tap Chŏn Iji ron mun sŏ*	答全履之論文書
T'aejong	太宗		
Taejongbaek	大宗伯	Tarŭlsŏng-hyŏn	達乙省縣
Taejungjae	大中齋	*tiansi*	天駟
taenae	大內	Tian Zifang	田子方
Taep'yŏng t'ongjae	太平通載	Tian Zongren	田宗仁
taesu	大手	*Tiaoxi yuying conghua*	苕溪漁隱叢話
taesuk	大叔	*Ting gongyin*	聽宮鶯
T'aewi	太尉	*Ti xiaoqiao qian xinzhu zhao ke*	題小橋前新竹招客
Taewŏn-gong	大原公		
Taewŏn wanggong	大院王公	*t'o*	兎
Taiping guangji	太平廣記	*todokpu*	都督府

t'oerak	磊落	*Tongsa kangmok*	東史綱目
Tohwasŏ	圖畫署	*tongsan*	東山
Tohwa-wŏn	圖畫院	Tongsan-jae	東山齋
Tojung mun aeng	途中聞鶯	*Tongsan-jae ŭngje si*	東山齋應製詩
tokhaeng	篤行	*tongtong*	統統
tokkwŏn'gwan	讀卷官	Tong Wu	童烏
Tok Ok	毒王	*Tongyu ki*	東遊記
Toksŏ-dang	讀書堂	*Tosa*	都事
tong	洞	*tou*	道友
Tongan kŏsa chip	動安居士集	Tŏkchŏn	德全
Tong chi gonggŏ	同知貢舉	Tŏkpyŏng	德柄
T'ongch'ŏn-gun	通川郡	Tŭgok	得玉
Tongdo	東都	*tui*	退
Tongdo hŭije	東都戲題	*tui*	推
Tongdo *Kwan'gi*	東都管記	*tuiqiao*	推敲
Tonggak	東閣	*t'uja sŏn*	骰子選
Tongguang	同光	Tŭkchŏng	得正
tongguk	東國	Tu Kyŏngsŭng	杜景升
Tongguk mun'gam	東國文鑑	*T'u mogwan*	投某官
Tongguk myŏngga sihwa chip	東國名家詩話集	*tŭnghwa*	燈花
		tŭngji	藤紙
Tongguk t'onggam	東國通鑑	*tŭngnong si*	燈籠詩
Tongguk Yi Sangguk chip	東國李相國集	*tuniu*	土牛
		tunjŏk	遁迹
Tongguk yŏji chi	東國輿地誌	*tuogong*	舵工
Tonggung	東宮	Turyu	頭留
Tonggung ryojwa	東宮寮佐	Turyu	頭流
tonggwan	東館	*U chŏngŏn*	右正言
t'onggwan (also *t'ongsa*)	通官	U-hu	牛後
Tonggwang	東光	*U-hu ka*	牛後歌
Tonggye chip	東溪集	*ŭi*	醫
Tonggyŏng *Changsŏgi*	東京掌書記	Ŭich'ŏn	義天
Tonggyŏng chapki	東京雜記	Ŭijong	毅宗
Tongin mun	東人文	Ŭijŏngbu	議政府
Tongin sihwa	東人詩話	Ŭi Kyejŏng	魏繼廷
Tongin sihwa sŏ	東人詩話序	*uin*	優人
tongjinsa	同進事	*ujung*	禹中
Tongmunsŏn	東文選	*U kanŭi taebu*	右諫議大夫
Tongmun-wŏn	同文院	*ŭlgwa*	乙科
Tongmyŏng-wang p'yŏn	東明王篇	*ullam chi*	雲藍紙
Tongnam-do	東南道	*ŭlmyo*	乙卯
tongnyŏn	同年	*ŭm*	陰
T'ongryemun	通禮門	*ŭm*	蔭
t'ongsa	通事	*Ŭndae chip*	銀臺集

192 GLOSSARY

ŭngje	應制
un'gŭn	雲根
ŭnha yŏlsu	銀河列宿
ŭnmun	恩門
un un	云云
Ŭn Wŏnch'ung	殷元忠
Unyang chip	雲養集
U san'gi sangsi	右散騎常侍
U sŭngsŏn	右承宣
uta monogatari	歌物語
u tonghwan	又東還
Uya yu hoe	雨夜有懷
Wadohyŏn	臥陶軒
waegu	倭寇
waidian	外典
wang	王
Wang Anguo	王安國
Wang Anshi	王安石
Wang Bing	王冰
Wang Bo	王播
Wang Chaji	王字之
Wang Chong	王充
Wang Dao	王導
Wang Dingbao	王定保
Wang Fu	王浮
Wang Fu (in 2:2)	王黼
Wanghai lou wanjing	望海樓晚景
Wang Huizhi zhuan	王徽之傳
Wang Huizi	王徽之
Wang Hun	王渾
Wang Hyo	王俲
Wang Ji	王績
Wang Jiefu	王介甫
Wang Kai	王愷
Wang Kexun	王可訓
Wang Mang	王莽
Wang Meng	王孟
Wangnyun-sa	王輪寺
Wang Rong	王戎
Wang Sŏ	王恕
Wang Sun	王詢
Wang Ŭi	王瑋
Wang Wei	王維
Wang Xianzhi	王獻之

Wang Xizhi	王羲之
Wang Zhu	王著
Wang Ziqiao	王子喬
Wang Ziyou	王子猷
wanhuhao	萬戶侯
Wanhui	萬回
Wanp'ok-tae	玩瀑臺
Wansan	完山
wazhu	瓦注
Wei Dan	韋誕
Wei *gong*	魏公
Wei *gongzi*	魏公子
Wei Ye	魏野
Wei Yingwu	韋應物
Wei Zheng	魏徵
wenfang sibao	文房四寶
Wenfang sipu	文房四譜
Wengong xu shihua	溫公續詩話
Wen Lugong	文潞公
wenming buru jianmian	聞名不如見面
Wen sang	問喪
Wen Tong	文同
wenxi er keqian	文細而刻淺
Wenxuan	文選
Wenying	文瑩
Wen Yuke	文與可
Wen Yuke hua Yundang Gu yanzhu ji"	文與可畫篔簹谷偃竹記
Wen Zhi	文摯
Wenzhong ji	文忠集
Wenzong	文宗
Wiwigyŏng	衛尉卿
wo	臥
Wŏlch'ul-san	月出山
Wŏllo	元老
Wŏlsŏng	月城
wŏn	院
Wŏnae Im Wŏnhu	元數 任元厚
Wŏn'gyŏng *kuksa*	元敬國師
Wŏnhyu	元休
Wŏnoerang	員外郎
Wŏn Yŏng	元穎
Wu	吳

GLOSSARY 193

wu	武	*Xikun ti*	西崑體
Wucheng	武成	*Xiliu ying*	細柳營
Wudai	五代	*xinfa*	新法
Wuling	吳綾	*Xinglu*	行錄
wuling	五陵	Xinling gongzi	信陵公子
wuling taoyuan	武陵桃源	Xinling jun	信陵君
Wuling yuan	武陵源	*Xinlun*	新論
Wuliu xiansheng ji	五柳先生集	*Xin Tangshu*	新唐書
Wuliu xiansheng zhuan	五柳先生傳	*Xi qian ying*	喜遷鶯
wushi	無事	*Xiqing shihua*	西┌詩話
wutong	梧桐	Xi Shi	西施
Wuyan	無鹽	Xitang	溪堂
Wuyi	無逸	*Xiti mudan*	戲題牡丹
xian, lan ye	閑,闌也	*Xiyouji*	西遊記
Xiangan liangcong	湘岸兩叢	Xi Zaochi	習鑿齒
xiang che	香車	*Xizeng Du Fu*	戲贈杜甫
xiang liu	巷柳	Xizhou-men	西州門
Xiang Xiu	向秀	Xizi	西子
Xiangyang ji	襄陽記	Xizong	熙宗
Xiang Yu	項羽	Xu	徐
Xianxiao huangdi	顯孝皇帝	*Xuanguai lu*	玄怪錄
Xianyun	獫狁	*Xuanhe fengshi gaoli tujing*	宣和奉使高麗圖經
Xiao Dezao	蕭德藻	*Xuanhe shupu*	宣和書譜
Xiaodu ji	小杜集	Xuanhua	玄華
Xiao Gou	蕭遘	Xuanzong	玄宗
Xiao He	蕭何	Xue'er	雪兒
Xiaoman	小蠻	*Xuehou shu beitai bi*	雪後書北臺壁
Xiao pan	小弁	*xuemai*	血脈
Xiaoshi baye	蕭氏八葉	Xue Rengui	薛仁貴
Xiao Tong	蕭統	*xuetang*	雪堂
Xiaowu	孝武	*Xuetangji*	雪堂記
Xiaoxiao	笑笑	*Xuetang jushi*	雪堂居士
Xiaoya	小雅	Xu *fei*	徐妃
Xiaoyao yu	逍遙遊	Xu Jing	徐兢
Xiao Yu	蕭瑀	*Xu Jin yangqiu*	續晉陽秋
Xia Wuqie	夏毋且	Xu Ling	徐陵
Xida Yuan Zhen	戲答元珍	*Xunzi*	荀子
Xie An	謝安	Xu You	許由
Xie An zhuan	謝安傳	Xu Zhaopei	徐昭佩
Xie Linchuan	謝臨川	*ya*	鴉
Xie Lingyun	謝靈運	*ya*	雅
Xie Yi	謝逸	*yadam*	野談
Xijiang yue	西江月	Yakch'ung	若沖
Xikun chouchang ji	西崑酬唱集		

194 GLOSSARY

yaksŏk	藥石	Yi Chadŏk	李資德
Yang	讓	Yi Chae	李載
Yang Chae	梁載	Yi Chagyŏm	李資謙
Yangch'ŏn-gu	陽川區	Yi Chahyŏn	李資玄
Yangch'ŏn-hyŏn	陽川縣	Yi Chasang	李子祥
Yangch'on sŏnsaeng munjip	陽村先生文集	Yi Chayŏn	李子淵
		Yi Chehyŏn	李齊賢
yanggap suk	羊胛熟	Yi Chijŏ	李之氐
Yang Guifei	楊貴妃	Yi Chisim	李知深
Yanggwang-do	楊光道	Yi Chiyŏng	李至榮
yanggye	兩界	*Yi Ch'ŏnggyŏng*	李淸卿見訪小
Yanggye pyŏngmasa	兩界兵馬使	*kyŏnbang soju yong*	酌用劉禹錫
Yang Huizi	楊徽之	*Yu Usŏk siun tongbu*	詩韻同賦
yanghwa ch'ŏn	養花天	Yi Chonggyu	李宗揆
Yanghwado	楊花渡	Yi Chonghwi	李種徽
Yangja-gang	楊子江	Yi Chongjun	李宗準
Yang Jiong	楊炯	Yi Chonyŏn	李兆年
Yang-ju	梁州	Yi Chunch'ang	李俊昌
Yangon sung	良醞丞	Yi Chungyak	李仲若
Yang Qiu	楊球	Yi Chuni	李俊異
Yangsuk	良淑	Yi Hŏgyŏm	李許謙
Yang Tan	羊曇	Yi Ik	李瀷
Yang Xiong	揚雄	Yi Illo	李仁老
Yangyanggong	襄陽公	Yi Insil	李仁實
Yang Yi	楊億	Yiji	益稷
Yang Yingcheng	楊應誠	*Yijia bie hushang ting*	移家別湖上亭
yansheng	厭勝	*Yijing*	易經
Yan Shi	楊時	Yi Ko	李高
Yan Yu	嚴羽	Yi Kok	李穀
Yan zhi	言志	Yi Kongsu	李公壽
Yao	堯	Yi Kongsŭng	李公升
Yebu nangjung	禮部郎中	Yi Kŭkton	李克敦
Yebu sangsŏ	禮部尚書	Yi Kŭngik	李肯翊
Yebu wŏnwoerang	禮部員外郎	Yi Kwangjin	李光縉
Yech'ŏn Im-*ssi*	醴泉林氏	Yi Kwangp'il	李光弼
Yejong	睿宗	Yi Kwe	李軌
Yejong ch'anghwa chip	睿宗唱和集	Yi Kyŏngbaek	李景伯
Ye Mengde	葉夢得	Yi Kyubo	李奎報
Yemun'gwan	藝文館	Yi Kyugyŏng	李圭景
yesang	霓裳	Yi Kyun	李困
Yesŏng-gang to	禮成江圖	Yi Mubang	李茂芳
Yeŭi	霓衣	*Yi Nangjung Illo, Son*	李郎中仁孫翰
yi	奕	*Hallim Tŭkji kyŏn*	林得之見和
Yi Am	李巖	*hwa, pogyong chŏn un*	復用前韻

GLOSSARY 195

Yi Nangjung Yuŭi tajŏm chusu	李郎中惟誼茶店畫睡	*Yŏ Hong Kyosŏ sŏ*	與洪校書書
Yingzhou	瀛州	Yoil	寥一
Yin Xi	尹喜	*yŏk*	驛
Yi Nyŏng	李寧	Yŏlban	涅槃
Yi O	李頴	*Yŏllyŏsil kisul*	燃藜室記述
Yi Ŏllim	李彦林	*yŏmin tong*	與民同
Yi Paeksŏn	李伯仙	*Yŏ Misu ron Tongp'a mun sŏ*	與眉叟論東坡文書
Yi Pok	李復	Yŏmju	鹽州
Yi Pokki	李復基	*yŏmju*	炎州
Yi Sangbo	李相寶	Yŏmsa	廉使
Yi Sanggang	李思絳	*yŏn*	然
Yi Sehwang	李世黃	Yŏndam	淵湛
Yi Sejang	李世長	*yŏndŭng hoe*	燃燈會
yishang lao	坭上老	*Yongch'ŏn tamjŏk ki*	龍泉談寂記
Yishan yuefu	遺山樂府	*yŏng*	映
Yishao	逸少	*yŏngdang*	影堂
Yishui ge	易水歌	*yongdu*	龍頭
Yi Sik	李軾	Yongdu Hoe	龍頭會
Yi Sugwang	李睟光	Yŏnggwang	永寬
Yi Sŭnghyu	李承休	*Yong hŭng*	龍興
Yi Sunu	李純祐	*Yongjae ch'onghwa*	慵齋叢話
Yi Sunu	李純佑	*Yong ju*	咏菊
Yi Tamji	李湛之	Yongman	龍灣
Yi Tŏgu	李德宇	*yongmun*	龍門
Yi Tŏgu	李德羽	Yŏngnak	亦樂
Yi Tŏngmu	李德懋	Yŏngnam	嶺南
Yi Ŭi	李儀	Yŏngnang	永郎
Yi Ŭibang	李義方	*yŏngni*	驛吏
Yi Ŭimin	李義旼	Yŏngnong	玲瓏
Yi Yangsil	李陽實	*Yŏngnyu si*	詠柳詩
Yi Ye	李預	*yongŏ*	龍馭
Yi Ye (1419–1480)	李芮	*yŏn'gok*	輦轂
Yi Yugyŏng	李惟卿	Yongŏn-gak	龍堰閣
Yi Yuin	李惟仁	Yongŏn-gung	龍堰宮
Yi Yujik	李惟直	*Yongshi shi*	詠史詩
Yi Yujŏk	李攸績	Yongshu	永叔
Yi Yuon	李惟溫	Yŏngsŏk	永錫
Yi Yuryang	李惟諒	*yongsŏn*	龍船
Yi Yuŭi	李惟誼	Yŏngt'ong-sa	靈通寺
Yi Yuwŏn	李裕元	Yŏngŭi	榮儀
yoch'e	拗體	*yongwu shi*	詠物詩
Yŏgong p'aesŏl	櫟翁稗說	Yŏngyun	永胤
yŏgwŏn	驛院	*yŏnju*	聯珠

196 GLOSSARY

yŏn kwan 捐舘
yŏnmun 聯文
Yŏnŭi-jŏng 漣漪亭
Yŏrha ilgi 熱河日記
you 酉
Youyang zazu 酉陽雜俎
Yŏ Wang Yakchu sŏ 與王若疇書
Yŏ Yi Misu hoe Tamji-ji ka 與李眉叟會湛之家
yuan 源
Yuan Ang 袁盎
Yuanchang 元長
yuan ci 怨詞
yuan tao 園桃
Yuanyou 遠遊
Yu Chaeyŏng 柳在泳
Yu Chiri-san 遊智異山
Yu Ch'unggi 劉沖基
Yue 越
Yue Guang 樂廣
Yueming 說命
Yuezhong mudan 越中牡丹
Yugam 有感
yugo 遺稿
Yugong 禹貢
yugou 御溝
yugung 幽宮
Yuhoe Misu 有懷眉叟
Yu Hŭi 劉義
Yu Hyŏngwŏn 柳馨遠
yuji 遺址
Yu Kwang 俞光
Yulinling 雨霖鈴
Yuljin-gun 栗津郡
yumyŏng 乳名
Yun Hae 尹諧
Yun-ju Chahwa-sa si 潤州慈和寺詩
Yun Kwan 尹瓘
Yun Ŏni 尹彦頤
Yun Uil 尹于一
yunwŏn 綸苑
Yunxi ji 筠溪集
Yunzhou 筠州
Yu P'aljŏn-san 遊八巓山

Yu Rang 豫讓
Yusŏn ka 儒仙歌
Yusu 留守
Yu Sŭngdan 俞升旦
Yutai xinyong 玉臺新詠
Yu Turyu-san kihaeng p'yŏn 遊頭流山紀行篇
Yuwŏn 留院
Yuyan 寓言
Yuyuan 虞淵
zaiyou 在宥
Zaoxing linxia 早行林下
Zhang Heng 章衡
Zhang Ji 張繼
Zhang Jie 張戒
Zhang Liang 張良
Zhang Shizhi Feng Tang liezhuan 張釋之馮唐列傳
Zhanguo si gongzi 戰國四公子
Zhao Guo 趙構
Zhao Meng 趙孟
Zhao Ming 昭明
Zhao Shouzong 趙守宗
Zhao Xiangzi 趙襄子
Zhejiang tongzhi 浙江通志
zhen 震
Zheng 鄭
Zheng fuma zhai, yan dong zhong 鄭駙馬宅宴洞中
Zhenjiang 鎮江
Zhenshuaihui 眞率會
Zhenzhong ji 枕中記
Zhenzong 眞宗
zhi 紙
Zhi Anjie yuanlai yezuo 姪安節遠來夜坐
Zhi Bo 智伯
Zhichuan 椎川
Zhinü 織女
zhong 中
Zhongdu Culai ji 重讀徂陳集
Zhonghang 中行
Zhonghui zhi gao 仲虺之誥
Zhong Lichun 鍾離春

GLOSSARY

Zhongshu	仲殊	Zhu Yun	朱雲
Zhongxian	仲先	Zichan	子產
Zhong Yi	仲翼	*Zi jing fu Fengxianxian yonghuai wubai zi*	自京赴奉先縣詠懷五百字
Zhongyong	中庸		
Zhongzai	冢宰		
Zhong Ziqi	鍾子期	Zimei	子美
Zhou Bo	周勃	*ziqi*	紫氣
Zhouli	周禮	*Zixia*	紫霞
Zhou Yafu	周亞父	*Zixu fu*	子虛賦
Zhou Yue	周越	Zi yi	緇衣
Zhou Yuling	周與齡	Ziyun	子雲
Zhou Zhu	周伫	*Zoubi xie Meng jianyi ji xin cha*	走筆謝孟諫議寄新茶
Zhou Zi	周顗		
Zhuangzi	莊子	Zuimo-tang	醉墨堂
Zhuangzong	莊宗	Zuiweng	醉翁
Zhu Gui	朱珪	*Zuixiang ji*	醉鄉記
Zhulin qixian	竹林七賢	*Zuo qian zhi Languan shi zhisun Xiang*	左遷至藍關示侄孫湘
zhuo	琢		
Zhu Xi	朱熹	Zu Ti	祖逖
zhuyou	杼柚		

Abbreviations

SHC	Sŏha chip
STYS	Sinjŭng tongguk yŏji sŭngnam
TMS	Tongmunsŏn
TYSC	Tongguk Yi Sangguk chip

Notes

Translator's Introduction

1. The following example from a very early stage of the Great East Asian War illustrates the extensive loss of primary sources from earlier times: after King Sŏnjo (r. 1567–1608) and hordes of his ministers fled the capital helter-skelter, slaves seized the opportunity to set government offices ablaze, burning all the documents and books stored therein (the targeted slave registers certainly, but all kinds of other archived literature as well). Countless sources from previous eras, texts that for centuries had been gathered and centralized at the courts of Koryŏ and Chosŏn, were lost during these few devastating years of war.

2. Rogers, "National Consciousness in Medieval Korea," 151.

3. The Koryŏ capital of Kaesŏng, where the royal libraries and archives were located, and the northwestern city of P'yŏngyang, which served as the center for the production of carved woodblocks used for printing, were invaded and looted repeatedly during these invasions. This had a far-reaching impact on the destruction of material culture. For the impact of the Red Turban invasions on the loss of books and collections, see Reynolds, "Culling Archival Collections," 248n57.

4. Reynolds, "Culling Archival Collections," 232.

5. Regarding the existence of late Koryŏ archival collections, as well as the specific selection and elimination of documents, records, and books from the "former dynasty" in the early years of the Chosŏn dynasty, see again Reynolds, "Culling Archival Collections." These major early Chosŏn writings must be approached with caution, for works such as *Koryŏsa* and *Tongmunsŏn* constitute secondary, partially agenda-driven pieces geared toward a necessary legitimization of the new dynasty, Chosŏn. Also, these works dealt with the predecessor dynasty selectively, in some ways distorting it, decades after Koryŏ had been downed from within by some of its chief military figures (who then went on to establish its dynastic successor) in an age of profound change throughout East Asia. Naturally, these works nonetheless constitute invaluable sources of information regarding the Koryŏ dynasty. *Koryŏsa*, created from a multitude of now lost Koryŏ annals and histories, served to shape the retrospective views of the preceding dynasty regarding such issues as its domestic and foreign politics, its various political crises, its social and religious customs, and especially its countless political actors. Meanwhile, the literature of Koryŏ was consciously selected in a large-scale canonization process that resulted in such works as *Tongmunsŏn*, the major collection of Chinese literary works from Korea, which was assembled by representatives of the early Chosŏn intellectual elite such as Sŏ Kŏjŏng (1420–1488) and No Sasin (1427–1498).

201

202   NOTES TO PAGES 4–5

6. The title has also been transcribed as *P'ahanjip, P'ahan-jip,* and *Pahanjip.* The meaning of the title is discussed later in the introduction, in the section "The Cure for an Illness, the Question of Audience and Readership, and the Destruction of Old Men's Idleness."

7. A number of Korean online encyclopedias (such as the *Han'guk hyŏndae munhak taesajŏn* and the *Tusan paekkwa*) have Wadohyŏn as Yi Illo's sobriquet. See, for instance, the entry on Yi Illo in the *Tusan paekkwa,* accessed June 17, 2023, https:// terms.naver.com/entry.naver?docId=1135331&cid=40942&categoryId=33382. I was not able to find this pen name in any of the relevant sources, however. Other secondary texts claim that Yi's pen name was Ssangmyŏng-jae, but this was, in fact, the sobriquet of Yi's acquaintance Ch'oe Tang (1135–1211).

8. *Koryŏsa,* vol. 102, "Yŏlchŏn" (Exemplary biographies).

9. The compilers of *Tongmunsŏn* selected and included the comparatively large number of 113 poems by Yi Illo. See Wei and Lewis, *Korea's Premier Collection of Classical Literature,* 8.

10. The majority of the selections are of a decidedly nonfictional character, but in some cases we can perhaps detect a heightened level of fictional storytelling. Episode 11 in fascicle 3 (3:11), in which Yi retells the humorous story of a young and jumpy scholar, serves as an example.

11. In Korean literary studies there is disagreement concerning the division of the episodes as well as the resulting overall number of entries. I have followed the most established structure, which is: twenty-five entries in fascicle 1 (K. *kwŏn sang*), twenty-five entries in fascicle 2 (K. *kwŏn chung*), and thirty-three entries in fascicle 3 (K. *kwŏn ha*). The word *kwŏn* I have chosen to render as "fascicle," a term usually denoting pieces of a larger work not bound together but stacked on top of one another separately. *Kwŏn* can also be translated as "chapter" or "volume."

12. In some sources, *P'ahan chip* is spoken of as a *sosŏl.* This term since the early twentieth century has come to refer specifically to the novel but in the case of *P'ahan chip* would best be understood as short for *p'ilgi sosŏl* (C. *biji xiaoshuo*), "random notes and trivial anecdotes." This categorization can, for instance, be found in a passage from *P'aegwan chapki,* quoted later in the introduction.

13. See especially the chapter "A New Poetry Criticism: The Creation of 'Remarks on Poetry' " in Egan, *Problem of Beauty,* 60ff. Also see Owen, "Remarks on Poetry: Shih-hua" and "Ts'ang-lang's Remarks on Poetry," in *Readings in Chinese Literary Thought,* 359–420. For the impact of *Canglang sihua* on later developments of poetry criticism, see Lynn, "The Talent Learning Polarity in Chinese Poetics." For short general introductions of poetry criticism, see Idema and Haft, *Guide to Chinese Literature,* 156; Chang and Owen, *Cambridge History,* 1:460–461.

14. McCann, *Early Korean Literature,* 4.

15. Cho goes on to say, " *P'ahan chip* is a collection of *sihwa.* There are anecdotes on the writing of poetry, garnished with poetry-criticism, supplemented now and then with a discussion of a writer or even discussions of literary theory — that is how [Yi Illo] prepared a book which no one had ever seen before." Cho, *Han'guk munhak t'ongsa,* 2:38. Here one must note that similar Chinese works of poetry criticism, such

as *Lengzhai yehua* (see 1:2), were clearly already circulating in Koryŏ when *P'ahan chip* was written.

16. See Egan, *Problem of Beauty*, 77.

17. In pentasyllabic or heptasyllabic quatrains, the last word of the second line and the last word of the fourth line rhyme (in longer poems this continues accordingly, six/eight, ten/twelve, etc.). The rhyme is generally made up of the same or a very similar vowel along with an ending consonant (if any). For clarification: since imitating the rhyme in the translation of Literary Chinese poems often leads to rather awkward results, I have chosen to disregard the rhyme in my English renderings of the verse compositions. I have paid close attention, however, to other characteristic features of poetry composed in Literary Chinese, such as parallelisms.

18. About a third of the poems in *P'ahan chip* were composed by Yi Illo himself. His compositions can be found in 1:2–1:20, 1:22–1:24, 2:1, 3:21, 3:23, 3:24, 3:27, and 3:28.

19. On the other hand, Yi also either failed to recognize or consciously omitted the works of several poets who are today counted among the most prominent writers of early to mid-Koryŏ, such as Kim Kŭkki (n.d.).

20. While Yi Illo in many instances supplements the works of not-so-famous Korean and Chinese poets, often giving the impression that he actually strove to outshine them, Du Fu, Su Shi, and Huang Tingjian appear as seemingly unreachable role models. In 1:19, Yi writes poems in reply to compositions by Su Shi and Wang Anshi, and regarding the quality of his own lines he apologetically states, "I hope that those who view [my poems] may forgive me for it."

21. In his early years, Yi does not seem to have had access to the collected writings of Su Shi. This is evidenced by a passage from *Pohan chip* (Collection of supplementary writings [for overcoming] idleness) 2:18, which reads,

> Teacher Im Ch'un sent a letter to Yi Misu, in which it said, "You and I, though we haven't yet read Su Shi, time and again there are [poems written by us] which generally resemble his in terms of the techniques of line-composition. [...]" Now when I look at Misu's poetry, sometimes there are seven words, sometimes five words that have come from the *Dongpo ji* [Collection of Dongpo]. And when I look at Master Munsun's [Yi Kyubo (1168–1241)] poems, there's not a single instance in which there would even be four or five characters taken from Dongpo's words—and still, the bold energy and the abundant style [in Yi Kyubo's poetry], they seem to have derived directly from Dongpo himself.

Later, however, Yi Illo did get to read Su Shi's collected writings. In *Pohan chip* 2:46 it says, "The Academician Yi Misu said, 'I closed my door and read the collected writings of both Su [Shi] and Huang [Tingjian], and it was only then that my words became strong and my rhymes became crisp. [By reading their works] I managed to reach the realm of perfect composition when writing poetry.' Master Munsun thereupon said, 'I don't copy the words of the people of old, I create and bring forth new meaning.'"

204 Notes to Pages 6–11

22. The *Shijing,* for example, is discussed and quoted from only in 3:21, an entry partly dealing with the inscriptions on the *shigu,* the ancient Stone Drums, which are closely interrelated with certain odes in the *Shijing.* The other classical poetry anthology, the *Chuci,* is not mentioned in *P'ahan chip* at all. On the other hand, some space is given to the classic recluse poet Tao Yuanming, another ancient model. In this, *P'ahan chip* is in line with Song Chinese predecessors from the *sihwa* genre. See Egan, *Problem of Beauty,* 80.

23. Interpreters, though they are hardly ever mentioned in diplomatic travel writings, were usually an indispensable and constant presence in these diplomatic meetings. As Sixiang Wang writes, "Before the thirteenth century, the Koryŏ dynasty already employed interpreters of spoken Chinese as well as the Khitan and the Jurchen languages. Although occasionally recruited through exams, these interpreters were not trained by the state. They were ready-made talent, such as political refugees of foreign origin or exceptional individuals. [...] The training of language experts by the Korean state only began with the establishment of the Translation Bureau (T'ongmungwan) in 1276." Wang, "Chosŏn's Office of Interpreters," 3.

24. Rogers, "The Regularization of Koryŏ-Chin Relations," 52.

25. See Tillman and West, *China under Jurchen Rule.*

26. Michael C. Rogers writes that Koryŏ, "the spiritual heirs of Koguryŏ, could never forget the ancestral lands in Liaotung and beyond," and that "for purposes of foreign relations [...] the Koryŏ court presented itself as heir of Koguryŏ." Rogers, "National Consciousness in Medieval Korea," 152–153.

27. Emperor Huizong of the Song dynasty did single out books for suppression. The first edict to this effect was issued in 1103. It said, "Burn the wooden printing blocks for Su Shi's *Dongpo Collection* and *Later Collection.*" A Southern Song source says that an official proposed also destroying steles with Su Shi's books, which was approved. The next order, on 1103/4/27, was not limited to Su Shi. It ordered the burning of the printing blocks for the collected works of the "Three Su" (meaning the brothers Su Shi and Su Che and their father, Su Xun) as well as those of Su Shi's disciples. Ebrey, *Emperor Huizong,* 118.

28. For the reading of the word *hwa* as "story," "tale," or "anecdote," see *Thesaurus Linguae Sericae,* s.v. "hua," accessed June 17, 2023, https://hxwd.org/char .html?char=%E8%A9%B1. Alternatively, the term "narrative" could also be used to translate *hwa,* in the sense of a telling of some event or a connected sequence of events.

29. Entry 3:33 also does not feature any poetry, but as explained later in the introduction, this entry might, in fact, constitute not an original entry but a later addition.

30. In his short but intriguing, actually quite debatable (especially concerning his claim that "Yi believes that a life spent writing poetry is preferable to an active life of glory") essay on *P'ahan chip* in *A History of Korean Literature,* Peter H. Lee translates the title as *Jottings to Break Up Idleness.* Lee, *History of Korean Literature,* 138–140.

31. Yi repeatedly speaks of people, organizations, customs, and events of Silla, but he does not refer to anybody or anything from the other ancient Korean states (only in 3:30 he states, "In times of old, the Western Capital served as the capital of

Koguryŏ"). Breuker explains that this fixation on Silla may have occurred because during the mid-Koryŏ period, no writings of Koguryŏ or Paekche of high stature were extant. Yet this focus on the idea of Silla heritage defining Koryŏ can also be found, for example, in *Samguk sagi* (History of the Three Kingdoms). The implications of this non-consideration of the other states in terms of Koryŏ self-identification have been discussed in Breuker, *Establishing a Pluralist Society*, 125; for a great discussion of this topic, see also Rogers, "National Consciousness in Medieval Korea." The notable absence of especially Koguryŏ-related information is discussed again toward the end of the introduction.

32. See King, *Mosaic Techniques and Traditions*, 9.

33. In this respect, *P'ahan chip* is seemingly in line with foundational works of the *sihwa* genre, such as *Liuyi shihua*. See Egan, *Problem of Beauty*, 60–61.

34. Yi, "Ryŏjo sanmunhak sogo," 27.

35. A crucial difference between *P'ahan chip* and *Ise monogatari* is, of course, that in the case of the Japanese work the short narratives as well as the acting characters are to a large extent fictional. For a comparison between *P'ahan chip* and *Ise monogatari*, see Sin, "Sihwa-wa uta monogatari-ŭi pigyo yŏn'gu." Entries in *Ise monogatari* that can be understood as pairs comprise episodes 14 and 15 and episodes 21 and 22. See MacMillan, *Tales of Ise*, 204–205.

36. In 3:23 it says, "Now it is the cyclic year *kisa*, it has been six years since our king ascended the throne, and Master Kim [Kunsu] went out to govern a southern prefecture." Here, the year in question is 1209. In 1:15 it says, "It has been eight years now since our current king ascended the throne." This *kŭmsang*, "current king," is Hŭijong, and the year in question is 1211. Entry 1:15 thus must have been written a few weeks before Hŭijong was dethroned. In an afterword to *Pohan chip* it is moreover stated that *P'ahan chip* was finished in 1212.

37. See Fong, *Herself an Author*, 197.

38. Chŏng, *P'ahan chip p'an'gak-e issŏsŏ-ŭi ch'ŏmsak munje-wa kŭ munhak sajŏk ŭiŭi*, 27.

39. Pak, *Yŏkchu Pohan chip*, 395–396.

40. Chŏng, *P'ahan chip p'an'gak-e issŏsŏ-ŭi ch'ŏmsak munje-wa kŭ munhak sajŏk ŭiŭi*, 27.

41. Pak, *Yŏkchu Pohan chip*, 437.

42. We do, however, find the relevant poem by Im Chongbi in a text by Yi Kyubo, where it says, "This practice, it was begun by Im Chongbi! Thus, Master Im presented some government official with an announcement, in which it said, 'Widespreading is the high talent, / [like] the jade from upon the ridges of Mount Kunlun, which are difficult to buy even with a thousand cash.'" See, for instance, *TMS* 59:22b.

43. Haedong, "[Country] East of the Sea," was a common Chinese and premodern Korean appellation for the Korean Peninsula.

44. For this, see Lee, "The Indigenous Religions of Silla," 61.

45. The relevant source mentioning this 1493 print is cited in the following section, "*P'ahan chip* in Chosŏn, Colonial Times, and the Koreas."

46. Breuker, *Establishing a Pluralist Society*, 327–328.

206   NOTES TO PAGES 19–22

47. See National Museum of Korea, accessed June 17, 2023, https://www
.museum.go.kr/site/main/relic/search/view?relicId=3186. This oldest extant
printed version of *P'ahan chip* is stored at the National Library of Korea. See *P'ahan
chip*, 1659, National Library of Korea, #Ko 3648-62-377, https://www.nl.go.kr.

48. See Huff, *Asami Library*, 371.

49. "Not wide-ranging enough" or "not broad enough" (K. *migwang*) can here
be understood as pertaining to the lack of mention of members of the ruling Ch'oe
house in *P'ahan chip*. This point is further elaborated upon toward the end of the
introduction.

50. *TMS* 84:2b. References to and borrowings from *P'ahan chip* in *Pohan chip* are
pointed out in this translation.

51. This *sang ha chil* may mean that in early-fifteenth-century Korea, there
existed a version of *P'ahan chip* consisting of only two fascicles, not three.

52. This entry in *Yongjae ch'onghwa*, which essentially constitutes a current-
status book catalogue, is a source that can shed a small light onto the question of
which works were extant in late-fifteenth–early-sixteenth-century Chosŏn and which
books were lost over the following decades. This issue is vital, I believe, because an
understanding of which carriers of knowledge were available and which were lost
allows us to gain an insight into the ways in which knowledge, cultures of remem-
brance, or self-perception in the light of Korean history transformed during the latter
half of the Chosŏn dynasty. The beginning of the relevant entry in *Yongjae ch'onghwa*,
where we find information especially on early Koryŏ literature, reads,

> In our country, writers have been scarce, and [extant] writings are even
> scarcer. [Here's what is circulating in the world:] The *Kyewŏn p'ilgyŏng*
> [Plowing the laurel grove with a writing brush] in several volumes was
> written by Ch'oe Ch'iwŏn of Silla, but all of it is in the four-six style; the
> *Tongin mun* [Easterners' literature] in several dozens of volumes was
> compiled by the *Sijung* Ch'oe Cha; the *Samhan kugam* [Turtle mirror of the
> Three Han; *kugam*, "turtle mirror," being the memory of an event from the
> past that is to serve as an example or a warning for the later-born] in one
> cased copy was compiled by Yesan Ch'oe Hae [1287–1340]; the *Tongguk
> mun'gam* [Mirror of the literature of the Eastern Country] in several dozens
> of volumes was compiled by the *Sijung* Kim T'aehyŏn [1261–1330]; the
> *Tongmunsŏn* in several dozens of volumes, which is a complete collection
> of the poetry and prose of [our country's] former worthies, was com-
> piled on royal order by Sŏ [Kŏjŏng] of Talsŏng; Minister of State Yi's
> former and latter collection in several dozens of volumes was written by
> Master Munsun Yi Kyubo, and it is most vigorous; the *Kim kŏsa chip* [Col-
> lection of Hermit Kim] in several dozens of volumes was written by the
> *Wŏnoerang* [assistant office chief] Kim Kŭkki, and an old print of it exists
> at the Kyosŏgwan [Office of Editorial Review], but half of [the original]
> was cut out; of the *Ŭndae chip* there exists only a single cased copy; then
> there is the *Ssangmyŏngjae* [*chip*], which is extant in one cased copy, as

well as the upper and lower cased copies [K. *sang ha chil*] of *P'ahan chip*—
all of these were written by Yi Illo; the upper and lower cased copies of
Pohan chip were written by the *Sijung* Ch'oe Cha; the *Sŏha chip*, fragments
[K. *tan'gan*] of which are extant in a single cased copy, was written by Im
Ch'un; the *Ikchae chip* in several volumes and the *Yŏgong p'aesŏl*, extant in
a single cased copy, were written by Yi Chehyŏn; the *Yejong ch'anghwa
chip* [Song and response collection from the reign of Yejong of Koryŏ] in
two cased copies was written when King Yejong and men such as Kwak
Yŏ exchanged poems [see 2:9]; the *Tongan kŏsa chip* [Collection of Hermit
Tongan] in one cased copy was written by Yi Sŭnghyu [1224–1301]; the
Chungsundang chip [Collection of Chunsundang] in one cased copy was
written by Na Hŭngyu [n.d.; late Koryŏ]; the *Sigyŏngam* in one cased
copy was written by a monk, but his name and lineage are unknown [not
Sigyŏngam but Sigam was the pen name of Yi Chahyŏn; see 2:8]. [...]

This list of books from *Yongjae ch'onghwa* can also be found in the fourteenth volume
of *Yŏllyŏsil kisul* (Narrations from Yŏllyŏ Study) by Yi Kŭngik (1736–1806). Inter-
estingly, in this volume of *Yŏllyŏsil kisul* there is another catalogue of earlier books,
which features a work entitled *P'ahan chapki* (Miscellaneous accounts for overcom-
ing idleness), written by the sixteenth-century scholar-official Cho Sik (1501–1572).
I was not able to find this work, which may have been a copy of the original *P'ahan
chip*, or perhaps an independent work modeled on *P'ahan chip*.

    53. *Sasukchae chip* 8:35b. Similar to the way it is referred to in *Tongin sihwa sŏ*,
P'ahan chip is also spoken of in Cho Wi's (1454–1503) preface to another literary
miscellany by Sŏ Kŏjŏng, namely, the *P'irwŏn chapki* (A miscellany of the brush
garden, 1487).

    54. The institution is here referred to as *nanp'a*.

    55. Yi, *Tongin sihwa*, 70. References to or borrowings from *P'ahan chip* in *Tongin
sihwa* can be found in 1:6, 1:10, 1:28, 1:36, 1:40, and 3:56. They are pointed out in this
translation.

    56. References to and borrowings from *P'ahan chip* in *Tongmunsŏn* are pointed
out in this translation.

    57. *Sŏngjong sillok*, twenty-fourth year (1493), twelfth month, twenty-eighth day.

    58. *Sŏngjong sillok*, twenty-fourth year (1493), twelfth month, twenty-ninth day.

    59. See Wuerthner, *Tales of the Strange by a Korean Confucian Monk*, 174n10.

    60. *Hŭiraktanggo* 8:415a.

    61. *P'aegwan chapki*, vol. 4.

    62. See, for instance, *STYS* 30:2b, which cites from *P'ahan chip* 1:1. References
to *P'ahan chip* in *STYS* are pointed out sporadically in this translation. The same
applies for *Yŏgong p'aesŏl*.

    63. Pak T'aesun goes on to say:

The first splendid flourishing of the literature of us Easterners occurred
during the Koryŏ dynasty, and concerning famous masters and talented

208   NOTES TO PAGES 26–27

scholars who dominated the field for a time, there was no lack of these men during that [mid-Koryŏ] period. Yet the remaining collections [by outstanding Koryŏ literati], which were passed down to posterity don't exceed those of some three masters — it's a shame, indeed! The poetry and prose that is still extant, it's only from the *sihwa* and the *sosŏl* genres! But fortunately we can at least rely on this here collection [*P'ahan chip*], the *Pohan,* and the *Yŏgong p'aesŏl,* for their dissemination has been long-lived. (*Tonggye chip* 7:1b–2a)

64. *Tongsa kangmok, purok* (appendix) 1:35a. See also *STYS* 21:29b.

65. *Maeho yugo* originally constituted a literary collection by Chin Hwa of Koryŏ, but it was printed with wooden movable type in 1784 after Hong Manjong (1637–1707) had collected Chin's writings quoted in other sources. In this 1784 version of *Maeho yugo* we find a quote from *P'ahan chip* 1:21. See *Maeho yugo* 1:14b.

66. In volume 12 of *Imha p'ilgi* we find a quote from *P'ahan chip* 3:17.

67. *Susan chip* (Collection of Susan, 1803), 10:3a–5a.

68. See Sin, "*P'ahan chip* sojae si-ŭi chŏn'go hwaryong-gwa hyŏngsanghwa-e kwanhan *koch'al,* 10; Hŏ, "Chong Such'arok kyŏn sipku segi hanjŏk kyoryu," 300.

69. See Ch'oe, "Ilche kangjŏmgi kojŏn-ŭi hyŏngsŏng-e taehan ilgoch'al," 174; Kim, *Bibliographical Guide to Traditional Korean Sources,* 25.

70. *Unyang chip* 3:9b.

71. For instance, around the same time, *Kŭmo sinhwa* by Kim Sisŭp appeared in a Japanese translation by Wada Tenmin (Wada Ichirō, b. 1881). Wada's translations of the five Korean tales of the strange were successively published in five volumes of *The Chōsen,* the monthly bulletin of the Office of the Government-General of Korea, from December 1926 (vol. 139) to April 1927 (vol. 143). For more information, see the introduction to Wuerthner, *Tales of the Strange by a Korean Confucian Monk.*

72. The available *Chungoe ilbo* issues feature the following *P'ahan chip* entries: 1929/11/05: 1:1 (complete), 2:1 (abridged), 1:8 (slightly altered); 1929/11/06: 1:13 (complete), 1:23 (complete), 1:21 (complete); 1929/11/08: 2:2 (abridged); 1929/11/09: 1:18 (abridged), 2:4 (abridged), 2:9 (abridged); 1929/11/10: 1:22 (complete); 1929/11/12: 2:13 (complete), 2:14 (complete), 2:10 (complete); 1929/11/13: 2:15 (complete), 2:17 (complete), 3:20 (complete); 1929/11/14: 1:12 (complete), 2:24 (abridged), 3:25 (complete); 1929/11/15: 3:6 (complete), 3:3 (complete), 2:5 (slightly altered); 1929/11/17: 3:12 (complete), 3:32 (complete), 3:19 (complete); 1929/11/19: 3:7 (complete), 3:8 (complete), 3:11 (complete), 3:31 (complete); 1929/11/21: 3:15 (complete), 2:23 (abridged), 3:17 (abridged). See National Institute of Korean History, Korean History Database, s.v. "P'ahan chip," accessed June 18, 2023, db.history.go.kr.

73. I have understood this line as pertaining to the rise and military expansion of the Jurchen Jin dynasty. It could, however, potentially also be read as relating to an envisioned military campaign of Koryŏ itself, as, "now is the time for an expansion of [our] territory, an extension of [our] boundaries." The line has been translated this way in Sim, "*P'ahan chip*-ŭi yŏksajŏk sŏnggyŏk," 107. However, against the backdrop of the overall power relations in mid-twelfth-century East Asia, as well as the fact

NOTES TO PAGES 28–30   209

that in the following line there is a reference to the figure of Lian Po (see following note), I find this reading of Koryŏ as the aggressor unconvincing.

74. Lian Po was a military general of the state of Zhao during the Warring States period. Even at the age of eighty he is said to have eaten large amounts of rice, which intimidated the rulers of the neighboring states so that they did not dare encroach upon the borders of his country.

75. Huo Qubing (140–117 BCE), a famed general of the Western Han during the rule of Emperor Wu of Han. After he had won merits in battle, the emperor wanted to present him with a magnificent mansion. Huo refused, stating that he could accept nothing until the enemy was not completely annihilated.

76. In a discussion of his "Chasan *sihwa*" published in a later volume of *Tong-gwang* (vol. 12 [1927/04/01]), An Hwak writes, "From ancient times there have been collections of Korean poetry composed in Literary Chinese [K. *hansi*] such as the *Tongmunsŏn* or the *Kia*; as for *sihwa*, there are books from the category of *P'ahan chip*, *Tongin sihwa*, and *Sohwa sip'yŏng*. These, however, are all critiques concerned with the art of [poetic] form — with regard to [poetic] ideas, there isn't a single work dealing with it over the last thousand years."

77. *Chosŏn sosŏlsa* appeared continuously in the *Tonga ilbo* from October 31, 1930, to February 25, 1931. There was also a Japanese version, *Chōsen shōsetsushi*, which appeared in *Chōsen tsūshin* (Korea news) from November 1930 to March 1931. It was first published as a book in 1933 by the publishing house Ch'ŏngjin Sŏgwan.

78. Kim T'aejun, *Chosŏn sosŏlsa*, 24–25.

79. At the same time, North Korean anthologies of premodern literature increasingly featured poems and entries from *P'ahan chip*. For instance, in the 1964 work *Uri nara kojŏn chakkadŭlŭi mihak kyŏnhae charyo chip* (Collected materials on the aesthetic views of our country's writers of premodern literature) we find passages from the following *P'ahan chip* entries: 3:22, 3:20, 1:21, 3:18, 3:4. See Ri and Ryu, *Uri nara kojŏn chakka*, 33–35.

80. This era of military rule is a well-researched one. In South Korea, studies of this period as well as the political, social, intellectual, and cultural transformations brought about by the revolt are legion. Examples include Yi Hŭngjong, "Koryŏ musin chŏnggwŏn'gi munin-ŭi sasang yŏn'gu" (PhD diss., Kŏn'guk University, 1991); Sin Sujŏng, "Musin chŏnggwŏn-gwa Mun Kŭkkyŏm," *Yŏksa-wa sirhak* 10 (1999): 115–150. In Western Korean studies, especially the works by Edward J. Shultz are of importance. They include *Military Revolt in Koryŏ: The 1170 Coup d'État; Twelfth-Century Koryŏ Politics: The Rise of Han Anin and His Partisans*, and his pivotal book, *Generals and Scholars: Military Rule in Medieval Korea*.

81. For another factor for this coup, namely, the frustration and anger of certain parts of the civil elite who had suffered under Ŭijong, see Shultz, "Twelfth-Century Koryŏ Politics," 30–31.

82. Rogers, "National Consciousness in Medieval Korea," 162.

83. The term "intellectuals-in-between" was coined by Professor Marion Eggert of Ruhr University Bochum for the 2019 conference "Korean Intellectuals-in-Between: Configuring Knowledge in Periods of Transition," held at Ruhr University Bochum.

210 NOTES TO PAGE 31

84. In the discussion of the literature of the tenth to thirteenth centuries it says,

The military revolt [of 1170] was achieved through wise actions taken by men of the military, such as Chin Chun [d. 1179] (the grandfather of Chin Yŏp), Rangjung Kim Pu (the father of general Kim Ch'wiryŏ [1172–1234]). Yet through this coup, the military officials' role in the dynasty was strengthened, while the civil officials, who until then had held power in their hands, were either killed or ousted. This incident could not but cast an influence on the literature of that age. The progressive literati of that age [...] felt the impact of the social conflicts that started to arise in the wake of this incident, and they took a critical stance. These historical realities reflect especially in the poetry composed in Literary Sinitic of that age. Those who enjoyed the greatest fame among the poetry groups of the time were the members of the Haejwa Ch'irhyŏn. [...] They were of one mind, and leaning on the brush and the ale, they worried about and lamented the affairs of the world. The two people who formed the core of the Haejwa Ch'irhyŏn were Ri Illo and Rim Ch'un. (Chosŏn minjujuŭi inmin konghwaguk kwahakwŏn, *Chosŏn munhak t'ongsa*, 1:103)

85. *Chosŏn munhak t'ongsa*, 1:105. Also see Ko et al., *Chosŏn munhak-esŏ-ŭi sajo mit pangbŏp yŏn'gu*, 56–61. Later North Korean studies also feature similar portrayals of Yi's literature. See, for instance, Chŏng, Chang, and Pak, *Chosŏn kodae chungse munhak chakp'um haesŏl 2*, 78–80. Yi Illo as well as certain episodes from *P'ahan chip* are taught to North Korean students to this day, evidenced through publications such as *Chosŏn-ŭi irŭmnan chakka-wa irhwa* (Famous authors and anecdotes of Korea). In this book, we find an entire section on Yi Illo and *P'ahan chip*, but also narrative retellings of specific anecdotes, such as 1:14, 2:6, 2:9, 2:22, and 3:6. The narratives in this relatively recent work (from 2006) are furthermore furnished with interesting illustrations.

86. I am aware of and have access to one vernacular Korean translation of *P'ahan chip* from North Korea. I would like to express my sincere gratitude to Dr. Vladimir Glomb for making this publication available to me. The thorough, slightly abridged translation, prepared by Ri Sŏng, is contained in the 2016 publication *Ri Illo, Rim Ch'un chakp'um chip* (Collection of works by Yi Illo and Im Ch'un), which is volume 95 of the reissued series *Chosŏn kojŏn munhak sŏnjip* (Selected works of Korean classical literature). Interesting renditions of *P'ahan chip* passages as appearing in *Ri Illo, Rim Ch'un chakp'um chip* are pointed out in this translation.

87. For South Korean articles arguing in this direction, see, for example: Kim, "*P'ahan chip* chŏsul-ŭi yŏksajŏk paegyŏng"; Chŏng, "*P'ahan chip* p'an'gak-e issŏsŏ-ŭi ch'ŏmsak munje-wa kŭ munhak sajŏk ŭiŭi"; Sim, "*P'ahan chip-ŭi* yŏksajŏk sŏnggŏk." In South Korean literary studies, studies on *P'ahan chip*, a core work of the Korean canon, are thematically diverse and vast in number. For a list of selected academic articles, see, for instance, Koryŏ taehakkyo han'guksa yŏn'guso koryŏ sidae yŏn'gusil,

NOTES TO PAGES 32–34   **211**

P'ahan chip yŏkchu, 4. There also exist many South Korean vernacular Korean translations of *P'ahan chip*, such as those created by literary scholars Ku Chagyun (Koryŏ taehakkyo minjok munhwa yŏn'guso, 1964), Yi Sangbo (Taeyang sŏjŏk, 1972), Yu Chaeyŏng (Iljisa, 1978), and Ku Inhwan (Sinwŏn munhwasa, 2002). While preparing this English translation, I have greatly profited from the annotated translations by Pak Sŏnggyu (*Yŏkchu P'ahan chip*) as well as the one by the Koryŏ taehakkyo han'guksa yŏn'guso koryŏ sidae yŏn'gusil (*P'ahan chip yŏkchu*). In South Korea, there exist storybook versions of *P'ahan chip* for young children, as well as editions designed for middle school students (for the latter, see Ku Inhwan, Sŏng Naksu, O Ŭnju, and Kim Sŏnhwa, trans., *Chunghaksaeng-i ponŭn P'ahan chip* [Seoul: Sinwŏn munhwasa, 2012]). Interestingly, between 2006 and 2008 there appeared a popular comic book series by South Korean artist Yun Chiun carrying the title *P'ahan chip* (published by Daewon C. I.). This *manhwa*, however, is set in the Tang dynasty, deals with exorcists and ghosts, and has (as far as I can tell) no direct relation to Yi Illo's work.

88. Kim remarks that he was given Yi Illo's work by a certain Kim Kyŏngsu and that he read it "in leisure." The "Sŏ *P'ahan chip* hu" is contained in the third volume of *Kukch'ang yugo* (Posthumous manuscripts of Kukch'ang).

89. Yi Chayŏn was the brother of Yi Illo's great-great-grandfather Yi Chasang.

90. A clan that also came to be known as the Kyŏngwŏn Yi-*ssi*. Today this clan is mostly referred to as the Inch'ŏn Yi-*ssi*. Yi Illo was an ancestor in the seventh generation of the progenitor Yi Hŏgyŏm (n.d.). The main line of this family lost much of its might in the wake of Yi Chagyŏm's failed rebellion.

91. In the case of Yi O, in *Koryŏsa* (vol. 95) it says,

> [Yi] O, upon passing the civil service examination he became Hallim academician. He served under six kings—Munjong, Sunjong, Sŏnjong, Hŏnjong, Sukchong, and Yejong—and was repeatedly promoted, serving as commander unequaled in honor, acting grand preceptor, grand guardian of the heir apparent. [...] When he passed away at the age of sixty-nine, business at the court was suspended for three days, and they conferred upon him the posthumous name Mullyang. [Yi] O was quiet and had few desires, and aside from his official salary he did not manage any property. Strongly he believed in the Buddha and had comprehensively read the various scriptures and theses. Since he enjoyed the *Kŭmgang-kyŏng* [Diamond-*sūtra*] the most, he styled himself Kŭmgang kŏsa [Recluse of Kŭmgang]. His son was [Yi] Kwangjin.

92. His three legitimate sons had all passed the civil service examinations by the time Yi finished *P'ahan chip* (see 3:10). His oldest son, Chŏng, had already received an office in Chindong in 1203 (see 2:21), which implies that he must have been roughly forty years of age in 1211. Yang and On must have been in their early to mid-thirties. Yi Sehwang, on the other hand, must still have been a child or at most

212 NOTES TO PAGES 34–35

a young man at that time, for he is known to have moved with the court to Kangdo in 1232 and to have still served in office when he handed his father's writings over to Duke Taewŏn in the late 1250s. His brothers, who must have been born around 1180 (Yi Illo was clearly married by 1182 when he followed his father-in-law to the north) were probably long dead by then.

93. "Left of the [Yellow] Sea" and "Left of the [Yalu] River" as appellations for Korea must be understood from a Chinese perspective, for the Chinese emperor's throne (and therefore his countenance) would always face south. From this position, the Korean Peninsula lay to the emperor's left.

94. The Zhulin Qixian consisted of Ji Kang, Liu Ling, Ruan Ji, Ruan Xian, Xiang Xiu, Wang Rong, and Shan Tao.

95. Yŏngnak Cho T'ong is mentioned in 1:13 and 1:24; Chajin Ham Sun (to whom Yi Illo later even lived next door in Hongdojŏng Village) features in 1:5, 1:7, 1:13, and 2:21; Yi Tamji appears in 1:7, 2:17, and 2:21; O Sejae is discussed in 3:22; Im Ch'un features in 1:22, 1:23, 2:15, 3:8, 3:18, and 3:25. The only member of the Chungnim Kohoe not spoken of in the extant *P'ahan chip* is Hwangbo Hang.

96. The life, literature, and thought of Im Ch'un have long since been subject to extensive research in South Korea. Examples of studies include Chin Sŏnggyu, "Im Ch'un-ŭi saengae-wa hyŏnsil insik," *Han'guksa yŏn'gu* 45 (1984): 29–57; Hwang Pyŏngsŏng, "Im Ch'un-ŭi kŏsaron-gwa chŏngch'igwan-ŭi sŏnggyŏk," *Yŏksahak yŏn'gu* 16 (2001): 77–100; Pak Sŏnggyu, "Im Ch'un-ŭi munhak segye," *Han'guksa simin kangjwa* 39 (2006): 135–148; Ŏm Yŏnsŏk, "Im Ch'un-ŭi yuhak sasang ihae-wa ch'ulch'ŏ ŭnhyŏn'gwan-ŭi t'ŭkching," *Inmun yŏn'gu* 72 (2014): 355–384; Kim Sut'ae, "Muin chipkwŏn'gi Im Ch'un-ŭi ŭn'gŏ kwannyŏm — pulgyo-rŭl chungsim-ŭro," *Han'guk chungsesa yŏn'gu* 62 (2020): 185–218.

97. Sem Vermeersch's wonderful English translation of one of the more prominent prose works by Im Ch'un, a satirical tale entitled *Kongbang chŏn* (The tale of Mr. Cash), is contained in Pettid, Evon, and Park, *Premodern Korean Literary Prose,* 21–25. In an introductory paragraph it is said that the collection of Im Ch'un's writings has been lost (see Pettid, Evon, and Park, *Premodern Korean Literary Prose,* 20), but that is not the case — the *Sŏha chip,* edited by Yi Illo, is extant.

98. Apart from Im Ch'un, Yi Illo in *P'ahan chip* speaks of only Yi Tamji as *ou,* "my friend." See 2:17, 2:21.

99. Yoil was Yi's father's younger brother, and there are no sources explaining why he did not move to the house of Yi Kwangjin after the revolt, though one may suspect that a temple in the mountains was a safer hideout. One poem by Yi Illo that can be assumed to have been composed when he lived in hiding at his uncle's monastery is a verse entitled *San'gŏ* (Living in the mountains), which reads,

> Spring has gone, but the flowers are still there;
> skies are clear, but the valley lies in shadow.
> The cuckoo cries in broad daylight;
> only now I realize that I sited my dwelling at a deep spot.
> (*TMS* 19:3b)

Especially the first two lines may be interpreted as alluding to the perilous situation the dynasty was in, with the sky (the royal house) still clear but the valley (the country) covered in dark shadows (cast by the military revolt).

100. Min Yŏngmo is known to have achieved office only because of his close ties with King Myŏngjong. See Shultz, "Ch'oe Ch'unghŏn: His Rise to Power," 81.

101. Tillman and West, *China under Jurchen Rule*, 4–5.

102. On the first page of *P'ahan chip* it says that he served as *chwa kanŭi taebu*, but in his biography in *Koryŏsa* it says that he was *u kanŭi taebu* (right grand master of remonstrance). It may be that he served in both offices, left and right.

103. Im Ch'un's biography in *Koryŏsa* (vol. 102) reads, "[Im] Ch'un, his courtesy name was Kiji. He was a person from Sŏha. On account of his literary writing, [his name] resounded in the world, but he repeatedly failed the civil service examinations. During Chŏng Chungbu's coup his entire family met disaster, but [Im] Ch'un got away and barely made his escape. In the end, however, he lived a life of abject poverty and died young. [Yi] Illo collected his posthumous manuscripts, turned them into six volumes, and entitled [the collection] *Sŏha sŏnsaeng chip*. It circulates in the world." The Im family may have met with disaster on account of their stance or behavior toward the military before the coup, which may not have been as respectful as that of Yi Illo's family. For this and an abundance of relevant information on Im Ch'un's life before and after the revolt, see Ryŏ, "Im Ch'un-ŭi saengae-e taehan chaegŏmt'o."

104. These peasant and slave revolts arose in reaction to the exploitation of the lower strata and an overall highly tense social climate in the early 1170s, a time when the traditionally underprivileged challenged and usurped the authority of those who had long since been in power. Such uprisings by agitated, overtaxed peasants and slaves against the new leaders with a military—and therefore in many people's eyes illegitimate—background took place, for example, in Ch'angju and Sŏngju in the northwest of the Korean Peninsula in 1172. Another massive rebellion was led by the slaves Mangi and Mangsoi in 1176 in the southwestern region of Kongju.

105. An example of such a poem appears toward the end of this introduction in the section "Walking Cane and Frosty Sword, Opposing Roles and Conflicting Obligations, and the Appropriation of a Dead Man's Poetry."

106. In *Koryŏsa* (vol. 19, third year of Myŏngjong [1173], eighth month, twentieth day) it says, "On the day *kyŏngjin*, the military commissioner for the Northeastern District Kim Podang mustered soldiers in the northeastern border region, aiming to attack Chŏng Chungbu and Yi Ŭibang and to restore the former king. [...] Han Ŏn'guk took his army and joined him, and commanding Chang Sunsŏk and others they arrived at Kŏje, where they showed their respect to the former king, and moved to Kyerim."

107. Edward Shultz interprets these two revolts as an expression of the disdain that had built up in the north toward the central government. Shultz, *Generals and Scholars*, 34–35.

108. Yi, *Han'guk myŏngjŏ taejŏnjip*, 383.

109. *TMS* 59:14a.

214   NOTES TO PAGES 39–40

110. This proverbial expression usually relates to Confucius or Mozi, and it can refer to people moving restlessly about to help the people of the world. Here, however, it seems as though it was primarily meant as "being driven here and there by poverty." See Owen, *Poetry of Du Fu*, 2:435.

111. A reference to Ruan Ji (210–263), one of the Seven Worthies of the Bamboo Grove. In his biography in *Jinshu* (vol. 49) it says that Ruan Ji often wandered out on his own without following any set road. When the trails he was walking on came to an end and he had to turn his cart around, he would wail bitterly and return home.

112. The *Pu Yi Misu che Im sŏnsaeng mun* is a crucial source regarding the relationship between Yi and Im, as well as Yi Illo's perception of Im's life and poetry. It says,

> Numinous one! Hermit, you were lone and pure; adjutant [K. *ch'amgun*], you were noble and free. Your literature was [surprising and daring] as if it had come forth from the side of the moon, your poems were standing tall like the bones of the mountains. [...] You had risen in a noble house of vermilion columns, with riches controlling the cave of gold, with matches of Qin and Jin [intermarriages between high families], with quarrels of Zheng and Xue. Heaven's avenues [in the capital] are very broad, reachable with frog-leap steps, but you never thought that the bustling splendor [of the metropolitan area] was pleasing. The well of sweet water was the first to be exhausted [a reference to "Shanmu" from *Zhuangzi*], a cultivated tree was the first to be removed; ten thousand matters burst, but you alone escaped and got away. Wherever you dwelled, you never had a blackened chimney, and when you were traveling you wailed at the end of each trail [when your cart could go no farther]. But you did not let poverty and peril alter any of your standards. Thereupon you sang in a high voice, which cracked rocks and had spirits and ghosts grieve. Dark anger filled your chest, meanderingly entwined like clouds and rainbows. You were melancholy in the same way as Master Liu [Zongyuan] [who also lived in poverty], and distressed like Duke [Xiang] of Song. Frowning, groaning, shouting, laughing, being right and being wrong, success and failure — all of this rested in your brush and in your tongue. [...] You galloped past [all the poets] from times of Han and Wei, mixed with Zhuan[zi] and Qu [Yuan]. This sharp-wittedness [of yours] could bore through wooden writing boards, [your] skillfulness could pierce a louse. [...] But it was just like [you were the man of Song who] went to Yue to sell his cap [to people who cut off their hair and tattooed their bodies, so that they had no use for a cap] [a reference to a passage from "Xiaoyao yu" from *Zhuangzi*], like selling sandals to someone whose feet have been amputated, like the fish hawks over the [Song] capital that flew backward and tumbled down [a reference to an anomalous event mentioned in *Zuozhuan* 16.1], like the anthill that leans over and crumbles [perhaps a reference to Im Ch'un's family, which crumbled], like the willow-leaf of [Yang] Youji that hasn't

yet been split, like [Lu] Guimeng's moon in a pond that suddenly burst. As a young man of thirty years you passed away, wearing commoners' clothes. The anger and resentment over you not having been granted the red cassia [success in the civil service examinations] shall remain until the end of Heaven and earth. Alas, in the world everyone said that you peered arrogantly at others, that you were relentless, hard-nosed, and that you would never bend, that you relied on your energy like Kong [Rong] or Mi [Heng] did, that you disdained [people and] things like Pan [Yue] and Zhang [Heng] did, but this was a tiny speck on the pure waters of the Huai River, a small black ant on a white wall — how could this be anything to be concerned about? There may be one with a glorious vermilion sash [the insignia of a high official] who is more vulgar than him dressed in linen and kudzu, and maybe he whose hair is streaked with brilliant gray really doesn't come close to him who died young. Turtles, snakes, trees, stones — they all live long, but what's it all worth? Though now your body, Master, is no more, your talent will twinkle on with the stars, and though your life was short, your fame shall be like Mount Tai and Mount Hua, never to perish. If one takes *this* [your poetry] and compares it to *that* [everybody else's verses], it's as big a difference as that between the sky and the soil. Early on we roamed the elegant rooms [of our homes], we were like glue and varnish, [...] but suddenly I lost my closest friend [the source here has a reference to Zhuangzi's best friend, Huizi]. Dust once stirred by an emotional song has already dispersed, fogs once stirred by clothes have come to a rest. My mad words — who will now reply to them? The errors in my poetry — who will now scold me for them? (*SHC* 6:27a–28b)

113. *TMS* 59:6a.

114. *SHC* 3:16a; *TMS* 13:4b.

115. In 3:23, Yi describes how he was a member of an exclusive club of principle graduates, a so-called Assembly of Dragon Heads (K. Yongdu Hoe). In these Yongdu Hoe, not even those who had successfully passed the examinations in second place, the so-called *awŏn* (C. *yayuan*), were allowed to join.

116. *SHC* 3:2b.

117. The civil service examinations were divided into two main categories, or "fields" (K. *kwa*): first, the *chesulgwa*, a highly prestigious examination testing literary and lyrical composition; second, the (at least during that age) less valued *myŏnggyŏnggwa*, an examination testing familiarity with the Confucian classics. Candidates in literary composition were tested in the composition of poetry, rhapsodies, odes, and essays in three stages. Over the course of the Koryŏ dynasty, the number of candidates in the *chesulgwa* (both overall as well as successful) was far higher than that in the *myŏnggyŏnggwa*.

118. *SHC* 1:12b.

119. This can be taken as a reference to a tale from *Jinshi* (History of Jin) about a fight between Shi Le, founder of the Later Zhao (319–351), and his neighbor Li Yang,

216   NOTES TO PAGES 41–44

during which Shi is reported to have said, "In former days I have had my fill of your old fists, and you, in turn, shall get enough of my venomous hand." See Cutter, *Brush and the Spur*, 181. This line may be understood as a reference to the aftermath of the 1170 military revolt.

120. *TMS* 4:4b–5a.

121. This is evidenced, for example, in Im Ch'un's poem *Misu pang yŏ ŏ-Kaeryŏng i arijiju wi hyang; chaksi saji* (Misu came to visit me in Kaeryŏng [Kimch'ŏn in present day Northern Kyŏngsang Province] and had me drink wine made of fine-skinned pears—Composing a poem to thank him). *SHC* 2:20a.

122. This does not only apply to high positions, but government offices in general. As Edward Shultz notes,

> One of the immediate developments [of the new emphasis put on education in the late eleventh century] was the gradual increase in the number of examination passers. Beginning from Sŏnjong's reign (1083–94), the average yearly number of passers nearly doubled. For example, in Munjong's reign 11.8 men passed the examination on a yearly average, compared to 19.4 men in Sŏnjong's reign and 22.5 under Yejong. Although the number of successful candidates increased, there was no appreciable change in the number of positions available in the government. The inevitable result was heightened competition among those who successfully passed the examination for the few existing government offices. (Shultz, "Twelfth-Century Koryŏ Politics," 7)

123. The *ŭm* privilege was held by higher officials and essentially meant that their sons would automatically be appointed to office after taking a pro forma examination. In mid-Koryŏ, this system still constituted the primary method of recruiting officials. See Seth, *Concise History of Premodern Korea*, 84–85.

124. O Sejae obviously had a keen interest in passing the civil service examinations, because he sat for them on several occasions. He was, however, repeatedly passed over in selection. When he finally did pass the *kwagŏ*, he was already past the age of fifty. In the end, however, he never received an office and seems to have lived in abject poverty until his death.

125. In his *Why Societies Need Dissent*, Cass Sunstein has debated issues surrounding conformity and dissent and has posed dissent as not "doing what others do." See Sunstein, *Why Societies Need Dissent*, 15ff.

126. This line is based on Confucius's comment on Yan Hui from *Lunyu* 6.11.

127. In *Zhuangzi* 8:3 it says that Robber Zhi died on top of Mount Dongling on account of his greed, and that he was later called a *soin*, a "small man" or "bad person."

128. *TMS* 6:1b.

129. For the dissident nature of Su Shi's poetry, as well as for the severe consequences Su Shi and his acquaintances had to suffer on account of his government or "new policies" (C. *xinfa*) critical writings, see Hartman, "Poetry and Politics in 1079."

130. One must concede, however, that the poem was included, and thereby recognized as worthy of preservation, in *Tongmunsŏn*.

131. Almost the same wording, i.e., people in attendance being "awed by someone's literary skillfulness," appears again in relation to the high civil official and influential intellectual Kim Puŭi in 2:2. At that later point in the text, however, the statement is meant not ironically but in earnest.

132. Cho, *Han'guk munhak t'ongsa*, 2:38.

133. See the section "Ch'oe Fiscal Policy: The *Sigŭp*" in Shultz, *Generals and Scholars*, 153–157.

134. The connection between Chinyang and the Ch'oe Clan in *P'ahan chip* is mentioned in Sim, "*P'ahan chip*-ŭi yŏksajŏk sŏnggŏk," 108–109.

135. For instance, the story "Qincheng bajiao" (The plantains of Qin fortress) from *Taiping guangji* (Extensive records of the Taiping era, vol. 140) tells of an army commander-in-chief in the cold region of Tianshu planting these *bajiao* in his pavilion and protecting them from the cold weather. As the climate changes and the plantains grow luxuriously, Tianshu becomes a visiting spot for crowds of people from the state of Shu, and before long, Qin's fortress is annexed by Shu forces. See Dudbridge, *Portrait of Five Dynasties China*, 65.

136. This "black peony flower" (K. *hŭk moktan*) may be understood as a reference to the tale of Liu Xun, a wealthy man during the Tang dynasty who invited guests to his home to view his peonies. At the time he had several hundred head of oxen tied up at a gate, and his guests pointed at them, inquiring whether they were "the black peonies of the Liu house." Fraleigh, *Plucking Chrysanthemums*, 393n67. *Hŭk moktan* here means "cow." Snow Hall was Su Shi's painting studio, which he built in the winter of 1082 during his exile in Huangzhou (1080–1084).

137. Thus it is stated, for instance, in an anecdote about Kim Sisŭp contained in Kim Allo's *Yongch'ŏn tamjŏkki*. See *Hŭiraktang ko* 8:8b–10a.

138. This interpretation of the cow episode is partly suggested in Na, "*P'ahan chip* yŏkchu sojae yŏnsasi-ŭi chaehaesŏk," 148.

139. See 1:13, note 154.

140. Babcock, "The Aesthetics of Non-Discrimination," 44.

141. See *Thesaurus Linguae Sericae*, accessed June 18, 2023, https://hxwd.org/concept.html?uuid=uuid-25118dda-1ad5-474a-bfb1-f766ef011637.

142. See Charles Muller, trans., *The Analects of Confucius*, accessed June 18, 2023, http://www.acmuller.net/con-dao/analects.html.

143. See *Thesaurus Linguae Sericae*, accessed June 18, 2023, https://hxwd.org/concept.html?uuid=uuid-729a57d0-5998-4529-bd38-9945388d0a7a.

144. For English proverbs of the idea of "idleness being the root of all evil," or "an idle brain being the devil's workshop," see Speake, *Oxford Dictionary of Proverbs*, 160. In his book *Early Korean Literature*, David McCann translates the title as "Collection for Overcoming Leisure."

145. See Kubin, *Die chinesische Dichtkunst. Von den Anfängen bis zum Ende der Kaiserzeit*, 192.

218 NOTES TO PAGES 51–53

146. My translation, on the basis of an authoritative English rendering in Waley, *Hundred and Seventy Chinese Poems,* 233.

147. *Mogǔn'go* 6:13a. The term *p'ahan* also appears in Yi Saek's poem *Pang Yu Milchik Pǒn. Kwi-i yuyǒng* (Having paid Yu Pǒn of the Bureau of Military Affairs a visit, upon my return I chanted). See *Mogǔn'go* 31:11a.

148. The term *hanja* has here been understood as meaning *hanin* (C. *xianren*), "unoccupied person" or "person with leisure," which could be taken as an allusion to a recluse. Yet it could also be translated simply as "when I speak of [the concept of] leisure."

149. The source says *hyǒnch'a,* "disengage the carriage [from one's horse]," which means to retire, traditionally at the age of seventy.

150. The ancient Chinese board game *liubo* and the chess-like game known in Korea as Paduk (in the West commonly under its Japanese pronunciation Go).

151. This sentence builds on *Lunyu* 17.22. Yet while in the *Analects* playing games is better than doing nothing, here it is the reading of *P'ahan chip* that is said to be better than playing these board games. The relevant *Lunyu* passage reads, "The Master said: 'What can be done with a man who stuffs his face with food all day, without exercising his mind. He could at least play cards or chess or something. It would be better than nothing.'" See Muller's translation of *Analects of Confucius.*

152. For example, on the basis of this quotation Peter H. Lee writes, "Yi Illo suggests that the primary condition that led him to write was leisure. Leisure is the product of disengagement—the scorn for wealth and rank of a solitary, private man who 'lives hidden in the mountains and forests' seeking peace of mind and his own identity." See Lee, *History of Korean Literature,* 138. In the Digital Library of Korean Literature by the Literature Translation Institute of Korea it says, "The title of the book, 'Pahan' [*sic*] means 'breaking up idleness.' Based on the title, it is said that the reason for writing *Pahanjip* [*sic*] was to pass his time, however, in reality, it can be assumed that he hoped to prevent the gradual disappearance of the poems and writings by prominent Korean figures." Digital Library of Korean Literature, s.v. "Lee Inro," https://library.ltikorea.or.kr. See also Cho, *Han'guk munhak t'ongsa,* 2:40.

153. Tai-jin Kim writes, "Lamenting the contemporary situation whereby outstanding Confucian scholars and poets were gradually fading away without passing their works on to succeeding generations, the author is said to have compiled the *P'ahan-jip,* the title meaning 'for leisurely reading.'" Kim, *Bibliographical Guide to Traditional Korean Sources,* 25.

154. See Koryǒ taehakkyo Han'guksa yǒn'guso, *P'ahan chip yǒkchu,* 3.

155. Ziporyn translates this sentence from *Zhuangzi* as "A large consciousness is idle and spacey; a small consciousness is cramped and circumspect." Ziporyn, *Zhuangzi,* 10. In Kalinke's new German translation, however, it somehow reads, "Wer viel weiß, hat Schwierigkeiten; wer wenig weiß, hat Muße" (He who knows much has troubles, he who knows little has idleness). Kalinke, *Zhuangzi,* 23. I have not found this understanding of *hanhan* as "troubles" or "problems" anywhere else. A term that seems to be semantically similar to *p'ahan* is *p'asu* (C. *poshui*), "overcome sleepiness" or "waking someone from his slumber."

NOTES TO PAGES 53–57 **219**

156. See Huang, "Xunzi's Criticism of Zisi," 295. Huang argues that Xunzi looks upon this living and thinking in leisure in a negative way.

157. My translation, based on Charles Muller, trans., *The Great Learning,* http://www.acmuller.net/con-dao/greatlearning.html.

158. It might be wise to point out that the *han* I am speaking of here is, of course, not the *han* (C. *hen*) that is oftentimes associated with Koreans today, i.e., an almost undefinable, supposedly uniquely Korean sense of melancholy. For this other kind of *han,* see Kang Minsoo's interesting essay "The Problem with 'Han,'" *Aeon,* March 18, 2022, https://aeon.co/essays/against-han-or-why-koreans-are-not-defined-by-sadness.

159. See Shultz, "Ch'oe Ch'unghŏn: His Rise to Power," 69.

160. *Koryŏsa,* vol. 21, second year of Sinjong (1199), sixth month, thirteenth day. The same happened again in 1203. See *Koryŏsa,* vol. 21, sixth year of Sinjong (1203), seventh month, second day.

161. It is clear that Yi Sehwang, who was still serving in office in the 1250s, cannot have been present when his father allegedly uttered these words to the other members of the Chungnim Kohoe. Hence, there is ample room for the hypothesis that there must have occurred some sort of error in the process of production of Yi Sehwang's afterword.

162. Ch'oe Sŏn was Ch'oe Tang's younger brother. He retired from office in 1206.

163. For the Haedong Kirohoe and its members, see e.g., Pak, "Koryŏ sigi Haedong kirohoe-ŭi kyŏlsŏng-gwa hwaltong"; O, "Koryŏ sidae Haedong kirohoe-ŭi sŏngnip-kwa 'kiro'-ŭi ŭimi pyŏnhwa."

164. *Yangch'on sŏnsaeng munjip* 19:12a.

165. The association is described in a similar way in the *Ssangmyŏng-jae ki* (Records of Ssangmyŏng Studio) by Yi Illo, where the history of the club is reiterated. Yi writes that the defender-in-chief, the master of Ch'angwŏn Ch'oe Tang, who was then not yet seventy years of age, presented a letter of resignation to the throne, begging to be permitted to withdraw from office, and eventually was allowed to retire. Yi states that in days gone by, Ch'oe had been very fond of a certain beautiful tree that stood atop a sharp-rising peak to the south of Sungmun-gwan (Noble Literary Pavilion), and that Ch'oe built a hall right next to that very tree. Together with eight people, all older scholar-officials (K. *sadaebu*) of that time, whose level of virtue was enormous, he would sojourn and rest therein. Day in and day out they would have zither performances, Paduk games, or poetry and ale as their merriment, and generally they agreed to model all of their regulations on the ancient model of the *zhenshuaihui* (true and simple gathering) of Sima Guang. See *TMS* 65:17b.

166. In her informative essay on the political philosophy and intellectual history of dissent, Barbara J. Falk states, "What makes resistance *political,* however, and perhaps *transforms* it into dissent, is its purposeful and public nature. Dissent requires entering public space." Falk, "The History, Paradoxes, and Utility of Dissent," 25.

167. This may have been the reason why Yi included so many of his own poems in the first fascicle of *P'ahan chip.* Yi may have meant for King Hŭijong to recognize his talent from the moment he picked up the manuscript.

220   NOTES TO PAGES 56–59

168. At the same time, by having the old men read many of his own poems, Yi may have meant to point out to the other Kirohoe members that their decision to let him participate in this meeting of poets had been the right one.

169. Yi Illo had clearly meant for *P'ahan chip* to be read by the king (either Hŭijong, Kangjong, who reigned from 1211 to 1213, or Kojong) and to be subsequently printed. By means of a woodblock print he could have exceeded the narrow boundaries of the Haedong Kirohoe, reached a larger readership, and stirred a broader literati audience.

170. A reference to the chapter "Neize" (The pattern of the family) from *Liji* (Book of rites), where the customs for the birth of a ruler's son are described.

171. The term *haojie [zhi] shi*, "outstanding person" or "scholars of heroic mold," derives from *Mengzi* 7A:10. See van Norden, *Mengzi*, 174.

172. A reference to *Lunyu* 17.7. See Slingerland, *Confucius: Analects*, 202–203.

173. This is an allusion to a story in the biography of Sima Xiangru (179–117 BCE) from *Shiji*. See fascicle 3, note 136 (where it relates to Chŏng Sŭmmyŏng [d. 1151]).

174. This line can certainly be understood as a reference to submissive, opportunistic Koryŏ civil officials who will do everything in the service of the military rulers (the first part could thus be taken as, "Who lick [the military rulers'] piles"). It is a reference to a passage from the chapter "Lie Yukou" of *Zhuangzi* (32:8): "Zhuangzi said, 'When the king of Qin falls ill, he calls for his doctors. The doctor who lances a boil or drains an abscess receives one carriage in payment, but the one who licks his piles for him gets five carriages. From the large number of carriages you've got, I take it you must have been treating his piles. Get out!'" Watson, *Complete Works of Zhuangzi*, 282.

175. A reference to *Mengzi* 2B:12:

> Mengzi said, "[...] To come a thousand leagues to see the king was something I wanted. To not find him suitable and to leave, how could this be something I wanted? I simply had no choice. [...] The king almost reformed things. If the king had reformed them, that would have definitely made me return. But I left Zhou and the king did not pursue me. Only then did I have, floodlike, a will to return home. Even so, have I deserted the king? The king still has the capability to do good. If the king would employ me, then would only the people of Qi be given peace? The people of the world would all be given peace." (Van Norden, *Mengzi*, 60)

176. In the poem *Fuchou* (Worried again) by Du Fu it says,

> When were the Hu barbarians ever really ascendant? —
> some just won't stop the clash of arms.
> I listened to young people by the village gate
> chat about seeking to be made a lord.
>   (Owen, *Poetry of Du Fu*, 5:242)

NOTES TO PAGES 59–60 **221**

177. In this book, "league" is a translation of the unit of distance *li* (K. *ri*), which is also widely known as the "Chinese mile." *Li* nowadays has the standardized length of five hundred meters.

178. The term *sun'gaeng* (C. *chungeng*), often appearing as *sun'gaeng nohoe* (C. *chungeng lukuai*), "watershield broth and sliced perch," refers to the special cuisine of one's home region as well as the nostalgia and the longing for home it evokes. The term derives from the biography of Zhang Han in *Jinshu* (vol. 92). Zhang Han, a native of the southern state of Wu, was serving in the capital, Luoyang. It says, "When [Zhang Han] saw the autumn wind rise, he thought of the small fungus, the water-shield broth, and the sliced perch of [his home region] of Wu. Thereupon he said, 'The most valuable thing in a person's life is that he gets to act according to his will. How could one be held down in officialdom several thousand leagues away [from one's home] only to seek fame and status?' And straightaway he commanded his coach drivers take him home [to Wu in the south]." Im Ch'un in this line may be hinting at his intention of moving to his ancestral home of Yech'ŏn (in present-day North Kyŏngsang Province), but I think he really bemoans the fact that he is incapable of following Zhang Han's example and turning around to go back to the place where he grew up, i.e., Kaesŏng.

179. The Eastern Jin military general and poet Liu Kun (270–318) was close friends with Zu Ti (266–321). There is a famous story that has become a four-character idiom: it seems that Zu and Liu were such good friends they slept under the same coverlet. In the middle of the night Zu Ti heard a cock crow. He kicked Kun awake and said, "This is not a disagreeable sound." (A cock crowing at night was considered a bad omen.) They then got up and began to dance. Hence the phrase *wen ji qi wu*, "rising at cockcrow to begin action." Knechtges and Chang, *Ancient and Early Medieval Chinese Literature*, 1:541.

180. This line is a reference to Zhang Liang of the Western Han, who during the wars between Qin and Han attempted to assassinate Qin Shihuangdi. The attempt on the emperor's life failed, however, and Zhang Liang was forced to escape to the garrison of Xiapi.

181. Zhang Liang is famously said to have encountered an old man by the name of Huang Shigong, a possibly legendary recluse, who helped him by presenting him with a treatise on military strategy entitled *Huang Shigong sanlue* (Three strategies of Huang Shigong). Zhang then went on to become a master tactician, and aided Liu Bang, the later emperor Gao and founder of Han, in establishing the Han dynasty in the wake of Liu Bang's victory over the forces of Xiang Yu (233–202 BCE) in the wars against the Western Chu. This *Huang Shigong sanlue* then became one of the major military texts of ancient China. The episode of Huang Shigong and Zhang Liang's initial encounter on Yi Bridge is vividly described in a much later masterwork of Chinese prose fiction, the *Xiyouji* (The journey to the West), where in chapter fourteen it reads,

> "The immortal in the painting," said the dragon king, "was named Huang Shigong, and the young man kneeling in front of him was called Zhang

222 NOTES TO PAGES 60–62

Liang. Shigong was sitting on the Yi bridge when suddenly one of his shoes fell off and dropped under the bridge. He asked Zhang Liang to fetch it, and the young man quickly did so, putting it back on for him as he knelt there. This happened three times. Since Zhang Liang did not display the slightest sign of pride or impatience, he won the affection of Shigong, who imparted to him that night a celestial manual and told him to support the house of Han." (Translation in Yu, *Monkey and the Monk,* 230)

Im Ch'un here thus refers to a well-known failed attack against the enemy from Chinese history, and this line, in turn, might be read as an allusion to his participation in the failed countercoups and unsuccessful assassinations attempted by Kim Podang and other counterrevolutionaries after the 1170 revolt. In addition, Im Ch'un may here imply that, just as Zhang Liang had to take refuge in a place on the periphery but later returned gloriously to overthrow the enemy, he likewise means to lie low and bide his time to reemerge and join the fight again, equipped with a great plan.

182. Xiang Yu was a warrior and prominent rival of Liu Bang. In death, the once seemingly invincible Xiang Yu burst out into a song: "My strength is such to move mountains and my vehemence covers the world, / Now that fate is not on my side, my dappled steed can run no more." Wang, " 'Making Friends with the Men of the Past,' " 86.

183. This "prominent nose" or "high-bridged nose" was the mark of Liu Bang.

184. The source says *changbu.* According to *Mengzi* 3B:2, this *tae changbu,* "great man" or "great fellow," is a person who, if necessary, will pursue his way alone for the good of the people, a man who is resolute and can never be "bent by authority or violence."

185. This final part is a quotation from *Zhuangzi* 1.1.

186. According to an anecdote in the *Jinshu* (vol. 62), Liu Kun purportedly wrote this about his friend Zu Ti. Liu Kun wrote in a letter, "Pillowed on a spear, I wait for dawn. My intention is to execute treacherous barbarians and expose their bodies to public view! But I always fear that Scholar Zu [Ti] will bring out his whip before me."

187. The source here has *poguk* (C. *baoguo*), which I have understood as "repay one's debt to the dynasty." It could also be taken in the sense of "serve the dynasty," or perhaps even "avenge the dynasty." For the entire poem, see *SHC* 1:19b–20b.

188. *SHC* 1:16b.

189. Yi Illo's patron was Mun Kŭkkyŏm. See 2:1.

190. Yet also to his other friends, people such as Cho T'ong, Yi Tamji, and Ham Sun, who were employed by the government of Ch'oe Ch'unghŏn and certainly would not have wanted Yi to rebel in any public way, thereby potentially derailing their careers.

191. The other four central, hierarchically structured relationships in Confucian society and thought are those between ruler and subject, father and son, husband and wife, and older and younger brothers.

192. See Muller's translation of *Analects of Confucius.*

NOTES TO PAGES 62–63 **223**

193. In the *Sūtrâlaṃkāra-śāstra,* for instance, a "verse on the four bests" (K. *sa cheil kye*) reads,

> Health is the best wealth,
> contentment the best riches,
> friendship the best relationship,
> nirvāṇa the best joy.
> (Muller, *Digital Dictionary of Buddhism*)

194. For a discussion of the notion and the implications of male friendship in premodern East Asia, see the chapter "Friendship" in Lee, *Celebration of Continuity,* 144–173.

195. This perhaps willful omission of the Ch'oes has already been noted in Kim, *P'ahan chip chŏsul-ŭi yŏksajŏk paegyŏng,* 192. For a convincing reading of Yi Illo's literature in relation to the Ch'oe house, and of *P'ahan chip* as a work of criticism, see Chŏng, "*P'ahan chip* p'an'gak-e issŏsŏ-ŭi ch'ŏmsak munje-wa kŭ munhak sajŏk ŭiŭi." For the relationship between the Ch'oe clan and *Pohan chip* by Ch'oe Cha, who appears to have had no dissenting views whatsoever with regard to the political power structures of the mid-thirteenth century, see Kim, "Ch'oe Cha-ŭi Pohan chip chŏsul tonggi," 147–148.

196. *Pohan chip* 2:27 says, "In mid-summer of the year *kimi* [1199], the pomegranate trees stood in full bloom at the house of Master Chin'gong [Ch'oe Ch'unghŏn], and so the master had invited the Hallim [academician] Yi Illo, the Hallim [academician] Kim Kŭkki, the official retained in the academy [K. *yuwŏn*] Yi Tamji, the rectifier [K. *sajik*] Ham Sun, [. . .] Yi Kyubo and others, and asked them to rhapsodize on the trees." Pak, *Yŏkchu Pohan chip,* 281. This information can also be found in the twenty-first entry of *Paegun sosŏl.* See Rutt, "The White Cloud Essays," 23. For the possible motives behind these poetry gatherings, see Kim, "Ch'oe Cha-ŭi Pohan chip chŏsul tonggi," 146.

197. According to Ch'oe Ch'unghŏn's biography in *Koryŏsa* (vol. 129), "One day, [Ch'oe] Ch'unghŏn wanted to go to Hŭngwang Temple to celebrate in front of the statue of the Buddha, but then somebody tossed him an anonymously written letter which read, 'Yoil, the monk superintendent of Hŭngwang Temple, together with the secretary director [K. Chungsŏryŏng] Tu Kyŏngsŭng [d. 1197] have conspired to murder [Ch'oe] Ch'unghŏn.' Thus he refrained from going [to Hŭngwang-sa]." As a consequence, the Great Sŏn Master Yŏndam and about a dozen other monks were sent into exile to Yŏngnam, and it may well be that Yoil was one of them. Chŏng Sŏnmo hypothesizes that Yi Illo may have had knowledge of the monks' and scholarofficials' plans to assassinate Ch'oe Ch'unghŏn. See Chŏng, "*P'ahan chip* p'an'gak-e issŏsŏ-ŭi ch'ŏmsak munje-wa kŭ munhak sajŏk ŭiŭi," 20.

198. Yi Illo speaks highly of several archenemies of Ch'oe Ch'unghŏn, not only his uncle Yoil, but also family members of Hŭijong, who tried to have Ch'oe killed in 1211 and was subsequently ousted. See 3:33.

224   NOTES TO PAGES 63–65

199. Next to Chŏng Yŏryŏng from 1:1, the only military official who is mentioned in (the extant version of) *P'ahan chip* is Pak Kongsŭp (d. 1196), a military official during Myŏngjong's reign who served under Yi Ŭimin. He is spoken of in a rather unfavorable way as an impoverished, almost pathetic drunkard who begs the monks of Yŏngt'ong Temple for wine and is eventually deceived by them. Pak fought for Yi Ŭimin when Ch'oe Ch'unghŏn rose to oust Yi in 1196. At the end of the battles with the forces of the Ch'oe Clan, Pak Kongsŭp committed suicide. Earlier, Pak had served as a member of the Kyŏllyong Army (K. Kyŏllyonggun), a special palace-guard unit commanded directly by the king.

200. Rogers, "National Consciousness in Medieval Korea," 165.

201. *SHC* 1:2a.

202. Ch'oe U's afterword is contained in the sixth volume of the 1713 Chosŏn dynasty woodblock-print edition of *Sŏha chip*. *SHC* 6:29a–b. Harvard Yenching Library owns volumes 4 and 5 of the original 1222 version of *Sŏha chip*, http://nrs .harvard.edu/urn-3:FHCL:2248688. Interestingly, Ch'oe U's *husŏ* here features at the end of volume 5. I would like to thank Professor Sun Joo Kim of Harvard University for pointing out this *Sŏha chip* version to me.

203. As an entry in *Chungjong sillok* (thirty-seventh year [1542], seventh month, twenty-seventh day) shows, Im Ch'un's posthumous manuscripts (K. *yugo*) were circulating in sixteenth-century Korea. Regarding the transmission of the *Sŏha chip*, Yi Ik (1681–1763) in *Sŏngho sasŏl* (Sŏngho's discourses on the minute) tells the following interesting story:

> The courtesy name of Sŏha Im Ch'un was Kiji, and he was the nephew of Koryŏ dynasty academician Im Chongbi. There is his collection [of writings] in six volumes, in the preface to which Yi Illo wrote, "In the final year of King Ŭijong, his entire family met disaster, and only [Kiji] himself barely managed to escape. He fled to a place of refuge in the southland, but a few years later he did return to the capital, gathering together from the embers what was left [of his family's former possessions]. He had made up his mind that he would wipe clean the shame of three failed attempts [in the civil service examinations], but in the end he could not make a name for himself. In the Country East of the Sea, there has only been a single person who wore a commoner's clothes and still stood out in his age." Later his collection [of writings] eventually vanished and was not transmitted. Recently, however, at Unmun Temple in Ch'ŏngdo, there was the monk Indam. In a dream he encountered a Daoist who pointed with his finger [toward a certain spot], saying, "If you dig right there, you can obtain a rare treasure of the world." He awoke and did as he had been told — [after digging a hole in the ground] he obtained a bronze stupa; in that stupa was a bronze vessel, and from inside that vessel he obtained the *Sŏha chip*. Words were inscribed on the stupa, saying it was something that the monk Tamin had stored. So the one who stored it there was Tamin, and the one who dug it up there was Indam — how strange! (*Sŏngho sasŏl* 29:22b)

NOTES TO PAGES 65–71 **225**

204. One should note that the Ch'oes had employed – and thereby were shown to have valued – Yi Illo himself, and Ch'oe U may therefore not have seen the need to select one of Yi's own collections, *P'ahan chip* or perhaps the now lost *Ŭndae chip, Hu chip,* or *Ssangmyŏng-jae chip,* to be printed and preserved.

205. An excellent study dealing with this very issue of the favor-currying, appeasing stance of the Ch'oe clan vis-à-vis the civil officials, as well as the Ch'oe leaders' influence on the production of literature composed on their command and in their favor and support, especially *Pohan chip* (which was written by Ch'oe order during the Mongol invasions when the Ch'oes' power was in danger and the military leaders were under pressure from the civil officials to move the capital from Kanghwa Island back to Kaesŏng), is Kim, "Ch'oe Cha-ŭi Pohan chip chŏsul tonggi."

206. See Tian, "Collections (*ji* 集)."

207. As evidenced in 1:5, Yi was able to show apparently well-structured stacks of his compositions upon request.

P'ahan chip—Fascicle 1

1. "Composed in writing" here is a translation of *ch'an* (C. *zhuan*).

2. *Chwa kanŭi taebu* (C. *zuo jianyi daifu*). In China, grand master of remonstrance was one of the categories of prestigious officials called remonstrance officials or speaking officials, whose principal function was to attend and advise the emperor, and especially to remonstrate with him about what they considered improper conduct or policy. Hucker, *Dictionary of Official Titles,* 148.

3. Pomun-gak, which was built by King Yejong, was located on the palace grounds in Kaesŏng and served as a royal library. It primarily stored imperial edicts of Song dynasty emperors. See 1:18.

4. *Chijego* were academicians who assisted in the important task of drafting royal pronouncements.

5. In *Koryŏsa* the entry on Chinju (vol. 57, *chi* 11, *chiri* 2, Kyŏngsangdo, Chinjumok) reads,

> The Chinju region [K. Chinju-*mok*] originally was Kŏyŏl Castle [K. Kŏyŏlsŏng] of Paekche (another name for it was Kŏt'a). In the second year of King Munmu of Silla [662] it was seized [by Silla] and established as a prefecture. In the fourth year of King Sinmun [684] they divided Kŏt'a Prefecture [...]; under King Kyŏngdŏk, [the region's name] was changed into Kangju, under King Hyegong it was again changed to Ch'ŏngju, and under T'aejo it was changed back to Kangju. The twelve regions [K. *mok*] were first established in the second year of Sŏngjong [983], and [Kang]ju was one of them. [...] An alternative name was Chin'gang ([an appellation] fixed during Sŏngjong's reign); also, it was called Ch'ŏngju; also, it was called Chinyang.

226 NOTES TO PAGES 71–72

In this initial entry, Yi Illo calls Chinyang an "ancient imperial capital" (K. *ko chedo*). He may have done so because Chinyang served as the capital of Koryŏng Kaya, one of the six chiefdoms of the Kaya Confederacy (K. Kaya yŏnmaeng) mentioned in *Samguk yusa* and *Samguk sagi*. More importantly, however (as was elaborated upon in the introduction), Chinyang became the *sigŭp* of the Ch'oe family in 1205 and thus was synonymous with military rule during the time when Yi finished his *P'ahan chip*.

6. This sentence on the scenic beauty of Chinyang also appears in the *Sinjŭng tongguk yŏji sŭngnam*, where it says, "Picturesque scenery [K. *hyŏngsŭng*] [of Chinju-mok]: in Yŏngnam it is the very best. [Commentary:] In [*P'ahan*] *chip* by Yi Illo it says, 'Chinyang, the scenic beauty of its glens and mountains is the very best in Yŏngnam.'" *STYS* 30:2b. Yŏngnam refers to the area of Kyŏngsang in the southeast of the Korean Peninsula.

7. "Minister of state" is a translation of *sangguk* (C. *xiangguo*). In China, from Tang times it was an unofficial reference to the highest-ranking officials of the central government. See Hucker, *Dictionary of Official Titles*, 232. *Sangguk* appears, for instance, in the title of the collected writings of Yi Kyubo, *Tongguk Yi Sangguk chip* (Collected works of Minister of State Yi [Kyubo] of Korea).

8. Yi Chijŏ was principal graduate in the civil service examinations in 1120. He served as *tong chi gonggŏ*, "associate examination administrator," in the civil service examinations of 1138, as well as *chi gonggŏ*, "examination administrator," in the civil service administrations of 1140. Furthermore, Yi Chijŏ held several high offices: for instance, in 1140 he became *Yebu sangsŏ* (C. *Libu shangshu*), minister of rites. He also went to the Jurchen Jin dynasty as an envoy. He is known to have been an adversary of Yi Chagyŏm, who famously staged a revolt against King Injong and tried to usurp power. Later, together with Kim Pusik, Yi Chijŏ became known for opposing the geomancer and monk Myoch'ŏng during the rebellion of 1135 (although, as Breuker points out, Yi Chijŏ's position toward Myoch'ŏng was not always unambiguous; Breuker, *Establishing a Pluralist Society*, 415). Yi positioned himself against the monk during a time when Myoch'ŏng was very powerful at Injong's court [...], a time in which the pro-Myoch'ŏng atmosphere in the capital seems to have been extremely intimidating. Breuker, *Establishing a Pluralist Society*, 415. Yi Chijŏ's upright character, his refusal to subordinate himself under crooked leaders, and his opposition to some of the most politically powerful people of his time is vividly portrayed in his biography in *Koryŏsa*, parts of which read:

> Chijŏ, his courtesy name was Chago. He liked reading books, and when he composed texts it seemed as if he had worked them out beforehand. He was chosen as the winner of the civil service examinations and went straight to the Hallim Academy. At the beginning of the reign of Injong he was appointed right censor [K. *u chŏngŏn*]. At the time, his discussions were public-spirited and correct, and [because of this] he came into conflict with the grand councilor of that age. Hence, he was transferred to the position of palace eunuch ceremonial secretary [K. *chŏnjung naegŭpsa*] and had to leave to serve [as surveillance commissioner] in Sŏhae Province.

NOTES TO PAGE 72 **227**

At the time, [Yi] Chagyŏm had taken charge of the dynasty, and those lusting for personal profit vied with each other to place themselves at his disposal—[Yi] Chijŏ alone [did not join in] and thus cannot be compared to that lot [of opportunistic traitors]. [Yi] Chagyŏm's subordinates were scattered throughout the provinces and districts, vying with each other to get a hold of riches and bribes, but [Yi] Chijŏ strictly prohibited [such behavior by government officials]. [Yi] Chagyŏm hated him for it, and [Yi Chijŏ] was demoted to the position of commissioner of P'yŏngju. When [Yi] Chagyŏm was subdued, [Yi Chijŏ] was summoned back [to the capital] and promoted several times, [eventually] becoming royal diarist [K. *kigŏju*]. When Myoch'ŏng and Paek Suhan [d. 1135; a court astronomer about whom almost nothing is known; Breuker, *Establishing a Pluralist Society*, 413] conspired to get close to the king, when by means of sorcery they bewitched the masses, [Yi] Chijŏ alone deeply reproached them, saying, "This lot will definitely harm the country."

In *P'ahan chip*, Yi Chijŏ is mentioned again in 2:5.

9. The term *sangjae hyang* (C. *sangzi xiang*), "mulberry and catalpa home," derives from the third stanza of the ode "Xiao pan" from the *Shijing*: "Even the mulberry trees and the *tsze* (*zi*) must be regarded with reverence; But no one is to be looked up to like a father; no one is to be depended on like a mother. Have I not a connection with the hairs [of my father]? Did I not dwell in the womb [of my mother]? O Heaven who gave me birth! How was it at such an inauspicious time?" Legge, *Chinese Classics*, 4:337. In the very influential commentary on the *Shijing*, the *Shi jizhuan* (Collected commentaries to the books of poetry) by Zhu Xi (1130–1200), the relevant passage in the explanation to this poem reads, "*Sang* and *zi* are two trees. If one plants them beside the wall of every household with five acres and leaves them for sons and grandsons, they will give them silkworms [for clothes] and food. [...]" Zhu Xi, *Shi jizhuan*, 140. This explanation by Zhu can in turn be read as being based on *Mengzi* 7A 22.2: "If one plants a mulberry tree beside the wall of every household with five acres, so that the wives can spin silk from the caterpillars, then the elderly will be able to wear silk clothes." Van Norden, *Mengzi*, 177. The mulberry and catalpa trees are thus metonyms of one's homeland and parental devotion.

10. This poem by Chŏng Yŏryŏng was referred to and quoted in later works from the Chosŏn dynasty. We find it, for instance, in the aforementioned entry on Chinju in *Sinjŭng tongguk yŏji sŭngnam*. The poem is also in *TMS* 19:21a–b.

11. Huihong, styled Juefan, was a Buddhist monk and Chinese Chan master of the Northern Song dynasty, who is known to have been a friend of Huang Tingjian. Huihong was a major proponent of "lettered Chan" (C. *wenzi chan*), which valorized belles lettres, and especially poetry, in the practice of Chan Buddhism. Because of Huihong's close ties to famous literati officials of his day, and particularly with the statesman and Buddhist patron Zhang Shangying (1043–1122), his own career was subject to many of the same political repercussions as those of his associates; indeed, Huihong himself was imprisoned, defrocked, and exiled multiple times in his life

228   NOTES TO PAGE 72

when his literati colleagues were purged. Compounding his problems, Huihong also suffered along with many other monks during the severe Buddhist persecution that occurred during the reign of Emperor Huizong (r. 1100–1125). Even amid these trying political times, however, Huihong managed to maintain both his monastic vocation and his productive literary career. Given his literary penchant, it is no surprise that Huihong was a prolific author. His works include the *Chanlin sengbao zhuan* (Chronicles of the Saṃgha Jewel in the Chan Grove), a collection of biographies of about a hundred eminent Chan masters important in the development of the lettered Chan, or the *Linjian lu* (Anecdotes from the Grove [of Chan]), completed in 1107 and offering a record of Huihong's own encounters with fellow monks and literati and his reflections on Buddhist practice. Buswell and Lopez, *Princeton Dictionary of Buddhism*, 401.

12. The miscellany collection *Lengzhai yehua*, put together in 1121, is written in the brush-note style and is comprised of ten fascicles. It covers a wide array of topics and themes, but most entries deal with poetry and poetic criticism. Each chapter of *Lengzhai yehua* has a title, but these often have nothing to do with the content—this might be the result of later revisions and changes. These revisions or alterations of the original text, the fact that Huihong quoted many poets from his lifetime, and the fact that he included works that were later considered to be bordering on forgery eventually led to *Lengzhai yehua* being regarded as a rather unoriginal work. This negative perception of the collection is addressed here, for Yi Illo points out that the majority of the *Lengzhai yehua*'s content constitutes original, innovative compositions by Huihong. A recent in-depth English-language study on *Lengzhai yehua* is Babcock, "Aesthetics of Non-Discrimination." Another study dealing with Huihong is Keyworth, "Transmitting the Lamp of Learning." Keyworth discusses *Lengzhai yehua* in section 7.6, "Treatises on Poetic Criticism" (469–480). A recent Korean-language study on the circulation of *Lengzhai yehua* in premodern Korea is Ryu Hwajŏng, "*Naengjae yahwa*-ŭi kungnae hwaryong yangsang," *Minjok munhwa* 61 (2022): 173–197.

13. *Ch'uljin* (C. *chuchen*), "rise from the [mundane] dust," is a figurative expression for excellence.

14. Against the backdrop of this sentence it may be assumed that Yi got to see a handwritten copy of *Lengzhai yehua* produced in Korea. Alternatively, he may have seen a later Chinese copy of the work when he was visiting the Jurchen Jin dynasty in 1182.

15. In the relevant secondary literature, it is stated that Huihong wrote *Lengzhai yehua* and another collection entitled *Tianchu jinluan* (Forbidden cutlets from the imperial kitchen; see Buswell and Lopez, *Princeton Dictionary of Buddhism*, 401). Yet the *Yunxi ji* mentioned in this *P'ahan chip* entry must also have been a collection of poetic works by this author. Yunxi was a nickname of Huihong (see Babcock, "Aesthetics of Non-Discrimination," 78), certainly deriving from the fact that he was from the prefecture of Yunzhou (modern Yifeng) and was a monk from Shimen Monastery in Yunxi, Jiangxi Province. In the nineteenth volume of the *Junzhai dushu zhi* (Records of books read in my studio in the province), the oldest surviving Chinese

book catalogue of a private library, compiled by the Southern Song collector and scholar Chao Gongwu (ca. 1105–1180), we find the entry "Hong Juefan's *Yunxi ji* in ten volumes." Thus, not only *Lengzhai yehua* but other collections by this Northern Song dynasty writer were obviously available in early-thirteenth-century Korea. There exists another, more famous collection by the title of *Yunxi ji,* by the Song dynasty literatus Li Mixun (1089–1153). However, against the backdrop of the entire episode—which critically deals with the literary value of different collections by Huihong—it does not make sense to understand the title *Yunxi ji* as referring to the collected writings of Li Mixun.

16. The source here says *wazhu* (K. *waju*), "betting for tiles," which is a term deriving from "Dasheng" (Fathoming life) of *Zhuangzi:* "When you're betting for tiles in an archery contest, you shoot with skill. When you're betting for fancy belt buckles, you worry about your aim. And when you're betting for real gold, you're a nervous wreck. Your skill is the same in all three cases—but because one prize means more to you than another, you let outside considerations weigh on your mind." Watson, *Complete Works of Zhuangzi.* At this point, the reference to the passage from *Zhuangzi* could imply that Huihong, while possessing extraordinary talents, in Yi Illo's view simply tried too hard to create great poetry in *Yunxi ji.* Yi thus seems to imply that self-imposed pressure diminishes the quality of literary writing.

17. The original proverb, "Knowing someone by his reputation isn't as good as meeting him face-to-face" (C. *wenming buru jianmian*) is here turned upside down.

18. This entry is significant insofar as it sheds a tiny light on the question as to which kind of books, or "transporters of literary knowledge," must have been circulating in Kaesŏng in the late twelfth and early thirteenth centuries. Yi Illo obviously had easy access to copies of relatively recent works from Northern Song China, and one may surmise that his reading of Chinese *sihua* collections such as *Lengzhai yehua* inspired him to create such a work of poems and stories of his own.

19. Pan Dalin (n.d.), a poet of the Northern Song. His courtesy name was Binlao; his literary name was Keshan.

20. Xie of Linchuan refers to Xie Yi (1066–1113), courtesy name Wuyi, pen name Xitang.

21. As can be seen in these lines, although Yi Illo valued *Lengzhai yehua* as a structural model and as a source for especially Su Shi's poetry, he is quite critical vis-à-vis Huihong's abilities, even going so far as to simply supplement and thereby "improve" the Chinese poet's work. For a discussion of the relationship between the works of Huihong and Yi Illo, see Sim, "*P'ahan chip*-ŭi yŏksajŏk sŏnggyŏk."

22. Chongyang (K. Chungyang), also known as Chongjiu (K. Chunggu), is the "Double Yang" or "Double Ninth Festival," which falls on the ninth day of the ninth month of the lunar calendar. It is a festival during which people are meant to appreciate and enjoy autumn, especially autumn leaves and chrysanthemums.

23. *Ch'ugwang* (C. *qiuguang*), "autumn light," here means the light of the moon. Only the first line of this poem, i.e., "Wind and rain filled the city, the Double Yang was near," features in an entry in the fourth volume of *Lengzhai yehua.* The next three lines of the quatrain were supplemented by Yi Illo. The relevant *Lengzhai yehua* entry

230   NOTES TO PAGE 72

on the emergence of the line in question reads, "Pan Dalin of Huangzhou was skilled in poetry [and he had written] many beautiful lines. Nevertheless, he was very poor. Dongpo [Su Shi] and Shangu [Huang Tingjian] were very fond of [Pan's poetry]. Xie Wuyi of Linchuan asked him in a letter, 'Are there any new compositions of yours?' The reply letter by Pan read, 'Autumn has come, and for each of the things of the scene I had a beautiful line. Regrettably, I was obstructed by mundane vapors. See, yesterday I lay with a pure mind, listening to the sounds of the forest [outside my window] as it was swaying in wind and rain. Delighted, I rose and wrote the following on the wall, 'Wind and rain fill the city, the Double Yang is near.' [As I was about to finish the poem,] a tax man suddenly came rushing in, eventually ruining my ideas. Hence, I had to stop, and this is the only line I can respectfully send to you.' All who heard this smiled at the way he had his head in the clouds."

24. The items traditionally classed as *munbang sabo* (C. *wenfang sibao*), also known as *munbang sau* (C. *wenfang siyou*), "four friends of a scholar's studio," are paper (K. *chi*), brush (K. *p'il*), ink stone (K. *yŏn*), and ink (K. *muk*). It is unclear when exactly these four writing implements came to be regarded as a coherent group of "friends," but the earliest treatise to deal with them as such is a text by Su Yijian (957–995), *Wenfang sipu* (Four guides to the scholar's study), which has a postface by Su dated 986. This text collects extracts from various sources that provide evidence of the history, manufacture, use and appreciation of the items. Ink, paper, and ink stone are treated in one *juan* (volume), while the brush is treated in two, presumably because of the addition of a section on brush force, dealing with calligraphy. Wright, "Chinese Decorated Letter Papers," 97. The expression "four treasures of a scholar's studio" was used in Korea until the end of the premodern period, as can be seen in an entry in Yi Yuwŏn's *Imha p'ilgi* (vol. 29) entitled "Homuk koje" (The ancient manufacture of fine ink), where it says, "Among the 'four treasures of a scholar's studio,' ink is used a great deal, but a good product is not easy to obtain. Li Tinggui of the Song dynasty was so skilled in the manufacture of ink, his ink wouldn't fall apart even if it was immersed in water for an entire month. This product was worth being considered precious."

25. The source here says *kyŏngsa* (C. *jingshi*), which is one appellation for the metropolitan area of Kaesŏng, the capital of Koryŏ. Other names include *kyŏngsŏng* and *kyŏngdo*.

26. Maengsŏng is present-day Maengsan-gun, Maengsan Lesser County, in P'yŏngan Province. It was also referred to as Maengju. During Koryŏ times, Maengju was known for its ink production. In the *Xuanhe fengshi gaoli tujing* (Xuanhe commissioner's illustrated account of Koryŏ; vol. 23, "Zasu 2," "Tuchan") by Xu Jing (1091–1153; a Song envoy dispatched to Koryŏ in 1123), Maengju is mentioned as a place renowned for the manufacture of ink: "The ink made of pine soot from Maengju is considered the most valuable, but the color is dull and contains little glue. It is still full of sand and grit." Vermeersch, *Chinese Traveler*, 162. Yi Illo was appointed magistrate of Maengsŏng in the seventh year of the reign of King Sinjong, 1203. As is hinted at in 2:21, his appointment to this post in a faraway northern region may be understood as a form of political exile, and it certainly is no coincidence that in the

NOTES TO PAGES 72–73 **231**

episode at hand he relates this time of quasi banishment during the early years of the Ch'oe regime with the fabrication of ink, for we can see the very same in the case of Su Shi, who also took up ink making and began to write poetry and colophones on the production of inksticks as the very foundation of literary invention during his own time of political exile in Huangzhou between 1080 and 1084. In his wonderful article on Su Shi's ink poetry, Thomas Kelly writes that "poets' autonomy, Su came to believe during his experiences of censorship and banishment, depends on defending their custodianship of the basic instruments that make writing possible. [...] After Su Shi, an inkstick was no longer simply a tool for the making of literature but a contested subject and substrate of literary art." Kelly, "Death of an Artisan," 317. Through this entry and the following one, Yi Illo establishes a connection between himself and *P'ahan chip* with the life, views, and poetry of his role model Su Shi.

27. The source here says *fu* (K. *pu*), which means a tally given to officials dispatched to the countryside as an object representing royal order.

28. *Todokpu,* "protectorate" or "area command," designating a regional military jurisdiction and its headquarters.

29. *Ŏmuk* (C. *yomu*) are inksticks for royal use. The measuring unit given in the source is *chŏng* (C. *ting*), which is a measure word for sticklike objects. Yi is to deliver five thousand *chŏng* of inksticks.

30. The source here merely says *sŭng* (C. *cheng*), "ride" or "drive," which could also imply that Yi Illo rode a horse to Mengju.

31. *Hu* (K. *kok*), "bushel," is a dry volume measurement. Some understand it to have corresponded to half a *dan,* whereas others believe it to have equaled 1 *dan* (equal to 10 *dou*). One *hu* thus equaled 10 *dou* and would amount to 20 liters. Major, *Heaven and Earth in Early Han Thought,* 932.

32. Pine-soot inksticks (K. *songyŏn muk;* C. *songyan mo*) are made from burned pine twigs or roots. Pine soot was traditionally the favorite pigment in ink, and pine-soot inksticks were considered the highest-quality inksticks. An ink-making formula attributed to Wei Dan (179–253) calls for the use of fine and pure soot, pounded and strained to remove any adhering vegetative substances. In Ming times, it is said that nine-tenths of all ink was made from pine soot and one-tenth from oil lampblack. Tsien, *Collected Writings on Chinese Culture,* 117.

33. *Shanteng* is fine paper made of rattan. The origin of the use of rattan for papermaking can be traced back to the third century at Shangxi (modern Shengxian, Zhejiang), where rattan plants were said to have spread over hundreds of miles on the mountains along the Shangxi River. This old paper made of rattan from Shanxi came to be known as Shanteng, "rattan paper of Shanxi." Rattan paper became most popular in the Tang dynasty, and the area of its production was greatly extended beyond Shanxi. Rattan paper — described as smooth, durable, with fine texture, and in different colors — was selected for documents, bookmaking, calligraphy, and other uses. After the Song, there was a gradual decline in the use of rattan paper. There were several reasons for this. One was the depletion of the material, and another was the growing use of bamboo, which replaced rattan and hemp as the chief raw material for papermaking. Tsien, *Collected Writings on Chinese Culture,* 76–77. Extant records

232 NOTES TO PAGE 73

show that rattan paper was also used in Koryŏ. For instance, in *Xuanhe fengshi gaoli tujing* (vol. 29, "Kongjang 2") it says that for the production of white folding fans (K. *paekchŏpsŏn*), rattan paper (K. *tŭngji*) was dried and stretched over sticks of bamboo.

34. *Qizhu*, the "bamboo of Qi," refers to a species of very fine bamboo produced at Qizhou (modern Qichun). The bamboo was used for mats, flutes, and walking canes.

35. *Shujin*, the "brocade of Shu," is a high-quality brocade originally produced in the Chengdu region in Sichuan.

36. *Wuling* is a thin damask silk.

37. *Mei nong* was written by Li Shen (772–846), a high official and noted poet of Tang. He served as chancellor during the reign of Emperor Wuzong (r. 840–846). In the following, the final couplet of this poem is cited.

38. In the translation by Burton Watson, this poem reads:

He hoes the grain under a midday sun,
sweat dripping down on the soil beneath the grain.
Who realizes that the food in the food bowl,
every last morsel of it, is bought with such toil?
(Mair, *Shorter Columbia Anthology*, 111–112)

39. Zhichuan is the courtesy name of Ge Hong (283–343), a Daoist of the Jin dynasty. Ge Hong, who was also called Baopuzi, is today best known for his work in the field of alchemy as well as his interest in techniques of longevity. Ge Hong's contribution to alchemy and early chemistry is contained in *Baopuzi neipian* (Inner chapters of the master who embraces simplicity). The sash can here be understood as the insignia of his position as an administrator.

40. Cinnabar grains play a role in preparing elixirs of immortality. Ge Hong had been offered high positions several times during his life, but he always refused. Yet when he heard that the area of Jiaozhi (north of modern Hanoi, Vietnam) was rich in cinnabar, in 333 Ge requested to serve as magistrate of Goulou. The emperor granted his wish, but eventually Ge was held up in Guangzhou by a regional inspector who persuaded him to stay there. Ge lived in reclusion on Mount Luofu until his death in 364. See Li, *Geschichte des chinesischen Daoismus*, 112. By referring to Ge Hong, Yi Illo appears to allude to the fact that he himself set out to take charge of a serious administrative position as magistrate of Maengju, but that he eventually ended up doing something entirely different, similar to Ge Hong, who set out to Goulou but ended up in Guangzhou.

41. The source says *kyŏngsa* (C. *jingshe*), "startled snake," a term that compares cursive calligraphic writing with the swift, gliding movements of a "startled snake sliding into the high grass" (K. *kyŏngsa ip ch'o*). The term appears again in the poem of the following entry. At this point, Yi Illo seems to point out that he has not lost all his fine writing abilities during this time of hard manual labor.

42. The source says *chwabu* (C. *zuofu*), which means the left half of a tally given to officials dispatched by the court to the provinces to carry out certain civil or mili-

NOTES TO PAGE 73   **233**

tary orders. This system originated in the Tang dynasty. With regard to this, the Tang Code says, "Tallies and ensigns both come from the Imperial Chancellery. Tallies are made of bronze. The left half of the tally is kept in the imperial palace while the right half is kept in the provinces by the people who are in charge of tallies. When there is some matter that must be carried out and the tallies matched, the emperor is to give out the left half of the tally in order that it may be joined with the right half." Johnson, *T'ang Code*, 99.

43. The poem can also be found in *TMS* 20:1b. This *P'ahan chip* entry has been partially translated under the title "Yi Illo: The Four Treasures of the Studio" by Hugh H. W. Kang and Edward Shultz. See Lee, *Sourcebook of Korean Civilization*, 1:309–310.

44. Kim Saeng (b. 711), courtesy name Chisŏ, was also known by his nickname, Ku. He was considered the most refined calligrapher of ancient Korea, yet no original examples of his work have survived. A stele preserved in Kyŏngbok Palace bears an inscription carved in the style of his artful running script. It was dedicated by Tamnok to his fellow monk Nanggong in 954. See Pratt and Rutt, *Korea*, 216; Lee, *New History of Korea*, 88. Kim Saeng's biography in *Samguk sagi* (vol. 48) reads,

> Kim Saeng's parents were of humble descent, and his genealogy is unknown. He was born in the second year of the Jingyun period [of Tang emperor Ruizong; 710–712]. From an early age he was skilled in writing, and for his entire life he never studied any other kind of art. Even when he was past the age of eighty, he still held the brush and never quit. Clerical script, draft script — in everything he reached a spirit-like level. Even today [in mid-Koryŏ times], original traces [of his calligraphy] can be found almost everywhere, and the scholars transmit them, considering them precious pieces. During the Chongning period [of Emperor Huizong of Song; 1102–1106], Academician Hong Kwan [d. 1126; see 3:19] followed an emissary to Song China, eventually lodging in Bianjing. At the time, the academicians awaiting orders [C. *hanlin daizhao*] Yang Qiu and Li Ge, having received the emperor's command, arrived at the hostel [where Hong Kwan was staying]. They wrote something on the margin of a painting, whereupon Hong Kwang took out a scroll carrying Kim Saeng's draft script and showed it to them. Greatly astonished, the two [Chinese academicians] exclaimed, "We really didn't expect to see original calligraphy written by the hand of [the Jin dynasty master-calligrapher] Wang Youjun [Wang Xizhi, 307–365] today!" "But that's not what this is," Hong Kwan replied. "This here was actually written by Kim Saeng, a man of our own Silla dynasty." The two [Chinese] scholars smiled wryly at him, saying, "Under heaven, how could there be any such marvelous writing that wasn't [Wang] Youjun's?" Hong Kwan repeatedly told them [that it was, in fact, the calligraphic writing of the Korean Kim Saeng], but they did not believe him to the end.

Regarding Kim Saeng, Yi Kyubo wrote,

234 NOTES TO PAGE 73

Generally, when it comes to the one person who is considered number one in our dynasty [in terms of calligraphy], him who is in no way different to Yishao [Wang Xizhi] [...] This number one, who might he be? It's Kim Saeng and no one else. This man, he had the brush of a spirit [K. *sinp'il,* "divine brush"]. How come I say that? Well, the following has been transmitted in the world: "Early on, someone suddenly appeared before Kim Saeng and asked him to copy the *Dishi-jing* [Indra *sūtra*]. When the copy was finished, [Kim Saeng] asked him where he had come from, and that person answered, 'I'm an agent of [the King of Heaven] Indra, and [Indra himself] commanded me to ask you to copy this. That's why I came here.' And then, suddenly, he vanished.' Also, he wrote the wooden board of Anyang Temple. Over a span of several years, the building onto which this wooden board was nailed leaned over toward the south, and so [Kim Saeng] was asked to write something for the northern side of the building. [...] Thus it is appropriate to take Kim Saeng as someone who possessed first-rate divine gifts." (*TYSC* 11:3b–4a)

45. Kyerim was a metonymic toponym for the Silla dynasty, based on a forest near the palace of the Silla court in Kyŏngju.

46. *Ch'osŏ* (C. *caoshu*), "draft script" or "grass script," and *haengsŏ* (C. *xingshu*), "running script." *Ch'osŏ* and *haengsŏ* were predominantly used in the writing of poetry and letters, and Korean calligraphers such as Kim Saeng evolved more individual styles of their own. In the Koryŏ period calligraphic art was stimulated by the court patronage of Buddhism and copying of scriptures. Calligraphy was taught at the Sŏnggyun'gwan. One of the greatest exponents in this period was Yi Am (1297–1364). Pratt and Rutt, *Korea,* 33.

47. *Chunhuage fatie* or *Chunhuage tie* is a comprehensive collection of model calligraphies contained in the library of Emperor Taizong (r. 976–997) of Song. The collection comprises hundreds of ancient calligraphies owned by Taizong. Ordered to copy the calligraphic works was Wang Zhu (ca. 928–969), an experienced calligrapher, and these were cut in wooden boards and stone, to serve as "model calligraphies" (C. *fatie*). Taizong ordered rubbings, which were put up in ten volumes in 992. The collection features many pieces by Wang Xizhi and his son Wang Xianzhi (344–386). Starr, *Black Tigers,* 26. Kim Saeng's calligraphic style is at this point said to be more innovative and masterful than any of the models contained in the authoritative Chinese collection.

48. The source says *ponjo,* "present dynasty" or "our dynasty." Today this entity is known under the name Koryŏ, but Yi Illo does not use the word "Koryŏ" at all in *P'ahan chip*. Instead, we find Ponjo, Haedong ([Country] East of the Sea), or Tongguk (Eastern Country).

49. Hwaŏm taesa (C. Huayan dashi). *Taesa* can here be understood as the title of a high monk of the Hwaŏm School.

50. There exist no other records mentioning a great Hwaŏm master by the name of Kyŏnghyŏk.

NOTES TO PAGE 73   **235**

51. Ipchi is the courtesy name of Kim Tonjung. He became principal graduate in the state examinations of 1144 and served in high government positions such as palace censor. Kim Tonjung is inseparably linked with the military officers' revolt of 1170, during which he and countless other civil officials were killed. See, e.g., Lee, *New History of Korea,* 139. Kim Tonjung was well versed in poetry, and some of his works are contained in *Tongmunsŏn* and *Sinjŭng tongguk yŏji sŭngnam* (sec. "Kyŏngjubu"). His son, Kim Kunsu, is mentioned in 1:9.

52. Ch'ubu can here be understood as an alternate name of the Chungch'uwŏn or Chungch'ubu, which has been rendered as Office of Ministers without Portfolio, or Security Council. The administrative structure of Koryŏ was built around the *samsŏng* (three chancelleries), i.e., the Chungsŏsŏng, the Munhasŏng, and the Sangsŏsŏng. Of these, the first two merged into a single organ called Chungsŏ Munhasŏng (Chancellery for State Affairs, or Directorate of Chancellors). Here, the officials made policy decisions and undersecretaries were entrusted with the functions of proposing policy and acting as censors. The third chancellery (Secretariat of State Affairs) was responsible for carrying out policy through the six boards subordinated to it that handled actual government administration. These were Personnel, Military Affairs, Taxation, Punishments, Rites, and Public Works. Another major organ of Koryŏ central government, ranking in importance with the three chancelleries, was the Chungch'uwŏn, or Chungch'ubu (from 1095 onward called the Ch'umirwŏn), which was also simply referred to as the [Chung]ch'ubu. It was established during the reign of Sŏngjong (r. 981–997) and its duties comprised the transmission of royal commands, the handling of urgent military matters, the protection of the palace, and the management of arms and weapons. See, e.g., Lee, *New History of Korea,* 114. At this point, Yi Illo implies that Kim Tonjung served at the Chungch'ubu, but there seems to be no textual evidence for this.

53. Zhong Yi (1023–1063) and Zhou Yue (n.d.), two Northern Song calligraphers from the eleventh century. Su Shi, with whom innovation emerged as a primary virtue in calligraphy, believed that his contemporary early Song calligraphers were unable to get beyond the studied approach. Su Shi especially criticized Zhong Yi and Zhou Yue for writing even cursive script slowly and painstakingly. Egan, *Word, Image, and Deed,* 275. Yet the sentence at hand, in which two Koryŏ calligraphers, Kyŏnghyŏk and Kim Tonjung, are portrayed as uninspired and inelegantly common, may primarily be understood as being based on a description of Zhong Yi and Zhou Yue in the second volume of *Laoxue an biji* (Notes from Laoxue Hut) by Lu You. In the relevant entry in *Laoxue an biji,* the earlier criticism by Su Shi is likewise referred to, for it says, "Zhong Yi had a name in calligraphy, but the predecessors mostly considered him common. However, in that respect he likewise matches Zhou Yue. Early on I also saw his *Feibai dazi shufu* [Several roles of large characters in the *feibai* (flying white) style]. It was made in a very skillful way, yet truly it couldn't escape the common."

54. King Ŭijong was the first son of King Injong. The year mentioned here is 1170, the year he was overthrown and sent into exile in the wake of the military coup d'état. According to traditional Confucian interpretations of the 1170 purge, the men

236 Notes to Pages 73-74

of the military thought the king lacking moral character and being misled by his ministers and eunuchs. Ŭijong, later historians also argued, not only was surrounded by incompetent and negligent flatterers and manipulators, but neglected his duties himself, placing too much emphasis on Buddhist practices and superstitions. This traditional interpretation of Ŭijong's role has, however, been challenged. Cf. Shultz, *Generals and Scholars*, 13–27; Shultz, "Military Revolt in Koryŏ." Hugh H. W. Kang and Edward Shultz's translation of the relevant *Koryŏsa* entry dealing with the military revolt of 1170 can be found in Lee, *Sourcebook of Korean Civilization*, 1:332–334.

55. Great Jin (C. *dajin*), the official title of the Jurchen Jin dynasty.

56. Neither the *Koryŏsa*, nor the *Koryŏsa chŏryo*, nor the *Jinshi* shed any light onto the questions as to who this Ge Yi was, or why he came to Koryŏ.

57. Ch'oe Tang was born in Ch'angwŏn (modern Ch'ŏrwŏn in Kangwŏn Province). Alongside his brother Ch'oe Sŏn he served in the State Council during the reign of King Myŏngjong. His biography in *Koryŏsa* reads,

> [Ch'oe] Tang, from youth he was intelligent and smart and excelled in literary composition. At the beginning of the reign of Myŏngjong he became a censor [K. *chŏngŏn*; officials who monitored documents passing to and from the throne for propriety of form and content]. When discussing certain matters he came into conflict with noble vassals, and lost his office. Eventually he was raised to become assistant office chief of the Ministry of Personnel [K. *ibu wŏnoerang*]. He went out to the southeastern province [K. *tongnam-do*] as surveillance commissioner [K. *anch'alsa*], and he had renown and achievements. He was promoted several times, reaching the position of assistant executive in political affairs. During the time of King Sinjong he served as vice director of the Royal Secretariat and Chancellery [K. *chungsŏsirang p'yŏngjangsa*] [...] Eventually he retired from his government position and lived in idleness, calling his study Ssangmyŏng-[jae], and together with his younger brother [...] Ch'oe Sŏn, [...] Chang Paengmok, [...] Ko Yŏngjung [1133–1208], [...] Paek Kwangsin, [...] Yi Chunch'ang [see also 3:20], [...] Hyŏn Tŏksu [d. 1215], [...] Yi Sejang, [...] Cho T'ong [see 1:13] and others he formed the Kirohoe. Together they were unfettered and content. At the time, people referred to them as "immortals upon the earth" [K. *chisang sŏn*]—their figures were carved in rock, and thus they were transmitted in the world. He passed away in the seventh year of King Hŭijong [1211] at the age of 77. His posthumous name was Chŏngan. [...] (*Koryŏsa*, vol. 99, "Yŏlchŏn" 12, *chesin*)

58. Dongshan, "East Mountains," here stands for Su Shi. It could be a reference to a note by Huang Tingjian, Su Shi's closest friend and disciple: "Though Master Dongpo wears ceremonial jade, his heart is tranquil like a withered tree. Though he stands in court, his mind is among the East Mountains." Yang, *Dialectics of Spontaneity*, 14.

59. The expression *hwaji wi pyŏng* (C. *huadi wei bing*), "a rice cake drawn on the

ground," derives from "Lu Yü zhuan" in volume 22 of *Sanguozhi* (Records of the Three Kingdoms): "Appointment should not be granted on the basis of fame, for fame is like a rice cake drawn on the ground — it cannot be eaten."

60. This is a line from the second of Su Shi's poems *Ciyun Mi Fu Er Wang shu bawei ershou* (Two poems matching Mi Fu's colophons to the Two Wang's Calligraphy).

61. Ch'oe Tang quoting Su Shi and then laughing off his loss of a precious, apparently authentic work of calligraphy (and his acquisition of an obvious fake) is in line with Su Shi's own stance toward art collecting. When Su's friend Wang Shen constructed a building to house his enormous collection of paintings and calligraphy, Su wrote an essay about it at Wang's request. In this essay it says,

> When I was young I was fond of calligraphy and painting. Whatever my family owned, I only worried we would lose. Whatever other men owned, I only worried they would not give me. Eventually, I had to laugh at myself, thinking: you slight riches and high position but give importance to calligraphy; you take life and death lightly but are serious about painting. Is not your thinking inverted and backward, causing you to lose all innate understanding of the order of things? From this time on I was no longer so fond of art works. When I found one that gave me pleasure I would occasionally keep it, but if someone carried it off I would not regret it. Calligraphy and painting became like the mists and clouds that pass before the eyes, or the song of the many birds that delight the ear. Of course you appreciate them as you encounter them. But once they have left, you do not give them another thought. After this, these two things became a constant source of pleasure for me but could no longer afflict me. (Translation in Egan, *Problem of Beauty*, 166)

In his chapter "Art Collecting and Its Discontents in the Lives of Su Shi, Wang Shen, and Mi Fu," Ronald Egan writes that Su Shi was also quite familiar with a situation similar to the one described in the *P'ahan chip* episode. For one of Su Shi's friends, the brilliant calligrapher and ingenious art collector Mi Fu, "was in the habit of borrowing famous paintings or calligraphy scrolls from acquaintances, making a close copy of them, and then returning the copy to the owner, keeping the original for himself. Some accounts say that the original owner might be asked to choose between the authentic piece and the copy, and that usually they could not tell which was which. 'In this way, Mi Fu came to acquire a great many ancient paintings and calligraphy from other men.' Su Shi is said to have known about Mi Fu's little game and, not surprisingly, disapproved." Egan, *Problem of Beauty,* 204. Thus, the issues raised in this entry about Ch'oe Tang — connoisseurship, collecting, ownership, authenticity, or the question as to which (original or copy) is ultimately superior — are founded on the lives, ideas, and poems of Su Shi and his acquaintances.

62. Ziyun was the courtesy name of the Han dynasty poet Yang Xiong (53 BCE–18 CE). He is considered the most important *fu* poet of the Han dynasty next to Sima Xiangru. He served under Emperor Chengdi (r. 32–6 BCE) and his successors.

238 NOTES TO PAGE 74

Later historians criticized him for having served under the usurper Wang Mang (r. 9–23). Hermann, Weiping, and Pleiger, *Biographisches Handbuch,* 325. In the biography of Wang Xizhi in the *Jinshu* (Book of Jin; vol. 80), Yang Xiong's style of calligraphy is criticized, for "his lines are as tangled up as spring worms [C. *chunyin*], while his characters are as bound up as autumn snakes [C. *qiushe*]." The expression "spring worms and autumn snakes" thus may allude to poor penmanship. Yet "spring worms" and "autumn snakes" also appear in the third line of the first of Su Shi's abovementioned *Ciyun Mi Fu Er Wang shu bawei ershou:*

> Once when the Three Institutes was sunning its calligraphy, to protect it
>   from insects,
> I chanced to see "Crabapple" and "Green Plum."
> Spring worms have long been mixed with autumn snakes,
> Who could decide which is more beautiful, the wild pheasant or domestic
>   chicken?
>   (Translation in Egan, *Problem of Beauty,* 207)

Ronald Egan comments on this line, "Works of different quality and authenticity were hopelessly mixed together. [...] The language is drawn from Tang Taizong's criticism of Wang Xianzhi's calligraphy. [...] But I believe that Su Shi uses the metaphors in an altered sense, meaning simply that works of different levels of quality and reliability had all become equally part of the imperial collection he viewed." Egan, *Problem of Beauty,* 208n98.

63. Huaisu (737–779), a Buddhist monk and famous calligrapher of the Tang dynasty who was especially noted as the originator of the "wild cursive script" (C. *kuangcao*). He is known to have enjoyed alcohol. For information on Huaisu and his calligraphy, see Schlombs, *Huai-su and the Beginnings. Kyŏngsa,* "startled snake," appeared in the previous entry.

64. In this couplet, the poor penmanship of Ziyun may be understood to stand for the copy of Ge Yi's calligraphy that Ch'oe Tang got back, while the calligraphic work of Huaisu may stand for the authentic piece that was taken from him.

65. This line can be understood as an allusion to somebody unrightfully taking something away from someone. It is a reference to a tale in the Daoist classic *Liezi* about a woodcutter who kills a deer and buries the carcass in a dry moat. When he later forgets where he buried it, he comes to believe that he must have dreamed the whole affair. A second man, however, overhearing the first man telling the story, discovers the deer and claims it as his own. Yi Illo alluded to this tale in another poem contained in *Tongmunsŏn,* saying, "What to celebrate even when you obtain a deer from the dry moat." Translation from Wei and Lewis, *Korea's Premier Collection,* 49.

66. This line is an allusion to another tale from *Liezi.* Here, Yangzi sends his neighbors and all his retainers to search for his one lost animal, a sheep. The sheep is eventually lost for good, as those who went looking for it claim that there were too many forked roads in the forked roads, so that they did not know which path

NOTES TO PAGE 74   **239**

to take. Although the original tale addresses the issue of an overabundance of divergences, the line at hand may perhaps best be understood as an allusion to Ch'oe Tang sighing upon losing the original of Ge Yi's marvelous calligraphy for good.

67. Chajin is the courtesy name of Ham Sun, who was from Hangyang, present-day Yangp'yŏng in Kyŏnggi Province. He was a member of the Chungnim Kohoe and a close friend of Yi Illo. He was also acquainted with the Koryŏ dynasty intellectual giant Yi Kyubo, who was many years his junior. Original texts by Ham Sun are unfortunately not extant. He is mentioned in not only *P'ahan chip*, but a variety of other Koryŏ sources as well: for instance, in *Sŏha chip* we find the poems *Song Ham Sun pu Ingnyŏng sŏ* (Sending off Ham Sun, who proceeds to his new post in Ingnyŏng [Yangyang in Kangwŏn Province]; contained in the fifth volume of *Sŏha chip*), or *Pang Ham Chajin san'gŏ* (Visiting Ham Chajin's place of dwelling in the mountains), where it says, "When it comes to the drinking of ale, you're quite capable; / when it comes to the chanting of poetry, I'm also rather good." SHC 1:8a. Ham Sun is also mentioned in *Tongguk Yi Sangguk chip, Tongmunsŏn,* and *Pohan chip.* The most significant source on his life, however, is the *Ham Su myojimyŏng* (Epitaph of Ham Su[n]). For information on this epitaph and other biographical sources dealing with Ham Sun, see Sŏ, "Ham Sun-ŭi saengae-e taehan koch'al."

68. Kwandong refers to the northeastern region of the Korean Peninsula, usually meaning the region of Kangwŏn Province.

69. Trading slaves for livestock seems to have been a common practice at the time. The buying and selling of slaves was, in fact, regulated by a 987 ruling by King Sŏngjong contained in the Koryŏ Code. In *Koryŏsa* it says, "In the case of a male slave [K. *no*] who is over the age of fifteen and under the age of sixty, the price is one hundred bolts of cloth [K. *p'o paekp'il*]; for a male slave under the age of fifteen or over the age of sixty the price is fifty bolts of cloth; for a female slave [K. *pi*] over the age of fifteen and under the age of fifty the price is one hundred twenty bolts of cloth; for a female slave under the age of fifteen or over the age of fifty, the price is sixty bolts of cloth." *Koryŏsa*, vol. 85, *chi* 39, sec. *hyŏngbŏp* 2 (criminal code), subsec. *nobi* (slaves). The practice of trading slaves for horses or cattle is mentioned and criticized in another entry of the same Koryŏ Code, for a 1391 ruling by King Kongyang (r. 1389–1392) says,

> Slaves, although they are lowborn [K. *ch'ŏn*, short for *ch'ŏnmin*], are nevertheless subjects of Heaven [K. *ch'ŏnmin*]. They are generally discussed as objects, with nonchalance they are bought and sold, and sometimes they are even traded for oxen or horses. Two or three slaves are often not even enough to pay for a single horse, and consequently an ox or a horse is more valuable than the life of a human being. In the past, when there was a fire in the stables, Confucius asked, "Was any person hurt?" He didn't ask about any of the horses [a reference to *Analects* 10.11]. Hence, the sages thought people high and livestock low. If it is like this, how can there be a rationale for taking people and trading them for horses?

240   Notes to Page 74

70. Possibly a reference to the poem *Yijia bie hushang ting* (Moving house, I bid farewell to the pavilion on the lake) by Rong Yu (744–800), which reads,

> In the spring breeze she bids farewell to the pavilion on the lake;
> willow branches and vine tendrils fasten our hearts.
> The golden oriole has long lived here, she knows me so well,
> as she prepares to leave, she cries rapidly again and again.

Rong Yu is said to have composed this poem as his lover was summoned away by his superior, Han Huang. The poem portrays a lovers' sadness at the moment of separation, with Rong Yu's beloved embodied in the image of a golden oriole about to take wing. See Hong, "Structural Study," 11. Upon reading the poem, Han Huang is said to have sent the girl back to Rong Yu. In the poem by Yi Illo, the oriole, which has already disappeared into the far distance, never to return, may represent the servant girl, whom Yi thinks Ham Sun may have fallen in love with but sent away regardless.

71. This line might be understood as a reference to the tale "Jiangfei ernü" (Two consorts of the river) from *Liexian zhuan* (Biographies of immortals). *Liexian zhuan* is a collection of short accounts by immortals such as Laozi or Dongfang Shuo (fl. 140–130 BCE), as well of stories of love affairs between men and female transcendents. The collection is traditionally attributed to Liu Xiang (79–8 BCE). See Knechtges and Chang, *Ancient and Early Medieval Chinese Literature*, 1:517–518. The relevant story, "Jiangfei ernü," the twenty-fourth entry in *Liexian zhuan*, reads,

> The two consorts of the river, it is not known where they were from. They came forth from [the water] and sojourned along the shores of the Han River, where they met [a man by the name of] Jiao Fu, a person from Cheng. He saw them and was delighted by their appearance, but he did not know that they were divine beings. "I want to go down there and ask them for their jade pendants [K. *p'ae;* C. *pei*]," he said. His servant replied, "The people around here are all well trained with words. If you do not obtain it, I fear you will regret it." But Jiao Fu did not listen to him, went down, and spoke to the women. "The two ladies must be exhausted!" he said to them, and the two women replied, "You, traveler, must be tired — what would we be tired of?" Jiao Fu answered, "Tangerines and grapefruits, I put them in a bamboo basket which I will let float down the waters of the Han. I will follow by its side, picking divine plants [mushrooms] and eating them. If you do then consider me someone who is not impertinent, I would like to ask you for your jade pendants." [...] Eventually with their hands they loosened their jade pendants. Jiao Fu happily received them and held them to his breast. He hurried away. When he had walked a few dozen steps, he meant to inspect the jade pendants, but his bosom was empty and the jade pendants had vanished. He looked back toward the two girls, but suddenly they were nowhere to be seen.

NOTES TO PAGES 74–75   **241**

The beautiful women who vanish in the end can again be understood as an allusion to the servant Ham Sun traded away.

72. *Yuan tao* (K. *wŏn to*), "peach in the garden," and *xiang liu* (K. *hang ryu*), "willow of the lane" should be understood as a reference to Crimson Peach and Willow Branch, the two concubines of Han Yu. They feature in a poem Han Yu composed in Shouyang postal station upon leaving the Tang capital:

> When the seasonal scene was about to change I left Chang'an,
> half of spring has passed at this border settlement, yet it remains unexpectedly cold.
> I see not the garden flowers or willow of the lane,
> only my horse's head, and the round, round moon.
>   (Translation in Davis, "Lechery, Substance Abuse," 84)

Crimson Peach and Willow Branch also appear in another quatrain, *Just back from Chen-chou*. Willow Branch is known to have tried to escape (fly) in Han Yu's absence, and Han Yu hereafter favored Crimson Peach. The poem reads,

> When I left the willows by the wayside,
> flirting with the spring breeze tried to fly.
> But the garden still has plum and peach buds,
> flowers as yet unopened they await my return.
>   (Hartman, *Han Yü and the T'ang Search for Unity*, 109

73. In Literary Chinese poetry, the lush, aromatically alluring peonies were typically associated with beautiful, seductive women. Here, however, we have a *hŭk moktan*, a "black peony," which alludes to a cow (as explained in the introduction). At this point, the term can be understood as a slightly impudent reference by Yi Illo to his friend's (cowish) wife. There is, however, also the theory that "black peony" may refer to yet another, perhaps dark-skinned servant girl of Chajin. See Na, "*P'ahan chip yŏkchu* sojae yŏnsasi," 144. Yi Illo's prior allusion to Han Yu's two concubines might serve to underpin this idea.

74. Hongdojŏng-ri, "Village by Red Peach Well," was a village in the vicinity of Kaesŏng. Yi Illo spent the final years of his life in Hongdojŏng-ri, and it was here where he passed away. Ham Sun apparently moved there as well, and the two friends seem to have lived in close proximity to each other. In the relevant entry in *Sinjŭng tongguk yŏji sŭngnam* (sec. "Kaesŏngbu sang"), the *Hongdojŏng pu* (Rhapsody on Red Peach Well) by Yi Illo is cited. See *STYS* 4:11b; also see *TMS* 2:8b–9a.

75. "Poetry sketches" here is a translation of *sigo* (C. *shigao*).

76. *Tokhaeng* (C. *duxing*), "earnest practice," appears in *Zhongyong* 20. The term refers to the earnest practice of the way to be sincere.

77. The winner of the civil service examinations, which were implemented in Koryŏ in 958 by King Kwangjong (r. 949–975). The system of recruitment, based on a Tang dynasty examination model, was established by Kwangjong with the help of

242 NOTES TO PAGE 75

the Later Zhou envoy Shuang Ji, who came to Koryŏ in 956 (then fell ill and stayed on). Kwangjong established the examination system to recruit well-trained scholars, who were given the opportunity to serve in high government offices on the basis of their knowledge and skill, not on the basis of their aristocratic family background. By selecting skilled and, most importantly, grateful, loyal future ministers, Kwangjong aimed to consolidate and expand monarchical authority and control over Koryŏ while limiting the political and bureaucratic influence of the major aristocratic clans. The examination administrators were called *chi gonggŏ, tokkwŏn'gwan,* and *kosigwan.* Courant and Roux, *Répertoire historique,* 255.

78. *Koryŏsa* has no entry on a person called Hwang Pinyŏn. One may assume that Pinyŏn is a courtesy or nickname, and that the person in question, a distinguished principal graduate and member of Hallim Academy during Ŭijong's reign, is either Hwang Munjang or his older brother Hwang Munbu. Hwang Munbu was selected principal graduate in 1146, the first year of Ŭijong's reign, by the examiners Yi Insil (1081–1153) and Ch'oe Ham (1094–1160). Hwang Munjang became principal graduate in 1156 (see *Koryŏsa,* vol. 18, tenth year of Ŭijong, sixth month, twenty-first day). For a pair of brothers to both finish top of their class within a decade was certainly a rare thing, and apart from these two, no other person by the surname of Hwang was selected principal graduate during Ŭijong's reign. In 1:9, Hwang Pinyŏn is said to have entered the Hallim-wŏn as principal graduate after Yu Hŭi, who was principal graduate in 1152. Thus, in all likelihood this Hwang Pinyŏn is Hwang Munjang.

79. The term Oktang (C. Yutang), "Jade Hall," here alludes to the Hallim-wŏn. In Koryŏ times, the Hallim-wŏn was an important Confucian institution that directly influenced the conduct of government. Patterned after the Hanlin Academy founded in Tang China in 725, it was established in the reign of T'aejo, the first king of Koryŏ. Initially called the Yemun-gwan (Hall of Writing Skills), it was renamed Hallim-wŏn during the reign of King Hyŏnjong in the early eleventh century. In a Confucian system of government, the creation of documents with appropriate forms of etiquette and the compilation of historical records were important bureaucratic functions. The Hallim-wŏn was charged with the execution of these tasks. Grayson, *Korea – A Religious History,* 91. In the Chosŏn dynasty, Oktang can be found as an alternate expression for the Hongmun-gwan, the Office of Special Advisers.

80. O Semun (n.d.) came from Koch'ang in Chŏlla Province and was from a family known for its Confucian scholarship. He passed the preliminary qualification examinations (K. *sŭngbo si*) in 1152. The *Tongguk Yi Sangguk chip* contains a poem by Yi Kyubo entitled "Cha O Nangjung Semun ka pang Kwangmyŏng-sa Mun changno ch'aun Mun-gong" (Visited Elder Mun of Kwangmyŏng Temple at the house of the office chief O Semun and replied to a poem by Master Mun), by means of which we can see that O Semun at one point in time held the office of *nangjung. TYSC* 3:9b–10a. Through another poem in *Tongguk Yi Sangguk chip,* the "Ch'aun O tonggak Semun chŏng kowŏn che haksa sambaek un si" (In reply to a poem of three hundred rhymes presented to the scholars of the Office for Drafting Proclamations by O Semun of the Eastern Hall), we can see that he was active at the Hallim-wŏn as well. O Semun

NOTES TO PAGES 75–76   **243**

was the elder brother of the renowned scholar O Sejae (for O Sejae, see especially 3:22). For Yi Kyubo's eulogy on O Semun's brother, "Eulogy on O Sejae," see Lee, *Sourcebook of Korean Civilization,* 1:343–345.

81. The source says *ji meng* (K. *kye maeng*), which refers to the first (C. *meng*) and third (C. *ji*) month of a season. The relevant season is, as mentioned at the beginning of the entry, autumn, and the character *shuo* (K. *sak*) is "the first day of each lunar month." Hence, it is the first day of the middle (C. *zhong*) month of the autumnal season, or the first day of the eighth month of the lunar year.

82. The source says *kŭmp'ung* (C. *jinfeng*), literally "metal wind." Metal, as one of the five elements, is associated with autumn, and *kŭmp'ung* thus means the autumn wind that sweeps the clouds that veil the moon from the sky.

83. Angam-sa was a temple located in Majŏn-hyŏn, Majŏn Lesser Prefecture (modern Kyŏnggi Province, Yŏnch'ŏn District), in the vicinity of Kaesŏng. During the reign of King Munjong (r. 1450–1452) of the Chosŏn dynasty, the Sungŭi-jŏn, a shrine dedicated to the kings of the Koryŏ dynasty and housing the ancestral tablets, was built at the spot where once had stood Angam Temple.

84. Tan-ju was an administrative district during the Koryŏ dynasty. It was called Changdan-hyŏn, Changdan Lesser County, during Silla times, and was elevated to the status of a prefecture (K. *chu*) in 1001. Later, however, it was again called Changdan Lesser County.

85. Tamji is Yi Tamji. His courtesy name was Ch'ŏnggyŏng, and he was the grandson of Yi Chungyak (d. 1122; for information on the pluralist literatus Yi Chungyak, see Breuker, *Establishing a Pluralist Society,* 284). Yi Tamji was friends with Yi Illo, and he was a member of the Chungnim Kohoe. He left the capital together with Im Ch'un in the wake of the 1170 coup but returned to Kaesŏng much earlier than Im. In Im's poem *Chŭng Tamji* (Presented to Tamji) it says,

> We left the capital and roamed around together;
> yet this morning you reentered the emperor's gates.
> Heaven instructed the twin swords to be united;
> but after the rebellion only one pearl returned.
> Years and months make my waning hair stick to my temples,
> wind and frost have altered my face of old.
> For all our lives our friendship is deep,
> joyfully looking forward to that day we meet again.
>   (*SHC* 3:16b)

When Yi Tamji successfully passed the civil service examinations, Im Ch'un (to a certain extent certainly jealous of Yi's return to the center and his scholarly success) wrote the poem *Mun Tamji t'akche, i si haji* (Heard that [Yi] Tamji passed the civil service examinations; congratulating him with a poem). As can be seen in another poem by Im, the *Yŏ Yi Misu hoe Tamji-ji ka* (Getting together with Yi Misu at [Yi] Tamji's house; *SHC* 3:3b), Yi Tamji and Im Ch'un saw each other even long after Yi had returned to the capital. Im Ch'un also wrote a poem on the occasion of Yi Tamji

244   NOTES TO PAGE 76

going to the Jurchen Jin dynasty as an envoy (*Song Tamji sa pukcho*, "Sending off [Yi] Tamji, envoy to the Northern dynasty"; *SHC* 3:10a). Later in life, Yi Tamji was also well acquainted with Yi Kyubo, and his name appears several times in *Tongguk Yi Sangguk chip*. There is the poem *Chujung chup'il chŭng Yi Ch'ŏnggyŏng* (Dashed off poetically while drunk on ale — presented to Yi Ch'ŏnggyŏng; *TYSC* 2:1b), as well as the poem *Yi Ch'ŏnggyŏng kyŏnbang soju yong Yu Usŏk siun tongbu* (Yi Ch'ŏnggyŏng came to visit me and have little drink; together we wrote rhapsodies using the poetic rhymes of Liu Yuxi [772–842]; *TYSC* 11:12a–b). Moreover, in the entry *Ron chup'ilsa yagŏn* (A discussion on the matter of dashing off poetically — some general words), Yi Kyubo talks about himself and Yi Tamji indulging in *changun chup'il*, "calling a rhyme and dashing off poetically," a sort of poetry for which one of them would call out a rhyme and then rhapsodize quickly while being drunk on alcohol. See *TYSC* 22:17a–b; for a translation, see Lee, *Sourcebook of Korean Civilization*, 345–346. Yi Tamji is also mentioned in *Paegun sosŏl* (see Rutt, *White Cloud Essays*, 12; also contained in *TYSC* 21:6a–b).

86. *Wuling yuan*, the "spring in Wuling," refers to the Peach Blossom Spring, the abode of the immortals, which is described in Tao Yuanming's *Taohuayuan ji*. This is discussed in detail in the notes to 1:14.

87. A reference to Xie Lingyun (385–433), a poet who is said to have been extraordinarily fond of hiking, often abandoning his official duties to climb high into the mountains. Purportedly, he invented special wooden hiking shoes with pegs on their soles. In the poem *Mengyou Tianmu yin liubie* (A dream journey to Tianmu), Li Bai also acknowledges Xie Lingyun, stating that he put on Xie's hiking clogs.

88. For Zhang Han, see note 178 of the introduction.

89. This line refers to the lore about Wang Ziqiao, allegedly Prince Jin, son of King Ling of Zhou (r. 571–545 BCE), i.e., a person of high rank with many official duties. He is said to have left the profane world behind and to have roamed the Yi-Luo region playing a syrinx to call forth a phoenix. A Taoist transcendent named Fuqiu Gong escorted him in his ascent of the mountain. About thirty years later, he reappeared on the mountaintop riding a white crane. People could see him but were unable to get close to him. Having thanked the folks there, he departed. To commemorate him, the local people built shrines at Mount Goushi and atop Mount Song. Wang, *Shaping the Lotus Sutra*, 149.

90. This *ch'ŏngsam* (C. *qingshan*), "blue coat," which is wet with tears in Penpu, is an allusion to the final lines of the famous long narrative poem *Pipa xing* (Song of the *pipa*) by Bai Juyi. Bai was demoted and sent to Jujiang Prefecture, and when he was seeing off a friend in Penpu, he heard an old *pipa* player's song. By way of this, Bai was reminded of his more successful days in the capital. Caught in nostalgic feelings, Bai wrote, "And who among the company cried the most? It was the marshal of Jiujiang, wetting his blue coat." Translation in Minford and Lau, *Classical Chinese Literature*, 893. On the contrary, Yi in this line states that in his view there really is no need to long for high office and official life in the capital. His own desire to stay in the calm, scenic mountain temple and turn his back on the obviously burdensome official life in Kaesŏng may be said to reflect in these two middle couplets.

Notes to Pages 76–77 **245**

91. The ten continents and three isles (C. *shizhou sandao*) are abodes of Daoist immortals.

92. Bones being exchanged usually alludes to a human being transformed into a Daoist immortal. Here it might be understood the other way around, as Yi Illo must now leave the enchanting, stimulating religious realm behind and return to the bustling city of Kaesŏng. This poem is contained in *Sinjŭng tongguk yŏji sŭngnam* (vol. 12; sec. "Kyŏnggi," subsec. "Changdan tohobu") as a lyrical reference to Angam Temple. It likewise features in *TMS* 13:7b.

93. This statement can be understood as an allusion to a tale of the high Tang dynasty official Wang Bo (759–830). When Wang Bo was young and poor, he lived among the monks of Mulan Monastery (Mulan-yuan) in Yangzhou. The monks, having grown tired of the young man's presence, played a trick on him, hitting the evening bell after they had already finished eating, and Wang Bo had to spend the night hungry. Thereupon he wrote a poem on a wall, voicing his disappointment. More than twenty years later, after having successfully passed the civil service examinations and having been appointed magistrate of Yangzhou, Wang Bo returned to the monastery where the monks had treated him badly. To his surprise he discovered that the monks had covered the poem he had written on the wall in green gauze to protect it from dust and filth. So he wrote a new poem on the wall, which read,

> Thirty years ago, when I sojourned in this monastery,
> magnolia flowers bloomed and the monastery had just been built.
> But now, as I return to this place where I used to walk up and down,
> the trees are old, the flowers are gone, and the monks all have white hair.

This story features, for instance, in *Taiping guangji* (vol. 199, "Wang Bo").

94. The source here says *fuzuo* (K. *pojwa*). *Fu*, an ornament in the shape of an axe or hatchet, is among the so-called *shier zhang*, the twelve emblems described in the "Yiji" section of the *Shujing* as ordained by the legendary emperor Shun to use on his ministers' robes. See Legge, *Chinese Classics*, 3:80. In Korea, these signs were not used together, but appeared singly. The "Guming" section of the *Shujing* mentions screens embroidered with axes (C. *fuyi*, K. *poŭi*). See Legge, *Chinese Classics*, 3:551. At this point, *fuzuo* means the ruler's seat, which was ornamented with figures of axes. The festival in question here is the *yŏndŭnghoe*, "lantern festival," a festival where congratulations between the king and his ministers were exchanged. Vermeersch states that this festival was originally held on the fifteenth of the first month, but that it was moved to the fifteenth of the second month after 1010. See Vermeersch, "The P'algwanhoe," 89. Yet Yi Illo was first appointed to serve at the Hallim Academy in 1185, and in this year the festivities were apparently still carried out on the fifteenth day (or full moon day) of the first month.

95. Such a *tŭngnong si* (C. *denglong shi*), "lantern poem," would be written on a piece of cloth or paper and fastened to the lantern.

96. *Jinbo* (K. *kŭmbak*), "cut gold foil," is a special type of surface decoration known best from Japanese and Korean Buddhist art. Gold foil was cut thinly and

246 NOTES TO PAGE 77

then applied to Buddhist works of art such as sculptures or paintings. The application of cut gold foil decorations requires careful technical preparation of the materials. Three layers of thin gold foil leaves are pressed together by means of heat. The foil thus becomes thicker and does not tear easily. A sharp bamboo knife is then used to cut threads of gold foil that are up to three millimeters wide. The gold foil threads are picked up with a brush and then carefully applied with a special glue made of seaweed to a colored surface or an unpainted wooden background. See Rösch, *Chinese Wood Sculptures,* 192–193.

97. The term *kŭmsin* (C. *jinjin*), "golden ashes," here refers to the ashes of a burning candle in one of the lanterns.

98. *Okch'ung* (C. *yuchong*), "jade worm," is a literary expression for the stub of a burned-down wick. A similar term is *tŭnghwa* (C. *denghua*), "wick flower."

99. *Chungdong* (C. *chongtong*), "double pupils," are the mark of a sage or a sage-like king. The term appears in *Shiji,* where it refers to Xiang Yu (232–202 BCE). The author Sima Qian cites the double pupil as possible "evidence" that Xiang Yu might have been descended from the sage-king Shun, who is also said to have had double pupils. See Hsia et al., *Columbia Anthology of Yuan Drama,* 99. At this point, "he with double pupils" is King Myŏngjong.

100. The source says *p'yŏngjang,* short for *p'yŏngjangsa,* manager of affairs. Hucker, *Dictionary of Official Titles,* 386. At this point, the person in question held the office of *sirang p'yŏngjangsa,* vice director of the Royal Secretariat and Chancellery.

101. Hŏ Hongjae (d. 1170) won first place in the civil service examinations presided over by Im Wŏnae (n.d.) in 1134. He served as *chwa chŏngŏn,* censor of the left, at the beginning of Ŭijong's reign. In 1164, when serving as *chwa sŭngsŏn,* commissioner of the left, he supervised the civil service examinations as associate examination administrator. Later he was town magistrate of Annam (K. Annam *tohobusa*). In 1169 he became vice director of the Royal Secretariat and Chancellery. Hŏ Hongjae was killed during the military coup of 1170.

102. *Kŭmbang su* (C. *jinbang shou*), "head of the Golden Roster," is the person whose name is written at the top of the list of those who successfully completed the state examinations.

103. The dates of Yu Hŭi are unknown. When King Ŭijong personally evaluated official candidates in the civil service examinations (K. *ch'insi*) of 1152, Yu Hŭi became principal graduate. *Koryŏsa,* vol. 17, sixth year of Ŭijong, eighth day of the fifth month.

104. The term *zaiyou* (K. *chaeyu*) derives from the first passage and chapter title of "Zaiyou" from *Zhuangzi.* The beginning of the chapter reads, "I have heard of letting the world be, of leaving it alone; I have never heard of governing the world." Translation in Watson, *Complete Works of Zhuangzi.* Here, the term may be understood as alluding to the military rule under Myŏngjong. Regarding Myŏngjong's time as king, Edward J. Shultz writes that during his reign, men of lower social status rose to political prominence as service barriers and class distinctions eroded, and men of little administrative experience began governing the dynasty. Myŏngjong was closely tied to the military leader Yi Ŭimin. Fearing a rebellion, Myŏngjong turned

NOTES TO PAGE 77 **247**

a blind eye to the fact that Yi Ŭimin and his sons plundered the kingdom from 1184 until 1196, when the later military strongman Ch'oe Ch'unghŏn assassinated him. See the chapter "Myŏngjong's Reign" in Shultz, *Generals and Scholars,* 28–53.

105. Yi Sunu (also Yi Sunu with a different character for *u,* d. 1196), courtesy name Palchi. He passed the civil service examinations in 1163 during the reign of Ŭijong but is known to have been a favorite of Myŏngjong, under whom he served as a high official. Yi was killed during Ch'oe Ch'unghŏn's coup.

106. The source says *myŏng* (C. *ming*), "call" or "singing," which may here perhaps be understood as short for *pong myŏng,* the "call of the phoenix." The singing of the phoenix usually stands for a man becoming principal graduate, for him being awarded a high office, as well as for him receiving the affection of a ruler. This derives from the *Shijing* ode "Juan a," parts of which read, "The phoenix is in flight, Clip, clip go its wings; It is here that it alights. In their multitude swarm the king's good men; But it is our lord that is chosen to serve, For by the Son of Heaven he is loved." Translation in Waley, *Book of Songs,* 184.

107. Yi Illo was appointed to serve at the Hallim Academy for the first time in 1185. As we can see in his poem *Oktang paek pu* (Fu on a cypress of the Jade Hall), which is contained in *Tongmunsŏn,* in 1189 he appears to have been reappointed to the academy, because at the beginning of this long poem it says, "The year is in *jiyou* [1189], / the winter months are drawing to an end. Master Longxi [Rongsŏja; i.e., Yi Illo] has entered service at the *jinluan* [the Hallim Academy]. [...]" *TMS* 2:9b. Yi Illo stayed at the Hallim Academy until 1194. Later he was appointed *nangjung.* This we can see in the title of a poem by Yi Kyubo, which reads *Yi Nangjung Illo, Son Hallim Tŭkji kyŏn hwa, pogyong chŏn un* (Office Chief Yi Illo and Hallim [Academician] Son Tŭkji see my reply; reusing the rhyme pattern of the last [poem]). *TYSC* 13:13b. This "last poem" by Yi Kyubo is the *Chaeip Oktang yujak sŏ pyŏksang* (A poem composed upon reentering the Jade Hall — writing it on a wall), which was penned by Yi Kyubo on the occasion of being reappointed to the Hallim Academy in 1212. This, in turn, implies that Yi Illo served as *nangjung* in his early sixties, in 1212. For Yi Illo's role as a Hallim academician, see especially Kim, "Yi Illo-ŭi sarye-ro pon Koryŏ chŏn'gi Chik Hallim-wŏn-ŭi unyŏng-gwa yŏkhal."

108. The dates of Kim Kunsu, styled Sŏldang, are unknown. A member of one of the most prestigious literati families of the age, the influential Kyŏngju Kim Clan, Kim Kunsu was the grandson of Kim Pusik and the son of Kim Tonjung. He was selected principal graduate in 1194, fourteen years after Yi Illo. *Koryŏsa,* vol. 20, twenty-fourth year of Myŏngjong (1194), sixth day of the fifth month. This implies that Kim Kunsu was appointed to the Hallim Academy immediately after having passed the civil service examinations. Of the forty-seven people who passed the civil service examinations as principal graduates during Yi Illo's lifetime (thirteen in Ŭijong's reign, seventeen in Myŏngjong's reign, six in Sinjong's reign, five in Hŭijong's reign, two in Kangjong's reign, four in Kojong's reign), Kim Kunsu was the only one with whom Yi Illo appears to have had a closer personal relationship. Yet Kim Kunsu was also acquainted with Im Ch'un, Yi Illo's best friend. This is evidenced by Im Ch'un's poem *Chŭng Kim kong (Kunsu)* (Presented to Master Kim

248 Notes to Page 77

[Kunsu]). See *SHC* 1:14b. Besides being selected principal graduate, Kim Kunsu also won first place in poetry examinations held personally by King Myŏngjong. *Koryŏsa*, vol. 20, twenty-fifth year of Myŏngjong, thirteenth day of the fourth month, 1195. His biography in *Koryŏsa* reads:

> [Kim] Kunsu, before he was even twenty years in age, [his ability in] literature was already abundant, and his peers respected him as a superior expert. During Myŏngjong's reign he was selected principal graduate, then straightaway became [an academician] at the Hallim Academy. At the beginning of Kojong's reign he was appointed vice director. At the time, ministers of the court were sent out as emissaries, and sometimes among them there were some filled with covetous greed who encroached on others, and the people were often complaining and sighing [on account of these corrupt and evil officials]. [Kim] Kunsu, together with Yi Chonggyu, Song An'guk, Kim Chujŏng, Ch'oe Chŏngbun, and others — eleven people over all — were chosen as commissioners for inspection in the various provinces [K. *chedo ch'albangsa*], and they questioned the people about their grievances while examining the officials' honesty or corruptness. Just then, Khitan troops attacked and he did not get to finish his investigations calmly. [...] [Kim] Kunsu was later appointed left grand master of remonstrance, then replaced Cho Ch'ung [1171–1220] as deputy commissioner of men and horses of the Northwest Frontier-District [K. sŏbungmyŏn *pyŏngma pusa*], and on account of his integrity and love for the people he was praised. When the Khitan troops arrived at the border of Sukju and Yŏngch'ŏn, [Kim] Kunsu led soldiers of several cities on to attack them, beheading some 430 men, taking twenty-one [enemy soldiers] as prisoners of war, and capturing about fifty horses. When Han Sun and Ta Chi rebelled [in 1219 in the north], [Kim] Kunsu went on to become deputy provincial military commander of men and horses [K. *chi chunggunbyŏng masa*] and suppressed [the insurrection]. By means of a scheme [of making them drunk on wine] he beheaded Han [Sun] and Ta [Chi], whereupon he put their heads in a box and sent them to the capital. Provincial Military Commander [K. Pyŏngmasa] Kim Ch'wiryŏ [d. 1234; for a translation of Yi Chehyŏn's "On Command of the Army by General Kim Ch'wiryŏ" from *Tongmunsŏn*, see Wei and Lewis, *Korea's Premier Collection*, 169] disliked his not reporting to him first, and imprisoned [Kim] Kunsu. The recorder who had jurisdiction over the case was a person called No Insu. Generally, there existed rifts in the relationship [between No and Kim] Kunsu, and due to this, [No] had several times slandered [Kim Kunsu] in front of [Kim] Ch'wiryŏ, and again he had slandered him in front of Ch'oe I [Ch'oe U]. Eventually, [Kim] Kunsu was exiled to Hannam. At the time, the people thought this utterly wrong. (*Koryŏsa*, vol. 98, "Yŏlchŏn" 11)

Kim Kunsu appears again in the following entry, as well as in 3:22.

NOTES TO PAGE 78   **249**

109. The source says *lun* (K. *ryun*), "cord," which here refers to the king's decrees (also *cheryun*, "imperial decree"). This meaning derives from the "Zi yi" chapter of *Liji*. According to his biography in *Koryŏsa*, Yi Illo worked at the Hallim Academy as history academician (K. *sahan*) for fourteen years. This entry was consequently written sometime in the mid- to late 1190s.

110. These *huazhuan* (K. *hwajŏn*) are stones with a surface molded with patterns of flowers, primarily used for paving. These paving stones were used in the Hanlin Academy during Tang times and became a symbol for the academy and its scholars. The term is used in this sense by Yi Illo at this point. In the section "Tangshu" in the sixth volume of the Qing dynasty *Huangchao cilin diangu* (Materials concerning the history of the Hanlin Academy; compiled by Zhu Gui [1731–1807] in 1805) it says, "During Tang times, by the stairs in front of the northern hall of the Hanlin Academy there was a path made of flower-patterned paving stones. In the winter, when the sun would reach the fifth paving stone, it would be time to go on duty." For the *Huangchao cilin diangu*, see Grimm, *Kaiser Qianlong*, 163.

111. The term *cheil in* (C. *deyi ren*), "foremost people," here refers to the top successful candidates in the examinations.

112. "Passing the Dragon Gate" (K. *yongmun*) synonymously stands for the successful passing of the civil service examinations.

113. The source says *mukkun* (C. *mojun*), "ink gentleman" or "ink painting of the noble." In East Asian art, *kun* stands for the bamboo, or, in a broader sense, also the "four nobles" or "four gentlemen" (K. *sa kunja;* C. *si junzi*): orchid, bamboo, chrysanthemum, and plum blossom. This entry deals especially with ink bamboo painting, yet in the North Korean translation of *P'ahan chip*, *mukkun* was understood by the translator Ri Sŏng as *maehwa*, "plum blossoms." See Ri, *Ri Illo*, 54.

114. In all likelihood this refers to the precious "mottled bamboo" (C. *banzhu;* K. *panjuk*) growing by the Xiang River. It is said to have been mottled by the tears of the two daughters of Emperor Yao, who mourned the death of their husband, Emperor Shun, on the banks of this river.

115. The source says *taejongbaek* (C. *dazongbo*), minister of rites. The core personnel for cultic service in the Department of Spring (C. Chunguan) was supervised by this minister of rites, who oversaw all sacrificial and ritual matters ranging from setting up altars for various sacrifices to distinguishing names and quantities of sacrificial grains and ritual vessels. See Lagerwey and Kalinowski, *Early Chinese Religion*, 854; Hucker, *Dictionary of Official Titles*, 473. It was an alternative title of *libu shangshu* from Tang times on. In Koryŏ, *taejongbaek* was likewise used as an alternative title for minister of rites. See Courant and Roux, *Répertoire historique*, 110. The Ministry of Rites became responsible for the coordination of educational affairs and examination matters, which means that the civil examination system fell under its jurisdiction. Hence, the term at this point can be understood as a reference to someone supervising the civil service examinations.

116. "Minister of State Ch'oe" most likely refers to Ch'oe Yuch'ŏng (1095–1174), who served as one of the two examiners in the civil service examinations Kim Tonjung passed as principal graduate in 1144. In these examinations, Han Yuch'ung

250   NOTES TO PAGE 78

(d. 1146) functioned as examination administrator, while Ch'oe Yuch'ŏng served as associate examination administrator. *Koryŏsa,* vol. 73, "kwagŏmok," "kwagŏjang," fifth month of 1144. The circumstances under which Kim Tonjung became principal graduate appear to have been somewhat unusual, because the examiners Han and Ch'oe had originally put him in second place. King Injong thereupon personally intervened, changed the result, and put Kim Tonjung in first place to console his utterly disappointed father, the meritorious subject Kim Pusik.

117. Traditional interpretations of this passage have it that Minister of State Ch'oe composed the following quatrain to thank Kim Tonjung for presenting him with the bamboo ink painting. If Ch'oe Sangguk is Ch'oe Yuch'ŏng, however, the creator of this poem may well have been Kim Tonjung himself, thanking his old examiner for his help.

118. "His late Majesty" here is a translation of *sŏnje* (C. *xiandi*), literally "former emperor" or "previous sovereign." Though he passed the civil service examinations under Injong, Kim Tonjung primarily served in office during the time of Ŭijong. The term *sŏnje* can thus be understood as a reference to Injong. The sentence at hand could alternatively be translated as "His late Majesty in his years praised [your ink gentleman] as a 'living bamboo.' " Nevertheless, the translation "His late Majesty in his years was praised 'a live bamboo,' " I think, makes more sense. This is the case because King Injong being likened to a bamboo may be taken as a reference to the *Shijing* ode "Qi ao," which describes the emergence of an elegant, charismatic, upright nobleman (traditionally interpreted as Duke Wu of Wei [r. 812–758 BCE]) on the bamboo-covered shores of the Qi River. Generally, the bamboo was in premodern China and Korea attributed with the quality of standing strong in the face of adversity, of refusing to crack even in times of terrible crisis, of being able to salvage desperate situations. Injong, in fact, faced such existential crises in 1126 during the coup attempted by his maternal grandfather, Yi Chagyŏm, as well as during the rebellion by the monk Myoch'ŏng, which unfolded in P'yŏngyang in 1135. Injong weathered both these storms (with the help of Kim Pusik), and the appellation *hwalchuk,* "live bamboo," may have derived from that.

119. If the two shrubs of mottled bamboo suddenly facing the palace balcony, i.e., the place where a king would show himself to his officials (see 2:7), are understood as representations of the mourning wives of the dead emperor Shun, the poem's third line could well be read as an allusion to King Injong's death. The poem's final line about a rootless trunk might consequently be taken as veiled criticism of Injong's unsettled son and successor, Ŭijong.

120. Ch'arwŏn, "Surveillance Office," here refers to the Ŏsadae, the Censorate, which was established by Sŏngjong and known under various names, such as Kŭmodae, Kamch'alsa, and Sahŏnbu. Courant and Roux, *Répertoire historique,* 83. The Censorate had the important duties of evaluating administrative performance and censuring the wrongdoings of officials. Lee, *New History of Korea,* 114.

121. Xuetang Jushi (K. *Sŏltang Kŏsa*), "Hermit of Snow Hall," is Su Shi.

122. This line can be understood as a reference to the black ink painting of snow that Su Shi painted on the walls of his Snow Hall. In *Xuetangji* (A record of Snow Hall)

NOTES TO PAGES 78–79   **251**

it says, "Master Su acquired a deserted garden by the East Slope. He constructed a fence around it and built a hall in it, calling the middle studio 'Snow Hall.' Since this hall was built in a heavy fall of snow, he painted snow on the four walls without a single space left blank. Wherever he was in activity or in repose, looking around, it was all snow. When Master Su dwelt in it, he was truly at home." Yang, *Dialectics of Spontaneity*, 69–70.

123. Xiaoxiao is one of the many sobriquets of the Northern Song dynasty painter Wen Tong (1018–1079; style name Yuke), a cousin, friend, and teacher of Su Shi. He received his *jinshi* degree in 1049 and held various posts in the provinces and at the central court. Wen Tong was especially renowned for his paintings of ink bamboo. He famously instructed Su Shi that the painter shall first "have a complete bamboo in the breast," then "holding a brush in hand, observing it long and thoroughly, he will see what he wants to paint." Yang, *Dialectics of Spontaneity*, 65.

124. This line is a reference to a letter sent by Wen Tong to Su Shi (who at the time stayed in Pengcheng, modern Xuzhou), which is cited in Su's *Wen Yuke hua Yundang Gu yanzhu ji* (Record of Wen Yuke's painting of the dipping bamboo of Yundang Valley):

> When Yuke first began painting bamboo, he did not consider it to be something of great value. But people from all corners began to arrive bearing fine silk and requests, so many that they were lined up waiting at his gate. Yuke despised this and threw the silk to the ground, angrily scolding, "I am going to use this to make socks!" Scholar officials have passed this story down as something he really said. When Yuke left Yangzhou [Shaanxi] to return to the capital, I was serving in office in Xuzhou [Jiangsu]. Yuke sent me a letter, writing, "I recently told these gentlemen that of late my school of ink bamboo painting is in Pengcheng and that they should go there in search of paintings. The sock material can be stored at your place!" (Translation from Sturman, "Su Shi Renders No Emotion," 18–19)

125. Pyŏngna noin, literally "Elder of Emerald Vines." It is unfortunately not clear to me who this person is. In Hwasun District, Southern Chŏlla Province, there is a village called Pyŏngna, and the name may have derived from that. Pyŏngna noin appears as Pyŏngna noin Kŏbi in 2:13, where it becomes clear that he must have been a contemporary and acquaintance of Yi Illo. In the later entry it also appears as if he were a Buddhist priest.

126. Su kŏsa, "Sleeping Hermit," was one of the style names of the Koryŏ scholar An Ch'imin (n.d.; courtesy name Sunji; other sobriquets include Kiam kŏsa and Ch'wisu sŏnsaeng). He lived in reclusion, but similar to his contemporary O Sejae (who lived in abject poverty and who An Ch'imin is known to have admired) was considered one of the great scholars and artists of the late twelfth and early thirteenth centuries in Korea. He was renowned for his poetry, and especially for his mastery in ink bamboo painting. Yi Kyubo wrote the *An kŏsa mukchuk ch'an* (A brief encomium on the ink bamboo of Hermit An), in which it says,

252   NOTES TO PAGE 79

"Kiam kŏsa, his [ink] bamboo reached the realm of the immortals. [...] The hand is the heart-mind's servant, and always it transmits as the heart-mind intends. The heart-mind shows, the hand responds, and the things, how could they escape from this? As for the bamboo, that is why when he looked at it, there was nothing by which it could have hidden its Heavenly nature, and every single joint, every single leaf, they all revealed their entirety to him. The man and the brush have both perished, and it already seems so long ago, as if a thousand years had passed. A piece of white silk a remnant of his art, its value no less than ten thousand coins. (*TMS* 51:1a)

Pohan chip 1:4 says in relation to An Ch'imin, "Thus they called the place where Master [Ch'oe Ch'iwŏn] had once resided Sangsŏjang, 'Hamlet where the letter was written.' Later, eminent scholars [K. *kosa*] such as Yi Nŭngbong, O Sejae, An Sunji and others resided there in succession." Pak, *Yŏkchu Pohan chip*, 49. *Pohan chip* 2:3 says, "[The poetry of] Teacher O Sejae and the Hermit An Sunji [K. An *kŏsa* Sunji] was abundant and profound, simple and vigorous." Interestingly, *Pohan chip* 2:24 suggests that Yi Illo was an ardent admirer of An Ch'imin's style of writing, but that An seems to have been bothered by Yi's constant approaches (in this episode, the screen bearing Su kŏsa's painted bamboo was also not given to Yi directly by An Ch'imin): "Kiam kŏsa An Sunji, as one of the rare masters [K. *taesu*] of his generation, was careful in commending others in terms of their literary writing. Yi Misu early on had sent him a letter with a poem, requesting him [An Ch'imin] to compose an account [to his poem] *Kŭpkodang*. [Yi Illo] asked several times, but never even got as much as a response. So, Yi [Illo] seriously put him under pressure, and since [An] in the end couldn't do otherwise, he composed the account. With it, however, he went against the meaning of Yi [Illo's] *Kŭpkodang* poem and negated it. Academician Kim Kŭkki came from the same district and was his contemporary, but in An's collected writings there isn't a single composition sung in unison with Kim. Only regarding Teacher O Sejae he ceaselessly sighed in admiration at first sight of his poetry. [...]" Pak, *Yŏkchu Pohan chip*, 268. An Ch'imin's poetry is further cited in *Pohan chip* 2:36. Pak, *Yŏkchu Pohan chip*, 306.

127. Bai Fu is the prominent Tang dynasty poet and official Bai Juyi.

128. These lines derive from the poem *Ti xiaoqiao qian xinzhu zhao ke* (Written on new bamboo before a small bridge, summoning guests) by Bai Juyi, which in Howard S. Levy's translation reads,

> Geese teeth, small rainbow bridge—
> hanging eaves, white room low. What is there before the bridge?
> One on another, the new bamboo.
> Bark opens, bursting forth brown brocade;
> joints revealed, drawing out green jade.
> The green skin seems eatable,
> the powdered frost can't bear touching.

Idly chanting poems without end,
lone pleasure heart hard to satiate.
In control of fine breeze and smoke,
impudent to grass and trees.
On a night of moon, can you too
make this your forest home? For you I'll tilt a glass, wildly sing the "Bamboo
   Branches" song.
(Levy, *Translations from Po Chü-i's Collected Works*, 75)

129. In premodern China and Korea, calligraphy reigned supreme in the hierarchy of the arts. And as Lothar von Falkenhausen writes, "handwriting was interpreted as a reflection of a person's inner self and taken as a basis for judging his or her character; however, [...] it was deemed possible to shape one's character by imitating, through assiduous practice, the calligraphy of a morally exemplary person." Von Falkenhausen, "Antiquarianism in East Asia," 42–43.

130. The source says *bi langgan* (K. *pyŏng nan'gan*), which can refer to a precious gemstone (often rendered as lapis lazuli). At this point, however, it is a literary expression for green bamboo.

131. *Tangdu* (C. *tangtou*), "chief monk," is the abbot of a monastery.

132. The source says *hwasa* (C. *huashi*). During the Chosŏn dynasty, *Hwasa* was the title of an office (rank 8 B) in the Tohwa-sŏ, the Bureau of Painting. During the Koryŏ dynasty, this Tohwa-sŏ was called Tohwa-wŏn (Academy of Painting). At this point, *hwasa* simply appears to mean *hwasa* (C. *huashi*), "painting master."

133. Pan Yue (247–300), courtesy name Anren, a major poet of the Western Jin. Next to Lu Ji (261–303) he is counted among the finest poets of his time, and anecdotes about him are recorded in the story collection *Shishou xinyu* (A new account of tales of the world) by Liu Yiqing (403–444). Purportedly, he was so good-looking that hordes of women would mob him whenever he roamed the streets. He was executed in 300 on account of his alleged involvement in a scheme. Twenty poems of his are still extant.

134. Yue Guang (d. 304), a famous *qingtan* ("free conversation") adept, was a literatus and contemporary of Pan Yue. This sentence alludes to an anecdote featured in "Yue Guang zhuan" (Biography of Yue Guang) contained in *Jinshu* (vol. 43). When Yue Guang, who was a skilled debater, was appointed to a high position, he was about to decline the position due to the fact that he was not skilled in brushwork. Then, however, he asked Pan Yue to write the memorial to the throne in his stead. Pan said, "I must first understand your main idea [behind your decision]." Thus, Yue Guang eloquently put his ideas in two hundred lines, which Pan then turned into an outstanding piece of brush writing. At the time, the people said, "If Guang had not borrowed Pan's brush, and if Yue had not received Guang's ideas, there would have been nothing by means of which this beautiful [piece of writing] could have been accomplished."

135. Zichan (580–522 BCE) was grand councilor of the state of Zheng and a man much admired by Confucius. He features in *Lunyu* 5.16, 14.8, and 14.9. *Lunyu* 14.9

254   NOTES TO PAGES 79–80

says: "Someone asked about Zichan. The Master said: 'He was a benevolent man.'"
Slingerland, *Confucius: Analects,* 157.

136. The state of Zheng (806–375 BCE) was a vassal state during the time of the Zhou dynasty (1046–221 BCE).

137. This sentence is a reference to *Lunyu* 14.8: "The Master said, 'In preparing diplomatic orders, Zichan of East Village would have Bi Chen go into the country and draft it, Shi Shu critique and discuss it, the foreign minister Ziyu edit and ornament it, and then finally Zichan himself would mark it with his own unique style.'" Slingerland, *Confucius: Analects,* 156.

138. The source here says *panbak* (C. *panbao*), which can be understood as an allusion to an ingenious draftsman featured in the *Zhuangzi* chapter "Tian Zifang" and who sits in this very position, with his legs outstretched:

> Lord Yuan of Song wanted to have some pictures painted. The crowd of court clerks all gathered in his presence, received their drawing panels, and took their places in line, licking their brushes, mixing their inks; so many of them that there were more outside the room than inside it. There was one clerk who arrived late, sauntering in without the slightest haste. When he received his drawing panel, he did not look for a place in line but went straight to his own quarters. The ruler sent someone to see what he was doing, and it was found that he had taken off his robes, stretched out his legs, and was sitting there naked. "Very good," said the ruler. "This is a true artist!" (Watson, *Complete Works of Zhuangzi*)

139. *Luchui* (K. *noch'u*), "stove and hammer" or "bellows and hammer," the two tools that have to work in complete unison to create something from steel. The term here alludes to the perfect unison of the bamboo branch painted by Yi Illo and the leaves drawn by the nameless painter.

140. This refers to the peoples in the far north and the far south of China, the Hu and the Yue.

141. Meaning that no traces of the painting having been worked on or improved can be discovered, and that the collaboratively painted bamboo appears highly homogeneous, as if painted by one hand.

142. The source says *pongsŏng* (C. *fengcheng*), "Phoenix City," which means the imperial compounds. In this case, the red leaf actually flows forth from inside the quarters of the palace ladies.

143. A *yugou* (K. ŏgu) is a palace canal, a stream of water that drains from a palace ditch or moat.

144. This lyrical work on the theme of the *hongye tishi* (K. *hongyŏp chesi*), the "poem written on a red leaf," is based on a famous eleventh-century tale: While taking a stroll through the gardens of the imperial compound, a young scholar by the name of Yu You discovered a red leaf onto which a poem had been written with ink in the waves of a canal flowing out of the palace ladies' quarters. The poem read,

Flooding water, where do you flow in such impetuous haste?
Deep in the palace, prisoner till the end of my days.
I will thank you incessantly, you red leaf,
If you can escape unharmed into the world of men.

Deeply moved by the poem bemoaning the female poet's loneliness and her longing for personal freedom, Yu eventually writes a response poem on yet another red leaf, which he sets adrift on the waters of a brook streaming into the palace. Plagued by desire and loneliness, he is not able to complete the civil service examinations successfully and finally ends up at a benefactor's house. One day, this benefactor informs him that three thousand palace ladies were released and told to marry, and that among them is the particularly beautiful Lady Han. The old benefactor arranges the marriage between the bachelor Scholar Yu and the released Lady Han. On the day after the wedding, Lady Han discovers the red leaf onto which she herself had written the poem lamenting her loneliness. Hereupon she opens her own casket and pulls out the red leaf bearing Scholar Yu's response poem, which she had picked up inside the palace. This story has been translated, for instance, under the title "Rotes Laub in den Wellen" (Red leaves in the waves) in Bauer and Franke, *Die Goldene Truhe*, 179–183.

145. "Grease splats" is a translation of *hanju* (K. *han'gu*), which is a fried dish. It is an allusion to a story related in Tan Daoluan's (fl. 459) *Xu Jin yangqiu* (Sequel to the Annals of Jin). Huan Xuan (369–404) liked to collect writings and paintings, and he enjoyed showing them to people. Once there was a guest who ate the fried dish *hanju*, which Huan Xuan had prepared for him, and eventually some of the frying fat sprinkled onto one of the precious paintings. Hereafter, Huan Xuan never offered *hanju* to his guests again. At this point the term simply alludes to multiple stains on the hanging scrolls.

146. The *yŏngsa si* (C. *yongshi shi*), "poem on historical themes," is a pervasive theme throughout the Chinese poetic tradition. In its most common form, the poet writes about a historical figure or a historical event. Poems on historical events can involve a simple retelling of history as a guide for the present. The poet may write about a historical figure to praise him or to criticize him. In some *yongshi* poems on historical personages, the poet identifies himself with a figure from the past. Knechtges and Chang, *Ancient and Early Medieval Chinese Literature*, 3:1947. In the case of the lyrical work at hand, the ancient tale on which Yi Illo based his poem (which, judging from the aged look of the scrolls, he most likely wrote during his younger years) essentially serves to criticize the state of affairs at the court, and Yi's poem could be interpreted as a lyrical piece critical of contemporaneous Korean political issues as well. Here one must bear in mind that the situation for intellectuals and civil officials in Korea after the military revolt of 1170 was precarious, and if Yi Illo had stepped forward and directly criticized the political and social upheavals, it would have made him a political threat whom those in charge would certainly have dealt with most severely. Thus, the literary form of the *yŏngsa si* may have offered him the means to artistically camouflage his disapproval of the state of affairs at court.

256   Notes to Pages 80–81

As a thought, the beholders gathered around the hanging scrolls may have been taken aback not so much by the artwork's seemingly ancient outer appearance as by the audacity as well as the only scarcely veiled display of dissent contained in the poem itself. Yi Illo states that he "answered slowly," which may indicate that at this moment he hesitated before cautiously telling them the truth about his authorship of the piece. In addition, when at the beginning of the entry Yi alleges that the scrolls in question were hanging "on the wall of some noble house," one may surmise that the house he is speaking of really was his own home.

147. As is evidenced also by the poem *Ki Misu ku ch'osŏ* (Sent to Misu asking for a piece of draft script; *SHC* 3:6a) by Im Ch'un, Yi Illo appears to have created such pieces of draft script upon request.

148. Yŏngnak is the courtesy name of Cho T'ong. He was born in 1143, he is known to have passed the civil service examinations during the early reign of Myŏngjong, and although it is not clear when he died, he lived much longer than some of Yi Illo's other close acquaintances. This is evidenced by the fact that, next to Yi Illo, Cho was the only member of the Chungnim Kohoe who was later likewise involved in the Haedong Kirohoe, and he also held a civil post after Ch'oe Ch'unghŏn's rise to power. Cho T'ong's biography in *Koryŏsa* reads,

> Cho T'ong, his courtesy name was Yŏngnak, he was a person from Okkwa County. His body was tall and sturdy, and with regard to the Classics, the Histories, and the Hundred Schools of Thought there was nothing he did not penetrate thoroughly. When King Myŏngjong heard of his name, he time and again summoned him to court to ask him questions. He passed the state examinations, progressively moved through the ranks, then became censor. [...] As an emissary he went to the Jurchen Jin dynasty, and just at the time there was a reproach, so that he was held in custody for three years, but the people of Jin cared for his talents and sent him back [to Korea]. When he became magistrate of the Northwest District [K. *chi sŏbungmyŏn yususa*] he was open-minded, humane, courteous and modest, treating others with trust. In terms of office he reached that of left grand master of remonstrance, headmaster of the National Academy [K. Kukchagam *taesasŏng*] and Hallim academician." (*Koryŏsa*, vol. 102, "Yŏlchŏn" 15)

During the reign of Sinjong, in 1199 he served as pacification commissioner in Kyŏngju in the wake of a local insurrection started by Kim Sun of Kyŏngju and Kŭm Ch'o of Uljin.

149. Yang-ju, present-day Yangsang in Southern Kyŏngsang Province, South Korea.

150. The construction of Ch'ŏnsu-sa was completed in 1116, the eleventh year of King Yejong. It was located in Chŏnch'e Village in Changdan District in the vicinity of Kaesŏng. Ch'ŏnsu Temple was frequently visited by various kings of the twelfth century.

NOTES TO PAGE 81 **257**

151. The word *kaek* (C. *ke*), which has here been understood as an informal term for "friend," could also be rendered as "traveler," referring to Yŏngnak Cho T'ong traveling to Yang Prefecture.

152. Yŏngnak Cho T'ong is in other texts by Yi Illo also referred to with the word *u* (C. *you*), "friend." This is the case, for instance, in Yi Illo's poem *Chŭng sau*, which is contained in *Tongmunsŏn*. Here, Yi Illo names the following four people as his friends: Im Ch'un; Cho T'ong, whom Yi Illo refers to as his "friend of mountains and rivers" (K. *sansu u*); Yi Tamji, who in the poem is called his "friend in ale" (K. *chu u*); and a monk by the dharma name of Chongnyŏng, his "friend of the Teachings of Emptiness (Buddhism)" (K. *kongmun u*). Aside from the earlier quoted verse about Im Ch'un, the poem reads,

> [Master] Taozhu [Fan Li], though he was grand councilor of the state of Yue,
>> drifted out to the dark sea in a single barge.
> When Anshi was at the court of Jin [Anshi is the Jin dynasty statesman and
>> military strategist Xie An (320–385), who chose to abandon his post to
>> become a hermit]
> he enjoyed the moon over the Eastern Mountains in a refined way.
> Now, me and you,
> how could we be fond of the hairpins and ribbons [of officials]?
> Spent entirely is the Donghai gold;
> just go on, pluck the ferns of the western mountains.
>> *[The poem] to the right [in the source] is for Cho Yŏngnak,*
>>> *my friend of mountains and rivers.*

> When I drink, I stop after a few cups,
> but when you drink, you surely [gulp down] a whole *dan* [a hundred liters].
> Then, when accordingly you're merrily drunk,
> our ultimate joys are in line with each other.
> Two faces, [reddishly beaming] like the warmth of spring,
> have a thousand sorrows melt away like ice.
> Why must one competitively vie whether [one drinks] little [and the other
>> drinks] much?
> Simply have each get what suits him best.
>> *[The poem] to the right [in the source] is for Yi Tamji, my friend in ale.*

> Zhidun [314–366] followed Anshi,
> while Bao Zhao [414–466] cared for the [poet-monk] Hui Xiu.
> From ancient times the group of dragons and elephants [i.e., outstanding
>> monks and bodhisattvas who possess great power in meditation]
> has always sojourned together with unicorns and phoenixes [noble and
>> worthy Confucian scholars].
> The *Odes* and the dharma [Confucianism and Buddhism] don't obstruct one
>> another;
> in old and new they're a single hill.

258   NOTES TO PAGE 81

Together in the light of perfect extinction,
why would they have to face the sorrows of separation?
> *[The poem] to the right [in the source] is for Chongnyŏng,*
> *my friend of the teachings of emptiness.*

(*TMS* 4:4b–5b)

153. *Cheho* (C. *tihu*), "lift the jug [of ale]," is a pun with the name of a bird, a sort of pelican, which is likewise called *cheho* (C. *tihu;* with different characters). The Chinese name of this bird derives from its distinctive call, "ti-hu, ti-hu." Another English translation of this poem, by Richard J. Lynn, reads,

I wait for a guest who does not come;
I look for a monk who is also out.
Only a bird beyond the grove
Welcomes me, urging me to drink.
(Lee, *Columbia Anthology of Traditional Korean Poetry,* 210.

In the sixty-third entry of the upper fascicle of *Tongin sihwa,* Sŏ Kŏjŏng discusses this poem in the following way:

> *Taegan* Yi Illo inscribed the following poem on a wall of Ch'ŏnsu Temple: "Waiting for a friend, but the friend hasn't arrived yet; / looking for a monk, but there're no monks here either. / Only a bird beyond the forest / calling a tune, urging us on: *che-ho,* 'lift the jug.'" In ancient times, someone who judged poetry remarked, "A poem ought to be something that has the ability to make scenery that is difficult to describe appear as if it was right in front your eyes, something that contains inexhaustible meaning which reveals itself beyond words — only then is it perfect." [This is a statement by Mei Yaochen (1002–1060) of the Song dynasty.] Now, when I look at this very poem [by Yi Illo], that's exactly what I see! Also, there is the following poem by Han Changli [Han Yu]: "I was called awake as the window was entirely filled with dawn; / I was urged to return as the sun was not yet in the west. / A bird amid the heartless flowers, / again it sings to its heart's content." *Cuigui* [K. *ch'oegwi;* "urged to return"] and *huanqi* [K. *hwan'gi;* "called awake"] both are the names of birds, and *cheho* [in Yi Illo's poem] is likewise a bird's name. Yi's poem, it naturally has Han's [poetic] technique. (Yi, *Tongin sihwa,* 120)

154. It is not entirely clear to me whether the term *kajip,* "collection of family writings," here refers to a separate collection or to *P'ahan chip* itself, although the fact that Yi Illo included the entry in the work at hand strongly suggests that he used *kajip* as an alternate name for *P'ahan chip.* As a matter of fact, the collection does contain a number of poems by his ancestors, his older family members, and even his children, so that that *kajip* as an alternative title is not entirely unfitting.

NOTES TO PAGE 81   **259**

155. Chiri-san, located in the southwest of the Korean Peninsula, is here said to have been known under the name Turyu. In *Koryŏsa*, Turyu appears with a different character for *ryu* ("flow"). Further names for Mount Chiri include Chiri and Pangjang. *Koryŏsa*, vol. 57, "Chiri 2," "Chŏlla-do Namwŏn-bu," "Yŏnhyŏk." Chiri-san was in the early Chosŏn dynasty still referred to as Turyu-san. This can be seen in the title of a poem written by Hwang Chullyang (1517–1563) during his travels through Mount Chiri in 1545, the *Yu Turyu-san kihaeng p'yŏn* (Travel notes [written] while sojourning Mount Turyu). While Paektu-san was considered the origin of the T'aebaek mountain range and the Korean Peninsula, Chiri-san was thought to be its end. This idea is reflected in the appellation "Mount Headstop."

156. At this point in time in the late twelfth, perhaps early thirteenth century, *pukcho* (C. *beichao*), "Northern dynasty" or "Northern court," from a Koryŏ perspective refers to the Jurchen Jin dynasty.

157. Taebang-gun, present-day Namwŏn in Northern Chŏlla Province. *Koryŏsa* says that during Paekche times it was originally called Koyong-gun but was then renamed Taebang-gun. After being named Namwŏn sogyŏng during Silla times, it was once again called Taebang-gun from the second year of King Ch'ungsŏn (r. 1298, 1308–1325) on. Hereafter, it was, again, renamed Namwŏn-gun.

158. Ch'ŏnghak-tong, the "Blue Crane Grotto." *Tong* (C. *dong*) is here translated as "grotto," because it stands for *tongch'ŏn* (C. *dongtian*), "grotto-heaven" (as in *dongtian fudi*, "grotto-heavens and blissful lands"), which are worlds believed to exist hidden within famous mountains and beautiful places. Grotto-heavens are secluded, possibly stone-walled or underground utopias. The inhabitants of these earthly paradises do not suffer from floods, wars, epidemics, illness, old age, or death. See Pregadio, *Encyclopedia of Taoism*, 368. Ch'ŏnghak-tong is the name of an actual place located in the Chiri mountains, but from early on it likewise gained a reputation as a secluded earthen paradise of the sort described in Tao Yuanming's *Taohuayuan ji*. Ch'ŏnghak Grotto features in many works of premodern Korean poetry and prose, for instance, Hwang Chullyang's poem "Ch'ŏnghak-tong" (contained in the first volume of Hwang Chullyang's collected writings *Kŭmkye chip*), which he wrote on a trip through the Chiri-san region in 1545. As for prose literature, the framing narrative of the late Chosŏn dynasty prose work *Oksŏnmong* (Dream of a jade immortal), a dream adventure tale partly based on *Kuunmong* (Dream of nine clouds), by Kim Manjung (1637–1692), is set in Ch'ŏnghak Grotto. Here, the main character Hŏ Kŏt'ong falls asleep inside a Buddhist prayer hall in Ch'ŏnghak Grotto and, just as is the case in respresentative Tang dynasty dream-journey works such as Shen Jiji's (ca. 740–ca. 803) *Zhenzhong ji* (Record within a pillow; see 2:3, note 71) or Li Gongzuo's (ca. 770–850) *Nanke taishou zhuan* (The prefect of the Southern Branch), lives a marvelously successful life as a great Chinese official within the span of a dream. When he awakes, Hŏ Kŏt'ong is back at Mount Chiri. It says,

> The heavens rose and sank, clouds and hazes darkened, his mind was paralyzed like a star in a well, swaying like smoke on the wind, as if he was there and as if he was not, and suddenly [...] it all took form and he

260 NOTES TO PAGES 81–82

awoke, lying in front of the statue of the Vajra-Buddha and underneath the incense-burner table. A yellow hat and straw-made shoes lay scattered by his side, and, just as before, he was the fallen, impoverished Hŏ Kŏt'ong. He took a look at the place where he was at, and it was Ch'ŏnghak Grotto on Mount Chiri. Though forty years of service had clearly passed before, he had now returned from a fantasy that had lasted only a moment. It had all been but a single dream. (Im, *Han'guk hanmun sosŏl chŏnjip,* 3:324)

Like the hermits who purportedly lived in Ch'ŏnghak Grotto, Hŏ Kŏt'ong also renounces the world at the end of the story. For a detailed discussion of *Oksŏnmong* and other late Chosŏn dynasty adaptations of *Kuunmong,* see Wuerthner, *Study of Hypertexts of Kuunmong.* This upcoming passage in *P'ahan chip* contributed greatly to the reputation of Ch'ŏnghak Grotto as a secluded, utopian place of wonder.

159. This depiction of the rough path that leads to Ch'ŏnghak Grotto was clearly inspired by the description of the way leading to the hidden land behind Peach Blossom Spring in *Taohuayuan ji.* In the work by Tao Yuanming it reads:

He (the fisherman) went on for a way with the idea of finding out how far the grove extended. It came to an end at the foot of a mountain whence issued the spring that supplied the stream. There was a small opening in the mountain, and it seemed as though light was coming through it. The fisherman left his boat and entered the cave, which at first was extremely narrow, barely admitting his body; after a few dozen steps it suddenly opened out onto a broad and level plain where well-built houses were surrounded by rich fields and pretty ponds. (Minford and Lau, *Classical Chinese Literature,* 515)

As can be seen, Chŏnghak-tong is not a cave-like grotto in the usual sense of the word *tong.* Related to this, Chŏng Yagyong (1762–1836) wrote in *Kyŏngse yup'yo* (Design for good government),

Also, the word *tong* designates a cave in a cliff — in the case of such places as Manp'ok-tong in the Kŭmgang Mountains or Ch'ŏnghak-tong in the Turyu Mountains it somehow still seems reasonable to call them that, but with regard to the people dwelling in the fields and farmhouses there, how can one speak of them while applying the word *tong*? The people from the neighboring villages refer to these people as "*tongnae ch'ŏmjon,*" "honorable gentlemen from inside the grotto," the village controller is called "grotto controller," the village chief is called "grotto chief," the village assembly is called "grotto assembly" [...] — how is that not wrong? (*Kyŏngse yup'yo* 8:7b–8a)

160. For instance, legend has it that Later Silla intellectual giant Ch'oe Ch'iwŏn withdrew to Ch'ŏnghak Grotto after his return from Tang China, eventually mount-

NOTE TO PAGE 82   **261**

ing a blue crane and flying off to become a Daoist immortal (he is otherwise believed to have died at Haein-sa). In a poem by mid–Chosŏn dynasty scholar Ki Taesŭng (1527–1572), entitled *Ip Ch'ŏnghak-tong pang Ch'oe Koun* (Entering Ch'ŏnghak Grotto, looking for Ch'oe Koun), the first lines read, "Koun [Ch'oe Ch'iwŏn], a person from a thousand years ago, / refined the form [C. *lianxing*] and rode off on a crane." *Kobong chip* 1:27b.

161. In *Kiŏn*, the collection of writings of the sixteenth-century scholar Hŏ Mok (1592–1682), we find interesting firsthand descriptions of the area and its legendary history in the entry "Chiri-san Ch'ŏnghak-tong ki" (Account of Ch'ŏnghak Grotto in the Chiri Mountains), which Hŏ Mok wrote when actually looking down upon Ch'ŏnghak-tong from on high. It reads,

> Of all the mountains in the southern region [of the peninsula], Chiri-san is the deepest and most remote, the faintest and darkest, and thus it is called Sin-san, "Spirit Mountain." Its secluded cliffs and supreme realms cannot be recorded comprehensively. Alone, the most extraordinary place [among all the natural sights of Chiri-san] is one referred to as "Chŏnghak-tong." It has been described in records from times of old, and it lies above the stone gates of Ssanggye[-sa], "Two Creek Temple." If one passes the ravine to the east of Okso, there are deep waters and great rocks all over, where humans cannot pass through. Setting out from the cliffs to the north of Ssanggye [Temple], if one follows the mountain slope upward, climbing cliffs and scarps, one reaches the top of the stone wall of the plateau in front of Puril-[am], "Buddha-sun Hut." And that's where, if one stands facing the south, one can gaze down upon Ch'ŏnghak-tong. It is a stone grotto, encircled by precipitous cliffs, and atop the cliffs and rocks there are many pines, lots of bamboo, and many maples. Long ago there was a crane nest on a rocky peak in the southwest, and the old people of the mountains transmit the following among each other: "The cranes [that nested here] had black wings, the crowns of their heads were red, while their lower legs were of a violet color. If one looked at them under the light of the sun, however, their wings and feathers all seemed to shimmer in a bluish hue. In the morning they spiraled upward, entering the faint and dark; in the evening they would return to their nests. But it has been more than a hundred years since they were seen here last." For this reason the peak is called Ch'ŏnghak-pong, "Blue Crane Peak," and the grotto itself is called Ch'ŏnghak-tong. In the south it faces Hyangno Peak, while in the east three rocky peaks stretch out. Its eastern ravines are all of layered rock and strange-looking cliffs. Yesterday evening it rained hard, and the ravines were filled with waterfalls. On a rock atop the plateau one can find the inscription *Wanp'ok-tae*, "Enjoying Waterfalls Plateau," and below there is a deep pond. In the thirteenth year of the reign of Sungjong [1640], the ninth month, the third day, coming from Agyang, I ventured upstream Sŏm[jin] River, passing Three Spirits Grotto [K. Samsin-tong].

262 NOTES TO PAGE 82

> In the morning light I looked at the stone gates of Ssanggye [Temple], and at Ssanggye Temple itself I looked at the Stone Tablet for Chan Master Chin'gam [K. Chin'gam Sŏnsa Pi] by the academician Ch'oe [Ch'iwŏn]. About a thousand years have passed since [it was created], but in between the moss it was still possible to make out and read the characters of the text. Thereupon I ascended to the plateau in front of Puril-[am], and there I composed the "Account of Ch'ŏnghak Grotto." (*Kiŏn* 28:1b–2a)

162. It is not entirely clear who this person is. He is referred to at this point as *tanghyŏng*, "paternal older male cousin." However, Yi Illo was married to the daughter of Ch'oe Yŏngyu, so it might be a person from his wife's side of the family.

163. That is, they wanted to give up their official careers and live as hermits.

164. *Sang mun* (C. *xiang wen*), "hear one another," might be an allusion to life in seclusion as described in *Daodejing* 80: "[...] Bring it about that the people will return to the use of the knotted rope, will find relish in their food, and beauty in their clothes, will be happy in the way they live and be content in their abode. Though adjoining states are within sight of one another, and the sound of dogs barking and cocks crowing in one state can be heard in another, yet the people of our state will grow old and die without having had any dealings with those of another." Lau, *Tao Te Ching*, 241. The expression also appears in *Taohuayuan ji*: "Mulberry, bamboos and other trees and plants grew there, and criss-cross paths skirted the fields. The sounds of cocks crowing and dogs barking could be heard [*sang mun*] from one courtyard to the next." Minford and Lau, *Classical Chinese Literature*, 515.

165. Hwaŏm-sa, located in present-day Hwangjŏn Village (K. Hwangjŏn-ri) in Kurye District (K. Kurye-gun) in Southern Chŏlla Province.

166. Hwagae-hyŏn, present day Hadong County (K. Hadong-gun) in Southern Kyŏngsang Province.

167. *Sinjŭng tongguk yŏji sŭngnam* (vol. 30; sec. "Kyŏngsang-do," subsec. "Chinju-mok") states that Sinhŭng-sa and Hwaŏm-sa were temples in the Chiri Mountains. It furthermore states that Sinhŭng-sa was located on Mount Pokch'i (K. Pokch'i-san; see vol. 40; sec. "Chŏllado," subsec. "Posŏnggun").

168. Chiri-san is here compared to the Chinese Kuaiji-shan, the mountain where legendary emperor Yu of Xia passed away while being on a tour of inspection. Qin Shihuangdi purportedly performed ritual sacrifice to the legendary emperor Yu on Kuaiji-shan, and he is said to have erected and engraved a stone stele. This writing on stone might be alluded to at this point by Yi Illo, who also states that he wrote his own poem on the rock.

169. The white monkey (C. *baiyuan*) is a transcendent, heavenly animal. It appears, for instance, in tales about the acquisition of Taoist texts, such as the one in which Sun Bin, a famous strategist of the Warring States period, one night encountered a white monkey that wanted to steal fruit. After threatening the animal with his weapon, Sun discovered that it was, in reality, a transcendent being charged with secret writs to transmit to him. Eventually, the monkey transformed itself into white light and vanished, only to return the following day, as agreed, to deliver secret

scrolls. Sun, not knowing their title, called them the "writs of the white monkey." See Mollier, *Buddhism and Taoism Face to Face,* 40. At this point, the white monkeys allude to the believed existence of an otherworldly realm, i.e., Ch'ŏnghak Grotto, somewhere close by, but Yi Illo and his cousin merely hear them howl from beyond the dark forests and are unable to reach the place from where they call out to them.

170. This might refer to the three mythical mountains/islands Penglai, Fangzhang, and Yingzhou, which synonymously stand for purest, otherworldly bliss. It can here be understood as an allusion to the all-too-distant Ch'ŏnghak Grotto.

171. It is not clear which four Chinese characters are meant here. One might surmise that Yi Illo wanted to allude to a blurred and faded stone inscription such as *wuling taoyuan,* "Peach Spring of Wuling," which would perhaps mark the entrance to the abode of the immortals. Since the characters are indecipherable, they cannot find the entrance to Ch'ŏnghak Grotto.

172. This spring (C. *yuan*) is of course the spring mentioned in *Taohuayuan ji,* i.e., the spring next to which the entry to the immortals' realm is located.

173. Another reference to *Taohuayuan ji,* for this alludes to the falling petals by the stream that the fisherman sails up until he reaches the spring. In the final lines of this poem, Yi Illo compares himself to the main character in the tale by Tao Yuanming: just as the fisherman was not able to find the magical realm amid the flurry of petals once he had left it, Yi Illo is not able to find Ch'ŏnghak Grotto. The abode of immortals, he implies, cannot be discovered by humans.

174. *Wuliu xiansheng ji* can here be understood as an alternate title of the *Tao Yuanming ji* (Collected works of Tao Yuanming), which was originally compiled and edited by Xiao Tong (501–531). Wuliu Xiansheng, "Master Five Willows," was Tao Yuanming's sobriquet. Tao Yuanming's quasi-autobiographical work is entitled *Wuliu xiansheng zhuan* (Biography of Master Five Willows). For a translation, see Minford and Lau, *Classical Chinese Literature,* 494–495.

175. The Qin dynasty lasted from 221 to 207 BCE.

176. Taiyuan era (376–397), the era of Emperor Xiaowu of Jin (r. 372–396).

177. *Changsaeng kusi* (C. *changsheng jiushi*), "longevity and everlasting vision," appears in *Daodejing* 59 and refers to Daoist immortals. See Lau, *Chinese Classics: Tao Te Ching,* 87.

178. Liu Ziji is the person who appears at the end of *Taohuayuan ji* and who wants to venture out and find the abode of the immortals: "A high-minded gentleman of Nanyang named Liu Ziji heard the story and happily made preparations to go there, but before he could leave he fell sick and died. Since then there has been no one interested in trying to find such a place." Minford and Lau, *Classical Chinese Literature,* 516.

179. Richard Rutt's magnificent 1972 translation of this entry can be found in Rutt, "Traditional Korean Poetry Criticism," 117–118.

180. *Munsaeng* is short for *munhasaeng,* which could be translated as "disciple."

181. *Chongbaek* here means *taejongbaek.*

182. In late Koryŏ, literati were often closely connected to one another through either familial ties or mentorship. This mentorship was not limited to actual

264 NOTES TO PAGE 83

teacher-disciple relations. Examination administrators and those who passed the examination formed a special relation in Koryŏ, as was the case in China, in which an examination passer, as a protégé (i.e., the *munsaeng*), honored an examination administrator (i.e., the *chongbaek*) as a mentor (K. *chwaju* or *ŭnmun*). This relation entailed a strong implication of a political contract, for the mentor would provide both guidance and sponsorship in the protégé's career, but this guidance and sponsorship were kept within the form of teacher-disciple bonds. Oh, *Engraving Virtue*, 51. Ch'ŏngun, "blue clouds," means high and prestigious official positions.

183. According to a tale in *Liezi*, Zhong Ziqi was the friend of the famous zither player Boya. Zhong Ziqi could immediately understand and appreciate the entire meaning of Boya's music, and Boya knew and valued this. When Zhong Ziqi died, Boya broke his zither and cut its strings, for now there was no one left who truly "understood the tune." See Kroll, "Aid and Comfort," 845. The relationship between the examiner, who reads and evaluates a text submitted within the framework of the civil service examinations, and the student, who writes and submits that text, is here said to be as intimate and full of understanding as that of Zhong Ziqi and Boya.

184. *Kyunhyŏng*, "guardian of measure," is an alternative expression for *chaesang* (C. *zaixiang*), grand councilor, a paramount executive official.

185. During the period of the Five Dynasties (Wudai, 907–960) in China, a time of short-lived dynasties founded in the north as successor states of the Tang empire, Pei Hao (856–940) had served the Later Liang dynasty (907–923) but eventually became known as the most celebrated examiner of the brief Later Tang dynasty (923–936). While serving the Later Tang as vice director of the Ministry of Rites, Pei Hao presided over the first examination during the reign of Emperor Mingzong, (r. 926–933) in 926. A total of eight candidates earned doctoral degrees in this examination, including Han Xizai (902–970), who later migrated south and became a leading statesman in the kingdom of Wu (902–937; one of the Ten States (Shiguo, 902–979), the southern successor states of the Tang). The examination in the twelfth month of 927, which produced twenty-three doctoral degree winners, was again presided over by Pei Hao. Davis, *From Warhorses to Ploughshares*, 144. Pei Hao served as examination administrator three times overall.

186. Tongguang is the era of Emperor Zhuangzong (923–926) of the Later Tang.

187. Ma Yisun (d. 953), courtesy name Qingxian. He served in high positions such as adviser to the heir apparent (C. *taizi binke*). Ma Yisun was Pei Hao's graduand.

188. The word *pang* (C. *bang*), "roster," is here short for Hwanggŭmbang (C. Huangjinbang), "Golden Roster," which refers to the plaque and hall where the names of successful civil service examination candidates were announced. The examinations in question are those of 936.

189. With respect to this poem as well as the attitude of Pei Hao toward his *munsaeng* during the gratitude ceremonies, Moore writes,

> Long into the Five Dynasties too, the ceremony of gratitude endured as the only ceremonial gathering in which overt inversions of status are known to have been such a major feature. Pei Hao [...] congratulated his former

NOTES TO PAGE 83   **265**

graduand Ma Yisun [...] with a verse concluding: "Three times I took charge of the Spring Apartment, and I am now eighty; Thus, within my disciple's gateway, I am granted an audience with his disciples." The self-deprecatory tone of this verse was intended as an affectionate tribute to Ma Yisun's career, if not also as a gentle reminder of who was owed what by whom. But, an allegedly casual remark by Pei Hao concerning another of his graduates reveals a more steely side to the examiner-graduand relationship. In this instance, Pei Hao was asked why he did not perform the elaborate formalities of greeting and farewell on behalf of a guest as important as the Latter Jin minister Sang Weihan (899–947), and he replied: "If I am granted an audience by his Excellency Sang in the secretariat, I am but a common functionary; today, when he was granted an audience with me in my own apartments, he was my disciple." (Moore, *Rituals of Recruitment*, 201)

190. The source says *sa* (C. *shi*), which is here short for *chinsa* (C. *jinshi*), "licentiate" or "presented scholar," a highly prestigious status conferred on successful candidates tested in knowledge and artistry of Chinese literary forms in the highest-level civil service examinations.

191. The actual official procedure and strict regulations of such a Koryŏ civil service examination are described, for instance, in the eighth entry of the first fascicle of *Yŏgong p'aesŏl*, where it says,

According to the ancient system, [...] on the day of the examination, even before the sky brightens, the examination administrator sits down on the northern seat facing the south, while the associate examination administrator sits down on the western seat facing the east. The inspection official [K. *kamch'al*], having received the king's command, sits down in the south, slightly to the west and elevated to the east, facing the north. Military officials of higher rank [K. *changgyo*], bearing flags, split up and stand at the bottom of the stairs. When the examination candidates [K. *kŏja*] have assembled, the doors are locked straightaway, the clerks of the examination call out the names of the examination candidates and divide them into two groups. Then wooden boards are erected to the east and the west of the two side halls, the examination topic [K. *sije*] is written down on them, and they are hung up above them. At 10 a.m. [K. *ujung*] the commissioner in the Security Council arrives after having received a golden seal [K. *kŭmin*] from the king. The associate examination administrator welcomes him in the courtyard, they bow to one another and then proceed. The examination administrator thereupon withdraws behind the northern wall, while the commissioner in the Security Council and the associate examination administrator ascend to the hall, prostrate themselves twice, inquire after their well-being, and then prostrate themselves two more times. The examination administrator then comes forth and sits down upon the mat

266   NOTES TO PAGE 84

below the northern seat, while the commissioner in the Security Council prostrates himself twice facing the north, and the associate examination administrator likewise prostrates himself two times. The commissioner in the Security Council moves forward, lies down prostrate, inquiring after [the examination administrator's] well-being, and the examination administrator, from his seated position, answers him. The commissioner in the Security Council withdraws, again prostrating himself twice, while the examination administrator also prostrates himself twice. Only then they bow to each other and sit down. The commissioner in the Security Council sits down on the eastern seat facing the west, while the associate examination administrator sits down on the opposite side. A clerk, holding the candidates' examination sheets [K. *napkwŏn*], steps forward, the commissioner in the Security Council opens the golden seal and stamps the papers. When a palace attendant [K. *naesi*] arrives with royal brew sent by the king, the examination administrator and the associate examination administrator together with the commissioner in the Security Council bow toward the royal gift, go to the mats, drink it up, and then bow again to express their gratitude. The commissioner in the Security Council then has to go back, and the associate examination administrator bows and sends him off in the courtyard. This is the way it is done at all three examination sites [K. *samjang*]. (Yi, *Han'guk myŏngjŏ taejŏnjip*, 372)

192. Han Ŏn'guk (d. 1173) functioned as associate examination administrator in the examinations of 1172. *Koryŏsa*, vol. 73, *ji* 27, "sŏn'go 1," "kwamok 1," 1172. The examination administrator was Kim Ch'ŏn (n.d.), and twenty-nine candidates successfully passed. As explained in the introduction, Han Ŏn'guk was involved in Kim Podang's restorational countercoup. Concerning this, *Koryŏsa* (vol. 19, third year of Myŏngjong [1173], eighth month, twentieth day) says, "On the day *kyŏngjin*, the military commissioner for the northeastern district Kim Podang mustered soldiers in the northeastern border region, meaning to attack Chŏng Chungbu and Yi Ŭibang and restore the former king. […] Han Ŏn'guk took his army and joined him, and commanding Chang Sunsŏk and others they arrived at Kŏje, where they showed their respect to the former king, and moved to Kyerim." Another entry says, "[Kim] Podang and the other [ringleaders] were arrested at Anbuk Regional Military Command and then sent [to the capital], where Yi Ŭimin [personally] killed them in a marketplace. All of the ordinary civil officials were simply put to death." *Koryŏsa*, vol. 19, third year of Myŏngjong (1173), ninth month, thirteenth day. Thus, Han Ŏn'guk was arrested and executed only a year after having presided over the civil service examinations. *Koryŏsa*, vol. 19, third year of Myŏngjong, fifteenth day of the tenth month, 1173.

193. Ch'oe Yuch'ŏng (mentioned in 1:10, as he served as one of Kim Tonjung's examiners in 1144) was already almost eighty years old when this incident took place. Ch'oe Yuch'ŏng, courtesy name Chikchae and literary name Munsuk, was a descendant of the meritorious subject Ch'oe Chunong, who had helped T'aejo Wang Kŏn

NOTES TO PAGE 84   **267**

establish the dynasty. He passed the civil service examinations during the reign of Yejong, served as an envoy to Song during Injong's reign in 1132, and ten years later, in 1142, when serving as grand master of remonstrance, he went to the Jurchen Jin dynasty. On the basis of his close ties to Kyŏng, the brother of King Ŭijong (i.e., the later King Myŏngjong), he was purged and demoted on two occasions. At the beginning of Ŭijong's reign, he often remonstrated against what he perceived to be royal misbehavior. In 1151 he lost his office when Ŭijong, suspicious of a purge, exiled his own brother to Ch'ŏnanbu, and was again demoted in 1157. His sons, In and Tang, were registrars in the capital armies and are said to have witnessed military grievances on the eve of the military coup of 1170. See Shultz, *Generals and Scholars*, 14–15. Ch'oe was reinstated and served in high office even in his old age during the early reign of Myŏngjong.

194. The term *kŭmsang* (C. *jinshang*) here means the current king and is thus a reference to Hŭijong (r. 1204–1211). The year in question is 1211.

195. *Sasŏng* (C. *sicheng*). Hucker has the translation "Rector." Hucker, *Dictionary of Official Titles*, 442.

196. Cho Ch'ung of the Hoengch'ŏn Cho Clan, courtesy name Tamyak and literary name Munhŏn, was the son of Cho Yŏngin, a civilian supporter of Ch'oe Ch'unghŏn, who took charge of the Ministry of Civil Personnel after Ch'oe came to power. For Cho Yŏngin, see Shultz, *Generals and Scholars*, 81. Cho Ch'ung, who also became a merit subject like his father under Ch'oe rule, passed the civil service examinations presided over by Im Yu (1149–1212) in 1190 alongside such literary greats as Yi Kyubo. As Hallim academician he functioned as associate examination administrator in the examinations of 1211, then once more as examination administrator in the examinations of 1219. Yi Illo at this point refers to the examinations of 1211.

197. Im Yu, whose literary name was Yangsuk, was of the Chŏngan Im Clan. He was the son of Grand Councilor Wŏnae Im Wŏnhu (1089–1156) and uncle to Kings Ŭijong, Myŏngjong, and Sinjong. He was an important civilian adviser to Ch'oe Ch'unghŏn after his rise to power. Im Yu advanced into the State Council after Ch'oe Ch'unghŏn took over, and played a prominent role in supervising the state examinations, recruiting and recommending many men to the Ch'oe leaders. Im Yu's son married one of Ch'oe Ch'unghŏn's daughters, further solidifying the relationship between the families of Ch'oe and Im. Im Yu's sons all served the house of Ch'oe. See Shultz, *Generals and Scholars*, 81.

198. The source says *ch'ongjae*, which means the *munha sijung*, i.e., the director of the Chancellery.

199. This passage could (and maybe ought to) be taken literally. It could, however, also be read as criticism regarding the transformation of long-established, time-honored traditions under the new leadership of the Ch'oe house.

200. During the Chosŏn dynasty, Hwanggak (C. *Hwangge*), Yellow Cabinet or Yellow Tower, meant the *Ŭijŏngbu*, the State Council. During the Koryŏ dynasty, it was an alternative appellation for the Chancellery for State Affairs.

201. This is an allusion to the aforementioned poem by Pei Hang. Spring

268   Notes to Page 84

Apartment (C. Chunwei) is an archaistic reference to the Ministry of Rites. In the poem by Pei Hao cited previously, the term used is Rites Apartment (C. Liwei), which likewise means the Ministry of Rites.

202. Im Yu not only functioned as one of the leading drafters of royal pronouncements for more than fifteen years, thereby having an influence on the stabilization of the dynasty under Ch'oe rule, but also served as examination administrator overall on four different occasions: in 1190 he served as associate examination administrator, but in 1198, 1200, and 1206, after Ch'oe Ch'unghŏn's accession to power, he served as examination administrator. *Koryŏsa*, vol. 73. These two lines thus allude to Im Yu's illustrious career under the Ch'oe house. In the eleventh entry of the first fascicle of *Pohan chip* it says, "Master Yangsuk Im Yu had examination passers on four [Golden] Rosters: Master Munjŏng [Cho Ch'ung], Master Munan [Yu Sŭngdan, 1168–1220], Master Munsun [Yi Kyubo], the two military affairs commissioners Han [Kwangyŏn, n.d.] and Chin [Hwa, n.d.], the assistant headmaster of the National Academy Yu Ch'unggi [n.d.], [...] and Yun Uil all [passed the civil service examinations] in the same year." Pak, *Yŏkchu Pohan chip*, 68.

203. This line, which hints at a subordinate's loyalty and the proper repayment of a *guoshi* (K. *kuksa*), a "gentleman of the state," can be understood as a reference to a story contained in "Cike liezhuan" (Biographies of the assassins) from *Shiji*. It is a story about the failed assassin Yu Rang, who was well treated by Zhi Bo. When Zhi Bo was killed by Zhao Xiangzi, Yu Rang wanted to avenge his late master Zhi Bo and assassinate Zhao Xiangzi. When Yu Rang fails and is arrested, Xiangzi asks him why he did not avenge his earlier lords Fan and Zhonghang, who were both killed by Zhi Bo, but rather chose to serve Zhi Bo instead. Hereupon Yu Rang answers: "When I served Fan and Zhonghang, they treated me like they treated everybody else. That is why I reciprocated them like everybody else did. As for Zhi Bo, he treated me as a gentleman of the state (*guoshi*). And that is why I repay him as a gentleman of the state." Chang, "Stories of the 'Others,' " 71. This line can be understood as referring to Ch'oe Ch'ung paying tribute to his former examiner.

204. The second part of this line about the Kun and the Peng is an allusion to the chapter "Xiaoyao you" from *Zhuangzi*: "There is a fish in the Northern Oblivion named Kun, and this Kun is quite huge, spanning who knows how many thousands of miles. He transforms into a bird named Peng, and this Peng has quite a back on him, stretching who knows how many thousands of miles. When he rouses himself and soars into the air, his wings are like clouds draped across the heavens. [...] When Peng journeys to the Southern Oblivion, the waters ripple for three thousand miles." Ziporyn, *Zhuangzi*, 3. At this point the transformation of the Kun into the mighty Peng symbolizes the transformation of Ch'oe Ch'ung from student / examination passer to teacher / examination administrator, from *munsaeng* to *chongbaek*.

205. *P'ogal*, "linen and kudzu," was the type of cloth that commoners were allowed to use (the use of silk, for instance, was restricted and allowed only for members of the higher social strata). "Linen and kudzu" essentially thus means the simple clothes worn by commoners or poor scholars from minor lineages without office. *Kongno*, "swans and egrets," i.e., birds with extraordinarily pretty feathers,

NOTES TO PAGE 84   **269**

is at this point an allusion to the *munsaeng*, who stand out from the ordinary crowd and need to be recognized by the mentors.

206. *Jinye* (K. *kŭmaek*), "gold liquor," is a magical liquor prepared from powdered gold and mercury, which are placed in a bamboo cylinder with saltpeter and realgar. The cylinder is sealed with silk and lacquer and soaked in vinegar. After one hundred days, the gold and mercury dissolve and form the gold water (C. *jinshui;* i.e., the golden liquor) and the mercury water, respectively. Both are ingested while facing the sun; one's body is said to take on a golden hue, and one is transformed into light (C. *guangming*) and ascends to Heaven. Pregadio, *Encyclopedia of Taoism*, 588.

207. *Sheng* (K. *saeng*) usually means a *shenghuang* (K. *saenghwang*), an ancient reed-pipe wind instrument. At this point, however, the pipe is said to have been made of jade.

208. The Tang dynasty tune "Xi qian ying" (Rejoicing that the oriole has flown) celebrates success in the civil service examinations. This poem by Yi Illo also features in *TMS* 13:6b. It is likewise partly contained in Yi Yuwŏn's *Imha p'ilgi* (vol. 12) under the title "Im Yu munsaeng" (The examination passer of Im Yu), where Yi Yuwŏn mistakenly writes that this incident is to have taken place "in the seventh year of the reign of Kangjong." Kangjong reigned from 1211 to his death in 1213, and Im Yu died in the second year of his reign. Furthermore, this poem also partly features in *Pohan chip* 1:12, an entry on examination administrators and examination passers clearly modeled after the *P'ahan chip* entry at hand. After Ch'oe Cha has reiterated the tale of Pei Hao and Ma Yisun, he tells the Korean story in the following way:

> In our dynasty, the Academician Han Ŏn'guk led on his examination passers to pay respect to Master Munsuk Ch'oe Yuch'ŏng, and the master composed the following poem: "Attached in lines they come to pay me a visit, what an honor it is for me; I am happy to see my *munsaeng*'s *munhasaeng*." Master Yangsuk [Im Yu] was the maternal uncle [K. *ku*] of three generations of sovereigns (the three generations of Ŭi[jong], Myŏng[jong], and Sin[jong]), and he held the position of Grand Councilor [K. *ch'ongchae*]. His examination passer Master Cho Munhŏn, as assistant headmaster of the National Academy, presided over the examinations, he commanded his *munsaeng* to go [with him] and pay respect to the drafter of proclamations [K. *Kowŏn*]. Yi Illo composed a poem to congratulate him: "Ten years in the Yellow Cabinet, he assisted in finding peace; three times he opened the Spring Apartment, presiding over the association alone. / A gentleman of the state, as always, repays like a gentleman of the state; a *munsaeng* has now, too, obtained his *munsaeng*." (Pak, *Yŏkchu Pohan chip*, 70–71)

This *Pohan chip* entry has been translated under the title "Ch'oe Cha: Teachers and Disciples" by Hugh H. W. Kang and Edward Shultz. See Lee, *Sourcebook of Korean Civilization*, 1:308–309.

209. *Hoemun si* (C. *huiwen shi*) are poems that can be read in any order (forward, backward, diagonally, etc.) and that make good sense in whichever direction they

270   NOTES TO PAGES 84–85

are read. The same poem thus can yield completely new meanings depending on the direction in which it is read. There are amazing grammatical and semantic shifts that occur in a Chinese palindrome depending on which direction it is read in. For in a Chinese palindrome, all Chinese syllable words, while staying in exactly the same place, are called upon to play quite different syntactic and semantic roles. Lotman, *Universe of the Mind,* 78. In the English language, palindromes can usually run to only a line or two. Yet Chinese palindrome poems may run to a sizable number of lines. Gu, *Chinese Theories of Reading and Writing,* 240. *Huiwen shi* have a long history in China. The form is mentioned by Liu Xie (465–522), and the earliest illustrious example is attributed to Su Hui, who is mentioned in the following sentence of this entry. From Song times there exists a poem that must count as a consummate *huiwen shi.* It consists of twenty characters and it makes sense if one starts with the first character, or the second or the third, etc., thus giving the reader effectively twenty poems. But it can also be read backward, again starting from the last, or the last but one character, etc., thus giving the reader yet another twenty poems. Harbsmeier, *Science and Civilization in China,* 143.

210. Meaning the Southern Qi dynasty (479–501) and the Liang dynasty (502–557) during the time of the Southern and Northern dynasties. The Qi dynasty lasted for little more than twenty years; many men of letters lived through the two dynasties of Qi and Liang, and the literary fashion and the way of composition of the two dynasties came down in one continuous line; hence there are the combined terms of the "Qi-Liang literature" or the "Qi-Liang style." Luo, *Concise History of Chinese Literature,* 214.

211. This refers to Su Hui (fourth century), courtesy name Ruolan, the wife of Duo Tao. Su Hui is arguably the most famous poet associated with the Former Qin period. According to the *Jinshu,* when Duo Tao was serving as magistrate of Qinzhou (modern Tianshui, Gansu), he was banished to the desert. To express her longing for him, Su Hui wrote a long, 841-character palindrome. She reputedly wove the palindrome onto brocade in a circular pattern. Scholars have long attempted to see how many poems they could find in this poetic maze. Li Wei claimed to discover 14,005 trisyllabic, tertasyllabic, pentasyllabic, hexasyllabic, and heptasyllabic poems in it. Knechtges and Chang, *Ancient and Early Medieval Chinese Literature,* 2:1034–1035. Su Hui became famous during the fifth century as an exemplar of a virtuous woman who could combine skill in the feminine arts with literary talent. In all likelihood, however, the palindrome may not have been the work of Su Hui. Later, the palindrome achieved wide circulation, especially during early Ming times. See Chang and Owen, *Cambridge History of Chinese Literature,* 47.

212. The source says *zhuyou* (K. *chŏch'uk*), which means a weaving loom. It is here used in a literary sense as the form of composition.

213. Song Sanxian, "Three Sages of the Song dynasty," may refer to Yan Shi (1053–1135), Luo Congyan (1072–1135), and Yi Tong (1093–1163). Luo Congyan was a student of Yan Shi; Yi Tong studied Confucianism under Luo Congyan.

214. It is not entirely clear which collection of poetry the title *Nanxu ji* (K. *Namsŏ chip;* Collected writings of Nanxu) refers to, but one can surmise that it is an alter-

NOTES TO PAGE 85   **271**

nate title of a book today known as *Yutai xinyong* (New songs from a jade terrace). *Yutai xinyong* is a collection of poems and songs from the Eastern Zhou (770–221 BCE) to the early Liang period collated by Xu Ling (507–583) of the Liang period. The Liang dynasty was the third of the so-called southern dynasties (420–589), and Xu Ling's last name appears in the title. Most importantly, however, the relevant palindrome poem at this point, the *Panzhong shi* (Poem on a tray), features in vol. 9 of the *Yutai xinyong*.

215. Usually this poem is referred to as *Panzhong shi*. It was composed by Su Boyu *qi*, literally the "wife of Su Boyu." The name, dates, and natal place of the wife of Su Boyu are not known. However, she is usually identified as having lived in the Jin period. Her husband, Su Boyu, had been sent off on official business to Shu (modern Sichuan), and she wrote a palindrome poem to express her longing for him. Knechtges and Chang, *Ancient and Early Medieval Chinese Literature,* 2:1031. She wrote the poem on a tray in the normal fashion of rows of characters forming a square, but the poem was palindrome and has thus been described as a spiral poem. For further information and a translation of the poem, see Lee and Stefanowska, *Biographical Dictionary of Chinese Women,* 334.

216. *Xuemai* (K. *hyŏlmaek*), the "network of the blood vessels," here means the network of literary context.

217. Yi Chisim (d. 1170), a civil official active mainly as a remonstrance official during the reign of Ŭijong. He served as palace steward (K. *kŭpsajung;* C. *jishizhong*) and presided over the civil service examinations of 1160, after which he became grand master of remonstrance. Yi Chisim was killed in the coup of 1170. He was the father-in-law of O Sejae, and although "O Sejae was proud, peevish, and arrogant, [...] Lord Yi Chisim valued his talent and did not speak ill of him." Lee, *Sourcebook of Korean Civilization,* 1:343. As a poet, Yi Chisim is mentioned in *Pohan chip* 1:33: "The academician Yi Chisim wrote a poem on the wall of P'ungju Castle:

> Heaven and ocean are boundless; gazing out into the vast distance, it goes on forever.
> In all four directions, the vision travels a thousand leagues; in the sixth month, a late autumn wind.
> In a painting it would be hard to catch such beauty; in a piece of writing, how could one obtain such skill?
> If only I could grow wings, so that my body could be in the Great Void."
> (Pak, *Yŏkchu Pohan chip,* 132.)

218. The source does not feature the relevant poem read backward. However, since it is a palindrome poem, it was meant to be read backward by any contemporary Koryŏ reader. For this reason it is translated here the other way around as well. The poem is likewise contained in *TMS* 9:3a–b.

219. This poem features in *TMS* 9:7a–b. The drying fish can be understood as a reference to a story from the *Zhuangzi* chapter "Waiwu" (External things; 26.2). Through the allusion to the drying and dying fish from *Zhuangzi,* Yi essentially states

272 NOTES TO PAGES 86–87

that in officialdom he has lost his proper element and cannot survive in this hostile environment any longer. Thus, with this poem he is asking the grand councilor for help — perhaps meaning a new position with a higher salary (to fill the rumbling empty stomach), or to be allowed to retire.

220. These five colors are red, yellow, green, white, and black. Generally they are associated with the five elements (metal, water, wood, fire, and earth) or the five directions — east, west, north, and south, respectively, correspond to blue, red, white, and black. Yellow, the color of the earth, is usually associated with the middle. For this reason the color yellow was always considered the central, most important of the five colors.

221. This couplet is taken from the poem *Yong ju* (Sung on the [theme of] chrysanthemums) by the Song dynasty poet Wei Ye (960–1020), courtesy name Zhongxian, who became famous for being a hermit poet.

222. In all likelihood this is Ch'oe Tang. Ch'oe Tang's studio was called Ssangmyŏng-jae.

223. This line refers to a tale in which an auspicious yellow swan is said to have appeared by Taiye Pond (C. Taiye Chi) in Jianzhang Palace (C. Jianzhang Gong) during the times of Emperor Zhao of Han (r. 87–74 BCE). There is the *Huanghu ge*, the "Song of the yellow swan," which is attributed to Emperor Zhao. In the *Songshu* (History of the Song dynasty; vol. 29) it says, "In the second month of the first year of the reign of Emperor Zhao of Han, a yellow swan lowered itself onto Taiye Pond in Jianzhang Palace." There is also an old-style song by the important Tang dynasty poet Wang Wei, in which the yellow swans appear: "From the Heavens' road comes — a pair of yellow swans. / They fly above the clouds — and spend the night on the water." For this song, see Fuller, *Introduction to Chinese Poetry*, 24. The auspicious yellow bird here stands for the yellow chrysanthemums.

224. Luo Fei (K. Rak Pi), the "Spirit of the Luo River" (C. Luoshen), is Fu Fei, the daughter of Fu Xi, an ancient culture hero. According to legend, she drowned in the Luo River and turned into its guardian goddess.

225. This latter part of the line is a shortened, reversed quotation from the *Luoshen fu* (Fu on the Luo River goddess) by Cao Zhi (192–232). The translation by Burton Watson says, "[Traversing the waves in tiny steps], her gauze slippers seem to stir a dust." Minford and Lau, *Classical Chinese Literature*, 317. At this point, the river goddess's graceful movements may be understood as an allusion to the chrysanthemums gently swaying in the wind.

226. *Samch'un*, "three springs," means the three months of spring (individually called *maengch'un, chungch'un,* and *kyech'un*).

227. Ch'ŏngyŏn-gak was an academic institution and royal library located on palace grounds in Kaesŏng. Through Ch'ŏngyŏn-gak as well as the royal library Pomun-gak, which were both established by Yejong around 1116 and which constituted institutions devoted to Chinese letters and learning, the king primarily promoted Confucianism. Pomun-gak was intended to store imperial Chinese edicts; Ch'ŏngyŏn-gak housed Confucian books and classics. Moreover, Ch'ŏngyŏn-gak provided a venue for lectures, some of which were even attended by the king himself.

NOTES TO PAGE 87   **273**

In the sixth chapter of his *Illustrated Account of the Xuanhe Embassy to Koryŏ*, Xu Jing quotes a text (purportedly) by Kim Injon (see 2:6), a leading diplomat and scholar of Yejong's reign, on the topic of Ch'ŏngyŏn-gak:

> [One of these pavilions] is called Pomun (precious letters) Pavilion and it enshrines the edicts bestowed by successive sages. To the west is the Ch'ŏngyŏn (bright banquet) Pavilion, which stores various works from the histories, philosophers, and miscellaneous collections. I once managed to obtain the record of the [Ch'ŏng]yŏn Pavilion, which reads as follows: Written by royal command of Kim Yŏn, custodial grand guardian with the prestige title equivalent to rank 1B, conjointly vice director of the Chancellery, editor of the state history, pillar of the state, merit baron of Kangnŭng district with a stipend village of 1,300 households, 300 of which are effective. [...] The king with acumen and resourcefulness devotedly implements resplendent virtue; worshipping the Confucian arts and music, he admires the Chinese customs. Therefore, on the side of the royal palace, north of the Yŏnyŏng book hall and south of Chahwa Hall, he separately built the pavilions of Pomun and Ch'ŏngyŏn. The former is intended to enshrine the edicts bestowed by the sagacious emperors of Song and the writings and paintings commissioned by them. [...] The latter is intended to gather the ancient and modern writings composed by the likes of the Duke of Zhou, Confucius, Mencius, and Yang Xiong." (Vermeersch, *Chinese Traveler*, 88)

In the twenty-first entry of the fourth fascicle (*hujip* 2:21) of *Yŏgong p'aesŏl*, Yi Chehyŏn mentions that "the *Ch'ŏngyŏn-gak ki* [Account of Ch'ŏngyŏn Tower] by *Sijung* Kim Injon is contained in the *Gaoli tujing* [K. *Koryŏ togyŏng*] by Xu Jing." Yi, *Han'guk myŏngjŏ taejŏnjip*, 461.

228. The source says Fendian (K. Punjŏn), which is an abbreviation for Sanfen Wudian (Three Prescripts and Five Canons), the books and writings of the sage-kings, the Three Sovereigns and Five Emperors. The term refers to the ancient Confucian canons.

229. In Xu Jing's illustrated account it says, "Oh, to discuss these daily with tutors and old scholars, to internalize the way of former kings — to store [these texts], to cultivate [one's mind], and to repose and seek pleasure there! Without having to go beyond this building, the teachings of the three bonds and five norms, the principle of nature's mandate and the virtuous way, are fully spread among the four walks of life. [...]" Vermeersch, *Chinese Traveler*, 88–89.

230. Sa-ru, "Sedge-Grass Tower." This incident, which took place in 1122, is likewise recorded in *Koryŏsa*, but here the building is called Sa-ru, "Gauze Tower." *Koryŏsa*, vol. 14, seventeenth year of Yejong, eighteenth day of the third month, 1122. "Sedge-Grass Tower" at this point may be understood as a reference to Ch'ŏngyŏn-gak.

231. It has to be kept in mind here that in Literary Chinese poetry, peonies typically stand for beautiful young women.

274   NOTES TO PAGE 87

232. The source says *kŭmsŏ cheyu*, which might be understood as a reference to the six education bureaus (K. *hakkwan*) in the forbidden inner palace (K. *kŭmnae*). The highly trained Confucian scholars of the *kŭmnae hakkwan* worked in the Pisŏ (Palace Library), the Sagwan (Bureau of Historiography or Bureau of State Records), the Hallim Academy, the Pomun-gak, the Ösŏ-wŏn (Institute of Calligraphy), and the Tongmun-wŏn (Chinese Relations Institute). See *Koryŏsa*, vol. 76, "Paekkwan," "T'ongmun-gwan." In the relevant entry in *Koryŏsa* it says that King Yejong called upon fifty-six literati to write their poems on the lyrical theme of the peony within the time limit set by a marked candle.

233. *Kakch'ok* (C. *kezhu*), "marked candle," refers to an ancient method of limiting time in poetry competitions. Candles were engraved and marked with a line, and once the fire had burned down to the mark, the time granted to the poets to finish their lyrical works had expired.

234. An Porin (d. 1126). In 1126, when serving as palace attendant overseer (K. *naesi roksa*), An Porin and others opposed Yi Chagyŏm and his followers. The coup initiated by the group surrounding An Porin was countered by Yi Chagyŏm, and An Porin died during the fighting. The source here has him as *tonggung ryojwa*, which seems to be an unidentifiable office in the Eastern Palace, the residence of the heir apparent (K. *t'aeja*). The relevant entry in *Koryŏsa* states that An Porin at this point in time served as secretary in the household administration of the heir apparent (K. *ch'ŏmsabu chubu*), an agency of the central government in charge of administrating the affairs of the heir apparent. Hence, the title named in *Koryŏsa* is in line with the Tonggung-related office mentioned in the present entry.

235. In spite of his apparent fame as a poet, lyrical works by Kang Iryong (n.d.) extant today are rather scarce. This, however, was apparently already the case during late Koryŏ times, as can be seen in the fifteenth entry of the fourth fascicle (*hujip* 2:15) of *Yŏgong p'aesŏl*, where Yi Chehyŏn writes, "In the world it is said, 'Teacher Kang Iryong and the Libationer [K. Chwaeju] Im Yujŏng [n.d.] were both skilled in the poetic forms of the Hundred Schools. Kang's poems, however, can hardly be found anywhere today, while Im's collected writings have been printed and are circulating." Yi, *Han'guk myŏngjŏ taejŏnjip*, 452.

236. *So hwangmun*, "junior attendants at the yellow gates."

237. At the age of forty, after his demotion in 1046, Song dynasty statesman, scholar, and poet Quyang Xiu (1007–1072) called himself Zuiweng, "Old Drunkard" (the pen name is well-known because of Ouyang's pavilion, the Zuiweng Ting, "Old Drunkard Pavilion," as well as his famous essay composed there, the "Zuiwen Ting ji").

238. In the fortieth entry of the upper fascicle of *Tongin sihwa*, Sŏ Kŏjŏng discusses both the incident and the poem at hand, writing,

> At the court of King Ye[jong] of Koryŏ, in front of the royal tower [K. ŏru], tree peonies once stood in full bloom, and thus [the king] commanded the various Confucian scholars of the [six] Inner Palace Offices to write poems on them. Teacher Kang Iryong merely managed to write, "His head

white, Old Drunkard glanced [at them] from behind the main hall; / his eyes sparkling, a Confucian Elder leaned [toward them] beside his fence." The elders [K. *sŏnbae*] then said that his use of allusions was precise and appropriate. I first chewed around [on these two lines] and didn't quite understand what their piquancy was supposed to be, but later I read that Changli [Han Yu] had chanted on the topic of peonies, [and in his poem entitled *Xiti mudan* (Playfully on the topic of peonies)] there was the line, "But today, beside my fence, my eyes sparkled for a while." And when Master Ouyang [Xiu] [who was by then already an old man] chanted on the peonies [i.e., young women] there was the line, "And I laugh at myself, for now I've become a white-haired old man." It was only then that I began to grasp that the origin [of the old man Kang Iryong's lines] and his use of allusions were indeed precise and fitting. The only disappointment is that the words are deep and unfamiliar, and that the rhyme is high but the talent short. In the case of someone like the teacher [Kang Iryong], how couldn't one point to what an ancient meant when he remarked: "He's a person skilled in the making of prescribed wine [K. *pŏpchu*], but he doesn't have the ingredients." (Yi, *Tongin sihwa*, 87)

The relevant poem by Han Yu, *Playfully on the Topic of Peonies,* reads,

> By good fortune they opened together, all in a blur,
> why must they rest on each other in contest of light charms?
> At the break of dawn they all have newly made up faces,
> facing visitors they show special reserve, passions unspoken.
> No designs on them, a pair of swallows again brushes past them,
> but roaming bees are full of longing and now busy at them.
> For an older person all such concerns have been entirely left behind,
> but today beside my fence my eyes sparkle for a moment.
> (Owen, *The Late Tang*, 455)

Hence, both lines by Kang Iryong allude to Chinese master poets of a rather advanced age feeling aroused — and thereby also embarrassed — by young women. This same embarrassment may have been the cause for Kang Iryong being unable to finish the poem and for him hiding in the palace canal.

239. Xi Shi (ca. 503–ca. 473 BCE) is traditionally considered the most beautiful of the "four most beautiful women of ancient China" (C. *sida meiren*). The slightly different basis for this saying can be found in the second entry of the tenth volume of a collection of short stories from the Tang period entitled *Tang zhiyan* (Collected statements of the Tang), which was written by Wang Dingbao (870–940). This work features many stories dealing with the civil service examination. The relevant story reads,

> During the Qianfu-era [of the Xizong emperor of Tang, 874–879], [a person by the name of] Jiang Ning took the preeminent *hongci* ["magnificent

276   NOTES TO PAGE 88

diction"] examination, and for a [long] rhapsody he stopped when he had written four rhymes. Eventually he pulled along [and handed in] an [almost] white sheet of paper, after which he left. [...] Soon thereafter, [when his writing] was compared with that of the various masters [who had also taken part in the examination], [it was seen] that Ning's [short poem] had something very special to it, and the examination officials sighed for a long time. In no time, word [about this extraordinary incident] had spread, and somebody called out [mockingly], "If, on a white head, flowery hairpins entirely fill the face, it still won't be like Consort Xu's face only half made up."

Xu Fei, "Consort Xu," was Xu Zhaopei, a concubine of Emperor Yuan of Liang known for her surliness and lack of beauty. On the rare occasion that the emperor visited her, she emerged from her room only half made up, and the emperor would depart in anger. The last part of the line on Consort Xu also features in the poem *Nanchao* (The southern dynasties) by the Tang dynasty master poet Li Shangyin (812–858), where it says,

> Earth's escarpment stretches on, Heaven's escarpment is long.
> The kingly aura of Jingling matches the Jasper Luminescence.
> Yet do not boast that this place divides all under Heaven;
> Just look at Consort Xu's face, with cosmetics half applied.

For the translation of this poem and the information on Consort Xu, see Rouzer, *Writing Another's Dream,* 117. King Yejong here appears to imply that even though Kang Iryong's verse is short and only half-finished (just like Xi Shi's makeup being only half-applied), it still beats anything a person without natural talent could have produced. It is important to note that Yi Illo portrays King Yejong as having had no difficulties understanding the allusions used by Kang Iryong—as can be seen in the previous note, the highly trained intellectual Sŏ Kŏjŏng in the early Chosŏn dynasty was in turn not able to do so on the spot.

240. The entry in *Koryŏsa* retelling this incident (which constitutes an almost one-to-one copy of the *P'ahan chip* episode at hand) ends at this point. See *Koryŏsa,* vol. 14, seventeenth year of Yejong, eighteenth day of the third month, 1122.

241. In volume 104 of *Zhejiang tongzhi* (Gazetteer of Jiejiang) it says, "When there are often light clouds and faint rain, that's [the period] referred to as the 'weather for cultivating flowers' [K. *yanghwa ch'ŏn*]." An annotation states that this information derives from the *Yuezhong mudan* (Peonies in the Yue region), a work by the Song dynasty monk Zhongshu.

242. The *jiegu* (K. *kalgo*) is a bucket-shaped drum that became popular in Tang China. Here, the reference to the *jiegu* can be understood as an allusion to the *cuihua gu* (K. *ch'oehwa ko*), the "drum that causes flowers to bloom," a *jiegu* that, as legend has it, belonged to Tang emperor Xuanzong (r. 712–755). According to the *Kaiyuan Tianbao yishi* (Anecdotes from Kaiyuan and Tianbao), Xuan-

NOTES TO PAGE 88 **277**

zong is said to have caused flowers and trees to bloom by beating on this special *jiegu* drum. In the entry "Kalgo" in the fourth volume of Yi Kyubo's *Tongguk Yi Sangguk chip,* Emperor Xuanzong's supernatural handling of the *jiegu* is described in the following way:

> In the *Jiegu lu* [*Jiegu* records; written by Nan Zhuo, ca. 850] it says: "[...] Emperor Ming [Xuangzong] liked it [the *jiegu* drum] very much. When the rains of spring began to clear and the scenery of the season was bright and beautiful, the Emperor took the drum, looked down over the balustrade and beat the drum to his heart's content." Also, in the [*Taiping*] *guangji* it says: "When he [Xuangzong] wanted willow trees and apricot trees to bloom inside [the garden of] a small palace pavilion, the emperor took the drum and beat it to his heart's content. The name of the song was "Chunguang hao" [K. "Ch'ungwang ho"], and when he looked back at the willow trees and the apricot trees which together were already in full bloom, he pointed at them laughingly [...]" (*TYSC* 4:4a–b)

243. *Baiwu* (K. *paeg'o*), "one hundred and five," refers to the Hanshi Jie (K. Hansik Chŏl), the "Cold Food Festival," an ancient festival traditionally associated with mid-spring. The date for the festival was a hundred and five days after the winter solstice, at the end of the second month, and thus it was often referred to as the "festival on the one hundred and fifth day." The one hundred fifth day here refers to the time in which the peonies are in bloom.

244. This refers to the three thousand ladies of the Han dynasty court, who are here said to all have worn peonies in their hair.

245. The source here says *un un,* "the above cited" or the "aforementioned verse," meaning, "His head white, Old Drunkard glanced [at them] from behind the main hall; / his eyes sparkling, Confucian Elder leaned [toward them] beside his fence."

246. Since there is no line break between the previous entry on King Yejong's poetry competition and the one at hand, this entry has by some been understood as a part of the previous entry. However, in the source, a small black dot in front of the first character indicates, I believe, that in seventeenth-century Chosŏn it was perceived as a new section and that it was indeed treated as episode 1:19.

247. This is because the one who harmonizes has to use the same rhyme categories and is consequently forced to adjust his or her own poem to that of the precursor.

248. Chulao is the literary name of the Northern Song political reformer and poet Wang Anshi (1021–1086).

249. Meishan is a mountain in Sichuan. Meishan here refers to Su Shi, who was a native of Meishan.

250. *Cha* (K. *ch'a;* "fork") is a character for which few sensible rhymes exist. One poem by Su Dongpo in which he used the rhyme category *cha*—with *cha* constituting the final character of the entire poem—is *Xuehou shu beitai bi* (Written after snowfall on a wall of the northern terrace), which reads as follows:

278   NOTES TO PAGES 88–89

> Early in the morning when the crows just fly off the city walls,
> And on the paths between the fields the carts get stuck in bright mire,
> From cold the shoulders [lit., jade towers] shrug; chillness makes the flesh
> creep,
> Brilliant light dazzles the eyes [lit., silver seas] with sparkles.
> The nymphs of the locusts must have retired into the ground a thousand
> feet deep.
> The wheat, sown last autumn, reaches to the clouds, enough for ten thousand
> households,
> Old and decrepit, I lament my waning poetic strength,
> In vain! I recite "Icicles" to commemorate Liu Cha.
> (Translation in Kovacs and Unschuld, *Essential Subtleties on the Silver
> Sea*, 123)

The personal name of the poet Liu Cha, who is mentioned in the last line of the poem, is the character *cha*. Liu Cha, author of the poem *Bingzhu* (Icicles), was a contemporary and protégé of Han Yu. Regarding the relationship between Su Shi and Wang Anshi, Ronald Egan writes,

> After years of dispute and mutual suspicion, Su Shi and Wang Anshi had their first direct contact in 1085. Their meetings together were private and, by all indications, extremely cordial. The origin of the personal relationship between the two political antagonists can be traced back to the late 1070s, and it began with poetry. In the winter of 1076, while serving in Mizhou, Su Shi had witnessed a great snowstorm and had written two poems about it, emphasizing the hardship it caused for the commoners. Su's poem circulated, and eventually reached Wang Anshi, who had by then resigned permanently from the government and was living in seclusion at Zhong Mountain, outside Jingling (Nanjing). Wang was impressed by Su's snow poems, and he praised and explicated them to his son-in-law. Then Wang wrote several poems in response and evidently sent them to Su Shi. The poems that survive compliment Su on the intricacy of his verses and present images of Wang poring over and savoring them in his study. [...] When Su's exile ended in 1084, [...] he paid several visits to Wang Anshi in his seclusion outside the city. This was apparently the first and only time the two men ever met. (Egan, *Word, Image, and Deed*, 91–92)

251. The poem through which Wang meant to express his affection for Su Dongpo's use of rhymes is entitled *Du Meishan ji ai qi xueshi neng yongyun fu ciyun yishou* (One verse of responding rhymes upon reading the *Meishan ji* and admiring the capability of using rhymes in his snow poems).

252. These five lyrical pieces by Wang Anshi are entitled *Du Meishan ji ciyun xueshi wushou* (Five verses upon reading responding rhyme snow poems in *Meishan ji*).

253. The final character and rhyme of the first lines in this poem, the *Xuehou*

shu beitai bi, as well as the *Du Meishan ji ciyun xueshi wushou* is *ya* (K. *a*), "crow." The first line of Su's poem reads, "Above the city-wall the rising sun, flying off are the crows." The first line in Wang Anshi's first of the five poems reads, "The Ruo Tree murky and dark, on the ends [of its branches] are [perching] crows."

254. The final character of the second line in the relevant poems is *che* (K. *ch'a*), "cart." In Su's poem the second line reads, "Bright mire on a field lane, already stuck is the cart."

255. The line ends with *chuzi* (K. *ch'ŏja*), which means an unmarried young girl who still lives at home. The virgin girl might at this point be understood as a reference to "Xiaoyao you" from *Zhuangzi,* which contains a description of a holy immortal that features the term *chuzi.* See Ziporyn, *Zhuangzi,* 7. In *Xuehou shu beitai bi* the final character of the third line is *su* (K. *sok*), "grain." It reads, "Frozen, hunched jade pavilions [shoulders], the cold gives me goose bumps." In *Du Meishan ji ai qi xueshi neng yongyun fu ciyun yishou* it is *gu* (K. *kol*), "bone."

256. The final character of the fourth line in all three poems is *hua* (K. *hwa*), "flower" or "blossom." The fourth line in Su Dongpo's poem reads, "Brilliant light agitates the silver seas, the eyes produce flowers."

257. The final character in this line is *zhi* (K. *chi*), "paper." The final character in this line in Su's poem is *chi* (K. *ch'ŏk*), "measure" or "feet." In the poem by Wang Anshi it is *li,* "league." In Su's poem it says, "Locust larvae have entered the earth for a thousand feet."

258. The final character in the fifth line of all three relevant poems is *jia* (K. *ka*), "house," "household," or "home."

259. "All around" is a translation of *doulu,* a term that may refer to an ancient state to the west of China. It can also, however, be understood in the sense of *tongtong* (K. *t'ongt'ong*), "wholly" or "completely."

260. The final character here is *jie* (K. *kye*), "world." In Su's poem it is *tui* (K. *t'oe*); in Wang Anshi's poem it is *wo* (K. *wa*).

261. The final character in this line in all three poems is, of course, *cha.*

262. This *xiang che,* or "fragrant cart," is a reference to the chariot ridden by the God of Thunder, for the Thunder God's chariot is pushed and steered by an immortal boy by the name of A Xiang. The second line in Wang Anshi's first of the five reply poems also features the thunder cart of A Xiang.

263. This line might be a reference to a tale about the Jin dynasty calligrapher and poet Wang Huizi (Wang Ziyou, d. 386) who one snowy day took his boat and set out to visit his friend Dai Kui (Dai Andao, 326–396). In *Shishuo xinyu* the story is recorded in the following way:

> Wang Ziyou lived in Shanyin. One night, it snowed heavily. He woke up from a sleep, opened the door to his room, and asked for wine. It was a shining white all around. He rose to walk back and forth, and chanted Zuo Si's "Poem to Call the Recluse to Service." He suddenly thought about Dai Andao who was living in Shan at the time, and just took a small boat and traveled to see him that night. He didn't arrive until the next morning.

280 NOTES TO PAGES 89–90

When he was about to reach the gate, he stopped moving and then turned back. When people asked him the reason, Wang said, "I took the trip on an impulse. Once the impulse was gone, I just returned. Why must I see Dai?" (Luo, *Concise History of Chinese Literature*, 264)

264. A *hwach'a* (C. *huacha*) is a wooden frame onto which paintings (or, in this case, coins with a hole on a string) could be hung.

265. The incident presented in this entry is likewise described in *Koryŏsa*, vol. 18, eighth year of Ŭijong, twenty-sixth day of the first month, 1154. The entry in *Koryŏsa* reads as follows: "In the cyclic year *kimyo*, the king resided at Kyŏngp'ung Palace Hall. He summoned his retinue of scholar officials and ordered them to write a poem on the topic of [*The functionary of*] *Ch'ŏnggyo-yŏk presents a blue cow*. Hallim Academician Kim Hyosun and fourteen others who met the standards and passed were bestowed upon with goods, and furthermore they were bestowed upon with wine and fruit."

266. The source says *ri* (C. *li*), "official" or "functionary," but it can here be taken as *yŏngni* (C. *yili*) or *chŏlli* (C. *zhuanli*), the "stationmaster" of a relay station.

267. According to the *Sinjŭng tongguk yŏji sŭngnam* (vol. 4; sec. "Kaesŏngbu"; subsec. "yŏgwŏn"), Ch'ŏnggyo-yŏk was a postal relay station (K. *yŏk*) located five leagues outside of Pojŏng-mun, the northern gate in Kaesŏng's fortification wall. It played a role in the coup of 1170, when Mubi, King Ŭijong's favorite courtesan, fled to Ch'ŏnggyo-yŏk to hide from Chŏng Chungbu and his men, who were out to kill her. She eventually survived and was allowed to follow King Ŭijong into exile to Kŏje.

268. *Ch'ŏngu* (C. *jingniu*), a blue (or perhaps greenish-colored) cow, is an animal purportedly ridden by immortals or Taoist masters.

269. *Sasin* (C. *cichen*), "rhetorical ministers," can here be understood as an allusion to the drafters of royal proclamations or the various Confucian scholars of the Six Inner Palace Offices, who always surrounded the king.

270. Apart from the *Koryŏsa* entry cited in note 265, Kim Hyosun (n.d.) is mentioned only one other time in *Koryŏsa*. In this second entry from 1162 he is said to have served as remonstrator (K. *sagan*).

271. The source here says Tonggwan (C. Dongguan), "Eastern Bureau." It is not entirely clear what specific institution is meant, but one can surmise that it refers to either the Hallim Academy or the Office for Drafting Proclamations. It may be an alternate designation for Hallim-wŏn, because in the previously cited *Koryŏsa* entry, Kim Hyosun is clearly said to have served as a Hallim-wŏn academician at the time in question. In addition, Sin Ŭngnyong, the participant who was awarded second place in this poetry competition, is also said to have been from the Hallim Academy. However, in 3:17, a clear distinction is made between the Tonggwan and the Oktang, for it says "that the Eastern Bureau is referred to as 'Mount Penglai' while the Jade Hall is called 'Turtle Head.' [...]" Against the background of this later entry, one can surmise that Eastern Bureau denotes the Office for Drafting Proclamations.

272. The phoenix, a mythical bird whose appearance is usually taken as a highly auspicious sign, comes to a virtuous ruler or worthy, noble men. This understanding derives from the *Shijing* ode *Juan a*. At this point, the phoenix is seemingly ashamed

to enter the palace compound where the virtuous king resides, because an even more auspicious animal, the blue cow, is already present at the tower. *Kak*, "tower," may here be taken as a reference to the Ch'ŏngyŏn-gak, the Tower of Pure Debate.

273. This is an allusion to the "constellation of the four heavenly horses" (C. *tiansi*), which is also known as the "constellation of the room" (K. *pangsŏng*; C. *fangxing*), the fourth of the twenty-eight lunar mansions (C. *ershiba xiu*). The celestial horses are here also said to be embarrassed to come forth in the presence of the blue cow, a divine animal.

274. Ningzi, "Master Ning," refers to Ning Qi, who lived during the Spring and Autumn Period. Before he was discovered, Ning Qi worked as a petty merchant. According to legend, he was feeding a cow one day when King Huan of Qi happened to pass by. Seeing him, Ning Qi attracted his attention by singing while striking the cow's horn. Something about the singing and drumming signaled to King Huan that the singer was an extraordinary person. He consequently elevated him to minister. See Sukhu, *Shaman and the Heresiarch*, 231–232. In *Huainanzi* (Masters of Huainan; a second-century BCE Chinese philosophical classic) 10.94 it says, "Ning Qi beat time on a cow's horn and sang, and Duke Huan raised him up with a great grant of land." Major, *Heaven and Earth in Early Han Thought*, 383.

275. This line is a reference to a person by the name of Hu He, who appears in *Mengzi* 1A 7.4, an entry in which Mengzi converses with King Xuan of Qi. It reads,

> The king said, "Can one such as Ourselves care for the people?" Mengzi said, "You can." The king said, "How do you know that We can?" Mengzi said, "I heard your attendant Hu He say, 'While the king was sitting up in his hall, an ox was led past below. The king saw it and said, 'Where is the ox going?' Hu He replied, 'We are about to ritually anoint a bell with its blood.' The king said, 'Spare it. I cannot bear its frightened appearance, like an innocent going to the execution ground.' Hu He replied, 'So should we dispense with the anointing of the bell?' The king said, 'How can that be dispensed with? Exchange it for a sheep.' " (Van Norden, *Mengzi*, 8)

276. Im Chongbi was the older brother of Im Kwangbi, the father of Im Ch'un. Im Chongbi, who served as Hallim academician, penned the epitaph for the prominent Koryŏ monk Chiin (1102–1158; courtesy name Kwangji). The epitaph is entitled *Kwangji taesŏnsa Chiin myojimyŏng* (Epitaph on a memorial tablet on the grave of the Great Sŏn Master Kwangji Chiin). The literature of Im Chongbi served as a model for literati even decades after his death, as can be seen in *Pohan chip* 3:19, where it says, "After I [Ch'oe Cha] had passed the civil service examinations, I admired the four-six [syllable texts] by Im Chongbi and Chŏng Chisang." Pak, *Yŏkchu Pohan chip*, 429.

277. "In Peach Grove you were let loose in spring" is an allusion to an entry in "Wucheng" (The successful completion of the war) from *Shujing*. Here, King Mu of Zhou released his warhorses and oxen after the victory over the Shang dynasty in order to demonstrate that he would never wage war again. A translation can be found in Legge, *Chinese Classics*, 3:308.

278. The "red room" (K. *hongbang*) stands for the palace. "Marched into" here is

282 NOTES TO PAGES 90–91

a translation of *ta* (K. *tap*), short for *cuta* (K. *ch'uktap*), which usually denotes the trampling movement of horses (or, in this case, oxen). In early Chinese texts, however, *cuta* is also associated with the movement of soldiers or armies. See Owen, *Poetry of Du Fu*, 1:429. The term appears, for instance, in the poem *Zi jing fu Fengxianxian yonghuai wubai zi* (Going from the capital to Fengxian County, singing my feelings) by Du Fu, and Stephen Owen's translation of the relevant lines (where *cuta* is rendered as "the tramp of armies") reads, "Where battle flags blocked a cold and empty sky, / Where slopes and valleys were worn smooth by the tramp of armies." Owen, "Tu Fu," 838.

279. This line is a reference to the legend of Niulang, the "Cowherd" or "Oxherd," and Zhinü, the Weaver Maid, i.e., the stars Altair and Vega. When the two of them got married, the Weaver Maid was so overjoyed that she neglected her duties of weaving the celestial cloth with its pattern of clouds. Her father, the Emperor of Heaven, grew angry and concluded that her husband was the cause of this. Thus he separated them and ordered that the Cowherd should move to the other side of the Silver Stream, the Milky Way. Afterward they were only allowed to meet once a year, on the seventh day of the seventh month. When the time comes, myriads of magpies are said to fly together and to form a bridge over the flood of stars to aid the two lovers' meeting.

280. Hangu Pass (C. Hangu-guan) was an ancient strategic pass near present-day Lingbao, Henan Province. When Laozi passed through Hangu Pass, he purportedly rode on the back of a blue/green cow. According to legend, on Hangu Pass, the border guard Yin Xi saw a purple vapor moving toward him from the east, and thus he knew that a sage was coming. He requested the *Daodejing* and subsequently became the first recipient of Laozi's teachings. When Laozi then disappeared westward to become an immortal, riding on the blue cow, the "purple *qi*" or "purple vapor" (C. *ziqi*) appeared again. For this *ziqi*, see Benn, *Burning for the Buddha*, 271.

281. The source here says *zhuo* (K. *t'ak*), which means to polish a jade stone or to cut and sculpt jade.

282. This is a couplet from Du Fu's poem *Hengzhou song Li daifu qizhang mian fu Guangzhou* (At Hengzhou seeing off Censor-in-Chief Li Mian on his way to Guangzhou). The poem reads,

> The axe descends from the blue darkness,
> his towered galley crosses Lake Dongting.
> The north wind brings an invigorating atmosphere,
> the Southern Dipper flees the Star of Letters.
> Days and months, a bird in a cage,
> Heaven and Earth, a duckweed on the waters.
> Our Prince in the position of a senior
> sees me, tossed and fallen, approaching old age.
> (Translation in Owen, *Poetry of Du Fu*, 6:39)

These lines in *P'ahan chip* are referred to and quoted in *Maeho yugo* (Posthumous manuscripts of Maeho, 1784). See *Maeho yugo* 1:14b.

NOTES TO PAGE 91   **283**

283. This is a line from Du Fu's long poem *Fengji zhouzhong fuzhen shuhuai sanshiliuyun fengcheng Hunan qinyou* (Lying on my sickbed in the boat with a "wind illness," writing my feelings in thirty-six couplets: Respectfully to be shown to my friends in Hu'nan). Translation in Owen, *Poetry of Du Fu*, 23:233.

284. Yan and Yue, the northernmost and southernmost Chinese states during ancient times.

285. To knock, *qiao* (K. *ko*), and to push, *tui* (K. *t'oe*). Usually, the term appears in the reverse order as *tuiqiao* (K. *t'oego*), which is the Chinese expression for "deliberation" and which literally means "to 'push' or to 'knock' [on the gate]." In the realm of poetry, *tuiqiao* alludes to how careful and deliberate ancient Chinese poets were in their choice of words in the process of creating poetry. The expression derives from the following anecdote about Jia Dao (779–843), a talented poet-monk and a member of Han Yu's circle:

> When Jia Dao first went to the capital for the examinations, he happened to hit upon a couplet of poetry while he was riding a donkey: "The birds roost in trees by the pool, / A monk knocks on a gate under the moon." At first he chose the word "push," but later he took a liking to "knock." He rehearsed both in his mind, undecided, reciting the line aloud from the back of his donkey. From time to time he put forth his hands and imitated the gestures of knocking and pushing. At this time Han Yu held a position in the Board of Public Office (metropolitan governor) in the capital, and Jia inadvertently blundered into his retinue. Han's servants seized him and brought him before their master. Jia then proceeded to explain the lines he had composed, and so forth; Han held his horse still for a long while, then finally said to Jia, " 'Knock' is better."

For the translation of the anecdote (which is suspiciously similar to the anecdote about the way in which Chŏng Chisang hit upon a couplet while riding his horse after having left the Eight-Foot-Room in 1:22), see Rouzer, *Writing Another's Dream*, 9. "Metropolitan governor" is a translation of *jingyin* (K. *kyŏngyun*), which is here short for *jingzhou yin* (K. *kyŏngjo yun*), "the office of metropolitan governor." Han Yu held this position when Jia Dao allegedly ran into him and asked him for his advice on the fitting expression in his poem.

286. This line can be understood as a reference to the poem *Xizeng Du Fu* (Addressed humorously to Du Fu) by Li Bai (701–762). *Xizeng Du Fu* was written by Li Bai upon meeting Du Fu on Fanke-shan, "Boiled Rice Mountain." In the translation by David Young, the poem reads:

> On Boiled Rice Mountain I met Du Fu
> wearing a big round bamboo hat in the hot noon sun
> Du Fu, how come you've grown so thin?
> you must be suffering from too much poetry.
>   (Minford and Lau, *Classical Chinese Literature*, 751–752)

284 NOTES TO PAGES 91–92

287. The term *sŏbong* (C. *xifeng*), "western peaks," might stand for *sŏsan* (C. *xishan*), "western mountains," and thereby perhaps to Du Fu's three poems *Xishan* (The western mountains), which are on the topic of the mountains on the Tibetan border. See Owen, *Poetry of Du Fu,* 3:276.

288. This might be an allusion to the poem *Fengqiao yebo* (Mooring at night by Maple Bridge) by Zhang Ji (mid-eighth century). Not much is known about the Tang dynasty poet Zhang Ji. Generally he is considered a minor poet of the golden age of Tang poetry. He is said to have passed the highest state examinations in 753. Though several dozen of his poems were transmitted over time, his lasting fame was founded predominantly on the poem *Fengqiao yebo.* Klöpsch, " 'Um Mitternacht der Glocke Ton,' " 65. In the translation by Stephen Owen, the poem *Fengqiao yebo* (Mooring by night at Maple Bridge) reads: "The moon is setting, crows cry out, and frost fills the sky. / River maples and fishermen's fires face someone who lies here melancholy. / Beyond the walls of Ku-Su, Cold Mountain Temple: / At midnight the sounds of its bell reach the traveler's boat." Owen, *Readings in Chinese Literary Thought,* 424. One of many other translations of this poem is the one by Wittner Bynner under the title *A Night-Mooring Near Maple Bridge.* Minford and Lau, *Classical Chinese Literature,* 852.

289. The poetry of Su Shi was immensely popular during mid-Koryŏ times. This is evidenced, for instance, in the fact that the names of the influential brothers Kim Pu*sik* and Kim Pu*ch'ŏl* were modeled after Su Shi (K. *sik*) and his younger brother Su Zhe (1039–1112; K. So Ch'ŏl). Concerning the popularity of Su Shi's poetry during this time, Yi Kyubo stated in the letter *Tap Chŏn Iji ron mun sŏ* (Letter in reply to Chŏn Iji's discussions on literature), "Also, those who are learning in this day and age, when they first practice the literary styles needed for the civil service examinations, they are much too busy devoting themselves to the study of elegant poetic writing. It's only after they have already passed the examinations that they actually get to learn how to write poetry. Since they're all extremely fond of reading [Su] Dong-po's poetry, each and every year, after the successful candidates have come forth in the [Golden] Roster, everyone thinks, 'This year, another thirty Dongpos have come forth again.' " *TYSC* 26:5a. Su Shi's literature was also enormously important to Yi Illo throughout his life. Yi Illo mentions the Song dynasty poet several times in *P'ahan chip,* but as can be seen in the letter *Yŏ Misu ron Tongp'a mun sŏ* (Letter discussing [Su] Dongpo's literature with Misu; *SHC* 4:10b–11a), a letter sent to Yi Illo by Im Ch'un, the two friends engaged in discussions of Su's poetry decades before the creation of the *sihwa* collection at hand.

290. The source here says Hwang Wŏn or Hwangwŏn. It appears reasonable to assume that the person meant is the high official and renowned poet Kim Hwangwŏn (1045–1117). Kim served in positions such as left reminder (K. *chwa sŭpyu*), royal drafter, and chancellor of the Directorate of Education (K. Kukja Cheju). According to his biography in *Koryŏsa* (vol. 97), during his day he was considered the best writer of old-style literature in all of Korea.

291. "Studio in the province" here is a translation of *kunje* (C. *junzhai*), a term appearing, for example, in the title of the Song dynasty book catalogue *Junzhai dushu zhi. Kunje* usually refers to the place of residence of a county magistrate. For two

Notes to Page 92   **285**

years, Kim Hwangwŏn served as magistrate of Kyŏngsan, present-day Sŏngju. The following poem was probably composed during his time in this office.

292. The source says *chami* (C. *ziwei*), "crape myrtle," which is an alternate designation for the Chungsŏ Munhasŏng, the Chancellery or Secretariat. At this point, the position of Yi Sunu (see 1:9), who served as drafter in the Secretariat, is being referred to. The second line in the next poem is a play on words with *chami* and *chungsŏ*.

293. Xiliu Ying, "Thin Willow Camp," is the name of the place where the Han dynasty general Zhou Yafu (d. 143 BCE) stationed his troops to ward off Xiongnu attacks from the north. Zhou Yafu was known as a man of great integrity who expected the highest form of disciplined response from troops under his command. He demanded such discipline that in later times any tightly run, disciplined army base became known as a *xiliu ying*. Idema and West, *Battles, Betrayals, and Brotherhood*, 183. At this point, the "newly appointed grand general" who comes to the military camp in Kwandong is Yi Sunu himself.

294. This line can be understood as a reference to the poem *Duange xing* (Short song) by Cao Cao (155–220, Emperor Wu of Wei) in which it says: "The moon is bright, stars are few; crows and magpies flying toward the south. Thrice they circle above the trees, but there is no branch that they could perch on." The first two of these lines from Cao Cao's poem are quoted in the former *Chibi fu* (Red cliff rhapsody) by Su Shi. Strassberg, *Inscribed Landscapes*, 186. The lines at hand constitute slight variations of two lines that are part of a longer congratulary poem written by Im Ch'un for Yi Illo entitled *Chaksi ha Yi changwŏn Misu* (Composing a poem to congratulate Principal Graduate Yi Misu), which is contained in the third volume of *Sŏha chip* and reads,

> Ice cold tip of the brush, a hundred victories achieved;
> already on three occasions selected as the worthy winner.
> Together we sojourned in the examination halls, but [in the national examination] you succeeded first;
> laughingly I point toward the mists and auroras [of the mountains], I shall return there alone.
> The wind blows hard, as the circling Peng rises from the north;
> the moon shines bright, as the startled magpie flies off toward the south.
> My wife in the mountains only finds it strange that my head is white as snow,
> and that in my prime years I am still wearing a commoner's clothes.
> (*SHC* 3:2b)

On the one hand, in this poem Im Ch'un certainly congratulates his friend Yi Illo on his success in the civil service examinations. On the other hand, he also clearly bemoans his own failure, stating that while Yi rises like the majestic Peng in the north (i.e., Kaesŏng), he himself must take flight like a magpie and escape toward the south.

295. "Rectifier of omissions" is a translation of *pogwŏl* (C. *buque*), which was one of several titles used for officials known generally as remonstrance officials. Hucker,

286 Notes to Page 92

Dictionary of Official Titles, 391. Though he is here not mentioned by name, the poetic lines that follow were penned by Chŏng Chisang. Chŏng, a native of P'yŏngyang, was a major political figure and one of the finest poets of Koryŏ times. He passed the civil service examinations in 1114 and subsequently became one of the most prominent political figures of the early twelfth century, serving in several high positions such as left remonstrator (K. *chwa sagan*), royal diarist (K. *kigŏju*), Hallim academician, and royal drafter. Well versed in Confucianism as well as Buddhism, he became friends with the Buddhist master Myoch'ŏng and the scholar-official Paek Suhan (d. 1135). In 1135, Chŏng was accused of being linked to the uprising initiated by Myoch'ŏng and was killed by troops led by Kim Pusik, Chŏng Chisang's chief political rival. See Han and Chu, "Twenty-Four Poems by Chŏng Chisang," 611. At the time, P'yŏngyang literati thought that Kim Pusik had been jealous of Chŏng Chisang's superior literary talents and had him executed on the pretext of having been behind the rebellion. See Jang, "Regional Identities of Northern Literati," 82.

296. P'alch'ŏk-pang appears to have been a tiny lodging room for wayfaring monks or travelers in Kaesŏng-sa on Ch'ŏnma-san.

297. The *Sinjŭng tongguk yŏji sŭngnam* (vol. 4, sec. "Kaesŏng-bu") states that Ch'ŏnma-san, "Heavenly Grindstone Mountain," stands to the north of Mount Songak. Its manifold peaks are said to tower high into the sky, they pierce the heavens, and when looked at from afar, a kingfisher-blue color purportedly amasses above and around it. The framing narrative of the dream-journey tale "Yonggung puyŏn rok" (Report of [Scholar Han] attending a banquet in the Dragon Palace), the fifth and final tale of Kim Sisŭp's *Kŭmo sinhwa,* is set at Ch'ŏnma-san. The opening passage of "Yonggung puyŏn rok" reads,

> Near Songdo lies Mount Ch'ŏnma. This mountain pierces [the sky], shooting up steeply, and for this reason it is called Ch'ŏnma, "Heavenly Grindstone." Amid the mountain there exists a dragon pond named Pagyŏn, which is narrow and so deep that no one knows how many fathoms downward it reaches. [This deep pool] flows out into a waterfall that may be several hundred fathoms in height. The scenery here is so pristine and beautiful that itinerant monks and passing wayfarers necessarily stop and admire the view. [There are tales of Pagyŏn] having early on brought forth a different, numinous [being]. [The stories are] contained in all transmitted records, and the country offers sacrificial animals to worship [the numinous being] every year in the appropriate season. (Translation in Wuerthner, *Tales of the Strange by a Korean Confucian Monk,* 128)

298. These lines are part of one of Chŏng Chisang's extant poems, the *Kaesŏng-sa p'alch'ŏk-pang* (The Eight-Foot Room in Kaesŏng Temple), which features in *Tongmunsŏn.* See *TMS* 12:16a–b. In Han and Chu's translation, the entire poem reads:

> Climbing one hundred steps and passing nine bends, I ascend the lofty mountain.

The temple in midair has only a few rooms.
The bubbly brook so crystal clear, its frigid water flows downhill.
The ancient cliffs bleakly dim, their walls are marked with green moss.
At the rock's edge a pine ages under a crescent moon.
At the sky's end clouds descend on a thousand crags below.
Myriad affairs of the dusty world cannot reach here.
The hermit alone earns the repose of years on end.
(Han and Chu, "Twenty-Four Poems by Chŏng Chisang," 624)

The two lines are likewise cited in *Tongin sihwa* as representative lines for Chŏng Chisang's outstanding irregular-style poetry. Yi, *Tongin sihwa*, 29. In addition, *Pohan chip* 1:34 deals with this incident and couplet in the following way:

In bygone times, Drafter [K. *Sain*] Chŏng Chisang wrote the following on the Eight-Foot Room, "At the top of the rocks a pine ages under a single slice of moon; / at the end of the earth a cloud descends upon a thousand dots of mountains." Early on I cared for the purity of meaning of this couplet's words, and from time to time I would chant and simply enjoy it. Then I became surveillance commissioner of Chŏlla Province. It was during the first days of the second month when I climbed up to the peak behind Pulsaŭi-bang, the "Room of Inconceivability," on Mount Pyŏn. Off to one side stood an old pine, piercing into the sky, while the new moon shone faintly. I gazed down upon the level plains, and saw a cluster of mountains on the horizon. [...] Suddenly, I thought of Master Chŏng's poem, and delved into chanting it, intoning it over and over again. And I thought to myself thus: if I hadn't reached this realm, how could I have ever gotten a sense of the place which Master Chŏng had obtained his inspiration from?" (Pak, *Yŏkchu Pohan chip*, 133)

299. The source says *wŏn* (C. *yuan*), which can be a general name for a Buddhist temple as well as a designation for a specific building within a temple compound. See Muller, *Digital Dictionary of Buddhism*. At this point, it is a reference to the Eight-Foot Room.

300. In the tenth entry of the upper fascicle of *Tongin sihwa*, Sŏ Kŏjŏng writes the following regarding this episode:

Teacher Kang Iryong wanted to rhapsodize a poem on the egret. Thus every day he braved the rain and [ventured out] to arrive above the creek south of Ch'ŏnsu Temple. As he was watching them, he suddenly happened to hit upon a single line, which went as follows: "It flies, slicing an emerald mountainside." Then he said to the people, "Today, at last I got to reach a place that even the ancients never reached." To this I say: he wanted to rhapsodize on the egret, braved the rain and went to the creek — that's quite an accomplishment, is it not? Later I got to see a poem by the

288 NOTES TO PAGE 93

Song dynasty poet Xiao Jianfu [Xiao Dezao], which read, "I happened to hit upon a line at the place where the egrets fly, / while looking at the mountains at the edge of the sky. / Still suspecting that it wasn't yet anything special, / again I ascended Yueyang Tower." Astonished, I sighed, thinking to myself, "If I could have made Teacher Kang see this very poem, certainly he would've said, 'I obtained a spiritual friendship with someone from inside the Nine Regions [of China]!' " (Yi, *Tongin sihwa*, 38)

301. This last sentence might be understood as an allusion to *Huainanzi* 16.4a (chap. "Shuoshan xun"), where it says, "Thus, if there is jade in the mountains, the plants and trees are enriched; if a pool produces pearls, its banks do not dry up." Major, *Heaven and Earth in Early Han Thought*, 627.

This anecdote about Kang Iryong in *P'ahan chip* essentially deals with a poet who simply tries too hard to come up with an original poem—a predicament that is already humorously spoken of in the very first collection of remarks on poetry, the *Liuyi shihua* by Ouyang Xiu, where it says, "There was also someone who recited a poem containing these lines, 'All day he searches but does not find it, / Yet occasionally it comes to him of its own accord.' The couplet describes the difficulty of composing good poetic lines when you are trying too hard. But someone said of it, 'It sounds like a poem about someone who lost his cat,' and everybody laughed." Egan, *Problem of Beauty*, 73.

302. *Soja* (C. *xiaozi*), "milk name" or "childhood name" (also appears as *yumyŏng* [K. *ruming*] or *somyŏng* [C. *xiaoming*]).

303. In a *Koryŏsa* entry (vol. 128) on the military leader and dictator Yi Ŭimin (the entry is cited in the first note of 3:12), a dancing girl (or concubine) by the name of Hwawŏnok (with slightly different Chinese characters) is mentioned. This would correspond with the Bureau of Music, the institution to which this woman is linked and where palace courtesans and *kisaeng* (female entertainers / concubines) were trained.

304. The source says *kyobang hwa*. Kyobang, the Bureau of Music or Royal Music School, was established under King Kwangjong. Musicians for the king's personal entertainment were instructed at the Kyobang. Especially the *kisaeng* were trained at this institution in singing, dancing, and the playing of instruments. *Hwa*, "flower," can here be understood as a euphemistic term for such a *kisaeng*.

305. See note 78 of 1:6. "Principal Graduate Hwang" in all likelihood refers to Hwang Munjang. In the earlier entry, he was mentioned together with Principal Graduate Yu Hŭi, and the same is the case in this episode.

306. This line can be understood as a reference to Yang Guifei (718–756), "Imperial Consort Yang," the favorite concubine of Emperor Xuanzong of Tang. In Korea, Yang Guifei was considered a nonpareil of tragic beauty. The emperor was seventy-two and she was thirty-eight when they fled from Chang'an during the rebellion of An Lushan (703–753). According to the famous *Changhen ge* (Song of lasting regret) by Bai Juyi, which narrates their tale, Xuanzong was forced to have his beloved beauty strangled in front of Mawei Postal Relay Station (C. Mawei-yi),

west of Xingping, Shaanxi. This line by Hwang Munjang clearly is an allusion to Bai Juyi's poem. In the translation by Paul W. Kroll, the relevant lines in *Changhen ge* read, "And then the Six Armies would go no farther — there was no other recourse / But the fluently curved moth-eyebrows must die before the horses." Kroll, "Po Chü-i's 'Song of Lasting Regret,'" 98.

307. What is suggested in this line is that the girl's parents named her U-hu in order to warn their daughter away from falling in love with the wrong man (or perhaps simply a powerful man), and thus prevent her from sharing the same sad fate as Yang Guifei.

308. Xizhi here, firstly, refers to Wang Xizhi. This line alludes to an episode contained in Wang's biography in *Jinshu* (vol. 80). Here, the high-ranking official Zhou Zi (269–322) is said to have cut off a slice of roasted cow heart, a rare and precious dish, and offered it to the yet unknown and young Wang Xizhi before giving any of it to other guests. By this, Zhou Zi acknowledged Wang Xizhi's outstanding talent. One must note that Yu Hŭi's line can be understood as featuring a witty play on words with the characters *hŭi* (C. *xi*) and *chi* (C. *zhi*), for, on the one hand, *hŭiji* (C. *xizhi*) could simply mean the name [Wang] Xizhi — if taken this way, the line would merely be a reference to the mentioned cow-related episode from Chinese antiquity. Yet on the other hand, *hŭi* could be read as Yu Hŭi's personal name, while *chi* would have to be taken as an object pronoun, "it." Read this way, Yu Hŭi would imply that the beautiful courtesan's heart, i.e., her love and affection, should only be given to himself, and the line would read, "The cow's heart, [she] should only offer it to Hŭi." I have attempted to incorporate both possible meanings by translating the line as, "The cow's heart, it should only be offered to me, Xizhi."

309. This line is another reference to the tale of the *qianniu*, the "oxherd," "herder boy," or literally "he who leads a cow by a rope," and Zhinü, the weaver woman. The tale was alluded to in 1:20.

310. The poem Im Ch'un wrote on this occasion on the dancing girl U-hu, whose milk name (as I understand it), alluding to a goddess representing conjugal faithfulness, is not in line with her rather licentious occupation as a concubine or singing girl, is still extant. It is entitled *Sok U-hu ka yŏ Misu tongbu* (Continuing the *Song of U-hu*; rhapsodizing together with Misu) and features lyrical variations of the two lines cited in the entry at hand. The poem (including an inter-lineary commentary) reads,

> In the Heavenly Palace the Weaver Woman had a husband;
> but still blocked in the far distance was the Silver Stream (the *Shenyi ji*
>   [Records of spirits and extraordinary beings; by the Jin dynasty Wang
>   Fu, third century]) says, "Guo Han encountered the Weaver Woman,
>   who had come down [from Heaven] to his house. 'But where is the
>   Cowherd Boy?' [Guo] Han asked, and the Weaver Woman replied, 'The
>   Stream of Stars is blocked, we cannot hear of each other anymore.' ").
> Arranged to meet in the seventh month, but how wide is [the river of stars] in
>   between;
> she spent her nights alone in an empty chamber, shedding tears.

290 NOTES TO PAGE 94

Then threw away her loom, couldn't bear to go to Mr. Guo;
did she ever realize that there is embarrassment and shame in the mortal
world?
[Heavenly] vermilion towers and alabaster pavilions, never thought of them
again;
sited a dwelling close to the village where [the Herder Boy] walks his cows.
Only because she once followed [a fine husband like] the Cowherd up there
in Heaven;
she called herself "Behind the Cow," taking these characters for her name.
How should she have known that on another day, when following behind
a cow,
she would intermingle [and have intercourse] with minor clerks all over the
palace?
Yet those matters related to gods and immortals, I'm not sure whether they
were real or not;
just have to ask the Pillar Scribe [Laozi] of Zhou again, who came riding on
a cow.
(*SHC* 3:9a)

311. Shi Chong (249–300) of the Jin dynasty was known as one of the richest
men of his time. This line is an allusion to the following anecdote concerning Shi
Chong's rivalry with Wang Kai:

When Shi Chong had bean gruel made for a guest, it would be ready as
soon as he called for it; and throughout the winter he had a supply of leek
and duckweed pickles. Moreover, although the appearance and vigor
of his carriage ox were inferior to Wang's, it ended by winning in races:
Whenever the two of them would go out, they would set out late and then
race each other back to the Luoyang city gates before they would shut for
the night. Shi would start out several dozen paces behind, but he would
always zoom ahead like a bird, and Wang's ox could never catch up, no
matter how hard it tried. (Rouzer, *Articulated Ladies,* 105–106)

312. Lüzhu, who was renowned for her beauty and musical talent, was Shi
Chong's favorite concubine. She killed herself to escape the unwanted attentions
of a powerful suitor and to die before her lover Shi Chong. Mostly because of his
wealth, but also partly because he refused to give Lüzhu up, Shi Chong was even-
tually executed himself. Lüzhu's name has traditionally been synonymous with
women faithful to their husbands. Lee and Stefanowska, *Biographical Dictionary of
Chinese Women,* 321–322. This couplet thus alludes to an ancient example of marital
fidelity, but most importantly it involves a virtuous woman and a cow.

313. Wei *gong,* "Duke of Wei," here refers to Li Mi (582–618) of the Sui dynasty,
who rebelled against the Sui and Tang. In spite of the title he inherited from his father,
Li Mi's family was so poor that they were unable to send him to school, and he had

NOTES TO PAGE 94   291

to earn a living by herding other people's cattle. He is said to have hung books on the horns of the cows, reading while traveling on their backs.

314. Xue'er was Li Mi's cherished concubine. Whenever Li happened on a memorable phrase, he set it to music for Xue'er to sing. Chang and Saussy, *Women Writers of Traditional China,* 385. This couplet, too, alludes to a gifted woman following a man riding a cow.

315. "Girls in patterned silk" refers to the two concubines Lüzhu and Xue'er, both of whom followed honorable men they dearly loved, i.e., Shi Chong and Li Mi.

316. This line could also be translated as "what they call you, does it correspond with your ideas or not?" This translation would, I believe, make sense if the woman had given the name "U-hu" to herself. Yet it is her milk name, most probably given to her by her parents. Also, in light of the overall entry, which deals with various scholars comparing their ideas on (and knowledge of) the possible origin of this woman's milk name, it seems more reasonable to assume that Yi Illo at this point is trying to verify whether or not his own thoughts and literary references to possible inspiriational model figures are correct or not.

317. In Koguryŏ times, this region was originally referred to as Chubut'o County (K. Chubut'o-gun). It was renamed Changje County (K. Changje-gun) during the reign of King Kyŏngdŏk of Silla (742–765), then Su Prefecture (K. Su-ju) in early Koryŏ. It was elevated to the status of Kyeyang Regional Military Command (K. Kyeyang tohobu) in 1215. Today it is Kyeyang District (K. Kyeyang-gu) in Puch'ŏn, near Inch'ŏn, South Korea. Yi Illo was sent south to become secretary of Kyeyang after he had accompanied his father-in-law to the Jurchen Jin dynasty. This trip to the Northern dynasty took place in the twelfth year of King Myŏngjong, 1182, which implies that he became an official in Kyeyang sometime in mid- to late 1183. Consequently, in the entry at hand, Yi Illo recalls what took place as he passed through the area of present-day Yongsan in Seoul on his way to the western coast more than thirty years prior to putting together *P'ahan chip.*

318. The source here says *Yŏmsa* (C. *lianshi*), which is short for *Allyŏmsa,* surveillance commissioner or anti-corruption commissioner. They were in charge of investigating officials and adjudicating court cases. This sentence could be translated as "Long ago I went out to assist in Kyeyang upon having received a surveillance commissioner's tally [myself]." In my understanding, however, Yi Illo, who was then comparatively young and still at the very beginning of his official carreer, did not receive such a *pu* (C. *fu;* "tally"), thereby becoming surveillance commissioner himself. I believe he rather politely received the invitation of the acting *Yŏmsa* to spend the night at Mount Yong as he was passing through the region of the Southern Capital on his way from Kaesŏng to Kyeyang. For this reason I have translated *pu* not as "tally" but as "call."

319. Yong-san, "Dragon Mountain," is located by the Han River. Today, Yongsan is a busy, well-known district in downtown Seoul.

320. As is stated in the first volume of the seventeenth century *Tongguk yŏji chi* (A geographical survey of Korea, 1656; sec. "Kyŏngdo" (Capital), subsec. "Hansŏngbu") by Yu Hyŏngwŏn (1622–1673), the Han River, on its way toward the west, forks at

292   NOTES TO PAGES 94–95

Yongsan. The two river forks reunite again at a village called Yanghwado. In the *Tongguk yŏji chi* entry, Yu Hyŏngwŏn cites the first line of Yi Illo's poem from this episode, "Two rivers, billowing, billowing, split like a swallow's tail," and says that this is the spot Yi was referring to. *Tongguk yŏji chi* was created a few years before the oldest extant Chosŏn dynasty version of *P'ahan chip* (1659), but Yu Hyŏngwŏn clearly seems to have had access to the work (the poem also features in *Tongmunsŏn*, but without the explanatory prose passage relating to Yong-san).

321. According to legend, three golden turtles carry the three mystical mountains of the holy immortals in the Eastern Sea (that is, the Yellow Sea), i.e., Penglai, Fangzhang, and Yingzhou, on their heads. For a detailed discussion, see Bauer, *China und die Hoffnung auf Glück*, 144–147.

322. This *kujang* (C. *jiuzhang*) is a walking cane with a handle shaped like the head of a turtledove. According to the *Hou Hanshu* ("zhi" [Treatises] 5, "Liyi zhong"), the king presented such canes to high-ranking officials who had passed the age of eighty or ninety. The reason for this, it says, was the following: "The turtledove is a bird that does not choke [on its food]. [The king] wishes that the old men will not choke, either."

323. In *Tongmunsŏn* we find this poem under the title *Suk Han Ŏn'guk sŏjae* (Spending the night at Han Ŏn'guk's studio) in the way it appears in *P'ahan chip* (*TMS* 20:4b), but also as part of a longer poem by Yi Illo entitled *Han Ŏn'guk kanggŏ* (At Han Ŏn'guk's dwelling by the river), which reads,

> Drilled a hole in the roots of the clouds [the rock of a mountain], constructed
> a small tower;
> the river and the mountains are boundless, entering the curtain hook.
> Master Xie did not begrudge having spent a thousand in gold;
> Grand Councilor Fan will surely take a trip in a barge.
> Two rivers, billowing, billowing, split like a swallow's tail;
> three mountains, faint, faint, carried on the turtles' heads.
> In those years, if I had been allowed to accompany [him who carries] the
> turtledove cane,
> together we would have headed toward the gray waves, grown familiar with
> the white gulls.
> (*TMS* 13:6a–b)

Hence, the one with the turtledove cane whom Yi Illo would have loved to spend time with is Han Ŏn'guk. This poem is intensively discussed in the North Korean textbook *Munhak* from 1955. See Wŏn Uhŭm, *Munhak*, 71–74.

324. It is basically impossible that Han Sangguk, "Minister of State Han," at this point refers to Han Ŏn'guk. It is not entirely clear when Cho T'ong passed the civil service examinations, but since he was born in 1143, theoretically he could have been one of the twenty-eight successful candidates who passed the examinations of 1172 (for which Han served as associate examination administrator) next to the principal graduate Chang Mun'gyŏng (n.d.). However, since Yi Illo in this passage states that

NOTES TO PAGE 95   **293**

his friend Cho T'ong recited the poem he himself composed at Han Ŏn'guk's study in the early 1180s to this minister of state Han, Han Sangguk cannot possibly be Han Ŏn'guk (who was executed in 1173). Hence, Han Sangguk could be understood as a reference to Han Munjun (d. 1190), who served as associate examination administrator in the examinations of 1176 and as principal examination administrator in 1178 and 1182. Cho T'ong must have passed one of these examinations in order to have told his *chongbaek* Han Munjun of Yi Illo's poem in the early 1180s.

325. Hanyang is the ancient designation for the city that became the capital of the Chosŏn dynasty, present-day Seoul.

326. The words by Minister of State Han can be understood as a reference to Su Shi's painting inscription *Shu Mojie Lantian yanyu tu* (Colophon to Mojie's [Wang Wei] painting on a drizzle in Lantian), in which Su Shi writes the following concerning the poetry and painting of Wang Wei (699–761): "When one savors Mojie's poems, there are paintings in them. When one looks at Mojie's paintings, there are poems there." Qian, *Patchwork,* 57.

327. The Huangtong period of Emperor Xizong of the Jurchen Jin dynasty lasted from 1141 to 1149. The year referred to at this point is 1143.

328. *Sŭngsŏn,* "royal secretary" or "commissioner," a rank 3A position in the Security Council. It is unclear which person by the surname of Kim is meant here.

329. "Two ministers" is a translation of *myŏnggong.*

330. Naksŏngjae Study Hall (K. Naksŏngjae Haktang) was one of nine academies founded by the early Koryŏ Confucian Ch'oe Ch'ung (984–1068), who was known as "Haedong kongja" (Confucius of Korea), because of his pioneer teaching program. When he retired in 1055 he established the first private Confucian school, Kujae Haktang (Nine Course Academy), so called because the many students who wanted to learn under him for the civil examinations were divided into nine groups according to the content of their teaching. See Pratt and Rutt, *Korea,* 72. The nine academic Confucian institutions, established at the foot of Mount Songak in the vicinity of Kaesŏng, were called Naksŏngjae, Taejungjae, Sŏngmyŏngjae, Kyŏngŏpchae, Chodojae, Solsŏngjae, Chindŏkchae, Taehwajae, and Taebingjae. Edward Shultz writes that many of Ch'oe Ch'ung's disciples founded similar institutions, which, together with Ch'oe's original school, came to be known as Sibido, "Twelve Assemblies." These schools became the primary training centers for the children of Koryŏ's elite families, while government-supported schools further declined. Shultz, "Twelfth-Century Koryŏ Politics," 6.

331. Irwŏl-sa, a temple on Mount Songak in the vicinity of Kaesŏng, was established in 922.

332. The term *kangsŭp* (C. *jiangxi*), literally "debate and practice," refers to the practicing of philosophical debates.

333. *Lianju* (K. *yŏn'gu*), "linked verse" or "joint lines," are poems on fixed topics composed jointly by multiple poets.

334. Ch'oe Sanbo (n.d.) is mentioned in *Koryŏsa* as having been sent by King Injong to Kim Pusik's house in 1145 upon Kim's compilation of the *Samguk sagi.* He appears to have been involved in the compilation project as well.

294 NOTES TO PAGES 95–97

335. The source says *hak hae* (C. *xue hai*), an expression that derives from Yang Xiong's *Fayan* (Exemplary sayings): "The hundred rivers study the sea and thereby reach it; the hills study the mountains, but do not reach them. Therefore evil is limited." Brokaw, *Ledgers of Merit and Demerit,* 85. The expression alludes to a student reaching the sea of learning by a constant flow of practice.

336. The poets' names, in this case the name of a person called Myŏngjong, are interlinear comments inserted in smaller characters in the source. It is highly doubtful whether the given name at this point ought to be understood as that of the actual later King Myŏngjong, who was born in 1131 as the third son of King Injong, which would have made him twelve years in age at this point in time. First, it seems a little unlikely that he spent time at a private *haktang* designed for future candidates of the civil service examinations. Second, aside from this entry, the name Myŏngjong does not appear again in *P'ahan chip,* and whenever Yi Illo speaks of the actual King Myŏngjong, he says Myŏng-*wang,* "King Myŏng" (see 1:8, 1:9, 1:15). Moreover, the younger brother of Ŭijong (whose kingship was far from certain at this point in time) would not have referred to himself under his later temple name (K. *myoho*), i.e., "Myŏngjong." Thus, as is the case with all the other poets who appear in this entry and who were the mentioned ministers and scholars present at the Naksŏngjae Study Hall (Kim Sukch'ŏng, Kim Chach'ing, Sang Yŏnggong, and Kim Sangsun), it is unfortunately unclear who this person is.

P'ahan chip—Fascicle 2

1. This is a reference to a story about the famed (but perhaps mythical) healer Bian Que and Lord Huan, originally contained in *Han Feizi* (Writings of Master Han Fei). At a court audience, Bian Que warned Lord Huan of a deadly ailment lodged between his lord's skin and flesh. As he was feeling well at the time, Marquis Huan scoffed. "You healers," the lord said with disdain, "like to treat those without sickness in order to accrue merit." Undeterred, Bian Que returned to repeat his warnings some days later, only to be ignored again. The healer nevertheless came back for two more audiences, meeting a chillier reception each time. Bian Que persisted in delivering his bad news, announcing that the illness had penetrated farther into the lord's body. The lord, the healer pleaded, had to take action against the illness immediately, before it was too late. Bian Que's pleas fell on deaf ears. Several days after the final visit, the lord began to feel unwell and sent for the healer. Yet by then Bian Que had fled the state, so the lord met his end. See Brown, *Art of Medicine in Early China,* 41.

2. Emperor Wen of the Han dynasty reigned from 180 to 157 BCE.

3. Jia Yi (201–169 BCE), an early Han dynasty writer and statesman. A high official under Emperor Wen, Jia Yi submitted proposals for institutional reforms, which the emperor did not dare implement early in his reign. Eventually, under factional pressure Emperor Wen ceased to seek Jia Yi's advice and dismissed him. The lamentations mentioned at this point refer to Jia Yi's plans for necessary reforms, which remained unheard.

NOTES TO PAGE 97   **295**

4. Tang Wenhuang is the posthumous title of Li Shimin (598–649), Emperor Taizong, the second emperor of Tang (r. 626–649). He is widely considered the co-founder of the dynasty for his role in encouraging his father to rebel against the previous dynasty, the Sui. He must be differentiated from the later emperor Wenzong (r. 826–840).

5. Wei Zheng (580–643), a high minister and chancellor under Taizong, who also served as the lead editor of the *Suishu* (History of the Sui dynasty).

6. *Shijian shu* (Memorial of the emperor's ten lapses), a daring memorial to the throne in which Wei Zheng respectfully but firmly criticized Taizong at the risk of losing not only his position but also his life. At first, Taizong is said to have been infuriated by the critical memorial, but later he realized what a good and honest minister he had in Wei Zheng.

7. The image of soft frost that turns into solid ice to symbolize a process of something building up slowly but steadily before reaching ultimate strength and danger already appears in the "First Yin" in the hexagram "Kun" (Pure Yin) of the *Yijing:*

> The frost one treads on reaches its ultimate stage as solid ice. What starts out as frost that one might tread on ultimately becomes hard ice. [...] Commentary on the words of the text: A family that accumulates goodness will be sure to have an excess of blessings, but one that accumulates evil will be sure to have an excess of disasters. When a subject kills his lord or a son kills his father, it is never because of what happens between the morning and the evening of the same day but because of something that has been building up for a long time and that should have been dealt with early — but was not. (Lynn, *Classic of Changes,* 145–146)

8. Ŭijong, one must note here, ascended the throne in 1146, a mere decade after the rebellious monk Myoch'ŏng had almost brought the dynasty to its knees. And a few years before that, the Yi Chagyŏm Rebellion had also posed a serious threat to the integrity of the royal house. Hence, the real political situation in the years leading up to Ŭijong's reign had not been "marked by plentifulness and peace" in the same way as Yi Illo would like his readers to believe. Yi, of course, at this point intends to underscore the righteousness of his mentor Mun Kŭkkyŏm, and therefore the overly positive depiction of the earlier ages, which were then purportedly ruined by Ŭijong, does make sense in the context of the overall entry.

9. Mun Kŭkkyŏm, courtesy name Tŏkpyŏng, a clansman of the Namp'yŏng Mun (originally a military household although it became a successful civilian lineage at the start of the twelfth century; Shultz, "Twelfth-Century Koryŏ Politics," 31), served under Ŭijong and Myŏngjong in high positions such as *chŏngŏn,* "censor." He was the son of Mun Kongyu (1088–1159) and the grandson of Han Anin. Moreover, he was related by marriage to Yi Ŭibang, one of the military leaders of the 1170 coup, for Mun's daughter had married one of Yi Ŭibang's brothers. Mun passed the civil service examination in 1158. When Mun was at the head of the Censorate in the early 1160s, in 1163 he remonstrated because of the improper behavior of certain

296 NOTE TO PAGE 97

influential figures at court, especially the eunuch Paek Sŏnyŏn and the geomancer Yŏngŭi, who wielded their power and, in Mun's mind, had a bad influence on King Ŭijong. With regard to such remonstrance by members of the Censorate, Edward J. Shultz writes,

> During Ŭijong's reign there was a vociferous barrage of criticism leveled against the king and his activities. The censorial agencies had reached their maturity as an institution and were exercising all the power they could muster to enforce their will. The Censorate criticized Ŭijong in countless statements attacking his poor administration, his reckless appointments, and his general deportment. [...] The Censorate not only criticized the general state of affairs. It also attacked repeatedly the king's enjoyment of polo (*kyŏkku*). [...] The men Ŭijong had recruited were suspect and unacceptable to the censors. Policy critics condemned the behavior of high-ranking officials who supported Ŭijong, as well as eunuchs and palace attendants. [...] Ŭijong resisted these attacks in a variety of ways. One tactic was simply to ignore the protest. When determined, Ŭijong would pit his will against the censors and force them to accept his decisions. On one occasion Ŭijong was so incensed over the effrontery of a memorial that he burned it before the censor's eyes. (Shultz, *Generals and Scholars*, 15–16)

This memorial is the one presented to the throne by Mun Kŭkkyŏm at this point in the episode. Shultz writes, "In 1163 the Censorate, under the leadership of Mun Kŭkkyŏm, chided the king for supporting the eunuchs and confidants who damaged the throne. When Mun referred to scandals in the palace, an enraged Ŭijong ignited the petition and banished Mun," Shultz, 213n32. It should be noted that Mun Kŭkkyŏm seems to have been acquainted with Yi Tamji, one of Yi Illo's closest friends.

10. This incident and Mun's memorial to the throne are described in *Koryŏsa* (vol. 99) in the following way:

> [Mun Kŭkkyŏm] was promoted several times until he reached the office of censor of the left. He prostrated himself in front of the palace gates and presented a memorial to the throne, which read, "The court eunuch Paek Sŏnyŏn [n.d.] tyrannically abuses his powers any way he pleases, and together with the palace lady Mubi he stealthily behaved in a scandalous fashion. The geomancer Yŏngŭi has taken hold of the wrong Way, has heaped flattery onto Your Majesty, and had the [monasteries on the grounds of the] two [detached] palaces Paeksun-gung and Kwanbuk-kung reinstalled. He has secretly amassed riches and goods, [...] and in taking control of these affairs he conspired with [the palace eunuch Paek] Sŏnyŏn. In general, when the provincial military commanders of the two realms [K. *yanggye pyŏngmasa*] and the surveillance commissioners of the five provinces [K. *odo anch'alsa*] take their leave and want to bid Your

NOTES TO PAGE 98   **297**

Majesty farewell, they are forced to have drinking parties and farewell dinners at these two [detached] palaces, and then they are commanded to each offer regional products [to Yŏngŭi and Paek Sŏnyŏn], and depending on whether the amount of their tributary offerings is large or small, they are graded as either good or bad. It has reached a state where [money and bribes] are collected even from [ordinary] families, and by that the wrath of the people is being aroused. Furthermore the administrator to the Security Council [K. *chi ch'umilwŏnsa*] Ch'oe P'och'ing [n.d.] [...] is greedy and insatiable, and those who do not butter him up will inevitably be slandered by him, and hence the riches he has amassed are enormous. Therefore, I request the following: behead [Paek] Sŏnyŏn [and the courtesan] Mubi; expel [the geomancer] Yŏngŭi and make his status equal to that of a herder boy; dismiss [Ch'oe] P'och'ing and have him apologize to the entire country." In addition, [in the memorial, Mun] spoke about some [delicate] matters which had [allegedly] taken place in the bedchambers of the [king's] forbidden inner palace. The king flew into a rage and burned the memorial. [Ch'oe] P'och'ing entered the palace to see the king and requested a clarification, so the king summoned [Mun] Kŭkkyŏm and had him clarify it to [Ch'oe's] face. [Mun] Kŭkkyŏm's words were very earnest. Eventually he was demoted to the position of executive administrator of Hwangju.

By lauding Mun Kŭkkyŏm's memorial, Yi Illo simultaneously hints at his critical stance toward the reign of Ŭijong.

11. Again a reference to the ode "Juan a" from the *Shijing*. See Waley, *Book of Songs*, 184.

12. After he had been already been overthrown by Chŏng Chungbu and Mun Kŭkkyŏm's relative Yi Ŭibang in 1170, Ŭijong is said to have bitterly regretted not having listened to Mun. Yi Illo at this point also appears to allude to the absence of a "culture of discussion" at court even for the remonstrance officials, whose job it traditionally was to criticize the ruler.

13. Zhu Yun (fl. 47–36 BCE) was a Han dynasty official. During the reign of Emperor Cheng (r. 32–7 BCE) of Han, Zhu Yun submitted a memorial in which he asked for the beheading of the imperial favorite, Zhang Yu (just like Mun Kŭkkyŏm had done in his memorial). The emperor flew into a rage and ordered Zhu Yun executed, but he clung so strongly to the palace balustrade that the guards broke the balustrade when they tried to pull him away. Intercession by other court officials saved Zhu Yun's life. See West and Idema, *Monks, Bandits, Lovers, and Immortals*, 176.

14. Yuan Ang was a Han dynasty official during the time of Emperor Wen. This line alludes to the following anecdote:

Yuan Ang was a man of fierce loyalty and was motivated in all his conduct by the highest principles. It happened that there was a eunuch named Zhao Tan who, because of his knowledge of numerology, had gained favor

298   NOTES TO PAGE 98

with Emperor Wen. This man took every opportunity to speak ill of Yuan Ang, until Yuan Ang began to fear that some misfortune would befall him. Yuan Zhong, the son of Yuan Ang's elder brother, was a horseman in the emperor's retinue and used to bear the imperial credentials and accompany the emperor's carriage. He advised his uncle, saying, "You had best have an open conflict with Zhao Tan and shame him before the court, so that the emperor will pay no more attention to his slander." Accordingly, when Emperor Wen left the palace one day in his carriage accompanied by Zhao Tan, Yuan Ang prostrated himself before the carriage and said, "I have always been told that only the most distinguished men of the empire are privileged to ride with the Son of Heaven in his six-foot carriage of state. Now although the Han may be lacking in worthy men, I cannot imagine why Your Majesty would deign to ride in the same carriage with a man who is no more than a remnant of the knife and saw!" The emperor laughed and ordered Zhao Tan to get down from the carriage. Weeping bitterly, Zhao Tan descended. (Watson, *Records of the Grand Historian,* 456)

15. This incident is also treated in *Pohan chip* 3:30, where its says, "King Ŭi[jong] held music and women near [to his heart], and he liked to roam around at ease. The loyal master Mun Kŭkkyŏm was censor at the time, and he presented a memorial to the throne in which he frankly remonstrated against it [the king's lifestyle and administration]. [Ŭijong, however,] did not follow [his advice]. Then, in the autumn of the cyclic year *kyŏngin,* the military officials started their revolt, and the king had to take a carriage and escape to the south." Pak, *Yŏkchu Pohan chip,* 456.

16. Mun was put back into office immediately after the takeover of the military in 1170, serving as commissioner of the right (K. *U sŭngsŏn*). See Shultz, "Twelfth-Century Koryŏ Politics," 3. He thus assisted in securing the dynasty in these tumultuous times. *Husŏl* (C. *houshe*), being the "throat and tongue" in the sense of speaking out loud the orders of the king, refers to the office of *sŭngsŏn,* commissioner. The term derives from the ode "Zhengmin" of the *Shijing.* See Waley, *Book of Songs,* 141.

17. Mun Kŭkkyŏm passed away in 1189, and the following poem was written in or around that year as well.

18. Changhe originally refers to the gates of the heavenly palace. It is mentioned in the section "*Zhuixing xun*" (4:6) of *Huainanzi.* It can here be understood as the gates of the palace in Kaesŏng.

19. The term *paeun* (C. *paiyun*), "push aside the clouds [blocking the sun]," here seems to refer to Mun Kŭkkyŏm remonstrating against ministers and eunuchs at court who, in his mind, led King Ŭijong astray or who failed to make him a more responsible ruler.

20. Yuyuan is the legendary place in the west where the sun sets. It is mentioned in the section "Tianwen xun" (3:25) of *Huainanzi.* Yuyuan and the setting sun here most likely stand for the decline of the royal house under Ŭijong. Alternately, as Yuyuan is associated with the western region, it could stand for the Western Capital, a city to which Ŭijong (the king, or, in this case, the "sun") often traveled

on his excursions. If understood in this way, the line may allude to Mun Kŭkkyŏm vehemently trying to convince the ruler to return to the capital Kaesŏng and to diligently apply himself to governing the dynasty instead of passing his time in idleness in P'yŏngyang.

21. Ponghwang Chi (C. Fenghuang Chi), "Phoenix Pool," was associated with the Secretariat and thus with the office of grand councilor. The phoenix can here be understood as an allusion to Mun Kŭkkyŏm and his continuous time in high office from the early 1170s to 1189.

22. This line can be understood as a reference to Xie An (320–385), whose dream about his own eventual death after having passed through Western Province Gate close to the city of Shitou is contained in "Xie An zhuan" (Biography of Xie An), *Jinshu* (vol. 79):

> Long ago, when Huan Wen [312–373] was alive, [...] in a dream I suddenly took [Huan] Wen's carriage and we traveled for sixteen miles. When I caught sight of a white chicken we halted. Taking [Huan] Wen's carriage [meant] that I would replace him in his position. [Having traveled] for sixteen miles and then stopping [meant] that until now sixteen years had passed. The white chicken meant *you* [K. *yu*; "chicken" or "tenth terrestrial branch"], and the present year is the cyclic year of the chicken. [This means that] I will contract a disease and that necessarily I shall not rise again.

The reference to *you*, "chicken," can be read as an allusion to 1189, which was the cyclic year *jiyou* (K. *kiyu*), and the year in which Mun Kŭkkyŏm died.

23. I have chosen to read this *taejŏl* (C. *dajie*), "large joints (of a bamboo)," in its possible meaning as "great crisis." The character *chŏl* (C. *jie*) can, of course, also be understood as one of the core values of Confucianism, namely "moderation" or "restraint." Furthermore, it could also mean "standard" or "integrity." If read as "great moderation" or "great standard," the passage at hand would have an entirely different, in fact contrary meaning. *Taejŏl* will appear again in 2:3, where it refers to the righteous, principled reign of Injong. In this latter case I have opted to translate the term as "great standard."

24. The "currents of [melted] ice and snow" (K. *pingsŏl p'a*) can here be understood as an allusion to an upright official's pure conduct in office. These lines seem to deal with the question of a possible lasting influence of Mun Kŭkkyŏm on the court and the country.

25. Tonggak (C. Dongge), "Eastern Tower," may be understood as a reference to the "eastern mountains" of Guiji, the place where Xie An lived in reclusion before he came to court and where he returned after his retirement. Eastern Tower here seems to stand for the place where Mun Kŭkkyŏm retired after his official career ended and which Yi Illo now finds overgrown and deserted.

26. The netherworld is oftentimes referred to as "Nine Springs" (C. Jiuquan; K. Kuch'ŏn).

27. The final four lines may be taken as yet another allusion to the aforementioned

300   NOTES TO PAGE 99

dream contained in "Xie An zhuan" of *Jinshu*. Before his death, Xie An dreamed that he would be carried through the Western Province Gate (C. Xizhou-men) and that he would die shortly thereafter. Yang Tan (late fourth century), a man from Taishan, was known as a fine scholar, and Xie An had deeply cherished his marvelous qualities. After Xie An passed away, Yang Tan mourned for several years and refused to travel on the road to the Western Province where his mentor had passed away. Then, when staying at Shitou, he got heavily drunk and eventually wandered along the road singing loudly. Not knowing where he had arrived, he asked the people to his left and right, and they said, "This is Western Province Gate!" Unable to bear his sadness, he began to beat the gate with his horsewhip. Then he recited two lines of the poem *Konghou yin* (Harp lay) by Cao Zhi, a poem dealing with the awareness of time and the acceptance of the inevitability of death. The two lines Yang Tan recited were: "Though we may live in splendid houses / Withered and wasted, we return to mountains and hills" (translation in Cutter, "Cao Zhi's [192–232] Symposium Poems," 22). Hereafter, Yang Tan cried bitterly and left. At this point, Yi Illo bewails the death of his mentor Mun Kŭkkyŏm at the place where he died in the same way Yang Tan bewailed the death of Xie An at the Western Province Gate.

28. Kim Puŭi, courtesy name Chayu. He passed the civil service examinations in 1097 and straightaway entered the Hallim Academy. His father was the high-ranking official Kim Kŭn, his three elder brothers were Kim Pup'il (n.d.), Kim Puil (1071–1132), and Kim Pusik. See Shultz, "Military Revolt in Koryŏ," 24. Alongside his brother Pusik, Kim Puŭi took part in the suppression of the rebellion of the monk Myoch'ŏng. With regard to this, in *Koryŏsa chŏryo* it says,

> The administrator to the Security Council Kim Puŭi has passed away. [...] When Myoch'ŏng requested the construction of a new palace in the Western Capital, [Kim] Puŭi presented a memorial to the throne in which he stated, in very strong words, that this must not be done. Thereupon, when Myoch'ŏng rebelled, troops were mobilized to suppress him, and [Kim Puŭi] presented a ten-point plan to pacify the west. The general outline of this plan said the following: "The terrain of the city of the Western Capital is rugged and provisions are sufficient, which makes it impossible to capture the city [quickly]. It would be appropriate to wait calmly for the enemy forces to exhaust themselves, [attack when they become tired and underfed], and to seize victory by means of this calculation." The king happily welcomed this [idea], and when the Western Capital was pacified, it all happened in accordance with [Kim Puŭi's] plan. The king thus especially bestowed upon him a golden belt. (*Koryŏsa chŏryo*, vol. 10, fourteenth year of the reign of Injong, tenth month.)

29. Kim Pusik is mentioned on several occasions in *P'ahan chip* (see, for instance, 2:11). For an introduction to the life and impact of Kim Pusik, see Shultz, "Introduction to the 'Samguk Sagi.'"

NOTES TO PAGES 99–100   **301**

30. In *Koryŏsa* (vol. 97) it says that in 1111 (sixth year of the reign of King Yejong), Kim Puŭi followed the vice commissioner of the Security Council (K. *ch'umirwŏn pusa*) Kim Yŏn as an envoy to Song China, holding the position of document officer. After having submitted some writings, his literary talent is said to have been praised by the Chinese emperor.

31. Emperor Zhenzong of Song reigned from 997 to 1022. The mention of Zhenzong at this point is obviously an error in the source. The Song dynasty emperor who ruled when Kim Puŭi went to China as an envoy was Emperor Huizong (r. 1100–1126), who is mentioned a bit later in the entry.

32. It can be surmised that these two people are similar to the *t'onggwan* (or *t'ongsa*) of later times, i.e., Chinese officials generally of Korean descent who (usually through the training of their parents) were capable of speaking Korean and thus were charged with dealing with the Korean envoys during their stay in the capital. In late premodern times, these *t'onggwan* were usually not of high rank, but still had some authority and power over the envoys and their movement in the Chinese capital. They were meant to assist the Korean envoys, and thus they operated directly on the premises of the official hostel (K. *kwan*) where the Korean embassy was stationed. Thus they were in constant contact with the foreigners, and it is likely that they also spent time with the Koreans when they were "off duty," when they had time to sit down, have a drink, and compose poetry with the guests from afar. This situation is portrayed in the entry at hand.

33. This drinking game, usually known as *juling* (K. *churyŏng*), is essentially a poetry competition. Each participant of the game has to come up with a couplet matching the one presented by his predecessor. If he is unable to do so, he must take a drink as a forfeit.

34. In a comment to a passage in *Huangdi neijing suwen* (Inner canon of Huangdi — basic questions), Wang Bing (710–805) says, " 'Six [times] six terms' are the degrees of heaven; 'nine [times] nine to set up calculations' is the number of qi terms. [...] One celestial cycle consists of 365 degrees plus one fourth of a degree. If this is paralleled with the *qi* of the twelve [thirty days] terms [of a year], then one year ends after 360 days." Unschuld and Tessenow, *Huang Di nei jing su wen*, 164.

35. Qi is the chess-like board game known in Korea as Paduk and in Japan as Go. On a Qi board there are nineteen vertical and nineteen horizontal rows, which make it 360 intersections plus one.

36. The stones in such a board game are often referred to as "horses."

37. Clay oxen (C. *tuniu*) or spring oxen (C. *chunniu*) were an essential part of an ancient Chinese ritual held to ensure good weather and harvest at the beginning of spring. During the ritual, the worshipping of the clay figure shaped like an ox was followed by its immediate destruction.

38. Chenxiang-ting, "Eaglewood Pavilion," was on the grounds of Xingqing Palace. According to legend, in 743 Tang emperor Xuanzong and his beloved Yang Guifei were enjoying the peonies at Chenxiang Pavilion and had Li Bai record his threefold poem *Qingping diao* (Qingping melody). The "new melody" heard at this

302 NOTES TO PAGE 100

point may be understood as an allusion to Li Bai's poem. Kim Puŭi appears to hint at the fact that he is offering a poem upon the emperor's request just as Li Bai did when ordered to compose a verse by Xuanzong.

39. Lili-wen, "Establishing Rites Gate," refers to the southern gates of the palace.

40. The Song capital Bianjing (Keifeng), located on the shores of the Bian River, was attacked, taken, and plundered by the Jurchen Jin in 1126 (the final year of Huizong's reign), and both the retired emperor Huizong as well as the reigning emperor Qinzong (r. 1126) were deported as prisoners of war to Manchuria. Huizong is known to have been an avid collector of art, calligraphy, and objects from nature, especially rocks. He was an aesthete, and in later times it was his apparent decadence that was blamed for the loss of the northern territories to the Jurchen Jin.

41. The Prince of Kang, Zhao Guo (1107–1187), was one of Emperor Qinzong's younger brothers. After the fall of the capital he fled south, organized a court, and ascended the throne as Emperor Gaozong (r. 1127–1187), the tenth emperor of the Song dynasty and the first emperor of what is today known as the Southern Song dynasty.

42. Yang Yingcheng, in his position as *Dajin Gaoli guoxinshi* (envoy with state message to Great Jin and Gaoli; see Rogers, "Regularization of Koryŏ-Chin Relations," 70n99) and garrison commander of Eastern Zhejiang, came to Koryŏ as an envoy of Song on the fourteenth day of the sixth lunar month of 1128. In the *Songshi* (History of Song, vol. 25, twenty-third day of the third month, 1128) it says, "On the day *dingwei* [the emperor] dispatched Yang Yingcheng as national diplomatic envoy to the Great Jin and to Gaoli [Koryŏ]." Yang stayed on in Korea for a rather long time, for he returned on the third day of the tenth month, 1128. In *Koryŏsa* it says that Yang came alongside the defense commissioner of Qizhou (C. Qizhou *fangyushi*), Han Yan. An account of the mission to Koryŏ prepared by Yang Yingcheng himself, the *Jianyan jiadao Gaoli lu*, was lost.

43. Huining, present-day Baichengzhi in the south of Acheng, Heilongjiang, was one of the five secondary capitals of Jin. The Jin court ruled there from 1115 to 1149.

44. Michael C. Rogers writes the following regarding Yang's mission:

> The Koreans [...] were not so imprudent as to entertain any idea of entering into relations with the new Sung [Song] court in Nanking. [...] It was with evident surprise and consternation that the Koreans greeted a fully accredited Sung envoy, Yang Ying-ch'eng [Yang Yingcheng], who arrived in their capital some three months later [in mid-July of 1128]. A unique feature of this mission is the fact that its ultimate destination was not Koryŏ, but the Supreme Capital of Chin [Jin], Hui-ning fu (south of Harbin); its objective was to communicate with the captive Sung emperors and if possible to obtain their release. Yang Ying-ch'eng was not the first Chinese adventurer, nor was he the last, who embarked on this rather far-fetched undertaking in response to Kao-tsung's [Gaozong] appeals for "envoys to the sundered region." But to him belongs the dubious credit for the idea of attempting to reach the Chin capital from the east, i.e., through

NOTE TO PAGE 100   303

Koryŏ, thereby circumventing the Jurchen filed commanders in North China. [...] Yang Ying-ch'eng stayed more than two months, and seems to have made rather a nuisance of himself. To the end the Koreans insisted that their consent to this request would have two consequences: it would suggest to the Jurchen the feasibility of a Korean (sea) route to Sung, and it would have a disruptive, possibly disastrous, effect on Koryŏ's precarious *modus vivendi* with Chin. Yang Ying-ch'eng's persistent efforts to refuse these ideas only elicited further elaborations of them. He was told that a new strategic vista would be opened to the Jurchen once they grasped the potentialities of the peninsula: they would use it as a springboard for naval operations against the Chinese coast. Nor could the Koreans refrain, in the face of Yang's importunities, from pointing out that the Chinese had already brought disaster on themselves by ignoring Koryŏ's advice regarding an alliance with the Jurchen. The two official missives from Koryŏ to Sung which came out of the affair are closely related. One was presented to Yang on Sep. 14; the other was sent via a Koryŏ envoy, Yun Ŏni [see 2:19], who was commissioned four days later. In the first the king used the ancient term "venerating the King'" [K. *chonwang*] to describe his attitude henceforth toward the Sung emperor, while the traditional Korean policy of "serving the greater" [K. *sadae*] would perforce be reserved for Chin. [...] (Rogers, "Regularization of Koryŏ-Chin Relations," 70–72)

Parts of the first missive given to Yang Yingcheng by the Korean king (contained in *Koryŏsa*, vol. 15, eighteenth day of the eighth lunar month of 1128) reads,

At the time, [Yang] Yingcheng and the others went back and forth, ceaselessly [insisting on their demand to be allowed to borrow a route], so that [King Injong] again answered [in a letter] in the following way: "[...] They [the Jurchen] were already aware of the deficient state that [Song] China was in, and once that prying heart had stirred, they galloped far and entered deep [into Song territory], wreaking havoc in the capital region. Our small country and the country of Jin share a border, we understand the situation with them, but now Your envoy [Yang Yingcheng] means to pass through here and go there—thus, [the Jurchen's] suspiciousness [with regard to us] would lead to cracks [in our relationship with them], and calamity would soon follow. Supposing that Your envoy would pass through here and go there, they would certainly also want to pass through here to repay the rites. Moreover, to the east their country touches the great sea, and they are very good at naval warfare. [...] If they were to send warships [from the Korean Peninsula], have them sail down the ocean and strike in a surprise attack, We fear that in the north you would be troubled with a war on land, while simultaneously you would be troubled with a naval war in the south. The head and the tail would then be under attack at the very same time, and Your problems would necessarily be enormous. If

304   NOTES TO PAGE 100

it came to this, You could regret it all you like, there would be no escape."
[...] [Yang] Yingcheng and the others said, "Your country's lord and
ministers, we believe that they will invariably suffer dire consequences."

45. Rogers states that "Kim Pusik was among the Korean officials who were
outspoken in their rejection of Yang's proposal." Rogers, "Regularization of Koryŏ-
Chin Relations," 71n101.

46. Yang Yingcheng is here said to have asked to "borrow a route/passage"
(K. *kado*) to go visit the captured Song emperors. Lo Jung-pang writes in the fourth
chapter of his *China as a Sea Power* that Yang had really devised the plan to establish a
naval base in Korea. He writes that the Song meant to use this base to launch attacks
against the Jurchen Jin, and to rescue the captured Song emperors. Lo states that
Yang's plan had been discussed at the Song court, and Yang had left for Korea in the
summer of 1128. At this point in time, however, Koryŏ feared the rising Jurchen Jin
more than the Song, and the request was denied by the Korean court. Injong pointed
out that Song had the Shandong peninsula from which to launch a naval invasion
against Jin, but Yang Yicheng insisted that Korea was closer. It was only during
this time that the Song first learned that the Jurchen had become proficient in naval
affairs. Lo writes, "The warning of the Korean kings was later justified, but at the
time Yang Yingcheng presented the letter, the Song emperor became very angry.
One councilor [...] suggested the sending of large warships with several thousands
of picked men to chastise the Koreans. Another councilor [...] urged that a naval
expedition be sent to attack Manchuria and rescue the two captured emperors. But
more prudent counsel prevailed and both of these suggestions were rejected." Lo,
China as a Sea Power.

47. With regard to this missive by Kim Puŭi, Michael C. Rogers states,

This was reinforced by the second missive, which begged the emperor to
have compassion of Koryŏ in its precarious position vis-à-vis Chin, and
to be satisfied with the king's "interior yearning." On the more practical
side, it contains an admission that the Koreans would be forced by their
Jurchen overlords to engage in espionage in any further contacts with
Sung. Finally, it brings the respective interests of Koryŏ and Sung into a
synthesis: if Koryŏ were to lose its political integrity (i.e., by Jurchen inva-
sion), it could no longer be useful to Sung as a buffer against Chin. The em-
peror's reaction to Yang Ying-ch'eng's report, as portrayed in the Chinese
sources, was one of bitter anger, which was not mitigated by an objective
and reasonable statement attributed to Chu Sheng-fei. But the rescript
which Yun Ŏni brought back to Kaesŏng acknowledged the sincerity of
the king's motives. (Rogers, "Regularization of Koryŏ-Chin Relations," 72)

The entire letter that Kim Puŭi wrote for King Injong is reproduced in *Tongmunsŏn*,
and parts of it read:

Humbly We venture to think: The benevolence of Heaven and earth brings each of the myriad things to completion. The virtue of emperors and kings should not hold the multitude of [base] people responsible for what causes them difficulties. How dare we spit out sincere expressions [of loyalty], and intrude upward, asking You to give a ready ear to it? We humbly remember that our country is located in a remote eastern border region, and that for ages we have served China. We have protected thousands of leagues of frontier, but We still have not yet personally bowed at a court audience. We have looked at two hundred years of grace [by emperors of Song], and merely swore loyal earnestness. Recently We heard that the two sages [Huizong and Qinzong] were moved to a different location [and held captive in the north], and the entire [country of the] Three Han was deeply saddened [by this news]. We have not been able to run and inquire about their well-being, thereby expressing the sincerity of the servant; also We did not get to be the first to lead a righteous army to die for the cause of [lifting] the [Song] dynasty's troubles [when the Jurchen Jin attacked Keifeng and abducted the emperors]. Now Emperor [Gaozong] has risen from the precincts of the commander-in-chief, illuminating the foundations of the previous kings, meaning to go out to meet the phoenix-belled palanquin [the two captive emperors] together with the ministers and people. When the imperial decree was handed down, the old and the young stooped over and cried, when the virtuous reputation took form, those near and far were stirred in their hearts. [...] Generally, that country of Jin is connected to us along the shores of the Yalu River. They are still controlling the power [that enabled them] to wreak havoc in China, and they still have it in their mind to harm their neighbors. Always they are commanding secret agents and spies, waiting for an opportunity to put an end to us [and our political integrity; I have understood this differently from Rogers] — if they now heard that a [Song] envoy with staff and tally [was allowed] to borrow an [eastern] route [through our country], they may respond to the times and create an incident [to invade our Country East of the Sea]. If soldiers were mustered, we may stand in awe of the penalty brought down upon us, and if they requested to move [toward the Southern Song] in the name of requiting the rites, this country of ours, which lies on the way there, how could we refuse [to let them pass through and thereby be taken by them]? They are many, we are few — that already makes it hardly possible for us to engage in battle with them. If the lips are missing, the teeth will be cold — again, how do we know that this won't turn out to be a blessing [for the Southern Song]? How could we only consider the hand-wringing of today? For we fear that in later times we shall be doomed to useless regret. [...] Leading the vassal lords and honoring the kings of Zhou — we dare not agree [to emulate] the ancient example of Qi and Jin. Defining the land and creating the Tribute of Yu — we hope

306 NOTES TO PAGES 100–101

not to lose the old righteousness of Jing and Xu. The loyal heart does not deceive, and August Heaven is our witness. (*TMS* 39:17b–18b)

48. "They are many, we are few" is being said with regard to the size of the relevant states' armies, i.e., the number of troops of the Jurchen Jin and of Koryŏ.

49. I understand this saying about missing lips and cold teeth in the following way: the lips represent the Koryŏ dynasty, while the teeth stand for the Southern Song. Kim Puŭi here implies that if Koryŏ were to crumble in the wake of a possible Jurchen Jin invasion, it could not serve as the buffer protecting the Song from the Jin anymore, which might lead to further military conflicts and potential danger for the Southern Song.

50. Through the words of Kim Puŭi, the Koryŏ court here clearly states that it will not follow the example of Qi and Jin, i.e., states that continued to honor the emperors of the Zhou dynasty although the Zhou were already in dynastic decline, and will rather primarily turn its gaze toward the barbaric (i.e., not Han-Chinese) but strong Jin dynasty.

51. A reference to the "Yugong" (Tribute of Yu) chapter from *Shujing,* where it is said that the ancient states of Jing and Xu offered articles of tribute to Yu. Kim Puŭi here implies that Koryŏ, while now "serving the greater" in the north, likewise vows to uphold, at least to a certain degree, tributary relations with the Southern Song. The overall writing, of course, aims to make clear that Koryŏ intends to withdraw from Song Chinese political influence.

52. According to Koryŏ law, close relatives were allowed to serve in the same offices at the same time, except for the Chancellery/Secretariat. Thus it is stated in "Mutual Avoidance" (K. *sangp'i*) in the section "Officials" (K. *kongsik*) in the "Penal Code" (K. *hyŏngbŏp*) contained in volume 84 of *Koryŏsa.* Kim Pusik and Kim Puŭi were consequently not allowed to work together at the same office.

53. Xiaoshi Baye, the "Eight Petals of the Xiao Clan," refers to the Xiao Clan of Lanling, which brought forth grand councilors for eight successive generations, starting with Xiao Yu (574–647) and ending with Xiao Gou (d. 887). They were the descendants of Xiao He (d. 193), the first grand councilor of the Han dynasty.

54. This practice—or at least the depiction of it—derives from a description of the same careful preparation for the act of poetic writing contained in the third volume of *Shihua zonggui* (General compendium of remarks on poetry; compiled by Ruan Yue between 1086 and 1100). In the *Shihua zonggui,* the monk Wenying says to Yang Huizi (921–1000) that he should cleanse his brush in the dews of the Heavenly Lake, which should be contained in a bowl of ice and a cup of snow, to make his poetry marvelous.

55. Yŏmju is the ancient name of present-day Yŏnan District in Hwanghae Province.

56. This pun with the words Yŏmju, "Salt District" (C. Yanzhou), and *wuyan* (K. *muyŏm*), "saltless," is an allusion to the tale of Zhong Lichun, a woman from Wuyan, a district during the Chinese Warring States period. Zhong Lichun was famous for being exceptionally ugly. Yet she was confident in her own learning and sagacity,

and thus she eventually became the chief consort of Prince Xuan of Qi. At this point, the allusion to the Chinese tale appears to hint not so much at the flavorlessness of the scenery as at the ugliness of the women in Yŏmju, women with whom Kim Puŭi, albeit being "full of passion," seemingly does not want to spend the night.

57. The source here says *im taebo* (C. *lin dabao*), "take over the great treasure," which refers to a ruler ascending the throne.

58. Chosŏn Kong, or rather Chosŏn Kukkong, "Duke of Chosŏn," was the title of Yi Chagyŏm, one of the most infamous political figures of the Koryŏ dynasty. Yi Chagyŏm's family (to a branch of which Yi Illo belonged himself), the Kyŏngwŏn Yi Clan, had had tight relations with the royal house for generations, and the clan dominated royal authority in the early twelfth century: Yi Chagyŏm's older sister, for instance, was Princess Changgyŏng (K. Changgyŏng Kongju), wife of King Sunjong; Yi Chagyŏm's second daughter became the wife of Yejong, and this aided Yi Chagyŏm's own official career, for he held several high posts, such as assistant grand councilor. Following the death of Yejong in 1122, Yi Chagyŏm successfully installed his grandson, the later Injong, as king. Yi then made his third and fourth daughters his grandson's wives, which led to predicaments with respect to the rites that Injong had to adhere to. After having heaved his grandchild and son-in-law onto the throne, Yi Chagyŏm himself became the most powerful political figure of his time. He accused other important figures at court such as Han Anin (d. 1122), the brother of Yejong, or Mun Kongin (d. 1137) of conspiring against the new king and had them either executed or sent into exile (for these power struggles at court, see Shultz, "Twelfth-Century Koryŏ Politics"). In the wake of these political upheavals he furnished his sons with high posts, placed partisans and henchmen in a number of key government positions, and de facto claimed control over the court. Yi Chagyŏm himself subsequently developed aspirations to usurp the throne and worked to overthrow his own grandson. When Injong ordered his grandfather's elimination, Yi Chagyŏm initiated an ultimately disastrous counterattack alongside his ally and lieutenant Ch'ŏk Chun'gyŏng (d. 1144; see 2:7), in the wake of which the palace in Kaesŏng was burned to the ground and many people lost their lives. However, when Ch'ŏk Chun'gyŏng learned that Yi planned to blame him for the destruction of the palace, he sided with Injong. Eventually, Yi Chagyŏm was captured and imprisoned in the fifth month of 1126. He died in exile in Yŏnggwang, Chŏlla Province, in 1126. One must note that Yi Chagyŏm was influential during a time when powers and relations in China and East Asia were in flux. Concerning Koryŏ foreign relations, Yi was a strong supporter of the position that recognition of the Jurchen Jin was essential for Koryŏ. In this respect, Yi Chagyŏm's opinion coincided with that of his archrival, Kim Pusik.

59. Ch'oe Sajŏn (1067–1139) was royal physician (K. *naeŭi*) under Yejong and a doctor with a rather dubious reputation. After Yejong died of a serious illness, Han Anin and Mun Kongin accused Ch'oe Sajŏn of having failed to act and wanted to sentence him to death, but through the intervention of Yi Chagyŏm, who slandered Han and Mun, Ch'oe was saved by Injong while Han and Mun were punished. Later, during the Yi Chagyŏm Rebellion, Ch'oe played an important role in the suppression

308 NOTES TO PAGE 102

of the rebellion as he persuaded Ch'ŏk Chun'gyŏng to change sides. Ch'oe was subsequently bestowed with high offices by Injong.

60. Ch'oe Sajŏn is here likened to Lu Jia (240–170 BCE) who according to his biography in *Hanshu* is said to have insinuated himself between the two high Han dynasty politicians Chen Ping (d. 187 BCE) and Zhou Bo (240–169 BCE) in order to reconcile these two rivals. Ping and Bo ended the dominance of the Lü Clan and helped Emperor Wen of Han to ascend the throne. Ch'oe Sajŏn being compared to Lu Jia can at this point be understood as a reference to his position between Yi Chagyŏm and Ch'ŏk Chun'gyŏng, and his role in the elimination of Yi Chagyŏm, which in turn secured the position of Injong.

61. There was a Kirin-gak, "Kirin Tower," in Kaesŏng. Injong went to this Kirin (C. Qilin) Tower, for instance, in 1132 to discuss the *Shujing* and the *Yijing* with his ministers. *Koryŏsa,* vol. 16, tenth year of Injong, eleventh day of the third month. However, at this point the term seems to refer to the Qilin Tower of Han times, a tower onto which Emperor Xuan of Han had his court painters draw the portraits of meritorious officials.

62. Kim Chonjung (d. 1156), a protégé of Ŭijong, who by way of his contact with the king rose through the ranks quickly, is in relevant sources generally portrayed negatively as an opportunistic minister. His biography in *Koryŏsa* reads,

> Kim Chonjung was a person from Yonggung County. By nature he was intelligent, and acquired fame as a poet. During the reign of Injong he became attendant in the Secretariat of the Heir Apparent [K. *ch'unbang sihak*], and upon passing the civil service examinations he was installed as overseer of the household administration of the heir apparent [K. *ch'ŏmsabu roksa*]. He was on good terms with the eunuch Chŏng Ham [see 3:6]. When Ŭijong ascended the throne it was on account of old favors [acquired while having worked] at the Secretariat of the Heir Apparent that he was appointed palace attendant, and he enjoyed special favors [by the king]. He was promoted several times. [...] When the head of the Security Council [K. *chi chusa*] Chŏng Sŭmmyŏng [again, see 3:6] passed away, the king wanted a renowned man to take his place, and [Chŏng] Ham forcefully recommended [Kim Chonjung], so that he became commissioner of the right. From then on he walked in and out of the forbidden inner parts of the palace, planned and commented upon national politics, and his power influenced both the court and the dynasty. (*Koryŏsa,* vol. 123, "Yŏlchŏn" 36)

63. Ma Heluo (whose surname was posthumously changed to Mang), a courtier under Emperor Wu of Han (Han Wudi, r. 141–87 BCE), had plotted to assassinate the emperor. When he was about to enter the emperor's bedchamber with a dagger, he accidentally bumped into a lute. He was thus seized and struck down by Jin Midi (134–86 BCE).

64. This is an allusion to a story recorded in *Shiji:*

The king said to Ching K'o (Jing Ke): "Get hold of the map Wuyang is car-rying," said the King of Qin. When Jing Ke had got hold of the map and offered it to him, the King of Qin unrolled the map. And when the map was completely unrolled, the dagger was revealed. Using his left hand, he grabbed the King of Qin's sleeve, and with his right hand he held the dagger to stab him. [...] At this time, the attendant physician, Xia Wuju [Wuqie], warded off Jing Ke with the bag in which he carried drugs. (Dawson, *Sima Qian*, 19–20)

65. Such *jinlei* (K. *kŭmnoe*) appear, for instance, in the ode "Juan er" from the *Shijing*. See Legge, *Chinese Classics* 4:8. This drinking vessel was made from wood, carved so as to represent clouds, and variously gilt and ornamented. Waley translates the term as "bronze ewer." Waley, *Book of Songs*, 45.

66. The source says *yŏn kwan* (C. *juan guan*), "abandon the house," which is a euphemism for a person's death.

67. Or "the first of them," meaning the gilded vase that Ch'oe Sajŏn had given to his first son, Pyŏl.

68. *Kangmun chihu*. Kangmun, the Office of Audience Ceremonies, was renamed T'ongryemun in 1274.

69. "Minister" is a translation of *sangsŏ*. Kim Sinyun (n.d.) was left grand master of remonstrance and in 1171 became examination administrator in the civil service examinations. Kim Sinyun appears several times over the course of *P'ahan chip*, and he is portrayed as an upright, dissident minister. Together with such ministers as Kim Podang, he was at odds with eunuchs and high officials such as Chŏng Ham or Mun Kŭkkyŏm at the beginning of Myŏngjong's reign, and as a result of this was eventually demoted.

70. *T'uja sŏn* (C. *touzi xuan*), "selection with dice," here alludes to the oftentimes arbitrary fortunes and chances in the selection of successful candidates in the civil service examinations, and ultimately in the acquisition of office.

71. "Yellow millet dream" is a reference to the Tang tale "Zhenzhong ji" by Shen Jiji. In the tale, a Taoist priest by the name of Old Man Lü meets an unsuccessful scholar and shows him the meaninglessness of an official career and the vacuity of constant struggle and striving for worldly honors by sending him into a dream of official glory, eventual failure, and bitter death. Though the dreamer feels as if he spent an entire life in the dream, in reality it is shorter than the time it takes for cooking a bowl of yellow millet. This line implies that a great official career should not be desired and pursued at all costs, and that a successful official life may turn out to not be as magnificent as it appears.

72. *Kŭpkŭp* (C. *jiji*) could perhaps be understood as a reference to "Wen sang" (Questions about mourning rites) from the *Liji*, which in the translation by James Legge reads, "[...] they looked forward, with an expression of eagerness, as if they were following someone, and unable to get up to him." Legge, *Sacred Books of China*, 376.

73. This poem and the overall entry can certainly be read as criticism of the state examination and recruitment system, because by relating this episode, Yi Illo

310   NOTES TO PAGES 103–104

makes it unequivocally clear that the government would do well to employ such a benevolent, righteous person and have him work for the benefit of the state, but that due to the inflexible selection criteria and process, Ch'oe Hyoin must remain unemployed. In the poem at hand, Kim Sinyun portrays the civil service examinations as arbitrary, and as useless for acknowledging and determining the true worth of a real Confucian scholar.

74. The source says *ya* (K. *a*), which means the sections "Xiaoya" (Minor Odes) and the "Daya" (Greater Odes) of the *Shijing*. *Feng* (K. *p'ung*) here means the "Guofeng," also a section of the *Shijing*.

75. These are two virtuous ministers who served under the sage-kings Yao and Shun.

76. A slightly altered quotation from *Mengzi* 5B:1: "Hence, when they hear of the style of Bo Yi, the unperceptive develop discretion, and the weak develop resolution." See van Norden, *Mengzi*, 131.

77. This sentence is a quote from *Fayan* by Yang Xiong. Translation in Nylan, *Exemplary Figures*, 131.

78. Together with Yi Sik, Kim Yŏngbu (1096–1172) went to the Jurchen Jin dynasty as an envoy in 1148. He served as assistant grand councilor and vice director of the Royal Secretariat and Chancellery.

79. Mount Tai and Mount Hua are two of the Five Great Mountains of Chinese Taoism, the others being Mount Song, Northern Mount Heng, and Southern Mount Heng.

80. The meaning of this final sentence as well as its relation to the overall entry is unfortunately not clear to me.

81. Remko Breuker writes,

> During the reign of Yejong, new palaces and temples were built in the Western Capital "to prolong the life span of the royal undertaking now that it has been more than 200 years since the establishment of the capital at Songdo." Injong continued the policies of his predecessors: he tried to benefit from the Western Capital's terrestrial force after the aftermath of Yi Chagyŏm's failed rebellion in 1126 had reduced his palace to ashes. Swayed by geomancer Myoch'ŏng's insistence that building new palaces in the Western Capital would restore order back to Koryŏ's badly shaken political structure, he issued the following edict: It has been thus from olden times on that palaces were not restricted to certain sites, but varied depending on the times and circumstances. An ancient sage from Haedong said that the life of the country would be prolonged if a palace would be built on a "force of great flowering." I intend to disseminate my benevolence by building a palace on a site already chosen and reside in it according to the seasons. (Breuker, *Establishing a Pluralist Society*, 379–380)

82. Yongŏn-gak was the name of the palace in the Western Capital, which was newly constructed at the ancient site of Yongŏn-gung, a palace of the kingdom of Koguryŏ. It was a site strongly associated with nativist ideology.

NOTES TO PAGE 104   311

83. This sentence is based on the fifth passage of "Shuogua" (Explanations on the trigrams) from *Yijing*, which says, "The Divine Ruler [*shangdi*] comes forth in *Zhen* [Quake] [...], has them do battle in *Qian* [Pure Yang]." Lynn, *Classic of Changes*, 121–122. *Zhen*, "thunder," is in this Yijing passage said to correspond to the east, while *Qian* is the trigram for the northwest. Consequently *Zhen* can be understood to stand in for Kaesŏng, from which King Injong came forth, while *Qian* in this context means P'yŏngyang, which lies northwest of the capital.

84. "The king is at home in Hao, and he is drinking his wine" is a shortened quotation of a line from the first stanza of the ode "Yuzao" from the *Shijing*. In the translation by Arthur Waley, the original reads, "The king is at home, at home in Hao, / content and happy he drinks his wine." Waley, *Book of Songs*, 202. This ode has been understood as a praise of the joyful life of King Wu of Zhou, but it can also be read as a hidden critique of a king's overly luxurious, carefree lifestyle. Hao, or Haojing, the capital of Zhou during King Wu's reign, was referred to as the Western Capital of the Zhou after the center of government had been relocated to Luoyang in the east. At this point, Hao can be understood to stand for P'yŏngyang, the "new home" of the Koryŏ royal house in the west.

85. The term *chung* (C. *zhong*), "the many" or "the crowds," may here be taken as an allusion to the crowds of people in P'yŏngyang, the envisioned new capital at this point in time before the rebellion of Myoch'ŏng. A similar poem by Yi Chijŏ, which likewise deals with P'yŏngyang and at the end of which he actually says *yŏmin tong*, "together with the people," is contained in the sixty-fifth entry of the lower fascicle of *Tongin sihwa*, where Sŏ Kŏjŏng writes,

When in the cyclic year *kyŏngjin* King Sejo [r. 1455–1468] went on a royal tour of the Western Capital, the provincial governor [K. *kamsa*] Master Cho Hyomun [d. 1462] asked me for a poem to accompany music. My talents are meager [and thus I couldn't write a piece of my own], but since I also wasn't able to refuse his command, I simply showed him the following [P'yŏngyang-related] poem by Yi Chijŏ: "The waters of the Taedong River, lapis lazuli in emerald; / the flowers of Changle Palace, embroidered brocade in red. / The jade carriage [of the ruler] has wandered out once, isn't it a good event? / Breeze and moonlight of the Great Peace, together with the people." Delighted, Ch'angnyŏng said, "Vice Director of the Royal Secretariat and Chancellery Yi [Chijŏ] had the same heart-mind as I already a thousand years ago." (Yi, *Tongin sihwa*, 221)

86. A slightly transformed quotation from "Zhonghui zhi gao" (Zhonghui's proclamation) from *Shujing*. Translation in Legge, *Chinese Classics*, 3:181.

87. A slightly altered quotation from *Mengzi* 1B.1, which reads, "Hearing the notes of Your Majesty's bells and drums, the sounds of Your pipes and flutes, the commoners all furrow their brows. With pained heads they say to one another, 'How has our king's fondness of musical performances driven us to this extremity?' " See van Norden, *Mengzi*, 17.

312   NOTES TO PAGES 104–105

88. A reference to *Mengzi* 1B:4. See van Norden, *Mengzi*, 20–21.

89. A reference to the ode "Luming" from the *Shijing*. See Waley, *Book of Songs*, 192.

90. Yi Kongsu's (d. 1137) participation in a royal tour of the Western Capital during King Yejong's times is fittingly mentioned in his biography in *Koryŏsa* (vol. 95), where it says,

> [Yi] Kongsu, his courtesy name was Wŏllo, the original name given to him was Su. When he was young, his maternal grandfather, the *Sijung* Ch'oe Yusŏn, stroked his head, saying, "This child shall certainly become a great vessel." [...] When King Yejong went on a royal tour to the Western Capital, Yi Kongsu entertained and looked after him, but never caused any trouble for the average people [who had to supply the food]. The king thought him excellent, and after the royal carriage had returned [to the capital], he ordered him to stay in attendance. [Yi Kongsu, however,] refused, saying, "From times of old it has been acted that after the return of the royal carriage only one administrative clerk [K. *chisa*] and a single regent [K. *yusu*] are to form the retinue—how could I venture to request any special favors and thereby go against the everlasting canons?"

91. Tongdo, "Eastern Capital," is Kŭmsŏng, present-day Kyŏngju, the erstwhile capital of Silla.

92. A slightly different version of this poem features in *Tongmunsŏn* under the title *Tongdo hŭije* (Written playfully in the Eastern Capital):

> Drunk I am, utterly befuddled, tumbling in and out of dreams at dawn;
> unaware that a jade-like beauty is sleeping beneath the curtain.
> Thus I can rhapsodize to the *Xijiang yue;*
> don't you laugh at me for my elegant expressions being inferior to those of
>   my youth.
> (*TMS* 19:21a)

93. Kim Yŏn is Kim Injon, one of the most prominent scholars and statesmen of mid-Koryŏ, who was admired not only by his countrymen but, as can be seen in this entry, also by foreigners visiting Koryŏ. In his biography in *Koryŏsa* it says, "Kim Injon, his courtesy name was Ch'ŏhu, his first name [K. *ch'omyŏng*] was Yŏn, he was a descendant of [Kim] Chuwŏn of the royal clan of Silla." *Koryŏsa*, vol. 96, "Yŏlchŏn" 9. Kim Injon was governor of Kangnŭng, worked under and served as a tutor to Yejong, and went to Song China as an emissary in 1111. Regarding this, in *Pohan chip* 1:24 it says,

> In the first year of the reign of Tianqing [of Liao; r. 1111–1120], the envoy of appreciations (K. *saŭnsa*) Kim Yŏn, Im Yumun [1056–1125], and others entered Song China, and Emperor [Huizong of Song] paid them respect by meeting them in person. When Kim, Im, and the others returned, the

king questioned them regarding the reception they had received by the Song emperor, and Kim [Yŏn] replied, "The emperor treated our country with abundant generosity, and the presentation of ritual ceremony was exceptional. However, everything there was excessively extravagant and special, and I may say [that, given the precarious international situation with the Northern dynasty] it was quite pathetic." (Pak, *Yŏkchu Pohan chip*, 109)

One must note that the year mentioned for Kim Injon's visit to Song China in *Pohan chip* is given in the periodization of the Liao dynasty. In 1105, Kim Injon went to Liao himself as a lamentation annunciation envoy [K. *koaesa*], to announce the death of King Sukchong (1095–1105). Kim Yŏn was an ancestor of the prominent early Chosŏn intellectual Kim Sisŭp, who in his extant letter "Sang Yu Yangyang chinjŏng sŏ (Chahan)" (Letter explaining my situation to Yu [Chahan], [magistrate of] Yangyang) writes, "My remote ancestors Kim Yŏn and Kim T'aehyŏn [1261–1330] were directors of the Chancellery of Koryŏ for generations. In the basic annals of Koryŏ there are detailed records [about them]!" The letter can be found in Kim Sisŭp's collected writings, *Maewŏltang chip* 21:19b–21b; for a study and annotated translation of Kim's letters to his benefactor Yu, see Dennis Wuerthner, " 'Thus I May Now Dare Explain My Actual Situation without Hiding Anything' — Autobiographical and Biographical Writings," in *The Lives and Legacy of Kim Sisŭp (1435–1493): Dissent and Creativity in Chosŏn Korea*, edited by Vladimir Glomb and Miriam Löwensteinová (Leiden: Brill, 2023), 33–73.

94. Kim Sanggi (b. 1031). In 1084 he served as associate examination administrator in the civil service examinations. When serving as minister of taxation (K. *hobu sangsŏ*), together with a person by the name of Ch'oe Samun he was dispatched to Song China as an envoy to offer condolences for the death of Emperor Shenzong in the fall of 1085.

95. "Escort commissioner" is a translation of *chŏppansa*.

96. This incident took place in 1102. In the relevant entry in *Koryŏsa* it says, "In the cyclic year *kyech'uk*, [the Liao] also sent the drafter in the Secretariat Meng Chu, who came to congratulate the king on occasion of his birthday." *Koryŏsa*, vol. 11, seventh year of Sukchong, twelfth month.

97. Horse, Thunder, feet, and Heaven — this line is packed with subtle references to the section "Shuogua zhuan" (Explanations of the hexagrams and trigrams) from the *Zhouyi*, which features glosses on the *Yijing* trigrams' corresponding natural forces, symbolic animals, parts of the human body, and members of a model family. According to this, "Qian is a horse" and "Zhen is the foot"; furthermore, "Zhen is thunder [...]; horses that neigh well, have white hind legs, are sprightly [...]," "Thunder (Zhen) for moving," and "In all moving, nothing is swifter than Thunder." See Rutt, *Book of Changes (Zhouyi)*, 445–449.

98. While it is obvious that Meng Chu's line is deeply rooted in ancient Chinese literature and thought, Kim's line does not seem to feature any such readily recognizable allusions to the ancient classics. It appears to have been taken by Meng as a

314 Notes to Page 106

beautiful composition, though it is doubtful whether the Liao envoy truly considered it on par with his own poetic line. Nevertheless, Meng is shown to have positively acknowledged that the Korean responded quickly and skillfully, and this seems to have functioned as the basis for their developing friendship. The positive impression Kim Injon apparently left on the Liao envoy is also discussed in the pioneering historiography of Sino-Korean literature *Chosŏn hanmunhaksa* (History of the study of Korean literature in the Literary Sinitic, 1931) by colonial modernity intellectual giant Kim T'aejun, who also penned the historiography of Korean narrative literature *Chosŏn sosŏlsa*. In the *Chosŏn hanmunhaksa* section "Pak Illyang-gwa Kim Injon (Yŏn)" (Pak Illyang and Kim Injon [Yŏn]) it says, "At the same time lived Kim Injon (first name Yŏn), a man of erudition, who penned the *Lunyu sinŭi* and the *Haedong pirok*. [...] He not only had many literary achievements, but also uttered the phrase 'Banners' tassels fluttering in the wind, [it is as if] blazing fires flew,' as a parallel phrase when the Liao envoy Meng Chu said, 'Horses' feet stomping the snow, in heaven Thunder is moving,' thereby stunning [the Liao emissary] — he seems to have been very wise and sagacious." Kim, *Chosŏn hanmunhaksa*, 57. A modern nationalistic, purpose-oriented interpretation of this medieval source — emphasizing the literary superiority of the Korean — can be found in the comparatively recent North Korean publication *Chosŏn-ŭi irŭmnan chakka-wa irhwa*.

99. "Horn for the Communication with Heaven" (C. Tongtian Xi) is usually understood as a fantastic rhinoceros horn. The horn's magical quality as an instrument for the parting of water is mentioned in *Baopuzi neipian*, for here it is said that if a fish were carved on a rhinoceros horn three inches or more in length, a person holding the horn in the mouth would be able to breathe normally under water, because water would recede three feet from the horn, forming a volume of air. Yoke, *Li, Qi and Shu*, 179. In Kim Injon's biography in *Koryŏsa* (vol. 96, biographies vol. 9) it says that Meng Chu loosened his *jindai* (K. *kŭmdae*), his "golden belt."

100. The story told here also appears in the "Yŏlchŏn" section of *Koryŏsa* (vol. 96, "Yŏlchŏn" 9). It is also contained in the twelfth volume of *Imha p'ilgi*. Later, when in the Liao capital as an envoy, Kim met Meng Chu again.

101. The source here says *kanwŏn* (C. *jianyuan*), which in China during the times of Song was an unofficial reference to the Censorate. See Hucker, *Dictionary of Official Titles*, 151. In his *Chosŏn hanmunhaksa*, Kim T'aejun cites this passage but says that Kim Injon was at the *siwŏn* (C. *shiyuan*). See Kim, *Chosŏn hanmunhaksa*, 57.

102. In the biography of Kim Injon in *Koryŏsa* we find the following explanation for this: "When Injong inherited the throne at a young age, Yi Chagyŏm took charge of power. Afraid that he might meet disaster, [Kim Injon] asked to be allowed to retire from office, but did not obtain permission. One day, as he was on his way to the office, upon the road he heard nursery rhymes [ridiculing the ruler as a puppet-king]. Thereupon he fell off his horse, [hurt himself,] and returned home [to Kangnŭng] to lie down." *Koryŏsa*, vol. 96, "Yŏlchŏn" 9. I could not find more detailed information on the specific content of these nursery rhymes.

103. A reference to the restoration of Injong's rule after Yi Chagyŏm's failed attempt to usurp power.

NOTES TO PAGE 106   315

104. According to his biography, Kim Injon's three sons were called Yŏngsŏk, Yŏngyun, and Yŏnggwang. All three are said to have passed the state examinations and to have reached high offices.

105. Kim Injon's family with its successive generations of successful, high-ranking scholar-officials is at this point compared to two powerful clans of the Eastern Jin, the Langya Wang Clan (C. Langya Wang-*shi*) and the Chenjun Xie Clan (C. Chenjun Xie-*shi*), which brought forth such statesmen as Wang Dao (276–339) and Xie An (320–385).

106. There is a page break in the source at this point, from 2:4b to 2:5a. In between these pages, however, we find a double page carrying densely handwritten poems and notes by a reader or owner of this 1659 *P'ahan chip* print.

107. Kim Injon was sent to the northern frontier regions in 1117, where he served as vice provincial military commander of the Northwest District (K. *p'an sŏbukmyŏn pyŏngmasa*). This happened during the final phase of the confrontations between the Khitan Liao and the Jurchen Jin. Though Koryŏ had originally taken a neutral stand during this conflict, by the mid-1110s Koryŏ was looking to push away the Liao (which they had reluctantly served as a vassal-state) and come to satisfactory diplomatic relations with the rising Jurchen Jin. In this precarious situation, the tested diplomat Kim Injon was charged with transmitting to the Liao that Koryŏ would not come to their aid and support them in their struggles with the Jurchen. For the Koreans, gaining possession of the border city of P'oju (later Ŭiju) was of utmost importance. The Jin attacked the two strategically important walled cities of Naewŏn and P'oju by the Yalu River, which had until then been held by the Liao, and stepped aside to have these walled towns taken by Koryŏ. It was Kim Injon who led his soldiers to take over P'oju in April 1117. Afterward Kim was also the person who informed the king about these events (see *Koryŏsa*, vol. 14, third day of the third month, 1117; for more information on the political developments, see Rogers, "Regularization of Koryŏ-Chin Relations," 58–59). As can be seen in the entry at hand, Kim Injon was one of the top diplomats of Koryŏ during this tumultuous era. Moreover, Kim Injon served as examination administrator in 1106 and 1114. The farewell celebrations organized by his 1114 *munsaeng* and the relevant poem are mentioned in the entry on Ŭiju in *Sinjŭng tongguk yŏji sŭngnam. STYS* 53:15b.

108. *Taegak* (C. *taige*) was used to designate both the departments of state and the highest-ranking ministers who served there. In the Tang histories, it is used primarily to refer to the three major departments of the central government: the Censorate, the Secretariat, and the Chancellery. Nienhauser, *Tang Dynasty Tales*, 89.

109. *Saryun* (C. *silun*), "reeling silk," a conventional reference to an imperial edict, derives from a passage in *Liji*: "The king's words are like silken threads; when they go forth it is like reeling them out." Owen, *Poetry of Du Fu*, 18:35.

110. The source here says *kon-oe sin*, "minister beyond the city gate," but this expression may be understood as a reference to a passage from "Zhang Shizhi Feng Tang liezhuan" (Biographies of Zhang Shizhi and Feng Tang) from chapter 102 of *Shiji*, in which the Han official Feng Tang speaks with Emperor Wen about giving the generals guarding the frontier regions free rein, saying, "I have heard that when

316 NOTES TO PAGES 107–108

the kings of ancient times deployed their generals, they would kneel down and push the wheels [of their war chariots]. Then they would say, 'That what lies within the city gates We control; that what lies beyond the city gates you, Generals, control.' "

111. The source has *kumun* (C. *qiumen*), which may be understood as a reference to *Lunyu* 11:15. See Slingerland, *Confucius: Analects*, 116.

112. The poem is also contained in *Tongmunsŏn* under the title *Ch'uljin Yongman ch'a simunsaeng* (Going out to guard Yongman, then see my examination passers). *TMS* 12:10a–b.

113. Kim Chaŭi (n.d.) was second examination administrator in 1147. In 1150 he was appointed right policy adviser (K. *u san'gi sangsi*; see *Koryŏsa*, vol. 17, fourth year of the reign of Ŭijong, twelfth month) in the Secretariat, and in 1152 became minister of rites (see *Koryŏsa*, vol. 17, sixth year of the reign of Ŭijong, fourth month).

114. The source says *chŏnye*, which has here been translated as "take up the struggle in the arts of writing" and which basically means "to take part in the civil service examination." Chunguan, "Department of Spring," is the Ministry of Rites.

115. *T'akche* (C. *zhuodi*), "being picked out for the ranks," refers to successfully passing the civil service examinations.

116. It is not exactly clear in which year Kim Chaŭi passed the civil service examinations, but judging from the fact that he held high offices in the 1140s under Ŭijong, the dreaming king referred to at this point can be surmised to have been Injong.

117. The two characters *ch'ang* (C. *chang*) and *chŏng* (C. *jing*) look very similar.

118. The source at this point says *sahae-ji ka*, which I have understood as meaning "all kinds of songs from here and there," but which could, in fact, also be the specific title of a certain song, i.e., the "Song of the Sea-Girt World."

119. This is a *ch'ŏlbal* (C. *tiebo*), an iron *pātra*, or alms bowl. Muller, *Digital Dictionary of Buddhism*.

120. Ch'ŏk Chun'gyŏng, a minister who played a part in the Yi Chagyŏm rebellion. Originally a Yi henchman, in 1115 Ch'ŏk had aggressively protested the dispatch of troops to help the Khitan, who were fighting the Jurchen. See Shultz, "Twelfth-Century Koryŏ Politics," 10. During the revolt of Yi Chagyŏm he changed sides, joined King Injong, and eventually arrested Yi Chagyŏm. The sentence at this point alludes to Chŏk Chun'gyŏng's banishment to Amt'a Island (present-day Amt'ae Island in South Chŏlla Province) in 1127, when he fell from Injong's grace and was impeached by then censor of the left Chŏng Chisang, who lauded Ch'ŏk for having arrested Yi Chagyŏm but simultaneously also attacked him for having been involved in the burning and invasion of the palace in the wake of the rebellion. Since Ch'ŏk Chungyŏng's place of banishment was in the following year changed to Kokchu in Northern Hwanghae Province, the sentence at this point must refer to 1127, when Ch'ŏk was banished to the south of the Korean Peninsula. Ch'ŏk was pardoned and reinstalled in 1144.

121. An allusion to a tale from *Shiji*. Han Xin (d. 196 BCE), who served Liu Bang, the first emperor of the Han dynasty, had periods of estrangement from his lord. At one point, he was trussed up and thrown into a cart, whereupon he declared: "When

NOTES TO PAGE 108   **317**

the cunning hares have died, the good dog is cooked. When the lofty birds are gone, the good bow is put away. When the enemy is broken, the adviser perishes. The empire is pacified; I shall be cooked." Sargent, *Poetry of He Zhu*, 133.

122. Another reference to Han Xin and Liu Bang. Since Liu Bang feared Han Xin's growing influence, he demoted him to the title of Marquis of Huaiyin. Later, Han Xin was accused of having taken part in a rebellion and was executed. At this point, the poet states that neither Han Xin nor Chŏk Chun'gyŏng revolted against their respective lords.

123. Yi Chahyŏn (1061–1125) was the son of one of Koryŏ's most powerful families, the Kyŏngwŏn Yi lineage. He retired from the profane world and became the most famous recluse of his time, living in hiding on Mount Ch'ŏngp'yŏng. Owing to his illustrious aristocratic family background, he would have been entitled to automatic entry into Koryŏ's capital bureaucracy. Instead, he decided upon a more difficult route by taking and passing the state examinations. He entered the bureaucracy and quickly rose in the ranks, but then chose to leave and concentrate on a contemplative life. Having read widely in Confucian, Buddhist, and Daoist texts, he renounced wealth and fame and lived the rest of his life as a Buddhist recluse. From time to time he counseled holders of high office, scholars, and, on two different occasions, even the ruler. See Breuker, *Establishing a Pluralist Society*, 189–190. Yi Chahyŏn's posthumous name was Chillak.

124. The term *zixia* (K. *chaha*), "purple-tinted clouds" or "purple twilight," refers to the realm of Daoist immortals. At this point, *zixia* means that Yi wished to live in reclusion.

125. Originally one of the portals of the western Han imperial palace in Chang'an. Adjacent to the Hanlin Academy, it was here where the academicians awaited imperial command, and where scholars met and conversed. Thus, by extension the term originally alludes to the Hanlin Academy of the Tang dynasty, and at this point to the Hallim Academy of Koryŏ where Yi Chahyŏn served as a young man.

126. "Daoist" here is a translation of *shushi* (K. *sulsa*). The geomancer Ŭn Wŏnch'ung (n.d.) is said to have been a teacher and friend of Yi Chahyŏn. He is mentioned in *Koryŏsa*, where, for instance, it says, "In the cyclic year *kyŏngo* [1103], King Sukchong summoned the recluse of Mount Mudŭng, Ŭn Wŏnch'ung." See *Koryŏsa*, vol. 12, eighth year of the reign of Sukchong, tenth month. He is also said to have been dispatched by Yejong in 1105 to go on an inspection of Tonggye (present-day Hamgyŏng Province). See *Koryŏsa*, vol. 12, first year of the reign of Yejong, eleventh month). He is a case in point to show that people of vastly different ideological, religious, and educational backgrounds (Buddhists, Confucians, Buddho-Confucians, Daoists) were simultaneously employed at the court of mid-Koryŏ before the military revolution, and that they worked together productively and harmoniously for the benefit of their shared society and government.

127. Yangja-gang here means the Pukhan River, which flows from the Kŭmgang Mountains toward the west and eventually forms the Han River, which runs through the city today known as Seoul.

128. *Taeaksŏ ryŏng*, "director of the Office of Music." Other designations for the

318 NOTES TO PAGE 108

Office of Music were "Taeaksa" and "Taeakkuk." In Xu Jing's *Illustrated Account of the Xuanhe Embassy to Koryŏ*, in the section on the music of Koryŏ it says, "There are three (administrative) levels: the Office of Music has 260 musicians, which are usually employed by the king; next, the Reeds and Strings Ward [K. Kwanhyŏnbang] has 170 musicians; next, the Bureau of Capital Markets [K. Kyŏngsisŏ] has more than 300 musicians." Vermeersch, *Chinese Traveler*, 243.

129. The source says "drumming against a basin," which is a reference to "Zhile" from *Zhuangzi* (18.2) and alludes to the process of mourning one's wife.

130. Ch'ŏngp'yŏng-san today is Obong-san in Kangwŏn Province.

131. In *Tongmunsŏn* we find the *Ch'ŏngp'yŏng-san Munsu-wŏn ki* (Account of Munsu Monastery on Mount Ch'ŏngp'yŏng) by Kim Puch'ŏl (Kim Puŭi), which retells this incident. It says,

> Hereafter, when Hŭiija left office and came to live in hiding at this place, thieves and robbers lay low while tigers and wolves vanished without a trace. Thereupon he renamed the mountain, calling it Ch'ŏngp'yŏng, "pure and peaceful." Also, after having twice seen Mañjuśrī Bodhisattva appear, [...] he changed the name of the monastery [from Pohyŏn Monastery (K. Pohyŏn-wŏn)] to Munsu [Mañjuśrī] Monastery [K. Munsu-wŏn]. He then added buildings and fixed [the broken ones]. Hŭiija was the eldest son of Master Yi [Ŭi], his name was Chahyŏn, his courtesy name Chinjŏng. His physical appearance was magnificent, his Heavenly endowed nature quiet and contented. In the sixth year of the Yuanfeng reign he passed the literary licentiate examination [K. *chinsagwa*], and in the fourth year of the Yuanyou reign he became assistant in the Office of Music, but then he abandoned office and escaped from the profane world. During his travels he reached the Imjin River, and as he crossed the river he swore to himself, "Now I am leaving, and never again will I enter the capital." In terms of his learning there was nothing he hadn't looked at—he had deeply investigated the principles of Buddhism, and he particularly cared for Sŏn meditation. [...] Then he traveled to all of the famous mountains of the Country East of the Sea, searching for remaining traces of the [Korean] sages and worthies of old. Later he met State Preceptor Hyejo, who was the abbot of Hwaak Monastery on a mountain in the vicinity, and when they were going back and forth he would consult and ask [Hyejo] with regard to the principles of Sŏn. (*TMS* 64:27b–28a)

132. This line may allude to the last part of the chapter "Waiwu" from *Zhuangzi*, where it says, "Words are there for the intent [meaning]. When you have got hold of the intent [meaning], you forget the words. Where can I find a man who has forgotten words, so I can have a few words with him?" Ziporyn, *Zhuangzi*, 114.

133. Taegam, or Taegam Kuksa (State Preceptor Taegam), is the posthumous epithet of the important Koryŏ monk Tanyŏn (1070–1159), who was also a noted calligrapher. He is mentioned again in 3:19.

NOTES TO PAGES 108–109   **319**

134. *Kuksa* (C. *guoshi*), "state preceptor" or "national teacher." In Koryŏ, there was usually one national teacher designated at a certain time. Muller, *Digital Dictionary of Buddhism.*

135. Sigam is also Yi Chahyŏn's pen name.

136. Kwak Yŏ (1058–1130), a Daoist and literatus who served in a number of government positions, and also as tutor of King Yejong. In terms of official position, he reached the office of vice director of the Ministry of Rites. After a distinguished official career, Kwak retired early to a scholar's retreat into eremitism but was recalled after the ascension of Yejong to become the king's royal tutor. When he retired for the second time, the king built him a studio in the mountains. The biography of Kwak Yŏ in *Koryŏsa* reads,

> [Kwak] Yŏ, as a child he had dreamt about someone giving him the name Yŏ, and eventually he considered this his name. His courtesy name was Mongdŭk [Obtained in a Dream]. From an early age he did not eat any meat, and never played with the other children, but would always stay in his room by himself, studying with all his might. He passed the civil service examinations, was appointed to Palace Domestic Service, […] and went out as commissioner of Hongju [present-day Hongsŏng County in Southern Ch'ungch'ŏng Province]. Right away he built a small temple on the shores of a brook in the countryside, which he called Changgye Ch'odang [Thatched hall by the long creek], and when there was some leisure time in his official business he would always go there to rest. When his appointment ended, he entered the office of vice director of the Ministry of Rites, but then went back into reclusion in Kŭmju. When Yejong was staying at the Eastern Palace [as crown prince] he learned about him, and when he then ascended the throne, he dispatched a special royal commissioner to call upon him. Hereafter he had [Kwak Yŏ] reside on the palace grounds at Sunbok Hall. [King Yejong] called him "teacher." Wearing a black kerchief and a crane-feather coat, he always served [the king] left and right, and unhurriedly they would talk and discuss about various matters or share poetry. At the time, people referred to him as the "Feathered Guest of the Golden Gates." The king thought that, since he had him stay on the palace grounds for such a long time, [Kwak Yŏ] might want to go out and sojourn a bit, and thus he commissioned the construction of a villa outside of Sŏhwa Gate [the western gate of the palace in Kaesŏng]. [Kwak] Yŏ then invited Wang Chaji [1066–1122] and Mun Kongyu [1088–1159], who were about to go to Song China as envoys, for a farewell banquet to this villa. The king bestowed upon them wine and fruit and had the eunuchs set up everything. […] A little while later, [Kwak Yŏ] forcefully requested to be allowed to withdraw from his place of residence [on the palace grounds], and the king bestowed upon him one peak of Mount Tuyak, which lies to the east [of the capital], where he built a room to live. He made his pen name "Tongsan *ch'ŏsa*" [Recluse of

320 NOTES TO PAGES 109–110

the Eastern Mountain], and his hall he called "Hŏjŏng," [Hall of emptiness and silence], his study he named "Yangji" [Study of cultivation]. The king himself wrote these characters on signboards and bestowed them upon him. One day, [King Yejong] went out incognito and arrived at his mountain-study, but Yŏ had gone out to the capital. The king lingered around for a long time, waiting for him [to come back], but then he wrote a poem on a wall and returned [to the palace]. [This incident is described in the following entry, 2:9]. Later [the king] came back to the mountain-study, held [Kwak's] hands, and had him call out a lyrical phrase—when they met, his affection for and [special] treatment of [Kwak] were such as this. [Kwak Yŏ] passed away in the eighth year of the reign of Injong [1130] at the age of seventy-two. (*Koryŏsa*, "Yŏlchŏn" vol. 10)

137. The fact that Yi Chahyŏn and Kwak Yŏ passed the civil service examinations in the same year is also mentioned in *Pohan chip* 1:10. According to this entry, the year in question would be 1083. It says, "In the cyclic year *kyehae*, the ninth year of the Dakang reign [of Liao (1075–1084)], among those who passed the civil service examination together that year there were later no successful officials. Yi Chahyŏn and Kwak Yŏ [both were great intellectuals, but] both abandoned their official positions to become hermits. At the time, people called [the class of 1083] the "hermit class" [K. *ch'ŏsa pang*]." Pak, *Yŏkchu Pohan chip*, 66.

138. In his biography it merely says that Kwak Yŏ was appointed to an office in Hongju, but apparently he also served in the Kangwŏn region.

139. This line suggests that their meeting took place around 1113, since both are said to have passed the state examinations in 1083.

140. The relevant term here is *wushi* (K. *musa*), "no business," "no problems," or "non-interference in affairs." It has here been understood as "free from the trouble of worldly affairs."

141. The Shang princes Boyi and Shuqi are said to have starved themselves to death in opposition to the overthrow of the Shang by the Zhou in Chinese antiquity.

142. Xie and Hou Ji, the purported ancestors of, respectively, the Shang (Yin) and the Zhou dynasties.

143. The meeting between Yi Chahyŏn and Kwak Yŏ as well as their poetic exchange is also contained in *Sinjŭng tongguk yŏji sŭngnam. STYS* 46:12a.

144. Kui was the minister who was charged by the sage-emperor Shun with the responsibility of overseeing ritual music. Long was appointed minister of communication.

145. Chao Fu and Xu You were hermits who lived during the time of Emperor Yao. They are described in note 152 following.

146. A reference to an anecdote contained in "Zhile" from *Zhuangzi*: the Marquis of Lu held a banquet for a seabird that had alighted there. He had music played and offered the bird various kinds of marvelous foods as sacrificial offerings. The bird, however, died within a few days after its capture, because it was not treated in accordance with its nature.

147. This is an allusion to the discussion on knowledge between Zhuangzi

NOTES TO PAGE 110   **321**

and Huizi, conducted on a dam of the Hao River, which is contained in the chapter "Qiushui" of *Zhuangzi*. See Ziporyn, *Zhuangzi*, 76.

148. Another reference to a passage in *Zhuangzi*, this time from the chapter "Dazhongshi." Ziporyn, *Zhuangzi*, 43.

149. The memorial to King Yejong by Yi Chahyŏn presented at this point in *P'ahan chip* is only an abridged version of the original. The memorial is contained in its entirety under the title *Che i p'yo* (Memorial, number 2) in the thirty-ninth volume of *Tongmunsŏn* (sec. "Memorials and Memorandums" [K. *p'yojŏn*]). Parts of the more detailed version read,

> The subject so-and-so ventures to say: This month, on the day so-and-so, I received the sagacious will transmitted to me by so-and-so of this-and-that office, and [by Your Majesty's] comforting affection, as You commanded me to come to the Southern Capital and meet You in person. [...] I have heard that birds enjoy staying in deep forests, and that fish enjoy staying in deep waters. It is impossible to think of a fish's love for the water, and to change a bird's place of residence to a deep pond; it is also impossible to think of a bird's love for the forest, and change a fish's place of residence to a deep marsh. To nourish a bird as a bird should be nourished, one must let it indulge in the joys of forests and marshes; to see a fish and know a fish, one must release it into the happiness of rivers and lakes. One is to ensure that not one animal loses its [correct] place, and that each and every sensitive being obtains what is right for it. This is a sagacious emperor's deep benevolence, a wise king's magnificent brilliance. (*TMS* 39:4a–5a)

150. The present South Korean capital of Seoul, which from the early fourteenth century on was known under the name Hansŏng or Hanyang, was during Koryŏ times referred to as Namdo, "Southern Capital."

151. A quotation from *Mengzi* 7B 35. See van Norden, *Mengzi*, 193.

152. The expression "The Way [*dao*] cannot be transmitted" derives from "Yuanyou" (Far-off Journey) of the *Chuci*: "The *dao* can be received, but it cannot be transmitted [or taught]." Xu You, a scholar hermit from Chinese antiquity famous for his extreme aversion to improper behavior, was asked by the sage-emperor Yao to take over the rulership from him. He was so appalled by the suggestion that he ran away to Ji Mountain. When Emperor Yao offered him the position of governor of the nine regions, Xu felt so corrupted by the request that he had to walk down to the Ying River to wash his ears free from this insult. Another hermit by the name of Chao Fu came along to water his ox in the same river. When Xu told him what had happened, Chao Fu turned away from the contaminated water of the river and led his ox upstream to drink. See Lagerwey and Marsone, *Modern Chinese Religion*, 531.

153. Almost the exact same story can also be found in Yi Chahyŏn's biography in *Koryŏsa*. The only difference is the information that "when the king himself went on a royal tour to the southern capital, he dispatched Yi Chahyŏn's younger brother, Yi Chadŏk, to order Yi Chahyŏn to come to the travel lodge where the king

322 Notes to Page 110

was staying. The king created a poem, wrote it down by hand and bestowed it upon him, and Chahyŏn heeded the call." *Koryŏsa,* "Yŏlchŏn" vol. 8.

154. *Chungch'ang ki* appears to be an alternative title of the previously quoted *Ch'ŏngp'yŏng-san Munsu-wŏn ki* by Kim Puŭi (whose first name was Puch'ŏl), which has survived in *Tongmunsŏn.* See note 131. This text has been translated in its entirety by Hugh H. W. Kang and Edward Shultz. One passage from Kim Puch'ŏl's text on "the disciplined life of Yi Chahyŏn," which is of relevance in light of the *P'ahan chip* entry at hand, reads,

> Yejong several times instructed his palace attendants to grant Master Hŭii [Hŭiija] royal gifts of tea, incense, and Buddhist paintings in large amounts and ordered him to come to the palace. But not wishing to abandon the vow made when he crossed the river, to the end Hŭii did not comply with this royal request. When the king went to the Southern Capital in 1117, he sent Master Hŭii's younger brother, Minister Yi Chadŏk, to ask Master Hŭii to come there. The king's summons was expressed in a poem: "The passing of each day increases my desire to see you. / Difficult though it is to override the will of a lofty sage, / What would I do with my own heart's desire?" Master Hŭii sent a letter respectfully declining the invitation, but there was no way to change the king's earnest desire, and so in the eighth month of that year he went to the Southern Capital to pay his respects. The king said, "Although I have wanted to see you, a gentleman of high morality, for several years, I could not receive you in the manner of an ordinary subject." The king commanded him to come up to the throne and bow. The king responded with a bow. Then they sat, had tea, and talked quietly. Thereupon the king ordered him to remain at Ch'ŏngnyang Monastery on Mount Samgak for a while, and the king visited him, inquiring about meditation teaching. Master Hŭii in the end wrote and presented an essay titled "Simyo" (Fundamentals of the Mind) and then firmly asked to return to the mountains. The king gave him tea, incense, Buddhist utensils, and clothes, blessing his departure. (Lee, *Sourcebook of Korean Civilization,* 1:315–316)

155. Tongsan-jae, "Tongsan Studio," is the name of the residence and studio (K. *chaeho*) of Kwak Yŏ, which was located east of Kaesŏng. As was mentioned in the notes to the previous entry, sources suggest that the hermit Kwak Yŏ was not only Yejong's tutor, but in fact also a mentor and close friend of the king. For instance, in a *Koryŏsa* entry from 1115 it says, "In the cyclic year *sinmi*, the king, under cover of night, secretly went to visit the hermit Kwak Yŏ, who lived on Ch'ŏngsim Terrace in Sunbok Hall. There he prepared some wine, and together with his close minister [Kwak] he discussed literature. Only at dawn did he leave." *Koryŏsa,* vol. 14, tenth year of the reign of Yejong, ninth month. Another entry says, "In the cyclic year *pyŏngin* [1116], the king summoned the hermit Kwak Yŏ. They sat together in the flower garden behind Sangan Palace Hall, where the king personally had wine

NOTES TO PAGES 110–111   **323**

and food with him. Just at that time they suddenly looked toward the southeastern horizon, where there were several wisps of white clouds, and in between there was a pair of cranes flying back and forth in the air. Therefore the king ordered Kwak Yŏ to compose a poem [on this sublime scenery], which the king personally then wrote a lyrical response to." *Koryŏsa,* vol. 14, eleventh year of the reign of Yejong, fourth month.

156. *Kŭmmun,* "golden gates," are the main gates of a palace. This appellation "Feathered Guest of the Golden Gates" appears in Kwak's biography in *Koryŏsa* (see note 136).

157. An entry in *Koryŏsa* (vol. 7, tenth year of Munjong, twelfth month) says that Changwŏn Pavilion (K. Changwŏn-jŏng), a detached palace (K. *igung;* C. *ligong*) used by the crown prince, was built in 1056 (tenth year of the reign of King Munjong) by the shores of the Western River.

158. This is both the title and the prefacing topic phrase of the poems that follow. King Yejong's pentasyllabic poem of twenty lines as well as the response poem by the hermit Kwak, which is likewise a five-character poem of twenty lines, can be understood as adaptations of a series of seven pentasyllabic poems of the same title by Bai Juyi, *Hechu nanwang jiu – qishou* (Wherever, [whenever,] it's hard to forget the ale—seven poems; in Chinese studies the title has been rendered as "Where is wine the hardest to forget." See Pease, *His Stubbornship,* 91). The poems are part of Bai's *Quanjiu shisi shou.* Bai Juyi, who wrote *Hechu nanwang jiu* in 830 at the age of fifty-nine, here describes seven settings—events and times in a person's life marked by either happiness or sorrow—during which the speaker is overcome by the urge to drink alcohol: successful completion of the civil service examinations and the first appointment to office in the capital; a meeting with an old friend after decades of separation; a festival or a banquet; cold days in late autumn marked by the melancholy and loneliness of old age; victory in battle; saying goodbye to loved ones outside the city gates; or the occasion of someone's return from exile. In the poems, the initial line as well as the first line of the final couplet (line 7), "If there wasn't a single cup [of ale] at a time like this," reappear continuously, and these lines are also picked up and cited in both King Yejong and Kwak Yŏ's poems. Some of Bai's relevant foundational poems read,

> [1] Wherever, [whenever,] it's hard to forget the ale;
> in Chang'an I rejoiced in the freshness of the atmosphere.
> The day I first climbed the heights of the state examinations,
> I was suddenly made a fine official.
> Looked at the wall, where the Roster had been brightly spread out;
> the court robe fitted perfectly to my body.
> If there wasn't a single cup [of ale] at a time like this,
> how was I to cope with spring in the Emperor's Castle?
>
> [2] Wherever, [whenever,] it's hard to forget the ale;
> at the ends of the earth we chat about old affections.

324 NOTES TO PAGES 111–112

Blue clouds, together we failed to reach them;
white hair, taking turns we're startled at the sight of it.
Twenty years ago we parted,
from three thousand leagues away I traveled.
If there wasn't a single cup [of ale] at a time like this,
how should we ever manage to talk about our entire lives?

[3] Wherever, [whenever,] it's hard to forget the ale;
[at a house with] vermilion gates I envy young men.
At Spring Equinox, after the flowers have bloomed;
at Cold Food Festival, before the moon has brightened.
In the small courtyard, circling are [those dressed in] gauze and silk;
in the deep chamber, arranged are [those people playing] wind and string
     instruments.
If there wasn't a single cup [of ale] at a time like this,
how should I pass [these days] of the gorgeous weather?

[4] Wherever, [whenever,] it's hard to forget the ale;
in a frosty yard, there's a sick old man.
Faint sounds of chirping crickets,
dried leaves falling down from *wutong* trees.
The hair on the temples has already turned white in anguish;
the face has shortly turned red in drunkenness.
If there wasn't a single cup [of ale] at a time like this,
by what means could I cope with the winds of autumn? […]

[7] Wherever, [whenever,] it's hard to forget the ale;
an exiled minister returns to the gardens of home.
A writ of pardon is encountered by relay riders;
friends with congratulations come out the capital's gates.
Half of the face covered in darkish marks of malaria;
all of the robe moistened by the tears I shed when thinking of home.
If there wasn't a single cup [of ale] at a time like this,
with what thing could I manage to call back my soul?

For further information on the reception and adaptation of Bai Juyi's series of poems in premodern Korea, see Kim, "Paek Kŏi *Kwŏnju sipsa su*-ŭi han'gukchŏk suyong-gwa pyŏnyong."

159. This can be understood as a reference to the ballad "Qiu feng ci" (Song of the autumn wind) by Han Wudi (156–87 BCE), whose first line reads, "Autumn winds rise, white clouds fly."

160. Fangzhang (K. *pangjang*) could here signify the private chamber of a monk and could mean the "abbot's chamber." I have here, however, understood it as an allusion to a paradisiacal Daoist realm, as a reference to the legendary isle Fangzhang.

NOTES TO PAGES 112–113 **325**

161. The term *chumun* (C. *zhumen*), "vermilion gates" or "crimson gates," alludes to the vermilion-painted doors of splendid houses owned by rich high officials in ancient China. In the poem *Zi jing fu Fengxianxian yonghuai wubaizi* (Going from the capital to Fengxian County, singing my feelings [five hundred words]) by Du Fu it says, "Crimson gates reek with meat and ale, while on the streets are bones of the frozen dead." Owen, *Poetry of Du Fu*, 4:215.

162. Such cinnabar stoves (K. *tanjo;* C. *danzao*) were commonly used by Daoists in the framework of alchemism.

163. The oldest extant version of *P'ahan chip* at this point has *chang* (C. *zhang*), "to rely upon," while in the version of this poem contained in *Tongmunsŏn* it says *chang* (C. *zhang*), "staff." *TMS* 11:1a. I have here chosen to follow the *Tongmunsŏn*.

164. Pengdao refers to one of the three mystical paradise islands of the immortals in the Eastern Sea. At this point, Pengdao alludes to Mount Yaktu, the place of dwelling of the Daoist Kwak Yŏ.

165. Luoyang, one of the great ancient capitals of China, here stands for Kaesŏng, the capital of Koryŏ.

166. *Ch'ŏngdong* (C. *qingtong*), "blue-clothed child," usually refers to a Daoist master's child-servant.

167. *Ogung* (C. *biegong*), "turtle palace," most likely refers to the Eastern Mountain Study of Kwak Yŏ.

168. *Yongŏ* (C. *longyu*), "dragon chariot," refers to the chariot of an emperor or ruler. The term also appears, for instance, in *Changhen ge*.

169. The term *irwŏl* (C. *riyue*), "sun and moon," alludes to the king.

170. This poem by Kwak Yŏ is also contained in *Tongmunsŏn* under the title "Tongsan-jae ŭngje si." *TMS* 11:1a–b. It can be surmised that these poems will also have featured in the now lost *Yejong ch'anghwa chip.*

171. Kyeŭng (n.d.), dharma name T'aebaek-san-in, "Man of the T'aebaek Mountain," styled Muaeji Kuksa (State Preceptor Muaeji), was a high-ranking monk of the mid-Koryŏ period.

172. Taegak Kuksa, the "State Preceptor of Great Awakening," is the son of King Munjong, named Hu, courtesy name Ŭich'ŏn (1055–1101), one of the most illustrious scholar-monks of the Koryŏ period, who was responsible for the cross-border transmission of Buddhist teachings and books from China to Korea. This can be seen in his biography in *Koryŏsa*, parts of which read,

> Taegak *kuksa* Hu, courtesy name Ŭich'ŏn; because of the naming taboo [of him having the same personal name as] Emperor Zhezong of Song [r. 1085–1100; personal name Xu (K. *hu*)], he is known in the world under his courtesy name. [His father, King] Munjong one day asked all of his sons, "Who of you is capable of becoming a monk and creating fields of merit to confer blessings?" Hu rose and spoke. "I have the intention to leave the profane world, if only Your Majesty order me to do so." "Good," the king said. Eventually, [Ŭich'ŏn] accompanied Buddhist masters and left the mundane world behind, living at Yŏngt'ong Monastery. By nature

326   NOTES TO PAGE 113

he was intelligent and very fond of learning, and he began by making the *Avataṃsaka-sūtra* [K. *Hwaŏm-kyŏng*] his business, and soon enough he penetrated the Five Teachings [K. *ogyo;* the five taxonomies of Huayan]. On the other hand he was also concerned with Confucianism, and there was nothing he did not essentially understand. [...] Hu wanted to enter Song dynasty China and search for the Buddha's teachings and scriptures, but the king did not allow it. During Sŏnjong's reign [r. 1083–1094] he requested to be allowed to go several times more, but the high ministers and officials all vehemently said that this would not be possible. In the fourth month of the second year [of Sŏnjong's reign], Hu, alongside two of his disciples, secretly followed a Song Chinese merchant by the name of Lin Ning, boarded his vessel, and left [Korea for China]. The king ordered the censor Ŭi Kyejŏng [d. 1107] and others to go on their way, board ships and chase after him, but it was to no avail. Thus [the king] dispatched Vice Director in the Office of Guest Affairs Chŏng Kŭn [n.d.] and others to inquire whether [Ŭich'ŏn's] crossing of the ocean had gone well or not. When Hu arrived in Song, the emperor presented himself at Chuigong Palace Hall, waiting on him with the rites of a [high] guest, treating him very favorably and in accordance with the rites. Hu requested to travel around and inquire about the teachings of the Buddha. [...] When he reached the various temples of Wuzhong, everyone welcomed him or saw him off as a king's minister. The [Korean] king sent a memorial to the emperor of Song, begging him to order that [Ŭich'ŏn] be sent back home to his native country, and by imperial order he was allowed to return to the east. When Hu arrived at the Yesŏng River, the king [...] went out to Pongŭn Temple to wait for him there. [...] Hu presented a thousand Buddhist scriptures and classics to the king, and asked to have the Directorate for Buddhist Scriptures established at Hŭngwang Monastery. Books he had bought in Liao and Song amounted to some four thousand volumes, and all of them were printed and circulated. He founded the Ch'ŏnt'ae Order [K. Ch'ŏnt'ae-chong] at Kukch'ŏng Temple. (*Koryŏsa,* "Yŏlchŏn" vol. 3)

For further information on Ŭich'ŏn, see McBride, Ŭich'ŏn.

173. *Pŏpki* (C. *faqi*), a "dharma vessel," is someone who is suitable to believe, understand, and transmit the teachings of Buddhism.

174. *Yŏn'gok* (C. *niangu*), literally the "ruler's carriage," has here been understood as referring to the capital. It could, however, also mean the king himself, that Kyeŭng was never allowed to leave the king's side.

175. *Pohan chip* 3:23 deals with this matter in the following way:

Aside from lecturing on the Way, State Preceptor Muaeji Kyeŭng was also well versed in literary writing. When King Ye[jong] invited him to the Inner Palace and strongly urged him to stay [on the palace grounds], the master created a poem, which read, "The sage-[king's] orders are strict

Notes to Pages 113–114 **327**

and clear, refusing them I cannot do; / the monkey on the rock and the crane on the pine, they have departed Kangdong. / For many years I had narrowly escaped being a fish swallowing bait, / but one morning I was turned into a bird in a cage. / An unbound traveler filled with worry [at the sight] of the moon from inside the palace grounds; / now and then in dreams of returning there is wind in the grotto. / Do not know on what day my Lord's grace will be repaid, / or when a monk may return to the blue-green peaks." Hereafter he went back into the T'aebaek Mountains straightaway, where he lived in seclusion, determined to end his days there. The king sent envoys to summon him time and again, and repeatedly issued royal decrees, but the royal summons were never received. (Pak, *Yŏkchu Pohan chip*, 446)

176. Kakhwa-sa, located in present-day South Korea, Northern Kyŏngsang Province, Ponghwa District.

177. Hŭngwang-sa was located on Mount Tŏkchŏk in Kyŏnggi Province, Kaep'ung District, present-day North Korea. It was established in 1067, during the reign of King Munjong. Ŭich'ŏn lived at this temple during the early reign of Sŏnjong. When a son was born to King Ŭijong, a devout Buddhist, the king repaired the walls at Hŭngwang-sa and stored two copies of sets of Hwaŏm scriptures there. See Shultz, "Military Revolt in Koryŏ," 26. Hereafter, especially between 1157 and 1162, King Ŭijong frequently traveled to and stayed at this temple. In fact, one of the king's brothers was a monk at Hŭngwang Temple. Hŭngwang-sa, which was a temple of the influential Kyo Buddhist sect, is mentioned in *Xuanhe fengshi Gaoli tujing,* where Xu Jing writes, "Hŭngwang Temple is located southeast of the capital. About two leagues outside the Changp'ae Gate, it faces towards a stream. Its scale is vast, and it houses a hemp-lined Buddha statue bestowed during the Yuanfeng era and a Tripitaka granted during the Yuanfu era (1098–1100). On both walls are paintings." Vermeersch, *Chinese Traveler,* 137.

178. Apart from the entry at hand there are no other extant sources dealing with a monk by the name of Chisŭng. The term *kuŭi* [C. *kouyi*], "lifting the front of one's garment," refers to a gesture to show respect in ancient China.

179. This poem by Kyeŭng is contained in *Tongmunsŏn* under the title *Song Chisŭng* (Sending off Chisŭng). *TMS* 9:9a–b.

180. Chanyue Guanxiu (832–913), a poet-monk of the Tang and Five Dynasties / Ten Kingdoms period. His sobriquet was Chanyu Dashi, "Great Master of the Moon in Meditation." His *Chanyue ji* (Collection of the moon of meditation) is one of the most important collections of Chan poetry.

181. Canliao is the courtesy name of the Song dynasty poet-monk Daoqian (1043–1106), who was a friend of Su Shi's. The poetic nimbleness and excellence of Canliao becomes evident in a statement by Su Shi, which says,

Canliao (a courtesy name of the monk Daoqian) came from Yuhang to visit Su Shi at Pengcheng. One day, [Su Shi] set up a banquet for the

328 NOTES TO PAGES 114–115

county officials and said to his guests: "Canliao doesn't participate in this gathering, but we must bother him. He sent a government courtesan Ma Panpan with paper and a brush to ask for a poem from Canliao. Canliao completed this poem instantly and there was a couplet. 'A mind of Zen like the catkin touched by mud / does not chase the eastern wind wildly up and down.'" Su Shi was very happy and said: "I once saw a willow catkin that had fallen in the mud and secretly said that it could be turned into poetry. By accident I have not sorted it out yet, and this person did it before I was able to. It is a pity." (Hao, *Reception of Du Fu*, 49)

182. This is a quotation of a piece of calligraphic writing by the Jin dynasty politician Wang Hun (223–297) contained in the early-twelfth-century Song dynasty treatise on calligraphy *Xuanhe shupu* (Notes on calligraphy from the Xuanhe reign). It features in the thirteenth volume of this work and refers to an unusually gifted person.

183. Hyeso (n.d.), a poet-monk of King Sukchong's time, was a disciple of Ŭich'ŏn.

184. According to *Sinjŭng tongguk yŏji sŭngnam,* another name for Kyŏnbu-sa, the temple where Hyeso was the abbot, was Kangsŏ-sa, "Monastery to the West of the River." See *STYS* 43:31a. Sŏho, "Western Lake," may therefore be an alternative name for Kyŏnbul-sa.

185. "Inner and outer canons" are the *neidian* (K. *naejŏn*), the "canonical scriptures," and the *waidian* (K. *oejŏn*), the "noncanonical writings." The term alludes to Buddhist and non-Buddhist teachings.

186. The term *sŭngsŏn* (C. *sengxuan*) refers to when a person meets the required standards for scripture recitation and obtains a passing grade in the administered exam to enter the clergy.

187. *Xinglu* (K. *haengnok*), "records of activities" or "accounts of conduct," are the chronicles of a monk's pilgrimages, his sayings and activities.

188. This refers to the *Koryŏguk Ogwan-san Taehwaŏm Yŏngt'ong-sa chŭngsi Taegak kuksa pimyŏng* (Inscription on the funerary stele of the posthumously titled state preceptor Taegak of Great Hwaŏm Yŏngt'ong Monastery on Mount Ogwan in the state of Koryŏ), which was composed by Kim Pusik in 1125 and erected in 1133. See McBride, Ŭich'ŏn, 900.

189. In *Tongmunsŏn* we find the poem *Kim Sijung sŭngno pang kangsŏ Hyeso sangin* (Riding on a donkey, Director of the Chancellery Kim [Pusik] visited the monk Hyeso at Kangsŏ [Monastery]), by Min Sap'yŏng (1295–1359), which deals with these visits by Kim Pusik. Here it says, "All alone sitting atop a grayish donkey, visiting emerald mountains; / this mountain monk may well be a descendant of [the monk] Fenggan. [...]" *TMS* 21:18a. Kim Pusik's visits are also referred to in the above-mentioned entry from *Sinjŭng tongguk yŏji sŭngnam.*

190. Naedojang, "Place of Practice in the Inner Palace," is a term referring to a temple or an altar on the palace grounds.

191. Kŭmnan is a different name for T'ongch'ŏn County [K. T'ongch'ŏn-gun] in Kangwŏn Province.

NOTES TO PAGE 115   **329**

192. Hansong-jŏng, "Cold Pine Pavilion," was a pavilion located in the city of Kangnŭng. Many lyrical works were written on the topic of Hansong Pavilion, for example, a *sijo* by the courtesan Hongjang. For this, see O'Rourke, *Book of Korean Shijo*, 155.

193. *Sasŏn*, "four immortals," alludes to four famous *hwarang* of Silla, namely, Yŏngnang, Sullang, Namnang, and Ansang. In the eighteenth volume of *Chibong yusŏl* it says, "Coming to the times of Silla, they chose beautiful men, adorned and decorated them, put them in groups and had them roam as a flock. Looking at their conduct and righteousness, they called them *hwarang* ["flower boys"], or *nangdo* ["followers of the boys"], or sometimes even *kuksŏn* ["immortals of the dynasty"]. Such [*hwarang*] as Yŏngnang, Sullang, and Namnang belonged to that kind. Nowadays it is customary to say that male shamans [K. *nammu*] became *hwarang*, but that's not in accord with their original purpose."

194. As is evidenced in the poem *Che Hansong-jŏng* (Written on Hansong Pavilion) by the late Koryŏ scholar An Ch'uk (1282–1348), the magnificent, lush pine trees allegedly planted by the three thousand retainers of the Four Immortals all burned down in a wildfire sometime in the middle of the fourteenth century. This poem, which is contained in *Tongmunsŏn*, reads,

> "The Four Immortals early on gathered here,
> their retainers were like the ones [who stood] at [the Lord of]
>   Mengchang's gate.
> Those with beaded shoes [the *hwarang*] are like the clouds, all gone without
>   a trace;
> the gray officials [the pine trees] have caught fire and have ceased to exist.
> Searching for those genuine ones [of Silla], longing for that azure thicket [of
>   pines];
> meditating on the past, standing there at dusk.
> Only left is Tea-Brewing-Well [K. Chŏnda-jŏng];
> still here as it has always been, by the root of the rocks. (The reason for this is
>   that the pines all burned down recently in a wildfire). (*TMS* 9:19a)

When the late-Koryŏ poet Yi Mubang (1319–1398) visited Hansong-jŏng, the pines were apparently still there. In his poem *Ch'a Hansong-jŏng un* (Rhymes upon reaching Hansong Pavilion) it says,

> The pavilion leans against the edge of pine-covered foothills;
> gazing out toward the east, the sea has no gates.
> The region is tranquil, the immortals' traces still exist;
> the sand is bright, the bird sealscript still there.
> At the heart of the memorial stele, a halo of moss is green;
> on the face of the rock, tracks of rain are dark.
> A small spring hasn't run dry,
> it flows forth from the roots of heaven and earth. (*TMS* 10:5b–6a)

330   NOTES TO PAGES 115–116

195. *Pohan chip* 1:38 says that Hyeso wrote an account [K. *ki*] on Ch'ongsŏk Pavilion in Kŭmnan, the *Kŭmnan ch'ongsŏk-chŏng ki,* which Kim Pusik later ridiculed as too lyrical in style. It might be this *ki* being alluded to at this point. See Pak, *Yŏkchu Pohan chip,* 139.

196. Pyŏngna noin was already mentioned in 1:11, but without the addition Kŏbi. Kŏbi, "Going into Not-Being" (or perhaps short for *pi kwagŏ pi mirae pi hyŏnjae,* "Neither past, nor future, nor present") may be the dharma name of a monk. The courtesy name of the late Koryŏ dynasty literatus Chŏng Sŏn (1251–1325) was Kŏbi, but his dates obviously do not coincide with the time of creation of *P'ahan chip.* Later in the present entry it says that Pyŏngna noin, alongside a "teacher" or "preceptor" [K. *sa*] by the name of Kwangch'ŏn, who in all likelihood was a Buddhist priest, followed renowned, probably Buddhist worthies from Korea. Thus, this Pyŏngna noin is likely to have been a Buddhist priest.

197. Plantains here is a translation of *bajiao* (K. *p'ach'o*), a kind of banana plant with large leaves that grows rapidly in a warm climate. The plant's large leaves tear easily in wind and rain, and, in contrast to the leaves of the bamboo, they wither in the frost.

198. The addressee of these words is the aforementioned plantain. *Ch'a kun* (C. *chi jun*), "this nobleman" or "this gentleman," is a reference to the bamboo. The expression derives from the "Wang Huizhi zhuan" (Transmitted record of Wang Huizhi) from *Jinshu* (vol. 80), where it says,

> At the time, in the state of Wu, in the house of a literatus there was a nice bamboo. He wanted to look at it, so he went out, sitting in a carriage, and halted right underneath the bamboo, where he recited and whistled for a good while. The owner came out to sprinkle and sweep [the courtyard], and he asked [Wang] to take a seat, but Huizhi didn't even look back at him. As he was about to leave, the owner [of the house] shut his door [and did not bid him farewell], upon which [Wang] said, "I appreciated this [bamboo], and I am leaving after having enjoyed myself entirely." Early on he had [temporarily] lodged at [another person's] vacant house, where he had [straightaway] ordered a bamboo to be planted. Someone asked what the reason for this was, but Huizhi only chanted and whistled. Then he pointed at the bamboo and said, "How could I live even a single day without this gentleman?"

199. Wangnyun-sa was located on Mount Songak near Kaesŏng. In an account by Im Ch'un contained in *Tongmunsŏn* it says, "West of Wangnyun-sa lies a hermitage, and the monk Teacher Ch'ŏn [K. Ch'ŏn-sa, as in Kwangch'ŏn-sa] resided there." *TMS* 65:10b. This Buddhist monk seems to have been well-connected and widely known—judging from the entry at hand he appears to have had a close relationship with Yi Illo, while in the following entry it is shown that he also served at the court in Kaesŏng.

200. The oriole could be understood as a bird representing the royal palace or

NOTES TO PAGE 116   **331**

even the ruler. In this sense it appears in Wang Wei's poem *Ting gongyin* (Listening to orioles in the palace), and also in the poems featured in 3:18.

201. Punhwang-*chong*, a Korean Buddhist doctrinal stream, the founding of which is attributed to Wŏnhyo. Muller, *Digital Dictionary of Buddhism*. It is also known as Haedong-chong, "Korean School," or Pŏpsŏng-chong, "Dharma-Nature School." The name Punhwang derives from Punhwang Monastery, where Wŏnhyo is said to have lived and worked.

202. Chogam is the dharma name of the monk Chongnyŏng (n.d.), a close friend of Yi Illo's. The last of Yi Illo's poem "Presented to the Four Friends" is dedicated to Chongnyŏng. It treats the productive fusion of poetry and Buddhism, of literature and religion.

203. Pattra leaves, or palm leaves, are an early Indian medium for the writing of Buddhist texts.

204. These *ch'ŏnhwa* (C. *tianhua*), "heavenly flowers," are said to have rained down from the sky when Shakyamuni lectured on the Buddhist scriptures.

205. *Anhwa* (C. *yanhua*), "flowers in the eyes" or "blossoms in the eyes," usually is a metaphor for blurred vision. At this point, the term can be understood as referring to the blurred vision of someone in a drunken stupor.

206. The "land of drunkenness" (K. *chuhyang;* C. *zuixiang*) was a popular trope in Tang dynasty poetry, a famous example being *Zuixiang ji* (Record of the land of drunkenness) by Wang Ji (590–644).

207. Wanhui (632–711), a monk of the Tang dynasty, at one point was appointed Duke Fayun. See Chen, "Complicated Figure," 148. In the biography of Wanhui contained in *Song gaoseng zhuan* (Biographies of eminent monks compiled during the Song dynasty; vol. 18) it says,

> The Buddhist monk Wanhui, by his worldly name he was a member of the Zhang family, and he was a man from Wenxiang County in Guo Prefecture. When he was still of a young age, [it became clear that] he was disabled [C. *baichi*, an "idiot"] who did not speak, and his parents lamented his turbid *qi*. He became the object of the neighborhood's children's scorn, and in the end there was no one he had the attitude to compete with. But since he called himself Wanhui, "Ten Thousand Repetitions," this became his name there. [...] At the age of ten, his elder brother became a guard in Liaoyang [...] and for a long time there was no news of him. Their mother was very worried about him, and eventually she offered a meal at a Buddhist ceremony and prayed for good fortune. Just then, Hui suddenly said to his mother, "It's very easy to find out whether elder brother is safe. Why worry?" Thus, he wrapped up a bundle of food, walked out the door, and went on his way. At nightfall he returned, holding a letter by his elder brother in his hands. It read, "I am in peace and doing well." When [his mother] asked him where that letter was from, he fell silent and did not answer. The way to and from [Liaoyang] was ten thousand leagues. Later, his elder brother returned, saying, "That day I spoke with Hui, he

332   NOTES TO PAGES 116–117

had come from home, we bought pastries to eat, and then he went back." The entire family was pleasantly surprised.

The line at hand says that Wanhui "feigned insanity" or "acted mad," which might be understood as a reference to Wanhui acting as if he were "dumb" while in reality being equipped with quasi-supernatural powers. By this, Chogam seems to imply that Teacher Kwangch'ŏn may at first glance may have looked like a dozing, drooling drunkard, but that in reality he is a great monk with magnificent abilities.

208. This poem by the so-called Buddhist Chongnyŏng Chogam (K. Sŏk Chongnyŏng Chogam) is also contained in *Tongmunsŏn* under the title *Hŭijŭng Ch'ŏn sa* (Playfully presented to Teacher Ch'ŏn). Certainly based on the *P'ahan chip* entry at hand, the explanatory subtitle in *Tongmunsŏn* reads, "The teacher early on went to the Place of Practice in the Inner Palace. Drunk [on ale] he had dozed off, with mucus and tears dribbling down [onto his clothes], and was expelled by an officer in charge." *TMS* 19:14b.

209. The late-twelfth–early-thirteenth-century Koryŏ monk Hwaŏm wŏlsa (n.d.) was also known under the names Hwaŏm wŏlsujwa, Kakhun, and Kagwŏl, as well as under his pen name, Koyang ch'wigon. He was the abbot of Yŏngt'ong Monastery. On King Kojong's royal order, in 1215 he served as compiler of the *Haedong kosŭng chŏn* (Biographies of eminent monks of Korea), which contains biographies of eminent Buddhist monks of the Korean Three Kingdoms period. Next to the *Samguk sagi* and the *Samguk yusa* (for the creation of which the author Iryŏn is known to have extensively used Kakhun's work as a source), the *Haedong kosŭng chŏn*, of which two chapters are still extant (the oldest manuscript was discovered only in the early twentieth century), counts among the most important sources dealing with figures from early Korean history. The work has been translated by Peter H. Lee as *Lives of Eminent Korean Monks: The Haedong Kosŭng Chŏn* (Cambridge, MA: Harvard University Press, 1969).

210. Koyang Ch'wigon (C. Gaoyang Zuiju) can here be understood as an allusion to the Western Han figure Li Yiji (268–204 BCE), an adviser to the founding emperor of Han, who styled himself Gaoyang Jiutu, "Drunkard of Gaoyang." By calling himself "Baldheaded Drunkard," Hwaŏm wŏlsa makes it clear that even as a monk he indulges heavily in alcohol, behaving in a rather unrestrained manner.

211. The Tang-dynasty poet-monk Jia Dao left the monastic order and went back to the lay life on the advice of Han Yu, whom he followed afterward. That Hwaŏm wŏlsa excelled in literary writing is also mentioned in *Pohan chip* 3:39, where it says, "Hwaŏm wŏlsujwa—with regard to other matters [than Buddhist ones], he also had a deep understanding of literary writing, and his collection of draft script poetry was transmitted among literati circles. Early on he had compiled the *Haedong kosŭng chŏn*." Pak, *Yŏkchu Pohan chip*, 478.

212. The entry at hand obviously deals with an incident that must have taken place many years in the past, and it seems to have been written decades prior to the completion of *P'ahan chip*, for Im Ch'un died around 1190, while *P'ahan chip* was finished about twenty years later.

NOTES TO PAGES 117–118 **333**

213. It is not exactly clear who this monk is, but he appears to have been a contemporary and acquaintance of Su Shi and Ouyang Xiu. For instance, Huiqin is mentioned in the title of a poem by Su Shi, *Lari you Gushan fang Huiqin Huisi erseng* (On the day of the winter sacrifice I roamed Lone Mountain, visiting the two monks Huiqin and Huisi). As was mentioned in note 238 of 1:18, Zuiweng, "Old Drunkard," is the pen name of Ouyang Xiu. The friendly relationship between the scholar Yi Illo and the Buddhist Hwaŏm wŏlsa is here compared to that of Ouyang Xiu and Huiqin.

214. No information can be found on a monastery called Kamak-sa directly, yet according to the "Chiri chi" (vol. 56, "Wanggyŏng Kaesŏngbu," sec. "Chŏksŏnghyŏn") of *Koryŏsa*, there was a shrine atop Mount Kamak where the court offered incense and formulaic invocations in writing (K. *ch'ungmun*) for memorial services in spring and autumn. It is furthermore said that the people of Silla performed ritual services for the Tang dynasty general Xue Rengui (614–683) at this place. Xue Rengui was viewed as the mountain god of Mount Kamak.

215. In light of the way in which Kim Sinyun is portrayed in other entries of *P'ahan chip* (see especially 3:29), namely as an upright, righteous, and frank minister, it can be assumed that he dared to criticize the king, here in all likelihood Ŭijong, and his ministers at the court. In the second entry of the fourth fascicle (*hujip* 2:1) of *Yŏgong p'aesŏl*, Yi Chehyŏn writes the following about Kim Sinyun's assessment of Ŭijong's apparently inappropriate idleness while revolution and murder unfolded all around:

> At Ŭi[jong's] court, on the ninth day of the ninth lunar month in the cyclic year *kyŏngin* [1170; when Chŏng Chungbu staged his coup], Minister Kim Sinyun wrote the following poem: "Beneath the ruler's coach, windblown dust [K. *p'ungjin;* a term alluding to revolt or war] rises; / the killing of men [civil officials] like tangled hemp. / But a good time just cannot be wasted [by the king and his decadent ministers]; / on white wine they float yellow flowers." [This poem also features in *Tongmunsŏn; TMS* 19:3a]. I can see that the events of that time [the military revolt] couldn't have been anything but inevitable. Yet the feelings this old man [Kim Sinyun] had in his breast, and also his high-minded presence [K. *t'oerak*] — they were quite unusual [during his day and age]. (Yi, *Han'guk myŏngjŏ taejŏnjip*, 441)

216. This sentence has been understood differently by Ri Sŏng, the North Korean translator of *P'ahan chip*, for he rendered this passage about writing (into) ashes in the following way: "Kim Sinyun stayed under his blanket all day long, not uttering a word, but then he happened to pick up a fire tong and drew the character *hoe* [C. *hui*], 'ashes,' [on the ground], and those who happened to sit close by all pointed and glanced at it, saying, 'That old man seems to understand characters quite well.'" Ri, *Ri Illo, Rim Ch'un chakp'um chip*, 79.

217. Kim On'gi (n.d.). Unfortunately no information on this person could be found.

218. Fan Sui (d. 255 BCE), a native of the state of Wei during the Warring States

334 NOTES TO PAGES 118–119

period, who was wrongly accused of treason by Xu Jia and had to flee to the state of Qin, where he impressed King Zhao and came to serve as grand councilor. Years later, when the state of Wei learned that Qin was about to mount an attack against them, they sent Xu Jia to make peace. Fan Sui, dressed in ragged clothes and using an alias, went to meet Xu Jia, who did not recognize him. Yet Xu Jia presented Fan Sui with a silk robe because he felt pity for the poor man. Later, when Xu Jia realized that Fan Sui had become grand councilor in Qin, he apologized and was forgiven.

219. Though it cannot be said with absolute certainty, judging from the name, this person is likely to have been a monk residing at Kamak Monastery at the time in question.

220. A reference to *Zhuangzi* 1:11. Ziporyn, *Zhuangzi*, 7.

221. A reference to *Feng fu* (Rhapsody on wind) attributed to Song Yu (ca. 290–ca. 223 BCE). Here it reads: "King Xiang of Chu was taking his ease in the Palace of the Orchid Terrace, with his courtiers Song Yu and Jing Cha attending him, when a sudden gust of wind came sweeping in. The king, opening wide the collar of his robe and facing into it, said, 'How delightful this wind is! And I and the common people may share it together, may we not?' But Song Yu replied, 'This wind is for Your Majesty alone. How could the common people have a share in it?' " Minford and Lau, *Classical Chinese Literature*, 270.

222. This story of Kim Sinyun and Pin Yŏn is also contained in *Sinjŭng tongguk yŏji sŭngnam*. STYS 11:42a–b.

223. The biography of Kim Hwangwŏn in *Koryŏsa* (vol. 97) reads,

> Kim Hwangwŏn, his courtesy name was Ch'ŏnmin, he was originally from Kwangyang County. He passed the civil service examinations at an early age, vigorously studied the ancient literary style, and was called the very best in all of Korea. He was upright and would not cling to the powerful. He was friends with Yi Kwe [d. 1122; see 3:14] — they were at the Hallim[-wŏn] together, making a name for themselves by means of their [superb] literary writings, and at the time they were simply referred to as "Kim & Yi." Once, when a Khitan Liao envoy had arrived [in Korea], during the inner-palace banquet [Kim] Hwangwŏn recited a poem, which included the line "Holding a silken thread in his mouth, the phoenix descends from the sky; / riding on Penglai [Island], the turtle crosses the ocean." The envoy gasped in admiration, asked to note down the entire piece, and left. Grand Councilor Yi Chawi hated that [Kim Hwangwŏn's] literature did not follow the popular style of the time, so he said, "If that lot is at the Hallim-wŏn for too long, they'll certainly have a bad influence on later students," and eventually he succeeded in having them expelled. [...] [King] Sŏnjong heard about this and selected him to serve as left reminder and drafter of royal pronouncements, but soon thereafter he was sent out to become magistrate of Kyŏngsan [present-day Sŏngju]. Once, a petty official captured and brought in [an alleged] robber and murderer. Master [Kim Hwangwŏn] took a closer look at the man and said, "He's

NOTE TO PAGE 119 **335**

not the thief." Then he quickly ordered him to be released. "But that thief has already confessed," Magistrate's Aide [K. P'an'gwan] Yi Sanggang exclaimed. Yet [Kim Hwangwŏn] wouldn't hear of it. Later they caught another thief, and, truly, he was the [real] murderer from the time before. The petty officials and the people all admired his spirited clarity [this story is also retold in the nineteenth-century manual for district magistrates *Mongmin simsŏ* (Admonitions on governing the people, 1821) by late Chosŏn dynasty intellectual giant Chŏng Yagyong; see *Mongmin simsŏ* 11:12b–13a]. He stayed in Kyŏngsan for two years, and manifold were the acts of benevolent government, but since the quality of the silver he offered as tribute was not correct, he was dismissed from office. During Yejong's reign he was repeatedly promoted, until he became drafter in the Secretariat [K. *chungsŏ sain*]. He was appointed envoy to the Khitan Liao, and on his way there in the northern regions he witnessed a great famine, with people eating one another. [Kim Hwangwŏn] [...] asked that the grain from the provincial granaries be distributed, and the king complied with his words. When he was on his way back, the people caught sight of him, calling out, "That's the master who saved our lives!" [...] In the twelfth year [of Yejong's reign] he passed away at the age of seventy-three. By nature he was not restrained or cautious, but rather fond of music and women. [...]

224. Regarding the office, the source here has *chwasa*, which may be understood as being short for *chwa sarangjung*, "bureau director of the left" or "left ministerial director." The courtesy name of Yi Chungyak (d. 1122) was Chajin; his pen name was Ch'ŏnghaja. He applied himself especially to the studies of Daoism, and in 1108 he traveled to Song China, accompanying the envoy Han Kyoyŏ, where he met the Daoist masters Huang Dazhong and Zhou Yuling, from whom he allegedly learned Daoist powers. See Breuker, *Establishing a Pluralist Society*, 284. Through the efforts of the Daoist geomancer Ŭn Wŏnch'ung (see 2:8) he was allowed to build a studio called Ilchae on Mount Wŏlch'ul (K. Wŏlch'ul-san). He was banished in 1122 and died in exile. In his *Ilchae ki* (Account of Ilchae studio), Im Ch'un wrote the following about Yi Chungyak:

> [...] A scholar who has the Dao in the world, someone who is the very embodiment of this Dao — in our our Country East of the Sea there has only been Left Ministerial Director Yi Chungyak and no one else. Chungyak was the teacher's name; Chajin was his courtesy name. Being Heaven on the inside while being human on the outside, that was the teacher's Dao; the golden hall and the jade room were the teacher's houses; the purple mansion and the cinnabar terrace were the teacher's offices. His ancestors came from the royal house of Kyerim, and reaching up to the teacher there had been seven generations of high literati. His late mother was from the Yi Clan, and in a dream she had seen a yellow cap, whereupon she had

336   NOTES TO PAGE 119

become pregnant. For this reason, from the time when the teacher was in his youth he was addicted to reading Daoist texts, and he deeply cared for the genuine ones' elegance. This was because he had been trained in the study of Confucianism and the Mysterious [Daoism] even before his birth. [...] He abandoned his house and went to live in seclusion on Mount Kaya, styling himself Ch'ŏnghaja. (See, for instance, *TMS* 65:6b–7a)

225. The second part of this line may be understood as an allusion to the *Dayan fu* (Fu on magniloquence) by Song Yu, which was composed in a situation similar to the one in this entry. When sitting together with King Xiang of Chu, Tang Le, and Jing Cuo, the king said, "Whoever can prevail in magniloquence for me gets the top seat." When it was Song Yu's turn to create a lyrical pair, he said, "I make square earth my chariot and circular heaven my canopy; / My long sword, shining brightly, hangs beyond the firmament." Song Yu eventually won the lyrical contest, because he invoked a realm beyond the king's control. For a translation and study of this, see Wang, *Age of Courtly Writing*, 19–22.

226. In his vernacular Korean translation of *P'ahan chip*, Pak Sŏnggyu here suggests that this line ought to be understood as a reference to General Deng Yu (2–58), who helped Liu Xiu, the future Guangwu emperor of the Later Han, devise plans and strategies. See Pak, *Yŏkchu P'ahan chip*, 159.

227. Three Mountains refers the three isles of the immortals in the Eastern Sea.

228. "Marquis of ten thousand households" is a translation of *wanhuhao* (K. *manhohu*), which is usually a general term for a powerful noble. Unfortunately it is not entirely clear to me what the line means.

229. This is a quotation from *Lunyu* 11.26. See Slingerland, *Confucius: Analects,* 123.

230. In *Pohan chip* 2:35 we find a description of a much later—yet in essence quite similar—poetry gathering involving Yi Chungyak's descendant Yi Tamji. In *Pohan chip*, however, the poetic excellence and creativity of Yi Tamji is actually called into question:

[...] One evening, as the moon shone radiantly in the autumnal sky, an invigorating atmosphere took hold of the people. There were the subordinate of Councilor-in-Chief Ham Sun, then Yi Tamji, who had passed the civil service examinations but hadn't yet received an office, and also Ok Hwau [n.d.]. They had brought along six or seven youths [their students] and had gathered on the stone bridge in front of Kwibŏp [Temple] for a few drinks. They started composing poems using a previous person's rhymes, and Yi Tamji said, "Summer heat, the wind sweeps it away; / autumn mood, the moon brings it along." Flabbergasted, Ham and Ok both fell onto their knees [in awe]. Someone who heard [this story] smiled and said, "These are Teacher Im Ch'un's poetic lines. I don't know whether Drunken Yi [K. Ch'wi Yi] secretly stole them, or whether this was some sort of weird coincidence. But how come Poisonous Ok [K. Tok Ok] did not know [that these weren't Yi Tamji's original lines] and even fell to his

NOTES TO PAGE 120   **337**

knees [in awe]?" [Explanation:] Yi [Tamji] was not frugal when it came to alcohol, and Ok [Hwau] was so frank that he actually came across as disrespectful toward others. For this reason, they were called "Drunken Yi" and "Poisonous Ok" at the time. (Pak, *Yŏkchu Pohan chip*, 312)

231. Yi Chayŏn (1003–1061) was of the Inju Yi Clan. His courtesy name was Yakch'ung. In his biography his *siho* appears as Changhwa, but here it reads Ch'anghwa. He passed the *mun'gwa* examination as principal graduate in 1024, and served, for example, as vice commissioner in the Security Council (K. *chungch'uwŏn pusa*). Several of his daughters were royal consorts. His first daughter, Queen Dowager Inye (K. Inye T'aehu), was the queen of King Munjong. She gave birth to Sunjong, Sŏnjong, Sukjong, and other princes. His sons also married into prestigious clans, and his sons' daughters married the three mentioned kings. By way of this, the family of Yi Chayŏn was closely connected to the royal house, and became the most prestigious and influential family of its time in Korea. Yi Chayŏn's close relationship with King Munjong (r. 1046–1083) and his political influence at court are described in the tenth entry of the first fascicle of *Yŏgong p'aesŏl* by Yi Chehyŏn, where it says, "King Munjong reigned for thirty-eight years. [...] Yi Chayŏn was of old age and high virtue, and always he was summoned to the Informal Hall of the palace [K. *p'yŏnjŏn*], where [King Munjong] would solicit his opinion concerning political matters. When they were done [talking about politics], they would set out ale, and when night came they would light the lamp and converse in its gleam. A lord and his minister, with bushy brows and hoary heads, facing one another in utter delight — looking at this from a distance, it must have been like in a painting." Yi, *Han'guk myŏngjŏ taejŏnjip*, 376.

232. *Namjo*, "Southern dynasty" or "Southern court," here means the Song dynasty. At this specific point in time in the eleventh century, its northern counterpart from a Koryŏ perspective were the Khitan Liao. There exist, in fact, no official records concerning this diplomatic mission, neither in Korean nor in Chinese sources. Koryŏ-Song diplomatic relations have traditionally been organized into the following chronological phases: an initial phase from the first embassy sent by Kwangjong in 962 to 1030; a second phase, when relations with Song were severed and when under the rising strength and pressure of the Khitan Liao no Korean missions to the Song court could be dispatched for more than forty years; and a third phase from 1071, when the connection was renewed on Song initiative as part of Wang Anshi's reform program, until the fall of the Northern Song in 1126. Concerning the final envoy to Koryŏ before the suspension of relations in 1030, the *Songshi* (History of the Song dynasty; vol. 487) says, "In the eighth year of Tiansheng [Emperor Renzong of Song, r. 1022–1063], Wang Sun [Koryŏ king Hyŏnjong] again sent [...] Wŏn Yŏng and 293 others to offer a petition for an audience at Changchun Hall. They brought vessels of gold, swords of silver, horses with saddles and reins, fragrant oil, ginseng, finest cloth, bronze vessels, [...] and hides as tributary gifts. When in the second month of the following year [1031] [the Koreans] took their leave and returned [to Koryŏ], [the emperor] bestowed upon them various [gifts] and accompanied the envoys to

338 NOTES TO PAGE 120

Dengzhou. Hereafter, relations [with Koryŏ] were severed, and there was no communication with China for forty-three years." Concerning this final mission before the Korean vassalage to the Khitan and the complete severance of official relations with Song, see Rogers, "Some Kings of Koryo as Registered in Chinese Works," 418–419. Except for this 1030 embassy, which was the first one received since 1022 (two years before Yi Chayŏn had obtained an office in 1024), there seems to have been only one further diplomatic mission to Song China during Yi Chayŏn's lifetime, namely, in 1032. In the *Songshi* (vol. 27) it says that Koryŏ sent a tributary mission on the third day of the fourth month, 1032. This means that Yi was either one of the "293 others" mentioned in the previously quoted *Songshi* entry of 1030 or a member of the 1032 mission, or that there may have been a later, perhaps unrecorded effort of Korean affiliation with Song. Since Yi Chayŏn was, in fact, a distant relative of Yi Illo, Yi Illo may have had access to certain sources telling of such an otherwise unrecorded mission that have not been transmitted. For a discussion of Yi Chayŏn's possible mission to the Song court and the *P'ahan chip* entry at hand, see, for instance, Yi, "Taesong woegyo hwaldong;" also see Chŏng, "Yi Chayŏn-ŭi puksong sahaeng ko."

233. Ganlu-si, "Sweet Dew Temple," was located on Mount Beigu (C. Beigu-shan), north of present-day Zhenjiang. There was an iron pagoda of nine stories at Ganlu Temple. Also, as can be seen in *Yŏrha ilgi* (The Jehol diary) by Pak Chiwŏn (1737–1805), there existed a marvelous lion painting at Ganlu Temple, for in the Korean travelogue it says, "A green lion painted on the wall opposite the entrance looked lifelike. It could have been copied from the lion painting in Ganlu si Temple." Translation in Choe-Wall, *Jehol Diary*, 187.

234. The source here says *samno* (C. *sanlao*), which is often a respectful designation for an elderly person or village head. It can also, however, refer to an old river hand, as can be seen in Du Fu's poem *Bomen* (Getting rid of melancholy; for a translation, see Owen, *Poetry of Du Fu*, 4:70). Furthermore, it is an alternate expression for a rudder worker or steersman on a ship (C. *tuogong*; K. *t'agong*). Yi Ch'angsŏp hypothesizes that this person may have been a member of Koryŏ's navy. Yi, "Taesong woegyo hwaldong," 37. It was not entirely unusual for military officials to accompany Korean envoys to China, and at this point it does make sense to understand the term *samno* in this way, because the person in question, who clearly must have been from Koryŏ, is at a later point referred to as a *chusa* (C. *zhoushi*), which usually alludes to a person active in the naval forces. Because of the lack of clarity regarding this man's actual duties, I decided to translate *chusa* as "boatman," but it could also be rendered "navy man."

235. Jiuyi-shan, "Nine Doubts Mountain," in Hunan Province, so called because of the confusing similarity of its peaks. The legendary emperor Shun is said to have been buried here, along the shores of the Xiang River.

236. Jingkou here refers to the aforementioned region of Runzhou.

237. Implying that the boatman received financial compensation for six years for essentially doing nothing but roaming around, and then "accidentally" finding the spot at a place in the immediate vicinity of Kaesŏng, this passage seems to me to have been meant in an amusing, perhaps even ridiculing way. It could be under-

Notes to Page 121 **339**

stood as portraying the boatman as sly, and Yi Chayŏn as a man with lofty ideas and knowledge of distant lands who did not even know the close surroundings of the city he lived in.

238. *Sinjŭng tongguk yŏji sŭngnam* says that Kamno-sa was located below Obong Peak in the vicinity of Kaesŏng. Hereafter, the present entry from *P'ahan chip* is cited in this Chosŏn dynasty geographic survey. See *STYS* 4:26a–b. This implies that Yi Chayŏn's journey to Song China was taken as a historical fact during the fifteenth century, despite the issue that there exist no records of an official diplomatic mission after 1030.

239. This poem by Kim Pusik, entitled *Kamno-sa ch'a Hyewŏn un* (In Kamno Temple replying to Hyewŏn's rhyme), has been transmitted in *Tongmunsŏn*. It reads,

> A place that visitors from the profane world cannot reach; I've ascended to it,
>   and my thoughts have become pure.
> The shape of the mountains, in autumn it is even better; the color of the river,
>   at night it seems even brighter.
> A white bird flies away, lonely; a lone boat darts off, all by itself.
> I feel ashamed, for atop a snail's antenna, I've spent half my life in search of
>   merit and fame. (*TMS* 9:2a–b)

240. The most famous of the poets who wrote companion pieces to these poems on Kamno-sa are mentioned in *Sinjŭng tongguk yŏji sŭngnam*. They include such master poets as Yi Kyubo, Yi Saek, and Kwŏn Kŭn. See *STYS* 4:27a. The poem by Yi Kyubo, entitled *Ch'aun tongnyŏn Mun Wŏnwoe che Kamno-sa* (Replying to the rhyme of Vice Director Mun's poem on Kamno Temple), is also contained in *Tongguk Yi Sangguk chip*. See *TYSC* 3:20a–b.

241. *Sinjŭng tongguk yŏji sŭngnam* says, "Anhwa-sa is located in Chaha Grotto [K. Chaha-dong] on Mount Songak. There is Yŏnŭi Pavilion [K. Yŏnŭi-jŏng] and Chach'wi Gate [K. Chach'wi-mun]." *STYS* 4:23a.

242. Anhwa-sa, or Chŏngguk Anhwa-sa (Temple of Tranquility in the Peaceful Country), as well as the cultured age of the kings Yejong and Injong, are likewise discussed in the thirteenth entry of the third fascicle (*hujip* 1:13) of *Yŏgong p'aesŏl*, where Yi Chehyŏn writes,

> At Chŏngguk Anhwa-sa there is a poem of four rhymes in the Tang-style by King Ye[jong] carved in stone. On the back of it there is an inscription that says, "Written down by Crown Prince so-and-so," [and the name given] is actually King In[jong's] taboo name. At that time, the king and the crown prince applied themselves grindingly to learning, and they would consult with cultured Confucian scholars. Yun Kwan [d. 1111], O Yŏnch'ong [1055–1116], Yi O, Yi Ye [n.d.], Pak Ho [n.d.], Kim Yŏn [see 2:6], Kim Puil, Kim Pusik, Kim Puŭi [see 2:2], Hong Kwan [see 3:19], In Pin [see 3:15], Kwŏn Chŏk [1094–1147; see 3:19], Yun Ŏni [1090–1149; mentioned later in the entry at hand], Yi Chijŏ [see 1:1], Ch'oe Yuch'ŏng [see 1:15],

340   NOTES TO PAGE 121

Chŏng Chisang [see 3:30], Kwak Tongsun [n.d.; see 3:1], Im Wan [n.d.], Hu Zongdan [mentioned again in the entry at hand] — all of these famous ministers and virtuous scholars were constantly present and brought forth at the court, they engaged in critical discussions [among themselves and with the rulers] and lent color [to literary writings], and it all had the elegance of Chinese [models]. In later ages, there hasn't been anything close to it [i.e., the fruitful cooperation between rulers and highly educated civil officials]. (Yi, *Han'guk myŏngjŏ taejŏnjip*, 428)

243. Xianxiao *huangdi* is the posthumous title of Emperor Huizong of the Northern Song, which was given to him in 1143.

244. Cai Jing (1047–1126), courtesy name Yuanchang, an official, grand tutor, and famed calligrapher of the Northern Song, who was one of the leading statesmen of his time. Cai Jing was appointed chief councilor in 1101 and almost continuously administered the central government in the first quarter of the twelfth century. Though traditional accounts depict him as an opportunist with a notorious reputation, in recent scholarship he is viewed increasingly as an innovative politician. In the early 1120s he lost the trust of Emperor Huizong of Song and was arrested and banished to southern China in 1125. He died on the journey to his place of banishment. See the entry on Cai Jing in Dillon, *Encyclopedia of Chinese History.*

245. According the relevant entry in *Koryŏsa* (vol. 14, thirteenth year of Yejong, fourth month, twentieth day), Koryŏ initially sent an envoy to Song, who specifically asked for such a plaque. It says,

In the cyclic year *imsin*, the king returned to the palace and passed down a written document of his royal decision to give different types of objects to the officials in charge of labor supervision as well as to the artisans. [...] Also, to the envoy going to the Song dynasty he decreed to ask [the Song emperor] for a plaque with marvelous calligraphy on it. When Emperor [Huizong] heard this, he wrote on a plaque the name for a Buddhist prayer hall with his own imperial brush. It read, "Hall of the Buddha." He had the Grand Tutor Cai Jing inscribe the following on the door board, "Temple of Tranquility in the Peaceful Country," in order to give it [to the temple as well]. He also gave [Anhwa Monastery] sixteen arhat-statutes.

246. Anhwa Monastery is described in great detail in the seventeenth chapter of Xu Jing's *Illustrated Account of the Xuanhe Embassy to Koryŏ*, where the Chinese envoy portrays it as the most prestigious in the Kaesŏng area. In the brilliant translation by Sem Vermeersch, the relevant passage reads,

[...] Then you enter Chŏngguk Anhwa temple gate and next the temple itself. The temple's name plaque was inscribed by the present grand preceptor, Cai Jing. West of the gate there is a pavilion with the name Naengch'ŏn (cold spring); further north you enter the Chach'wi (purple-emerald) Gate, and the Sinho (spirit protection) Gate. In the eastern wing of this gate there is a statue of the god Indra, while in the western wing is a hall called Hyangjŏk (incense accumulated). In the middle [of the temple compound] has been built the Muryangsu Hall with a pavilion on each side. The one to the east is called Yanghwa (harmony of yang) and the one to the west Chunghwa (respecting China). Behind this building, three gates are lined up next to each other. The eastern gate is called Sinhan (divine brush). Behind it is a hall called Nŭngin (Buddha [literally "the humane one"]) Hall. Both plaques [of the hall and the gate] are embellished with imperial writings bestowed by the current emperor. The middle gate is called Sŏnbŏp (good dharma) and behind it is the Sŏnbŏp Hall. The western gate is called Hyosa (filial thoughts) Gate, and behind its courtyard there is a hall called Mit'a (Amitābha) Hall. Between the Sŏnbŏp and Mit'a Halls there are two rooms, one for worshiping Avalokiteśvara and the other, the Medicine Buddha. The eastern wing [of the Mit'a Hall] has portraits of the patriarchs, and the western wing, portraits of Kṣitigarbha [and the Ten] Kings. The other [buildings] are the living quarters of the monastic community. To the west there is a fasting complex; whenever the king visits this temple, he comes to this complex via the Simbang (finding fragrance) Gate. The front gate is called Ŭngsang (gathering blessings); the north gate is called Hyangbok (expecting blessings). In the middle is the Insu (benevolent long life) Hall and behind it the Cheun (clouds joining) Tower. (Vermeersch, *Chinese Traveler*, 134–135)

247. "Royal Flower Garden" is a translation of *ŏhwawŏn*. In *Xuanhe fengshi Gaoli tujing*, Xu Jing writes,

A spring emerges halfway up the mountain with sweet, pure, and delicious water. A pavilion has been built around it with a plaque bearing the name "Anhwa Spring." Flowers, plants, bamboo, trees, and strange rocks have been planted there to make this a place for relaxation and amusement. The skill of constructing and decorating the garden was not special, but it was done in imitation of Chinese models [of landscaping]; moreover the scenery was clear and beautiful, as if one were in a screen [painting]. The Koryŏ people keep the imperial writings as well as compositions by kings in this place and uphold them with special solemnity. (Vermeersch, *Chinese Traveler*, 135)

248. The valley where Anhwa Monastery was located was also referred to as Chaha-dong, "Grotto of purple auroras." Yŏnha-dong appears to have been an alternative designation.

249. Yun Ŏni was styled Kŭmgang Kŏsa, "Recluse of Kŭmgang." As the son of the influential commander and director of the Chancellery Yun Kwan (d. 1111), he was a politician and scholar who served in such high positions as *chŏngdang munhak*

342 NOTE TO PAGE 122

(assistant executive in letters). Alongside Kim Pusik he helped suppress the rebellion of Myoch'ŏng, yet it is known that Kim and Yun were bitter rivals who very much disliked one another (see Shultz, "Twelfth-Century Koryŏ Politics," 22). Yun Ŏni was later also demoted because of his connection to Chŏng Chisang. *Pohan chip* 1:25 deals with Yun Ŏni as a Buddhist and poet, and this is of interest in the framework of the entry at hand. It reads,

> Master Mun'gang Yun Ŏni, toward the end of his life he became very fond of the taste of meditation, and thus he retired to Kŭmgang Study in Yŏngp'yŏng Prefecture, styling himself "Kŭmgang Kŏsa." Whenever he entered the capital he would do so riding on a yellow ox, and everybody would recognize him straightaway. He had become friends with Sŏn Master Kwansŭng [d. 1149], a disciple of Hyeso, and the two of them treated each other with great affection. At the time, Kwansŭng had gone to Kwangmyŏng Monastery, where he had built a grass-hut hermitage, so small that only a single person could sit in it. [Thereupon the two friends] promised each other, "Whoever of us is about to die first, shall sit in here and pass away in meditation." One day, [Yun Ŏni] rode out on his ox in order to pay Kwansŭng a visit. They ate together, and then [Yun Ŏni] said, "I must return now, for the time [of my death] is not far away. I only came here to tell you that from now on we must part." Said it and left immediately. Kwansŭng dispatched somebody to run after him, sending him to the grass-hut hermitage. When the master saw this he laughed, saying, "The teacher hasn't forgotten our promise. I shall move on now!" He hurriedly picked up his brush and wrote the following Buddhist verse, "Spring, then autumn again; flowers bloom, leaves fall. / East, then west again; well supported a true gentleman. / Today I'll be on my way, looking back at this life. / In the infinite sky of ten thousand miles, a single wisp of an idle cloud." When his writing was finished he sat down in the hermitage and passed away. (Pak, *Yŏkchu Pohan chip*, 115)

250. Hu Zongdan (K. Ho Chongdan; n.d.), a person originally from Song China who is said to have come to Koryŏ aboard a merchant vessel. He was naturalized in Korea, was appointed Hallim academician, and eventually rose to the rank of chief chronicler (K. *kigŏ sain*) under Yejong and Injong. His biography in *Koryŏsa* depicts him rather negatively as a manipulative foreign geomancer, a person who employed Daoist techniques to control and seduce Korean rulers, especially Yejong, possibly particularly with regard to the king's foreign policy in opposition to Khitan Liao. The entry reads,

> Hu Zongdan, likewise, was a person from Fuzhou in Song China. Early on he had entered the National Academy [C. Taixue], where he became a student in the Upper Hall [C. Shanhshe Sheng]. Later he sojourned in the two Zhe [C. *liang zhe*; meaning Zhedong and Zhexi, present-day Shaan

NOTES TO PAGE 122 **343**

xi], and eventually came [to Korea] aboard a merchant vessel. Yejong was very enthusiastic about him, installing him as overseer of the left and right guards [K. *chwauwi roksa*], and successively as Hallim academician. Quite unexpectedly he was thereupon promoted to the office of edict attendant at the Tower of Treasuring Literature [K. Pomun-gak *taeje*]. At the time, the king was quite fond of music, and the courtesans Yŏngnong and Arun were good at singing—hence they were often bestowed with the king's blessings. Ko Hyoch'ung [n.d.], a student at the National Academy, wrote a poem entitled *Kam inyŏ* [Touched by two women], satirizing it [the king's relationship with these *kisaeng*]. Drafter in the Secretariat Chŏng Kŭgyŏng [1067–1127] informed the king about it, and the king was displeased [regarding this specific incident, see also 3:2]. When [Ko] Hyoch'ung was to participate in the civil service examinations, the king ordered that he be expelled, and eventually even had him thrown in prison. [Hu] Zongdan thereupon offered a memorial to the throne to rescue [Ko Hyoch'ung], and they released him. [Hu] Zongdan: by nature he was intelligent, erudite, and capable in writing, neat, and fond of himself. Moreover he was well versed in several arts and crafts, was advanced in the [Daoist] techniques of domination [C. *yansheng*]—the king couldn't help but be deluded [by him]. Later he took care of Injong and became chief chronicler [in 1126]. (*Koryŏsa*, vol. 97, "Yŏlchŏn" 10)

Hu Zongdan is also mentioned in the twenty-eighth entry of *Pohan chip*, where it says,

> [...] Uhwa Gate at Hwangnyong Temple [in Kyŏngju] was built in times of old by the group of the [four] immortals [see 2:12], but this scenic spot has become ruinous and desolate. Among those who pass by [this place] there is no one who does not feel saddened [by the wretched state it is in]. When Academician Hu Zongdan, riding in an emissary's carriage, passed by this gate, he caught sight of a poem that had been left here by Advanced Scholar Ch'oe Hongbin: "Ancient trees, howling in northern winds; rippling waves, swaying in waning sunlight. / Lingering on, I think of bygone matters; unaware that tears moisten my robe." Startled, Hu exclaimed, "Now these are truly otherworldly talents!" Upon his return [to the capital], the king asked him about any memorabilia in the Eastern Capital, and eventually [Hu] brought forth this poem, considering it an exemplary poetic work. (Pak, *Yŏkchu Pohan chip*, 120)

Hu Zongdan is furthermore mentioned in the twentieth entry of the fourth fascicle (*hujip* 2:20) of *Yŏgong p'aesŏl*, where Yi Chehyŏn writes,

> Zhou Zhu [K. Chu Chŏ, n.d.; he came to Korea on a merchant vessel in 1005] and Hu Zongdan were both people of Min [i.e., Fujian Province in eastern China]. During the time of King Hyŏn[jong], many of the writings

344   NOTES TO PAGE 122

that went back and forth between the Northern dynasty [and our dynasty] were created by Zhou Zhu. With regard to [Hu] Zongdan, there were writings that he formally submitted to King In[jong], and while he couldn't match [Zhou] Zhu in terms of learnedness [K. *pakhŭp*; C. *boqia*], […] he was clever, and well versed in a variety of arts. For this reason, even to this day no one has been able to determine who was the better one of the two. (Yi, *Han'guk myŏngjŏ taejŏnjip*, 460)

251. These *oun* (C. *wuyun*), "five-colored clouds," are auspicious clouds.

252. The picturesque beauty of this mountainous area, as well as the natural appeal of Ch'ŏnsu Temple and its main gate, Ch'ŏnsu-mun, which both fell into ruin and eventually vanished at the end of the Koryŏ dynasty, is also described in *Sinjŭng tongguk yŏji sŭngnam* in a passage dealing with Ch'ŏnsu Station (K. Ch'ŏnsu-wŏn), a postal relay station that in the late fifteenth century was located at the spot where Ch'ŏnsu-sa had once stood. The entry reveals that Chosŏn officials were well aware that this place had in the past served as a gathering place for Koryŏ nobility and literati. It reads,

Relay stations [K. *yŏgwŏn*]: […] Ch'ŏnsu-wŏn is located east of the city [of Kaesŏng] at the spot where Ch'ŏnsu-sa once stood. During the reign of the Chenghua emperor of Ming, in the cyclic year *pyŏngsin* [1476], Magistrate [K. Yusu] Yi Ye [1419–1480] had built a pavilion next to the station at the foot of Ch'wijŏk Peak. Thereupon he recorded the following, "Early on I heard that Koryŏ Drafter Ch'oe Sarip [n.d.] wrote the following poem: 'In front of Ch'ŏnsu Temple willow catkins are flying about; with a bottle of ale I am waiting for an old friend to return. / My eyes pierce through the [light of the] setting sun, [gazing down at people] at the far edge of the long road; a few travelers [are coming my way], but as they draw closer, [I see] he's not [among them].' Musing over it now I remember that Ch'ŏnsu-mun during Koryŏ times was a place where visitors were welcomed and guests were bid farewell for some five hundred years. During the Chenghua reign, in the cyclic year *kabo* [1474], when I came here as magistrate, I saw that of this so-called Ch'ŏnsu-mun only ruins remained. In what had become thick undergrowth there were heaps of tiles and gravel. The people of the prefecture, still following matters of ancient times, have turned a piece of land by the western peak into a terrace, and whenever there is a high visitor or guest, he is necessarily brought there to be [properly] welcomed [in accordance with the ancient traditions]. One day, after I had sent off one of my guests at this location, I ascended on high and gazed out into the far distance, and when I asked [a bystander] regarding the name of that spot [high up the mountain], he answered, 'That's Ch'wijŏk Peak.' This is how I came to know the place where at the height of the Koryŏ dynasty the literati had bid one another farewell, where they welcomed each other, and where they had once sojourned." (*STYS* 4:17a)

NOTES TO PAGES 122–123   **345**

253. The biography of the painter Yi Nyŏng (n.d.) in *Koryŏsa* reads,

Yi Nyŏng was a person from Chŏnju. From an early age he was well-known for [his outstanding talent in] painting. During the reign of Injong he followed Military Affairs Commissioner [K. Ch'umilsa] Yi Chadŏk [1071–1138] to Song China. Emperor Huizong [of Song] ordered the academicians awaiting orders Wang Kexun, Chen Dezhi, Tian Zongren, Zhao Shouzong, and others to follow [Yi] Nyŏng around and learn how to paint from him. Furthermore he commanded [Yi] Nyŏng to paint a [motif] from our country, the *Yesŏng-gang to* [Painting of Yesŏng River]. Then, [when Yi Nyŏng was finished and] brought it forth, Huizong sighed in admiration and said, "In recent times, painting masters from Koryŏ have often come here following in the wake of [Korean] emissaries! But only you, Nyŏng, are a skilled hand!" Then he bestowed him with wine and foods, clothes of embroidered brocade, as well as finest silk. In his youth, [Yi] Nyŏng [had studied under] teacher […] Yi Chuni [n.d.], but [Yi] Chuni was jealous of those who came after him, and even if there were able painters [among his students] he scarcely ever commended them. King Injong summoned [Yi] Chuni and showed him a landscape that [Yi] Nyŏng had painted. Amazed, Chuni said, "If this painting was in a different country, I'd readily give a thousand pieces of gold to purchase it." Also, a Song merchant once offered a painting [to the court], and Injong, believing it to be a rare piece of art from China, was pleased with it. He summoned [Yi] Nyŏng, meaning to show off [his new acquisition], but [Yi] Nyŏng said, "This is actually one of my own paintings." Injong refused to believe him, but [Yi] Nyŏng took the painting, peeled a layer off the back, and truly, there was his name. The king cared for him even more after that. Then, during the reign of Ŭijong, all the painting matters in the inner palace were taken over by him. (*Koryŏsa*, vol. 122, "Yŏlchŏn" 35)

Yi Nyŏng's son, Yi Kwangp'il [n.d.], was also a famous painter.

254. The source here says Hwaguk, "Department of Painting," which I have understood as an alternate designation for the Tohwa-wŏn, the Koryŏ office responsible for the production of paintings and artifacts.

255. As can be seen in note 253, in Yi Nyŏng's biography in *Koryŏsa* it is not King Yejong but his son and successor Injong who requested the painting from the Song merchant.

256. King Sinjong, the twentieth king of Koryŏ, was born in 1144 as the fifth son of King Injong and younger brother to kings Ŭijong and Myŏngjong. The seventh year of his reign corresponds to 1203.

257. Yi Illo had three sons. Adae refers to his eldest son, Chŏng.

258. Chindong refers to present-day Chinsan in Kŭmsan County, Southern Ch'ungch'ŏng Province.

259. This line features the character of the name of Yi Illo's first son, *chŏng* (C. *cheng*), "journey."

346 NOTES TO PAGE 124

260. Ko Chumong (also known as King Tongmyŏng), the mythical founder of the ancient state of Koguryŏ, is said to have resided at Kuje-gung, "Nine Stepladder Palace," his legendary residence. Yŏngmyŏng-sa, "Eternal Light Temple," was allegedly built at the site of this Kuje-gung, west of Mount Kŭmsu and above Kirin Cave, overlooking the Taedong River in the direct vicinity of the city of P'yŏngyang. The temple became famous for lodging Ado, the monk who transmitted Buddhism to Koguryŏ. During the Koryŏ dynasty, monarchs would frequently visit it whenever they came to the Western Capital. See Breuker, *Establishing a Pluralist Society*, 73–74.

261. Sŏgyŏng, the "Western Capital," is the city of P'yŏngyang.

262. A picture postcard of Yŏngmyŏng Temple (https://museum.seoul.go.kr/archive/archiveNew/NR_archiveView.do?ctgryId=CTGRY874&type=D&upperNodeId=CTGRY874&fileSn=300&fileId=H-TRNS-80607-874), produced in 1921, shows Yŏngmyŏng-sa and Pubyŏk Pavilion (the temple at the bottom, and the pavilion on the top of the hill at the picture's left upper margin). It is this exact scenery that is described in this passage.

263. Magnificent, long-lasting poetry as well as the zither were traditionally both said to have the tones of "metal and stone." See Owen, *Readings in Chinese Literary Thought*, 367.

264. Yi O passed away in 1110, which means that he served under King Yejong for the last five years of his life. According to *Koryŏsa* (vol. 12, eleventh and twelfth months of 1107), during this time Yejong went to the Western Capital only a single time, namely, in the eleventh month of the second year of his reign, 1107. In the relevant entry it says, "On the day *kyŏngo*, the king went on a royal tour to the Western Capital. At the time, a court astrologer [K. *ilgwan*] said, 'When Your Majesty goes to the Western Capital, it would be appropriate to dispatch a military general.' Hence there was this practice." Over the course of the journey, Yejong and his ministers held banquets, for instance, on Chabi Ridge (K. Chabi-ryŏng) in Hwanghae Province on the twenty-second day of the eleventh month. The party arrived in P'yŏngyang on the twenty-fourth day of the eleventh month, and successively there were also a number of feasts in the Western Capital: at Changnak Hall (K. Changnak-chŏn; third day of the twelfth month), or in a dragon boat (K. *yongsŏn*) on the Taedong River (fifth day of the twelfth month). The feast at Pubyŏng-nyo is not recorded in *Koryŏsa*, but it is likely to have taken place around this time. As is stated in the *P'ahan chip* entry at hand, at this stage of his life Yi O served as vice director of the Royal Secretariat and Chancellery, and it is not exactly clear how he was simultaneously affiliated with the Hallim-wŏn.

265. Pubyŏng-nyo is usually known as Pubyŏk-chŏng or Pubyŏng-nu (Pubyŏk Tower). *Sinjŭng tongguk yŏji sŭngnam* states that Pubyŏk Tower is located beneath Ŭlmil Rock (K. Ŭlmil-tae) and east of Yŏngmyŏng Temple. Pubyŏk Pavilion, which was built in 393, is mentioned in an abundance of premodern Korean sources, for example, the *Pubyŏng-nu ch'aun* (Matching rhymes on Pubyŏk Tower) by Kwŏn Han'gong (d. 1349; in *TMS* 7:17a) or *Pubyŏng-nu* (Pubyŏk Tower) by Yi Saek, which reads as follows:

Yesterday I passed by Yŏngmyŏng Temple, and for a while ascended to
   Pubyŏk Tower.
The city was empty, the moon a slice; stones were ancient and the clouds
   have seen a thousand autumns.
The wondrous horse has gone and will not return, where might the Descen-
   dant of Heaven [King Tongmyŏng] sojourn?
Whistling long notes while leaning on a windswept flight of stone stairs,
   mountains are green and the river flows along by itself.
   (*Mogŭn'go* 2:14b)

266. The source here says *sŏp'an*, "writing tablets" or "writing boards," but I
have understood this term as referring to *sip'an* (C. *shiban*), "poetry boards," which
were often hung up in monasteries, postal relay stations, or pavilions such as
Pubyŏk-chŏng for the public posting of lyrical works. Several times in *P'ahan chip*
it is said that people, on a whim, would simply write poems on doors or walls, and
it can be assumed that these *sip'an* were hung up in public places so that traveling
poets could write on them and the walls would not have to be whitewashed over
and over again. See Denecke, Li, and Tian, *Oxford Handbook of Classical Chinese Lit-
erature*, 53, 67. After a while, when the poetry boards were filled with poems written
by scores of visitors and travelers, they must in all likelihood have been collected
and either stored or destroyed. It may be that this is the procedure described at this
point. However, in an entry in *Tongin sihwa* dealing with Kim Hwangwŏn and this
very incident (see the following note), Sŏ Kŏjŏng states that the poems of old and
new that Kim Hwangwŏn found at the top of Pubyŏk Tower simply "did not fill his
mind" (K. *pulman ki ŭi*), i.e., that they were not to his liking or did not satisfy him.
Thus, he may have simply burned the poetry boards out of spite or some feeling of
perceived superiority. In addition, by burning the writing boards of old and new at
Pubyŏk Pavilion, Kim Hwangwŏn probably also had the poem by Yi Illo's ancestor
Yi O destroyed, and this could be the reason why Kim is portrayed in such an unfa-
vorable way in the entry at hand.

267. This couplet by Kim Hwangwŏn is discussed in the chapter "Kwannae
chŏngsa" (Keeping track of the route within the pass) from *Yŏrha ilgi* by Pak Chiwŏn.
Here it reads:

Outside the city wall at Yongping, a large river flows in curves and em-
braces the city. The geographical situation is similar to that of P'yŏngyang,
but much more majestic and expansive, only that Yongping does not have
the Clear River Taedong. An old story tells of how *haksa* Kim Hwangwŏn
ascended Pubyŏk Tower, where he thought up the couplet "like one long
wall the gently flowing water; at the eastern rim of the great plain dots of
mountains," but after he had laboriously sung these lines, his imagination
dried up and he left the place in tears. Those who tell the story want to say
that the beauty of the P'yŏngyang landscape is fully expressed by these

348   NOTES TO PAGE 125

two lines, and for a thousand years nobody was able to add a verse. But I never thought of these as successful verse. "Gently flowing" [billowing, billowing] is not the characteristic of a big river, and the mountains that "dot the eastern rim" are no more than forty *li* away; could one call this a "great plain"? Now these verses are written on the pillars of Yŏn'gwang Pavilion; when the imperial ambassadors ascend this pavilion, they will certainly laugh at the words "great plain."

The translation of the fourth, fifth, and sixth chapters of *Yŏrha ilgi* by Marion Eggert of Ruhr University Bochum is forthcoming in the Korean Classics Library series. Kim Hwangwŏn's haughtiness and his laboriously chanted, yet in reality apparently somewhat mediocre poem, are also discussed in the sixth entry of the upper fascicle of *Tongin sihwa*, where Sŏ Kŏjŏng states,

> When Academician Kim Hwangwŏn ascended Pubyŏk Tower, he caught a glimpse of the inscribed poems of old and new, and they weren't to his satisfaction. So he immediately had all of the poetry boards burned. All day long he then leaned against the railing and painstakingly managed to chant the following: "On one side of the long wall — billowing, billowing waters; on the eastern rim of the great plain — dots and dots of mountains." Then his imagination dried up, and wailing bitterly he went away. In the past, Jia Langxian [Jia Dao] obtained a single verse upon chanting for three years. It went as follows: "Going alone, my shadow at the bottom of the lake; / often resting my body by the edge of the trees." And then his tears ran down unawares. Now, when I look at this, I must say that Langxian's poem is poor and meager, rough and ordinary — so, how could it have come so far that he shed tears over it? And [Kim] Hwangwŏn's verse is [in terms of style and content] something that the old Confucians always chat on and on about — so how come he wailed bitterly and suffered for himself the way he did? (Yi, *Tongin sihwa*, 31)

In the twenty-third entry of the upper fascicle of *Tongin sihwa*, Sŏ Kŏjŏng goes on to say, "The 'Pubyŏk Tower Poem' [K. *Pubyŏk-nu si*] by Principal Graduate Kim Hwangwŏn reads, 'On one side of the long wall — billowing, billowing waters; on the eastern rim of the great plain — dots and dots of mountains.' Later there was Ilchae Kwŏn Han'gong [d. 1349], who continued it, writing, 'On the waves a white gull — gusts and gusts of rain; / on the south of the slopes a yellow calf — dots and dots of mountains.' [...]" Yi, *Tongin sihwa*, 62.

268. This magnificent piece is not cited, and Yi Illo's remark may well have been meant ironically.

269. Song Yu is credited with the "Jiubian" (Nine arguments) in the *Chuci*. He was an official at the court of King Qingxiang of Chu until he was banished. In the *Nine Arguments*, Song Yu regrets his dismissal from court and vents his fury at those who had slandered his good name. The opening sections of the *Nine Arguments* use

NOTES TO PAGE 125 **349**

autumn as a figure for his career in decline and for the approaching end of his life. Murck, *Poetry and Painting in Song China*, 13.

270. This refers to the first lines of "Jiubian," where it says, "Alas for the breath of autumn! Wan and drear: flower and leaf fluttering fall and turn to decay." Hawkes, *Songs of the South*, 209.

271. In the North Korean publication *Chosŏn-ŭi irŭmnan chakka-wa irhwa*, in which the episode at hand is retold in a narrative fashion, we can find an interesting interpretation of Kim Hwangwŏn's failure to come up with a corresponding couplet to his first two lines. It says,

> When he wasn't able to finish the poem, he finally threw away his brush and sobbed bitterly. "Ah, I'm not talented enough to sing a poem on this superb scenery!" Kim Hwangwŏn sighed, wailed deep into the night, and then went on his way. Later, the people of P'yŏngyang hung his couplet on one of the pillars of Pubyŏk Pavilion, it was passed on, and eventually [the poetry board] was moved and hung up on a pillar of Ryŏn'gwang Tower. This not only happened because the unfinished couplet was so very well written, but also because [the people of P'yŏngyang] wished to proudly show that even a famous poet [such as Kim Hwangwŏn] lacked the words to describe the marvelous beauty of P'yŏngyang. (Ri and Ch'oe, *Chosŏn-ŭi irŭmnan chakka-wa irhwa*, 95)

Hence, from an early-twenty-first-century North Korean standpoint, the original *P'ahan chip* entry is twisted around, and the reader is left with the impression that it was the magnificence of (the current North Korean capital) P'yŏngyang that so overwhelmed Kim Hwangwŏn that he was unable to finish his verse. The original entry, however, does not lead to this conclusion. The importance of tackling the source when dealing with premodern Korean literature can be viewed herein.

272. Munch'ang (Literary Noble) Ch'oe Ch'iwŏn, perhaps the most prominent intellectual and scholar-poet of the Later Silla period (668–935), won literary fame not only in his native country of Silla but also in Tang China. The biography of Ch'oe Ch'iwŏn from *Samguk sagi* reads:

> Ch'oe Ch'iwŏn, whose polite name was Koun, was from the Saryang district of the capital of Silla. Since historical records have been destroyed, we know nothing of his genealogy. From his youth onward he was precocious, capable and loved learning. When, at the age of twelve, he went to board a ship to study in Tang China, his father said to him, "If you cannot pass the examination in ten years, you're not a worthy son of mine. Go and study hard!" Once in China he studied diligently under a teacher. In the first year, *kabo*, [...] the examiner [...] passed Ch'oe on his first attempt, and Ch'oe was appointed chief of personnel. [...] At that time, the Huang Chao Rebellion broke out, and Gao Pian was appointed circuit field commander. Gao appointed Ch'oe as his secretary, and the memorials, letters,

350   NOTES TO PAGE 125

and manifestos that Ch'oe wrote at the time are still extant. (Lee and de Bary, *Sources of Korean Tradition*, 71)

He retired to Haein Temple on Mount Kaya at the end of his life, and it is not clear whether he still served under the new dynasty, Koryŏ. However, as an intellectual and poet Ch'oe Ch'iwŏn was undoubtedly held in high esteem during early Koryŏ. For instance, in the eleventh century he was posthumously promoted to office: in 1020, during the reign of King Hyŏnjong (r. 1009–1031), the high title of *naesaryŏng* was conferred upon him while memorial services were held in his honor at the Confucian shrine in Kaesŏng (*Koryŏsa*, vol. 4, eighth month of the eleventh year of Hyŏnjong). Three years later, in the fourteenth year of Hyŏnjong, he conferred upon him the title *munch'ang-hu*, "Duke Literary Noble," on account of his exalted literary reputation in Tang China (*Koryŏsa*, vol. 5, second month of the fourteenth year of Hyŏnjong). Ch'oe Ch'iwŏn is in the entry at hand called Munch'ang-gong, "Master Literary Noble."

273. *Bingong ke*, "guest and tributary examinations," were the civil service examinations designed for foreigners in Tang dynasty China. Silla began to send students to Tang China in 640. In 821 the first candidate from Silla, a certain Kim Un'gyŏng, passed these examinations; by 837, the number of Silla students in China amounted to as many as 216. By the Late Tang, fifty-eight candidates had passed the *Bingong ke*, and a further thirty-two succeeded during the Later Liang and Later Tang dynasties. Most of them came from the "head-rank six" class, like Ch'oe Ch'iwŏn. See Denecke, Li, and Tian, *Oxford Handbook of Classical Chinese Literature*, 536–537. Ch'oe Ch'iwŏn went to Tang in 868 and passed the "guest and tributary examinations" supervised by the executive at the Ministry of Rites (C. *libu shilang*, K. *yebu sirang*) Pei Zan (n.d.) in 874. Thereupon he was appointed to different offices by the emperor, such as defender of Lishui County (C. Lishui-xian *wei*). In the second entry of the upper fascicle of *Tongin sihwa*, Sŏ Kŏjŏng writes with regard to Ch'oe Ch'iwŏn,

Duke Literary Noble Ch'oe Ch'iwŏn entered Tang and successfully passed the civil service examinations. On account of his literary writings he brought forth his name [at the Chinese court]. He wrote the *Yun-ju Chahwa-sa si* [Poem composed at Cihe Temple in Runzhou], where it says, "To the sound of the painted horn [K. *hwagak*; a bamboo instrument used to rouse sleepers at dawn], waves of morning and night; in the shadow of the green mountains, men of old and new." Later, when there was a traveling merchant of Kyerim who had entered Tang to purchase a poem, there was someone who wrote down this very verse and showed it to him. (Yi, *Tongin sihwa*, 25)

274. Gao Pian (821–887), a famed Late Tang dynasty military general. When an affluent commoner named Huang Chao (d. 884) started a rebellion in 875, Gao Pian was made commanding general and began a long campaign to subdue this rebel-

NOTES TO PAGE 125   **351**

lion. Huang Chao's revolt was eventually subdued, but it significantly destabilized the central government.

275. This information on Ch'oe Ch'iwŏn's role in the military campaigns of Gao Pian is missing in the 2016 North Korean translation of *P'ahan chip*, both in the supplied original text as well as in the vernacular Korean rendition. Ri, *Ri Illo, Rim Ch'un chakp'um chip*, 86–87.

276. Ch'oe Ch'iwŏn returned to Silla in 885.

277. The Tang poet Gu Yun, courtesy names Chuixiang and Shilong, was born in 851 in Chizhou. Like Ch'oe, he had passed the civil service examinations in 874. Together with Ch'oe Ch'iwŏn he was employed at the military camp of Gao Pian, and the two of them are known to have been friends. He died in 894. See Yi, "Ko Un-i Ch'oe Ch'iwŏn-ege," 334.

278. In the relevant entry in the biography of Ch'oe Ch'iwŏn in Kim Pusik's *Samguk sagi* (vol. 46), the poem Gu Yun wrote for Ch'oe Ch'iwŏn is different. The entry reads,

> Also, he was good friends with Gu Yun, who had passed the civil service examinations in the same year [K. *tongnyŏn;* not referring to the year they were born]. When he was about to go back [to Silla], Gu Yun bid him farewell with a poem, a summary of which reads, "As I heard there are three golden turtles in the [eastern] sea [in China the golden turtle was a synonym for Korea] / the golden turtles carry mountains on their heads which rise up high. / On the mountains, palaces of pearl, seashell towers, and halls of yellow gold. / Below the mountains, great waves for thousands, ten thousands of miles. / To their sides a single dot of Kyerim in deepest blue; turtle mountain, pregnant with gracefulness, gave birth to a strange and unique [person]. / At the age of twelve he took a ship and sailed across the ocean to come here; his literary writings moved the entire country of China. / At the age of eighteen he went out to the place where they fight with words; a single arrow was shot, breaking the Golden Gate's [examination] standards."

In *Tongguk Yi Sangguk chip* we find the entry *Tangsŏ purip Ch'oe Ch'iwŏn yŏlchŏn ŭi* ("Discussion on the topic of the *Book of Tang* not containing an exemplary biography of Ch'oe Ch'iwŏn"), where it says, "Gu Yun, who had passed the civil service examinations in the same year, gave him the *Yusŏn ka* [Song for a Confucian immortal; C. *Ruxian ge*] as a present. A summary of it says, 'At the age of twelve he took a ship and sailed across the ocean to come here; his literary writings moved the entire country of China.'" *TYSC* 22:7b (the same entry is contained in *Tongmunsŏn; TMS* 106:20b). The two poems by Gu Yun cannot be found in relevant Chinese sources such as the *Quan Tangshi* (Complete Tang poems, 1705) but only in the Korean sources. In fact, Ch'oe went to Tang and back to Korea on two occasions. In *Samguk sagi* it says, "Hereafter [i.e., after having returned to Silla] Ch'iwŏn yet again received commission to go to Tang as an envoy, only we do not know at which point in time this took

352 NOTES TO PAGE 125

place." Hence, some scholars have hypothesized that the *Koun p'yŏn* was written by Gu Yun on the occasion of the two friends' second and final parting (the final line of the poem reads, *u tonghwan*, "again you go back to the [country in the] east). Yi Illo, however, presents the poem — which clearly differs from the *Yusŏn ka* — at this point in the entry as if Gu Yun had written it on the first occasion. It is not exactly clear when Ch'oe went back to Tang, but there is a theory that he returned to China after Gu Yun's death in 894, which could imply that the *Koun p'yŏn* was not written by Gu Yun at all. These questions are debated in Yi, "Ko Un-i Ch'oe Ch'iwŏn-ege."

279. This refers to the twelve peaks of Mount Wu and thus implies that he was twelve years old when he left for Tang China.

280. The term *ŭnha yŏlsu* means the twenty-eight mansions in the Chinese constellation system. Ch'oe Ch'iwŏn was twenty-eight years old when he returned to Silla (apparently after his first stay).

281. *Yong hŭng,* the "dragon arises," here alludes to T'aejo Wang Kŏn having ascended the throne of Koryŏ.

282. Wang Kŏn ousted Kungye, the founder of Hu-Koguryŏ (Later Koguryŏ, also known as Koryŏ), and rose to power in 918, approximately twenty years after the Later Silla scholar and statesman Ch'oe Ch'iwŏn had retired from office. Ch'oe Ch'iwŏn's biography in *Samguk sagi* nevertheless has an entry on a purported connection between the scholar-poet and the founder of the new dynasty. It reads, "At first, when T'aejo of our dynasty rose to power, [Ch'oe] Ch'iwŏn knew that [T'aejo] was no ordinary person and that he would necessarily receive the mandate and establish the country. Therefore [Ch'oe] Ch'iwŏn wrote a letter, asking [for acceptance by T'aejo], and there was the line, 'In Kyerim are yellow leaves, in Kongnyŏng [Kaesŏng, i.e., Koryŏ] are green pines.'" While Koryŏ is here portrayed as a healthy green tree, the term *hwangyŏp,* "yellow leaves," alludes to the Later Silla dynasty withering away in the early tenth century (Silla surrendered to Koryŏ in 935). There exists, however, the theory that another person, pretending to be Ch'oe Ch'iwŏn, "defected" to Koryŏ and asked for acceptance by T'aejo.

283. Here it says that Ch'oe "sited a dwelling to live in reclusion" (K. *pogŭn*), which appears differently in other sources. For instance, in his biography in *Samguk sagi* it says, "At the end he took his family and lived in reclusion at Haein-sa on Mount Kaya, where he formed a friendship of the same Way [K. *tou;* alluding to a close relationship based on shared intellectual and religious convictions] with his older brother, the Buddhist monk Hyŏnjun, as well as the Buddhist Master Chŏnghyŏn." Family relations thus apparently played a decisive role in his decision to settle down at this particular temple on Mount Kaya. The abovementioned poetic line, which Ch'oe is said to have addressed to Wang Kŏn, "In Kyerim are yellow leaves, in Kongnyŏng are green pines" (K. *Kyerim hwangyŏp Kongnyŏng ch'ŏngsong*), is also mentioned in *Pohan chip* 1:4, even alongside an inter-lineary commentary in which Ch'oe Ch'iwŏn's escape to Mount Kaya is mentioned as well. It reads,

When our T'aejo rose to power, Ch'oe Ch'iwŏn of Silla knew that [T'aejo] would necessarily receive the mandate. He presented a letter in which

NOTES TO PAGE 125 **353**

there were the words, "In Kyerim are yellow leaves, in Kongnyŏng are green pines." When the king of Silla heard about this he despised him, and so [Ch'oe Ch'iwŏn] took along his family to live in hiding at Haein Temple on Mount Kaya, to stay there until the very end. The brightness of [Ch'oe Ch'iwŏn's] reflection and understanding [of the state of things] could be seen in the letter, and the people of Silla deeply admired him. Thus they called the place where Master [Ch'oe Ch'iwŏn] had once resided Sangsŏ-jang, "Hamlet Where the Letter Was Written" [a building that today ranks forty-sixth on the list of prestigious heritage sites of Northern Kyŏngsang Province, South Korea]. Later, eminent scholars such as Yi Nŭngbong, O Sejae, An Sunji, and others resided there in succession. (Pak, *Yŏkchu Pohan chip*, 49)

284. Regarding this Toksŏ-dang, Ch'oe Ch'iwŏn's "Hall of Study" or "Hall of Reading Books," the *Sinjŭng tongguk yŏji sŭngnam* says, "Tansok Temple [Tansok-sa] lies east of Mount Chiri. At the entrance to the valley is a rock onto which Ch'oe Ch'iwŏn carved the four characters *kwangje ammun* [Kwangje Stone Gate]. Also there is [Ch'oe] Ch'iwŏn's Reading Hall. Later it became the monk Taegam's hall of images [K. *yŏngdang;* a hall containing images or paintings of eminent or illustrious monks of the temple]." *STYS* 30:15a. In the section on Hapch'ŏn County (K. Hapch'ŏn-gun) it says, "In the world it is transmitted that when Ch'oe Ch'iwŏn hid on Mount Kaya, one morning he rose early, walked out the door, left his cap and shoes in the forest, and no one knows where he returned to. [...] The place where the hall once stood [K. *yuji*] is west of the temple [Haein-sa]." *STYS* 30:35a.

285. The source here says Munŭng-nu, "Munŭng [C. Wuling] Tower." In the "Remains of Old" (K. *kojŏk*) section of the entry on Hapch'ŏn County in *Sinjŭng tongguk yŏji sŭngnam* we find the following information: "Chesi-sŏk [Inscribed poem rock]: The valley of Haein-sa is commonly called Hongnyu-dong [Grotto of Red Currents]. At the entrance of the valley is Munŭng-gyo [Munŭng Bridge]. When you cross the bridge and walk toward the temple for five or six leagues, there will be a rock upon which Ch'oe Ch'iwŏn inscribed a poem. [...] People of later times referred to this rock as Ch'iwŏn-dae, 'Ch'iwŏn's Terrace.'" *STYS* 30:35a.

286. In an article entitled "Note on Ch'oe Ch'i-wun" contained in the June 1903 issue of the *Korea Review* (no. 6, 245), edited by Homer B. Hulbert, it says with regard to this couplet, "Near a bridge in that vicinity, called Mu-reung Bridge, there is a high cliff on which is inscribed one of his sayings, [the lines at hand], which seems to mean that the water falling over the precipice without any conscious effort makes the whole valley resound with its roar so that even though people stand beside each other not a word can be heard. This is interpreted to mean that the commotion and senseless turmoil of Silla politics makes it impossible to hear the voice of reason." In his *History of Korean Literature,* Peter H. Lee writes, "Are tranquility and solitude worth the suffering they entail? Ch'oe seems to think so in 'Inscribed at the Study on Mount Kaya,' which delights in a mountain torrent as it rushes down jumbled rocks and drowns out the cacophony of the world below. The speaker scorns distinctions,

354   NOTES TO PAGE 126

all petty disputes, for he is no longer affected by life and death, benefit and harm. Thus by nondiscrimination he has withstood the onslaught of time. He has not asked great questions but offers a Daoist solution to his problems." Lee, *History of Korean Literature*, 97.

287. This poem is also contained in *Tongmunsŏn* under the title "Che Kayasan Toksŏ-dang" (Written on the reading hall on Mount Kaya). See *TMS* 19:14a. An abundance of premodern Korean lyrical works feature allusions to Ch'oe Ch'iwŏn, Hongnyu-dong, and his "poem inscribed on the rock," such as *Suk Yŏnho-sa sa chae ruhu* (Lodged at Yŏnho Temple; the temple is located behind the tower; contained in the fourth volume of *Pŏnam chip*, the *munjip* of the eighteenth-century scholar Ch'ae Chegong [1720–1799]), where the last lines read, "From here it isn't far to Munŭng [C. Wuling] Bridge / covering the river, [peach] blossoms have fallen—one could take a fishing boat." *Pŏnam chip* 4:1b. Hongnyu-dong is here likened to the utopian "Peach Blossom Spring," which in the Chinese legend is discovered by a fisherman from Wuling. In *Sŏngho sasŏl*, for example, it says, "Koun abandoned office and sojourned beyond the realm; to this day his immortal traces have remained on [Mount] Kaya." *Sŏngho sasŏl* 7:16b.

288. The previous entry discussed the life and poetry of Silla intellectual Ch'oe Ch'iwŏn, and the present entry yet again deals with a person from this earlier dynasty. Kim Yusin was a noble, scholar, general, and statesman of Silla who rose to fame in the unification wars and Silla's conquest of Paekche and Koguryŏ in the middle of the seventh century. His biography in *Samguk sagi* comprises three full chapters (vols. 41, 42, and 43). There exist many stories and legends about his bravery and noble character. He is known to have been an illustrious *hwarang*-leader with many followers, and the name of his band of flower boys was "Dragon Flower Aspirants." For a discussion of Kim Yusin's biography, see, for example, McBride, "Structure and Sources." The term *kuksa*, "Histories of the [Three] States," here most likely refers to the biographical entries contained in *Samguk sagi*.

289. His mother, Manmyŏng, played an influential role in Kim Yusin's life. Against the backdrop of the entry at hand it is interesting to note that she herself had an illicit sexual relationship with Kim Yusin's father, Kim Sŏhyŏn, with whom she eloped. In the first volume of Kim's biography in *Samguk sagi* (vol. 41), it says about the relationship of his parents,

> At the beginning, as [Kim] Sŏhyŏn was walking upon the road, he caught a glimpse of Manmyŏng, the daughter of [Kim] Sukhŭlchong, the son of Ipchong *kalmunwang*. In his heart, [Kim Sŏhyŏn] was overjoyed, and glanced at her longingly. Without even waiting for a matchmaker the two of them simply united. When Sŏhyŏn then became governor of Manno County, he wanted to go together with Manmyŏng. Sukhŭlchong knew that his daughter had illicitly united with Sŏhyŏn, and he simply hated it. Thus he put [his daughter] in an annex and ordered some people to guard it. Suddenly, however, thunder struck the door of the house, which shocked the guards and threw them in a state of utter confusion, where-

NOTES TO PAGES 126–127   **355**

upon Manmyŏng was able to climb through the hole in the door and get away. Eventually, together with Sŏhyŏn she hurried to Manno. Sŏhyŏn, in the *gengchen* night, dreamed that the two stars Yinghuo and Zhen fell down toward him from the sky. Manmyŏng, too, in the *xinchou* night, in a dream caught a glimpse of a child dressed in golden armor who entered her hall riding on a cloud. She then got pregnant, and after twenty months gave birth to [Kim] Yusin.

290. This sentence could also be translated as, "In the Eastern Capital lies Ch'ŏn'gwa-sa, which once was this [singing] girl's house." According to *Sinjŭng tongguk yŏji sŭngnam*, Ch'ŏn'gwan-sa was located east of the Orŭng, the five royal tombs of Silla in Kyŏngju. In South Korean scholarship on the subject, it has been determined that Ch'ŏn'gwan-sa was only five hundred meters away from the residence of Kim Yusin. Moreover, there exists the theory that, since Ch'ŏn'gwan-sa was a temple, the woman may not have been an ordinary singing girl, but rather a person who had been raised in a religious realm and therefore constituted a sort of priestess. This, in turn, may have been at the root of Kim's mother's rejection of her son's relationship with this woman. See Yi, "Kim Yusin kwallyŏn yŏsŏngdŭl-ŭi munhakchŏk hyŏngsang-gwa hudaejŏk pyŏnhwa," 337–341.

291. Yi Kongsŭng (1099–1183). His courtesy name was Talbu; his *siho* (poetic name) was Munjŏng. He passed the civil service examinations during Injong's reign and traveled to the Jurchen Jin dynasty as an envoy in 1148. During the political upheavals of the 1170s, he was saved from harm by the influence of his examination passer Mun Kŭkkyŏm, whom Yi Illo also knew well.

292. The source says Tongdo *Kwan'gi*, but what is most likely meant is the office of Tonggyŏng *changsŏgi*, "Eastern Capital [Kyŏngju] regional commissioner" or "Eastern Capital secretary."

293. The source has *sŏm t'o*, "toad and rabbit," which are symbols for the moon. I have interpreted the first part of this line as one line from the lost *Song of Resentment* composed by the woman Ch'ŏn'gwan on the relationship with Kim Yusin.

294. This poem by Yi Kongsŭng is contained in *Tongmunsŏn* under the title *Ch'ŏn'gwan-sa*. TMS 12:14a–b. The poem as well as the story of Kim Yusin and the — as it is put in the Chosŏn dynasty source — "prostitute" [K. *ch'angnyŏ*] also features in *STYS* 21:29b.

295. Ch'ŏn'gwan, the woman of lower social status who, as the present entry strongly suggests, had a love affair with the glorious Kim Yusin, is not mentioned in Kim's exemplary biography in *Samguk sagi*. The term *ch'ŏn'gwan*, however, does appear there, for in the first part of the biography (vol. 41) we can find the story of Kim receiving spiritual help from a "celestial official," who "let down his glory and descended in spirit into [Kim Yusin's] precious sword. [...] The sword appeared to be moving and shaking." Translation in McBride, "Structure and Sources," 516. Yet one has to bear in mind the following statement by Kim Pusik regarding the process of composition of his biography in *Samguk sagi* (vol. 43): "[Kim] Yusin's great-grandson, Gentleman of the Chancellery (*chipsarang*) of Silla, Changch'ŏng, wrote Yusin's

356   NOTES TO PAGE 127

Account of Conduct (*haengnok*), in ten rolls, while he traversed the mundane world. So many were the fomented words that it had to be cut and reduced. I chose those things that were worth writing and made them his biography," McBride, "Structure and Sources," 511. Kim Changch'ŏng lived in the eighth century, and his *Kim Yusin haengnok*, which unfortunately has not been transmitted, clearly served as a major source for Kim Pusik's *Kim Yusin chŏn* (Biography of Kim Yusin). It is very possible that Yi Illo, when writing the entry at hand for *P'ahan chip*, had access to the original source, the *haengnok* by Kim Changch'ŏng—a source that may have featured this very story about Kim Yusin and the woman Ch'ŏn'gwan. For Kim Pusik, on the other hand, the anecdote about the Silla hero and a prostitute was obviously not "worth writing down" in his royally commissioned work *Samguk sagi.*

296. The source says Myŏng *hwang* (C. Ming *huang*). It is here not a reference to Emperor Xuanzong of Tang, who is commonly known as "Tang Ming *huang*," but can rather be understood as referring to King Myŏngjong.

297. The text says *taesuk* (C. *dashu*), which means the eldest of one's father's younger brothers. I have understood this term as relating to Yi Illo himself, i.e., "my paternal uncle Yoil." In the 2016 North Korean translation of *P'ahan chip*, however, the translator Ri Sŏng writes *Myŏngjong taewang-ttae kŭ-ŭi samch'on in chung Ryoil*, meaning "The monk Yoil, King Myŏngjong's uncle." See Ri, *Ri Illo, Rim Ch'un chak-p'um chip*, 88.

298. In Koryŏ times, the official position of *sŭngt'ong*, "sangha overseer" or "monk superintendent," was similar to that of a medieval Christian bishop. See Sørensen, "Investigation of Two Buddhist Tomb-Inscriptions," 82. It was an administrative office in the temple system, first established in China during the Northern Wei, designating the person in charge of the affairs of all monks and nuns in the country. Muller, *Digital Dictionary of Buddhism*. As Sem Vermeersch points out, Yoil was the abbot of Hŭngwang Temple, and Yi Illo was a frequent guest there during his early years. See Vermeersch, "Buddhist Temples or Political Battlegrounds?," 209.

299. It is not exactly clear what position Yoil held at the palace, but these lines clearly show that he was close to the ruler Myŏngjong. Myŏngjong's brother, Ch'unghŭi, better known as the monk State Preceptor Wŏn'gyŏng (Wŏn'gyŏng *kuksa* [d. 1183]), also served as monk superintendent at Hŭngwang Monastery, a few decades before Yoil held the same position (cf. *Koryŏsa*, vol. 90, "Yŏlchŏn" 3). The close relationship between the king and the monk may have derived from this connection.

300. *Ogyŏng*, the "fifth watch," denotes the time from three to five a.m., i.e., daybreak. Yet since the term also alludes to the last part of the night, it can likewise refer to the final phase of a person's life. *Songgwan*, "pinewood gates" or "gate of pine," can allude to the gate of a temple. Here, however, it may be understood as referring to the gates of Songdo, the "Pine Capital" (i.e., Kaesŏng), or, even more specifically, the gates of the palace, where Yoil had had to stay for the last ten years.

301. Chagŭm, "Purple Precincts," alludes to the forbidden parts of the palace complex, the chambers where the king resides.

302. *Chagoban*, "partridge feather design," can here, on a first level, be under-

stood as a blackware tea bowl. The black glaze of such teacups, which were *en vogue* during the Song, was occasionally designed with white spots to resemble elegant partridge feathers. On a subtextual level, in these two lines Yoil may be alluding to his early years at the royal court, when, at least in his personal view, the tea he poured out to the king, meaning the words of advice he offered, were as brilliant as phoenixes and as elegant as partridges. Lines three and four thus stand in contrast to the first two lines, in which the monk bemoans the fact that he is forced to hang around in the capital against his own will in the final phase of his life.

303. The gaunt crane and the hungry monkey, unfed and uncared-for by the monk for a decade, are here said either to have departed or to be feeling resentful because of Yoil's absence. Cranes and monkeys were generally associated with hermits living in inaccessible mountains.

304. This expression can be found in the section "Shenxian zaji" (Various accounts of spirits and transcendents) contained in *Tiaoxi yuying conghua* (Miscellanies by a fisherman recluse by Tiao Stream) compiled in the mid-twelfth century by Hu Zhai. Here it reads,

> In *Xiqing shihua* [Remarks on poetry from the Hall of Western Purity] it says, 'Fan Zhixu [d. 1129] lived in Fangcheng. [...] He said of himself that he had once belonged to the white-haired elderly; then he had [accidentally] met a [Daoist] teacher who had taught him how to make spiritual medicine. [...] Thus his facial color became like that of a child again. Already long ago he had taken his leave, but he left a verse, the final couplet of which read, 'Don't be astounded if I go back early one morning, goosefoot-staff in hand; my old [instead of the character *ku*, "old" (or in this case "home"), the *P'ahan chip* entry at hand features the character *ko*, "for this reason"] mountain is idly holding back a cloud above a brook.

King Myŏngjong's words can at this point be understood as a rejection of Yoil's request, because the king does not consider a "cloud hanging on a mountain" to be a valid reason for wanting to leave the court and his side. King Myŏngjong seems to imply that the Way does not necessarily have to be taught in the deep mountains, but that Yoil—as Myŏngjong states in the following poem—may offer religious instruction to the ignorant people of the mundane world in the palace as well.

305. The term *simin* (C. *xinyin*), "mind-seal," means the mental impression, intuitive certainty, that the mind is the Buddha-mind in all, which can seal or assure the truth. The term indicates the direct approach of Chan, asserting independence from language. Muller, *Digital Dictionary of Buddhism*.

306. The source says *kigwan*, "motive force" or "opportunity." The term has been translated as "main gates" to preserve the parallel structure with the term *songgwan* in the first line of Yoil's poem.

307. The *chin'gong* (C. *zhenkong*), "absolute void" or "complete vacuity," is said to be the nirvana of the Hīnayāna. Muller, *Digital Dictionary of Buddhism*.

308. The term *haengjang* (C. *xingcang*), "serving and hiding," means "to be

358   NOTES TO PAGES 128–129

active in society or politics, or to stay away in seclusion," or "to take office and to retire from office." Muller, *Digital Dictionary of Buddhism*. The term derives from *Lunyu* 7.11, where it says, "The Master remarked to Yan Hui, 'It is said, 'When he is employed, he moves forward; when he is removed from office, he holds himself in reserve.' Surely this applies to you and me.' " Slingerland, *Confucius: Analects*, 67. Thus, in *Lunyu*, the term *xingcang* actually implies that both serving and hiding are appropriate modes of conduct at the proper time, but over time the term became commonly associated with "timely withdrawal from public life."

309. The South Korean scholar of literature Chŏng Sŏnmo interprets this entry in the following way: by praising the unusually close relationship between King Myŏngjong and Yoil as well as the two figures' poetic excellence, Yi Illo meant to criticize the military ruler Ch'oe Ch'unghŏn, who had dethroned Myŏngjong and probably sent Yoil into exile. Chŏng furthermore hypothesizes that Yi Illo may have had knowledge of the monks' and scholar-officials' plan to assassinate Ch'oe Ch'unghŏn, and that he may have meant to inform Hŭijong of this. Hŭijong was then later involved in a failed assassination of Ch'oe, after which he himself was dethroned. See Chŏng, "*P'ahan chip* p'an'gak-e issŏsŏ-ŭi ch'ŏmsak munje-wa kŭ munhak sajŏk ŭiŭi," 20.

P'ahan chip—Fascicle 3

1. For further information on the *hwarang*, see, for instance, Vladimir Tikhonov, "*Hwarang* Organization: Its Functions and Ethics," *Korea Journal* 38, no. 2 (1998): 318–338; Richard D. McBride, "Silla Buddhism and the *Hwarang segi* Manuscripts," *Korean Studies* 31 (2007): 19–38; Kyoung-hwa Kim, "Reevaluating Hwarang Images: National Scholarship in Korea and Its Traditional Sources," *Oriental Archive* 78 (2008): 177–193.

2. These figures are the so-called *zhanguo si gongzi*, the "Four Lords of the Warring States period." Having served as both military strongmen and high officials, they were considered perfect embodiments of the martial and the civil realms. The *hwarang* are through the comparison here said to have been both well-trained warriors and well-learned intellectuals.

3. These four *hwarang* (see 2:12 note 193) are also mentioned in *Pohan chip* 1:28, where it says, "The Eastern Capital was originally situated in the dynasty of Silla. In times of old there were the Four Immortals — upon each of them came more than a thousand followers, and their laws of music were very popular. [...] Uhwa Gate at Hwangnyong Temple was constructed in times of old by the followers of the [Four] Immortals, but this once elegant sight now lies in ruins and among those who pass by [the gate] there is no one who is not saddened by this." Pak, *Yŏkchu Pohan chip*, 120.

4. These steles were known as *sasŏn-bi*, the "Steles of the Four Immortals." In *Sinjŭng tongguk yŏji sŭngnam* (vol. 44, sec. "Kangwŏndo," subsec. "Kangnŭng tadohobu") we find the following entry: "Munsu Monastery is located on the eastern seashores of the prefecture. In Yi Kok's [1298–1351] *Tongyu ki* [Account of sojourning in the east; contained in *TMS* 71:20a] it reads, 'People have told me: Two stone

NOTES TO PAGES 129–130 **359**

statues of Mañjuśri and Samantabhadra shot up out of the earth [at this place]. To the east [of these stone statues] once stood the steles of the Four Immortals, but they were thrown into the waters [of the ocean] by the court [under the control] of Hu Zongdan [see 2:19], and now only their bases in the forms of turtles [K. *kwibu*] still remain.'" *STYS* 44:18a.

5. P'algwan *Sŏnghoe,* the "Magnificent Assembly of the Eight Commandments." Usually simply known as P'algwanhoe, "Festival of the Eight Commandments," this event was a principal Buddhist memorial rite that was first held during the reign of the Silla king Chinhŭng in the sixth century. In Koryŏ it later transformed into an annual festival held in the middle of the eleventh month, often in honor of local spirits. The festival was held in P'yŏngyang and Kaesŏng and involved both visits to temples and large-scale enactments of various ancient Korean traditions. As it took place on a day close to the winter solstice, the ritual was probably meant to propitiate Heaven so that the days would lengthen again. See Vermeersch, *Chinese Traveler,* 17; Vermeersch, "P'algwanhoe."

6. *Yeŭi* (C. *niyi*), "rainbow clothes," are the kinds of clothes purportedly worn by Daoist immortals. Another term for these garments is *yesang* (C. *nichang*), "rainbow skirt." One should note that there existed the "Yesang uŭi kok" (C. "Nishang yuyi qu"), the "Melody of the Rainbow Gown and Feathered Robe," a piece of Tang dynasty music that is said to have been created by Tang emperor Xuanzong. He purportedly memorized the music during a journey to the moon. The song is mentioned, for example, in *Changhen ge* by Bai Juyi: "But suddenly comes the roll of the fish-skin war-drums, breaking rudely upon the air of the 'Rainbow Skirt and Feather Jacket.'" Minford and Lau, *Classical Chinese Literature,* 885. The four young Koryŏ men selected at this point in the narration may have danced to this "Melody of the Rainbow Gown and Feathered Robe."

7. Kwak Tongsun (n.d.), who held the office of *taeje* (edict attendant) went to the Jurchen Jin dynasty as an envoy in 1135 in his role as grand academician (K. *t'aehak paksa,* C. *taixue boshi*), and in 1144 in his position as director of the Palace Library. He was the nephew of Kwak Yŏ. He is also mentioned in a number of entries in *Pohan chip,* e.g., 1:36, where it says, "Behind the guesthouse in Tongnae lies Chŏkch'wi Pavilion. Surveillance Commissioner Kwak Tongsun left a verse here." Pak, *Yŏkchu Pohan chip,* 137. In *Pohan chip* 1:38, Kwak Tongsun appears alongside other leading intellectuals of his age, such as the monk Hyeso and Kim Pusik.

8. Fuxi is a Chinese cultural hero who, according to legend, created mankind and invented hunting, fishing, cooking, and writing.

9. A reference to *Zhuangzi* 1:11.

10. Wŏlsŏng, or Panwŏlsŏng, was the royal palace compound of Silla and Later Silla in the capital of Kŭmsŏng. Wŏlsŏng here stands for Silla, while the term "four sons" (K. *saja*) means the four *hwarang.*

11. The first part of this line is a quotation from Li Bai's poem *Shanzhong wenda* (Questions and answers in the mountains). The relevant couplet reads: "Peach blossoms floating in a stream vanish into the distance; there's another Heaven and earth there which is not the human world." In the translation by James Liu the poem reads,

360 NOTES TO PAGES 130–131

"You ask me why I nestle among the green mountains; I smile without answering, my mind, by itself, at ease. / Peach blossoms on flowing water are going far away: there is another cosmos, not the human world." Liu and Lynn, *Language-Paradox-Poetics*, 60. The "other cosmos" mentioned in the present line can be taken as the long-gone era of Silla.

12. This is a slightly abbreviated quotation from *Mengzi* 2A:1: "Traces of the venerable families, surviving customs, prevailing trends, and good government of the earlier times persisted." Van Norden, *Mengzi*, 34.

13. A shortened quotation from *Lunyu* 9.5: "When under siege in K'uang, the Master said, 'With King Wen dead, is culture [*wen*] not here with me? Had Heaven intended that This Culture of Ours [*siwen*] should perish, those who died later would not have been able to participate in This Culture of Ours. Heaven is not yet about to let this Culture of Ours perish, so what can the men of K'uang do to me?'" See Bol, *This Culture of Ours*, 1.

14. The source says *ko* (C. *gao*), but meant is legendary emperor Yao (K. Yo). King Chŏngjong's (r. 945–949) personal name had been Yo, and because of the naming taboo, Yi Illo therefore wrote *ko* instead of *yo*.

15. This is an allusion to a line in "Shundian" (Canon of Shun) from *Shujing*. See Legge, *Chinese Classics*, 3:49.

16. This line, which alludes to Wang Kŏn, the founder of Koryŏ, is a reference to the final stanza of the ode "Siqi" from the *Shijing*. See Legge, *Chinese Classics*, 4:448.

17. Sanho-jŏng, "Sanho Pavilion." "Grand Interior" is a translation of *taenae* (C. *danei*), the forbidden inner palace where the king's sleeping quarters usually were located. Kwak Yŏ had access to these royal inner quarters because he had served as King Yejong's tutor.

18. The term *ch'ŏngdam* (C. *qingtan*), "pure conversation," means broad, serious discussions unconstrained by formalities.

19. This statement alludes to a tale about Emperor Xuanzong (who is here referred to under his style name Ming Huang) and the Tang dynasty poet Meng Haoran (689–740), the core of which is similar to the related content of the entry at hand. When Meng Haoran went to meet Wang Wei at his quarters in the palace, Emperor Xuanzong arrived unexpectedly and unannounced. Meng Haoran then quickly dove under a couch, but Wang Wei had to admit that Meng was present. Xuanzong asked to hear one of Meng's poems, whereupon the poet tactlessly obliged with a verse on his rejection by the court. Taking him at his word, Xuanzong sent him back to his retreat in the mountains. See Moore, *Rituals of Recruitment in Tang China*, 334.

20. During Yejong's reign we find such *ch'insi*, i.e., examinations personally conducted by the king, at irregular intervals, and overall on six occasions: in the third, fourth, ninth, tenth, eleventh, and fifteenth years. The first of these examinations overseen by Yejong took place in 1108 (sixth month, seventh day), the final one in 1120 (fifth month). The source here says *mae kanse* (C. *mei jiansui*), which I have therefore understood not as "biannually" but rather "every other year."

21. "Candidate in the departmental examinations" is a translation of *kŏja* (C. *juzi*).

NOTES TO PAGE 131   **361**

22. Ko Hyoch'ung (n.d.) appears to have been a scholar who was very frank and who cared little about the sentiments of high officials or even the king. In the eighth volume of *Koryŏsa chŏryo* we find the following entry involving this person: "At the time, the king was quite fond of music. The concubines Yŏngnong, Arun, and others were considered good singers, and thus they were summoned time and again and bestowed with gifts. The scholar of the National Academy Ko Hyoch'ung created the *Kam inyŏ si* [Poem on being touched by two women] to satirize it. Drafter in the Secretariat Chŏng Kŭgyŏng informed the king about it, and the king was quite displeased. [Ko] Hyoch'ung participated in the state examinations, but the king ordered him expelled, and eventually he had him thrown in prison." *Koryŏsa chŏryo*, fifteenth year of Yejong (1120), fifth month, twentieth day.

23. This *Sa muik si* by Ko Hyo'chung has not been transmitted. Yet *Sa muik si* appears to be an alternative title for the abovementioned *Kam inyŏ si*.

24. Im Kyŏngch'ŏng (n.d.) served, for example, as palace attendant under Yejong (in 1115), then as vice commissioner of the Security Council (appointed 1128) and administrator to the Security Council (appointed 1130) under Injong. He was forced to retire in 1135 because of his allegedly sympathetic stance toward the rebellious monk Myoch'ŏng. He is mentioned in Xu Jing's *Illustrated Account of the Xuanhe Embassy to Koryŏ*. See Vermeersch, *Chinese Traveler*, 100.

25. The document submitted by Hu Zongdan to rehabilitate Ko Hyoch'ung is a *ch'aja* (C. *zhazi*), an "appeal" or "abbreviated memorial." Hu must have had a close personal relationship with Ko to rush to the court and speak up for the young scholar.

26. Ko Hyoch'ung passed the civil service examinations in 1124. See *Koryŏsa*, vol. 73.

27. Unfortunately, there is no information on this person in *Koryŏsa*, but in *Tongmunsŏn* we can find a poem by Ch'ae Pomun (n.d.; passed the civil service examinations in 1163), in which a clerk by the name of Pak Wŏn'gae is mentioned. The poem, entitled *Che Naju kwan* (Written in a guesthouse in Naju), features an explanatory note: "In the cyclic year ŭryu [1165], while studying away from home, I arrived at this place [Naju], and the clerk [K. *sŏgi*; perhaps short for *changsŏgi*, an office in the staff of a regional commissioner, responsible for records and documents] Pak Wŏn'gae especially opened a banquet at the public guesthouse to comfort me. Now, having received a province surveillance commissioner's orders, I am again passing by [this guesthouse], remembering the past, being stirred by the present. Therefore, I am making these four rhymes." The poem itself reads,

That I came here and sojourned was more than ten years ago; this autumn I
again made a wild goose's flight to the south.
As the hanging curtain is drawn at sundown, [I see that] rivers and mountains are still the same; as the mirror-case is opened at sunrise, [I see that] teeth and hair aren't the same anymore.
The courtyard is quiet, the shine of the moon rests on white sand; the garden lies deep, the light of spring intoxicates the green bamboo.

362   NOTES TO PAGES 131–132

> Yellow [sash around my] waist and red eyes, the new honor is heavy; coming
> and going, who'd say I was that commoner [from long ago]?"
> (*TMS* 13:1b)

This poem we also find in *Pohan chip* 1:42, where it is introduced with the following passage: "Reminder [K. Sŭbyu] Ch'ae Pomun's literary fame was heavy at one point in time. [...] Early on he had studied away from home in Kŭmsŏng [Naju]. Later he became province surveillance commissioner and arrived [back at this place], and wrote a poem on the wall of a public guesthouse." Hereafter follows the poem." Pak, *Yŏkchu Pohan chip*, 149. As can be seen, there is no mention of a lower official by the name of Pak Wŏn'gae in the *Pohan chip* entry at all.

28. "Announcement" here is a translation of *kyesa* (C. *qishi*).

29. According to his biography in *Koryŏsa* (vol. 95, "Yŏlchŏn" 8, "Ch'oe Ch'ung"), Ch'oe Yunŭi (1102–1162) was the great-great-grandson of Ch'oe Ch'ung. He passed the civil service examinations in 1128 and subsequently held several high offices. In 1136 he was dispatched to the Jurchen Jin as an envoy. Ch'oe Yunŭi is known to have collated the *Sangjŏng kogŭm yemun* (Prescribed ritual texts of the past and present), which much later, in 1234, was brought out as the first work to have been printed using cast metal type (this work has not been transmitted).

30. Like so many other poems in this collection, the poem at hand is a pentasyllabic quatrain, in which the last word of the second and the last word of the fourth line make a rhyme. The rhyme is generally made up of the same or a very similar vowel along with an ending consonant (if any) — here it is *hyang* (C. *xiang*) and *wang* (C. *wang*).

31. *Moran*, the "tree peony," was traditionally viewed as the most beautiful of all flowers, the "king of all flowers."

32. "Triennial lower civil service examinations" is a translation of *samasi*. The term could also be rendered as "preliminary examinations for classics and literary licentiates."

33. Emperor Yao's successor was not his son Danzhu, but rather Shun, whom he persuaded to leave behind farming and take over power for him. Shun then was likewise not succeeded by Shangjun or any of his other apparently unworthy sons, but rather by the worthy Yu. In the eyes of Confucian scholars, these designations of capable, thoughtful, virtuous successors marked a precedent for the important concept of meritocracy. The purported succession of Yao and Shun was exemplary, for it underpinned the Confucian notion that the power to govern and rule was earned through ability, intelligence, and effort rather than simply being handed out through inheritance or taken by force through military strength. This can be seen, for instance, in *Mengzi* 5A5. See van Norden, *Mengzi*, 123.

34. The founder of the Shang, King Tang, established the dynasty by overthrowing Jie, the last ruler of the Xia dynasty. The Zhou dynasty, in turn, was founded by King Wu, who overthrew the Shang and thus established merit.

35. This *P'ahan chip* entry is fictionalized and creatively retold in the chapter "Sonyŏn siin Pak Wŏn'gae" (The boy-poet Pak Wŏn'gae) contained in the 2012

NOTE TO PAGE 132   **363**

North Korean publication *Chosŏn kojŏn chakka irhwa chip* (A collection of anecdotes of writers of classical Korean literature) by Pak Killam. This book, which is quite interesting in the framework of the question as to how knowledge of *P'ahan chip* is preserved in present-day South and North Korea, is meant for students of literature and writers in North Korea. It says,

> The following incident happened during the time of Koryŏ king Ŭijong (1147–1170). One day, an emotional meeting, which caught the eyes of all government officials present, took place in the courtyard of Hoegyŏng-jŏn Hall at the royal palace. "Wŏn'gae, say, how long has it been?" "Sir Vice Director, is it really you?" How the two people were standing there, holding each other's hands, was quite a touching sight to see. One of the two was Pak Wŏn'gae, principal graduate of the last *samasi* [the preliminary examinations for classics and literary licentiates] [...], the other was Ch'oe Yunŭi, a descendent of Ch'oe Ch'ung, the man who was known as the progenitor of historical studies in Koryŏ. "Back then I already knew that one day you'd be in this position," Ch'oe Yunŭi said with a bright smile, and Pak Wŏn'gae blushed. Among those who had witnessed this scene, the *chi gonggŏ* in charge of the present civil service examinations as well as the *tong chi gonggŏ* [...] were the ones most taken aback by it. They were wondering: what kind of relationship might exist between some nameless young scholar and the renowned high minister Ch'oe Yunŭi for the two of them to be so delighted by their meeting. Spurred by their curiosity, the officials stepped closer, and when they asked them for the reason, Ch'oe Yunŭi replied, "When this man here was eleven years old...," and then, overcome by emotion, he told them the whole story: on a spring evening many years before, as he had come home from the office, Ch'oe Yunŭi had unexpectedly received a sheet of paper, an announcement, which had been sent to him. (But an announcement, that's something that ought to be brought to the office—who'd ever send such a document to a high minister's private residence? Goodness, some people really don't know east from west!) Though at first he was displeased, it had nevertheless been sent to him personally, and thus Ch'oe Yunŭi tore the envelope open. But what a short piece of writing inside: "There is one man who has not been granted your grace—it is only my father. / He who can make all things obtain their proper place—truly, it is only you." (What sort of request for an office is that supposed to be?) Ch'oe Yunŭi hurriedly called his servant. "Who brought this in?" he asked. The servant, carefully watching his master's unusually agitated expression, replied, "This was brought in by some boy who said he was Pak Wŏn'gae from Songak-dong." "A boy, you say?" "Yes, and in fact he was quite pushy about wanting to meet you in person, sir, but I only took this writ from him and then made use of some force to send him away." Ch'oe Yunŭi, still suspicious, read the piece of writing over again more closely. [...] He had

364   NOTE TO PAGE 132

seen all kinds of talented people throughout his life, but never had he seen anything like this, and Ch'oe Yunŭi needed to take a look at [the boy] with his own eyes, for otherwise he would have been incapable of believing in his talent. Therefore, the next day he sent someone to call Pak Wŏn'gae to his house. When he then actually met him face-to-face, the boy turned out to be much younger-looking than he had expected. There was still downy hair on his skin, his body wasn't yet sturdy, and his shining bright eyes flickered as if they were covered with the dew of morning. At first sight, Ch'oe Yunŭi knew that this was no ordinary child, and intentionally putting on a stern expression he said to him, "Kid, do you perhaps think that the affairs of the state are some sort of children's game? It's absolutely clear that your father put this writ together, so what's all this nonsense?" The boy, instantly wide-eyed, quickly replied, as if in protest, "Your Excellency's words are entirely untrue. I may be young, but how could I wretchedly borrow someone else's hand? I have heard that you, Master, are fair and just when it comes to appointments to office, and as a son I meant to help my father. If it is not sufficient, you may simply refuse, but please do not construct such terrible accusations." Upon hearing Wŏn'gae's reasonable words, Ch'oe Yunŭi (this boy's the real thing; [. . .]) inwardly clicked his tongue in admiration. And in a much more gentle tone he asked him, "All right, but how old are you?" "I turned eleven this year." Ch'oe Yunŭi, whose curiosity had been stirred even more by the boy's tough demeanor, was now seriously determined to put him to the test. "Very well then. If it's true that you wrote this announcement all by yourself, let's give that talent of yours another try, shall we? If you succeed, I will award your father with an office, just the way you asked me to; but if you fail, I'll imprison him for fraud — be mindful of that." "I hope you mean what you say," Wŏn'gae retorted forcefully. Ch'oe Yunŭi chuckled and pointed at a peony blooming in the courtyard's flower garden. "Write a poem on that Chinese peony over there — your rhymes should be 'fragrance,' *hyang*, and 'king,' *wang*. You have time until I've finished my tea here." And with that he slowly brought the teacup that had stood on the table to his lips. Yet Ch'oe Yunŭi had barely taken two sips when Wŏn'gae's crystal-clear voice already rang in his ears: "On the Chinese peony still remain the colors of spring; / in front of the porch it emits a strange *fragrance*. / The tree peony, if it was by its side, / would surely be ashamed for being the 'hundred flowers' *king*.'" At that moment, Ch'oe Yunŭi was so shocked, he almost choked on the tea in his mouth and was on the verge of spitting it all over the floor. Barely having managed to swallow the liquid, with the teacup still in hand, he stared at Wŏn'gae as if with new eyes. His lyrical talent was truly amazing. The poetic idea to compare the Chinese peony with the tree peony was incredible — this boy had composed a perfectly round poem in a single instant. "Very elegant!" Ch'oe Yunŭi exclaimed in spite of himself. "You really are a boy-poet, there's no question about

NOTES TO PAGES 132–133   365

it. And I'm the one who lost." Pak Wŏn'gae also beamed with joy, saying, "So, you are going to keep your promise?" When Ch'oe Yunŭi gave a nod, Wŏn'gae bowed and then ran out the door without even putting his shoes on. Ch'oe Yunŭi's heart rejoiced in this display of youthfulness (That rascal will certainly become a great writer). Only a few years after this incident Pak Wŏn'gae had stood out in the preliminary examinations, just like Ch'oe Yunŭi had predicted. The examiners who had listened to Ch'oe Yunŭi's story were all deeply impressed by the fairy-tale-like talents of Pak Wŏn'gae. Later, however, when the age was in chaos because of Ŭijong's rotten politics and the subsequent military revolt, Pak Wŏn'gae left office and spent the rest of his life in some remote village. Hence, the light of this brilliant boy-poet's talent was never to be seen in the world again. (Pak, *Chosŏn kojŏn chakka irhwa chip*, 122–125)

It is very interesting to see here, I think, that Pak Wŏn'gae's eventual inability to serve in high office is portrayed as having been brought about by King Ŭijong's mismanagement of the state, for the original *P'ahan chip* entry does not readily suggest this conclusion.

36. *Chŏmgwi pu* (C. *diangui bu*) means a kind of poetry in which personal names of deceased people or events of ancient times are frequently referred to. The reader must have extensive knowledge of these dead people and long-gone matters in order to understand the allusions in the relevant poem. The poetry by Yang Jiong (650–695) of the Tang dynasty especially was referred to as *diangui bu*.

37. The *xikun ti*, literally "Western Kunlun Mountain Style," was an influential new style of poetry especially during the Northern Song in the early eleventh century. The name derived from the anthology *Xikun chouchang ji* (Collection of verses on the same themes from the Western Kunlun Mountain). The collection was compiled by Yang Yi (974–1020) in the autumn of the first year of the Dazhong Xianfu reign period (1008). It included around 250 poems. The poets took Li Shangyin's poetry as their chief model and also learned from Tang Yanqian (fl. 875) so that they composed poetry in an embellished and erudite style with many complicated allusions. Originally, Xikun Style referred to the poetic style of poems in the *Xikun chouchang ji*, but some later critics and scholars also employed it to refer to Li Shangyin's poems since the contributors to the *Xikun chouchang ji*, especially the three leading poets, took Li as their model. Jin, "Formation of the Xikun Style Poetry," 1.

38. The Xikun Style is also discussed in Ouyang Xiu's *Liuyi shihua*. In the translation by Stephen Owen the relevant entry reads,

In these days when literature is in full flower, Secretary Ch'en Ts'ung-yi [Chen Congyi, d. 1031] is uniquely praised for his old-style learning. His poems are very much like those of Po Chü-yi [Bai Juyi]. After Yang Yi and Liu Yün [Liu Yun] wrote their series of group compositions and the "His-k'un [Xikun] Collection" became current, aspiring writers did their best to imitate that style. Because of this, the poetry collections of the great T'ang

366   NOTES TO PAGE 133

[Tang] masters were virtually abandoned and not in common circulation. At one point Ch'en chanced to obtain an old edition of Tu Fu's [Du Fu's] poetry, the text of which was full of errors and lacunae. In Tu Fu's poem *Sending off Waterworks Commissioner Ts'ai* [Seeing Commander Cai Xilu Off on His Return to Longyou, By This I Write to Secretary Gao; Owen, *The Poetry of Du Fu*, 1:185], there was the line, "His body light: a single bird ..." One character had been lost. Thereupon Ch'en and several of his friends tried to fill in the missing space with a word. One tried, "[His body light: a single bird] goes swiftly." Another tried, "[His body light: a single bird] sinks." And another, "[His body light: a single bird] rises." And another, "[His body light: a single bird] descends." No one could get it just right. Later Ch'en got hold of a good edition, and found that the line was, in fact, "His body light: a single bird in passage." Ch'en accepted his defeat with a sigh: as he saw it, even though it was a question of one word, neither he nor any of his friends could equal Tu Fu's choice. (Owen, *Readings in Chinese Literary Thought*, 369–370; for another translation, see Egan, *Problem of Beauty*, 74)

In this episode in *Liuyi shihua*, Ouyang Xiu reminds readers of the excellence of the Tang poets and goes against the overemphasis of current literary fashions. Yi Illo likewise criticizes the Xikun Style for its overinflated use of allusions, and thereby he also disparages Li Shangyin. In this, he is in line with the way in which Northern Song intellectuals viewed the now famous Tang dynasty poet. As Ronald Egan writes,

Today, we think of Li Shangyin as a major poet. [...] That is not the way he was thought of in Northern Song times. Owing largely to the fact that certain early Song poets adopted him as their model and proceeded to develop a narrow but highly distinctive style, known for its challenging diction and density of allusions, that claimed him retrospectively as its leader (the Xikun Style), Li Shangyin was thought of in a peculiar way. Once the Xikun Style fell out of favor, in the mid–Northern Song, Li Shangyin tended to be thought of disparagingly, as the inspiration of a movement that eventually had to be abandoned and renounced. (Egan, *Problem of Beauty*, 98–99)

39. This line is an allusion to the first line of *Xunzi* (Writings of Xunzi), where it says, "Blue comes from the indigo plant but is bluer than the plant itself." The expression refers to a secondary object being better than the original.

40. This is a reference to a legend about the master poet Li Bai, who is said to not simply have passed away but rather to have ridden to Heaven astride a whale. This legend is mentioned, for example, in the tale "Li Zhexian zuicao he Man shu" (Li the banished immortal writes in drunkenness to impress the barbarians), which is contained in the Ming dynasty vernacular story collection *Jingshi tongyan* (Stories to caution the world). See Yang and Yang, *Stories to Caution the World*, 141. The image of

NOTES TO PAGE 133   **367**

Li Bai riding the whale can also be found in Du Fu's poem *Song Kong Chaofu xiebing guiyou Jiangdong jian cheng Li Bai* (Seeing off Kong Chaofu, who has resigned on account of an illness and will go back to visit east of the Yangzi; also for Li Bai), in which a variant of the second-to-last line reads, "If you meet Li Bai astride a whale [...]." Owen, *Poetry of Du Fu*, 1:401.

41. This is a reference to the following tale about Wang Meng (325–375) from the *Jinshu*: When as a young man he traveled to the capital of Ye, no one appreciated him except for Xu Tong [...], who tried to recruit him to serve in the Labor Section of his administration. Wang Meng did not respond to this offer and went into hiding. He eventually became a recluse in the Huayin Mountains. [...] However, he hoped one day to be of service to the state. In the meantime, he kept a low profile and waited for the right opportunity. When the Eastern Jin strongman Huan Wen (312–373) entered the mountain pass near Huayin, Wang Meng went to welcome him. Rather than being overawed by such an important person, Wang Meng casually chatted with him while picking lice from his clothes. Before returning home, Huan Wen gave Wang Meng a chariot and horses and offered him the position of protector-general. Wang Meng declined the appointment. See Knechtges and Chang, *Ancient and Early Medieval Chinese Literature*, 2:1204. These two lines are from Su Dongpo's poem *He Wang You* (Reply to Wang You).

42. This is a quote from Su Dongpo's poem *Zhi Anjie yuanlai yezuo* (My nephew Anjie comes from far away and sits with me in the night), in which Su alluded to the poem *Zuo qian zhi Languan shi zhisun Xiang* (Demoted I arrive at Lantian Pass and show this poem to my brother's grandson Han Xiang) by Han Yu, which Han had dedicated to his grandnephew. Han Yu's poem reads,

> A sealed memorial submitted at dawn to Ninefold Heaven —
> Exiled at dusk to Chaozhou, eight thousand leagues to travel.
> Wishing to save his Sagacious Brilliance from treacherous evils,
> could I have cared for the years that remain in my withered limbs?
> Clouds straddle the mountains of Qin: where is my home?
> Snows crowd the Lantian Pass, horse will not move.
> I know what the reason must be for you coming so far:
> The better to gather my bones from the shores of miasmic water.

This translation of Han Yu's poem can be found in Murck, *Poetry and Painting in Song China*, 257–258.

43. "This" is a translation of *ado* (C. *edu*), which is an abbreviation for *adomul* (C. *eduwu*), "that thing," a euphemism for money.

44. The term *kyŏgo* (C. *gewu*), "rolling a five," means a lucky roll of the dice, a lucky throw.

45. The expression *chosam mosa* (C. *zhaosan musi*), "three in the morning, four at night," means that there are no essential differences between things, that, at the core, everything is the same. The expression derives from a story about a monkey trainer that can be found in *Zhuangzi*. Ziporyn, *Zhuangzi*, 14.

368   Notes to Page 134

46. The expression *yanggap suk* (C. *yangjia shu*) derives from a description of the Kurykan tribes in *Xin Tangshu* (New history of Tang; vol. 217), where it says,

> Kurykans live north of the Baikal Lake [C. *hanhai*]. Their battle-ready troops consist of five thousand men, and since their grasslands are wide, they breed fine horses there. [...] The northern parts of this land are far away from the ocean, and farthest away from our capital. If one goes even farther north and crosses the ocean, [one reaches parts of the world where] the days are long and the nights are short [referring to the white nights (K. *paegya*) of Siberia]. When the sun sets, [the people there] boil a sheep's shoulder blade, and when it is well cooked, the eastern [sky] already brightens, and all is close to where the sun rises.

Hence, this line features an allusion to a passage from a Chinese text dealing with the quick passing of time.

47. The source here says *fengsao* (K. *p'ungso*), which literally means "wind sorrow" but can be understood as a reference to the "Guofeng" from the *Shijing*, and the "Lisao" from *Chuci*. It thus means the style of ancient poetry.

48. These lines are from Im Ch'un's poem *Yŏ Yi Misu hoe Tamji-ji ka*, which reads,

> For a long time now I've been a-wandering, having left the capital;
> in vain I had learned the *Sounds of the South* [the *Chuci*], wearing the cap of Chu.
> [The quick passing of] years and months often has me stunned, like when a
>   sheep's shoulder blade was well cooked [so rapidly];
> with ancient-style poetry we get together again, as the high skies are cold.
> After ten years of separation and hardship we again light the lamp and chat;
> the legacy of merit and fame for half my life: I often look [at my gaunt] face in
>   the mirror.
> And I laugh at myself, for in my old age I've come to follow the younger
>   generation;
> cultured thoughts, official ambitions — both disappeared at the very
>   same time.
>   (*SHC* 3:3b; also in *TMS* 13:3:3b–4a)

49. These are lines from the second stanza of Im Ch'un's poem *Misu pang yŏ ŏ-Kaeryŏng i arijiju wi hyang; chaksi saji*, where it says,

> The Purple Tenuity leisurely carries a single bottle [on the waist] and travels,
> sometimes I hear a knock on the door.
> Asking me to return home [to the capital] from short reclusion,
> but then I make you stay to talk and laugh, delaying your journey back.
> In the belly: early I knew that the spirit is full there;
> in the bosom: nothing vulgar is born there. [...]
>   (*SHC* 2:20a)

NOTES TO PAGES 134–135 **369**

50. The source says *so-sa* (C. *xiao-si*), which is the name for monasteries in the Liang dynasty (502–557), because Liang Wudi built so many of them that they were named after his surname, Xiao. Muller, *Digital Dictionary of Buddhism*. It has here been understood as a small, solitary, out-of-the-way temple located on Mount Ch'ŏnma.

51. Ch'ŏnma-ryŏng, "Heavenly Grindstone Ridge."

52. There exists the theory that this poem may have been written by Yi Illo's contemporary and acquaintance O Sejae. See Cho, "O Sejae-ŭi salm," 27.

53. The term *akchŏk* (C. *yueji*), "music register," refers to registers containing the names and personal specialties of the so-called *kwan'gi*, "provincial office courtesans," i.e., *kisaeng* who were registered as belonging to provincial government offices and officers. There indeed were also private *kisaeng* (the so-called *sagi*), yet the term *kwan'gi* is usually understood as referring to the opposite of the government-employed *kisaeng* in the capital, the so-called *kyŏnggi*, who performed during ceremonies at court. The provincial office courtesans had to offer performances of song and dance at the local government agencies, but much like the *kyŏnggi*, they were generally also forced to provide sexual services for local officials — while this may not have been written law, it unquestionably was common practice. This system and network of courtesans employed by the court, the government, and its local branch offices, which also flourished during the Chosŏn dynasty, was essentially nothing but a system of state-sponsored, organized prostitution, sexual exploitation, and sexual slavery. Oftentimes overly blunt sexual overtures or vicious fits of jealousy by officials led to serious predicaments and violent conflicts, as is evidenced in a drastic way in the framework of the present episode.

54. "Southern prefecture" here is a translation of *namju*, which in all likelihood refers to the region of present-day Chŏnju in Northern Chŏlla Province. This can be deduced from an entry in *Koryŏsa* (vol. 1) where it says that "Kyŏnhwŏn [the founder of the state of Hu-Paekche (892–936)] started a rebellion [against Silla] while leaning on the southern region." Kyŏnhwŏn's basis for operation and the original center of the state of Hu-Paekche was the Chŏnju region. *Namju* can also be found in *Pohan chip* 3:35.

55. Chŏng Sŭmmyŏng (d. 1151), a high official of the mid-twelfth century and one of Kim Pusik's most trusted protégés, who next to Kim also served as one of the chief compilers of the *Samguk sagi*. Chŏng had fought alongside Kim Pusik in P'yŏngyang during the suppression of the Myoch'ŏng Rebellion and was appointed to a high post in the wake of this incident. Breuker, *Establishing a Pluralist Society*, 438. He was known to be an extremely upright and frank minister, and he was held in high esteem by King Injong, as is evidenced in his biography in *Koryŏsa*. It says,

> Chŏng Sŭmmyŏng was a man from Yŏngil Lesser Prefecture [present-day Northern Kyŏngsang Province]. His casual, unruffled manner was strange and grand. He exerted himself in studying, became able and cultured, and as provincial applicant he passed the civil service examination, whereupon he was appointed palace attendant. [...] Chŏng Sŭmmyŏng for a long time served as a remonstrance official, and he had

370   NOTES TO PAGE 135

the elegant bearing of a minister who dares to speak frankly before his king. Injong deeply valued his [upright] character [...], and when the king was not in good health anymore he said to [his son] Ŭijong, "When you govern the country, you ought to make use of the words of [the royal tutor Chŏng] Sŭmmyŏng." [Chŏng] Sŭmmyŏng himself, believing that he had been specifically asked to do so by the previous king [Injong], never held back his words when he understood something, and Ŭijong gradually came to fear him. [Moreover,] Kim Chonjung and [the eunuch] Chŏng Ham slandered him both day and night. In time, Sŭmmyŏng announced that he was ill, and [Kim] Chonjung temporarily was appointed to serve as a substitute in his office. But [Chŏng] Sŭmmyŏng could surmise what the king's [true] intentions were. So he drank [poisonous] medicine and died. From then on, the number of those who flattered and spoiled [the king] grew with each passing day, King [Ŭijong] indulged in his personal pleasures more and more, and there was no limit to his indolence. Early on the king had once gone on a royal tour to Kwibŏp Temple. He had galloped his horse and arrived at Ta-wŏn [Tea Courtyard] on Tallyŏng [Peak] when none of the ministers in his retinue had yet reached the place. Thereupon the king, leaning alone against a pillar, spoke to his attendants, 'If Chŏng Sŭmmyŏng was still alive, how could I have managed to get here [all by myself and ahead of everybody else]?' (*Koryŏsa* vol. 98, "Yŏlchŏn" 11)

56. This fine paper is called *ullam chi* (C. *yunlan zhi*).

57. Otter marrow (K. *talsu*; C. *tasui*) was a precious medicine used especially for tissue repair and for healing crusted wounds or scars.

58. *Wuling* (K. *onŭng*) here refers to the five tombs of the earliest sovereigns of the Han dynasty, located north of the Wei River. Esteemed families and the young nobility lived in the vicinity of these five tombs. In the line at hand, the term can be understood as alluding to the nobles and rich officials of the southern region, who are to feel sorry for the girl and financially support her. The final character in this line, *kung* (C. *qiong*), which can mean "destitute," I have understood as "exhaust one's energies." This poem also features in the sixth entry of the fourth fascicle (*hujip* 2:6) of *Yŏgong p'aesŏl,* where Yi Chehyŏn writes,

[The poem which] Section Chief [K. Ch'ongnang] Hong Kan [d. 1304] enjoyed the most was the following by Commissioner Chŏng ([his name was] Sŭmmyŏng, he was a man from the time of King Ŭijong): "Amid a hundred flowery shrubs a serene, blossoming countenance; / suddenly struck by maddest wind, bereaved of its deepest red. / Even otter marrow could not mend her cheeks of jade; / noble sons of Wuling, boundless ought to be your efforts." But since [this poem] has been chewed around in people's mouths for such a long time now, how could there be any flavor left in it? Yi, *Han'guk myŏngjŏ taejŏnjip,* 446

NOTES TO PAGES 135–136 **371**

59. Richard Rutt's wonderful translation of this entry can be found in Rutt, "Traditional Korean Poetry Criticism," 139.

60. It is unfortunately not clear who this person by the name of Hwang Sunik is. He is not mentioned in other sources, and while he is here said to have been remarkably talented, he apparently never reached any higher office. The present entry speaks of his relation with the high minister Kim Chonjung, who is referred to as an official at the Security Council. Judging from this information, the relevant time frame would most likely be the 1140s or early 1150s.

61. *Jiancha,* as the source has it, is Fujian Jianzhou tea. This tea grown in the Fujian region was thought of highly especially during the Song dynasty.

62. A reference to a tea-related poem by the tea-loving Tang dynasty poet Lu Tong (795–835), entitled *Zoubi xie Meng jianyi ji xin cha* (Written in haste to thank Censor Meng for his gift of new tea), which reads,

The first bowl moistens my lips and throat.
The second bowl banishes my loneliness and melancholy.
The third bowl penetrates my withered entrails, finding nothing there but
    five thousand scrolls of writing.
The fourth bowl raises a light perspiration, as all the inequities I have suf-
    fered in my life are flushed out through my pores.
The fifth bowl purifies my flesh and bones.
The sixth bowl allows me to communicate with immortals.
The seventh bowl I need not drink, I am only aware of a pure wind rising
    beneath my two arms.
The mountains of Penglai, what is this place?
I, Master of the Jade Stream, ride this pure wind and wish to return home.

For the poem, see Benn, *Tea in China,* 14–15.

63. "Minister of State Wang" is Wang Anshi. Pingfu is the courtesy name of his younger brother, Wang Anguo (1028–1074).

64. A slightly altered quotation of the first line of Wang Anshi's poem *Jicha yu Pingfu* (Sending tea to Pingfu).

65. *Sikchi* (C. *shizhi*), literally "eating-finger," is an expression for the index finger. "The eating-finger moves" means that "appetite is whetted." The term derives from *Zuozhuan* 4.2. See Durant, Li, and Schaberg, *Zuo Tradition,* 608.

66. Sŏngsan is present-day Sŏngju-gun in Northern Kyŏngsang Province.

67. This line can be understood as a reference to the legend of the two lovers Nongyu and Xiao Shi. Xiao Shi, a "master of the pipes," was able to summon peacocks and cranes to the courtyard with his music. Nongyu, one of the daughters of Duke Mu of Qin, fell in love with him, and he took her as a wife. He taught her to imitate birdcalls on the flute, and after several years she could imitate the cry of the phoenix. She drew these auspicious birds there in flocks, and Xiao built a dais for the birds where the couple also lived. After a period of time, Xiao Shi and Nongyu flew away on the backs of the phoenixes. In addition, in classical Chinese literature,

372   NOTES TO PAGE 137

flutes can be taken as phallic symbols, while the blowing of flutes often alludes to sexual intercourse. The "climbing up [to the upper storey of] the tower" can likewise be interpreted as an allusion to the sex that is to be performed in this private space.

68. A reference to Heng'e, also known as Chang'e, a mythological figure commonly called the Goddess of the Moon. In *Huainanzi* it says that Heng'e stole the elixir of immortality from the Queen Mother of the West and fled to the moon. Major, *Heaven and Earth,* 152. This line thus alludes to the woman having escaped.

69. The information given in this episode also appears in the entry on Sŏngju-mok in *Sinjŭng tongguk yŏji sŭngnam,* where it says, "[Ch'ŏngun Tower] — Im Ch'un early on sojourned here for a short while after arriving in the prefecture, and the prefecture chief [K. *chuswi*] ordered a famous singing girl to sleep with him, but at night she ran off and went back. The next morning, [Im Ch'un] went to the office straightaway and wrote the following poem. [...]" *STYS* 28:23a. The poem that then follows in *Sinjŭng tongguk yŏji sŭngnam* (and which features the lines from the *P'ahan chip* entry at hand) is also contained in *Sŏha chip* and *Tongmunsŏn* (13:3b), yet in both collections the poem is entitled *Hŭijŭng Milchu swi* (Playfully presented to the chief of Milchu). Milchu, where Im Ch'un apparently really stayed when this incident happened, is present-day Miryang in Southern Kyŏngsang Province. In *Sŏha chip* we find the following explanatory note: "The [*Sinjŭng tongguk yŏji*] *sŭngnam* has Sŏngju — I fear this is a mistake." *SHC* 2:18a. The poem contained in *Sŏha chip* and *Tongmunsŏn* reads,

> With rouge awaited dawn, put in the golden hairpin;
> was rapidly forced to appear, ascended to the magnificent feast.
> Unafraid of the senior official's stern command;
> insulted and upset over a bad fated relationship with an [ugly old] wayfarer.
> Climbed a tower, but she failed to act as the partner who blows the pipe;
> fleeing to the moon, to no good purpose she became the immortal who stole
>   the elixir.
> I send word to the esteemed scholar of Ch'ŏngun —
> [look upon her with] a benevolent heart, and be careful not to apply the
>   cattail-whip.
>   (*SHC* 2:18a–b)

In *Tongmunsŏn* the final line of this poem is different, and it can be read in two different, in fact contrasting, ways: first, "[Look upon her with] a benevolent heart, do not make use of and show her the cattail-whip"; second, "The benevolent heart you should not use, show her the cattail-whip." Im Ch'un's longer poem also features in the fifty-sixth entry of the lower fascicle of *Tongin sihwa,* where Sŏ Kŏjŏng retells the story of Kiji and the singing girl and goes on to say,

> In recent times, there was the Confucian Han Kwŏn [n.d.], who arrived in P'yŏngyang upon having been sent on a mission. [In P'yŏngyang] lived a singing girl by the name of Sŭngso Man, whose beauty and artistry were

NOTE TO PAGE 137 **373**

both amazing. Han Kwŏn had fallen madly in love with her [the wording in this *Tongin sihwa* passage very much resembles *P'ahan chip* 3:6], and the magistrate of the prefecture commanded Man to share the pillow with him. Man, however, had another client [K. *apkaek*] at the time, and she loathed Han for being ugly and old. Carrying the lamp on her back she sat down, and in a moment she fled and was gone. Han then composed the following poem: "The beautiful child of P'yŏngyang, Sŭngso Man; / her age just two times eight, with a complexion of jade. / Even though the mandarin-duck dream couldn't be fulfilled, / it was better than to have seen her in a Gaotang dream." Now, compared with Im's poem, [this poem by Han] is inferior by far [...]. (Yi, *Tongin sihwa*, 209)

70. Sinjun is the dharma name of a late-twelfth-century Koryŏ monk whose real name, at least according to *Pohan chip* 1:40, was O Chŏngsŏk. His sobriquet being Paegunja, this person had been a Confucian and had served as a minister, but he became a Buddhist monk after the military seized power in 1170. He left a record dated 1156, which can be found in *Samguk yusa*. In a passage in the biography of Yi Chehyŏn in *Koryŏsa* (vol. 110) we find the following information on this person:

Unfortunately, in the final year of the reign of King Ŭijong, the men of the military started a revolt and rose to power, indiscriminately burning both jade and common stones. Those who by a stroke of luck were able to escape from the tiger's mouth fled into remote mountains, cast off their [Confucian] caps and girdles, and put on the patchwork robes of monks [K. *kari*] to spend the rest of their lives [as itinerant monks]. Sinjun and Osaeng belonged to that group of people. Later, when the country somewhat restored official selection by literature [i.e., the civil service examinations], there were scholars who had the intention to learn, but there was nowhere they could obtain that learning. Thus they all followed this group [of former ministers who were now living as monks].

Hence, Sinjun left the government, but although he did not return to the laity, he still offered Confucian learning to later-born students. The aforementioned *Pohan chip* entry 1:40 reads,

Lecturer [K. *chikkang*] Ha Ch'ŏndan [d. 1259] recited the poem *Yu P'aljŏnsan* [Sojourning on Mount P'aljŏn] by Paegunja O Chŏngsŏk. "Streams are long, the shadows of mountains distant; forests are dense, the cries of birds deep. / Weary servant boy, don't you whip the horse; the slower we proceed, the longer I get to chant." Thereupon he said, "The [second] line, 'Forests are dense, the cries of birds deep,' is really most excellent." I replied, "The meaning of this poem is far-reaching, and only after chanting all four lines in succession can one get a taste of its marvelous piquancy. How could one cut out only a single line by itself? For instance, in the

374 NOTES TO PAGE 137

case of 'Forests are dense, the cries of birds deep' — that line alludes to Du Zimei's line 'Beyond the bamboo, the cries of birds are deep' [this line was, in fact, not written by Du Fu, but by Bai Juyi; it is from Bai's poem *Zaoxing linxia,* "Walking under the trees at dawn"]." Pak, *Yŏkchu Pohan chip,* 144–145)

There are three poems by O Chŏngsŏk contained in *Tongmunsŏn:* "Chŭng Taegwang-sa tangdu" (Given as a present to the chief monk of Taegwang Temple; *TMS* 13:1a), "Sanch'on haedang" (On a crab apple tree in a mountain village; *TMS* 13:1a), and "Tojung mun aeng" (On the road, hearing an oriole; *TMS* 19:21b). The poem "Tojung mun aeng" features in 3:18, where Sinjun is mentioned again.

71. The term *kwae kwan,* "hang up the cap," alludes to a Confucian retiring from or refusing an office. Sinho-mun, "Spiritual Tiger Gate," was the northern gate of the palace in Kaesŏng. Other intellectuals living at the same time as Paegunja Sinjun were also highly critical of the Confucians and their standards during this age of political and social turmoil. Im Ch'un, for instance, wrote in a letter,

> Well, those people that in our generation are referred to as "distinguished Confucians" [K. *myŏngyu*], they're merely skilled in section and sentence commentary, by which they seize the ranks in the civil service examinations, nothing more. Really, if one takes these kind of [incapable] people and regards them as "distinguished Confucians" — how tumultuous would everything be from the sheer mass of all those "distinguished Confucians." It's not only that [true Confucians] can't be seen in the present age, but in times of old, too, they were exceedingly rare. Jia Yi [of the Western Han], Sima Qian [of the Han dynasty], Han Yu, or Liu Zihou [Liu Zongyuan] — such people certainly belong to this group [of true *myŏngyu*]. [...] In recent times, moreover, there was Ouyang Yongshu [Ouyang Xiu] [...], who may well be called the Han Yu of this day and age, Wang Jiefu [Wang Anshi], who writes based on the Three Scriptures and Five Canons and enlightens the Way of the ancient sages, as well as Su Zizhan [Su Shi], who captures the hundred clans and through investigation brings forth and creates their origins — they, too, are truly distinguished Confucians. But those who don't have the substance of a distinguished Confucian and merely thievishly take possession of such a title, they really are the criminals of Our [Korean] Confucian Way. I sincerely don't want to become anything like it, and if anyone refers to me in such a way, I'd respectfully make my bows and decline. I would never dare to think of [this appellation] as appropriate [for someone like me], and I'd never dare accept it. (*SHC* 4:11b–12a)

72. Xinling jun, Lord Xinling, who is here named Xinling Gongzi (d. 243 BCE), Ducal Son Xinling, was also known as Wei Gongzi, Ducal Son Wei. He was a prominent statesman and general of the state of Wei during the Warring States period. He

Notes to Pages 137–138   **375**

and two other members of the Four Lords of the Warring States period won great military fame when they lifted the Qin siege of Handan, the capital of the state of Zhao, and consequently defeated the Qin. "Ducal Son" is here in all likelihood an allusion to the son of the county magistrate of Kong Prefecture, while the "fine soldiers mustered by him" may represent the superb literary abilities he acquired under the guidance of his teacher Paegunja.

73. According to the *Shiji*, Hou Ying was an old and impoverished gatekeeper in the Wei capital who was known to be a wise man. Lord Xinling treated him with respect, and when he was about to go to war against the state of Qin, he received crucial advice from Hou Ying that enabled Lord Xinling to relieve the Qin siege of Handan. This final line of the poem could imply that Hou Ying was too old to follow into battle himself, or it could mean that he was capable of traveling behind the ruler's carriage but nevertheless refused to do so. Hou Ying, of course, represents Paegunja Sinjun, who did not accompany his student back to Kaesŏng, where the new ruler Myŏngjong had been installed as the military leaders' puppet-king. Another poem by Sinjun that can be interpreted as offering a glimpse into Sinjun's stern refusal to leave the countryside, return to the capital, and go back to serving the regime under Myŏngjong features in 3:18.

74. The term *hongji* (C. *hongzhi*), "red paper" or "crimson paper," refers to the certificate of success in the civil service examinations. This certificate is also often referred to as *hongp'ae* (C. *hongpai*).

75. Koyang wŏlsa appears to be a combination of Kakhun's two style names, Koyang ch'wigon and Hwaŏm wŏlsa. See 2:15.

76. The term *yŏnju* (C. *lianzhu*), "stringed pearls" or "linked pearls," can here be understood as a reference to the poetry composed by Yi Illo's sons during the civil service examinations, or perhaps specifically even to the poetic technique of *yŏnmun* (C. *lianwen*), "linked texts," in which the last word in a line is repeated as the first word of the following line.

77. According to legend, there is a great cassia tree on the moon that is a source of longevity and which no amount of chopping can fell or shorten. The term was used in the sense of majestic, long-lasting success in the civil service examinations.

78. Xixing is a village with a ferry station by the Qiantang River west of Zhejiang in eastern China. In the third of the five poems *Wanghai lou wanjing* (Nightfall scenery at Wanghai Pavilion) by Su Shi it says, "Where the green mountains end, a tower stands layer upon layer; a house on the other shore, and if I called out, there should be an answer. / Autumn winds upon the river, nightfall approaching rapidly; sounds of bells and drums sending us on our way to reach Xixing."

79. Information on this person named No Yŏngsu is unfortunately sparse. A single poem of his, entitled *T'u mogwan* (Relying on some office), is contained in *Tongmunsŏn*. It reads,

On the sea of officialdom, winds and waves are fierce; for a fish out of the
    water, all ways are blocked.
The old wife's countenance desolate; the young child's tears dripping down.

376 NOTES TO PAGES 138–139

Thin hair on the temples [as white as] a crane of a thousand years; remaining
    life [as short as that of] a firefly in the tenth month.
Indebted, know that the grace wasn't light; Ruan [Ji's] eyes once turned blue
    [as he showed his pupils].
    (*TMS* 9:6a)

80. This line is a slightly abbreviated quotation of a line from the poem *Yulin-ling* (A bell in driving rain) by the Song dynasty poet Liu Yong (987–1053): "[…] A thousand miles of fog and waves; mists at dusk engulfing, the Chu sky is vast."

81. The source says *sŏnjin* (C. *xianzhen*), which is similar to the Taoist term *sinsŏn* (C. *shenxian*), "divine immortal."

82. Apart from the entry at hand, I was not able to find any other sources mentioning this person named Ryu Su.

83. Pak Kongsŭp served under Yi Ŭimin, one of the paramount military leaders of the late twelfth century. He is mentioned in connection with Yi Chiyŏng (d. 1196), one of the infamous sons of Yi Ŭimin. In the biography of the "rebellious subject" Yi Ŭimin in *Koryŏsa* (vol. 128) it says,

> Whenever [Yi Chiyŏng] heard that someone had a beautiful wife, he would wait until her husband would leave the house, whereupon he would necessarily threaten and violate her. Whenever he encountered a beautiful married woman upon the road, he would always make his attendants grab and bring her along, and he would only stop after having defiled her. Once he had vied with the special palace guard Pak Kongsŭp over the singing girl Hwawŏnok [see 1:23], and, holding a grudge, [Yi] had drawn his sword, chasing [Pak] Kongsŭp all the way to the gates of the palace. [Yi] Ŭimin requested [Yi] Chiyŏng to be punished, but the king did not allow it. Then he requested Hwawŏnok to be exiled, upon which the king sent the palace attendant Yi Tŏgu to capture and imprison the singing girl. [Yi] Chiyŏng then broke into the prison, chased out [Yi] Tŏgu, and left with the singing girl. Furthermore he molested the king's favorite concubine, but here the king again did not get to punish him. Those at court as well as the ordinary people thoroughly detested him.

Later, Pak Kongsŭp served as a general under Yi Ŭimin and fought for him in the 1196 battles surrounding the usurpation of power by Ch'oe Ch'unghŏn and his younger brother Ch'oe Ch'ungsu (d. 1197). The relevant entry in *Koryŏsa* (vol. 129) reads,

> At the time, Kil In [d. 1196] was staying at Such'ang Palace when he heard of the uprising [by Ch'oe Ch'unghŏn], and together with the generals Yu Kwang [d. 1196] and Pak Kongsŭp he took ahold of all of the weapons in the arsenal. By deploying the palace guard, eunuchs [K. *hwan'gwan*], and slaves they mustered an army of about a thousand men. He ordered,

NOTES TO PAGE 139   **377**

"Right now, [Ch'oe] Ch'unghŏn has staged a rebellion, and he has killed many innocent people. Disaster will fall upon you soon, so you must rise up to establish great merit!" Thus they led the masses out through the palace gates. [...] Ch'oe Ch'unghŏn aligned his soldiers and met them head on. He selected about ten death-defying soldiers to serve as a vanguard, and had them dash forward at full speed, whirling their swords and screaming at the top of their lungs. [Kil] In's group saw them coming from afar, and dispersed in all four directions. Atop their horses, [Kil] In, [Yu] Kwang, and [Pak] Kongsŭp rode into Such'ang Palace, where they shut the gates and put up resistance. [...] [Yu] Kwang and [Pak] Kongsŭp committed suicide by cutting their own throats.

84. Yŏngt'ong-sa was located at the foot of Mount O'gwan in Kyŏnggi Province, in the vicinity of Kaesŏng. It is first mentioned in 946 and may have been erected by T'aejo as early as 919. See Vermeersch, "Yŏngt'ong-sa and Its Reconstruction," 2. It was one of the monasteries most frequently visited by the members of Koryŏ royalty, and State Preceptor Ŭich'ŏn stayed and studied at this temple as well. In *Sinjŭng tongguk yŏji sŭngnam* we find the following entry: "Yŏngt'ong Temple lies at the foot of Mount Ogwan. [...] The magnificence of its western pavilion really is the very best in all of Songdo. At the temple there is the *Sŭngt'ong Ŭich'ŏn t'ammyŏng* [Stele of Monk Superintendent Ŭich'ŏn], written by Kim Pusik. Moreover, the portraits of Munjong of Koryŏ as well as of Hong Chabŏn [n.d.] are stored there." *STYS* 12:9b. For a history of Yŏngt'ong-sa and an academic discussion of its recent reconstruction, see Vermeersch, "Yŏngt'ong-sa and Its Reconstruction."

85. Chen Wang, "King of Chen," is Cao Zhi. He was a son of Cao Cao and the brother of Cao Pi, the later emperor of the state of Wei. A prince in the state of Cao Wei during the Three Kingdoms period, Cao Zhi was considered one of the finest poets of his time. In his poem *Mingdu pian* (Song of the renowned capital) there is the line "Fine wine costs ten thousand cash for each gallon (*dou*)." Swartz et al., *Early Medieval China*, 264. This statement by Pak Kongsŭp can be understood as a reference to a couplet from Li Bai's poem *Jian jin jiu* (Urging forth the wine):

> From ancient times the sages and worthies are silent, there are only great
>   drinkers to leave behind their names.
> In days of old the King of Chen feasted in the Pingle Hall.
> Dippers of wine worth ten thousand cash, unrestrained pleasure and jest.
>   (Translation in Palumbo-Liu, *Poetics of Appropriation*, 43)

86. These lines constitute a slightly altered quotation of the final couplet of Du Fu's poem *Bizixing zheng Bi Yao* (So close by: A ballad for Bi Yao). Owen, *Poetry of Du Fu*, 6:29.

87. Luye *jiu* (K. Yŏak *chu*), "Wine of Lu Peak," alludes to a tale about the monk Huiyuan (334–416), who at the end of his life lived at Mount Lu, where he is said to have violated the Buddhist rules by offering wine to the famous Tao Yuanming.

378 NOTES TO PAGES 139–140

88. Huishan *quan* (K. Hyesan *ch'ŏn*), "Huishan spring water," is water from a spring located at the foot of Mount Hui in Wuxi, Jiangsu. The waters of Huishan Spring were famous for being ideally suited for brewing wine.

89. Li Guang (d. 119), a general of the Western Han, went hunting one time when he spied a rock in the grass, which he mistook for a tiger. He shot an arrow at the rock and hit it with such force that the tip of the arrow embedded itself in the rock. Later, when he discovered that it was nothing but a rock, he tried shooting at it again but was unable to pierce it a second time. Birch, *Anthology of Chinese Literature*, 128.

90. In the biography of the politician and calligrapher Yue Guang in *Jinshu* (vol. 43) there is the story of Yue meeting a friend who had not visited him in quite some time. Yue eventually learns that the last time this person was at his house, he had believed he had spotted a snake inside a cup of wine offered to him by Yue. Yue Guang later realized that what his friend had seen was not a snake but only the reflection of the string of his bow hanging on a wall.

91. A reference to a passage from *Xinlun* (New Discourses) by Huan Tan, in which Huan uses the butcher-shop metaphor to express admiration and vicarious pleasure: "The smell of meat is pleasant, so they stand in front of a butcher's shop, chewing vigorously." Cutter, "Letters and Memorials," 312.

92. This poem by Pak Kongsŭp is contained in *TMS* 9:5b.

93. It is not entirely clear who this person named P'aeng Chojŏk is. The name is mentioned in *Samguk yusa*, specifically in an entry on the Silla monk Poyo *sŏnsa* and the foundation of Haeryongwang Temple. Here it says, "In the Dading era [of Emperor Shizong of Jin, r. 1161–1189], Secretary of Hannam [Suwŏn] P'aeng Chojŏk left a poem." There exists the hypothesis that Chojŏk may be the sobriquet of P'aeng Hŭimil [n.d.]. According to a relevant entry in *Koryŏsa* (vol. 73), P'aeng Hŭimil passed the civil service examinations alongside twenty-six other candidates in the eighteenth year of King Injong's reign, 1140. The examination administrator in these particular examinations was Yi Chijŏ (see 1:1), who at the time served as administrator to the Security Council, while the second examination administrator was Im Kwang [n.d.]. At a later point in the entry at hand, however, Han Ŏn'guk is mentioned in his role as second examination administrator, who led his examination passers to pay a visit to his mentor, and P'aeng Chojŏk is said to have been among Han Ŏn'guk's examination passers. Han Ŏn'guk oversaw the state examinations in 1172, when twenty-nine candidates successfully passed. When taking all available sources into account, it may be that P'aeng Chojŏk served as a secretary in Hannam between 1172 and 1189. Furthermore, the present entry states that P'aeng served at the Kowŏn, the Office for Drafting Proclamations, when Yi Kwangjin (who passed away in 1178) was still in office at the end of his life, which implies that P'aeng probably served at the Kowŏn in the late 1160s or in 1170. Of interest with regard to this person and his name is an entry entitled "P'aeng Chojŏk, Chang Kŭngmaeng" in *Angyŏp ki* (Records of Angye, vol. 7), contained in *Ch'ŏngjanggwan chŏnsŏ* (Complete works of Ch'ŏnjanggwan, vol. 60) by Yi Tŏngmu (1741–1793), where it reads, "In *P'ahan chip* (written by Yi Illo) it says, 'The Academician P'aeng Chojŏk had an obsessive desire for books.' In *Koryŏsa* [vol. 5] it says, 'During Tŏkchong's reign [1031–1034] Chang Kŭngmaeng became senior executive [K. *Sangsŏ chwabokya*]. These persons' names can be said to make a

NOTES TO PAGE 140   **379**

fitting pair [with their predecessors]." Yi Tŏngmu here alludes to two figures from Chinese history, namely, the Jin dynasty general Zu Ti (in the Korean pronunciation Cho Chŏk; 266–321) as well as the powerful Han dynasty knight-errant Ju Meng (again, in the Korean pronunciation Kŭk Maeng; n.d.). This source, in turn, suggests that the name Chojŏk, in fact, was a style name.

94. The source says *maegye ch'wiok* (C. *maigui chuiyu*), which can be understood in the same way as *ch'angye ch'wiok* (C. *cuangui chuiyu*), "burning firewood is the same as burning cassia, cooking rice is the same as cooking jade." The phrase alludes to a person living in abject poverty.

95. Yi Kwangjin's biography in *Koryŏsa* (vol. 95) reads,

[Yi] Kwangjin, his initial name was Wŏnhyu. Through the *ŭm* [privilege of hereditary rank system] he was appointed official in the Office of Fine Wines [K. *yangon sung*], held office in the center and in the periphery, and eventually rose to the Security Council. During the rebellion of Chŏng Chungbu he was able to preserve his life by means of his mild and cautious character. At the beginning of the reign of Myŏngjong he became assistant grand councilor, then was appointed vice director of the Royal Secretariat and Chancellery, where he was authorized to control the assessment and selection of officials. When he passed away, his posthumous name was Chŏngŭi [Upright and Virtuous]. His sons were [Yi] Yuin, [Yi] Yuŭi, [Yi] Yujik, [Yi] Yuryang, [Yi] Yugyŏng, and [Yi] Yuon. Yi Kwangjin went to the Jurchen Jin in 1157 as an envoy.

96. This sentence shows that the high-ranking members of Yi Illo's family had acted in a more humble, perhaps more submissive manner toward the men of the military prior to the coup.

97. The source says *yunwŏn* (C. *lunyuan*), which can be understood as a reference to the office responsible for the drafting of the "silken threads," i.e., the royal edicts and proclamations. These officials were usually referred to as the *chijego,* working at the Office for Drafting Proclamations. I have not found the term *yuwŏn* in *Koryŏsa* or any other source but *P'ahan chip.*

98. This is a quotation from a passage in *Lunyu* 1.10, where it says, "Ziqin asked Zigong, 'When our Master arrives in a state, he invariably finds out about its government. Does he actively seek out this information? Surely it is not simply offered to him!' Zigong answered, 'Our Master obtains it through being courteous, refined, respectful, restrained and deferential. The Master's way of seeking it is entirely different from other people's way of seeking it, is it not?' " Slingerland, *Confucius: Analects,* 4. Yi Kwangjin's behavior was thus different from that of other civil elites.

99. In the North Korean translation of *P'ahan chip,* the word *kong,* "master," has been understood as a reference to Ch'oe Yuch'ŏng. See Ri, *Ri Illo, Rim Ch'un chakp'um chip,* 96. Since the overall episode, and especially the final passage, deal with P'aeng Chojŏk, however, I believe that the poet of the following verse composition must have been P'aeng, not Ch'oe.

100. This line contains a play on words with the term *saja,* which is here written

380 NOTES TO PAGES 140–141

with the words for "teacher" and "disciple," *saja* (C. *shizi*). Yet in combination with the cave, it can be read as *saja* (C. *shizi*), "lion." This second *saja* is also an epithet for Śākyamuni Buddha, who is king among humans in the same way that the lion is the king of beasts. See Muller, *Digital Dictionary of Buddhism*. The line at hand implies that a lion/leader-like teacher has brought forth a lion/leader-like disciple.

101. This line can be read as an allusion to the phrase *chŏl kyeji* (C. *zhe guizhi*), "snapping cassia branches" or "breaking cassia boughs," which means successfully passing the state examinations.

102. I could not find this Master Changgwan of the Huayan school in any other sources.

103. *Huayan fajie guanmen* (K. *Hwaŏm pŏpkye kwanmun*), a writing by Dushun (557–640), the first patriarch of the Chinese Huayan lineage.

104. The source has *yaksŏk*, "medicine and [acupuncture needles made of] stone" or "medicine and minerals," which at this point means "healing words of remonstrance pointing out the ruler's lapses." The term derives from *Zuozhuan* 23.5. See Durant, Li, and Schaberg, *Zuo Tradition*, 1117.

105. *Ch'ŏn* (C. *tian*), "Heaven," here alludes to the king, in this case King Sŏnjong.

106. Punhaeng-yŏk was located in Ansŏng, Kyŏnggi Province.

107. Yi Chae is the high official Yi Kwe (see 2:17, note 233). His biography in *Koryŏsa* (vol. 97) reads,

> [Yi] Kwe, his courtesy name was Kongje, his first name Chae. He was a person from Ch'ŏngju and his father, [Yi] Yujŏk, was executive at the Ministry of Rites. Kwe, during Sŏnjong's reign, [...] by royal edict proofread a memorial that was to be brought to the court of the Chinese Song dynasty, but by mistake he wrote the era name Da'an [1085–1094] of the Khitan Liao dynasty [onto the document]. The Song returned this memorial, and [Yi Kwe] had to retire from office. In the sixth year of the reign of Sukchong [1101], as office chief in the Ministry of Rites [K. *yebu nangjung*] he went as an envoy to the Khitan Liao. Taegak Kuksa [Ŭi'chŏn] was acquainted with Chief Clerk Yi Pok, and he asked to be allowed to offer a golden bell [to the Liao court through the embassy]. Upon the embassy's return [to Korea], the Ministry of Justice investigated [Yi] Pok's crime, and since [Yi] Kwe had had knowledge [of the affair] but had not prevented it, he was yet again dismissed from office. During Yejong's reign he switched office several times, [...] and since he was ill, he offered memorials to the throne on several occasions, asking to be allowed to retire from his post. The king then decreed that he was allowed to do so. He passed away in the seventeenth year [of Yejong, 1122], his posthumous name being Mun'gan.

108. The term Ch'ŏnwŏn, "Celestial Institute," appears several times in *Tongguk Yi Sangguk chip* (e.g., 2:18b, 9:12b) and seems to allude to the Hallim-wŏn. It might, however, also allude to the Naesi-wŏn, the Institute of Palace Attendants.

109. "Southern state" here is a translation of *namguk*, but it is not clear what exact region this term alludes to. The present entry's content also features in an entry

NOTES TO PAGE 141   **381**

on the topic of Punhaeng Relay Station in *Sinjŭng tongguk yŏji sŭngnam* (vol. 8, sec. "Kyŏnggi," subsec. "Chuksanhyŏn"), where it simply says that Yi Chae "returned from the south" (K. *chanam hwan*). *STYS* 8:19a. Yi Chae was thus on his way back to Kaesŏng from a southern part of the Korean Peninsula, probably Kyŏngsang or Chŏlla. The introductory passage in *STYS* reads, "When Kim Hwangwŏn of Koryŏ became grand master of remonstrance, he time and again spoke up in regard to certain matters, going against the king's command, and thus he was sent out to become magistrate of Sŏngju." *STYS* 8:18b.

110. The source says Punhaeng-nu, "Punhaeng Tower." This place-name has been translated as "Punhaeng Station's upper chamber" in Han and Chu, "Twenty-Four Poems," 617.

111. The source says *huanghua* (K. *hwanghwa*), which usually refers to an imperial envoy and could thus be read as an allusion to Yi Kwe's role as an envoy to the Khitan Liao. The term can, however, also be understood as a reference to the *Shijing* ode "Huanghuangzhe hua," which praises a man in service. *Huanghua* can thus also stand for an official in service. See Owen, *Poetry of Du Fu*, 1:147.

112. The source says *susin*, "who would believe," while *Sinjŭng tongguk yŏji sŭngnam* says *susin*, "have to believe." *STYS* 8:19a.

113. A reference to Jia Yi, a famous poet and reform-minded official under Emperor Wen of Han. He was dismissed from the court and exiled to become grand tutor of the king of Changsha (modern Hunan) upon speaking his mind. He is today mainly known for his two rhapsodies *Funiao fu* (Rhapsody on the owl) and *Diao Qu Yuan fu* (Rhapsody lamenting Qu Yuan). See Knechtges and Xiao, *Wen Xuan*, 376. Kim Hwangwŏn here alludes to himself as an official who spoke his mind and was sent away to the margins as a consequence.

114. "Members of the gentry" is a translation of *chinsin* (C. *jinshen*). Literati who composed reply poems include such master poets as Chŏng Chisang and Yi Kyubo. Chŏng Chisang's poem *Punhaeng-yŏk ki ch'ungju chasa* (From Punhaeng Relay Station. A letter to the Ch'ungju prefect) reads,

> In the evening I passed through the trail at the foot of Mt. Yŏnggok.
> In the morning I arrived at the Punhaeng Station and chanted in its upper
>   chamber.
> Red blossoms, caressed by bees' feelers, are half-bloomed. Green willows,
>   hiding parrots' wings, begin to turn greener.
> Viewing from this balcony, spring colors are in endless exuberance. After a
>   ten-thousand-*li* royal mission, I am eager to return home.
> Turning towards the central plain, no one is in sight, only lowlands covered
>   in white clouds, and growths of trees.
>   (Original in *TMS* 12:15b–16a; translation in Han and Chu, "Twenty-Four
>   Poems," 617)

The poem by Yi Kyubo is entitled *Punhaeng-yŏk rusang ch'a Kim haksa Hwangmun siun* (Matching the academician Kim Hwangmun's poem atop the tower at Punhaeng Station) and reads,

382   NOTES TO PAGE 141

[The man of] Kyerim did a good thing, being the first to chant his poem; the
   writing he left is full of emotions, it's on my mind both day and night.
When the horse in the stable neighs at the waning moon at dawn, or when
   the birds gather twitteringly on branches at the time of darkening mists.
From the north to the south, what limit has the road? From the old to the
   new, man grieves for himself.
The sun sinks, the waters flow, at this heartbreaking place;
at the postal station I am without words, reviewing flourishing and decline.
   (*TYSC* 10:7b–8a)

In the entry on Punhaeng Station in *Sinjŭng tongguk yŏji sŭngnam*, another poem by
Yi Kyubo is cited as his reply poem. It is the poem *Punhaeng-yŏk ch'a p'ansangun ŏkku*
(Matching rhymes written on a poetry board at Punhaeng Station while remember-
ing days of old), which reads,

Behind a yellow clay wall there is a poem that was left a long time ago;
   washed and wiped out, hardly any traces remain, and no one who takes
   notice.
Willows still drooping over that road I once walked on; rivers and mountains
   just as in the time when I formerly sojourned here.
Where is [that young girl of] dark brows, recall her uselessly; with white hair
   I've come once more, but there is only gloomy sadness.
Holding a tally I might get to return [to Punhaeng Station] some other year;
   but the muscle strength to climb up this tower, I fear it'll have left me
   by then.
   (*TYSC* 15:16a)

Other poets whose lyrical works are cited in the *Sinjŭng tongguk yŏji sŭngnam* entry
are Kim Kŭkki and Chŏng Io (1347–1434).

   115. This *Punhaeng chip* has not been transmitted. It is mentioned in the seven-
teenth-century *Haedong munhŏn ch'ongnok* (Annotated catalogue of Korean docu-
ments) collated by Kim Hyu (1597–1638). See Kim, "Haedong munhŏn ch'ongnok
sojae Koryŏ munjip yŏn'gu," 65.

   116. Pak Sŭngjung—his name is, in fact, usually spelled with a different charac-
ter for *chung* ("middle" [C. *zhong*] instead of "to infuse" [C. *chong*]) —was a specialist
in the study of Confucian ritual and an influential minister. His great-grandfather
had been a merit subject because of his support for King Hyŏnjong. See Vermeersch,
Chinese Traveler, 288. As becomes apparent in his biography, which features in the
"treacherous subjects" (K. *kansin*) section of *Koryŏsa* (vol. 125), on account of his
support of the rebellious Yi Chagyŏm, Pak Sŭngjung was well acquainted with both
Kim Hwangwŏn and Yi Kwe through their mutual service at the Hallim Academy.
Parts of his biography read, "Pak Sŭngjung's courtesy name was Chach'ŏn, and he
was from Muan Lesser Prefecture in Naju. [...] At Yejong's court he was excluded
from becoming Hallim academician reader-in-waiting [K. *hallim sidok haksa*], but

NOTES TO PAGES 141–142   **383**

together with Yi Chae, Pak Kyŏngjak, Kim Hwangwŏn, Ch'oe Sŏn, Yi Tŏgu, and others he became editor [K. *Sangjŏnggwan*]." Hence, Pak Sŭngjung, who alongside fellow academicians Kim Injon, Ch'oe Sŏn, and Yi Tŏgu also compiled the work of geomancy *Haedong pirok* (Secret records of Korea, 1106), was chosen to compose the foreword of the *Punhaeng chip* because he was well acquainted with both the original poet, Kim Hwangwŏn, and the original recipient (of the initial poem), Yi Kwe.

117. Lord Taewŏn (d. 1170; K. Taewŏn-gong), whose name was Wang Hyo, was the fifth son of King Sukchong. He was banished to the south in the wake of the Yi Chagyŏm Rebellion but reinstalled in 1129.

118. The *wutong*, i.e., the phoenix tree or Chinese parasol, is famous for its large leaves, which are said to produce mournful sounds in the rain. It functions as a symbol for a sad parting in autumn and appears frequently in Chinese poetry.

119. This poem is also contained in the ninth volume of *Tongmunsŏn* under the title *Uya yu hoe* (Having thoughts on a rainy night). The final two words in the *Tongmunsŏn* version read *sŏk chŏng*, "feelings this evening." *TMS* 9:4a.

120. The poet In Pin (n.d.) appears to have been long dead but still quite famous by Yi Illo's times. I have unfortunately not found any further information on this person.

121. During the Chosŏn dynasty, the area referred to here as Kongam-hyŏn was known as Yangch'ŏn-hyŏn. Today it is Yangch'ŏn-gu in Seoul. The relevant entry in *Sinjŭng tongguk yŏji sŭngnam* reads, "Originally, in Koguryŏ it was called Chech'ap'aŭi-hyŏn. Kyŏngdŏk of Silla changed [the name] to Kongam, and made it a lesser prefecture under the jurisdiction of Yuljin-gun. In the ninth year of Hyŏnjong of Koryŏ it was incorporated into Su Prefecture, and in the second year of King Ch'ungsŏn [r. 1308–1313] the name was changed to its present one [Yangch'ŏn]." *STYS* 10:8b.

122. During the Chosŏn dynasty, the area referred to here as Haeng-ju, "Haeng Prefecture," was known as Koyang-gun. The relevant entry in *Sinjŭng tongguk yŏji sŭngnam* reads, "Kobong-hyŏn originally in Koguryŏ was called Tarŭlsŏng-hyŏn, but Kyŏngdŏk of Silla changed its name to Kobong, and he made it a lesser prefecture under the jurisdiction of Kyoha-gun. Haeng-ju originally in Koguryŏ was called Kaebaek-hyŏn. [...] At the beginning of Koryŏ the name was changed to Haeng-ju. In the ninth year of Hyŏnjong of Koryŏ the two lesser prefectures were both incorporated into Yang Prefecture." *STYS* 11:27b.

123. *Sinjŭng tongguk yŏji sŭngnam* says, "Sohwa-sa is located fifteen leagues to the south of [Koyang] district by a lake." *STYS* 11:32b.

124. This poem is discussed in *Chibong yusŏl* by Yi Sugwang, where in the ninth volume it says,

> Long ago there lived a hermit—his name has since been lost. He inscribed a poem onto the place where he lived, which read, "Plantains resounding beyond the reed-screen, I know it is the mountain rain; / sails emerging atop the mountain-peaks, I see it is the ocean wind." Among the people were those who sought out that man's place of dwelling, but

384 NOTES TO PAGES 142–143

[from that location] they couldn't see any windblown sails. Therefore they thought that [the words of the poem] were not words of truth. In an instant, however, they spotted a fragment of a sail [the wisp of a cloud] revolvingly emerge atop the mountain-peaks, and thus they came to understand [the poem's] magnificence.

125. Kaegol, "All Bone," is an alternate name for the Kŭmgang Mountains in Kangwŏn Province. The term was particularly used to describe the mountain range's raggedness in winter, when the trees were stripped of their leaves and only the bare, bone-like rock formations were visible. *Sinjŭng tongguk yŏji sŭngnam* says, "These mountains have five names. The first is Kŭmgang, the second is Kaegol, the third is Yŏlban, the fourth is P'ungak, the fifth is Chidal, and they are the southern range of Mount Paekdu. […] Piro Peak [K. Piro-bong] is the primary peak of the Kŭmgang Mountains. […] They look like the color of snow, [like white bones,] and the name 'Kaegol' derives from that." *STYS* 17:2b; 17:8a.

126. Chŏn Ch'iyu (d. 1170) was a Hallim academician who, in the final year of his life, also served as palace attendant. In *Koryŏsa* (vol. 19, first day of the first month, 1169) it says, "In the twenty-third year [of the reign of Ŭijong], […] the king received new year's congratulations. […] The king was delighted and bestowed upon [his ministers] wine and fruits, and Hallim Academician Chŏn Ch'iyu, who had served as the headman [mainly responsible for the memorial to the throne], was assigned to the office of palace attendant." Alongside fifty other palace attendants he was killed during the military revolt of 1170.

127. As explained in note 272 of fascicle 1, Tonggwan, "Eastern Bureau," and Oktang, "Jade Hall," stand for two institutions, the Office for Drafting Proclamations and the Hallim Academy. As for the designations "Mount Penglai" and "Turtle Head," one can point to Gu Yun's poem for Ch'oe Ch'iwŏn. See note 278 of fascicle 2. The giant turtles originally appear in the Chinese creation myth of Nüwa.

128. The term *samda* [C. *sanduo*], "three often," has a number of meanings, but here it can be understood as referring to "reading often, writing often, and consulting what was written often."

129. Cao Zhi is traditionally considered the creator of the *Qibu shi* (Poem composed in seven paces). In *Shishuo xinyu,* the poem is the climax of an anecdote concerning Cao Zhi and his brother Cao Pi: "Emperor Wen [Cao Pi, r. 220–226] once ordered the King of Donge [Cao Zhi] to compose a poem in the time it took to walk seven paces. Should he not complete it, the death penalty would be carried out. Quick as an echo Cao Zhi composed the following poem: 'Boiling beans and taking them to make a soup, / Straining legumes to make a stock, / Beanstalks under the kettle burn, / Beans in the kettle cry, / Originally born from one root, / Why hurry us to fry?' The emperor looked profoundly ashamed." Cutter, "On the Authenticity of 'Poem in Seven Paces,'" 3.

130. The expression *hyŏlchi hanan* (C. *xuezhi hanyan*), "bloody fingers and sweaty face," refers to a person who is unskilled, someone who starts bleeding (probably from the nose) and breaking into a sweat when faced with a difficult task. At this

NOTES TO PAGES 143–144 **385**

point, it alludes to a person with minor literary abilities who nevertheless holds a high office at the Eastern Bureau or the Hallim Academy.

131. "Impoverished and unsuccessful scholar" is a translation of *chodae* (C. *cuoda*). For Chŏng Sŭmmyŏng, see 3:6.

132. The source says *kangnam*, literally "south of the river," which in Koryŏ times may have referred to Kangnam Province (K. Kangnam-do), today's Chŏlla Province. In *Koryŏsa* (vol. 57) it says, "Chŏlla was originally the territory of Paekche. [...] In the fourteenth year of the reign of Sŏngjong [995], Chŏnju, Sunju, Maju, and other prefectures and lesser prefectures were turned into Kangnam Province, while Naju, Kwangju, Chŏngju, Sŭngju, P'aeju, Tamju, Nangju, and other prefectures and lesser prefectures were turned into Haeyang Province [K. Haeyang-do]. In the ninth year of the reign of Hyŏnjong [1018] these [two provinces] were united and turned into Chŏlla Province." As was shown earlier, Chŏng Sŭmmyŏng was from Yŏngil Lesser Prefecture, present-day Northern Kyŏngsang Province, and appears to have had no personal relation to the province Kangnam-do. Hence, it seems reasonable to assume that *kangnam* at this point simply alludes to a region south of the capital, Kaesŏng.

133. This poem, which is also in *Tongmunsŏn* (*TMS* 9:2a), can naturally be understood as autobiographical, with Chŏng Sŭmmyŏng in the final lines alluding to his great ability going to waste in the countryside and his hope to be recognized and called to the court.

134. The source says *taehon* (C. *daihun*), "grand doorkeeper" or "grand porter," which refers to an office created in the state of Chu. See Durant, Li, and Schaberg, *Zuo Tradition*, 184.

135. The term *sinch'ong* (C. *chencong*), "Blessed Percipience," refers specifically to the aural faculties of the ruler.

136. The king's words and his summoning Chŏng Sŭmmyŏng to court are an allusion to a story in the biography of Sima Xiangru from *Shiji*. Around 137 BCE, the young emperor Wu summoned Sima Xiangru to an audience in the capital of Chang'an. One day the emperor chanced upon a poem Sima Xiangru had written at the Liang court, a poem entitled *Zixu fu* (Rhapsody of Sir Vacuous). This poem so impressed the emperor, he exclaimed to the keeper of the hounds, Yang Deyi, "Why do I not have the privilege of being this man's contemporary?" Yang Deyi, who was a Shu native, informed the emperor that his fellow townsman Sima Xiangru was the author of this piece. Emperor Wu immediately issued a summons for Sima Xiangru to appear at court. Knechtges and Chang, *Ancient and Early Medieval Chinese Literature*, 2:972.

137. The source says *hyŏllyang* (C. *xianliang*), a recommendation category for men nominated by local officials to be considered at the capital for selection and appointment to government posts. Hucker, *Dictionary of Official Titles*, 242.

138. Although he was apparently at first rather unsuccessful, Hwangbo T'ak (n.d.; see Shultz, *Generals and Scholars*, 197), who obviously was quite imperturbable in his determination, was finally made principal graduate in the state examinations of 1154, the eighth year of the reign of Ŭijong. Hereafter he did, in fact, have

386   NOTES TO PAGE 144

a successful career. In 1178, when serving as royal diarist, Hwangbo was chosen as commissioner for inspection in Ch'unju Province in present-day Kangwŏn Province to question the people about their sufferings. See *Koryŏsa,* vol. 19, eighth year of Myŏngjong, first month, twenty-second day. In 1186 he served next to Im Minbi as second examination administrator in the state examinations, and in the same year he was made headmaster of the National Academy. The passage at hand suggests that while numerous examination administrators were unable to recognize Hwangbo Tak's outstanding talents, King Ŭijong himself recognized his abilities in an instant.

139. Edward J. Shultz writes that Ŭijong was more an aesthete than a politician, a man "who enjoyed poetry and frequently wrote about the marvels of nature. He surrounded himself with gardens and artificial ponds. If he heard of a region that was said to be especially picturesque, he would visit it or try to embellish it further by planting rare trees. [...] On another occasion a flickering light was spotted moving through the forest at night behind the royal palace. Neighboring residents were alarmed until they discovered that the light was caused by Ŭijong strolling through the trees after dark." Shultz, *Generals and Scholars,* 19.

140. This poem can also be found under the title *Chagyak* (On Chinese peonies) in *TMS* 9:3b. Interestingly, the poet mentioned in *Tongmunsŏn* is Cho T'ong, not Hwangbo T'ak.

141. Sŏnbu, "Selection Ministry," can here be taken as an alternate name for the Ijo, the Home Office or Ministry of Personnel.

142. "Command poem" here is a translation of ŭngje (C. *yingzhi*), a highly prestigious kind of poetry. Poems would be written on personal order of the king in his very presence, sometimes even to match his own compositions.

143. This episode about Ŭijong and Hwangbo T'ak can also be found in the twelfth volume of *Imha p'ilgi.* At the time when Yi Illo wrote this episode, i.e., after the military revolt, the reigning rulers had turned into puppet-kings who had lost the right to make bureaucratic appointments. By describing how the kings Yejong and Ŭijong had used their power to personally appoint worthy yet unrecognized scholars to high office before the revolt, Yi Illo may be criticizing the loss of royal authority, as well as the military strongmen who appointed in the kings' stead.

144. The source says *ch'uaek,* which I have understood as an alternative name for the Chungch'uwŏn.

145. Edward J. Shultz states that "when Ŭijong was still crown prince, both his father Injong and his mother Lady Im questioned his right to succeed the throne. Injong harbored serious misgivings about Ŭijong's talent and ability to govern; his mother openly favored her second son, Ŭijong's brother Prince Kyŏng. Ŭijong won the throne only because of the staunch support of the royal tutor, Chŏng Sŭmmyŏng, who assured the royal parents that he would personally guide and instruct Ŭijong once he became king." Shultz, *Generals and Scholars,* 13. In *Koryŏsa chŏryo* (vol. 11) it says,

At first, when the king was still crown prince and [Chŏng] Sŭmmyŏng was reader-in-waiting [K. *sidok*], Injong feared that the crown prince could not continue his father's reign. Queen Im [1109–1183] likewise [predominant-ly] cared for her second son, and she meant to install him [Prince Kyŏng] as crown prince. Yet [Chŏng] Sŭmmyŏng took care of and protected [the crown prince], and for this reason he was not ousted. Chŏng Sŭmmyŏng for a long time served as a remonstrance official, and he had the elegant bearing of a minister who dares speak frankly before the king. Injong deeply valued his [upright] character, especially selected him as *sŭngsŏn*, commissioner in the Security Council, and made him tutor [of the crown prince] in the Eastern Palace.

146. "Conjunctions of wind and cloud" alludes to the meeting between a king and a worthy subject.

147. This is a reference to legends about rulers who obtained information on future great ministers through dreams or divination. Classic examples include Gaozhong of Shang, who dreamed that he would obtain a sage to assist him, where-upon he found Yue in Fuyan; or King Wen of Zhou, who divined before going hunting, whereupon he met Lu Shang, his later treasured adviser.

148. Paegunja Sinjun's refusal to serve the military regime as well as the new king but to become a wayfaring monk instead may have been an act of conscious dissidence. Yet his turn to Buddhism may also have been born out of utter necessity, for he simply may have been forced to flee from the capital and hide in the moun-tains to save his life. Whatever his motivation may have been, Paegunja Sinjun might have served as a model for dissident intellectuals in later centuries. Especially Kim Sisŭp, a major philosopher and poet of early Chosŏn, comes to mind in this frame-work. For Kim Sisŭp likewise chose to lead the life of a wayfaring monk in reaction to the usurpation of the throne by Prince Suyang, the later King Sejo. Judging from a number of descriptions in his collection of tales *Kŭmo sinhwa*, it can be assumed that Kim Sisŭp was aware of *P'ahan chip* and thus may have known about the life and dissidence of Paegunja Sinjun. Then again, Sinjun's turn toward Buddhism does not seem as surprising as that of Kim Sisŭp—Koryŏ was a Buddhist state in which Confucian ministers were all well trained in Buddhist teachings, and therefore the decision to become a monk in order to escape the regime would have come quite nat-urally to Sinjun. In Kim Sisŭp's case, the situation may seem contrary at first glance, since Chosŏn is often perceived as a thoroughly Neo-Confucian state and textbook narratives frequently characterize early Chosŏn Korea as a time of fierce conflict between Confucianism and Buddhism, where from the early sixteenth century on, after a short period of Buddhist restoration especially under Sejo, Buddhism was completely marginalized. Yet more recent research has shown that more hybrid, synchronized views on Confucianism and Buddhism did exist during these first decades after the fall of the Koryŏ dynasty. Sŏlcham Kim Sisŭp is known to have been educated in Buddhism during the early 1450s at Songgwang Temple, and thus he also possessed the necessary foundation to be able to turn to Buddhism as dissent or as escape. His decision as such, however, may in fact have been triggered by his reading about the way Sinjun had "hung up his Confucian cap" to express his refusal

388   NOTES TO PAGE 145

to lend his service to the new king and regime after 1170, which is described in the entries in *P'ahan chip* dealing with this person. For further information on the dissidence and life of Kim Sisŭp, see the introduction in Wuerthner, *Tales of the Strange by a Korean Confucian Monk.*

149. In a Chinese context, *hongqiang* (K. *hongdam*), "red walls" (which may here be "amid, i.e., overgrown by the light-green trees") are the walls of the imperial palace, or, more specifically, the perimeter walls of the forbidden city.

150. This poem, which is also contained in *TMS* 19:21b, offers different possible interpretations. One may understand it simply as a poem on a certain kind of bird. Also, the speaker may be Sinjun himself, essentially asking why he is not being made use of and why he has to live on the periphery (interpreted this way, the present episode would constitute a fitting contrast to the previous entry about Chŏng Sŭmmyŏng and Hwangbo T'ak). Yet one could also interpret the oriole as representing Sinjun, while the speaker may be understood to be the king, who is calling out to him time and again, telling him to leave the tumbledown village, shed his shabby Buddhist garments, come back to the court inside the "crimson walls," and boast with his colorful, elegant official attire while offering his service and learning to the king. Sinjun had left the capital in the wake of the military revolt, which implies that the king calling out to him from afar, from "[the capital] beyond the forest," would be Myŏngjong. Sinjun, however, apparently refused to heed the call.

151. In Yi Illo's preface to Im Ch'un's collected writings, the "Sŏha sŏnsaeng chip sŏ," Im Ch'un's escape from the capital to the south of the peninsula, as well as his frustrating failure in the civil service examinations, is described:

> Nobleness and long life are what every human heart longs for. Yet for a superior man [K. *kunja*; C. *junzi*] nobleness lies in virtue, not necessarily in high office or rank. And that what is called "long-lasting," that what does not decay, [for the superior man] it lies in his reputation [as a poet], not necessarily in long life. Long ago, [Confucius's favorite disciple] Yan Hui put his pillow high [and did not worry] while living [in abject poverty] in a back alley, yet for all eternity he will enjoy the same great reputation as the [legendary] emperors Yao and Shun. Boyi and Shuqi felt ashamed to eat the grain of Zhou, and so they picked wild beans on Mount Shouyang — yet [though they also lived in abject poverty,] their names vie for illustriousness with the sun and the moon. Thus when Laozi said, "To die, but to not disappear, that is long life," he was in principle speaking about this. Be that as it may, if one is not righteous yet becomes wealthy and noble, if one lives a long life by [spending money to] take care of one's body to become as long-lasting as the turtle or the snake, then that is exactly what Master Liu [Zongyuan] spoke of when [in his *Ku Zhang Houyu ci* (Ci to bewail Zhang Houyu)] he wrote, "[Living a] glittering [life] is a disgrace; and even if you are white-haired, you will die." How would this not be sad? Teacher Sŏha, already from an early age he was famous as a poet in the world. When he read his books, at first it seemed as though he wasn't very mindful (the text

is incomplete at this point) [but when he picked up his brush] every single word had root and stem, and it truly was as if he had directly obtained the [poetic] rules left by Su [Shi] and Huang [Tingjian]. He looked proudly upon the field of letters [i.e., the civil service examinations], thinking that he could hit the willow leaf from a hundred paces away [like the marksman Yang Youji], yet although he repeatedly took the civil service examinations, he never got to pass a single one. In the final year of King Ŭijong, his entire family met disaster, and only [Im Ch'un] himself barely managed to escape. He fled to a place of refuge in the southland, but a few years later he did return to the capital, gathering together from the embers what was left [of his family's former possessions]. He had made up his mind that he would wipe clean the shame of three failed attempts [in the *kwagŏ*], but in the end he just couldn't make a name for himself. The examination administrator, Minister of State Yi, gave him a poem as a present, which read, "Don't sigh because the red cassia has wronged you for so long; people are saying that next year you shall make principal graduate. [...]" Though he was poor, though he stumbled and fell, his name still shook the members of the gentry in such a way. [...] In our country, there has only been a single person who wore a commoner's clothes and still stood out [as a great poet and scholar] in his age, [and that was Im Ch'un]. It already has been twenty years now that he passed away, but among the learned people there is no one who does not recite his poetry with his mouth, admire him with his heart, and venerate him next to [such exemplars of unrightfully banished ministers at odds with the rulers of their times as] Qu Yuan and Song Yu. What a superior man calls "noble" and "long-lasting," it lies herein, does it not?" (*SHC* 1:1a-2a)

When Im Ch'un lived "in the southland," i.e., predominantly in the Kyŏngsang area, Yi Illo appears to have frequently visited him, as can be seen in Im Ch'un's poem *Misu pang yŏ ŏ-Kaeryŏng i arijiju wi hyang; chaksi saji*:

> Often you have visited me after I left to go into the mountains,
> upon the road there's the clinging sound of your steel cane.
> One hundred purple pears coming from the Great Gorge;
> one bottle of purest wine exchanged for Wucheng.
> For so long there hasn't been the good matter of searching out Master Yang
> > [Xiong],
> but suddenly I enjoy discussing literature and seeing Scholar Yi.
> Want to be buried in the land of drunkenness, finally never to return;
> who's out there on the road, waiting for [Tao] Yuanming? [...]
> > (*SHC* 2:20a)

The friends' meetings and partings are also described in the poem *Song Misu* (Sending off Misu):

390   NOTES TO PAGE 145

At the end of the earth, the border of heaven, solitary shadows separate;
how should I know whether I'll ever hear your voice again?
Cast adrift in an age of turmoil, who'll be the one to survive? Of all my old
 friends, the only one left is you.
Drifting about till we meet again, leaves adrift on the ocean;
clouds in the mountains, coming and going without will.
Keep the promise to come find me again in the winds of spring,
be diligent about letting fly the walking cane and setting out on the road.
 (*SHC* 2:21b)

152. This line is a reference to the poem *Xida Yuan Zhen* (Playfully in reply to Yuan Zhen) by Ouyang Xiu, which the poet wrote to express his disappointment with his own career.

The spring wind, I suspect, will not reach this place at the edge of the world;
 in the second month, flowers are not yet to be seen in this mountain city.
Remnant snow pushes down the branches, still covers the tangerine trees. Icy
 thunder rattles the bamboo shoots that were just about to sprout.
At night I hear [the sounds] of wild geese returning, and it makes me think
 of home; in bad health I enter the new year, but still I'm moved by the
 season's splendor.
Once I was a guest under the flowers of Luoyang; no need to sigh that wild-
 flowers are becoming fragrant so late.

153. This poem by Im Ch'un also features in the seventeenth entry of the fourth fascicle (*hujip* 2:17) of *Yŏgong p'aesŏl*, where Yi Chehyŏn writes,

Sŏha Im Ch'un heard an oriole and wrote the following poem: "By a farming home, mulberries ripen and barley gets dense; / from among the light-green trees I first hear the yellow bird. / As if it knew the traveler [who once was] under the flowers in Luoyang, / it solicitously warbles, unable to quit." Master Munch'ŏng Ch'oe Cha, while on night duty, heard a crane call out on Ch'aejin Peak and wrote the following poem: "Clouds swept away in the long sky, the moon is properly bright; / a drowsing crane in its pine-tree nest, purity beyond enduring. / Gibbons and birds fill the mountains, those who know these sounds are few; / alone preening its rough pinions, crying out at midnight." Both of these poems are compositions marked by the painful feeling of not meeting [the right times]. However, the mettle in [Master] Munch'ŏng's [poem] is overwhelming, and it's not comparable to Im's [poem]. (Yi, *Han'guk myŏngjŏ taejŏnjip,* 454)

Im Ch'un's poem is also in *Tongmunsŏn* under the title *Moch'un mun aeng* (In late spring, hearing an oriole). *TMS* 19:26b–27a. In *Tongmunsŏn* (as in *Yŏgong p'aesŏl*), the last part of the final line is slightly different, saying *minŭng hyu,* "unable to quit,"

Notes to Page 146   **391**

instead of *mijŭng hyu,* "never taking a rest." In *Sŏha chip,* the last line likewise says *minŭng hyu,* while the first line has *samwŏl maek ch'ojo,* "in the third month, barley gets dense for the first time," instead of *ch'imsuk maek changjo,* "mulberries ripen, barley gets dense." In *Sŏha chip* the complete first line thus reads, "By a farming home, in the third month, barley gets dense." See *SHC* 3:12b.

154. This entry and these poems are commented upon in an entry in the collection of essays and poems *Somun swaero* by Cho Sin (1454–1529). In Richard Rutt's translation the relevant entry reads,

> The Koryo monk Sinjun wrote a quatrain about hearing golden orioles: "The farmer's mulberries ripen, the barley begins to grow thick, / You do well to sing to the pink wall among the green trees. / But why in this deserted village, this desolate place, / Do you sing through the woods such short snatches of song?" Im Ch'un, a scholar, wrote: "The farmer's mulberries ripen, the barley begins to grow thick, / Now first I hear the golden birds singing among the green trees, / Like travelers returning from the pleasures of the capital, / Earnestly they sing away, and never seem to pause." Yi Inno remarked: "Although the two poems have very little in common, they are both melancholy and might have come from the lips of the same man." I do not agree. Sinjun's verses speak only of things and are exaggeratedly delicate; Im's verses speak of his feelings, and the technique is sturdy. The atmosphere of the two poems is so different that I cannot see how they could both have been written by the same man. Im's poem is modelled on a stanza by Ou-yang Hsiu: "In May the farmers' barley begins to grow thick, / The mulberry branches are fruiting and birds are crying there. / I do not know how many green trees are in Feng-ch'eng, / Nor whence they come, these fluttering golden birds." He did not simply copy the idea; he borrowed many of the words too. (Rutt, *Traditional Korean Poetry Criticism,* 128–129)

155. The biography of Hong Kwan (who was mentioned in note 44 of fascicle 1) in *Koryŏsa* (vol. 121) says,

> Hong Kwan, courtesy name Mudang, was a man from Tangsŏng District. Upon passing the civil service examinations, he was appointed vice censor-in-chief [K. *ŏsa chungsŭng*] and academician in both the Mundŏk[-kak] [Tower of the cultured and virtuous] and the Pomun[-gak]. King Yejong had early on read the [historiography] *Biannian tongzai* [of Zhang Heng (1025–1099)], and he ordered Hong Kwan to compile and gather the important remnants [of Korean history] from the time of the Three Han onward in order to bring them forth [as a book]. Furthermore he ordered him to compose judgments and argumentative essays on yin-yang writings together with Yi Kwe, Hŏ Chigi, Pak Sŭngjung, Kim Pusu, Yun Hae, and others. […] [Hong] Kwan put a lot of effort into learning, and he excelled in [calligraphic]

392   NOTES TO PAGES 146–147

writing, imitating the calligraphic writing techniques [K. *p'ilbop;* C. *bifa*] of Kim Saeng of Silla.

In 1113, when serving as minister of rites, he went to Khitan Liao as an envoy alongside Kim Ŭiwŏn. He also went to Song as a member of the entourage of an envoy. With regard to Hong Kwan the calligrapher, Yi Kyubo writes, "Academician Hong Kwan of a previous court was both an able poet as well as an able calligrapher, but in the world everybody merely thought of him as an able calligrapher, and Hong Kwan quite bemoaned this. He was not renowned for his poetry, and Hong Kwan was always infuriated by this. I personally would say that in the case of Lord Hong, poetry and calligraphy were equal to one another, and for this reason his [calligraphic] art was able to blend over and cover up [his skill as a poet]. But the case of the academician's poems, they were inferior to none." *TYSC* 5:17b–18a.

156. "Sacrificial address" is a translation of *chemun* (C. *jiwen*).

157. "Three perfections" is a translation of *samjŏl* (C. *sanjue*).

158. In the North Korean translation of *P'ahan chip* it says at this point, "its sharpness could put a hole in a tree." See Ri, *Ri Illo, Rim Ch'un chakp'um chip,* 103.

159. Kwŏn Chŏk (1094–1147). His courtesy name was Tŭkchŏng. Alongside Kim Tan, Kyŏn Yujŏ, and Cho Sŏk he was sent to Song China in 1115, where he studied at the National Academy. He passed the civil service examinations in Song China two years later and was sent back to Korea in 1118. In 1129 he served as right censor when Chŏng Chisang served as left remonstrator and Yun Ŏni as imperial diarist (K. *kigŏryang*). In the fourth month of 1141, when serving as executive at the Ministry of Rites, he was sent to the Jurchen Jin as an envoy but was not granted entry into the country on account of a possible disturbance of the farming season, whereupon he had to return to Korea. Kwŏn Chŏk, however, was again sent to the Jurchen Jin five months later. After having become a recluse at the end of his life, he passed away in 1147. In *P'ahan chip* his name is written with the character *chŏk* (C. *di*), "to enlighten," while in *Koryŏsa* his name is in many entries spelled with the character *chŏk* (C. *shi*), "suitable."

160. Yi Yugyŏng is here referred to by Yi Illo as his *tangje* (C. *tangdi*), "paternal younger male cousin." It is not clear when he held the position of *sangsŏ*. Upon his death, Yi Kyubo wrote a sacrificial address entitled *Che Taebugyŏng Yi-gong Yugyŏng mun* (Sacrificial address to Taebugyŏng Master Yi Yugyŏng), which is in *Tongmunsŏn.* Here, Yi Yugyŏng is addressed as *taebugyŏng,* chamberlain for the Palace Bursary. See *TMS* 109:14b–15a. According to the sacrificial address, Yi Yugyŏng was extremely fond of alcohol.

161. Sangch'un-jŏng, the "Pavilion for Admiring Spring," was located in the forbidden garden in the northern part of the palace grounds. Banquets and concerts were held at this place.

162. Yi Yangsil (n.d.) served as inspector of the granaries of Myŏngju Province (K. *Myŏngju-do Kamch'angsa*) in 1141. In 1146 he was sent to the Jurchen Jin dynasty as a gratitude envoy. Later, in 1163, when serving as chief minister of the Court of the Imperial Regalia (K. *wiwigyŏng*), he was promoted to chief provincial military commander of the Northwest District (K. *chi sŏbukmyŏn pyŏngmasa*).

NOTES TO PAGE 147   **393**

163. Longxi is the ancestral region of this Li/Yi family lineage, the Longxi Li Clan. The Longxi Li were one of the most prestigious clans in the Tang dynasty, whose members included the imperial family. See Nienhauser, *Tang Dynasty Tales* 2, 32. It is here, of course, a reference to Yi Yugyŏng and Yi Illo's lineage.

164. Luocheng, "City of Luo," means the ancient Chinese capital Luoyang. It here stands for the capital of Koryŏ, Kaesŏng.

165. Huang Tianjing here explains the techniques of making new use of poetic predecessors. Yi Illo in all likelihood took this quotation from the first volume of *Lengzhai yehua* (1:32; for *Lengzhai yehua,* see 1:2), where specifically in relation to Tao Yuanming and Du Fu it says, "Shangu said, 'Poetic meaning [C. *shiyi*] is boundless, but human talent does have its limits. To strive for this boundless meaning with limited talent, not even [Tao] Yuanming or Shaoling would have had that skill. However, not changing [a poem's] meaning but creating [poetry] with their words, that is referred to as the technique of *swapping the bones;* imitating their meaning and giving it [new poetic] shape and form is referred to as the method of *appropriating the embryo.*" For the introduction of Huang Tingjian's poetry and thought into Korea through such works as *P'ahan chip,* see Ryu, "Ryŏ-mal cho-ch'o Hwang Chŏnggyŏn siron-ŭi suyong yangsang." For a study of Huang Tingjian's poetic techniques as visible in *Lengzhai yehua,* see Babcock, "Aesthetics of Non-Discrimination," 170ff.

166. The expression *huobo shengtun* (K. *hwalbak saengt'an*), "stripping off an animal's hide and swallowing it raw" means indiscriminate plagiarism in poetry, stealing the ancients' poetic works and claiming them to be one's own creations.

167. Ssangmyŏng-jae not only served as Ch'oe Tang's personal study and reading room, but was also the place where some of the leading intellectuals of the early thirteenth century gathered. For more information on the importance and meaning of the study halls for the intellectual movements of this age, see Hwang, "Koryŏ sidae yusaeng-ŭi sŏjae-wa kŭ munhwa."

168. The biography of Yi Chunch'ang in *Koryŏsa* (vol. 100) reads,

Yi Chunch'ang became vice director of the Department of Justice [K. *hyŏngbu sirang*] during the time of the reign of King Myŏngjong. There was someone who at night threw an anonymous letter toward the gates of Such'ang Palace, and when the night guard got a hold of it, it was found to be [a writ] slandering [Yi] Chunch'ang and his brother. The king was weak by nature, all matters were decided by the various generals, and the king normally merely nodded his head to everything. The various generals gave credence to the writ and subsequently meant to put [Yi] Chunch'ang and the others to death. But when the king heard about this, he summoned the great general Chŏng Pangu and scolded him, saying, "Since the year *kyesa* [1173], a lot of innocent people have been harmed, and I haven't been able to save any of them. The fault, indeed, lies with me. But now, [Yi] Chunch'ang and the others [slandered in that letter], if they had really planned to commit any act of treason, the one [who wrote the letter] would certainly step forth and speak up in the open. Why

394   NOTES TO PAGES 147–148

would he throw an anonymous letter [in front of the palace gates] in the middle of the night? The fault lies with that man, so how can the various generals want to execute [Yi] Chunch'ang and the others?" The various generals tortured and questioned the man, and truly he confessed that he had falsely accused [the brothers Yi]. He was then exiled to some remote island. That man had been someone who had held a grudge against [Yi] Chunch'ang, because a number of his fields had been taken away [by Yi] at an earlier point in time. [...] In terms of office he reached the office of *ch'umilwŏnsa.*

169. The source has *mo* (C. *mou*), "so-and-so," but the word has here been understood as a reference to Yi Chunch'ang himself. Nevertheless, the sentence could also be translated as, "My late father gave this very poem to so-and-so as a present."

170. *Xiaodu ji* refers to the collection of poems by the Tang dynasty poet Du Mu (803–852).

171. The *shigu* are ten granite, roughly drum-shaped dolmens bearing engraved lyrical texts that constitute the oldest known Chinese "stone inscriptions." These Stone Drums were unearthed in Tianxing in northern China sometime before the seventh century during the Tang dynasty and are traditionally believed to have originally been inscribed sometime during the Eastern Zhou period (770–256 BCE). Texts are engraved on these cylinder-shaped stones, in the style that was used before the unification of characters under the first emperor of Qin. The content is singing praise of the emperors of Qin hunting. Due to erosion, most of these lyrical texts have become obscure. Many major poets of Chinese literary history wrote songs and odes on the topic of these Stone Drums.

172. Qiyang is Fengxiang, Shaanxi Province. The Stone Drums were placed in the Confucian temple there for protection by Zheng Yuqing (748–820), a friend of Han Yu, who responded to the plea Han Yu made in his "Song of the Stone Drums." Fuller, *Road to East Slope,* 102.

173. In the case of the *Shijing,* especially the odes "Cai qi," "Jiang han," and "Che gong" are of relevance in terms of their relationship with the stone inscriptions.

174. Wei Yingwu (737–792), a Tang dynasty bureaucrat and poet.

175. Han Yu wrote a long song entitled *Shigu ge* (Song of the stone drums). Su Shi later took this poem as a model for his own poem on the *shigu.*

176. For a translation and discussion of Han Yu's *Song of the Stone Drums,* see Owen, *Poetry of Meng Chiao and Han Yü,* 247–254.

177. King Xuan of the Western Zhou reigned from 827 to 782 BCE.

178. Ouyang Xiu wrote a substantial commentary on the Stone Drums, in which he raised three concerns regarding the fact that Wei Yingwu and Han Yu in their songs of the Stone Drums had unequivocally attributed them to King Xuan of the Western Zhou. Jeffrey Moser writes,

Ouyang's commentary begins with a lengthy reflection on the history of the Drums' reception, in which he discusses their rediscovery in the

Tang and explains that both Wei Yingwu (737–792) and Han Yu attributed their inscriptions to King Xuan [...] of the Western Zhou. He then proceeds with a critical analysis of the evidence for and against this traditional attribution: 'Of all the writings in my collection, this is the oldest. And yet there are a few reasons for concern: Of all the stele inscriptions that survive from the time of the Han emperors Huan (r. 146–168 CE) and Ling (r. 168–189 CE), none are more than a thousand years old, and all are carved deeply in large characters. Yet little more than one in ten survive.' By contrast, Ouyang continues, more than nineteen-hundred years had passed since the Drums were purportedly incised, and their inscriptions are not large and deep like those of the Han, but instead 'fine-lined and shallow' (*wenxi er keqian*). Would it not be reasonable to expect that an older, shallow inscription would show greater signs of wear and tear than a younger, deeper inscription? 'This,' he concludes, 'is the first reason for concern.' Ouyang then turns from the materiality of the inscriptions to their absence from the annals of classical scholarship. 'The characters are archaic and well-composed, the language matches the Elegantiae and the Paeans. Except for the texts transmitted in the *Odes* and *Documents*, these [Drum texts] are the only genuine traces of the literature of the Three Dynasties, and yet of all the learned and inquisitive scholars who have lived since the Han dynasty, not a single one has mentioned them. This is the second reason for concern.' [...] 'The book collections of the Sui were larger than all others. Their bibliographies include even the inscriptions of the First Emperor of Qin and the foreign books of the Brahmans. And yet they contain no record of the Stone Drums. It would be peculiar to omit what was close at hand, while recording what was distant. This is the third reason for concern.'" Moser, "Learning with Metal and Stone," 138–140.

179. "Library" here is a translation of *sŏru* (C. *shulou*), literally "tower of writings/books."

180. This alludes to the wooden shoes or sandals allegedly worn by Confucius.

181. The term Pyŏkkyŏng (C. Bijing), "Classics from the Wall," alludes to one of the most spectacular discoveries of texts in Chinese history. At one point, the old house of Confucius was to be demolished in the wake of the expansion of the palace of Prince Gong of Lu. When the people started tearing down the walls of Confucius's house, they unexpectedly discovered many bamboo-strip manuscripts, texts that were probably stashed away by a descendant of Confucius in order to escape the bibliocaust ordered by the first emperor of Qin. Many texts were discovered inside the walls of Confucius's old house, including the *Lunyu, Shangshu,* and *Liji.* They are celebrated as the *Kongbi zhong jing,* the "Classics from Confucius's Wall." Liu, *Introduction to the Tsinghua Bamboo-Strip Manuscripts,* 15–16.

182. *Fuzi* (K. *puja*), "Master," is again a reference to Confucius. "Dark Palace" (C. *xuangong;* K. *hyŏn'gung*) can be understood as an allusion to the Confucius Shrine, where the Stone Drums were kept.

NOTES TO PAGE 148

183. Fang Shu, a high minister serving under King Xuan of Zhou. He led the expedition against the state of Chu, and his military endeavors are extolled in the ode "Cai qi" (Pluck white millet) of the *Shijing*, where it says,

[...] Lo, we were plucking the white millet
In that new field,
In this middle patch,
When Fang-shu arrived
With three thousand chariots,
With banners shining bright.
Yes, Fang-shu came
With leather-bound nave and metal-studded yoke,
His eight bells jingling,
Wearing his insignia —
The red greaves so splendid,
The tinkling onion-stones at his belt. [...] Yes, Fang-shu has come
With his bandsmen beating the drums,
Marshalling his armies, haranguing his hosts.
Illustrious truly is Fang-shu, deep is the roll of his drums,
Shaking the hosts with its din.
(Waley, *Book of Songs*, 128–129)

184. Zhao Hu is mentioned in the ode "Jiang han" of the *Shijing*, which tells of King Xuan of Zhou ordering Zhao Hu to lead a punitive expedition against the tribes of Huai. Zhao Hu gains the victory and subsequently receives many precious gifts from the king and has a bronze pot made with an inscription commemorating the events. See Waley, *Book of Songs*, 131–132.

185. A reference to the aforementioned ode "Cai qi," where in the third stanza it says,

Swoop flew that hawk
Straight up into the sky,
Yet it came here to roost.
Fang-shu has come
With three thousand chariots
And a host of guards well-trained.
(Waley, *Book of Songs*, 128)

186. The Xianyun were a nomadic people that engaged the Zhou in battle for the first time during King Xuan's reign. The military victory over the Xianyun is said to have stabilized the country and contributed to King Xuan's restoration of central monarchical authority.

187. The Yue were a people and kingdom to the south of Zhou, in the area of present-day Zhejiang and southern Jiangsu.

NOTES TO PAGES 148–149   **397**

188. Meant are the kings Wen and Wu (Wen's son and successor), the founders of the Zhou dynasty, which itself was the longest-lived dynasty in Chinese history. Instead of *wu* (K. *mu*), the source at this point has *hu* (K. *ho*), "tiger." This is owing to the naming taboo, because the personal name of King Hyejong of Koryŏ (r. 943–945) was Mu, which meant that the character *wu* could not be used and a similar one had to be selected, in this case *hu*.

189. A quotation from "Cai qi" of the *Shijing*. James Legge translates the relevant couplet, "Deep rolled the sound of his drums; / With a lighter sound he led the troops back." Legge, *Chinese Classics,* 4:287.

190. This may be understood as a reference to the ode "Ji ri" of the *Shijing,* which tells of an auspicious day for a Zhou king's hunt and directly follows the two odes mentioned previously.

191. This oath, here *heshan zuoshi* (K. *hasan chaksŏ*), usually appears as *heshan daili* (K. *hasan taeryŏ*), "until the Yellow River becomes as thin as a girdle and Mount Tai as small as a grindstone." The phrase can describe an everlasting country with strong borders, or an oath of everlasting fealty.

192. The source says *un'gŭn* (C. *yungen*), "cloud-roots," but what is meant are a mountain's rocks, which lie below the clouds, at their roots. These rocks, or boulders, can be taken as an allusion to the inscribed dolmens, the Stone Drums.

193. *Kedou,* "tadpole script," refers to the ancient curvy Chinese script of books discovered in the ruins of Confucius's house. It is suggested here that the stone inscriptions adequately ought to have been contained in the collection of songs by Confucius, not merely coarsely inscribed in stone.

194. "Song collectors" (C. *shiguan*) refers to the *cai shiguan,* the officials who according to legend were sent out to collect songs from every part of the Zhou kingdom for the "Guofeng" section of the *Shijing*.

195. *Shelong* (K. *saryong*), "serpents and dragons," can here be understood as an allusion to the squiggly tadpole script.

196. "Our chariots are well crafted, our horses are well matched" constitutes the first couplet of the *Shijing* ode "Che gong," which itself is said to be based on the inscription of one of the Stone Drums. For a translation of "Che gong," see Waley, *Book of Songs,* 287. The inscription on the relevant Stone Drum reads,

Our chariots are well crafted,
Our horses are well matched,
Our chariots are in order,
Our horses are sturdy.
Our lord goes hunting, goes roaming about,
The does and deer so alert and agile,
Our lord seeks them out.
Well adjusted are our horn bows;
With horn and string we await [the animals].
We drive away the bulls who
approach with clattering hoofs,

398 NOTES TO PAGES 149–150

scampering and moving in droves.
Now we drive, now we stop.
The does and deer tread warily,
Their advance is ever so wild.
We drive out the tall ones;
They come with thud of hoofs.
We shoot the full-grown ones.
(Translation in Sterckx, *Animal and the Daemon,* 127)

197. *Siwen*, "this inscription" or "this writing," in all likelihood refers to the inscription on the *shigu*. However, as mentioned earlier, the term *siwen* also prominently features in *Analects* 9.5, where it means "This Culture of Ours" (i.e., Confucianism), which could also be meant here.

198. The term *juntian*, "Center of Heaven" or "Harmonious Heaven," is a legendary piece of ceremonial music.

199. For this "bird in flight" (or in passage) and the idea that the ancients cannot be matched, that masterful old poetry cannot be supplemented by the later-born, see note 38 of fascicle 3.

200. This line may be understood as an allusion to the hexagram *Li* (Cohesion) from *Yijing,* where it says, "Cohesion (*Li*) means "to cling" (*li*). [...] The sun and the moon cohere to Heaven." Lynn, *Classic of Changes,* 324.

201. Zhao Meng, a chief minister of the Jin dynasty. He is mentioned in *Mengzi* 6A:17. Van Norden, *Mengzi,* 157.

202. Yongshu is the courtesy name of Ouyang Xiu.

203. This is a quotation of a passage from "Zhongdu Culai ji" (Upon reading *Culai ji* [by Shi Jie] again), contained in volume 3 of *Wenzhong ji,* the collection of Ouyang Xiu's writing. Here it says, "Confucius and Mencius were indeed judged throughout their entire lives, were slandered and cast away, as they came across all sorts of difficult matters. If later generations hadn't been fair [in the judgment of Confucius's and Mencius's writings], there wouldn't be any Sages today." The quotation underpins Yi Illo's idea that the value of thought, poetry, and literary writing ought not to be judged against the backdrop of an author's poor living conditions or his inability to acquire an office.

204. The source says Sejae (with a different character for *chae*) of Puyang (in present-day Henan Province, China), but meant is O Sejae. His biography in *Koryŏsa* (vol. 102, Biography of Yi Illo) reads,

> O Sejae, his courtesy name was Tŏkchŏn, and he was a man from Koch'ang Lesser Prefecture. His ancestor was Hallim Academician O Hangnin [b. 1009]. Sejae studied hard from an early age—he, for instance, copied the *Six Classics* by hand in order to read them, and every day he recited the *Zhouyi*. He passed the civil service examinations during the time of King Myŏngjong, but by nature he was exceptional and knew little restraint. This [sort of free and unrestrained behavior] was not tolerated during his

age. Three times [his acquaintance] Yi Illo served as minister, and each time he recommended [O Sejae], but in the end he never obtained an office. He came to reside in the Eastern Capital, where he died in abject poverty. He was close friends with [Yi] Kyubo despite their difference in age, and [Yi] Kyubo privately conferred upon him the posthumous name "Teacher Mysterious and Calm" [K. Hyŏnjŏng *sŏnsaeng*].

As is alluded to here, O Sejae, though many years his senior, was close friends with the later much more famous Yi Kyubo. In the preface to *Tongguk Yi Sangguk chip* penned by Yi Su (n.d.; courtesy name Nagun) it says,

> There was Teacher O Sejae, who in the age was called a "renowned Confucian." For all his life he had rarely ever permitted anyone [to get to know him on a personal level], but when he met [Master Yi Kyubo] for the first time, he thought him extraordinary, and allowed [him in], forgetting the [great difference in] age. Someone criticized him for that, saying, "Teacher, you're older than this Yi by more than thirty years. How come you show interest in that naughty child, thereby encouraging him to act in an all too haughty a manner?" Teacher [O Sejae] replied, "It really isn't anything you lot could understand. This kid is no ordinary man. Later on he'll certainly go very far!"

Only a handful of poems by O Sejae are still extant. There is, for instance, the poem *Kŭgam* (Spear cliff; contained in the eighth entry of *Paegun sosŏl* as well as *TMS* 9:6b), which purportedly stunned a Mongolian envoy on account of its literary brilliance, or the poem *P'ung Ŭijong mihaeng si* (Poem recited on occasion of [King] Ŭijong traveling incognito), in which O Sejae sarcastically portrays Ŭijong as a dangerous dragon that is roaming around, out to harm the people and the country (see note 208 following). For interpretations of O Sejae's extant poetry, see Cho, "O Sejae-ŭi salm." Other studies on O Sejae include Yun Yŏng'ok, "O Sejae soron," *Han'guk minjok ŏmunhak* 8 (1981): 109–124; Pak Sŏnggyu, "O Sejae ron," *Ŏmun nonjip* 27 (1987): 113–130.

205. O Sejae obviously had a keen interest in passing the civil service examinations, because he sat for them on multiple occasions. He was, however, repeatedly passed over in selection, eventually never received an office, and seems to have lived in poverty. In *Tongguk Yi Sangguk chip* we find an entry titled "Kimyŏng sŏl" (Explanations on despising fame), which features a conversation between Yi and O, in which O Sejae touches upon the subject of the failed examinations and the poverty he lived in:

> Master Yi [Kyubo] asked O Tŏkchŏn, "In our country, since times of old there have been many who made a name for themselves in the world on account of their literary writing! Yet few are those whose names have also been known by the likes of cowherd-boys and servants. Your name alone—it is the only one that even all the women and children are aware

400   Notes to Page 150

of. How is that possible?" Teacher [O Sejae] smiled, saying, "Early on I became an old scholar; eating other people's food I roamed all over, and there wasn't a place I didn't reach. That's why many people got to know me. Also, several times in a row I took [the civil service examinations] at the Spring Office, but I was never successful. So the people all pointed their fingers at me, saying, 'That so-and-so hasn't passed this year, either!' That's how people became well acquainted with me. It certainly wasn't because I was so talented or anything. Moreover, being without truth and feeding off of an empty name is just like being without merit and eating up a salary of thousand bells [a reference to *Shiji,* "Wei shijia"]. For this reason I live in such poverty, because what I've despised for all my life is fame." [O Sejae] was humble and modest in this way, but then there were some who thought that the master merely relied on his talents and behaved arrogantly toward the other creatures — these people, however, did not know the first thing about the teacher. (*TYSC* 21:2a–b)

206. Xuanhua, literally "black blossom," is the name of a deity believed to be residing in the head. The term can here be understood as a reference to his eyes.

207. *Chasŏk* (C. *zhisi*), "purple stones," here means the pupils of the eyes.

208. The final word of this poem, *ki* (C. *ji*), has here been understood in the sense of *kisim* (C. *jixin*), meaning the high hopes and plans O Sejae held for his (perhaps financially well-off) future life in the wake of the desired successful completion of the examinations. The final lines can thus be read as an expression of O Sejae abandoning profane desires, his hopes for a better personal future, by closing his hurting eyes, thus shutting out the world. This poem, which Yi Illo here inserts to strengthen his point that literature and art are detached from personal wealth and that unemployed, ailing scholars in commoners' clothes such as O Sejae can, in terms of their erudition, literary writing, and state of philosophical awakening still tower high above the well-off yet narrow-minded scholar-officials employed by the contemporaneous military government, is also contained in *Tongmunsŏn* under the title "Pyŏngmok" (Ailing eyes). *TMS* 9:6a–b. A slightly different version of this poem furthermore features in the third entry of the fourth fascicle (*hujip* 2:3) of *Yŏgong p'aesŏl,* where Yi Chehyŏn writes,

Senior Supplicator [K. Taech'uk; see Hucker, *Dictionary of Official Titles,* 464] O Sejae recited a poem on the occasion of [King] Ŭijong traveling incognito, which read, "How can it be that on a day so clear and bright / black clouds are hanging low above the ground? / People of the capital, don't you go any closer [to those dark clouds], / for a dragon is traveling inside of them." Using someone else's rhymes he rhapsodized on Spear Cliff. [...] And on the topic of his ailing eyes he wrote, "Old age and illness accompany one another; I finish out the year, wearing commoners' clothes. / Black flowers [K. *hwa,* "flower," instead of *hwa,* "blossom"] have more and more veils, needs to treat [K. ŭi, "medical treatment," instead of *yŏng,* "shine"]; / purple stones have less and less glowing light. / Afraid of staring at words before the lamp; / ashamed of looking at sunglow behind the snow. / Waited to see the Golden Roster finished; / close my eyes, learn [K. *hak,* "learn," instead of *chwa,* "sit"] to forget [all lofty] plans." (Yi, *Han'guk myŏngjŏ taejŏnjip,* 443)

209. Since the subject of this sentence is not entirely clear, it could also be understood the other way around, i.e., "[O Sejae] had married three times, but [all of his wives] abandoned him and left."

210. In a lament in honor of O Sejae penned by Yi Kyubo (see note 212 following) it says that O Sejae was fifty-three years of age when Yi Kyubo was eighteen years old. Yi Kyubo was born in 1168, which means that O Sejae may have passed the civil service examinations of 1182, where Mun Kŭkkyŏm and Han Munjun served as the chief administrators. Moreover, this implies that O Sejae, who was the oldest member of the Chungnim Kohoe, must have been Yi Illo's senior by about twenty years.

211. O Sejae staying in Kyŏngju, where his maternal grandfather's home had been, is also mentioned in the ninth entry of *Paegun sosŏl.* Yi Kyubo (whose authorship of *Paegun sosŏl* is disputed) had close ties with the ruling Ch'oe House, especially Ch'oe U, and here he writes that at one point he was offered O Sejae's place in the gathering of the Chungnim Kohoe. Yi, who was still rather young at this point, states that he behaved in an inappropriate, arrogant manner on that occasion, which may hint at the political rifts between Yi Kyubo and such scholars as Im Ch'un, who despised the military. See Rutt, "White Cloud Essays," 12.

212. As can be seen in *Pohan chip* (1:44, 1:46), O Sejae's fame as a poet even transcended the borders of Korea:

> The grandsons of Academician [O Hangnin] were the three brothers [O] Segong, [O] Semun, and [O] Sejae, who were all masters of literary writing. Among them, Sejae was the best, and Semun came after him. The poetry sketches he penned throughout his life were as lofty as mountains, but all of them have been scattered and lost, and haven't been transmitted into the present age. [...] O Sejae rhapsodized on "Spear Cliff" of the Northern Mountain [Ch'ŏnma-san], [...] and there was someone from the Song dynasty who caught a glimpse of this poem. He sighed in admiration and asked, "The man who wrote this, is he still alive? If so, which office has he reached by now? If there was a man who could compose such a poem in our Song dynasty, he'd invariably be promoted to a very high office. This poem here wasn't written and recited in leisure—probably someone else came up with that difficult rhyme-pattern and commanded [the poet] to rhapsodize with it." (Pak, *Yŏkchu Pohan chip,* 153–154; 162)

After O Sejae's death, Yi Kyubo penned a lament (K. *aesa;* C. *aici*) for his mentor and friend O, which he supplemented with the following explanatory preface:

402   NOTE TO PAGE 150

Teacher Pogyang [K. Pogyang *sŏnsaeng*] O Sejae—his courtesy name was Tŏkchŏn, he was the grandson of the famous academician [O] Hangnin and came from a prominent Confucian family. They were three brothers— [O] Segong, [O] Semun, and he [O Sejae] was the youngest. Segong and Semun both were renowned Confucians of that age, but the Master was the most outstanding one of them, and his two brothers also believed that they could never match him. The academician Yi Chisim made his daughter [O Sejae's] wife, and although he sometimes acted sulky or aloof, Master Yi loved his talent and never dared to speak badly of him. Moreover, he put his energy in avidly mastering the *Six Classics,* had learned the complete *Zhouyi* by heart, and though he did not agree to learning all the other classics by heart as well, he could repeat about half of them simply from memory, because [the expressions] were so familiar to his mouth that they came flowing forth without him even being aware of it. Early on he had copied the *Six Classics* by hand, saying to the people, "When it comes to embedding a text in one's mind, reading it a hundred times is nothing compared to copying it only once." When writing poetry and literature he took on the form of Han [Yu] and Du [Fu], and even among the cowherd-boys and servants there wasn't anyone who did not know his name. In his youth he had been free-spirited, bold, knowing little restraint; in his later age he succeeded in the civil service examinations—he had curbed his principles, put in enormous effort, and was a nobleman of sincerest courtesy. Still, he was not made use of in his age, and as he stumbled and fell over [into dire straits and poverty], he was not rescued. Early on he had written letters to the two masters Cho and Yu, and the words [of these pleading letters] had been sad and mournful, the tone tactful—he really had the elegance of one of the ancients, and whoever read [these missives] would not even be aware of the tears streaming down his face. Nevertheless, he did not receive any support from them. It was terrible! The suppression and narrow-mindedness of the world—that's just how it is. Teacher [O Sejae] predicted that he would not be made use of until the very end, and so he made up his mind to depart for good. His maternal grandfather had been from the Eastern Capital, and [O Sejae] had wished to go back there, to grow old [in Kyŏngju], but since the road was long, going [to the south] on foot was not an easy undertaking. Eventually he requested to become supplication scribe [K. *ch'uksa*] [...], which enabled him to go [to Kyŏngju] riding on a post-horse. Thus he stayed there, and never got to return to the capital. In the Eastern Capital, however, there was no one who could have wielded his power to protect [and financially support] him, either, so in the end he died in abject poverty. The day before he passed away, a friend of his dreamed that he saw the Master flying off atop a white crane, and when he went to visit him the next morning, the teacher had already transformed. *Alas!* Long ago, although Qu Yuan and Jia Yi may have been neglected and rejected [at the end of their lives], at the beginning they did enjoy the favors of their lords and were able to develop what was hidden in them. With Li Taibo [Li Bai] it was the same, and in the case of Du Fu, he may have been poor, but he did become supernumerary vice minister. Alone Master [O Sejae] died without having been moistened by a single royal command—was it Heaven, was it his Mandate? If indeed it was Heaven, why did it make a talented worthy endure such ill-fatedness? Where is the principle in that? In the past, when the Master had not yet gone to the east [to Kyŏngju], he once came to visit me on my estate west of the city. He stayed for more than ten days, and we discussed what was on our minds in an intimate, close manner. At the time I was eighteen years old, had not yet earned the right to wear a hat [by reaching the age of twenty], while the Master had already been fifty-three years in age! I meant to respectfully treat him as my high senior, but the Master would not hear of it and allowed me to forget the difference in age. [...] Hereafter we spent our time with poetry and ale, and whenever we went to gatherings of renowned scholars, he would always boast about having acquired me [as a friend]. Once there was someone who ridiculed him, saying, "You're an aged Confucian master—how can you consider a kid like that your friend, and even boast with that [strange] sentiment?" The Master, however, replied at once, "That's really nothing you lot could understand." That way he praised me already during a time when my literary ability was not yet visible at all. Barely three years I got to sojourn with him, and though I was not able to fully grasp the orchid's fragrance, in many respects I was moistened by his grace. Long ago, after Tao Qian had died, his disciples privately composed his posthumous name, Teacher Jingjie. I, too, obtained the teacher's influence from an early age, and though I'm not worthy of calling myself his disciple, I still privately composed his posthumous name: Hyŏnjŏng *sŏnsaeng*. And eventually, I wrote this lament. (*TYSC* 37:1a–2b)

213. According to the ancient model system of Zhou, provincial examinations (C. *dabi*) were carried out every three years. Over the course of the entire Koryŏ period, however, civil service examinations were held exactly 251 times, which means that the *kwagŏ* were in fact carried out at closer intervals, almost every second year.

214. For a contemporaneous account of official dresses in Koryŏ, see Vermeersch, *Chinese Traveler*, 96–99.

215. These lines derive from a memoir to the throne quoted in *Hanshu*: "Heaven shares out its gifts: the beast which is endowed with sharp teeth is deprived of horns, the bird which is endowed with wings has only two feet. The principle is that anyone who receives great advantages must not capture small ones. In antiquity, anyone who was receiving emoluments would not eat the fruit of farming labor, and would not get involved in mercantile activity. It is the same idea as for heaven: anyone who receives great advantages must not capture small ones." L'Haridon, "Merchants in *Shiji*," 17.

404 NOTES TO PAGES 151–152

216. Yangzi refers to the Han dynasty poet, philosopher, and statesman Yang Xiong (53 BCE–18 CE).

217. Liu Zongyuan (773–819), a master poet of the Tang dynasty.

218. This saying, which refers to something being extremely rare and hard to accomplish, is an allusion to the rich and wealthy who are selected into high office. It is based on the following tale: "Some men were travelling together, and each expressed his ambition. One wanted to be the prefect of Yangzhou, one wanted to be wealthy, and one wanted to ascend to the heavens on a crane. One of them said, 'With 100,000 strings of cash at my waist I'll ride a crane to Yangzhou.' He combined the three." West and Idema, *Orphan of Zhao*, 262.

219. Ch'oe Hong'yun (d. 1229) reached the office of vice director of the Royal Secretariat and Chancellery and served as examination administrator on multiple occasions. Kŭgŭi is the initial name given to the mid-Koryŏ scholar-official Kŭm Ŭi (1153–1230). Kŭm Ŭi's courtesy name was Chŏlchi. He passed the civil service examination as principal graduate in 1184 and subsequently also reached the office of manager of affairs. Ch'oe Hong'yun and Kŭm Ŭi are together mentioned in this framework in *Pohan chip* 1:48, where it says,

> Master Kyŏngmun Ch'oe Hong'yun, as principal graduate of the Golden Roster, became assistant executive in letters, then entered the Chancellery, and the room he was on duty in was room number four. Master Yŏngnyŏl Kŭm Ŭi, likewise as principal graduate, became attending scholar and subsequently followed [Ch'oe Hong'yun] by entering that very same room. One night when he [Kŭm] was on duty, he created the following poem, "Number four in the Chancellery is the Prime Minister [K. *chaesin*] Room; / how many times did vice directors of the Royal Secretariat and Chancellery scholars pass through here? / Today's glory, who could obtain anything similar? / A young master principal graduate has filled in for a young master principal graduate." (Pak, *Yŏkchu Pohan chip*, 166)

220. Kowŏn, "Garden of Proclamations," can be understood as a reference to the Office for Drafting Proclamations.

221. The cyclic year *kisa* here corresponds to 1209, when Koryŏ was reigned by King Hŭijong.

222. It is not clear where exactly this Hoe-ri, "Juniper Village," was located, but most likely it was situated somewhere in the southern vicinity of Kaesŏng.

223. Concerning these Dragon Head Assemblies, the late-Koryŏ poet Yi Saek wrote, "In the past, the principal graduates of the civil service examinations held banquets, and they would refer to these as *Yongdu hoe*. Generally, occasions of welcoming and farewell, celebrations or condolences were always [held by the principal graduates] in accordance with the relevant rites." *Mogŭn'go* 25:3b. The *Yongdu hoe* constituted a highly exclusive club for a select few, and not even those who had successfully passed the examinations in second place were allowed to join. This can be seen in *Pohan chip* 2:5, where it says,

NOTES TO PAGE 152 **405**

Those who do not have the proper qualifications cannot participate in the *Yongdu hoe*. When this assembly was about to be held at the house of Principal Graduate Hwangbo Kwan, the nephew of Master [Kim In'gyŏng], the master did not get to go, because he had passed the civil service examinations in second place. Thereupon he brought forth a quatrain and sent it to them [the Dragon Heads]. It went as follows: "I've heard that venerable guests are at Your house, / in the cassia forest all of them were a single branch of spring. / Today I won't get to participate in the grand gathering; / I regret that back then I was only among the secondary men." (Pak, *Yŏkchu Pohan chip*, 201)

224. A reference to the "Fifth Yang" from the hexagram "Qian" of *Yijing*, which hints at the position of a true ruler or leader: "Fifth Yang [Nine]: When a flying dragon is in the sky, it is fitting to see the great man." The relevant commentary reads: "A sovereign's position depends on his virtue to prosper, and a sovereign's virtue depends on his position to have practical expression. When this grand and noble position is filled by someone with such paramount virtue, all under Heaven will go to him and look up to him with hope — is this not indeed appropriate!" Commentary on the images: "'When a flying dragon is in the sky': a great man takes charge." See Lynn, *Classic of Changes*, 137. The dragon, i.e., the "great man who takes charge," alluded to here is Kim Kunsu.

225. Li Ying (110–168), a leading court official of the Later Han. He was an exemplar of literati men, and a phrase alluding to success in the civil service examinations, "ascending the dragon's gate" (C. *deng longmen*), is associated with him. As Linda Rui Feng writes,

In *New Account of Tales of the World* (*Shishuo xinyu*) it says, "[Li Ying's] manner and style were outstanding and proper. He maintained a haughty dignity, and wished to take upon himself the responsibility for the Moral Teaching and right and wrong for the whole realm. Among the junior scholars, if anyone succeeded in 'ascending to his hall,' it was said that they had climbed through the Dragon Gate (Lung-meng)." In its early medieval usage, to "reach the dragon's gate" is the natural consequence of "ascending the hall" in the home of Li Ying. This usage can also be put in the context of its original meaning. In the *Analects* (XI 15), "ascending Confucius' hall" denotes a crucial milestone in learning. From the home of Confucius to the home of Li Ying, the metaphor of the dragon gate instills the milestone with a new element of sociality: beyond the accumulative study under a teacher-sage, it emphasizes inclusion in the circles of an enlightened patron conferring recognition. (Feng, *City of Marvel and Transformation*, 28)

226. A reference to the chapter "Yueming" (The charge to Yue) of *Shujing*. Emperor Gaozong of the Shang (Yin) had dreamed that he would find a great minister.

406 Notes to Pages 152–153

He had his servants search for this man throughout the entire empire, and they finally found Fu Yue, a humble man living in a hole. The emperor recognized him, made him prime minister, and according to a passage in the first chapter "Yueming" of *Shujing* said to him, "Morning and evening present your instructions to aid my virtue. Suppose me a weapon of steel—I will use you for a whetstone. Suppose me crossing a great stream—I will use you for a boat with its oars. Suppose me in a year of great drought—I will use you as a copious rain." Legge, *Chinese Classics*, 3:252.

227. Hua Xin (157–232), an official mainly of the state of Wei during the Three Kingdoms period. Together with his friends Bing Yuan and Guan Ning, Hua Xin passed the civil service examinations, and hence they were referred to as the "One Dragon." Hua Xin, the best of them in terms of the relevant examination score, formed the "Dragon's Head" (C. *longtou*), Bing Yuan and Guan Ning were, respectively, the "Dragon's Belly" (C. *longfu*) and the "Dragon's Tail" (C. *longwei*). The three figures are mentioned as the "One Dragon" in "Hua Xin zhuan" (Biography of Hua Xin; in "Weishu," vol. 13) of *Sanguozhi*. The reference to Hua Xin, the "Dragon Head," here points to the principal graduates who have come together on this occasion, while the "bellies" and the "tails" are those candidates in the civil service examinations who did not make first place and consequently were excluded from the lofty gathering.

228. A reference to the section "Dongguan Kaogong ji" (Artificer's record of the Winter Ministry) from *Zhouli*, where it says that a number of things must come together to make a fine artifact: a favorable season, the right local *qi* (energy), the quality of the material, and the skill of the craftsman. The relevant passage reads, "[When] despite beautiful materials and ingenious skill, an artefact is not excellent, it was made in the wrong season or did not partake of the local *qi* (*diqi*). The [thin-skinned] tangerine [of the south], when it is planted across the Huai, becomes the [thorny-skinned] orange." Translation in Hanson, "Robust Northerners and Delicate Southerners," 285. In ancient China, the *ju* tree, "sour peel tangerine," was for a long time cultivated in the warm climate of the south, and its fruit was considered particularly delicious. The *zhi* tree, "trifoliate orange," traditionally grew in the north, but its fruit was much smaller and not edible. It was believed that the *ju* tree became the *zhi* when it was transplanted to the north, thereby becoming a lesser variety of the citrus fruit. For an example of the use of this metaphor in classical Chinese literature, see Knechtges, "Sweet-Peel Orange or Southern Gold?," 36–37.

229. The term *kŭmgyu* (C. *jingui*), "Golden Boudoir," can here be understood as a reference to the Hallim Academy.

230. These words can be taken as referring to the social class of officials, i.e., whether they are from an important aristocratic lineage, or whether they have a military (near) or civil (distant) background. Yi Illo here stresses that individual talent and ability ought to be more valuable to a ruler than lineage or social background.

231. This sentence clearly shows that Yi Illo envisioned *P'ahan chip* (or at least some of its entries) as well as his own poetry being read and appreciated by the king. Therefore, the entry at hand may be understood as an admonition, a piece of literary remonstrance.

NOTES TO PAGE 153 **407**

232. The term *yŏmju*, translated here as "fiery prefecture," may be taken as a reference to a warm southern part of the Korean Peninsula, a region where the seedling of the tangerine tree is from. One must note that this is not the same Yŏmju as in 2:2.

233. The source says by *changhae* (C. *zhanghai*), which usually alludes to bodies of water in the hot and humid Chinese southwest, a region often associated with malaria. See Hua, Buell, and Unschuld, *Ben Cao Gang Mu Dictionary II*, 318. At this point it refers to the south of the Korean Peninsula, or perhaps to the periphery per se.

234. In the aforementioned passage from "Dongguan Kaogong ji" of the *Zhouli*, the relevant part reads, "The [thin-skinned] tangerine [of the south], when it is planted across the Huai [River], becomes the [thorny-skinned] orange."

235. The term *ch'ŏnno* (C. *qiannu*), "thousand slaves," is a reference to Xi Zaochi's (d. 384) *Xiangyang ji* (Account of Xiangyang), where it says that Li Heng (third century), magistrate of Danyang (in modern Jiangsu Province), left a thousand orange trees—which he referred to as "wooden slaves" (K. *mongno*)—to his sons to provide for their livelihood and ensure their economic independence. See Yang, *Dialectics of Spontaneity*, 191.

236. This line may be understood as a reference to the tale "Baqiong ren" (A man from Baqiong [present-day Sichuan]) from the third volume of the Tang dynasty collection of strange tales *Xuanguai lu* (Reports of the mysterious and odd) by Niu Sengru (778–847). The tale reads as follows:

> Once there was a Baqiong man, whose name we do not know. He had an orchard of tangerine trees next to his house. When, on account of the frost, all of the tangerines had been harvested, there were two large tangerines remaining, which were as big as pots. The Baqiong man thought this strange, and thus he climbed up the tangerine tree and brought them down. [Although they were huge], their weight was that of regular tangerines. He cut them open [and saw that] in each of the tangerines were two old men. Their hair and eyebrows were white, their bodies ruddy, [...] and they talked and laughed cheerfully. [The old men] were not surprised in the least even after [their tangerines] had been cut open, but only played board games with one another. [...] Another old man said: "[...] The happiness inside the tangerines wasn't lower than Mount Shang, but since [tangerines] don't have deep roots or a strong stem, we were picked and brought down by that foolish man." Another old man said: "I am hungry! I need to have some dragon-root jerky and eat it up!" Thereupon he took a grass-root from the pocket in his sleeve, [...] the shape of which was coiled and curling, just like a dragon. [...] He cut it into slices and ate it. [...] After he had eaten it, he spat it back out with water and [instantly] transformed into a dragon. The other old men took [the dragon] and from below they rose to the clouds. [...] It is not known where they are.

The allusion to this story implies that there are otherworldly abilities at the core of the tangerine trees (or the people resembling these trees).

408 Notes to Page 154

237. The "old man on Yi [bridge]" (C. *yishang lao*) is Huang Shigong, a possibly legendary recluse who helped General Zhang Liang by presenting him with a treatise on military strategy entitled *Huang Shigong sanlue* (Three strategies of Master Yellow Stone). Zhang went on to become a master tactician and aided Liu Bang, the later emperor Gao of Han, in establishing the Han dynasty in the wake of Liu Bang's victory over the forces of Xiang Yu in the wars against the Western Chu. This *Huang Shigong sanlue* then became one of the major military texts of ancient China. The entry at hand can be interpreted in different ways. It could be hypothesized that the great strategist Huang Shigong here represents Yi Illo himself, while Emperor Gao, a ruler in dire need of assistance and guidance, might stand for King Hŭijong. With the poem, Yi could have meant to ask the king to assign him to a meaningful office, to gain political power himself. As we know, Hŭijong was ousted in 1211, and Yi Illo's plans and ambitions thereby also came to naught. Alternatively, in light of the fact that many entries in *P'ahan chip* ought to be viewed as pairs or series, and bearing in mind that the following entry deals with Im Ch'un, one could construct the hypothesis that the king mentioned in this episode is not Hŭijong but rather Myŏngjong, and that the person who ought to receive an office is not Yi Illo himself but rather his friend Im Ch'un. If understood this way, Yi's conscious decision to specifically refer to a tangerine tree, a tree from the deep south that can also bloom and bear fruit in the north if treated and appreciated the right way, would make perfect sense, because at the beginning of the next entry Im is said to have returned to the capital in the north after having "sought refuge in the southland for about ten years." This interpretation would imply that the episode at hand was written at some point in the late 1180s or early 1190s.

238. With regard to his stay in the southern region, Im Ch'un stated in a letter entitled "Sa Sangju Chŏng Sŏgi So kye" (Notes to thank Secretary Chŏng So of Sangju), "So-and-so [I myself] ran into some bad luck, the family was in decline, the body was ruined, and the house was destroyed—he only wanted to save his fields and ask for a dwelling, but unexpectedly he had to leave the capital and part from his home, then scrape a meager living in the southland for a very long time." *TMS* 46:5a. After living in Yech'ŏn, Im Ch'un dwelled somewhere in the region of Sŏngju, then moved to Miryang. Around 1182 he returned to the capital, most likely to again participate in the civil service examinations. The entry at hand most likely deals with an incident that occurred in the early 1180s.

239. As extant sources suggest, though he lived a poor man's life, was unsuccessful in the civil service examinations, and had no office, Im Ch'un was known to be very aware of his intellectual capacities and his talents as a poet. Thus he seems to have come across as a rather arrogant, rude person. This can be seen, for instance, in Yi Kyubo's letter "Sang Min Sangsi Sik sŏ" (Letter presented to the attendant-in-ordinary Min Sik), where it says, "Two or three times you said to me, 'A scholar appropriately has to be modest [...], but in the present age there was the poet Im Ch'un, who relied on his talents and peered at everything around him in a jaunty manner. He finally didn't pass the civil service examinations a single time, and eventually died poor and hungry. As I see it, your talents aren't inferior to those of Scholar Im

[K. Im-*saeng*], but you're always modest and never appear rude or arrogant.'" *TYSC* 26:14a–b. One must note, however, that in spite of this source, which suggests a bad relationship, Im Ch'un and the much younger Yi Kyubo appear to have been on friendly terms. In his *Pu Yi Misu che Im sŏnsaeng mun*, Yi Illo likewise wrote that Im Ch'un peered at the world arrogantly, spoke harshly, and would never bend (see the introduction, note 112). In the extant letter "Yŏ Wang Yakchu sŏ," Im Ch'un himself writes, "This aspiration I held was very high, [...] and by that I did insult and affront people and things. Truly, there naturally was something like that. Hence, those who laughed at me, mocked me, hated me, and were jealous of me, they chided my unpretentious behavior, and when there is one barking dog, the sound of a thousand dogs barking can quickly be heard, and that way, by and by they turned me into a monster." In *TMS* 59:6b; *SHC* 4:14b–15a.

240. The original heptasyllabic poem consists of twenty-eight Chinese characters.

241. *Kongmun* (C. *kongmen*), "teachings of emptiness" or "gates of emptiness," is a general expression for Buddhism. The term alludes to the teaching that regards everything as unreal, immaterial. See Muller, *Digital Dictionary of Buddhism*. These lines by Im Ch'un, as well as perhaps the entire episode, are based on a story about the Tang poet Du Mu, which is contained, for example, in the chapter "Gaoyi" of the Tang dynasty collection of novellas *Benshishi* (Stories in verses) by Meng Qi. It goes as follows:

> When Drafter Du Mu was twenty years of age he had already achieved fame. For that year he had passed the court examinations, and his name had shaken the capital. Once he went out sightseeing to the south of the city with a few people who had passed the examinations the same year, and eventually they reached Wengong Temple. At the temple, they encountered a Chan monk who was sitting there all by himself, wrapped in rough robes. [...] When he asked Du about his name, he told him. The monk again asked: "And what is your profession, son?" The people standing next [to Du Mu] praised and lauded him [to the skies], [but the monk merely] glanced at him, smiled, and said, "I don't know any of that." Du [Mu] sighed in astonishment, and because of this incident composed the following poem: "My home is by Duqu, south of the city; / two branches of the immortal's cassia were fragrant simultaneously. / The Chan master has never heard of my name; / I've come to understand that the meaning of the Gates of Emptiness is superior."

242. Paek Kwangsin (n.d.) served as drafter of proclamations and was a member of the Haedong Kirohoe. In the second entry of the lower fascicle of *Pohan chip* he is mentioned in the following way: "At the time when Ŭimyo [King Ŭijong] conducted a royal tour of the Western Capital, Academician Paek Kwangsin was secretary in Hwang Prefecture [in Hwanghae Province]. He presented a song, which went as follows: 'The waters in the mountain streams of Tongsŏn carry the color of a thousand years; / the winds in the pines of Chŏllyŏng [Chabi Ridge] carry the sounds of

410 NOTES TO PAGES 154–155

ten thousand ravines.'" Pak, *Yŏkchu Pohan chip,* 374. He is also mentioned in *Koryŏsa* (vol. 129) in an episode with the military leader Ch'oe Ch'unghŏn:

> [Ch'oe] Ch'unghŏn built a thatched pavilion next to his home in Namsan Village, then planted two pine trees beside it. The examination passer Ch'oe I hereafter rhapsodized a *Poem on two pines* [K. *Ssangsong si*], and the men of letters from the two groups of drafters all wrote reply poems to this. [Ch'oe] Ch'unghŏn thereupon summoned the Confucian Paek Kwangsin, who was then already past the age of sixty, and others, and had them rank the poems. The poem by the examination passer Chŏng Kongbun was awarded first place. [Ch'oe] Ch'unghŏn presented his poem to the king, and the king eventually called upon him [Chŏng Kongbun] to become palace attendant.

We find a poem dedicated to Paek Kwangsin by Yi Kyubo in *TYSC* 5:18a–b.

243. In *Koryŏsa* (vol. 73) it says that Paek Kwangsin served as associate examination administrator in the examinations of 1200. The *chi gonggŏ* in these examinations was Im Yu (see 1:15). On this occasion they selected Cho Munbal (d. 1227) as principal graduate.

244. It is not clear where this Oksun-jŏng was located. The term *oksun* (C. *yusun*), "bamboo shoots of jade," can refer to outstanding young scholars, or, in this case, the successful candidates in the civil service examinations. This, in turn, may imply that the pavilion served as a traditional, fixed gathering place for examiners and successful candidates after examinations.

245. The Buddhist exegete Wŏnhyo ("Break of Dawn," 617–686) was an influential monk and vaunt-courier in the Hwaŏm/Huayan school of East Asian Buddhist thought. He served as a key propagator during Buddhism's formative period in Korea during the Later Silla. See Buswell, "Wŏnhyo: Buddhist Commentator *Par Excellence.*" Wŏnhyo had a son with a Silla princess, the famous Sŏl Ch'ong (ca. 660–730), who in his life primarily studied and taught Confucianism. Sŏl Ch'ong's *Hwawang kye* (Admonition for the Flower King), the earliest recorded parable of Korean literature, is contained in *Samguk sagi.*

246. This episode can also be found in Iryŏn's biography of Wŏnhyo in *Samguk yusa,* where it reads,

> After breaking his Buddhist vow and begetting Sŏl Ch'ŏng, Wŏnhyo put on lay clothes and dubbed himself a "Humble Householder." One day he met an actor who danced with a gourd mask, which struck him as uncanny. He made himself a gourd mask and called it "unhindered" after a passage in the *Flower Garland Scripture,* which says that "All unhindered men leave birth and death through a single path," and then composed a song and sang it until many people knew it. He used to tour thousands of villages and myriads of hamlets singing and dancing to convert the people, so that even the poor and the ignorant soon knew the name of the

NOTES TO PAGE 155   **411**

Buddha and called on Amitābha in order to be reborn in his Pure Land. Such was the conversion of the masses." (Translation in Lee, *Sourcebook of Korean Civilization*, 1:143–144)

247. "Enthusiasts" here is a translation of *hosaja* (C. *haoshizhe*).

248. "Scriptures and treatises" is a translation of *kyŏngnon* (C. *jinglun*).

249. "Buddhist *gāthās*" is a translation of *kyesong* (C. *jiesong*).

250. While the entry from *Samguk yusa*, written by the Buddhist monk Iryŏn in the middle of the thirteenth century, creates the impression that Wŏnhyo traveled the Korean Peninsula alone, singing and dancing to convert the ordinary people all by himself, the present passage suggests that the missionary work was, in fact, primarily done by many enthusiastic later Buddhists who spread the word (or song), following in Wŏnhyo's footsteps.

251. A reference to a passage from "Xiaoyao you" of *Zhuangzi*. See Ziporyn, *Zhuangzi*, 7.

252. This line can most likely be understood as a reference to *Daodejing* 1: "The Tao [Dao] that can be told of is not the eternal Tao; The name that can be named is not the eternal name. The Nameless is the origin of Heaven and Earth; The Named is the mother of all things." Wing-tsit Chan, trans., *Daodejing* (*Tao Te Ching*), in *A Source Book in Chinese Philosophy* (Princeton, NJ: Princeton University Press, 1969).

253. The term *sanin* (C. *shanren*), "mountain man," refers to a recluse or wayfaring monk. Guanxiu (832–912) was a poet-monk and painter of the Late Tang. A native of Wuzhou in present-day Zhejiang Province, Guanxiu entered a Buddhist temple when he was seven years old and took the tonsure to become a monk in his early twenties. During the unsettled later years of the Tang, he traveled to many provinces in southern China. In 902 he went to Sichuan and became an honored guest at the court of the Shu Kingdom. The King of Shu also bestowed on him the title of Chanyue dashi (Master of the Dhyana Moon) as well as the Purple Robe, the highest rank granted to a Buddhist clergyman. He died ten years later in Chengdu, Sichuan. See Hsu, *Monks in Glaze*, 104.

254. In Buddhism, the term *ijang* (C. *erzhang*), "two hindrances" or "two obstructions," first refers to the "obstruction of the defilements," which means the obstruction of wisdom caused by greed, anger, ignorance, and other forms of mental defilement; and, second, to "cognitive obstructions," which means obstructions caused by knowing too much, a hindrance to the development of wisdom. Muller, *Digital Dictionary of Buddhism*.

255. In Buddhism, *samgye* (C. *sanjie*), "three worlds," means the three realms of saṃsāra: the desire realm, the form realm, and the formless realm. Muller, *Digital Dictionary of Buddhism*.

256. These lines also appear in an entry on *hyangak*, "native music" (meaning "court music"), in the encyclopedia *Sŏngho sasŏl* by Yi Ik. In this entry, Yi Ik cites from a local gazetteer, the *Tonggyŏng chapki* (Miscellaneous accounts of the Eastern Capital), yet this quote, in fact, originally derives from the present *P'ahan chip* entry. In *Sŏngho sasŏl* it says,

412   NOTES TO PAGES 155–156

The section "Sogak" [Folk music] of *Akhak kwebŏm* [Guide to the study of music, 1493] contains the name *muae*. According to *Koryŏsa*, "The playful performance [K. *hŭi*] named *muae* originated in the western region. Its words frequently utilize Buddhist terminology, and now there exists a rhythmic performance." In the *Chasŏ* [Writings on words] it says that "*Ae* ["hindrance"] is the same as *ae* ["obstruction"; C. *ai*]." *Muae* thus corresponds to "the non-existence of what could serve as an obstruction or blockage" [K. *mu so aejang*]. The Silla monk Wŏnhyo, after the Jasper Palace had caught on fire [a reference to Wŏnhyo's sexual relationship with the Princess of the Jasper Palace during the reign of King Muyŏl (r. 654–661)], changed into lay clothes, from then on styling himself Sosŏng kŏsa. By chance he obtained a large gourd, which an entertainer [K. *uin*, a sort of jester or clown] used for dancing and playing around with. The shape of it was extraordinary and weird, and so he made it into a prop. Leaning on the following words from *Hwaŏm kyŏng*, "All unhindered men leave birth and death through a single path," he named [that object] *Muae*, and he even created a song, which streamed out into the world. Early on, when he was staying at Punhwang Monastery, composing [the commentary on] the [*Kŭmgang*] *sammae kyŏng* [*Vajrasamādhi-sūtra*], he had placed his brush and inkstone atop the horns of an ox. [...] Also, according to the [local gazetteer] *Tonggyŏng chapki*, "Wŏnhyo, long ago, beating on a [mask made of an uncanny-looking] crookneck bottle gourd, sang and danced on markets. [The mask] he named *Muae*, the 'Unhindered.' Later there were enthusiasts who attached golden bells to the top [of such gourd masks] and hung bright-colored silk at the bottom." When it is said, "The belly [hollow], resembling a cicada's in autumn; / the neck [outstretched], like a turtle's in summer," that is what is meant. (*Sŏngho sasŏl*, vol. 15, sec. "Insamun")

257. Han Xiangzi (b. 794), purportedly a nephew of Han Yu, was counted among the Eight Immortals revered by followers of Daoism. He is often seen as a patron saint of musicians. The present line may be understood as an allusion to a couplet in the poem "Yan zhi" [Speaking of intentions] contained in *Quan Tangshi*, which is ascribed to Han Xiangzi. It reads, "One gourd contains the entire world, / With my sword I behead evil monsters." Translation in Nienhauser, *Tang Dynasty Tales* 2:110.

258. Another reference to a passage from *Zhuangzi*. Ziporyn, *Zhuangzi*, 8.

259. Sosŏng kŏsa, "Humble Householder," is the sobriquet Wŏnhyo used after putting on lay clothes.

260. Rongsŏ t'ari, "Hunchbacked Yi of the Longxi Li Clan," is Yi Illo.

261. In the early Chosŏn dynasty, another so-called divine child [K. *sindong*], Kim Sisŭp, also learned to read Literary Chinese with these very two lines. We find this information in a letter he wrote toward the end of his life to his benefactor Yu Chahan [n.d.]. It says:

NOTES TO PAGE 156   **413**

I was born in the cyclic year ŭlmyo [1435], north of the *pan'gung* [the Sŏnggyun'gwan and the Munmyo Shrine] in the capital. My maternal grandfather at first did not teach me any Korean, but only taught me by means of the *Liang ch'ŏnmun* [Thousand-character classic of the Liang dynasty]. Though my mouth only brought forth chirping noises, I comprehended its meaning entirely. Hence, growing up I stammered and wasn't really able to speak, but when I was handed brush and ink, I was capable of writing down all of my intentions. For this reason I was already able to compose texts at the age of three. When they called me the "Five-year-old" [*ose*], that's when I was said to have greatly comprehended the structure of writing. In the spring of the cyclic year *pyŏngjin* [1436], my maternal grandfather instructed me with selected verses, but at the time I wasn't able to speak. Still he taught me, saying, "Flowers laugh before the railing, yet sounds cannot be heard." I pointed at a painting of flowers on a folding screen and said, "A, a." Again he taught me, saying, "Birds cry in the woods, yet tears are hard to see." I pointed at a painting of birds on a folding screen and said, "A, a." He then knew that I was able to comprehend. Thus, that year he selected about a hundred verses as well as poetry collections by masters of the Tang and Song dynasties and had me read them all. (*Maewŏltang chip* 21:20a–b)

This couplet about flowers and birds is also the first one contained in *Paengnyŏn ch'ohae*. See Hilker, *Paengnyŏn ch'ohae*, 210.

262. In this episode, Yi Illo, in a rather self-confident manner, portrays himself as an able poet in his early youth. In *Pohan chip* 2:46, however, Ch'oe Cha paints a different picture of the child prodigy and his self-perception:

Yi Misu composed his *Songch'un si* [Poem on sending off spring] as well as his *Kosŏk Pyŏngna-jŏng si ki* [Account of a poem on a lone rock by Pyŏngna Pavilion] when he was young in years, and they were in everyone's mouth. By this, in terms of fame [as a child prodigy], he strode alone [during that age]. After he had then become a Hallim [academician], he looked at what he had composed earlier in his life, and found [this poetry from his childhood days] very crude. Among the people there were those who spoke about [his early works], and he grew increasingly embarrassed — [in the end it reached a point where] he simply burned all of it. This is why none of his [early poetry] is contained in his collection of family writings [again, *kajip* is perhaps a reference to *P'ahan chip*]. (Pak, *Yŏkchu Pohan chip*, 347)

263. The *P'ahan chip* entry at hand is yet again fictionalized and reworked in *Chosŏn kojŏn chakka irhwa chip* under the title "Ri Yillo-ŭi ŏrilchŏk chaenŭng" (Yi Illo's childhood talents).

264. During Koryŏ times, Korea was divided in the *odo*, "five circuits," and the *yanggye*, "two realms." The *odo* consisted of Sŏhae Province (K. Sŏhae-do) in the

414 NOTES TO PAGES 156–157

northwest, Kyoju Province (K. Kyoju-do) in the northeast, Yanggwang Province (K. Yanggwangdo) in the middle, Chŏlla Province (K. Chŏlla-do) in the southwest, and Kyŏngsang Province (K. Kyŏngsang-do) in the southeast. The *yanggye*, "two realms," were the two northern border regions in the west (K. Sŏgye; also known as the Pukkye, "Northern Realm") and in the east (K. Tonggye). The organization into the five circuits and two border regions happened during King Hyŏnjong's reign (r. 1009–1031). One of the earliest maps of Korea was entitled *Odo yanggye to* (Map of the Five Circuits and Two Border Regions). For this, see Han, Ahn, and Bae, *Artistry of Early Korean Cartography*, 4–5.

265. The source says *ŏbu*, here understood as "royal archive" or "royal storehouse." It is not entirely clear which exact institution this term refers to, though it may be assumed that it is an alternative designation for the Ŏsŏwŏn, the Royal Library, which was located on palace grounds and stored rare and valuable books and writings. The poems ordered to be collected are most likely those on the "poetry boards," which were often hung up in such places for the public posting of lyrical works.

266. "Local folk songs" is a translation of *p'ungyo* (C. *fengyao*).

267. The hardworking yet utterly poor poet here implies that under his present living conditions he would, in fact, be better off dead. Thus, at the core this song is highly critical of contemporaneous political and social issues. In *Chosŏn munhak-esŏ-ŭi sajo mit pangbŏp yŏn'gu*, a 1963 North Korean study of developments in the history of Korean literature, this poem is cited and put into (a North Korean) context in the following way: "The farmers of that time, as is visible through the local folk songs, were mercilessly exploited, had to live under terrible conditions, and the hatred they felt for the ruling elite reached extreme levels. [Here the relevant poem is quoted in vernacular Korean translation.] This song is contained in fascicle 3 of Ri Illo's *P'ahan chip*, and it was sung among the ordinary people during the time when Ŭijong was overthrown and banished in the wake of the military revolt of Chŏng Chungbu." Ko et al., *Chosŏn munhak-esŏ-ŭi sajo mit pangbŏp*, 57.

268. This line may be read as an allusion to the *Shijing* ode "Min lao," where it says,

> Let us give no indulgence to the wily and obsequious,
> In order to make the unconscientious careful,
> And to repress robbers and oppressors,
> Who have no fear of the clear will [of Heaven].
> (Legge, *Chinese Classics*, 4:495)

In other *Shijing* translations, the relevant term *guisui* [K. *kwesu*], "the wily and obsequious," has simply been rendered as "swindlers" or "imposters." See Simon, *Shijing. Das altchinesische Buch der Lieder*, 629.

269. This is a reference to King Min of Qi (r. 300–284 BCE), a king prone to violence who apparently suffered from serious depression. The renowned physician Wen Zhi from the state of Song is said to have cured the king of an illness by deliber-

NOTES TO PAGE 157   **415**

ately infuriating him. Once the king recovered, however, he could not be dissuaded from executing the physician. Eventually, King Min of Qi boiled Wen Zhi alive, and although it took three days and nights, Wen Zhi eventually died. Through these lines, Kim Sinyun severely criticizes King Ŭijong, likening him to King Min of Qi while implying that he himself could offer a treatment for the illnesses of the dynasty and would also be willing to die for this.

270. P'yŏngyang was the capital of Koguryŏ during the latter half of the state's history. The capital was moved there from Ji'an (by the upper reaches of the Yalu River) in 427 in the wake of Koguryŏ's southward expansion on the Korean Peninsula and the military campaigns against the states of Paekche and Silla.

271. This "exceptionally talented" (K. *chunjae*) man, whose given name Yi Illo quite flimsily claims to have simply forgotten, is, of course, the famous poet and P'yŏngyang native Chŏng Chisang. Since Chŏng was a rebellious minister who was alleged to have taken part in a revolt that shook the dynasty to its core only a few decades earlier, Yi Illo apparently was not able to mention him by his full name throughout *P'ahan chip*. In terms of a modern reception and evaluation, already during the very early twentieth century Chŏng Chisang was singled out as the most significant and gifted poet of the mid-Koryŏ period. For instance, in the article "Sangha panmannyŏn-ŭi uri yŏksa — c'hong-ŭro pon Chosŏn-ŭi charang" (Five thousand years of our history — a linear look at the pride of Korea) in the popular magazine *Pyŏlgŏn'gon* (vols. 12–13, May 1928), it says, "[...] Hereafter, Paegun kŏsa Yi Kyubo was the 'tip of the brush,' as a group of master-poets such as Kim Hwangwŏn, Ch'oe Yuch'ŏng [1093–1174], Kim Pusik, Yi Illo [...] appeared, but from all these, the poems by Chŏng Chisang were especially pure, and time and again they were even presented to the Chinese Music Ministry." Moreover, Chŏng Chisang, as *the* medieval P'yŏngyang poet, enjoys high esteem particularly in North Korean literary studies. The passage at hand, and Yi Illo's almost ridiculous claim to be unable to remember the former great poet's name, are discussed in an interesting way in the influential early North Korean historiography of Korean literature *Chosŏn munhak t'ongsa*, where in the chapter "10–13 segi munhak" (The literature of the tenth to thirteenth centuries) it says,

> With regard to poetry composed in Literary Chinese, after the eleventh century a number of highly talented poets began to distinguish themselves. Among these poets, the representative figure was Chŏng Chisang. [...] Chŏng Chisang was a native of the Western Capital, i.e., P'yŏngyang, and he was active in the first half of the twelfth century. He served in office during the sixteenth king of the dynasty, Yejong, and the seventeenth king of the dynasty, Injong, first holding the office of retainer, then serving as Hallim academician and drafter of royal proclamations. Chŏng Chisang, however, was by nature free-spirited and warm-hearted. With a character such as this, he loathed the restrictions set by Confucianism, and consequently was treated with contempt by the Confucians, especially the *yangban* aristocracy from the capital of Kaesŏng. This was the reason why

416   Note to Page 157

he was forced into the Myoch'ŏng revolt and eventually murdered. Even after he had been killed, the feudalistic *yangban* bureaucrats somehow seem to have hated him, for even in Ri Illo's laboriously created work *P'ahan chip* it says, "During Yejong's reign there lived an exceptionally talented man by the surname of Chŏng—his first name is unknown," [which shows that Yi Illo] shied away from mentioning his name. His works, however, are highly regarded in the present day. (Chosŏn minjujuŭi inmin konghwaguk kwahakwŏn, *Chosŏn munhak t'ongsa*, 1:79)

Yet one must note that, although Yi Illo certainly does refrain from giving Chŏng's full name in *P'ahan chip* (also in 1:22), if one takes all the relevant entries into consideration, there can be no doubt that he held Chŏng Chisang in very high esteem both as a man and as a poet.

272. This poem by Chŏng Chisang is also in *Tongmunsŏn* under the title *Song in* (Sending someone off). In *Tongmunsŏn* the second line is slightly different, reading, "As I am sending you off toward the southern bank [K. *namp'o*], I am moved by sad singing." The second-to-last character in the fourth line is different as well, for it says, "[...] they shall swell its *green* waves." *TMS* 19:19b. In the early twentieth century, this poem appears to have been known under the title *Namp'o* (Southern bank). In the article "Sŏgyŏng-ŭi ch'ŏnjae siin, kamch'uŏjin kŭdŭr-ŭi myŏnsang ch'usangham" (The ingenious poets of the Western Capital—remembering their hidden appearances) in *Samch'ŏlli* (vol. 11, November 1934) the poem is cited, whereupon it reads, "It cannot be said with certainty at what age he composed the poems *Namp'o* and *Sŏdo*, but it is clear that it must have been during a time when his poetic imagination had already fully ripened." In North Korean publications, this poem has been referred to under the title *Taedong kang* (The Taedong River). See Kim, *Uri nara kojŏn munhak*, 47. In this historiography by Kim Hamyŏng it says with regard to the poem, "The poem shows the lyrical narrator standing on a long embankment on the shores of the Taedong River, on which the colors of the grass have become richer, greener after the rain. And it stresses the sadness felt by the narrator upon having sent off a friend by likening it to the ever-flowing waters of the Taedong River and the eternal nature of time." Kim, *Uri nara kojŏn munhak*, 47. The poem is likewise translated under the title *Taedong kang si* (Poem on the Taedong River) in early North Korean textbooks, such as the middle and high school textbook for first-year use *Munhak* (Literature), where the poem is also said to be a prime example of Koryŏ landscape poetry in Literary Chinese. Wŏn, *Munhak*, 74. An English translation of this poem by Peter H. Lee, entitled *Parting*, reads,

> After a rain on the long dike, grasses are thick.
> With a sad song I send you off to the South Bank.
> When will the Taedong River cease to flow?
> Year after year my tears will swell the waves.
>   (Lee, *Anthology of Korean Literature*, 58)

NOTE TO PAGE 158 **417**

Han and Chu's translation reads,

When rain stops, the long riverbank turns luxuriantly green.
Seeing you off at Namp'o moves me to sing sad tunes.
When will the waters of the Taedong River run dry?
Tears at parting each year add more blue swells."
(Han and Chu," Twenty-Four Poems," 622)

273. This and other poems by Chŏng Chisang are also discussed in the first entry of the fourth fascicle (*hujip* 2:1) of *Yŏgong p'aesŏl,* where Yi Chehyŏn writes,

A poem by Remonstrator Chŏng Chisang reads, "As the rain subsides over the long embankment, plants' colors are plentiful; as I am sending you off to South Bank, I am moved to sorrowful singing. The waters of the Taedong River, when will they be at an end? My tears of parting, year after year they shall add to and make rise its waves." Yŏnnam Yang Chae [n.d.] early on copied this poem, but for [the final line he put down], "My tears of parting, year after year they shall swell its green waves." I would say that the two words *chak* ["make rise" or "make something emerge"] and *ch'ang* ["swell"] both aren't perfect. Appropriately [Chŏng Chisang's original wording] must have been *ch'ŏm nokp'a,* "add to its green waves." Chŏng [Chisang] also had [the following poems]: "Land and dark blue sky do not seem far apart; / people and white clouds face each other in idleness." "Drifting clouds and flowing waters, a traveler arrives at a temple; / red leaves and green moss, a monk closes the gates." "By the light green willows are eight or nine houses, their doors shut; / under the bright moon are three or four people, leaning in a tower." "Above grinding into the Big Dipper, a house with triangular roof; / half reaching into the void, a tower with one room." "At the top of the rocks a pine ages under a single slice of moon; at the end of the earth a cloud descends upon a thousand dots of mountains." These [poems show] that the poet enjoyed using this method [of rhyming]. (Yi, *Han'guk myŏngjŏ taejŏnjip,* 441)

With regard to the wording in this last line of the poem *Song uin,* Sŏ Kŏjŏng writes in *Tongin sihwa:*

Yŏnnam Hong Chae [in *Yŏgong p'aesŏl* his name appeared as Yang Chae] early on copied this poem, but [as the final three words of the last line] he had *ch'ang nokp'a,* "swell its green waves." Teacher Ikchae [Yi Chehyŏn] thereupon wrote, "The two words *chak* and *ch'ang* both aren't perfect. Appropriately [Chŏng Chisang's original wording] must have been *ch'ŏm nokp'a,* 'add to its green waves.' In my personal humble opinion, that old man [Chŏng Chisang] simply must have enjoyed making use of the 'distorted off-rhyme style' [K. *yoch'e;* C. *aoti*]. Moreover, in [Du Fu] Shaoling's

NOTES TO PAGE 158

poem *Fengji Gao changshi* [Respectfully sent to Attendant Gao (Shi)] it says, 'Spring's colors here on the horizon hurry my twilight years, / far away tears of parting add to the waves of Brocade River' [translation in Owen, *Poetry of Du Fu*, 3:364]. The words *chŏm chakp'a*, 'add to and make rise its waves,' by and large are of the same elegance and rhyme as this very source [by Du Fu], and thus [the words *chŏm chakp'a*] would likewise have an origin [in Tang dynasty poetry] — it's just sad that I'm not able to catch a glimpse of the original [of Chŏng's poem to determine which exact words he put down]." (Yi, *Tongin sihwa*, 82)

Furthermore, in *Pohan chip* 1:30 we find the following related discussion:

The Taedong River is the river of parting for the people of the Western Capital. The scenery of its mountains and rivers is splendid, and it really is one of the most marvelous sights under heaven. When Retainer Chŏng Chisang sent off a friend there, he said, "The waters of the Taedong River, when will they be at an end? / My tears of parting, year after year they shall add to and make rise its waves." At the time, this poem was considered a "warning whip" [K. *kyŏngch'aek*; C. *jingce*; a concise text focusing on the essentials]. However, Du Shaoling says [in the final line of the poem *Respectfully Sent to Attendant Gao [Shi]*, "Far away tears of parting add to the waves of Brocade River." Li Taibo says [in his poem *Liu Yelang Yonghuasi ji Xunyang qunguan* (On my way into exile in Yelang, at Yonghua Monastery, sent to all the officials of Xunyang)], "Wishing to form good ties with the waves of Nine Rivers, / I add to them ten thousand streams of tears." All of these [lines] originate from one and the same pattern. (Pak, *Yŏkchu Pohan chip*, 125)

274. Chen Zhong and Lei Yi, two model friends from the Han dynasty. They were described as being closer than glue and varnish. See de Crespigny, *Biographical Dictionary of Later Han*, 83.

275. A reference to *Lunyu* 4.19: "While your parents are alive, [you should not travel far], and when you do travel you must keep to a fixed itinerary." A son may not travel or go abroad while his parents are alive, because a journey would entail neglecting his filial duties. Slingerland, *Confucius: Analects*, 36. Yet the line might also be understood as a reference to *Liji*, "Quli, shang" 17, which in the translation by Legge reads, "A son, when he is going abroad, must inform [his parents where he is going]; when he returns, he must present himself before them. Where he travels must be in some fixed [region]; what he engages in must be some [reputable] occupation." Legge, *Sacred Books of China*, 68 (bracketed information in the original).

276. Another translation of this poem can be found in Han and Chu, "Twenty-Four Poems," 623. In this poem, Chŏng Chisang impersonates and adopts a female voice and persona, but this is nothing extraordinary in Literary Chinese poetry. For a discussion of this literary phenomenon, see Chang, "Chinese Authorship," 204–205.

NOTES TO PAGES 158–159 **419**

277. The source here says *sangdo,* which is another name for the capital, Kaesŏng.

278. The incident when Chŏng Chisang, together with the hermit Kwak Yŏ, was part of the retinue that followed King Injong to Changwŏn Pavilion is also described in *Pohan chip* 1:21, where it says, "During King Injong's reign, Drafter Chŏng Chisang was praised on account of his poetry. Early on, together with Teacher Kwak [Yŏ] he had joined the king's entourage, spending the night at Changwŏn Pavilion." Pak, *Yŏkchu Pohan chip,* 98. Hereafter, several of Chŏng Chisang's poems are quoted.

279. Yi Illo here quoted only parts of an originally longer poem by Chŏng Chisang. Han and Chu's translation of this poem entitled "Changwŏn Pavilion" reads,

> Two soaring palatial watchtowers stand on the riverbank.
> On a clear night in the capital, there is not a speck of dust.
> Gusty winds press the sails of itinerant boats like fleeting clouds.
> Frost forms on palace roof tiles shimmering like scales of jade.
> Among the green willows are eight or nine houses with closed gates.
> Under the bright moon sit two or three people behind the rolled up curtains.
> Where is the mystical Penglai Island?
> When the dream ends, orioles sing of new spring.
> (Han and Chu, "Twenty-Four Poems," 612)

The poem is also in *Tongmunsŏn. TMS* 12:15b.

280. Chinjŏng was Kwak Yŏ's posthumous name. Kwak died in the year 1130, which means that the king who at this point ordered Chŏng Chisang to write an account was Injong. Only five years later, Chŏng rebelled against this ruler and was executed as a consequence. Yet his negative attitude toward Injong may already be detected in the following memorial.

281. Texts on a "serpent head" or "hornless dragon head" (K. *idu;* C. *chitou*) are ornamentations and writings on a gravestone.

282. The source says *chungsu* (C. *zhongshou*), "mid-range old age," a term relating to certain age-groups. It has been interpreted in various ways in different classical sources. For instance, in the chapter "Dao Zhi" of *Zhuangzi* it refers to the group of people above the age of eighty: "The greatest longevity man can reach is a hundred years; a medium longevity is eighty years [*chungsu*]; the lowest longevity is sixty." James Legge's translation as appearing in Xie, "Das Dao kennt weder Anfang noch Ende," 79. In *Huainanzi,* however, *chungsu* refers to the group of seventy-year-olds: "How do I know this is so? For most people, through a life span of about seventy years [*chungsu*] until they reach their death; they pursue things and then reject them; they divide things and then reassemble them; and daily they regret what they are doing." Major et al., *Huainanzi,* 61. In *Zuozhuan* it is also understood as a span of life between sixty and seventy. See Durant, Li, and Schaberg, *Zuo Tradition,* 443.

283. The source says *samch'ŏn,* which in all likelihood means *samch'ŏn'gye* (C. *sanqian jie*), a world system consisting of a triple-thousand worlds, i.e., the universe. See Muller, *Digital Dictionary of Buddhism.*

420   NOTES TO PAGE 159

284. The Daoist term *sangch'ŏng*, "unsurpassed purity," may be understood as an allusion to Heaven, or here perhaps the Jade Emperor.

285. Suong (C. Shouwen; "Old Man") appears to be a pen name, but unfortunately it is unclear who it refers to. The late-thirteenth–early-fourteenth-century scholar Ch'oe Hae's (1287–1340) sobriquet was Suong, but his lifetime obviously does not correspond with the time of creation of *P'ahan chip*. Kyerim is the common designation for Silla, and thus it can be assumed that the person in question was of Silla descent.

286. Wansan refers to the region of Chŏnju in Northern Chŏlla Province.

287. The source here clearly says Ch'oe Ku. A person by this name, let alone an exceptionally talented one who later served in high offices, is not mentioned anywhere else. At the end of the entry at hand, however, a number of poetic lines by this person are cited. These lines, in fact, also appear in *Tongmunsŏn*, but in this fifteenth-century anthology the relevant poet's name appears as Ch'oe Kyun (*TMS* 12:15a). Ch'oe Kyun (d. 1174), in turn, did serve in a number of high offices, such as executive at the Ministry of Rites. He also went abroad as an emissary and was renowned for his bureaucratic qualities (which he may have learned when serving as a minor clerk). Moreover, he was not only from the Ch'oe Clan of Chŏnju (or Wansan); he clearly lived in Wansan and was associated with the area in the mid-twelfth century. Hence, it seems reasonable to assume that the name given in the source, Ch'oe Ku, is actually a mistake made by either the copyist or the printer (the characters *ku* (C. *gou*), "to hook," and *kyu* (C. *jun*), "equal," look alike to a certain degree) in seventeenth-century Chosŏn, or perhaps even prior to that. The biography of Ch'oe Kyun in *Koryŏsa* (vol. 99) reads,

> Ch'oe Kyun, his courtesy name was Kanyu, and he was a person from Chŏnju. From early childhood he was talented in learning and stood out from the crowd. He passed the civil service examinations at Injong's court, was transferred several times, and eventually became secretary in the Directorate for Manufactories. At the time, Grand Councilor Ch'oe Yunŭi received the king's order to select men of letters [...], and [Ch'oe] Kyun resided at the top of this selection. When Yunŭi unexpectedly fell gravely ill, King Ŭijong sent a eunuch to ask whether there was anything he would still like to say, and he stated, "I have received the heavy favor of the dynasty, was allowed to reach the position of grand councilor, and even my sons and sons-in-law have been granted to brilliantly reveal themselves in office—again, there is nothing more to wish for. [Nevertheless,] when it comes to someone who will be of great use for our dynasty, there is no one else but Ch'oe Kyun." The king thus straightaway appointed him audience gate usher. When the Jurchen Jin dispatched an envoy to ask about the reasons for [Myŏngjong] having ascended the throne, [Ch'oe] Kyun was ordered to serve as escort commissioner. The Jin envoy inquired [about the regime change and the military revolt] time and again, but each question [Ch'oe Yun] was able make out and solve

NOTES TO PAGES 159–160 **421**

exactly, and there was never any miscommunication. The Jin envoy thus had nothing but admiration for his nimble control of speech. When Cho Wich'ong rose with his army in the Western Capital [in 1174], [Ch'oe] Kyun became commander-in-chief of the Northeastern Circuit, and he went out to bring order to various cities. [Ch'oe] Kyun visited Tŭngju, Hwaju, and a dozen other cities, and on his way back he arrived at Poryong Postal Relay Station. The king sent out Yi Kyŏngbaek [d. 1179] and gave him the authority to award [Ch'oe] Kyun with the office and title of executive at the Ministry of Rites [...] and have [Ch'oe] together with the commanders jointly attack the Western Capital. [Ch'oe] Kyun heard the order and said to [Yi] Kyŏngbaek, "As far as I have seen, the various cities are all connected with [Cho] Wich'ong, but they have two hearts beating in their breasts. If the enemy forces were to arrive [when we strike down upon the cities], it's hard to tell in which direction they would lean. But how could one's lord's command be avoided?" Thus he moved forward into the Hwaju camp. That night, [Cho] Wich'ong's generals Kim Paksŭng, Cho Kwan, and others came to attack, and the battalion commandant Yi Kŏ opened the city gates to let them in. [Ch'oe] Kyun, General-in-Chief Yi Ŭi, and Censor Chi Injŏng were captured. [Ch'oe] Kyun scolded [the insurrectionists], [...] and since there was no end to his scolding, [Ch'oe] Kyun and [Yi] Ŭi, as well as their aids, advisers, and comrades-in-arms all met their deaths. [Ch'oe] Kyun had been skilled in draft script and clerical script calligraphy. His talents in writing and his bureaucratic qualities were both superior. He had not been made use of to a great extent, and the people all thought this very regrettable.

288. The term *mongnol* (C. *mune*), "straightforward and reticent," may be understood as a reference to *Lunyu* 13.27, where it says, "The Master said, 'Resolute, decisive, straightforward, and reticent — these qualities are close to Goodness.' " *Mok* is "tree-like," meaning "simple," "honest," and "unpretentious," while *nol*, "reticent," is, according to *Lunyu* 4.24, a nobleman's quality to speak slowly but act quickly. See Slingerland, *Confucius: Analects,* 151.

289. The source here says *feiran* (K. *piryŏn*), which may be understood as a reference to a passage from "Kongzi shijia," Confucius's biography in *Shiji,* where it says, "The youngsters in my school are crazy madly unsophisticated, and though they are brilliant in completing writings, I have no idea how to trim them."

290. In terms of examination results, Koryŏ dynasty civil service examinations were divided into different ranks or grades: *kapkwa* ("first grade"), *ŭlgwa* ("second grade"), *pyŏnggwa* ("third grade"), and *tongjinsa.* The best examination passers originally belonged to the *kapkwa*-category, but this grade was discontinued after a while. Henceforth, the three best examination passers belonged to the *ŭl*-grade, while the seven best examination passers hereafter, meaning places four to ten of that year's class, belonged to the *pyŏng*-grade. Ch'oe was thus not at the absolute top of his class, but still a highly successful candidate in literary composition. In 1460,

422   NOTES TO PAGE 160

already during the Chosŏn dynasty, the number of examination passers awarded the *pyŏng*-grade increased to twenty-three.

291. The source says *sŏkkŏ* (C. *shiqu*), "stone canal," which originally refers to the *Shiqu ge*, "Stone Canal Pavilion," a pavilion located inside the western Han imperial palace at Chang'an. A major conference of Confucian scholars dealing with a reinterpretation of the Confucian canon was held there in 51 BCE. Thus the term can be understood as referring to the royal palace library where canonized books were stored. Another name for this palace library is Pisŏ-gak.

292. The characters are not entirely clear at this point. It may read *jianjian* (K. *kŏn'gŏn*), which makes sense if understood in the way it appears in "Lisao" of *Chuci*: "How well I know that loyalty [*jianjian*] brings disaster; yet I will endure: I cannot give up." Hawkes, *Songs of the South*, 69. However, if one takes the following two characters, *feigong* (K. *pigung*) into consideration, it may also read *jianjian* (K. *kŏn'gŏn*). *Jianjian feigong* could then be understood as an abbreviated quotation from hexagram "Jian" of *Yijing*, where it says, "The minister of the king suffers Adversity upon Adversity, but it is not on his own account." Lynn, *Classic of Changes*, 376. The present translation attempts to reflect both possible readings.

293. This *Yŏngnyu si* belongs to the genre of "Poems on things" (C. *yongwu shi*; K. *yŏngmul si*), i.e., poems dealing with particular objects, plants, or animals, waterways, buildings, or food and drink. *Yongwu shi* were especially popular during the Qi-Liang period (479–557), and they normally constitute poetic works of some more intent.

294. Xizi is another name for Xi Shi, one of the four famous beauties of Chinese history.

295. Xiaoman was one of two concubines of the Tang dynasty poet Bai Juyi, the other being Fansu. While Fansu is said to have been a great singer, Xiaoman was a renowned dancer. In a poem, Bai Juyi wrote "Cherries are Fansu's lips, a willow Xiaoman's waist."

296. These two lines appear in a slightly altered way as part of a longer poem contained in *Tongmunsŏn*. The author named in *Tongmunsŏn* is the aforementioned Ch'oe Kyun. The poem reads,

> Creation had manifold feelings when it brought forth the willow's branches;
> trimming what comes out with scissors again makes it even more enticing.
> When snow melts, it is dimly coated in colors of gold;
> when days are warm, it lightly drags threads of green.
> Xizi's brows were knitted, as if she had a bitterness;
> Xiaoman's waist was slender, she was of unrivaled charm.
> Holding a sinecure in a desolate place, where people are few;
> how carefree did it sway when blown by the breeze of spring.
> (*TMS* 12:15a–b)

297. This line is an allusion to the *Dengtuzi haose fu* (Fu on the lechery of Master Dengtu) from *Wen xuan*. In the story, when Song Yu is accused of lechery by Master

NOTES TO PAGES 160–161 **423**

Dengtu and threatened with expulsion from court, he replies, "Of all the women in the world none is more beautiful than those in Ch'u [Chu]. Of the women in Ch'u, none is more beautiful than the daughter of my eastern neighbor. […] For three years this girl has been climbing my garden wall and peeping at me, but I have never succumbed." Translation in Knechtges, "Wit, Humor, and Satire," 87. The young woman from the story is here likened to a yet unopened beautiful peony.

298. This is a reference to the tale of the poet Sima Xiangru and his wife, Zhuo Wenjun, which, for example, appears in *Shiji* 117. Zhuo Wenjun had been married, but when her husband died, she returned to the home of her wealthy father, Zhuo Wangsun, in the western commandery of Shu. At the same time, Sima Xiangru, a member of the literati who had just lost his patron, likewise stayed in Shu. Zhuo Wangsun hosted a banquet at which Sima Xiangru agreed to play the *qin* (a seven-stringed instrument similar to a zither). Sima Xiangru had apparently heard how beautiful and talented Zhuo Wenjun was and thus he used the banquet to gain access to the house. Zhuo Wenjun was quickly seduced by the sound of the zither and, secretly peering at him from her room, i.e., the other side of the wall, instantly fell in love with Sima Xiangru. Sima Xiangru then bribed a servant to declare on his behalf his love to Zhuo Wenjun, who responded by running off with Sima Xiangru. Infuriated, her father swore to cut them off. The couple lived in poverty and later opened a wine shop. When her father heard of their standard of living, he pardoned them and they were able to marry. Lee and Stefanowska, *Biographical Dictionary of Chinese Women*, 257–258.

299. Sŏ Munwŏn (n.d.). It is unclear who this person was.

300. Kwŏn Tollye (n.d.) was a Confucian official who became a recluse in the wake of the 1170 coup. Thus, he probably belonged to the same group of dissident intellectuals as Paegunja Sinjun. He appears to have been the eldest son of Kwŏn Chŏk, an official who served during Yejong's reign. Kwŏn Tollye is mentioned in *Pohan chip* 1:46 and 2:35.

301. Taizhen is the Taoist name of Yang Guifei, whose love affair with Emperor Xuanzong of Tang is the topic of Bai Juyi's *Changhen ge*. The emperor fell in love with her when he saw her bathing in Huaqing hot spring. In Bai's poem it says, "In the coolness of springtime, she was permitted to bathe in the Hua-ch'ing pools, / Where the slickening waters of the hotsprings washed over her firm flesh." Kroll, "Po Chü-i's 'Song of Lasting Regret,' " 97.

302. A reference to a passage from *Han Feizi* dealing with the officials Ximen Bao and Dong Anyu. Here it says that Ximen Bao was quick-tempered and purposely wore hide on his feet to make himself slow; Dong Anyu, being slow-minded, wore bowstrings on his feet to make himself quick. See Smith, *Declarations of the Perfected*, 233.

303. A quote from *Mengzi* 2B:15: "Gongsun Chou continued, 'May I ask what is meant by "floodlike *qi*"?' Mengzi replied, 'It is difficult to explain. It is a *qi* that is supremely great and supremely unyielding. […] It is produced by accumulated righteousness. It cannot be obtained by a seizure of righteousness.' " Van Norden, *Mengzi*, 39.

304. In the source we here find an inserted slip of paper (which at one point

424 NOTES TO PAGES 161–162

was apparently pasted onto the page) with a handwritten quote of a passage from the fourth volume of Ŏ Sukkwŏn's *P'aegwan chapki* on it. It reads,

> There was a superintendent [K. *Pyŏljwa*] by the name of Yi who said, "Early on I obtained a medical formula which read: 'If a person unexpectedly dies a sudden death, one simply has to pierce his ring-finger, withdraw some of the blood, and write the character *kwi* ["ghost"] onto his forehead — then he will be revived.' At first I didn't give this any credence, but then there was a man who contracted a serious disease and died a sudden death. After about half a day had passed, the entire area below his heart was ice-cold. I pierced the ring-finger of his left hand, and after quite some time there finally trickled out some of his blood. Eventually I leaned on the medical formula, just to test whether it would really result in reviving him. All in all, I managed to bring three people back to life." Although I didn't get to investigate deeper into the underlying principle, I did get to see this result. It was strange, indeed!

This quote from *P'aegwan chapki* seems to lack any readily discernable content-related connection to the *P'ahan chip* entry it is attached to, and thus one may assume that the slip of paper was put between the pages accidentally or for unclear reasons.

305. *Sagong*, "minister of works," a title of great prestige from antiquity. One of the three dukes (C. *sangong*) who were paramount dignitaries of the central government. See Hucker, *Dictionary of Official Titles*, 450.

306. The person whose name Yi Illo cannot openly mention at this point is Wang Ŭi (d. 1216), the eldest son of Prince Yangyanggong (n.d.). Prince Yangyanggong was the second son of King Sinjong and the older brother of King Hŭijong. His name was Wang Sŏ. The source here refers to him as *hwangdae che*, which I have understood as *t'aehwang che*, "Mighty Sovereign's younger brother" or "younger brother of the Crown Prince." When Hŭijong was dethroned by Ch'oe Ch'unghŏn in 1211, the king's older brother Yangyanggong was likewise exiled. Due to Wang Ŭi's relation to the overthrown Hŭijong (his uncle), Yi Illo obviously cannot call him by his name in the entry at hand.

307. This sentence implies that the entry at hand must have been written and inserted after Wang Ŭi's death, i.e., after 1216.

308. It is not clear who this Kwano is, and also whether Kwano was this person's sobriquet, his courtesy name, or his dharma name. Since he was able to stay at Wang Ŭi's mansion and look for the poet's surviving manuscripts, it appears as though he was well acquainted with Wang before his death.

309. It is not entirely clear to me who meant to have these poetic pieces carved on woodblock in the future (and who consequently wrote the following text), Yi Illo or Kwano, but I have taken this sentence to mean that Yi wanted to commission the carving.

310. When a Chinese ruler would pass on the realm and his power, he would wrap earth from every region in reeds and present it to his heir.

Epilogue

1. *Nanhuapian* means the *Zhuangzi*, which is also known as *Nanhua zhenjing* (Pure classic of Nanhua).

2. This sentence is from the chapter "Yuyan" (Metaphorical language) from *Zhuangzi*.

3. *Daijing* is a reference to the *Dadai liji* (Records of the rites of the elder Dai).

4. Accordingly, in *Zhongyong* 18 it says, "Confucius said: "The only one who didn't suffer from grief was King Wen, since his father was King Chi and his son was King Wu. His father set him up and his son continued his ways." See Charles Muller, trans., *The Doctrine of the Mean* (accessed June 26, 2023), http://www.acmuller.net/con-dao/docofmean.html.

5. *Taixuanjing* (Classic of supreme mystery) is a divinatory text written by the mid–Han period Confucian Yang Xiong. Yang Wu was Yang Xiong's son.

6. *Lulun*, the "*Lun[yu]* of Lu," refers to the *Lunyu*.

7. This is a quotation from *Lunyu* 1.11. See Charles Muller, trans., *The Analects of Confucius* (accessed June 26, 2023), http://www.acmuller.net/con-dao/analects.html.

8. The Tiande era of the Jurchen Jin dynasty lasted from 1149 to 1152. The fourth year is 1152, which corresponds to the sixth year of the reign of King Ŭijong of Koryŏ.

9. *Saŏp*, director of studies at the T'aehak, the National Academy.

10. Yi Illo's poem is filled with allusions to the An Lushan rebellion as it is portrayed in Bai Juyi's *Changhen ge*. In Paul W. Kroll's translation, the relevant part reads,

> The high sites of Mount Li's palace reached into clouds in the blue,
> And transcendent music, wafted on the wind, was heard there everywhere.
> Measured songs, languorous dancing merged with sound of strings and
> bamboo,
> As the sovereign king looked on all day long, never getting enough.
> Until, out of Yi-yang, horse-borne war-drums came, shaking the earth,
> To dismay and smash the melody of "Rainbow Skirts and Feathered
> Vestments."
> (Kroll, *Po Chü-i's Song of Lasting Regret*, 98)

"Pig-dragon" is a reference to An Lushan, who purportedly dreamed one day that he had been transformed into a black pig with the head of a dragon. Someone told this to Emperor Xuanzong, who said, "This dragon-headed pig is incapable of becoming an emperor." Strassberg, *Wandering Spirits*, 225. Another interpretation would be that when he was drunk, An Lushan revealed his true nature (that of a pig) as well as his true ambition (i.e., an imperial ambition, represented by the dragon). Yi Illo's poem is also contained in *TMS* 20:6a under the title "Kwa Ŏyang" (Upon passing Yuyang).

11. Yan is modern-day Beijing. The Jurchen Jin had established their central capital there.

426 NOTES TO PAGES 165–167

12. This is a reference to a sentence in "Xici zhuan" (Commentary on the appended phrases; also known as "Dazhuan," "Great Commentary") from *Yijing*. The quotation is often used to describe a strong and productive friendship. See Lynn, *Classic of Changes*, 58.

13. A reference to the thirtieth chapter of *Han Feizi*.

14. The jade of Mount Jing. The term derives from a tale contained in *Han Feizi*, chapter "Heshi" (Mr. He). It is a legend about a certain Bian He, a native of the state of Chu, who is said to have discovered a fabulous jade stone at Mount Jing. He attempts to present the object to Kings Wu, Wen, and Cheng of Chu. The first two were doubtful, and their jewelers opined that it was an ordinary stone and not fine jade. Regarding Bian He as a liar, they had first his left and then his right foot cut off in punishment for attempting to deceive the king. Finally King Chen, hearing of Bian's lamentation of the libel of his fine stone and of his own reputation, had the stone polished and discovered that it was indeed a fabulous treasure. The stone was used to show that the natural attributes of a treasure must be "polished" before its merits are obvious. See Knoblock, *Xunzi*, 206–207. Bian He's story became the standard allusion to a talented and upright person whose true worth, symbolized by the precious jade, is unrecognized by his ruler and the world at large. See Tian, *Tao Yuanming*, 164.

15. An allusion to *Mengzi* 7B 38. See van Norden, *Mengzi*, 196.

16. Pak Illyang (d. 1096) went to China as an envoy and was praised there for his poetic skills.

17. In all probability, this king is Hŭijong.

18. The source here says *hyŏng* (C. *heng*), here short for *munhyŏng*, which can be understood as a reference to the highly prestigious position of *chi gonggŏ*, "examination administrator."

19. The source here says Kyojang-dang, but meant is the Kyojang togam, the "Directorate for Buddhist Scriptures" or "Directorate for Printing the Sūtras," a large monastic library and printing office that was established by Ŭich'ŏn at Hŭngwang-sa in 1086.

20. Kangdo was situated on Kanghwa Island, off the western shore of Korea, not far away from Kaesŏng and present-day Seoul. In the thirteenth century, Kangdo came to serve as the new capital of Koryŏ after Kaesŏng had been abandoned during the Mongol invasions. Kangdo was inaccessible to the Mongol army because they lacked a functioning navy and could not cross the strait. During this time, the coffin and the portraits of the dynasty's founder, T'aejo, were relocated to Kangdo, and the court only returned to Kaesŏng after the end of Ch'oe rule in 1270.

21. Kijang-*hyŏn* is present-day Kijang-gun in the city of Pusan in the southeast of the Korean Peninsula.

22. It is unfortunately not clear who this person Taewŏn wanggong (or perhaps even Taewŏn Wang gong, with the last name being Wang) is.

23. Chŏng Sŏnmo convincingly argues that the final entry of *P'ahan chip*, 3.33, was in fact a text that was among these three hundred miscellaneous writings, and that Duke Taewŏn added this text to *P'ahan chip* prior to having the work carved

NOTES TO PAGE 168   **427**

on woodblock. See Chŏng, "*P'ahan chip* p'an'gak-e issŏsŏ-ŭi ch'*ŏmsak munje-wa kŭ munhak sajŏk ŭiŭi*," 28.

24. The term *yugung* (C. *yougong*), "dark palace," appears in *Hou Chibi fu* (Latter red cliff rhapsody) by Shu Si as the water palace of Feng Yi, i.e., He Bo, the Earl of the Yellow River. Yet the term can also refer to a person's grave. In this sense it appears in *Guo shihuang mu* (Passing the tomb of the [Qin] Shi Huang) by Wang Wei. The term here refers to Yi Illo's grave.

25. *Kangmun chihu*, audience usher, refers to a member of the Office for Audience Ceremonies.

Bibliography

Babcock, Sarah Jane. "The Aesthetics of Non-Discrimination: Chinese Poetics and Social Critique in Huihong's Night Chats from Chilly Hut (c. 1121)." Ph.D. diss., University of California, Santa Barbara, 2020.

Bauer, Wolfgang. *China und die Hoffnung auf Glück: Paradiese, Utopien, Idealvorstellungen in der Geistesgeschichte Chinas.* Munich: Deutscher Taschenbuch Verlag, 1974.

Bauer, Wolfgang, and Herbert Franke. *Die Goldene Truhe: Chinesische Novellen aus zwei Jahrtausenden.* Munich: Carl Hanser Verlag, 1988.

Benn, James A. *Burning for the Buddha: Self-Immolation in Chinese Buddhism.* Honolulu: University of Hawai'i Press, 2007.

———. *Tea in China: A Religious and Cultural History.* Honolulu: University of Hawai'i Press; Hong Kong: Hong Kong University Press, 2015.

Birch, Cyril, ed. *Anthology of Chinese Literature: From Early Times to the Fourteenth Century.* New York: Grove Press, 1965.

Bol, Peter K. *This Culture of Ours: Intellectual Transition in T'ang and Sung China.* Stanford, CA: Stanford University Press, 1992.

Breuker, Remco E. *Establishing a Pluralist Society in Medieval Korea, 918–1170: History, Ideology, and Identity in Koryŏ Dynasty.* Leiden: Brill, 2010.

Brokaw, Cynthia Joanne. *The Ledgers of Merit and Demerit: Social Change and Moral Order in Late Imperial China.* Princeton, NJ: Princeton University Press, 1991.

Brown, Miranda. *The Art of Medicine in Early China: The Ancient and Medieval Origins of a Modern Archive.* Cambridge: Cambridge University Press, 2015.

Buswell Jr., Robert E. "Wŏnhyo: Buddhist Commentator *Par Excellence.*" *Journal of Korean Religions* 8, no. 1 (2017): 131–160.

Buswell Jr., Robert E., and Donald S. Lopez Jr. *The Princeton Dictionary of Buddhism.* Princeton, NJ: Princeton University Press, 2014.

Chang, Kang-i Sun. "Chinese Authorship." In *The Cambridge Handbook of Literary Authorship,* edited by Ingo Berensmeyer, Gert Buelens, and Marysa Demoor, 201–217. Cambridge: Cambridge University Press, 2019.

Chang, Kang-i Sun, and Stephen Owen, eds. *The Cambridge History of Chinese Literature.* Vol. 1, *To 1375.* Cambridge: Cambridge University Press, 2010.

Chang, Kang-i Sun, and Haun Saussy, eds. *Women Writers of Traditional China: An Anthology of Poetry and Criticism.* Stanford, CA: Stanford University Press, 1999.

Chang, Shirley. "Stories of the 'Others': The Presentation of Unconventional Characters in Tang (618–907) *chuanqi.*" Ph.D. diss., University of Wisconsin–Madison, 1993.

Chen, Jinhua. "A Complicated Figure with Complex Relationships: The Monk

BIBLIOGRAPHY

Huifan and Early Tang Samgha-State Interactions." In *The Middle Kingdom and the Dharma Wheel: Aspects of Relationship between the Buddhist Samgha and the State in Chinese History,* ed. Thomas Jülch, 140–221. Leiden: Brill, 2016.

Cho Kyuik. "O Sejae-ŭi salm-gwa kŭ-ŭi munhak-e nat'anan sŏjŏngsŏng." *Onji nonch'ong* 21 (2009): 7–33.

Cho Tongil. *Han'guk munhak t'ongsa 2. Chungse hugi munhak.* Seoul: Chisik sanŏpsa, 2003.

Ch'oe Hyeju. "Ilche kangjŏmgi kojŏn-ŭi hyŏngsŏng-e taehan ilgoch'al: Chaejo ilbonin-gwa Chosŏn Kwangmunhoe-ŭi kojŏn kanhaeng-ŭl chungsim-ŭro." *Han'guk munhwa* 64 (2013): 157–195.

Choe-Wall, Yang Hi, trans. *The Jehol Diary:* Yŏrha ilgi of Pak Chiwŏn (1737–1805). Folkestone, UK: Global Oriental, 2010.

Chŏng Honggyo, Chang Kwŏnp'o, and Pak Ch'unmyŏng. *Chosŏn kodae chungse munhak chakp'um haesŏl 2.* P'yŏngyang: Kwahak, paekkwasa ch'ulp'ansa, 1986.

Chŏng Sŏnmo. "*P'ahan chip* p'an'gak-e issŏsŏ-ŭi ch'ŏmsak munje-wa kŭ munhak sajŏk ŭiŭi—*P'ahan chip* p'yŏnch'an sigi mit p'yŏnch'an ŭido-ŭi singoch'ar-ŭl pat'ang-ŭro." *Hanmun hakpo* 10 (2004): 3–42.

———. "Yi Chayŏn-ŭi puksong sahaeng ko. *P'ahan chip* surok Kamno-sa simun-ŭl chungsim-ŭro." *Taedong munhwa yŏn'gu* 106 (2019): 225–251.

Courant, Maurice, and Pierre-Emmanuel Roux. *Répertoire historique de l'administration coréenne de Maurice Courant.* HAL Open Science. https://hal.science/hal -01149446.

Cutter, Robert Joe. *The Brush and the Spur: Chinese Culture and the Cockfight.* Hong Kong: Chinese University Press, 1989.

———. "Cao Zhi's (192–232) Symposium Poems." *Chinese Literature: Essays, Articles, Reviews* (CLEAR) 6, no. 1/2 (1984).

———. "Letters and Memorials in the Early Third Century: The Case of Cao Zhi." In *A History of Chinese Letters and Epistolary Culture,* edited by Antje Richter, 307–331. Leiden: Brill, 2015.

———. "On the Authenticity of 'Poem in Seven Paces.'" In *Studies in Early Medieval Chinese Literature and Cultural History: In Honor of Richard B. Mather and Donald Holzmann,* edited by Paul W. Kroll and David R. Knechtges, 1–26. Provo, UT: T'ang Studies Society, 2003.

Davis, Richard L. *From Warhorses to Ploughshares: The Later Tang Reign of Emperor Mingzong.* Hong Kong: Hong Kong University Press, 2014.

Davis, Timothy M. "Lechery, Substance Abuse, and … Han Yu?" *Journal of the American Oriental Society* 135, no. 1 (2015): 71–92.

Dawson, Raymond, trans. *Sima Qian. The First Emperor. Selections from the Historical Records.* Oxford: Oxford University Press, 2007.

De Crespigny, Rafe. *A Biographical Dictionary of Later Han to the Three Kingdoms (23–220).* Leiden: Brill, 2007.

Denecke, Wiebke, Wie-yee Li, and Xiaofei Tian, eds. *The Oxford Handbook of Classical Chinese Literature (1000 BCE–900CE).* Oxford: Oxford University Press, 2017.

Dillon, Michael, ed. *Encyclopedia of Chinese History.* London: Routledge, 2016.

Dudbridge, Glen. *A Portrait of Five Dynasties China: From the Memoirs of Wang Renyu (880–956)*. Oxford: Oxford University Press, 2013.

Durant, Stephen, Li Wei-yee, and David Schaberg. *Zuo Tradition: Zuozhuan. Commentary on the "Spring and Autumn Annals."* Seattle: University of Washington Press, 2016.

Ebrey, Patricia Buckley. *Emperor Huizong*. Cambridge, MA: Harvard University Press, 2014.

Egan, Ronald C. *The Problem of Beauty: Aesthetic Thought and Pursuits in Northern Song Dynasty China*. Cambridge, MA: Harvard University Press, 2006.

———. *Word, Image, and Deed in the Life of Su Shi*. Cambridge, MA: Harvard University Press, 1994.

Falk, Barbara J. "The History, Paradoxes, and Utility of Dissent: From State to Global Action." In *Dissent! Refracted: Histories, Aesthetics and Cultures of Dissent*, edited by Ben Dorfman. Political and Social Change 3. Frankfurt: Peter Lang, 2016.

Feng, Linda Rui. *City of Marvel and Transformation: Chang'an and Narratives of Experience in Tang Dynasty China*. Honolulu: University of Hawai'i Press, 2015.

Fong, Grace S. *Herself an Author: Gender, Agency, and Writing in Late Imperial China*. Honolulu: University of Hawai'i Press, 2008.

Fraleigh, Matthew. *Plucking Chrysanthemums: Narushima Ryūhoku and Sinitic Literary Traditions in Modern Japan*. Cambridge, MA: Harvard University Asia Center, 2016.

Fuller, Michael A. *An Introduction to Chinese Poetry: From the Canon of Poetry to the Lyrics of the Song Dynasty*. Cambridge, MA: Harvard University Asia Center, 2017.

——— *The Road to East Slope: The Development of Su Shi's Poetic Voice*. Stanford, CA: Stanford University Press, 1990.

Grayson, James Huntley. *Korea – A Religious History*. New York: Routledge, 2005.

Grimm, Martin. *Kaiser Qianlong (1711–1791) als Poet: Anmerkungen zu seinem schriftstellerischen Werk*. Stuttgart: Steiner, 1993.

Gu, Ming Dong. *Chinese Theories of Reading and Writing: A Route to Hermeneutics and Open Poetics*. Albany: State University of New York Press, 2005.

Han, Christina, and Wing S. Chu, trans. "Twenty-Four Poems by Chŏng Chisang." *Acta Koreana* 16, no. 2 (2013): 611–627.

Han Young-woo, Ahn Hwi-Joon, and Bae Woo Sung. *The Artistry of Early Korean Cartography*. Translated by Choi Byonghyon. Larkspur: Tamal Vista Publication, 2008.

Hanson, Marta. "Robust Northerners and Delicate Southerners: The Nineteenth-Century Invention of a Southern Medical Tradition." In *Innovation in Chinese Medicine*, edited by Elisabeth Hsu. Cambridge: Cambridge University Press, 2001.

Hao, Ji. *The Reception of Du Fu (712–770) and His Poetry in Imperial China*. Leiden: Brill, 2017.

Harbsmeier, Christoph. *Science and Civilization in China*. Vol. 7, part 1, *Language and Logic*. Cambridge: Cambridge University Press, 1998.

Hartman, Charles. *Han Yü and the T'ang Search for Unity*. Princeton, NJ: Princeton University Press, 1986.

432 BIBLIOGRAPHY

———. "Poetry and Politics in 1079: The Crow Terrace Poetry Case of Su Shih." *Chinese Literature: Essays, Articles, Reviews* 12 (1990): 15–44.

Hawkes, David, trans. *The Songs of the South: An Ancient Chinese Anthology of Poems by Qu Yuan and Other Poets*. London: Penguin Classics, 2011.

Hermann, Marc, Huang Weiping, and Henriette Pleiger, eds. *Biographisches Handbuch chinesischer Schriftsteller: Leben und Werke*. Berlin: de Gruyter, 2011.

Hilker, Joyefina E. *Paengnyŏn ch'ohae: Charakteristika eines koreanischen Lehrbuchs der Parallelvers-Dichtung. Zusammenstellung, Quellen, Urheberschaft, Entstehungszeitraum und Entwicklung*. Wiesbaden: Harrassowitz Verlag, 2010.

Hŏ Pang. "Chong *Such'arok* kyŏn sipku segi hanjŏk kyoryu." *Han'gukhak nonjip* 73 (2018): 285–306.

Hong, Yue. "A Structural Study of Ninth Century Anecdotes on 'Original Events.'" *T'ang Studies* 26 (2008): 65–84.

Hsia, C. T., Li Wai-Yee, and George Kao, eds. *The Columbia Anthology of Yuan Drama*. New York: Columbia University Press, 2014.

Hsu, Eileen Hsiang-ling. *Monks in Glaze: Patronage, Kiln Origin, and Iconography of the Yixian Luohans*. Leiden: Brill, 2017.

Hua Linfu, Paul D. Buell, and Paul U. Unschuld, eds. *Ben Cao Gang Mu Dictionary*. Vol. 2, *Geographical and Administrative Designations*. Berkeley: University of California Press, 2017.

Huang, Kuan-yun. "Xunzi's Criticism of Zisi—New Perspectives." *Early China* 37 (2014): 291–325.

Hucker, Charles O. *A Dictionary of Official Titles in Imperial China*. Stanford, CA: Stanford University Press, 1985.

Huff, Elizabeth, ed. *The Asami Library: A Descriptive Catalogue, by Chaoying Fang*. Berkeley: University of California Press, 1968.

Hŭiraktanggo. n.d. Konkuk University Library. Database of Korean Classics. http://db.itkc.or.kr.

Hwang In'gyu. "Koryŏ sidae yusaeng-ŭi sŏjae-wa kŭ munhwa." *Han'guk kyoyuk sahak* 28, no. 2 (2006): 169–196.

Idema, Wilt L., and Lloyd Haft. *A Guide to Chinese Literature*. Ann Arbor: University of Michigan Press, 1997.

Idema, Wilt, and Stephen H. West, eds. and trans. *Battles, Betrayals, and Brotherhood: Early Chinese Plays on the Three Kingdoms*. Indianapolis, IN: Hackett Publishing, 2012.

Im Hyŏngsu. "Munjip-ŭl t'onghae pon Yi Illo-ŭi kyoryu kwan'gye." *Sach'ong* 83 (2014): 65–100.

Im Myŏngdŏk, ed. *Han'guk hanmun sosŏl chŏnjip*, 9 vols. Seoul: Kukhak charyowŏn, 2010.

Jang Yoo-Seung. "Regional Identities of Northern Literati: A Comparative Study." In *The Northern Region of Korea: History, Identity, and Culture*, edited by Kim Sun Joo. Seattle: University of Washington Press, 2010.

Jin Qian. "Formation of the Xikun Style Poetry." Master's thesis, University of Massachusetts, 2009. https://scholarworks.umass.edu/cgi/viewcontent.cgi?article=1289&context=theses.

BIBLIOGRAPHY 433

Johnson, Wallace Stephen. *The T'ang Code.* Princeton, NJ: Princeton University Press, 1979.

Kalinke, Viktor, trans. *Zhuangzi: Das Buch der daoistischen Weisheit. Vollständige Ausgabe.* Stuttgart: Reclam, 2021.

Kelly, Thomas. "The Death of an Artisan: Su Shi and Ink Making." *Harvard Journal of Asiatic Studies* 80, no. 2 (2020): 315–346.

Keyworth, George Albert. "Transmitting the Lamp of Learning in Classical Chan Buddhism: Juefan Huihong (1071–1128) and Literary Chan." Ph.D. diss., University of California, Los Angeles, 2001.

Kim Hamyŏng. *Uri nara kojŏn munhak.* P'yŏngyang: Kungnip munhak yesul sŏjŏk ch'ulp'ansa, 1959.

Kim Kŏn'gong. "*Haedong munhŏn ch'ongnok* sojae Koryŏ munjip yŏn'gu. Pujŏn munjip-ŭl chungsim-ŭro." *Changsŏgak* 18 (2007).

Kim Kyŏngdong. "Paek Kŏi *Kwŏnju sipsasu*-ŭi han'gukchŏk suyong-gwa pyŏnyong." *Chungŏ chungmunhak* 59 (2014): 27–54.

Kim Pogwang. "Yi Illo-ŭi sarye-ro pon Koryŏ chŏn'gi *Chik Hallim-wŏn*-ŭi unyŏng-gwa yŏkhal." *Sach'ong* 83 (2014): 101–137.

Kim, Taejun. *Chosŏn hanmunhaksa.* Kyŏngsŏng: Chosŏn ŏmun hakhoe, 1931.

———. *Chosŏn sosŏlsa.* Kyŏngsŏng: Ch'ŏngjin sŏgwan, 1933. Sogang University Loyola Library. www.library.sogang.ac.kr.

Kim, Tai-jin, ed. and trans. *A Bibliographical Guide to Traditional Korean Sources.* Seoul: Asiatic Research Center, Korea University, 1976.

Kim Tangt'aek. "Ch'oe Cha-ŭi Pohan chip chŏsul tonggi." *Chindan hakpo* 65 (1988): 143–152.

Kim Yongsŏn. "*P'ahan chip* chŏsul-ŭi yŏksajŏk paegyŏng." *Chindan hakpo* 73 (1992): 189–196.

King, Sonia. *Mosaic Techniques and Traditions: Projects and Designs from around the World.* New York: Sterling Publishing, 2003.

Klöpsch, Volker. "'Um Mitternacht der Glocke Ton' und andere Ungereimtheiten in der Wahrnehmung des Dichters." In *China und die Wahrnehmung der Welt,* edited by Antje Richter and Helmolt Vittinghoff. Wiesbaden: Harrassowitz, 2007.

Knechtges, David R. "Sweet-Peel Orange or Southern Gold? Regional Identity in Western Jin Literature." In *Studies in Early Medieval Chinese Literature and Cultural History: In Honor of Richard B. Mather & Donald Holzmann,* edited by Paul W. Kroll and David R. Knechtges, 27–79. Provo, UT: T'ang Studies Society, 2003.

———. "Wit, Humor, and Satire in Early Chinese Literature (to A.D. 220)." *Monumenta Serica* 29 (1970–1971): 79–98.

Knechtges, David R., and Taiping Chang, eds. *Ancient and Early Medieval Chinese Literature: A Reference Guide.* 4 vols. Leiden: Brill, 2014.

Knechtges, David R., and Tong Xiao. *Wen Xuan or Selections of Refined Literature.* Vol. 3, *Rhapsodies on Natural Phenomena, Birds and Animals, Aspirations and Feelings, Sorrowful Laments, Literature, Music, and Passions.* Princeton, NJ: Princeton University Press, 1996.

Knoblock, John. *Xunzi: A Translation and Study of the Complete Works.* Vol. 3. Books 17–32. Stanford, CA: Stanford University Press, 1994.

434 BIBLIOGRAPHY

Ko Chŏnguk, Ri Ŭngsu, Han Ryongok, and Ŏm Hosŏk. *Chosŏn munhak-esŏ-ŭi sajo mit pangbŏp yŏn'gu.* P'yŏngyang: Kwahagwŏn ch'ulp'ansa, 1963.

Koryŏ taehakkyo han'guksa yŏn'guso koryŏ sidae yŏn'gusil, trans. *P'ahan chip yŏkchu.* Seoul: Kyŏng'in munhwasa, 2013.

Kovacs, Jürgen, and Paul U. Unschuld, trans. *Essential Subtleties on the Silver Sea. The Yin-hai jing-wei: A Chinese Classic on Ophthalmology.* Berkeley: University of California Press, 1998.

Kroll, Paul W. "Aid and Comfort: Lu Zhaolin's Letters." In *A History of Chinese Letters and Epistolary Culture,* edited by Antje Richter, 829–852. Leiden: Brill, 2015.

———, trans. "Po Chü-i's 'Song of Lasting Regret': A New Translation." *Tang Studies* 8/9 (1990–1991): 97–105.

Kubin, Wolfgang. *Die chinesische Dichtkunst. Von den Anfängen bis zum Ende der Kaiserzeit. Geschichte der chinesischen Literatur.* Vol. 1. Munich: K. G. Saur, 2002.

Lagerwey, John, and Marc Kalinowski, eds. *Early Chinese Religion. Part One: Shang through Han (1250 BC–220 AD).* Leiden: Brill, 2009.

Lagerwey, John, and Pierre Marsone. *Modern Chinese Religion: Song-Liao-Jin-Yuan (960–1368 AD).* Leiden: Brill, 2015.

Lau, D. C., trans. *Chinese Classics: Tao Te Ching.* Hong Kong: Chinese University Press, 1982.

Lee, Ki-baik. *A New History of Korea.* Cambridge, MA: Harvard University Press, 1984.

Lee, Kidong. "The Indigenous Religions of Silla: Their Diversity and Durability." *Korean Studies* 28 (2004): 49–74.

Lee, Lily Xiao Hong, and A. D. Stefanowska, eds. *Biographical Dictionary of Chinese Women: Antiquity through Sui. 1600 B.C.E.–618 C.E.* Armonk, NY: M. E. Sharpe, 2007.

Lee, Peter H., ed. *Anthology of Korean Literature: From Early Times to the Nineteenth Century.* Honolulu: University of Hawai'i Press, 1981.

———. *Celebration of Continuity: Themes in Classic East Asian Poetry.* Cambridge, MA: Harvard University Press, 1979.

———, ed. *The Columbia Anthology of Traditional Korean Poetry.* New York: Columbia University Press, 2002.

———, ed. *A History of Korean Literature.* Cambridge: Cambridge University Press, 2003.

———, ed. *Sourcebook of Korean Civilization.* Vol. 1, *From Early Times to the Sixteenth Century.* New York. Columbia University Press, 1993.

Lee, Peter H., and Theodore de Bary, eds. *Sources of Korean Tradition.* Vol. 1, *From Early Times through the Sixteenth Century.* New York: Columbia University Press, 1997.

Legge, James, trans. *The Chinese Classics with a Translation, Critical and Exegetical Notes, Prolegomena, and Copious Indexes by James Legge.* Vol. 1, *Confucian Analects, The Great Learning, and the Doctrine of the Mean;* Vol. 2, *The Works of Mencius;* Vol. 3, *The Shoo King;* Vol. 4, *The She King;* Vol. 5, *The Ch'un Ts'ew with The Tso Chuen.* Teipei: Southern Materials Center, 1985.

———, trans. *The Sacred Books of China: The Texts of Confucianism. Part III, The Li Ki, XI–XLVI.* Oxford: Clarendon Press, 1885.

BIBLIOGRAPHY 435

Levy, Howard S., trans. *Translations from Po Chü-i's Collected Works*. Vol. 3, *Regulated and Patterned Poems of Middle Age (822–832)*. San Francisco: Chinese Materials Center, 1976.

L'Haridon, Béatrice. "The Merchants in *Shiji*: An Interpretation in the Light of Later Debates." In *Views from Within, Views from Beyond: Approaches to the Shiji as an Early Work of Historiography*, edited by Hans van Ess, Olga Lomová, and Dorothee Schaab-Hanke. Wiesbaden: Harrassowitz Verlag, 2015, https://doi.org/10.2307/j.ctvc771cb.11.

Li Yangzheng. *Geschichte des chinesischen Daoismus*. Vienna: Lit Verlag, 2020.

Liu Guozhong. *Introduction to the Tsinghua Bamboo-Strip Manuscripts*. Leiden: Brill, 2016.

Liu, James J. Y., and Richard John Lynn, eds. *Language-Paradox-Poetics: A Chinese Perspective: A Chinese Perspective*. Princeton, NJ: Princeton University Press, 1988.

Lo, Jung-pang. *China as a Sea Power, 1127–1368: A Preliminary Survey of the Maritime Expansion and Naval Exploits of the Chinese People during the Southern Song and Yuan Periods*. Edited, and with commentary, by Bruce A. Elleman. Singapore: National University of Singapore Press, 2013.

Lotman, Yuri M. *Universe of the Mind: A Semiotic Theory of Culture*. London: I. B. Tauris, 2001.

Luo, Yuming. *A Concise History of Chinese Literature*. Translated, with annotations and an introduction, by Ye Yang. Leiden: Brill, 2011.

Lynn, Richard John, trans. *The Classic of Changes: A New Translation of the I Ching as Interpreted by Wang Bi*. New York: Columbia University Press, 1994.

———. "The Talent Learning Polarity in Chinese Poetics: Yan Yu and the Later Tradition." *Chinese Literature: Essays, Articles, Reviews* 5, no. 1/2 (1983): 157–184.

MacMillan, Peter, trans. *The Tales of Ise*. London: Penguin, 2016.

Mair, Victor, ed. *The Shorter Columbia Anthology of Traditional Chinese Literature*. New York: Columbia University Press, 2000.

Major, John S. *Heaven and Earth in Early Han Thought: Chapters Three, Four, and Five of the Huainanzi*. Albany: State University of New York Press, 1993.

Major, John S., Sarah A. Queen, Andrew Seth Meyer, and Harold D. Roth, eds. and trans. *The Huainanzi: A Guide to the Theory and Practice of Government in Early Han China*. Translations from the Asian Classics. New York: Columbia University Press, 2010.

McBride II, Richard D. "The Structure and Sources of the Biography of Kim Yusin." *Acta Koreana* 16, no. 2 (2013): 497–535.

———. "Ŭich'ŏn." In *Brill's Encyclopedia of Buddhism*, edited by Jonathan A. Silk, vol. 2, Lives, 900–902. Leiden: Brill, 2019.

McCann, David R. *Early Korean Literature: Selections and Introductions*. New York: Columbia University Press, 2000.

Minford, John, and Joseph S. M. Lau, eds. *Classical Chinese Literature: An Anthology of Translations*. Vol. 1, *From Antiquity to the Tang Dynasty*. New York. Columbia University Press, 2000.

Mogŭn'go. 1626. Seoul National University Kyujanggak Institute for Korean Studies Library. #Kyu4277. Database of Korean Classics. http://db.itkc.or.kr.

436   BIBLIOGRAPHY

Mollier, Christine. *Buddhism and Taoism Face to Face: Scripture, Ritual, and Iconographic Exchange in Medieval China.* Honolulu: University of Hawai'i Press, 2008.

Moore, Oliver. *Rituals of Recruitment in Tang China: Reading an Annual Programme in the Collected Statements by Wang Dingbao (870–940).* Leiden: Brill, 2004.

Moser, Jefferey. "Learning with Metal and Stone: On the Discursive Formation of Song Epigraphy." In *Powerful Arguments: Standards of Validity in Late Imperial China,* edited by Martin Hoffmann, Joachim Kurtz, and Ari Daniel Levine. Leiden: Brill, 2020.

Muller, A. Charles, ed. *Digital Dictionary of Buddhism.* Accessed June 18, 2023. http://buddhism-dict.net/ddb.

Murck, Alfreda. *Poetry and Painting in Song China: The Subtle Art of Dissent.* Cambridge, MA: Harvard University Press, 2000.

Na Ch'ŏnsu. "*P'ahan chip yŏkchu* sojae yŏnsasi-ŭi chaehaesŏk." *Sach'ong* 83 (2014): 139–166.

Nienhauser Jr., William H. *Tang Dynasty Tales: A Guided Reader.* Singapore: World Scientific Publishing, 2010.

———. *Tang Dynasty Tales: A Guided Reader.* Vol. 2. Singapore: World Scientific Publishing, 2016.

Nylan, Michael, trans. *Exemplary Figures: Fayan.* Seattle: University of Washington Press, 2013.

O Ch'ihun. "Koryŏ sidae Haedong kirohoe-ŭi sŏngnip-kwa 'kiro'-ŭi ŭimi pyŏnhwa." *Sach'ong* 83 (2014): 3–28.

Oh, Young Kyun. *Engraving Virtue: The Printing History of a Premodern Korean Moral Primer.* Leiden: Brill, 2013.

O'Rourke, Kevin, trans. *The Book of Korean Shijo.* Cambridge, MA: Harvard University Press, 2002.

Owen, Stephen. *The Late Tang: Chinese Poetry of the Mid-Ninth Century.* Cambridge, MA: Harvard University Press, 2006.

———, trans. *The Poetry of Du Fu.* Boston: De Gruyter, 2016.

———. *The Poetry of Meng Chiao and Han Yü.* New Haven, CT: Yale University Press, 1975.

———. *Readings in Chinese Literary Thought.* Cambridge, MA: Harvard University Press, 1992.

———. "Tu Fu." In *Critical Readings on Tang China,* edited by Paul W. Kroll, vol. 2, 825–893. Leiden: Brill, 2018.

P'ahan chip. 1659. National Library of Korea. #Ko 3648-62-377. https://www.nl.go.kr.

Pak Chongjin. "Koryŏ sigi Haedong kirohoe-ŭi kyŏlsŏng-gwa hwaltong." *Yŏks-wa hyŏnsil* 66 (2007): 303–336.

Pak Killam. *Chosŏn kojŏn chakka irhwa chip.* Vol. 1. P'yŏngyang: Munhak yesul ch'ulp'ansa, 2012.

Pak Sŏnggyu, trans. *Yŏkchu P'ahan chip.* Seoul: Pogosa, 2012.

———, trans. *Yŏkchu Pohan chip.* Seoul: Pogosa, 2012.

Palumbo-Liu, David. *The Poetics of Appropriation: The Literary Theory and Practice of Huang Tingjian.* Stanford, CA: Stanford University Press, 1993.

BIBLIOGRAPHY 437

Pease, Jonathan. *His Stubbornship: Prime Minister Wang Anshi (1021–1086), Reformer and Poet.* Leiden: Brill, 2021.

Pettid, Michael J., Gregory N. Evon, and Chan E. Park, eds. *Premodern Korean Literary Prose: An Anthology.* New York: Columbia University Press, 2018.

Pratt, Keith, and Richard Rutt. *Korea: A Historical and Cultural Dictionary.* Richmond, Surrey: Curzon Press, 1999.

Pregadio, Fabrizio, ed. *The Encyclopedia of Taoism.* London: Routledge, 2008.

Qian Zhongshu. *Patchwork: Seven Essays on Art and Literature.* Leiden: Brill, 2014.

Reynolds, Graeme G. "Culling Archival Collections in the Koryŏ-Chosŏn Transition." *Journal of Korean Studies* 24, no. 2 (2019): 225–253.

Ri Ch'ŏlhwa and Ryu Suoe, trans. and eds. *Uri nara kojŏn chakkadŭl-ŭi mihak kyŏnhae charyo chip.* P'yŏngyang: Chosŏn munhak yesul ch'ongdongmaeng ch'ulp'ansa, 1964.

Ri Kiwŏn and Ch'oe Ryŏnsil, eds. *Chosŏn-ŭi irŭmnan chakka-wa irhwa (1).* P'yŏngyang: Paekkwa sajŏn ch'ulp'ansa, 2006.

Ri Sŏng, trans. *Ri Illo, Rim Ch'un chakp'um chip.* P'yŏngyang: Munhak yesul ch'ulp'ansa, 2016.

Rogers, Michael C. "National Consciousness in Medieval Korea: The Impact of Liao and Chin on Koryŏ." In *China among Equals: The Middle Kingdom and Its Neighbors, 10th–14th Centuries,* edited by Morris Rossabi, 151–172. Berkeley: University of California Press.

———. "The Regularization of Koryŏ-Chin Relations (1116–1131)." *Central Asiatic Journal* 6, no. 1 (1961): 51–84.

———. "Some Kings of Koryo as Registered in Chinese Works." *Journal of the American Oriental Society* 81 (1961): 415–422.

Rösch, Petra. *Chinese Wood Sculptures of the 11th to 13th centuries: Images of Watermoon Guanyin in Northern Chinese Temples and Western Collections.* Stuttgart: Ibidem, 2014.

Rouzer, Paul F. *Articulated Ladies: Gender and the Male Community in Early Chinese Texts.* Cambridge, MA: Harvard University Press, 2001.

———. *Writing Another's Dream: The Poetry of Wen Tingyun.* Stanford, CA: Stanford University Press, 1993.

Rutt, Richard, trans. *The Book of Changes (Zhouyi).* London: Routledge Curzon, 2002.

———. "Traditional Korean Poetry Criticism: Fifty *Sihwa* Chosen and Translated by Richard Rutt." *Transactions of the Korea Branch of the Royal Asiatic Society,* 47 (1972): 105–143.

———, trans. "The White Cloud Essays of Yi Kyubo." *Transactions of the Royal Asiatic Society* 52 (1977): 1–37.

Ryŏ Unp'il. "Im Ch'un-ŭi saengae-e taehan chaegŏmt'o." *Han'guk hansi yŏn'gu* 4 (1996): 203–245.

Ryu Hwajŏng. "Ryŏ-mal cho-ch'o Hwang Chŏnggyŏn siron-ŭi suyong yangsang." *Han'guk hanmunhak yŏn'gu* 77 (2020): 375–398.

Sargent, Stuart H. *The Poetry of He Zhu (1052–1125): Genres, Contexts, and Creativity.* Leiden: Brill, 2007.

438 BIBLIOGRAPHY

Sasukchae chip 私淑齋集. 1805. Han'gukhak chungang yŏn'guwŏn Changsŏgak. 4-6092. Database of Korean Classics. http://db.itkc.or.kr.

Schlombs, Adele. *Huai-su and the Beginnings of Wild Cursive Script in Chinese Calligraphy.* Stuttgart: Franz Steiner Verlag, 1998.

Seth, Michael J. *A Concise History of Premodern Korea: From Antiquity through the Ninteenth Century.* Vol. 1. 3rd ed. Lanham, MD: Rowman and Littlefield, 2020.

Shultz, Edward J. "Ch'oe Ch'unghŏn: His Rise to Power." *Korean Studies* 8 (1984): 58–82.

———. *Generals and Scholars: Military Rule in Medieval Korea.* Honolulu: University of Hawai'i Press, 2000.

———. "An Introduction to the 'Samguk Sagi.'" *Korean Studies* 28 (2004): 1–13.

———. "Military Revolt in Koryŏ. The 1170 Coup d'État." *Korean Studies* 3 (1979): 19–48.

———. "Twelfth-Century Koryŏ Politics: The Rise of Han Anin and His Partisans." *Journal of Korean Studies* 6 (1988–1989): 3–38.

Sim Hot'aek. "*P'ahan chip*-ŭi yŏksajŏk sŏnggyŏk. Ch'allok ŭido-ŭi sidaejŏk paegyŏng." *Hanmun kyoyuk yŏn'gu* 1 (1986): 89–120.

Simon, Rainald, trans. *Shijing: Das altchinesische Buch der Lieder.* Stuttgart: Reclam, 2015.

Sin Ŭn'gyŏng. "Sihwa-wa uta monogatari-ŭi pigyo yŏn'gu: *P'ahan chip*-kwa *Ise monogatari*-rŭl chungsim-ŭro." *Tongyanghak* 43 (2008): 49–69.

Sin Yŏngju. "*P'ahan chip* sojae si-ŭi chŏn'go hwaryong-gwa hyŏngsanghwa-e kwanhan koch'al." *Tongbang hanmunhak* 87 (2021): 7–33.

Slingerland, Edward, trans. *Confucius: Analects. With Selections from Traditional Commentaries.* Indianapolis, IN: Hackett Publishing, 2003.

Smith, Thomas E. *Declarations of the Perfected. Part One: Setting Scripts and Images into Motion.* St. Petersburg, FL: Three Pines Press, 2013.

Sŏ Chuyŏng. "Ham Sun-ŭi saengae-e taehan koch'al." *Yŏngnamhak* 68 (2019): 173–194.

Sŏha sŏnsaeng chip. 1713. Seoul National University Kyujanggak Institute for Korean Studies Library. #Ko-3428–466. Database of Korean Classics. http://db.itkc .or.kr.

Sørensen, Henrick H. "An Investigation of Two Budhdist Tomb-Inscriptions from 12th Century Koryŏ." *International Journal of Buddhist Thought and Culture* 12 (2009): 79–94.

Speake, Jennifer, ed. *Oxford Dictionary of Proverbs.* 6th ed. Oxford: Oxford University Press, 2015.

Starr, Kenneth. *Black Tigers: A Grammar of Chinese Rubbings.* Seattle: University of Washington Press, 2008.

Sterckx, Roel. *The Animal and the Daemon in Early China.* Albany: State University of New York Press, 2002.

Strassberg, Richard E., trans. *Inscribed Landscapes: Travel Writing from Imperial China.* Berkeley: University of California Press, 1994.

———, trans. *Wandering Spirits: Chen Shiyuan's Encyclopedia of Dreams.* Berkeley: University of California Press, 2008.

Sturman, Peter C. "Su Shi Renders No Emotion." *Journal of Chinese Literature and Culture* 6 (2019): 15–55.

Sukhu, Gopal. *The Shaman and the Heresiarch: A New Interpretation of the Li Sao.* Albany: State University of New York Press, 2012.

Sunstein, Cass R. *Why Societies Need Dissent.* Cambridge, MA: Harvard University Press, 2003.

Swartz, Wendy, Robert Ford Campany, Yang Lu, and Jessey J. C. Choo, eds. *Early Medieval China: A Sourcebook.* New York: Columbia University Press, 2014.

Tian, Xiaofei. "Collections (*ji* 集)." In *The Oxford Handbook of Classical Chinese Literature (1000 BCE–90 CE),* edited by Wiebke Denecke, Wai-Yee Li, and Xiaofei Tian, 219–234. New York: Oxford University Press, 2017.

———. *Tao Yuanming and Manuscript Culture: The Record of a Dusty Table.* Seattle: University of Washington Press, 2005.

Tillman, Hoyd Cleveland, and Stephen H. West, eds. *China under Jurchen Rule.* Albany: State University of New York Press, 1995.

Tongguk Yi Sangguk chip. N.d. Seoul National University Kyujanggak Institute for Korean Studies Library. #Kyu5270. Database of Korean Classics. http://db .itkc.or.kr.

Tsien, Tsuen Hsuin. *Collected Writings on Chinese Culture.* Hong Kong: Chinese University Press, 2011.

Unschuld, Paul U., and Hermann Tessenow. *Huang Di nei jing su wen: An Annotated Translation of Huang Di's Inner Classic – Basic Questions.* Vol. 1. Berkeley: University of California Press, 2011.

Van Norden, Bryan W., trans. *Mengzi: With Selections from Traditional Commentary.* Indianapolis, IN: Hackett Publishing, 2008.

Vermeersch, Sem. "Buddhist Temples or Political Battlegrounds? Kaesŏng Temples in Relation to Court and Aristocracy." *Bulletin de l'École française d'Extrême-Orient* 94 (2007).

———, trans. *A Chinese Traveler in Medieval Korea: Xu Jing's Illustrated Account of the Xuanhe Embassy to Koryŏ.* Honolulu: University of Hawai'i Press, 2016.

———. "The P'algwanhoe: From Buddhist Penance to Religious Festival." In *Religions of Korea in Practice,* edited by Robert E. Buswell, 86–99. Princeton, NJ: Princeton University Press.

———. "Yŏngt'ong-sa and Its Reconstruction. A Medieval Buddhist Site as a Space for North-South Cooperation." 2005, 1–8. congress.aks.ac.kr.

Von Falkenhausen, Lothar. "Antiquarianism in East Asia: A Preliminary Overview." In *World Antiquariansim,* edited by Alain Schnapp et al., 35–66. Los Angeles: Getty Research Institute Press, 2013.

Waley, Arthur, trans. *The Book of Songs.* London: George Allen & Unwin, 1954.

———, trans. *A Hundred and Seventy Chinese Poems.* New York: Knopf, 1919.

Wang, Eugene Y. *Shaping the Lotus Sutra: Buddhist Visual Culture in Medieval China.* Seattle: University of Washington Press, 2005.

Wang, Ping. *The Age of Courtly Writing: Wen xuan Compiler Xiao Tong (501–531) and His Circle.* Leiden: Brill, 2012.

———. "'Making Friends with the Men of the Past': Literati Identity and Literary Remembering in Medieval China." In *Memory in Medieval China: Text, Ritual, and Community*, edited by Wendy Swartz and Robert Ford Campany. Leiden: Brill, 2018.

Wang, Sixiang. "Chosŏn's Office of Interpreters: The Apt Response and the Knowledge Culture of Diplomacy." *Journal for the History of Knowledge* 1, no. 1 (2020): 1–15. http://doi.org/10.5334/jhk.17.

Watson, Burton, trans. *The Complete Works of Zhuangzi*. New York: Columbia University Press, 2013.

———, trans. *Records of the Grand Historian: Han Dynasty*. Vol. 1. New York: Columbia University Press, 1993.

Wei, Xin, and James B. Lewis, trans. *Korea's Premier Collection of Classical Literature: Selections from Sŏ Kŏjŏng's Tongmunsŏn: Korean Classics Library*. Honolulu: University of Hawai'i Press, 2019.

West, Stephen H., and Wilt L. Idema, trans. *Monks, Bandits, Lovers, and Immortals: Eleven Early Chinese Plays*. Indianapolis, IN: Hackett Publishing, 2010.

———. *The Orphan of Zhao and Other Yuan Plays: The Earliest Known Versions*. New York: Columbia University Press, 2015.

Wŏn Uhŭm. *Munhak: Kogŭp chung hakkyo che 1 hangnyŏn yong*. P'yŏngyang: Kyoyuk tosŏ ch'ulp'ansa, 1955.

Wright, Suzanne E. "Chinese Decorated Letter Papers." In *A History of Chinese Letters and Epistolary Culture*, edited Antje Richter, 97–135. Leiden: Brill, 2015.

Wuerthner, Dennis. *A Study of Hypertexts of Kuunmong, focusing on Kuullu/Kuun'gi. Nine Clouds in Motion*. Frankfurt: Peter Lang, 2017.

———, trans. *Tales of the Strange by a Korean Confucian Monk: Kŭmo sinhwa by Kim Sisŭp*. Honolulu: University of Hawai'i Press, 2020.

Xie Jinliang. "Das Dao kennt weder Anfang noch Ende: Konzeptionen von Zeit in *Zhuangzi*." In *Zeit, Raum und die Wirklichkeiten Chinas*, edited by Clemens von Haselber and Stefan Kramer. *Berliner China Hefte* 48 (2016).

Xin Wei and James B. Lewis, trans. *Korea's Premier Collection of Classical Literature: Selections from Sŏ Kŏjŏng's Tongmunsŏn*. Honolulu: University of Hawai'i Press, 2019.

Yang, Shuhui, and Yunqin Yang, trans. *Stories to Caution the World: A Ming Dynasty Collection*. Vol. 2. Compiled by Feng Menglong. Seattle: University of Washington Press, 2005.

Yang, Zhiyi. *Dialectics of Spontaneity: The Aesthetics and Ethics of Su Shi (1037–1101) in Poetry*. Leiden: Brill, 2015.

Yi Ch'angsŏp. "Taesong woegyo hwaldong-e ch'amyŏhan Koryŏ sugun. *P'ahan chip*-kwa *Koryŏ togyŏng*-e nat'ananŭn sarye-rŭl chungsim-ŭro." *Sach'ong* 83 (2014): 29–63.

Yi Hwangjin. "Ko Un-i Ch'oe Ch'iwŏn-ege chun songbyŏngsi *Koun p'yŏn*-e taehan chinwi kojŭng. Koun-p'yŏn-gwa Ch'oe Ch'iwŏn-ŭi chaeiptang sigi-e taehan hanjung yŏn'gusa-rŭl kyŏmhayŏ." *Inmun nonch'ong* 65 (2011): 331–352.

Yi Kidae. "Kim Yusin kwallyŏn yŏsŏngdŭl-ŭi munhakchŏk hyŏngsang-gwa hudae-jŏk pyŏnhwa." Ŏmun nonjip 62 (2015): 321–348.

Yi Sangbo, trans. *Han'guk myŏngjŏ taejŏnjip: Yi Illo, Ch'oe Cha, Yi Chehyŏn. P'ahan chip, Pohan chip, Yŏgong p'aesŏl.* Seoul: Taeyang sŏjŏk, 1972.

Yi Sangik. "Ryŏjo sanmunhak sogo. *Paegun sosŏl, P'ahan chip*." *Kugŏ kyoyuk* 18 (1972): 15–31.

Yi Wŏryŏng, trans. *Tongin sihwa.* Seoul: Wŏrin, 2000.

Yoke, Ho Peng. *Li, Qi and Shu: An Introduction to Science and Civilization in China.* Hong Kong: Hong Kong University Press, 1985.

Yu, Anthony, trans. *The Monkey and the Monk: An Abridgment of The Journey to the West.* Chicago: University of Chicago Press, 2006.

Zhu Xi. *Shi jizhuan.* Beijing: Zhonghua shuju chuban, 1958.

Ziporyn, Brook, trans. *Zhuangzi: The Essential Writings. With Selections from Traditional Commentaries.* Indianapolis, IN: Hackett Publishing, 2009.

Index

Page numbers in *italics* indicate artwork

akchŏk, 369n53
alchemy, 112, 232, 325n162
Amsŏ, 52
An Ch'imin, 79, 251n126
Angam Temple, 43, 76, 243n83
anhwa, 331n205
Anhwa Temple, 121–122, 339nn241–242,
    340nn245–246, 341nn247–248
An Lushan, 164, 288n306, 425n10
An Porin, 87, 274n234

Bai Fu, 79, 252n127
Bai Juyi, 6, 244n90, 288n306
baiwu, 277n243
Bianjing, 302n40
Bian Que, 97, 294n1
Bi Chen, 79
bilanggan, 253n130
Bingong ke, 350n273
Bizixing zheng Bi Yao, 377n86
black peony flower, 48, 74, 90, 217n136,
    241n73. *See also* peonies
blue cow, 47, 89–90, 281nn272–273, 282n280
Blue Crane ("Ch'ŏnghak") Grotto, 43–44,
    81–83, 259n158, 263n170
Bomen, 338n234
brush talks, 8

Cai Jing, 121, 340n244
Cai qi, 148, 394n173, 396n183, 396n185,
    397n189
cai shiguan, 397n194
calligraphy, 11, 73–74, 80, 119, 146, 234nn46–
    47, 235n53, 237n61, 253n129, 328n182.
    See also drunken ink calligraphy
Canglang sihua, 5
Canliao, 114, 327n181
Cao Zhi, 377n85, 384n129

censorship, 204n27, 231n26, 296n9
cha, 88, 277n250
Ch'ae Chegong, 354n287
Ch'ae Pomun, 360n27, 361n27
chagoban, 356n302
Chagyak, 385n140
Chajin, 74–75, 76–77, 123
Chaksi ha Yi changwŏn Misu, 40
chami, 285n292
ch'ang, 8, 316n117
changbu, 222n184
Changgŏm haeng, 58–60
changhae, 407n233
Changhe, 98, 298n18
Changhen ge, 288n306, 325n168, 359n6,
    423n301, 425n10
changsaeng kusi, 263n177
Chang Yunmun, 55
Chanyue Guanxiu, 327n180
Chao Fu, 110, 320n145, 321n152
chasŏk, 400n207
cheho, 258n153
cheil in, 249n111
chemun, 392n156
Che Naju kwan, 360n27, 361n27
Chen Ping, 308n60
Chen Wang, 377n85
Chen Zhong, 418n274
Che P'ahan chip hu, 26
Chibong yusŏl, 45, 383n124
chijego, 37, 225n4, 379n97
Chillak Yi Chahyŏn, 108
Chindong, 123, 211n92, 345n258
chin'gong, 357n307
Chinju, 23, 45, 46, 225n5, 227n10
chinsa, 264n190
ch'insi, 360n20
chinsin, 381n114

443

444 INDEX

Chinyang, 45–46, 62, 71, 217n134, 225n5, 226n6
Chisŭng, 113, 327n178, 327n179
Cho Ch'ung, 84, 267n196, 268n203
chodae, 385n131
Ch'odo Maengju, 23
Ch'oe Cha, 16, 17, 21, 25, 47
Ch'oe Ch'iwŏn, 14, 125–126, 260n160, 349–354nn272–288
Ch'oe Ch'unghŏn, 15, 30, 36, 56, 57, 62–63, 223nn196–198, 376n83, 410n242
Ch'oe Hae, 420n285
Ch'oe Hong'yun, 151, 404n219
Ch'oe Ku, 420n287
Ch'oe Kyun, 420n287, 422n296
Ch'oe Sajŏn, 102, 307n59, 308n60
Ch'oe Sanbo, 95, 293n334
Ch'oe Sŏn, 55, 219n162
Ch'oe Tang, 54, 74, 236n57, 237n61, 272n222
Ch'oe U, 21, 30, 62–66, 224n202
Ch'oe Yŏngyu, 33, 164
Ch'oe Yuch'ŏng, 84, 140, 249n116, 266n193
Ch'oe Yunŭi, 131–132, 362n29, 363n35
Chojŏk posal song, 141
Ch'ŏk Chun'gyŏng, 307n58, 308n59, 316n120, 317n122
ch'ŏlbal, 316n119
chŏl kyeji, 379n101
Ch'ŏllim, 79
chŏmgwi pu, 365n36
Chŏn Ch'iyu, 143, 384n126
chongbaek, 36, 83, 263n181, 264n182, 268n204, 293n324
Chŏng Chisang, 13, 44, 286n295, 381n114, 415n271, 416n272, 417n273, 418n276, 419nn278–280
Chŏng Chungbu, 30, 38, 44–45
ch'ŏngdam, 119, 130, 360n18
ch'ŏngdong, 112, 325n166
Ch'ŏnghak ("Blue Crane") Grotto, 43–44, 81–83, 259n158, 263n170
Chŏng Insŏ, 28
ch'ongjae, 267n198
Chŏng Kasin, 20
Chongnyŏng Chogam, 41, 118, 257n152, 331n202, 332n208
Ch'ŏngp'yŏng-san Munsu-wŏn ki, 108, 318nn130–131, 322n154

ch'ŏngsam, 244n90
Chŏng Sŏnmo, 358n309, 426n23
Chŏng Sŭmmyŏng, 135, 142, 144, 369n55, 385n136, 386n145
ch'ŏngu, 280n268
Ch'ŏn'gwan Temple, 127, 355n290, 355n295
Chŏng Yagyong, 260n159
Ch'ŏngyŏn-gak, 87, 272n227, 280n272
Chŏng Yŏryŏng, 23, 44–45, 46, 71, 227n10
ch'ŏnhwa, 331n204
ch'ŏnno, 407n235
Ch'ŏnsu-sa, 256n150, 341n252
Ch'ŏnsusa nammun to, 25
Ch'ŏnsu Temple, 13, 14, 25, 123
Ch'ŏnsu-wŏn to, 25
chŏnye, 316n114
chosam mosa, 367n45
Chōsen Kosho Kankōkai, 27
Cho Sin, 391n154
Cho Sok, 19
Chosŏn dynasty (1392–1897), 3–5, 201n5, 339n238
Chosŏn kojŏn chakka irhwa chip, 363n35, 413n263
Chosŏn munhak-esŏ- ŭi sajo mit pangbŏp yŏn'gu, 413n267
Chosŏn munhak t'ongsa, 31
Chosŏn sosŏlsa, 28–29, 209n77
Chosŏn-ŭi irŭmnan chakka-wa irhwa, 349n270
Cho T'ang, 55, 56
Cho Tongil, 5
Cho Wich'ong, 38
chrysanthemum, 72, 86, 229n22, 249n113, 272n223
ch'uaek, 385n144
chuanqi, 25
Chuci, 6, 348n269, 368n47
Chulao, 88
Ch'uljin Yongman ch'a simunsaeng, 316n112
chumun, 325n161
chung, 311n85
chunggan-pon, 18
Chŭng Kim kong (Kunsu), 247n108
Chŭng Misu che sŭng Ch'anji, 33–34
Chungnim Kohoe, 4, 31, 34, 54–55
Chungoe ilbo, 27–28
Chŭng sau, 41, 257n152
chungsu, 419n282

Chŭng Tamji, 243n85
Chunri, 51
chusa, 338n234
chuzi, 279n255
chwabu, 232n42
chwasa, 335n224
civil service examinations, 42, 215n117, 241n77, 249n112, 309n73, 421n290
Ciyun Mi Fu Er Wang shu bawei ershou, 237n60, 238n62
Classics from the Wall, 149, 395n181
clay oxen, 99, 301n37
Crimson Peach (person), 241n72
cultural heritage loss, 3

Daijing, 163, 425n3
Dajin Gaoli guoxinshi, 302n42
Daodejing, 411n252
Daxue, 53
Dayan fu, 335n225
Dengtuzi haose fu, 422n297
Dong Anyu, 423n302
doulu, 279n259
drunken ink calligraphy, 119, 121, 126. See also calligraphy
drunkenness, 331nn205–206, 332n210
Duange xing, 285n294
Du Fu, 6, 13, 91, 220n176, 377n86
Duke Taewŏn, 167
Du Meishan ji ai qi xueshi neng yongyun fu ciyun yishou, 88, 278n251, 278n253
Dushun, 380n103
Du Zimei, 103, 139

Eastern Capital, 105, 127, 150, 312nn91–92
Egan, Ronald, 238n62
Er shun yin, 51

Fang Shu, 396n183
Fangzhang, 324n160
Fan Sui, 333n218
Fascicle 1, P'ahan chip, 71–96, 202n11. See also P'ahan chip
Fascicle 2, P'ahan chip, 97–128, 202n11. See also P'ahan chip
Fascicle 3, P'ahan chip, 129–162, 202n11. See also P'ahan chip
feiran, 421n289

Feng fu, 334n219
Fengji Gao changshi, 418n273
Fengji zhouzhong fuzhen shuhuai sanshiliuyun fengcheng Hunan qinyou, 283n283
Fengqiao yebo, 284n288
fengsao, 368n47
Five Dynasties era (907–960), 264n185
Five Great Mountains of Chinese Taoism, 310n79
Four Immortals, 115, 129, 329nn193–194, 358nn3–4
fu, 231n27
Fuchou, 220n176
Fuxi, 359n8
fuzi, 149, 395n182
fuzuo, 244n94

Ganlu Temple, 338n233
Gao Pian, 125, 350n274, 351n275
Gaozong (emperor), 302n41, 405n226
gāthās, 116, 155, 411n249
Ge Hong, 232nn39–40
Ghost Registers, 132–133
Golden Chambers, 108, 317n125
Great East Asian War, 201n1
Guanxiu, 411n253
guoshi, 268n203, 319n134
Gu Yun, 125, 351n278, 384n127

Haedong Kirohoe, 4, 54–58
haengjang, 357n308
hak hae, 95, 294n335
Hallimwŏn, 4
Ham Sun, 239n67, 241n71, 241n74
han, 51, 52, 53, 219n158
Han Feizi, 294n1, 423n302, 426nn13–14
Han'guk munhak t'ongsa, 5, 45–46
Hangu Pass, 48, 90, 282n280
hanja, 218n148
hanju, 255n145
Han Kwŏn, 372n69
Han Ŏn'guk, 38, 140, 266n192, 292nn323–324, 378n93
Han Ŏn'guk kanggŏ, 292n323
Han River, 240n71, 291nn319–320, 317n127
Hansong-jŏng, 329nn192–194
Han Wudi, 324n159
Han Xiangzi, 412n257

446 INDEX

Han Xin, 316n121, 317n122
Han Xizai, 264n185
Hanyang, 19, 95, 293n325, 321n150
Han Yu, 6, 148–149, 241n72, 274n238, 367n42, 394n175
haojie shi, 220n171
Hechu nanwang jiu, 323n158
Heng'e, 372n68
Hengzhou song Li daifu qizhang mian fu Guangzhou, 282n282
heshan zuoshi, 397n191
hoemun si, 84–86, 269n209
Hŏ Hongjae, 77, 246n101
Hŏ Mok, 261n161
Hongdojŏng-ri, 241n74
hongji, 375n74
Hong Kwan, 146, 391n155
hongqiang, 388n149
Hong Sŏkchu, 27
hongye tishi, 254n144
hosaja, 411n247
Houshan shihua, 4
Hou Ying, 375n73
hu, 231n31
hua, 279n256
Huaisu, 238n63
Huangdi neijing suwen, 301n34
huanghua, 381n111
Huang Shangu, 138
Huang Shigong, 408n237
Huang Tingjian, 6, 91–92, 133, 147
Huan Xuan, 255n145
Hua Xin, 406n227
huazhuan, 249n110
Hu He, 281n275
Huihong, 6, 72, 227n11, 228n12, 228n15, 229n16
Hŭijong (king), 15, 17, 219n167, 404n221, 426n17
Huiyuan, 377n87
Huizong (emperor), 8, 100, 204n27, 228n11, 233n44, 301n31, 302n40, 305n47, 312n93, 340nn243–245, 345n253
Hu-Kiyŏnghoe sŏ, 55–56
Hundred Schools of Thought, 148, 163–164, 256
Hŭngwang Temple, 35, 42, 113, 223n197, 327n177, 356n298, 426n19

huobo shengtun, 393n166
Huo Qubing, 209n75
Hu Zhai, 357n304
Hu Zongdan, 122, 131, 341n250, 360n25
hwach'a, 280n264
hwaji wi pyŏng, 235n59
Hwangbo T'ak, 144, 385n138, 386n143
Hwang Munbu, 242n78
Hwang Munjang, 242n78, 288n305
Hwang Pinyŏn, 75, 117, 118, 242n78
Hwang Sunik, 135–136, 371n60
Hwaŏm taesa, 234n49
Hwaŏm taesa Kyŏnghyŏk, 73
Hwaŏm wŏlsa, 116–117, 332n209, 332n211
hwarang, 129, 329n193, 354n288, 358nn1–3, 359n10
hwasa, 253n132
hyangak, 411n256
Hyejong (king), 397n188
Hyeso, 121, 328nn183–184, 330n195
hyŏlchi hanan, 384n130
hyŏllyang, 385n137
hyŏnch'a, 218n149
Hyŏn Tŏksu, 55

ijang, 411n254
illness of idleness, 53, 57, 166, 294n1
Illustrated Account of the Xuanhe Embassy to Koryŏ (Xu Jing), 340n246, 341n247, 361n24
Im Chongbi, 48–49, 205n42, 281n276
Im Ch'un, 14, 34–35, 37, 39, 40–42, 58–61, 63, 212n96, 213n103, 214n112, 221n181, 285n294, 368n48, 388n151, 408nn237–239
Imha p'ilgi, 26, 386n143
Imjin War (1592–1598), 3, 19, 26
Im Kiji, 165
Im Kyŏngch'ŏng, 360n24
im taebo, 307n57
Im Yu, 84, 154, 267n197, 268n202
Injong (king), 30, 96, 101, 314nn102–103
Inju Yi-ssi sebo, 33
In Pin, 142, 383n120
intellectuals-in-between, 30–31, 54, 209n83
irhwa, 5
irwŏl, 112, 325n169
Irwŏl-sa, 95, 293n331
Ise monogatari, 12, 205n35

jia, 279n258
Jia Dao, 13, 117, 283n285, 332n211
Jiangfei ernü, 240n71
jianjian, 422n292
Jia Yi, 97, 294n3, 381n113
jie, 279n260
jiegu, 276n242
ji meng, 243n81
jinbo, 245n96
Jingkou, 120, 338n236
Jin Midi, 308n63
Jinshu, 214n111, 253n134, 270n211, 299n22,
 330, 367n41, 378n90
jinye, 269n206
Jiubian, 348n269, 349n270
Juefan Huihong, 6
juling, 301n33
juntian, 398n198
Jurchen Jin dynasty (1115–1234), 9, 33, 36,
 100, 208n73, 236n55, 293n327, 315n107,
 425n8, 425n11

kaek, 257n151
Kaesŏng, 17, 29, 201n3
Kaesŏng-sa p'alch'ŏk-pang, 286n298
kajip, 49, 258n154
kakch'ok, 87, 274nn232–233
Kamak-sa, 333n214, 334n219
Kamno-sa, 339nn239–240
Kamno-sa ch'a Hyewŏn un, 339n239
kamsa, 18, 311n85
Kangdo, 426n20
Kang Iryong, 13, 16, 87, 93, 274n235,
 274n238, 276n239, 287n300, 288n301
kangmun chihu, 427n25
kangnam, 385n132
kangsŭp, 95, 293n332
kanwŏn, 314n101
kedou, 397n193
Khitan Liao dynasty (916–1125), 3, 8–9
ki, 400n208
kigwan, 357n306
Kiji Im Ch'un, 19, 145–146, 154
Kim Allo, 25
Kim Chach'ing, 95
Kim Chaŭi, 107, 316n113, 316n116
Kim Chonjung, 102, 136, 308n62, 371n60
Kim Hamyŏng, 416n272

Kim Hwangwŏn, 92, 119, 124, 141, 284n290,
 334n223
Kim Hyosun, 90, 280n270
Kim I, 20
Kim Injon. *See* Kim Yŏn (Kim Injon)
Kim Ipchi, 73
Kim Kunsu, 13, 77–78, 151–152, 247n108
Kim On'gi, 118
Kim P'irhyŏng, 32
Kim Podang, 38
Kim Puch'ŏl, 322n154
Kim Pusik, 30, 99, 114–115, 121, 300n29,
 342n249
Kim Puŭi, 8, 99, 101, 141, 217n131, 300n28,
 301n30, 304n47, 306nn49–52, 318n131
Kim Saeng, 9, 73, 146, 233n44
Kim Sanggi, 105, 313n94
Kim Sijung sŭngno pang kangsŏ Hyeso sangin,
 328n189
Kim Sim, 23–25
Kim Sinyun, 44, 102, 117, 157, 309n69,
 333n215, 334n222
Kim Sisŭp, 25, 412n261
Kim Sukch'ŏng, 95
Kim T'aejun, 29
Kim Tonjung, 30, 78, 235n51, 250nn116–118
Kim Yŏn (Kim Injon), 7, 8–9, 105, 106,
 301n30, 312n93, 314nn101–102,
 315nn104–107
Kim Yŏngbu, 28, 103, 310n78
Kim Yunsik, 27
Kim Yusin, 14, 26, 126–127, 354nn288–289
Kiŏn, 261n161
Kirin-gak, 308n61
kisaeng, 288nn303–304
Ki Taesŭng, 261n160
Ko Chumong, 346n260
Ko Hyoch'ung, 131, 361nn22–25
Kojong (king), 15, 28–29
Kollyun'gang-sang, 17
kong, 379n99
Kongam-hyŏn, 383n121
Konghou yin (Harp lay), 300n27
kongmun, 409n241
Kongyang (king), 239n69
kon-oe sin, 315n110
Koryŏ dynasty (918–1392), 3–5, 29–30,
 204n23, 204n26, 337n232

448 INDEX

Koryŏguk Ogwan-san Taehwaŏm Yŏngt'ong-sa chŭngsi Taegak kuksa pimyŏng, 328n188
Koryŏsa, 3, 21, 35–37, 49, 201n5, 242n78, 266n192
Koun p'yŏn, 125
Koyang ch'wigon, 116, 332nn209–210
Koyang wŏlsa, 137–138, 375n75
Ko Yŏngjun, 55
kujang, 292n322
kuksa, 319n134, 354n288
Kŭmbang su, 246n102
kŭmgyu, 406n229
Kŭm Kŭgŭi, 151, 404n219
kŭmmun, 323n156
Kŭmnan, 328n191
Kŭmo sinhwa, 25
kŭmp'ung, 243n82
kŭmsang, 267n194
kŭmsin, 246n97
kŭmsŏ cheyu, 274n232
Kŭm Ŭi, 404n219
kumun, 316n111
kunje, 284n291
kŭpkŭp, 309n72
kwae kwan, 373n71
Kwak Tongsun, 129–130, 359n7
Kwak Yŏ, 109, 110–111, 112–113, 119, 159, 319n136, 320nn136–138, 419nn278–280
Kwangch'ŏn (teacher), 115–116
kwan'gi, 369n53
Kwangjong (king), 83, 241n77, 288n304
kwi, 20
Kwŏn Chŏk, 146, 392n159
Kwŏn Kŭn, 55–56
Kwŏn Tollye, 20, 160, 423n300
Kyerim Suong, 159
kyesa, 131, 132, 135, 362n28
Kyeyang, 94, 291nn317–318
Kyobang, 288n304
kyŏgo, 367n44
kyŏnggi, 369n53
kyŏngnon, 411n248
kyŏngsa, 232n41

Later Tang dynasty (923–936), 264nn185–186Lei Yi, 418n274
Lengzhai yehua, 6, 72, 228n12, 229n21, 393n165

li, 221n177
Liang dynasty (502–557), 270n210
lianju, 95, 119, 293n333
Lian Po, 209n74
Lianzhu shige, 22
Li Bai, 283n286, 301n38, 366n40
Liexian zhuan, 240n71
Liezi, 238nn65–66, 264n183
Li Guang, 378n89
Li He, 15
Liji, 220n170, 249n109
Li Mi, 290n313, 291n314
Li Shangyin, 133, 365n37
Li Shen, 232n37
Li Shimin, 97, 295n4
Liu Bang, 222n183, 316n121, 317n122
Liu Kun, 221n179, 222n186
Liu Xiang, 240n71
Liu Xihai, 27
Liu Xiu, 335n226
Liu Yiqing, 253n133
Liuyi shihua, 4, 50, 288n301, 365n38
Liu Ziji, 263n178
Liu Zongyuan, 151, 404n217
Li Yiji, 332n210
Li Ying, 405n225
Longxi Li clan, 393n163
luchui, 254n139
Lu Ji, 253n133
lun, 249n109
Lunheng, 52
Lunyu, 51, 62, 163, 216n126, 254n137, 314n98, 358n308, 360n13, 379n98, 418n275, 421n288, 425n6
Luo Fei, 272n224
Luoshen fu, 272n225
Luoyang, 145, 221, 290n311, 311n84, 325n165, 390n152, 393n164
Lu Tong, 135, 371n62
Lu You, 51–52
Lüzhu, 290n312

maegye ch'wiok, 379n94
Maeho yugo, 26, 208n65
Maengsŏng, 36, 72, 73, 123, 230n26
Ma Heluo, 102, 308n63
Ma Yisun, 264n187
Mei nong, 73, 232n37

Meng Chu, 7, 8, 105–106, 313n98, 314nn98–100
Mengyou Tianmu yin liubie, 244n87
Mengzi, 220n175, 227n9, 281n275, 311n87, 359n11, 360n12, 423n303, 426n15
Min (king), 413n269, 414n269
Min Yŏngmo, 36, 213n100
Misu pang yŏ ŏ-Kaeryŏng i arijiju wi hyang, 368n49, 389n151
mo, 394n169
Moch'un mun aeng, 390n153
mongnol, 421n288
Mongol invasions, 3, 16, 17, 30, 167, 225n205, 426n20
moran, 362n31
mottled bamboo, 78, 249n114, 250n119
Mount Beigu, 338n233
Mount Chiri, 43, 81–83, 259n155, 259n158, 262n168
Mount Ch'ŏngp'yŏng, 108–109, 146, 317n123, 318n130, 322n154
Muae, 155, 411n256
Muae ka, 155
mukkun, 249n113
Munbang sabo, 72, 230n24
munhyŏng, 426n18
munjip, 64
Munjong (king), 337n231
Mun Kŭkkyŏm, 44, 97–98, 222n189, 295n9, 296n10, 297n12, 298–299nn15–22
munsaeng, 36, 61, 83–84, 140, 263n180, 264n189, 268nn204–205
Mun Tamji t'akche, i si haji, 243n85
Myoch'ŏng, 30, 342n249
myŏng, 247n106
Myŏng (emperor), 127
Myŏngjong (king), 14, 30, 35, 61, 77, 84, 95, 98, 140, 294n336, 356n296, 356n299

Naedojang, 328n190
Naksŏngjae Study Hall, 95, 293n330
namguk, 380n109
Namp'o, 416n272
Nanhuapian, 163
Nanke taishou zhuan, 259n158
Nanxu ji, 85, 270n214
neidian, 328n185
Nine Springs, 99, 299n26

Niulang, 90, 282n279
Northern Song dynasty China (960–1127), 4, 229n18, 337n232
No Yŏngsu, 7, 138, 375n79

ŏbu, 413n265
O Chŏngsŏk, 373n70
odo, 413n264
Office of Music, 108, 317n128
ogung, 112, 325n167
ogyŏng, 356n300
Oju yŏnmun changjŏn san'go, 18
okch'ung, 246n99
oksun, 410n244
Oksun-jŏng, 410n244
Oktang, 242n79
Oktang paek pu, 247n107
Ŏm Chŏnggu, 19
ŏmuk, 231n29
oriole, 330n200
O Sejae, 14, 41–42, 150, 165, 369n52, 398n204, 399n205, 401nn209–212
O Semun, 242n80
Ŏ Sukkwŏn, 20, 424n304
otter marrow, 135, 370n57
Ouyang Xiu, 4, 5, 6, 15, 148–149, 274n237, 275n238, 288n301, 333n213, 365n38, 390n152, 394n178, 398nn202–203
Ouyang Yongshu, 150
oxen, 49, 50, 99, 121, 217n136, 239, 281n277, 282n278, 301n37

Paegunja Sinjun, 14, 137, 387n148
P'aegwan chapki, 20, 25, 424n304
Paek Kwangsin, 55, 154–155, 409n242, 410n243
P'aeng Chojŏk, 140–141, 378n93
Paengnyŏn ch'ohae, 413n261
paeun, 298n19
p'ahan, as term, 51
P'ahan chip, 4, 5–7, 12–16, 202n15, 202nn10–12; circulation of, 16–17; editions of, 18–20, 50; epilogue of, 163–168; fascicle 1, 71–96; fascicle 2, 97–128; fascicle 3, 129–162; historical context of, 21–33; intended audience of, 56–57, 219n167, 220nn168–169; as poetic criticism, 43–49; sequels of, 16, 17, 21; titles of, 49–53, 57–58, 202n6. *See also* Yi Illo

450 INDEX

Pak Chiwŏn, 338n233, 347n267
Pak Illyang, 426n16
Pak Insŏk, 55
Pak Kongsŭp, 139, 376n83, 378n92
Pak Sŏnggyu, 335n226
Pak Sŭngjung, 141, 382n116
Pak T'aesun, 26, 207n63
Pak Wŏn'gae, 131–132, 361n27, 363n35, 365n35
P'algwan Sŏnghoe, 129
palindrome poems, 84–86
panbak, 254n138
Pan Dalin, 72, 229n19
pang, 264n188
Pan Yue, 79, 253n133
Panzhong shi, 85, 271nn214–215
pattra leaves, 331n203
peasant and slave revolts, 37–38, 213n104, 213n107
Pei Hang, 267n201
Pei Hao, 83, 84, 264n185, 264n189, 269n208
Pengdao, 112, 325n164
peonies, 87, 144, 217n136, 241n73, 273n231, 274n238, 277nn243–244, 301n38. *See also* black peony flower
phoenix, 90, 111, 158, 244n89, 247n106, 280n272, 299n21, 334n223, 357n302, 371n67
Pin Yŏn, 334n222
Pipa xing, 244n90
P'irŏn kakbi, 27
plantain, 330nn197–198
poetry boards, 124, 347n266
poets' societies, 4
p'ogal, 268n205
poguk, 222n187
pogwŏl, 92, 285n295
Pohan chip, 16, 17, 21, 203n21, 223n196, 225n205, 251n126, 268n202, 269n208, 271n217, 281n276, 286n298, 298n15, 312n93, 320n137, 326n175, 332n211, 336n230, 341n249, 342n250, 352n283, 358n3, 361n27, 373n70, 401n212, 404n219, 404n223, 409n242, 413n262, 417n273
pongsŏng, 254n142
ponjo, 234n48
pŏpki, 326n173

Pubyŏng-nyo, 346n265
pukcho, 259n156
p'ungyo, 413n266
Punhaeng chip, 141, 382n115
Punhaeng-nu, 381n110
Punhwang, 331n201
Pu Yi Misu che Im sŏnsaeng mun, 214n112
Pyŏkkyŏng, 149, 395n181
p'yŏngjang, 246n100
Pyŏngjung yu kam, 40
Pyŏngna noin Kŏbi, 115, 251n125
P'yŏngyang, 29, 201n3, 415n270

qi (energy), 406n228, 423n303
Qi (game), 99, 301n35
Qian Hanshu, 118
Qi dynasty, 306n50
Qin dynasty (221–207 BCE), 43–44, 263n175
Qingping diao, 301n38
Qingxiang (king), 348n269
Qinzong (emperor), 302n40
Qizhou, 232n34
qizhu, 232n34
Quanjiu shisi shou, 323n158

rainbow clothes, 359n6
Ransaeng pyŏngjŭngsŏl, 18
rattan paper, 73, 231n33
rebellious ministers, 43–44
Red Turbans, 3*ri*, 280n266
Ri Sŏng, 333n216
Rogers, Michael C., 63, 302n44, 304n45, 304n47
Rong Yu, 240n70
Royal Flower Garden, 43, 121, 152–153, 340n247
Ruan Ji, 34, 214n11
Ryu Su, 139, 376n82

Sagong, 424n305
sahae-ji ka, 316n118
saja, 379n100
samasi, 362n32
samch'ŏn, 419n283
samch'un, 87, 272n226
samda, 384n128
Samguk sagi, 18, 354n288, 355n295, 369n55
Samguk yusa, 411n250

samgye, 411n255

samjŏl, 392n157

samno, 338n234

Sa muik si, 131

sanfen wudian, 87, 163–164, 273n228

sangch'ŏng, 420n284

Sangch'un-jŏng, 392n161

sangdo, 419n277

sangjae hyang, 227n9

Sangjŏng kogŭm yemun, 362n29

sang mun, 262n164

San'gŏ, 212n99

Sang Yŏnggong, 96

sanin, 411n253

Saŏp, 425n9

Sa-ru (Gauze Tower), 87, 273n230

saryun, 315n109

sasin, 280n269

sasŏn-bi, 358n4

Seven Worthies of the Bamboo Grove, 34, 214n11

shanteng, 231n33

Shanzhong wenda, 359n11

shelong, 397n195

sheng, 269n207

Shen Jiji, 309n71

Shi Chong, 94, 290n311, 291n315

shigu (Stone Drums), 148, 204n22, 394nn171–178, 395n182, 397n192, 397n196

Shihua zonggui, 306n54

Shiji, 7, 308n64

Shijian shu, 97, 295n6

Shijing, 6, 45, 46, 149, 204n22, 227n9, 397nn189–190, 414n268

Shilin shihua, 5

Shi Shu, 79

Shishuo xinyu, 279n263

Shizong (emperor), 36

shujin, 232n35

Shujing, 105, 245n94, 281n277, 306n51, 308n61, 311n86, 360n15, 405n226

Shultz, Edward J., 213n107, 216n122, 246n104, 293n330, 296n9, 386n139, 386n145

Shu Mojie Lantian yanyu tu, 293n326

Shuowen jiezi, 50

si, as genre, 5

sihwa, as genre, 4, 5, 10–11

sijung hwa, 95

Silla dynasty, 14, 204n31, 233n44, 234n45, 352n282

Sima Xiangru, 144, 423n298

simin, 357n305

sinch'ong, 385n135

Sinhŭng-sa, 262n167

Sinjong (king), 36, 154, 342n256

Sinjun, 373n70, 388n150

Sinjŭng tongguk yŏji sŭngnam, 4, 26, 245n92, 280n267, 286n297, 320n143, 334n222, 339nn240–241, 372n69, 382n114, 384n125

sip'an, 124, 347n266

sisŭng, 14

siwen, 398n197

Sixiang Wang, 204n23

slave trade, 239n69

sŏbong, 284n287

Sŏdo, 416n272

Sŏha chip, 35, 58–68, 224n203, 391n153

Sŏha Kiji, 136–137

"Sŏha sŏnsaeng chip sŏ," 388n151

soja, 288n302

Sŏkchukhwa, 143–144

Sok haengno nan, 42

sŏkkŏ, 422n291

Sŏ Kŏjŏng, 18, 22–23, 207n53, 274n238, 287n300, 311n85, 348n267, 417n273

Sok P'ahan chip. See *Pohan chip*

Sok P'ahan chip sŏ, 21

Sok U-hu ka yŏ Misu tongbu, 289n310

Sŏl Ch'ong, 155

sŏm t'o, 355n293

Somun swaero, 391n154

Sŏ Munwŏn, 20, 160–161

Song Chisŭng, 327n179

Song gaoseng zhuan, 331n207

Sŏngho sasŏl, 224n203, 354n287, 411n256

Sŏng Hyŏn, 21–22

Sŏngjong (king), 18, 23–25

Sŏngjong sillok, 23–24

Song Misu, 389n151

Song p'ung, 118

Song uin, 417n273

songyŏn, 231n32

Song Yu, 125, 334n221, 348n269

sŏnje, 250n118

452 INDEX

sŏnjin, 376n81
sŏrhwa, 12
so-sa, 369n50
sosŏl, as genre, 4
Sŏ Tamji ka pyŏk, 61
Southern Qi dynasty (479–501), 270n210
Southern Song dynasty (1127–1279), 5, 100,
  306n51, 337n232
Sŏ Yugu, 27
Ssangmyŏng-jae, 393n167
Ssangmyŏngjae chip, 21, 22, 26, 219n165,
  306n51
steles, 114, 129, 204n27, 233n44, 262n168,
  329n194, 358n4
Su Dongpo, 133, 138, 146
Su Hui, 84, 270n211
Suihantang shihua, 5
Sukchong (king), 19
Suk Han Ŏn'guk sŏjae, 292n323
sun'gaeng, 221n178
sŭngsŏn, 293n328, 328n186
sŭngt'ong, 356n298
Su Shi, 6, 9, 13, 14, 44, 48–49, 88–89, 91–92,
  237nn60–61, 284n289
susin, 381n112
Sūtrâlaṃkāra-śāstra, 223n193

T'aebaek-san-in Kyeŭng, 113–115, 325n171
Taebang-gun, 259n157
taegak, 315n108
Taegak Kuksa, 113, 114, 325n172, 328n188,
  380n107
taehon, 385n134
T'aejo, 129
taejŏl, 299n23
taejongbaek, 249n115
Taewŏn-gong, 17, 383n117
Taiyuan era (376–397), 263n176
Taizong (emperor), 97, 234n47, 238n62, 295n4
t'akche, 316n115
Tang (king), 362n34
tangdu, 253n131
Tan-ju, 243n84
Tanyŏn, 108, 146, 318n133
Taohuayuan ji, 43–44, 260n159, 263nn172–
  173, 263n178
Tao Yuanming ji, 263n174
tea, 135, 371nn61–62

"Tea Well," 115
Tiande era (1149–1152), 425n8
Tiaoxi yuying conghua, 357n304
Ti xiaoqiao qian xinzhu zhao ke, 252n128
todokpu, 231n28
Tohwa-wŏn, 342n254
Tokhaeng, 241n76
Tongdo hŭije, 312n92
Tonggak, 99, 299n25
Tongguk t'onggam, 18
Tongguk Yi Sangguk chip, 242n80, 244n85,
  277n242, 339n240, 351n278, 380n108,
  399–400
t'onggwan, 301n32
Tonggwang, 28
Tonggye chip, 26
Tongin sihwa, 22, 27, 207n55, 258n153,
  274n238, 287n300, 311n85, 347n267,
  372n69, 417n273
Tongin sihwa sŏ, 22
Tongmunsŏn, 3, 22–23, 42, 49, 202n9
Tongsa kangmok, 26
Tongsanjae ki, 159
t'uja sŏn, 309n70
T'u mogwan, 375n79
tŭngnong si, 245n95

U-hu, 93, 289n307, 289n310, 291n316
Ŭijong (king), 29–30, 38, 44, 73, 77, 89–90, 97,
  140, 156, 235n54, 386n139, 386n145
ŭm privilege, 42, 216n123
ŭngje, 385n142
un'gŭn, 397n192
ŭnha yŏlsu, 352n280
Ŭn Wŏnch'ung, 108, 317n126
Unyang chip, 27
uta monogatari, as genre, 12
Uya yu hoe, 383n119

Wang Anshi, 277n248, 279n257, 371n63
Wang Bing, 301n34
Wang Bo, 244n93
Wang Chong, 52
Wang Huizi, 279n263
Wang Hun, 328n182
Wang Hyo, 383n117
Wang Kai, 290n311
Wang Kŏn, 352nn281–282

INDEX   **453**

Wang Meng, 367n41
Wangnyun-sa, 115, 330n199
Wang Shen, 237n61
Wang Ŭi, 15, 17, 424nn306–308
Wang Wei, 272n223, 293n326, 331n200
Wang Zhu, 234n47
Wang Ziqiao, 244n89
wanhuhao, 335n228
Wanhui, 116, 331n207
wazhu, 229n16
Wei Dan, 231n32
Wei Gongzi, 374n72
Wei Yingwu, 394n174
Wei Zheng, 97, 295nn5–6
Wen (emperor), 97, 294nn2–3, 297n14
Wengong xu shihua, 4
Wen Tong, 251nn123–124
Wen Yingwu, 148–149
Wen Zhi, 413n269
white monkey, 82, 262n169
Willow Branch (person), 241n72
Wŏlsŏng, 129, 359n10
wŏn, 287n299
Wŏnhyo, 155, 410nn245–246, 412n259
wuling, 232n36, 370n58
Wuling yuan, 244n86
Wuliu xiansheng ji, 82–83
wushi, 320n140
wutong, 383n118

xian, 51
xiang che, 279n262
Xiangyang ji, 407nn235–236
Xiang Yu, 222n182, 246n99
Xianxian (emperor), 121
Xiaodu ji, 394n170
Xiao He, 306n53
Xiaoman, 160, 422n295
Xiao Shi, 371n67
Xiaoxiao, 251n123
Xiao Yu, 306n53
Xida Yuan Zhen, 390n152
Xie An, 257n152, 299n22, 299n25, 300n27,
    315n105
Xie Lingyun, 244n87
Xie Yi, 229n20
Xikun chouchang ji, 133, 365n37
Xikun Style, 133, 365nn37–38

xikun ti, 365n37
Ximen Bao, 423n302
xinglu, 328n187
Xin Tangshu, 368n46
Xishan, 284n287
Xi Shi, 160, 275n239, 422n294
Xizeng Du Fu, 283n286
Xizi, 160, 422n294
Xuan (king), 394n177, 396nn183–184,
    396n186
Xuanhe shupu, 328n182
Xuanhua, 400n206
Xuanzong (emperor), 301n38, 360n19
xuemai, 271n216
Xuetangji, 250n122
Xu Jing, 230n26, 273n227, 273n229, 327n177,
    340n246, 341n247, 361n24
Xu Jin yangqiu, 255n145
Xu Ling, 271n214
Xunzi, 366n39
Xu You, 110, 320n145, 321n152
Xu Zhaopei, 276n239

ya, 309n74
yanggap suk, 368n46
Yang Guifei, 288n306, 301n38, 423n301
yanggye, 413n264
Yangja-gang, 108, 317n127
Yang Xiong, 237n62
Yangyanggong (prince), 15, 161–162
Yang Yi, 365n37
Yang Yingcheng, 100, 302n42, 302n44,
    304nn46–47
Yangzi, 151, 238n66, 404n216
Yejong (king), 14, 25, 87, 109–112, 121,
    131, 157, 319n136, 321n149, 323n158,
    346n264
Yellow Cabinet, 84, 267n200, 269n208
yeŭi, 359n6
Yi Chae, 141
Yi Chagyŏm, 33, 226n8, 307n58, 316n120
Yi Chahyŏn, 109–110, 146, 317n123, 319n135,
    320n137, 321n153
Yi Chayŏn, 33, 120, 337n231, 338n232,
    339n237
Yi Chehyŏn, 38, 274n235, 370n58
Yi Chijŏ, 45, 46, 104–105, 226n8, 311n85,
    378n93

454 INDEX

Yi Chisim, 85, 271n217
Yi Chiyŏng, 376n83
Yi Chongjun, 23
Yi Chonyŏn, 20
Yi Chunch'ang, 55, 147, 393n168
Yi Chungyak, 119, 335n224
Yi Hŭijong, 57
Yi Illo, 4, 21, 31, 33–49, 52–53, 203nn18–21.
  See also *P'ahan chip*
Yijia bie hushang ting, 240n70
Yi Kongsu, 312n90
Yi Kongsŭng, 127, 355n291, 355n294
Yi Kŭkton, 18–19, 23
Yi Kwangjin, 33, 140, 379n95
Yi Kwe, 380n107, 381n109, 381n111
Yi Kyubo, 31, 233n44, 381n114, 401nn210–
  211, 408n239
Yi Kyugyŏng, 18
Yi Kyun, 34
Yi Misu, 413n262
Yi Mubang, 329n194
Yi Nyŏng, 25, 342n253, 345n255
Yi O, 33, 211n91, 346n264
Yi Ŏllim, 33
Yi Paeksŏn, 33
Yi Saek, 52, 404n223
Yi Sehwang, 16–17, 34, 49, 52, 67, 168,
  219n161
Yi Sejang, 55
Yishui ge, 7
Yi Sugwang, 45, 383n124
Yi Sunu, 77, 92, 247n105
Yi Tamji, 119, 243n85, 335n230
Yi Tŏngmu, 378n93
Yi Ŭibang, 38
Yi Ŭimin, 30, 288n303, 376n83
Yi Yangsil, 147, 392n162
Yi Yugyŏng, 33, 147, 392n160
Yi Yuwŏn, 26
Yŏgong p'aesŏl, 21, 25, 38–39, 265n191,
  390n153, 400n208
Yŏ Hong Kyosŏ sŏ, 39
Yŏkchu Pohan chip, 362n27
Yŏmju, 101, 306nn55–56, 407n232
Yongch'ŏn tamjŏk ki, 25
Yongdu hoe (Assembly of Dragon Heads),
  152, 215n115, 404n223
yong hŭng, 352n281

Yongjae ch'onghwa, 21–22, 206n52
Yong ju, 272n221
Yŏngnak, 80–81, 95
Yŏngnak Cho T'ong, 256n148, 257nn151–152
Yŏngnyu si, 160, 422n293
yongŏ, 112, 325n168
yŏn'gok, 326n174
Yongŏn-gak, 104, 310n82
Yong-san, 291n319
yŏngsa si, 255n146
Yŏngt'ong-sa, 377n84
yŏnju, 375n76
yŏn kwan, 309n66
Yŏrha ilgi, 347n267
Yŏ Wang Yakchu sŏ, 40
Yŏ Yi Misu hoe Tamji-ji ka, 368n48
Yuan Ang, 297n14
Yu Chiri-san, 23
Yue Guang, 253n134, 378n90
Yugam, 28, 103
yugou, 254n143
yugung, 427n24
Yuhoe Misu, 41
Yu Hŭi, 93–94, 246n103, 288n305
Yulinling, 376n80
Yun Kwan, 341n249
Yun Ŏni, 122, 304n47, 341n249
yunwŏn, 379n97
Yunxi ji, 72, 228n15
Yu P'aljŏnsan, 373n70
Yutai xinyong, 271n214
Yu You, 254n144
Yuyuan, 98, 298n20

zaiyou, 246n104
Zhang Han, 76, 221n178
Zhang Ji, 284n288
Zhang Liang, 221n181
zhanguo si gongzi, 129, 358n2, 375n72
Zhao (king), 334n218
Zhao Guo, 302n41
Zhao Hu, 396n184
Zhao Meng, 150, 398n201
Zheng Yuqing, 394n172
Zhenzhong ji, 259n158, 309n71
Zhenzong (emperor), 301n31
zhi, 279n257
Zhi Anjie yuanlai yezuo, 367n42

INDEX 455

Zhong Lichun, 306n56
Zhong Yi, 235n53
Zhou Bo, 308n60
Zhou dynasty (1046–221 BCE), 253n136,
306n50, 311n84
Zhou Yafu, 285n293
Zhou Yue, 235n53
Zhou Zi, 289n308
Zhuangzi, 42–43, 53, 216n127, 220n174,
229n16, 425n1
zhuo, 90, 282n281

Zhuo Wenjun, 423n298
zhuyou, 270n212
Zhu Yun, 297n13
Zichan, 253n135, 254n137
Zigong, 379n98
Zi jing fu Fengxianxian yonghuai wubai zi,
282n278
zixia, 317n124
Zoubi xie Meng jianyi ji xin cha, 371n62
Zuo qian zhi Languan shi zhisun Xiang, 367n42
Zu Ti, 221n179

About the Translator

Dennis Wuerthner is assistant professor of East Asian literature in the Department of World Languages and Literatures, Boston University. His main field of research is premodern and contemporary Korean literature, history, and culture in a broader East Asian context. He is the author of *A Study of Hypertexts of* Kuunmong, *Focusing on* Kuullu/Kuun'gi (2017). His most recent contribution in the field of premodern Korean literature is *Tales of the Strange by a Korean Confucian Monk* (2020), an in-depth study and fully annotated translation of the *Kŭmo sinhwa* by Kim Sisŭp (1435–1493), published in the Korean Classics Library: Historical Materials series.

Korean Classics Library: Historical Materials

Imperatives of Culture: Selected Essays on Korean History, Literature, and Society from the Japanese Colonial Era
edited by Christopher P. Hanscom, Walter K. Lew, and Youngju Ryu

A Chinese Traveler in Medieval Korea: Xu Jing's *Illustrated Account of the Xuanhe Embassy to Koryŏ*
translated, annotated, and with an introduction by Sem Vermeersch

Seeking Order in a Tumultuous Age: The Writings of Chŏng Tojŏn, a Korean Neo-Confucian
translated and with an introduction by David M. Robinson

Korea's Premier Collection of Classical Literature: Selections from Sŏ Kŏjŏng's *Tongmunsŏn*
translated, annotated, and with an introduction by Xin Wei and James B. Lewis

A Korean Scholar's Rude Awakening in Qing China: Pak Chega's *Discourse on Northern Learning*
translated and annotated by Byonghyon Choi, Seung B. Kye, and Timothy V. Atkinson

Tales of the Strange by a Korean Confucian Monk: *Kŭmo sinhwa* by Kim Sisŭp
translated, annotated, and with an introduction by Dennis Wuerthner

The Encyclopedia of Daily Life: A Woman's Guide to Living in Late-Chosŏn Korea
translated, annotated, and with an introduction by Michael J. Pettid and Kil Cha

Record of the Seasonal Customs of Korea: *Tongguk sesigi* by Toae Hong Sŏk-mo
translated, annotated, and with an introduction by Werner Sasse

Poems and Stories for Overcoming Idleness: *P'ahan chip* by Yi Illo
translated, annotated, and with an introduction by Dennis Wuerthner

Korean Classics Library: Philosophy and Religion

Salvation through Dissent: Tonghak Heterodoxy and Early Modern Korea
George L. Kallander

Reflections of a Zen Buddhist Nun
Kim Iryŏp, translated by Jin Y. Park

A Handbook of Buddhist Zen Practice
translated by John Jorgensen

Korea's Great Buddhist-Confucian Debate: The Treatises of Chŏng Tojŏn (Sambong) and Hamhŏ Tŭkt'ong (Kihwa)
translated and with an introduction by A. Charles Muller

A Korean Confucian Way of Life and Thought: The *Chasŏngnok* (Record of Self-Reflection) by Yi Hwang (T'oegye)
translated, annotated, and with an introduction by Edward Y. J. Chung

Numinous Awareness Is Never Dark: The Korean Buddhist Master Chinul's *Excerpts on Zen Practice*
translated, annotated, and with an introduction by Robert E. Buswell, Jr.

Doctrine and Practice in Medieval Korean Buddhism: The Collected Works of Ŭich'ŏn
translated, annotated, and with an introduction by Richard D. McBride II

The Foresight of Dark Knowing: *Chŏng Kam nok* and Insurrectionary Prognostication in Pre-Modern Korea
translated, annotated, and with an introduction by John Jorgensen

A Place to Live: A New Translation of Yi Chung-hwan's *T'aengniji,* the Korean Classic for Choosing Settlements
translated, annotated, and with an introduction by Inshil Choe Yoon

The Master from Mountains and Fields: Prose Writings of Hwadam, Sŏ Kyŏngdŏk
translated, annotated, and with an introduction by Isabelle Sancho

A Korean Confucian's Advice on How to Be Moral: Tasan Chŏng Yagyong's Reading of the *Zhongyong*
translated, annotated, and with an introduction by Don Baker